W9-BEH-080

Exploring Literature

GINN LITERATURE SERIES

Robert A. Bennett, *Senior Author*

INTRODUCTION TO LITERATURE

EXPLORING LITERATURE

UNDERSTANDING LITERATURE

TYPES OF LITERATURE

AMERICAN LITERATURE

ENGLISH LITERATURE

THE OLD STAGECOACH OF THE PLAINS *Frederic Remington* Amon Carter Museum

Exploring Literature

Louise Grindstaff
California State University, Northridge

Robert A. Bennett
San Diego City Schools

CONSULTANTS

Robert E. Beck, *English Consultant*
John Swett Unified School District
Crockett, California

Sharon L. Belshaw, *English Instructor*
Hopkins Junior High School
Fremont, California

Mary Gloyne Byler, *Consultant*
Association on American Indian Affairs
New York, New York

Kenneth L. Chambers, *Asst. Professor*
Black Studies Department
Wellesley College
Wellesley, Massachusetts

Barbara Z. Chasen
Instructional Support Team
Boston Public Schools
Boston, Massachusetts

Paula Grier, *Education Consultant*
Intercultural Development Research Association
San Antonio, Texas

Nicolás Kanellos, *Editor*
Revista Chicano-Riqueña
University of Houston
Houston, Texas

Ann Rayson, *Asst. Professor*
Department of English
University of Hawaii at Manou
Honolulu, Hawaii

Ginn and Company

Acknowledgments

Grateful acknowledgment is made to the following publishers, authors, and agents for permission to use and adapt copyrighted materials:

Atheneum Publishers, Inc., for "The Long Way Around" by Jean McCord from *Deep Where the Octopi Lie,* which is reprinted by permission of Atheneum Publishers. Copyright © 1968 by Jean McCord.

Brandt & Brandt Literary Agents, Inc., for "All You've Ever Wanted" by Joan Aiken. From *Smoke from Cromwell's Time,* Doubleday & Co., Inc. Copyright 1959, 1966, 1970 by Joan Aiken. Reprinted by permission of Brandt & Brandt Literary Agents, Inc. Also for the poems "Nancy Hanks" and "Thomas Jefferson 1743–1826" by Rosemary & Stephen Vincent Benet. From *A Book of Americans* by Rosemary & Stephen Vincent Benet. Copyright, 1933 by Rosemary & Stephen Vincent Benet. Copyright renewed ©, 1961 by Rosemary Carr Benet. Reprinted by permission of Brandt & Brandt Literary Agents, Inc.

Curtis Brown, Ltd., New York, for "The Ugly Duckling" by A. A. Milne. Reprinted by permission of Curtis Brown, Ltd./New York City. Copyright © 1941 by A. A. Milne.

Coward, McCann & Geoghegan, Inc., for the poem "Desert Noon" by Elizabeth Coatsworth. Reprinted by permission of Coward, McCann & Geoghegan, Inc. from *Compass Rose* by Elizabeth Coatsworth. Copyright 1929 by Coward-McCann, Inc.; renewed © 1957 by Elizabeth Coatsworth.

Doubleday & Company, Inc., for "Four Years in a Shed" from *Madame Curie* by Eve Curie, translated by Vincent Sheean. Copyright 1937 by Eve Curie. Reprinted by permission of the publisher. Also for "The Ransom of Red Chief" copyright 1907 by Doubleday & Company, Inc. from *The Complete Works of O. Henry*. Reprinted by permission of the publisher. Also for "Roberto Clemente—A Bittersweet Memoir" from *Great Latin Sports Figures* by Jerry Izenberg. Copyright © 1976 by Jerry Izenberg. Reprinted by permission of Doubleday & Company, Inc. Also for "How I Learned to Speak" by Helen Keller from her book *The Story of My Life,* copyright 1902, 1903, 1905 by Helen Keller. Also for the poem "Aesop Revised By Archy" from *Archy and Mehitabel* by Don Marquis. Copyright 1927, 1930 by Doubleday & Company, Inc. Reprinted by permission of the publisher. Also for the poem "Highway: Michigan" copyright 1940 by Theodore Roethke from *The Collected Poems of Theodore Roethke*. Reprinted by permission of Doubleday & Company, Inc.

Farrar, Straus & Giroux, Inc., for "Battle in the Depths" from *Pride of Lions and Other Stories* by Paul Annixter. Copyright © 1960 by Hill and Wang, Inc. (a division of Farrar, Straus and Giroux, Inc.). Reprinted by permission of Farrar, Straus & Giroux, Inc.

Greenbaum, Wolff & Ernst for the excerpt based upon *A Peculiar Treasure* by Edna Ferber. Copyright 1938, 1939 by Edna Ferber. Copyright © 1960 by Morris L. Ernst, et al Trustees. Copyright © Renewed 1966 by Edna Ferber. All Rights Reserved. Reprinted by permission.

Grosset & Dunlap, Inc., for "That Legendary Ride" from *Duke Kahanamoku's World of Surfing* by Duke Kahanamoku. Copyright © 1968 by Duke Kahanamoku. Used by permission of Grosset & Dunlap, Inc.

Harcourt Brace Jovanovich, Inc., for "Paul Bunyan of the North Woods" from *The People, Yes* by Carl Sandburg, copyright, 1936, by Harcourt Brace Jovanovich, Inc.; renewed, 1964, by Carl Sandburg. Reprinted by permission of the publishers. Also for the poem "To Look at Any Thing" by John Moffitt. © 1961 by John Moffitt. Reprinted from his volume *The Living Seed* by permission of Harcourt Brace Jovanovich, Inc. Also for the poem "Fog" from *Chicago Poems* by Carl Sandburg, copyright 1916 by Holt, Rinehart and Winston, Inc.; copyright 1944 by Carl Sandburg. Reprinted by permission of Harcourt Brace Jovanovich, Inc.

Harper & Row, Publishers, Inc., for "The Revolt of 'Mother'" from *A New England Nun and Other Stories* by Mary E. Wilkins Freeman, Harper & Row. Also for "A Measure of Freedom" abridged from pp. 121–132 in *Fifth Chinese Daughter* by Jade Snow Wong. Copyright 1950 by Jade Snow Wong. Also for the poem "Zuni Prayer" in *The Epic of the American Indian,* Rev. Ed. by D'Arcy McNickle (J. B. Lippincott). Copyright © 1949, 1975 by D'Arcy McNickle. Also for the poem "Carriers of the Dream Wheel" from *The Gourd Dancer* by N. Scott Momaday. Copyright © 1976 by N. Scott Momaday. Also for the poem "The Highwayman" from *Collected Poems* by Alfred Noyes (J. B. Lippincott). Copyright 1906, 1934 by Alfred Noyes. Also for the poem "Fifteen" from *Stories That Could Be True* by William Stafford. Copyright © 1964 by William Stafford. All used by permission of Harper & Row, Publishers, Inc.

Holt, Rinehart and Winston for "A Wild Strain" from *Great River* by Paul Horgan. Copyright 1954 by Paul Horgan. Reprinted by permission of Holt, Rinehart and Winston, Publishers. Also for "Going to Run All Night" from *All Your Idols* by Harry Sylvester. Copyright 1948 by Harry Sylvester. Reprinted by permission of Holt, Rinehart and Winston, Publishers. Also for the poem "A Time to Talk" from *The Poetry of Robert Frost* edited by Edward Connery Lathem. Copyright 1916, © 1969 by Holt, Rinehart and Winston. Copyright 1944 by Robert Frost. Reprinted by permission of Holt, Rinehart and Winston, Publishers.

Acknowledgments continue on page 655.

©Copyright, 1981, by Ginn and Company (Xerox Corporation)
All Rights Reserved
Home Office: Lexington, Massachusetts 02173

0–663–37139–2

Table of Contents

3 Plot

7 Nonfiction Narrative

8 The Novel

Exploring Literature

Encounters

ENCOUNTERS

Encounter—the word rings of romance, danger, and excitement. An encounter means something important is happening. Perhaps it is meeting someone who will change your life, or maybe it is attempting to do something terrifying like climbing a hazardous mountain or conquering a great fear. An encounter is coming face to face with someone or something. It is an experience that often leaves you different in some way.

   This unit is all about encounters—encounters of many different kinds. One story, for instance, tells about an encounter between a boy and a herd of wild horses. There is also a suspenseful encounter between a plantation owner and miles upon miles of killer ants.

   Much of literature, of course, is based on encounters. As you read this unit, you will discover how different writers take an encounter and transform it into a story or poem for you to enjoy.

A horde of soldier ants—ten miles long and two miles wide—is moving toward Leiningen's plantation. Having already defeated drought, flood, and plague, he surely can outwit these little insects, or can he?

Leiningen versus the Ants

CARL STEPHENSON

"UNLESS THEY ALTER their course and there's no reason why they should, they'll reach your plantation in two days at the latest."

Leiningen sucked placidly at a cigar about the size of a corn cob and for a few seconds gazed, without answering, at the agitated District Commissioner. Then he took the cigar from his lips, and leaned slightly forward. With his bristling gray hair, bulky nose, and lucid eyes, he had the look of an aging and shabby eagle.

"Decent of you," he murmured, "paddling all this way just to give me the tip. But you're pulling my leg, of course, when you say I must do a bunk. Why, even a herd of saurians[1] couldn't drive me from this plantation of mine."

The Brazilian official threw up lean and lanky arms and clawed the air with wildly distended fingers. "Leiningen!" he shouted. "You're insane! They're not creatures you can fight—they're an elemental—an 'act of God!' Ten miles long, two miles wide—ants, nothing but ants! And every single one of them a fiend from hell; before you can spit three times they'll eat a full-grown buffalo to the bones. I tell you if you don't clear out at once, there'll be nothing left of you but a skeleton picked as clean as your plantation."

Leiningen grinned. "Act of God, my eye! Anyway, I'm not going to run for it just because an elemental's on the way. And don't think I'm the kind of fathead who tries to fend off lightning with his fists, either. I use my intelligence, old man. With me, the brain isn't a second blind gut; I know what it's there for. When I began this model farm and plantation three years ago, I took into account all that could conceivably happen to it. And now I'm ready for anything and everything—including your ants."

The Brazilian rose heavily to his feet. "I've done my best," he gasped. "Your obstinacy endangers not only yourself, but the lives of your four hundred workers. You don't know these ants!"

Leiningen accompanied him down to the river, where the government launch was

---

1 **saurians** (sôr′ē ənz): lizards and lizardlike extinct forms such as dinosaurs.

moored. The vessel cast off. As it moved downstream, the exclamation mark neared the rail and began waving its arms frantically. Long after the launch had disappeared round the bend, Leiningen thought he could still hear that dimming, imploring voice. *"You don't know them, I tell you! You don't know them!"*

But the reported enemy was by no means unfamiliar to the planter. Before he started work on his settlement, he had lived long enough in the country to see for himself the fearful devastations sometimes wrought by these ravenous insects in their campaigns for food. But since then he had planned measures of defense accordingly, and these, he was convinced, were in every way adequate to withstand the approaching peril.

Moreover, during his three years as a planter, Leiningen had met and defeated drought, flood, plague, and all other "acts of God" which had come against him—unlike his fellow-settlers in the district, who had made little or no resistance. This unbroken success he attributed solely to the observance of his lifelong motto: *The human brain needs only to become fully aware of its powers to conquer even the elements.* Dullards reeled senselessly and aimlessly into the abyss; cranks, however brilliant, lost their heads when circumstances suddenly altered or accelerated and ran into stone walls; sluggards drifted with the current until they were caught in whirlpools and dragged under. But such disasters, Leiningen contended, merely strengthened his argument that intelligence, directed aright, invariably makes man the master of his fate.

Yes, Leiningen had always known how to grapple with life. Even here, in this Brazilian wilderness, his brain had triumphed over every difficulty and danger it had so far encountered. First he had vanquished primal forces by cunning and organization. Then he had enlisted the resources of modern science to increase miraculously the yield of his plantation. And now he was sure he would prove more than a match for the "irresistible" ants.

That same evening, however, Leiningen assembled his workers. He had no intention of waiting till the news reached their ears from other sources. Most of them had been born in the district; the cry "The ants are coming!" was to them an imperative signal for instant, panic-stricken flight, a spring for life itself. But so great was the Indians' trust in Leiningen, in Leiningen's word, and in Leiningen's wisdom, that they received his curt tidings, and his orders for the imminent struggle, with the calmness with which they were given. They waited, unafraid, alert, as if for the beginning of a new game or hunt which he had just described to them. The ants were indeed mighty, but not so mighty as the boss. Let them come!

They came at noon the second day. Their approach was announced by the wild unrest of the horses, scarcely controllable now either in stall or under rider, scenting from afar a vapor instinct with horror.

It was announced by a stampede of animals, timid and savage, hurtling past each other; jaguars and pumas flashing by nimble stags of the pampas, bulky tapirs, no longer hunters, themselves hunted, outpacing fleet kinkajous, maddened herds of cattle, heads lowered, nostrils snorting, rushing through tribes of loping monkeys, chattering in a dementia of terror; then followed the creeping and springing denizens of bush and steppe, big and little rodents, snakes, and lizards.

Pell-mell the rabble swarmed down the hill to the plantation, scattered right and left before the barrier of the water-filled ditch, then sped onwards to the river, where, again hindered, they fled along its banks out of sight.

This water-filled ditch was one of the defense measures which Leiningen had long since prepared against the advent of the ants. It encompassed three sides of the plantation like a huge horseshoe. Twelve feet across, but not very deep, when dry it could hardly be described as an obstacle to either man or beast. But the ends of the "horseshoe" ran into the river which formed the northern boundary, and fourth side, of the plantation. And at the end nearer the house and outbuildings in the middle of the plantation, Leiningen had constructed a dam by means of which water from the river could be diverted into the ditch.

So now, by opening the dam, he was able to fling an imposing girdle of water, a huge quadrilateral with the river as its base, completely around the plantation, like the moat encircling a medieval city. Unless the ants were clever enough to build rafts, they had no hope of reaching the plantation, Leiningen concluded.

The 12-foot water ditch seemed to afford in itself all the security needed. But while awaiting the arrival of the ants, Leiningen made a further improvement. The western section of the ditch ran along the edge of a tamarind wood, and the branches of some great trees reached over the water. Leiningen now had them lopped so that ants could not descend from them within the "moat."

The women and children, then the herds of cattle, were escorted by peons[2] on rafts over the river, to remain on the other side in absolute safety until the plunderers had departed. Leiningen gave this instruction, not because he believed the noncombatants were in any danger, but in order to avoid hampering the efficiency of the defenders.

Finally, he made a careful inspection of the "inner moat"—a smaller ditch lined with concrete, which extended around the hill on which stood the ranchhouse, barns, stables, and other buildings. Into this concrete ditch emptied the inflow pipes from three great petrol tanks. If by some miracle the ants managed to cross the water and reach the plantation, this "rampart of petrol" would be an absolutely impassable protection for the besieged and their dwellings and stock. Such, at least, was Leiningen's opinion.

He stationed his men at irregular distances along the water ditch, the first line of defense. Then he lay down in his hammock and puffed drowsily away at his pipe until a peon came with the report that the ants had been observed far away in the south.

---

2 **peons:** laborers.

Leiningen mounted his horse, which at the feel of his master seemed to forget its uneasiness, and rode leisurely in the direction of the threatening offensive. The southern stretch of ditch—the upper side of the quadrilateral—was nearly three miles long; from its center one could survey the entire countryside. This was destined to be the scene of the outbreak of war between Leiningen's brain and 20 square miles of life-destroying ants.

It was a sight one could never forget. Over the range of hills, as far as eye could see, crept a darkening hem, ever longer and broader, until the shadow spread across the slope from east to west, then downward, downward, uncannily swift, and all the green herbage of that wide vista was being mown as if by a giant sickle, leaving only the vast moving shadow, extending, deepening, and moving rapidly nearer.

When Leiningen's men, behind their barrier of water, perceived the approach of the long-expected foe, they gave vent to their suspense in screams and imprecations. But as the distance began to lessen between the "sons of hell" and the water ditch, they relapsed into silence. Before the advance of that awe-inspiring throng, their belief in the powers of the boss began to steadily dwindle.

Even Leiningen himself, who had ridden up just in time to restore their loss of heart by a display of unshakable calm, even he could not free himself from a qualm of malaise.[3] Yonder were thousands of millions of voracious jaws bearing down upon him, and only a suddenly insignificant, narrow ditch lay between him and his men and being gnawed to the bones "before you can spit three times."

---

3 **qualm of malaise:** a little discomfort.

Hadn't his brain for once taken on more than it could manage? If the blighters decided to rush the ditch, fill it to the brim with their corpses, there'd still be more than enough to destroy every trace of that cranium of his. The planter's chin jutted; they hadn't got him yet, and he'd see to it they never would. While he could think at all, he'd flout both death and the devil.

The hostile army was approaching in perfect formation; no human battalions, however well-drilled, could ever hope to rival the precision of that advance. Along a front that moved forward as uniformly as a straight line, the ants drew nearer and nearer to the water ditch. Then, when they learned through their scouts the nature of the obstacle, the two outlying wings of the army detached themselves from the main body and marched down the western and eastern sides of the ditch.

This surrounding maneuver took rather more than an hour to accomplish; no doubt the ants expected that at some point they would find a crossing.

During this outflanking movement by the wings, the army on the center and southern fronts remained still. The besieged were therefore able to contemplate at their leisure the thumb-long, reddish-black, long-legged insects; some of the Indians believed they could see, too, intent on them, the brilliant, cold eyes, and the razor-edged mandibles,[4] of this host of infinity.

It is not easy for the average person to imagine that an animal, not to mention an insect, can *think*. But now both Leiningen and the Indians began to stir with the unpleasant foreboding that inside every single

one of that deluge of insects dwelled a thought. And that thought was: Ditch or no ditch, we'll get to your flesh!

Not until four o'clock did the wings reach the "horseshoe" ends of the ditch, only to find these ran into the great river. Through some kind of secret telegraphy, the report must then have flashed very swiftly indeed along the entire enemy line. And Leiningen, riding—no longer casually—along his side of the ditch, noticed by energetic and widespread movements of troops that for some unknown reason the news of the check had its greatest effect on the southern front, where the main army was massed. Perhaps the failure to find a way over the ditch was persuading the ants to withdraw from the plantation in search of spoils more easily obtainable.

An immense flood of ants, about a hundred yards in width, was pouring in a glimmering black cataract down the far slope of the ditch. Many thousands were already drowning in the sluggish creeping flow, but they were followed by troop after troop, who clambered over their sinking comrades, and then themselves served as dying bridges to the reserves hurrying on in their rear.

Shoals of ants were being carried away by the current into the middle of the ditch, where gradually they broke asunder and then, exhausted by their struggles, vanished below the surface. Nevertheless, the wavering, floundering hundred-yard front was remorselessly if slowly advancing toward the besieged on the other bank. Leiningen had been wrong when he supposed the enemy would first have to fill the ditch with their bodies before they could cross; instead, they merely needed to act as stepping-stones, as they swam and sank, to the hordes ever pressing onward from behind.

---

4 mandibles: jaws.

10

Near Leiningen a few mounted herdsmen awaited his orders. He sent one to the weir[5]—the river must be dammed more strongly to increase the speed and power of the water coursing through the ditch.

A second peon was dispatched to the outhouses to bring spades and petrol sprinklers. A third rode away to summon to the zone of the offensive all the men, except the observation posts, on the nearby sections of the ditch, which were not yet actively threatened.

The ants were getting across far more quickly than Leiningen would have deemed possible. Impelled by the mighty cascade behind them, they struggled nearer and nearer to the inner bank. The momentum of the attack was so great that neither the tardy flow of the stream nor its downward pull could exert its proper force; and into the gap left by every submerging insect hastened forward a dozen more.

When reinforcements reached Leiningen, the invaders were halfway over. The planter had to admit to himself that it was only by a stroke of luck for him that the ants were attempting the crossing on a relatively short front: had they assaulted simultaneously along the entire length of the ditch, the outlook for the defenders would have been black indeed.

Even as it was, it could hardly be described as rosy, though the planter seemed quite unaware that death in a gruesome form was drawing closer and closer. As the war between his brain and the "act of God" reached its climax, the very shadow of annihilation began to pale to Leiningen, who now felt like a champion in a new Olympic game, a gigantic and thrilling contest, from which he

was determined to emerge victor. Such, indeed, was his aura of confidence that the Indians forgot their stupefied fear of the peril only a yard or two away; under the planter's supervision, they began fervidly digging up to the edge of the bank and throwing clods of earth and spadesful of sand into the midst of the hostile fleet.

The petrol sprinklers, hitherto used to destroy pests and blights on the plantation, were also brought into action. Streams of evil-reeking oil now soared and fell over an enemy already in disorder through the bombardment of earth and sand.

The ants responded to these vigorous and successful measures of defense by further developments of their offensive. Entire clumps of huddling insects began to roll down the opposite bank into the water. At the same time, Leiningen noticed that the ants were now attacking along an ever widening front. As the numbers both of his men and his petrol sprinklers were severely limited, this rapid extension of the line of battle was becoming an overwhelming danger.

To add to his difficulties, the very clods of earth they flung into that black floating carpet often whirled fragments toward the defenders' side, and here and there dark ribbons were already mounting the inner bank. True, wherever a man saw these, they could still be driven back into the water by spadesful of earth or jets of petrol. But the file of defenders was too sparse and scattered to hold off at all points these landing parties, and though the peons toiled like madmen, their plight became momentarily more perilous.

One man struck with his spade at an enemy clump, did not draw it back quickly enough from the water; in a trice the wooden haft swarmed with upward-scurrying insects. With a curse, he dropped the spade into the

---

5 **weir** (wir): a dam used to raise or lower the level of water.

ditch; too late, they were already on his body. They lost no time; wherever they encountered bare flesh, they bit deeply; a few, bigger than the rest, carried in their hindquarters a sting which injected a burning and paralyzing venom. Screaming, frantic with pain, the peon danced and twirled like a dervish.

Realizing that another such casualty, yes, perhaps this alone, might plunge his men into confusion and destroy their morale, Leiningen roared in a bellow louder than the yells of the victim: "Into the petrol, idiot! Douse your paws in the petrol!" The dervish ceased his pirouette as if transfixed, then tore off his shirt and plunged his arm and the ants hanging to it up to the shoulder in one of the large open tins of petrol. But even then the fierce mandibles did not slacken; another peon had to help him squash and detach each separate insect.

Distracted by the episode, some defenders had turned away from the ditch. And now cries of fury, a thudding of spades, and a wild trampling to and fro, showed that the ants had made full use of the interval, though luckily only a few had managed to get across. The men set to work again desperately with the barrage of earth and sand. Meanwhile an old Indian, who acted as medicine man to the plantation workers, gave the bitten peon a drink he had prepared some hours before, which, he claimed, possessed the virtue of dissolving and weakening ants' venom.

Leiningen surveyed his position. A dispassionate observer would have estimated the odds against him at a thousand to one. But then such an onlooker would have reckoned only by what he saw—the advance of myriad battalions of ants against the futile efforts of a few defenders—and not by the unseen activity that can go on in a man's brain.

For Leiningen had not erred when he decided he would fight elemental with elemental. The water in the ditch was beginning to rise; the stronger damming of the river was making itself apparent.

Visibly the swiftness and power of the masses of water increased, swirling into quicker and quicker movement its living black surface, dispersing its pattern, carrying away more and more of it on the hastening current.

Victory had been snatched from the very jaws of defeat. With a hysterical shout of joy, the peons feverishly intensified their bombardment of earth clods and sand.

And now the wide cataract down the opposite bank was thinning and ceasing, as if the ants were becoming aware that they could not attain their aim. They were scurrying back up the slope to safety.

All the troops so far hurled into the ditch had been sacrificed in vain. Drowned and floundering insects eddied in thousands along the flow, while Indians running on the bank destroyed every swimmer that reached the side.

Not until the ditch curved toward the east did the scattered ranks assemble again in a coherent mass. And now, exhausted and half-numbed, they were in no condition to ascend the bank. Fusillades of clods drove them round the bend toward the mouth of the ditch and then into the river, wherein they vanished without leaving a trace.

The news ran swiftly along the entire chain of outposts, and soon a long scattered line of laughing men could be seen hastening along the ditch toward the scene of victory.

For once they seemed to have lost all their native reserve, for it was in wild abandon now they celebrated the triumph—as if there were no longer thousands of millions of merciless, cold, and hungry eyes watching them from the opposite bank, watching and waiting.

The sun sank behind the rim of the tamarind wood and twilight deepened into night. It was not only hoped but expected that the ants would remain quiet until dawn. But to defeat any forlorn attempt at a crossing, the flow of water through the ditch was powerfully increased by opening the dam still further.

In spite of this impregnable barrier, Leiningen was not yet altogether convinced that the ants would not venture another surprise attack. He ordered his men to camp along the bank overnight. He also detailed parties of them to patrol the ditch in two of his motor cars and ceaselessly to illuminate the surface of the water with headlights and electric torches.

After having taken all the precautions he deemed necessary, the farmer ate his supper with considerable appetite and went to bed. His slumbers were in no wise disturbed by the memory of the waiting, live, 20 square miles.

Dawn found a thoroughly refreshed and active Leiningen riding along the edge of the ditch. The planter saw before him a motionless and unaltered throng of besiegers. He studied the wide belt of water between them and the plantation, and for a moment almost regretted that the fight had ended so soon and so simply. In the comforting, matter-of-fact light of morning, it seemed to him now that the ants hadn't the ghost of a chance to cross the ditch. Even if they plunged headlong into it on all three fronts at once, the force of the now powerful current would inevitably sweep them away. He had got quite a thrill out of the fight—a pity it was already over.

He rode along the eastern and southern sections of the ditch and found everything in order. He reached the western section, opposite the tamarind wood, and here, contrary to the other battlefronts, he found the enemy very busy indeed. The trunks and branches of the trees and the creepers of the lianas, on the far bank of the ditch, fairly swarmed with industrious insects. But instead of eating the leaves there and then, they were merely gnawing through the stalks, so that a thick green shower fell steadily to the ground.

No doubt they were victualing columns sent out to obtain provender[6] for the rest of the army. The discovery did not surprise

---

6 **provender** (prov'ən dər): food.

Leiningen. He did not need to be told that ants are intelligent, that certain species even use others as milch cows, watchdogs, and slaves. He was well aware of their power of adaptation, their sense of discipline, their marvelous talent for organization.

His belief that a foray[7] to supply the army was in progress was strengthened when he saw the leaves that fell to the ground being dragged to the troops waiting outside the wood. Then all at once he realized the aim that rain of green was intended to serve.

Each single leaf, pulled or pushed by dozens of toiling insects, was borne straight to the edge of the ditch. Even as Macbeth watched the approach of Birnam Wood in the hands of his enemies, Leiningen saw the tamarind wood move nearer and nearer in the mandibles of the ants. Unlike the fey Scot, however, he did not lose his nerve; no witches had prophesied his doom, and if they had, he would have slept just as soundly.[8] All the same, he was forced to admit to himself

that the situation was now far more ominous than that of the day before.

He had thought it impossible for the ants to build rafts for themselves—well, here they were, coming in thousands, more than enough to bridge the ditch. Leaves after leaves rustled down the slope into the water, where the current drew them away from the bank and carried them into midstream. And every single leaf carried several ants. This time the farmer did not trust to the alacrity of his messengers. He galloped away, leaning from his saddle and yelling orders as he rushed past outpost after outpost: "Bring petrol pumps to the southwest front! Issue spades to every man along the line facing the wood!" And arriving at the eastern and southern sections, he dispatched every man except the observation posts to the menaced west.

Then, as he rode past the stretch where the ants had failed to cross the day before, he witnessed a brief but impressive scene. Down the slope of the distant hill there came toward him a singular being, writhing rather than running, an animallike, blackened statue with a shapeless head and four quivering

---

7 **foray** (fôr′ā): raid.
8 "**Even as Macbeth . . . as soundly**": In Shakespeare's play *Macbeth,* the king's castle was attacked by soldiers disguised with branches and trees.

feet that knuckled under almost ceaselessly. When the creature reached the far bank of the ditch and collapsed opposite Leiningen, he recognized it as a pampas stag, covered over and over with ants.

It had strayed near the zone of the army. As usual, they had attacked its eyes first. Blinded, it had reeled in the madness of hideous torment straight into the ranks of its persecutors, and now the beast swayed to and fro in its death agony.

With a shot from his rifle Leiningen put it out of its misery. Then he pulled out his watch. He hadn't a second to lose, but for life itself he could not have denied his curiosity that satisfaction of knowing how long the ants would take—for personal reasons, so to speak. After six minutes the white polished bones alone remained. That's how he himself would look before you can—. Leiningen spat once, and put spurs to his horse.

The sporting zest with which the excitement of the novel contest had inspired him the day before had now vanished; in its place was a cold and violent purpose. He would send those vermin back to where they belonged, somehow, anyhow. Yes, but *how* was indeed the question; as things stood at present, it looked as if the devils would raze him and his men from the earth instead. He had underestimated the might of the enemy; he really would have to bestir himself if he hoped to outwit them.

The biggest danger now, he decided, was the point where the western section of the ditch curved southward. And arriving there, he found his worst expectations justified. The very power of the current had huddled the leaves and their crews of ants so close together at the bend that the bridge was almost ready.

True, streams of petrol and clumps of earth still prevented a landing. But the number of floating leaves was increasing ever more swiftly. It could not be long now before a stretch of water a mile in length was decked by a green pontoon over which the ants could rush in millions.

Leiningen galloped to the weir. The damming of the river was controlled by a wheel on its bank. The planter ordered the man at the wheel first to lower the water in the ditch almost to vanishing point, next to wait a moment, then suddenly to let the river in again. This maneuver of lowering and raising the surface, of decreasing then increasing the flow of water through the ditch, was to be repeated over and over again until further notice.

This tactic was at first successful. The water in the ditch sank, and with it the film of leaves. The green fleet nearly reached the bed and the troops on the far bank swarmed down the slope to it. Then a violent flow of water at the original depth raced through the ditch, overwhelming leaves and ants, and sweeping them along.

This intermittent rapid flushing prevented just in time the almost completed fording of the ditch. But it also flung here and there squads of the enemy vanguard simultaneously up the inner bank. These seemed to know their duty only too well, and lost no time accomplishing it. The air rang with the curses of bitten Indians. They had removed their shirts and pants to detect the quicker upward-hastening insects; when they saw one, they crushed it; and fortunately the onslaught as yet was only by skirmishers.

Again and again, the water sank and rose, carrying leaves and drowned ants away with it. It lowered once more nearly to its bed; but this time the exhausted defenders waited in vain for the flush of destruction. Leiningen sensed disaster; something must have gone wrong with the machinery of the dam. Then a sweating peon tore up to him—

"They're over!"

While the besieged were concentrating upon the defense of the stretch opposite the wood, the seemingly unaffected line beyond the wood had become the theater of decisive action. Here the defenders' front was sparse and scattered; everyone who could be spared had hurried away to the south.

Just as the man at the weir had lowered the water almost to the bed of the ditch, the ants on a wide front began another attempt at a direct crossing like that of the preceding day. Into the emptied bed poured an irresistible throng. Rushing and swarming across the ditch, they attained the inner bank before the Indians fully grasped the situation. Their frantic screams dumbfounded the man at the weir. Before he could direct the river anew into the safeguarding bed, he saw himself surrounded by raging ants. He ran like the others, ran for his life.

When Leiningen heard this, he knew the plantation was doomed. He wasted no time bemoaning the inevitable. For as long as there was the slightest chance of success, he had stood his ground, and now any further resistance was both useless and dangerous. He fired three revolver shots into the air—the prearranged signal for his men to retreat instantly within the "inner moat." Then he rode toward the ranchhouse.

This was two miles from the point of invasion. There was therefore time enough to prepare the second line of defense against the advent of the ants. Of the three great petrol cisterns near the house, one had already been half emptied by the constant withdrawals needed for the pumps during the fight at the

water ditch. The remaining petrol in it was now drawn off through underground pipes into the concrete trench which encircled the ranchhouse and its outbuildings.

And there, drifting in twos and threes, Leiningen's men reached him. Most of them were obviously trying to preserve an air of calm and indifference, belied, however, by their restless glances and knitted brows. One could see their belief in a favorable outcome of the struggle was already considerably shaken.

The planter called his peons around him.

"Well, lads," he began, "we've lost the first round. But we'll smash the beggars yet, don't you worry. Anyone who thinks otherwise can draw his pay here and now and push off. There are rafts enough to spare on the river, and plenty of time still to reach 'em."

Not a man stirred.

Leiningen acknowledged his silent vote of confidence with a laugh that was half a grunt. "That's the stuff, lads. Too bad if you'd missed the rest of the show, eh? Well, the fun won't start till morning. Once these blighters turn tail, there'll be plenty of work for everyone and higher wages all round. And now run along and get something to eat; you've earned it all right."

In the excitement of the fight the greater part of the day had passed without the men once pausing to snatch a bite. Now that the ants were for the time being out of sight, and the "wall of petrol" gave a stronger feeling of security, hungry stomachs began to assert their claims.

The bridges over the concrete ditch were removed. Here and there solitary ants had reached the ditch; they gazed at the petrol meditatively, then scurried back again. Apparently they had little interest at the moment for what lay beyond the evil-reeking barrier; the abundant spoils of the plantation were the main attraction. Soon the trees, shrubs, and beds for miles around were hulled with ants zealously gobbling the yield of long weary months of strenuous toil.

As twilight began to fall, a cordon of ants marched around the petrol trench, but as yet made no move toward its brink. Leiningen posted sentries with headlights and electric torches, then withdrew to his office, and began to reckon up his losses. He estimated these as large but, in comparison with his bank balance, by no means unbearable. He worked out in some detail a scheme of intense cultivation which would enable him, before very long, to more than compensate himself for the damage now being wrought to his crops. It was with a contented mind that he finally betook himself to bed where he slept deeply until dawn, undisturbed by any thought that next day little more might be left of him than a glistening skeleton.

He rose with the sun and went out on the flat roof of his house. And a scene like one from Dante[9] lay around him; for miles in every direction there was nothing but a black, glittering multitude, a multitude of rested, sated, but nonetheless voracious ants: yes, look as far as one might, one could see nothing but that rustling black throng, except in the north, where the great river drew a boundary they could not hope to pass. But even the high stone breakwater, along the bank of the river, which Leiningen had built as a defense against inundations, was, like the paths, the shorn trees and shrubs, the ground itself, black with ants.

So their greed was not glutted in razing that vast plantation? Not by a long shot; they were all the more eager now on a rich and certain booty—four hundred men, numerous horses, and bursting granaries.

At first it seemed that the petrol trench would serve its purpose. The besiegers sensed the peril of swimming it, and made no move to plunge blindly over its brink. Instead they devised a better maneuver; they began to collect shreds of bark, twigs and dried leaves and dropped these into the petrol. Everything green, which could have been similarly used, had long since been eaten. After a time, though, a long procession could be seen bringing from the west the tamarind leaves used as rafts the day before.

Since the petrol, unlike the water in the outer ditch, was perfectly still, the refuse stayed where it was thrown. It was several hours before the ants succeeded in covering an appreciable part of the surface. At length, however, they were ready to proceed to a direct attack.

Their storm troops swarmed down the concrete side, scrambled over the supporting surface of twigs and leaves, and impelled these over the few remaining streaks of open petrol until they reached the other side. Then they began to climb up this to make straight for the helpless garrison.

During the entire offensive, the planter sat peacefully, watching them with interest, but not stirring a muscle. Moreover, he had ordered his men not to disturb in any way whatever the advancing horde. So they squatted listlessly along the bank of the ditch and waited for a sign from the boss.

The petrol was now covered with ants. A few had climbed the inner concrete wall and were scurrying toward the defenders.

"Everyone back from the ditch!" roared Leiningen. The men rushed away, without the slightest idea of his plan. He stooped

---

9 **Dante** (dän' tā): a 14th century Italian poet who wrote horrifying descriptions of hell.

forward and cautiously dropped into the ditch a stone which split the floating carpet and its living freight, to reveal a gleaming patch of petrol. A match spurted, sank down to the oily surface—Leiningen sprang back; in a flash a towering rampart of fire encompassed the garrison.

This spectacular and instant repulse threw the Indians into ecstasy. They applauded, yelled, and stamped, like children at a pantomime. Had it not been for the awe in which they held the boss, they would infallibly have carried him shoulder high.

It was some time before the petrol burned down to the bed of the ditch, and the wall of smoke and flame began to lower. The ants had retreated in a wide circle from the devastation, and innumerable charred fragments along the outer bank showed that the flames had spread from the holocaust in the ditch well into the ranks beyond, where they had wrought havoc far and wide.

Yet the perseverance of the ants was by no means broken; indeed, each setback seemed only to whet it. The concrete cooled, the flicker of the dying flames wavered and vanished, petrol from the second tank poured into the trench—and the ants marched forward anew to the attack.

The foregoing scene repeated itself in every detail, except that on this occasion less time was needed to bridge the ditch, for the petrol was now already filmed by a layer of ash. Once again they withdrew; once again petrol flowed into the ditch. Would the creatures never learn that their self-sacrifice was utterly senseless? It really was senseless, wasn't it? Yes, of course it was senseless—provided the defenders had an *unlimited* supply of petrol.

When Leiningen reached this stage of reasoning, he felt for the first time since the arrival of the ants that his confidence was deserting him. His skin began to creep; he loosened his collar. Once the devils were over the trench, there wasn't a chance for him and his men. What a prospect, to be eaten alive like that!

For the third time the flames immolated the attacking troops and burned down to extinction. Yet the ants were coming on again as if nothing had happened. And meanwhile Leiningen had made a discovery that chilled him to the bone—petrol was no longer flowing into the ditch. Something must be blocking the outflow pipe of the third and last cistern—a snake or a dead rat? Whatever it was, the ants could be held off no longer, unless petrol could by some method be led from the cistern into the ditch.

Then Leiningen remembered that in an outhouse nearby were two old disused fire engines. Spry as never before in their lives, the peons dragged them out of the shed, connected their pumps to the cistern, uncoiled and laid the hose. They were just in time to aim a stream of petrol at a column of ants that had already crossed and drive them back down the incline into the ditch. Once more an oily girdle surrounded the garrison, once more it was possible to hold the position—for the moment.

It was obvious, however, that this last resource meant only the postponement of defeat and death. A few of the peons fell on their knees and began to pray; others, shrieking insanely, fired their revolvers at the black, advancing masses, as if they felt their despair was pitiful enough to sway fate itself to mercy.

At length, two of the men's nerves broke: Leiningen saw a naked Indian leap over the north side of the petrol trench, quickly followed by a second. They sprinted with incredible speed toward the river. But their fleetness did not save them; long before they could attain the rafts, the enemy covered their bodies from head to foot.

In the agony of their torment, both sprang blindly into the wide river, where enemies no less sinister awaited them. Wild screams of mortal anguish informed the breathless onlookers that crocodiles and sword-tooth piranhas were no less ravenous than ants, and even nimbler in reaching their prey.

In spite of this bloody warning, more and more men showed they were making up their minds to run the blockade. Anything, even a fight midstream against alligators, seemed better than powerlessly waiting for death to come and slowly consume their living bodies.

Leiningen flogged his brain till it reeled. Was there nothing on earth that could sweep this devils' spawn back into the hell from which it came?

Then out of the inferno of his bewilderment rose a terrifying inspiration. Yes, one hope remained, and one alone. It might be possible to dam the great river completely, so that its waters would fill not only the water ditch but overflow into the entire gigantic "saucer" of land in which lay the plantation.

The far bank of the river was too high for the waters to escape that way. The stone breakwater ran between the river and the plantation; its only gaps occurred where the "horseshoe" ends of the water ditch passed into the river. So its waters would not only be forced to inundate the plantation, they would also be held there by the breakwater until they rose to its own high level. In half an hour, perhaps even earlier, the plantation and its hostile army of occupation would be flooded.

The ranchhouse and outbuildings stood upon rising ground. Their foundations were higher than the breakwater, so the flood would not reach them. And any remaining ants trying to ascend the slope could be repulsed by petrol.

It was possible—yes, if one could only get to the dam! A distance of nearly two miles lay between the ranchhouse and the weir—two miles of ants. Those two peons had managed only a fifth of that distance at the cost of their lives. Was there an Indian daring enough after that to run the gauntlet five times as far? Hardly likely; and if there were, his prospect of getting back was almost nil.

No, there was only one thing for it, he'd have to make the attempt himself; he might just as well be running as sitting still, anyway, when the ants finally got him. Besides, there *was* a bit of a chance. Perhaps the ants weren't so almighty, after all; perhaps he had allowed the mass suggestion of that evil black throng to hypnotize him, just as a snake fascinates and overpowers.

The ants were building their bridges. Leiningen got up on a chair. "Hey, lads, listen to me!" he cried. Slowly and listlessly, from all sides of the trench, the men began to shuffle toward him, the apathy of death already stamped on their faces.

"Listen, lads!" he shouted. "You're frightened of those beggars, but you're more frightened of me, and I'm proud of you. There's still a chance to save our lives—by flooding the plantation from the river. Now one of you might manage to get as far as the weir—but he'd never come back. Well, I'm not going to let you try it; if I did, I'd be worse than one of those ants. No, I called the tune, and now I'm going to pay the piper.

"The moment I'm over the ditch, set fire to the petrol. That'll allow time for the flood to do the trick. Then all you have to do is wait here all snug and quiet till I'm back. Yes, I'm coming back, trust me"—he grinned—"when I've finished my slimming-cure."

He pulled on high leather boots, drew heavy gauntlets over his hands, and stuffed the spaces between breeches and boots, gauntlets and arms, shirt and neck, with rags soaked in petrol. With close-fitting mosquito goggles he shielded his eyes, knowing too well the ants' dodge of first robbing their victim of sight. Finally, he plugged his nostrils and ears with cottonwool, and let the peons drench his clothes with petrol.

He was about to set off, when the old Indian medicine man came up to him; he had a wondrous salve, he said, prepared from a species of chafer[10] whose odor was intolerable to ants. Yes, this odor protected these chafers from the attacks of even the most murderous ants. The Indian smeared the boss's boots, his gauntlets, and his face over and over with the extract.

Leiningen then remembered the paralyzing effect of ants' venom, and the Indian gave him a gourd full of the medicine he had administered to the bitten peon at the water ditch. The planter drank it down without noticing its bitter taste; his mind was already at the weir.

---

10 chafer: a large beetle.

He started off toward the northwest corner of the trench. With a bound he was over—and among the ants.

The beleaguered garrison had no opportunity to watch Leiningen's race against death. The ants were climbing the inner bank again—the lurid ring of petrol blazed aloft. For the fourth time that day the reflection from the fire shone on the sweating faces of the imprisoned men, and on the reddish-black cuirasses[11] of their oppressors. The red and blue, dark-edged flames leaped vividly now, celebrating what? The funeral pyre of the four hundred, or of the hosts of destruction?

Leiningen ran. He ran in long, equal strides, with only one thought, one sensation, in his being—he *must* get through. He dodged all trees and shrubs; except for the split seconds his soles touched the ground, the ants should have no opportunity to alight on him. That they would get to him soon, despite the salve on his boots, the petrol on his clothes, he realized only too well, but he knew even more surely that he must, and that he would, get to the weir.

Apparently the salve was some use after all; not until he had reached halfway did he feel ants under his clothes, and a few on his face. Mechanically, in his stride, he struck at them, scarcely conscious of their bites. He saw he was drawing appreciably near the weir— the distance grew less and less—sank to five hundred—three—two—one hundred yards.

Then he was at the weir and gripping the ant-hulled wheel. Hardly had he seized it when a horde of infuriated ants flowed over his hands, arms, and shoulders. He started the wheel—before it turned once on its axis, the

swarm covered his face. Leiningen strained like a madman, his lips pressed tight; if he opened them to draw breath. . . .

He turned and turned; slowly the dam lowered until it reached the bed of the river. Already the water was overflowing the ditch. Another minute, and the river was pouring water through the nearby gap in the breakwater. The flooding of the plantation had begun.

Leiningen let go of the wheel. Now, for the first time, he realized he was coated from head to foot with a layer of ants. In spite of the petrol, his clothes were full of them, several had got to his body and were clinging to his face. Now that he had completed his task, he felt the smart raging over his flesh from the bites of sawing and piercing insects.

Frantic with pain, he almost plunged into the river. To be ripped and slashed to shreds by the piranhas? Already he was running the return journey, knocking ants from his gloves and jacket, brushing them from his bloodied face, squashing them to death under his clothes.

One of the creatures bit him just below the rim of his goggles; he managed to tear it away, but the agony of the bite and its itching acid drilled into the eye nerves; he saw now through circles of fire into a milky mist, then he ran for a time almost blinded, knowing that if he once tripped and fell. . . . The old Indian's brew didn't seem much good; it weakened the poison a bit, but didn't get rid of it. His heart pounded as if it would burst; blood roared in his ears; a giant's fist battered his lungs.

Then he could see again, but the burning girdle of petrol appeared infinitely far away; he could not last half that distance. Swift-changing pictures flashed through his head, episodes in his life, while in another part of

---

11 **cuirasses** (kwi ras′ əz): bony structures protecting ants' bodies.

his brain a cool and impartial onlooker informed this ant-blurred, gasping, exhausted bundle named Leiningen that such a rushing panorama of scenes from one's past is seen only in the moment before death.

A stone in the path . . . too weak to avoid it . . . the planter stumbled and collapsed. He tried to rise . . . he must be pinned under a rock. . . . It was impossible . . . the slightest movement was impossible. . . .

Then all at once he saw, starkly clear and huge, and, right before his eyes, furred with ants, towering and swaying in its death agony, the pampas stag. In six minutes—gnawed to the bones. He *couldn't* die like that! And something outside him seemed to drag him to his feet. He tottered. He began to stagger forward again.

Through the blazing ring hurtled an apparition which, as soon as it reached the ground on the inner side, fell full length and did not move. Leiningen, at the moment he made that leap through the flames, lost consciousness for the first time in his life. As he lay there, with glazing eyes and lacerated face, he appeared a man returned from the grave. The peons rushed to him, stripped off his clothes, tore away the ants from a body that seemed almost one open wound; in some places the bones were showing. They carried him into the ranchhouse.

As the curtain of flames lowered, one could see in place of the illimitable host of ants an extensive vista of water. The thwarted river had swept over the plantation, carrying with it the entire army. The water had collected and mounted in the great "saucer," while the ants had in vain attempted to reach the hill on which stood the ranchhouse. The girdle of flames held them back.

And so, imprisoned between water and fire, they had been delivered into the annihilation that was their god. And near the farther mouth of the water ditch, where the stone mole[12] had its second gap, the ocean swept the lost battalions into the river, to vanish forever.

The ring of fire dwindled as the water mounted to the petrol trench and quenched the dimming flames. The inundation rose higher and higher: because its outflow was impeded by the timber and underbrush it had carried along with it, its surface required some time to reach the top of the high stone breakwater and discharge over it the rest of the shattered army.

It swelled over ant-stippled shrubs and bushes, until it washed against the foot of the knoll whereon the besieged had taken refuge. For a while an alluvium of ants tried again and again to attain this dry land, only to be repulsed by streams of petrol back into the merciless flood.

Leiningen lay on his bed, his body swathed from head to foot in bandages. With fomentations[13] and salves, they had managed to stop the bleeding, and had dressed his many wounds. Now they thronged around him, one question in every face. Would he recover? "He won't die," said the old man who had bandaged him, "if he doesn't want to."

The planter opened his eyes. "Everything in order?" he asked.

"They're gone," said his nurse. He held out to his master a gourd full of a powerful sleeping draught. Leiningen gulped it down.

"I told you I'd come back," he murmured, "even if I am a bit streamlined." He grinned and shut his eyes. He slept.

---

12 **mole:** a stone structure used as protection against waves.
13 **fomentations:** hot medicines.

Discussion	1. What defenses do Leiningen and his men construct to fight the attack of the ants?
	2. What counterstrategies do the ants use to overcome Leiningen's defenses?
	3. What is Leiningen's final solution for destroying the ants? Is this plan necessary?
	4. What does Leiningen do to prepare himself for his run to the dam? What one thing aids him most in his final effort to return to the safety of the main house?
	5. As it turns out, Leiningen only saves the buildings and his men. How would the result have been different if Leiningen had followed the advice of the District Commissioner to evacuate the plantation?
	6. What words would you choose to characterize Leiningen: arrogant? stubborn? foolhardy? heroic? intelligent? Explain your choices.
	7. In what way might a person with less self-pride than Leiningen face the encounter with the ants? Remember that modern machinery, insecticides, and aircraft were unavailable to the plantation.
Composition	1. Retell what happened in the story "Leiningen versus the Ants" as though you were writing for someone who had not read the story. Tell the events in the same order that the story does, but you should include only enough information to make clear what happened. To keep your retelling brief, you do not need to include dialogue or describe setting and characters in any detail.
	2. Leiningen is a man—both good and bad—who performs a heroic deed. He kills the ants at the risk of his own life. Yet, he also risked the lives of others. Pretend you are the District Commissioner. You know all the facts of Leiningen's actions against the ants. Write him either a letter of praise for his heroism or a letter of reprimand. Explain why you agree or disagree with his actions.
Vocabulary	A SYNONYM is a word that means the same, or nearly the same, as another word. For example, *big* is a synonym for *large*, and *doctor* is a synonym for *physician*.

On a separate sheet of paper, copy all the *italicized* words from the sentences below. Then write a synonym for each word from the list below. If you need help, use a dictionary.

greedy   pit
floods   calmly
destruction   required
jaws   thin
grass   countless

EXAMPLE: The Brazilian official threw up lean
          and *lanky* arms and clawed the air.
ANSWER: lanky—thin

1. Leiningen sucked *placidly* at a cigar and for a few seconds gazed without answering.
2. He had lived long enough in the country to see for himself the devastation wrought by these *ravenous* insects in their campaigns for food.
3. Dullards reeled senselessly and aimlessly into the *abyss*.
4. All the green *herbage* of that wide vista was being mowed as by a giant sickle.
5. As the war between his brain and the "act of God" reached its climax, the very shadow of *annihilation* began to pale to Leiningen.
6. An onlooker would have reckoned only by what he saw—the advance of *myriad* battalions of ants against the futile efforts of a few defenders.
7. The high stone breakwater, along the bank of the river, which Leiningen had built as a defense against *inundations,* was black with ants.
8. He tore off his shirt and plunged his arm and the ants hanging to it into one of the large open tins of petrol. But even then the fierce *mandibles* did not slacken; another peon had to help him squash and detach each separate insect.

Who is special in your life? Who has helped you and, perhaps, even changed your life? For Maya Angelou, one of those special people was almost a stranger.

from I Know Why the Caged Bird Sings

MAYA ANGELOU

WHEN I WAS THREE and Bailey four, we had arrived in the musty little town, wearing tags on our wrists which instructed—"To Whom It May Concern"—that we were Marguerite and Bailey Johnson, Jr., from Long Beach, California, en route to Stamps, Arkansas, c/o Mrs. Annie Henderson.

Our parents had decided to put an end to their calamitous marriage, and Father shipped us home to his mother. A porter had been charged with our welfare—he got off the train the next day in Arizona—and our tickets were pinned to my brother's inside coat pocket.

I don't remember much of the trip, but after we reached the segregated southern part of the journey, things must have looked up. Negro passengers, who always traveled with loaded lunch boxes, felt sorry for "the poor little motherless darlings" and plied us with cold fried chicken and potato salad.

Years later I discovered that the United States had been crossed thousands of times by frightened Black children traveling alone to their newly affluent parents in Northern cities, or back to grandmothers in Southern towns when the urban North reneged on its economic promises.

The town reacted to us as its inhabitants had reacted to all things new before our coming. It regarded us a while without curiosity but with caution, and after we were seen to be harmless (and children) it closed in around us, as a real mother embraces a stranger's child. Warmly, but not too familiarly.

We lived with our grandmother and uncle in the rear of the Store (it was always spoken of with a capital *s*), which she had owned some twenty-five years.

Early in the century, Momma (we soon stopped calling her Grandmother) sold lunches to the sawmen in the lumberyard (east Stamps) and the seedmen at the cotton gin (west Stamps). Her crisp meat pies and cool lemonade, when joined to her miraculous ability to be in two places at the same time, assured her business success. From being a mobile lunch counter, she set up a stand between the two points of fiscal interest and supplied the workers' needs for a few years. Then she had the Store built in the heart of the Negro area. Over the years it became the lay center of activities in town. On Saturdays, barbers sat their customers in the shade on the porch of the Store, and troubadours on their ceaseless crawlings through the South leaned across their benches and sang their sad songs of The Brazos while they played juice harps and cigar-box guitars.

The formal name of the Store was the Wm. Johnson General Merchandise Store. Customers could find food staples, a good variety of colored thread, mash for hogs, corn for chickens, coal oil for lamps, light bulbs for the wealthy, shoestrings, hair dressing, balloons, and flower seeds. Anything not visible had only to be ordered.

Until we became familiar enough to belong to the Store and it to us, we were locked up in a Fun House of Things where the attendant had gone home for life.

Each year I watched the field across from the Store turn caterpillar green, then gradually frosty white. I knew exactly how long it would be before the big wagons would pull into the front yard and load on the cotton pickers at daybreak to carry them to the remains of slavery's plantations.

During the picking season my grandmother would get out of bed at four o'clock (she never used an alarm clock) and creak down to her knees and chant in a sleep-filled

voice, "Our Father, thank you for letting me see this New Day. Thank you that you didn't allow the bed I lay on last night to be my cooling board, nor my blanket my winding sheet. Guide my feet this day along the straight and narrow, and help me to put a bridle on my tongue. Bless this house, and everybody in it. Thank you, in the name of your Son, Jesus Christ, Amen."

Before she had quite arisen, she called our names and issued orders, and pushed her large feet into homemade slippers and across the bare lye-washed wooden floor to light the coal-oil lamp.

The lamplight in the Store gave a soft make-believe feeling to our world which made me want to whisper and walk about on tiptoe. The odors of onions and oranges and kerosene had been mixing all night and wouldn't be disturbed until the wooded slat was removed from the door and the early morning air forced its way in with the bodies of people who had walked miles to reach the pickup place.

"Sister, I'll have two cans of sardines."

"I'm gonna work so fast today I'm gonna make you look like you standing still."

"Lemme have a hunk uh cheese and some sody crackers."

"Just gimme a coupla them fat peanut paddies." That would be from a picker who was taking his lunch. The greasy brown paper sack was stuck behind the bib of his overalls. He'd use the candy as a snack before the noon sun called the workers to rest.

In those tender mornings the Store was full of laughing, joking, boasting and bragging. One man was going to pick two hundred pounds of cotton, and another three hundred. Even the children were promising to bring home fo' bits and six bits.

The champion picker of the day before was the hero of the dawn. If he prophesied that the cotton in today's field was going to be sparse and stick to the bolls like glue, every listener would grunt a hearty agreement.

The sound of the empty cotton sacks dragging over the floor and the murmurs of waking people were sliced by the cash register as we rang up the five-cent sales.

If the morning sounds and smells were touched with the supernatural, the late afternoon had all the features of the normal Arkansas life. In the dying sunlight the people dragged, rather than carried their empty cotton sacks.

Brought back to the Store, the pickers would step out of the backs of trucks and fold down, dirt-disappointed, to the ground. No matter how much they had picked, it wasn't enough. Their wages wouldn't even get them out of debt to my grandmother, not to mention the staggering bill that waited on them at the white commissary downtown.

The sounds of the new morning had been replaced with grumbles about cheating houses, weighted scales, snakes, skimpy cotton and dusty rows. In later years I was to confront the stereotyped picture of gay song-singing cotton pickers with such inordinate rage that I was told even by fellow Blacks that my paranoia[1] was embarrassing. But I had seen the fingers cut by the mean little cotton bolls, and I had witnessed the backs and shoulders and arms and legs resisting any further demands.

Some of the workers would leave their sacks at the Store to be picked up the following morning, but a few had to take them home for repairs. I winced to picture them sewing the coarse material under a coal-oil

---

1 **paranoia** (par' ə noi' ə): a feeling of being persecuted or punished.

lamp with fingers stiffening from the day's work. In too few hours they would have to walk back to Sister Henderson's Store, get vittles and load, again, onto the trucks. Then they would face another day of trying to earn enough for the whole year with the heavy knowledge that they were going to end the season as they started it: without the money or credit necessary to sustain a family for three months. In cotton-picking time the late afternoons revealed the harshness of Black Southern life, which in the early morning had been softened by nature's blessing of grogginess, forgetfulness and the soft lamp-light. . . .

Weighing the half-pounds of flour, excluding the scoop, and depositing them dust-free into the thin paper sacks held a simple kind of adventure for me. I developed an eye for measuring how full a silver-looking ladle of flour, mash, meal, sugar or corn had to be to push the scale indicator over to eight ounces or one pound. When I was absolutely accurate, our appreciative customers used to admire: "Sister Henderson sure got some smart grandchildrens." If I was off in the Store's favor, the eagle-eyed women would say, "Put some more in that sack, child. Don't you try to make your profit offa me."

Then I would quietly but persistently punish myself. For every bad judgment, the fine was no silver-wrapped Kisses, the sweet chocolate drops that I loved more than anything in the world, except Bailey. And maybe canned pineapples. My obsession with pineapples nearly drove me mad. I dreamt of the days when I would be grown and able to buy a whole carton for myself alone.

Although the syrupy golden rings sat in their exotic cans on our shelves year round, we only tasted them during Christmas. Momma used the juice to make almost-black fruit cakes. Then she lined heavy soot-encrusted iron skillets with the pineapple rings for rich upside-down cakes. Bailey and I received one slice each, and I carried mine around for hours, shredding off the fruit until nothing was left except the perfume on my fingers. I'd like to think that my desire for pineapple was so sacred that I wouldn't allow myself to steal a can (which was possible) and eat it alone out in the garden, but I'm certain that I must have weighed the possibility of the scent exposing me and didn't have the nerve to attempt it.

Until I was thirteen and left Arkansas for good, the Store was my favorite place to be. Alone and empty in the mornings, it looked like an unopened present from a stranger. Opening the front doors was pulling the ribbon off the unexpected gift. The light would come in softly (we faced north), easing itself over the shelves of mackerel, salmon, tobacco, thread. It fell flat on the big vat of lard and by noontime during the summer, the grease had softened to a thick soup. Whenever I walked into the Store in the afternoon, I sensed that it was tired. I alone could hear the slow pulse of its job half done. But just before bedtime, after numerous people had walked in and out, and argued over their bills, or joked about their neighbors, or just dropped in "to give Sister Henderson a 'Hi y'all'," the promise of magic mornings returned to the Store and spread itself over the family in washed life waves.

Momma opened boxes of crispy crackers and we sat around the meat block at the rear of the Store. I sliced onions, and Bailey opened two or even three cans of sardines and allowed their juice of oil and fishing boats to ooze down and around the sides. That was supper. In the evening, when we were alone like that, Uncle Willie didn't stutter or shake or give any indication that he had an "affliction." It seemed that the peace of a day's ending was an assurance that the covenant God made with children, Negroes and the crippled was still in effect.

Throwing scoops of corn to the chickens and mixing sour dry mash with leftover food and oily dish water for the hogs were among our evening chores. Bailey and I sloshed down twilight trails to the pig pens, and standing on the first fence rungs we poured down the unappealing concoctions to our grateful hogs. They mashed their tender pink snouts down into the slop, and rooted and grunted their satisfaction. We always grunted a reply only half in jest. We were also grateful that we had concluded the dirtiest of chores and had only gotten the evil-smelling swill on our shoes, stockings, feet and hands. . . .

"Thou shall not be dirty" and "Thou shall not be impudent"[2] were the two commandments of Grandmother Henderson upon which hung our total salvation.

Each night in the bitterest winter we were forced to wash faces, arms, necks, legs and feet before going to bed. She used to add, with a smirk that unprofane people can't control when venturing into profanity, "and wash as far as possible, then wash possible."

We would go to the well and wash in the ice-cold clear water, grease our legs with the equally cold stiff Vaseline, then tiptoe into the house. We wiped the dust from our toes and settled down for schoolwork, cornbread, clabbered milk, prayers and bed, always in that order. Momma was famous for pulling the quilts off after we had fallen asleep to examine our feet. If they weren't clean enough for her, she took the switch (she kept

one behind the bedroom door for emergencies) and woke up the offender with a few aptly placed burning reminders.

The area around the well at night was dark and slick, and boys told about how snakes love water, so that anyone who had to draw water at night and then stand there alone and wash knew that moccasins and rattlers, puff adders and boa constrictors were winding their way to the well and would arrive just as the person washing got soap in her eyes. But Momma convinced us that not only was cleanliness next to Godliness, dirtiness was the inventor of misery.

The impudent child was detested by God and a shame to its parents and could bring destruction to its house and line. All adults had to be addressed as Mister, Missus, Miss, Auntie, Cousin, Unk, Uncle, Buhbah, Sister, Brother and a thousand other appellations indicating familial relationships and the lowliness of the addressor. . . .

[Bailey and Marguerite went to live with their Mother in St. Louis. But after a brief time they returned to Stamps, Arkansas.]

For nearly a year, I sopped around the house, the Store, the school and the church, like an old biscuit, dirty and inedible. Then I met, or rather got to know, the lady who threw me my first lifeline.

Mrs. Bertha Flowers was the aristocrat of Black Stamps. She had the grace of control to appear warm in the coldest weather, and on the Arkansas summer days it seemed she had a private breeze which swirled around, cooling her. She was thin without the taut look of wiry people, and her printed voile dresses and flowered hats were as right for her as denim overalls for a farmer. She was our side's answer to the richest white woman in town.

Her skin was a rich black that would have peeled like a plum if snagged, but then no one

---

2 **impudent:** smart-alecky.

Momma had a strange relationship with her. Most often when she passed on the road in front of the Store, she spoke to Momma in that soft yet carrying voice, "Good day, Mrs. Henderson." Momma responded with "How you, Sister Flowers?"

Mrs. Flowers didn't belong to our church, nor was she Momma's familiar. Why on earth did she insist on calling her Sister Flowers? Shame made me want to hide my face. Mrs. Flowers deserved better than to be called Sister. Then, Momma left out the verb. Why not ask, "How *are* you, *Mrs.* Flowers?" With the unbalanced passion of the young, I hated her for showing her ignorance to Mrs. Flowers. It didn't occur to me for many years that they were as alike as sisters, separated only by formal education. . . .

She appealed to me because she was like people I had never met personally. Like women in English novels who walked the moors[3] (whatever they were) with their loyal dogs racing at a respectful distance. Like the women who sat in front of roaring fireplaces, drinking tea incessantly from silver trays full of scones and crumpets. Women who walked over the "heath" and read morocco-bound books and had two last names divided by a hyphen. It would be safe to say that she made me proud to be Negro, just by being herself.

She acted just as refined as white folks in the movies and books and she was more beautiful, for none of them could have come near that warm color without looking gray by comparison.

It was fortunate that I never saw her in the company of powhitefolks. For since they tend to think of their whiteness as an evenizer, I'm certain that I would have had to hear her

would have thought of getting close enough to Mrs. Flowers to ruffle her dress, let alone snag her skin. She didn't encourage familiarity. She wore gloves too.

I don't think I ever saw Mrs. Flowers laugh, but she smiled often. A low widening of her thin black lips to show even, small white teeth, then the slow effortless closing. When she chose to smile on me, I always wanted to thank her. The action was so graceful and inclusively benign.

She was one of the few gentlewomen I have ever known, and has remained throughout my life the measure of what a human being can be.

---

3 **moors**: a broad area of open, sometimes swampy, land.

spoken to commonly as Bertha, and my image of her would have been shattered like the unmendable Humpty-Dumpty.

One summer afternoon, sweet-milk fresh in my memory, she stopped at the Store to buy provisions. Another Negro woman of her health and age would have been expected to carry the paper sacks home in one hand, but Momma said, "Sister Flowers, I'll send Bailey up to your house with these things."

She smiled that slow dragging smile, "Thank you, Mrs. Henderson. I'd prefer Marguerite, though." My name was beautiful when she said it. "I've been meaning to talk to her, anyway." They gave each other age-group looks.

Momma said, "Well, that's all right then. Sister, go and change your dress. You going to Sister Flowers's."

The chifforobe[4] was a maze. What on earth did one put on to go to Mrs. Flowers' house? I knew I shouldn't put on a Sunday dress. It might be sacrilegious. Certainly not a housedress, since I was already wearing a fresh one. I chose a school dress, naturally. It was formal without suggesting that going to Mrs. Flowers' house was equivalent to attending church.

I trusted myself back into the Store.

"Now, don't you look nice." I had chosen the right thing, for once.

"Mrs. Henderson, you make most of the childen's clothes, don't you?"

"Yes, ma'am. Sure do. Store-bought clothes ain't hardly worth the thread it take to stitch them."

"I'll say you do a lovely job, though, so neat. That dress looks professional."

Momma was enjoying the seldom received

compliments. Since everyone we knew (except Mrs. Flowers, of course) could sew competently, praise was rarely handed out for the commonly practiced craft.

"I try, with the help of the Lord, Sister Flowers, to finish the inside just like I does the outside. Come here, Sister."

I had buttoned up the collar and tied the belt, apron-like, in back. Momma told me to turn around. With one hand she pulled the strings and the belt fell free at both sides of my waist. Then her large hands were at my neck, opening the button loops. I was terrified. What was happening?

"Take it off, Sister." She had her hands on the hem of the dress.

"I don't need to see the inside, Mrs. Henderson, I can tell. . . ." But the dress was over my head and my arms were stuck in the sleeves. Momma said, "That'll do. See here, Sister Flowers, I French-seams around the armholes." Through the cloth film, I saw the shadow approach. "That makes it last longer. Children these days would bust out of sheet-metal clothes. They so rough."

"That is a very good job, Mrs. Henderson. You should be proud. You can put your dress back on, Marguerite."

"No, ma'am. Pride is a sin. And 'cording to the Good Book, it goeth before a fall."

"That's right. So the Bible says. It's a good thing to keep in mind."

I wouldn't look at either of them. Momma hadn't thought that taking off my dress in front of Mrs. Flowers would kill me stone dead. If I had refused, she would have thought I was trying to be "woman-ish." . . . Mrs. Flowers had known that I would be embarrassed and that was even worse. I picked up the groceries and went out to wait in the hot sunshine. It would be fitting if I got a sunstroke and died before

---

4 **chifforobe:** a cabinet to store clothes.

they came outside. Just dropped dead on the slanting porch.

There was a little path beside the rocky road, and Mrs. Flowers walked in front swinging her arms and picking her way over the stones.

She said, without turning her head, to me, "I hear you're doing very good schoolwork, Marguerite, but that it's all written. The teachers report that they have trouble getting you to talk in class." We passed the triangular farm on our left and the path widened to allow us to walk together. I hung back in the unasked and unanswerable questions.

"Come and walk along with me, Marguerite." I couldn't have refused even if I wanted to. She pronounced my name so nicely. Or more correctly, she spoke each word with such clarity that I was certain a foreigner who didn't understand English could have understood her.

"Now no one is going to make you talk—possibly no one can. But bear in mind, language is man's way of communicating with his fellow man and it is language alone which separates him from the lower animals." That was a totally new idea to me, and I would need time to think about it.

"Your grandmother says you read a lot. Every chance you get. That's good, but not good enough. Words mean more than what is set down on paper. It takes the human voice to infuse them with the shades of deeper meaning."

I memorized the part about the human voice infusing words. It seemed so valid and poetic.

She said she was going to give me some books and that I not only must read them, I must read them aloud. She suggested that I try to make a sentence sound in as many different ways as possible.

"I'll accept no excuse if you return a book to me that has been badly handled." My imagination boggled at the punishment I would deserve if, in fact, I did abuse a book of Mrs. Flowers'. Death would be too kind and brief.

The odors in the house surprised me. Somehow I had never connected Mrs. Flowers with food or eating or any other common experience of common people. There must have been an outhouse, too, but my mind never recorded it.

The sweet scent of vanilla had met us as she opened the door.

"I made tea cookies this morning. You see, I had planned to invite you for cookies and lemonade so we could have this little chat. The lemonade is in the icebox."

It followed that Mrs. Flowers would have ice on an ordinary day, when most families in our town bought ice late on Saturdays only a few times during the summer to be used in the wooden ice-cream freezers.

She took the bags from me and disappeared through the kitchen door. I looked around the room that I had never in my wildest fantasies imagined I would see. Browned photographs leered or threatened from the walls and the white, freshly done curtains pushed against themselves and against the wind. I wanted to gobble up the entire room and take it to Bailey, who would help me analyze and enjoy it.

"Have a seat, Marguerite. Over there by the table." She carried a platter covered with a tea towel. Although she warned that she hadn't tried her hand at baking sweets for some time, I was certain that like everything else about her the cookies would be perfect.

They were flat round wafers, slightly browned on the edges and butter-yellow in the center. With the cold lemonade they were sufficient for childhood's lifelong diet. Remembering my manners, I took nice little lady-like bites off the edges. She said she had made them expressly for me and that she had a few in the kitchen that I could take home to my brother. So I jammed one whole cake in my mouth and the rough crumbs scratched the insides of my jaws, and if I hadn't had to swallow, it would have been a dream come true.

As I ate she began the first of what we later called "my lessons in living." She said that I must always be intolerant of ignorance but understanding of illiteracy. That some people, unable to go to school, were more educated and even more intelligent than college professors. She encouraged me to listen carefully to what country people called mother wit. That in those homely sayings was couched the collective wisdom of generations.

When I finished the cookies, she brushed off the table and brought a thick, small book from the bookcase. I had read *A Tale of Two Cities* and found it up to my standards as a romantic novel. She opened the first page and I heard poetry for the first time in my life.

"It was the best of times and the worst of times . . ." Her voice slid in and curved down through and over the words. She was nearly singing. I wanted to look at the pages. Were they the same that I had read? Or were there notes, music, lined on the pages, as in a hymn book? Her sounds began cascading gently. I knew from listening to a thousand preachers that she was nearing the end of her reading, and I hadn't really heard, heard to understand, a single word.

"How do you like that?"

It occurred to me that she expected a response. The sweet vanilla flavor was still on my tongue and her reading was a wonder in my ears. I had to speak.

I said, "Yes, ma'am." It was the least I could do, but it was the most also.

"There's one more thing. Take this book of poems and memorize one for me. Next time you pay me a visit, I want you to recite."

I have tried often to search behind the sophistication of years for the enchantment I so easily found in those gifts. The essence escapes but its aura remains. To be allowed, no, invited, into the private lives of strangers, and to share their joys and fears, was a chance to exchange the Southern bitter wormwood for a cup of mead with Beowulf or a hot cup of tea and milk with Oliver Twist. When I said aloud, "It is a far, far better thing that I do, than I have ever done . . ." tears of love filled my eyes at my selflessness.

On that first day, I ran down the hill and into the road (few cars ever came along it) and had the good sense to stop running before I reached the Store.

I was liked, and what a difference it made. I was respected not as Mrs. Henderson's grandchild or Bailey's sister but for just being Marguerite Johnson.

Discussion

1. Describe how Marguerite and Bailey are treated on their train ride to Stamps.

2. The author gets angry at people who picture cotton pickers as

from *I Know Why the Caged Bird Sings* 33

carefree, "song-singing" people. Describe the Black cotton pickers she saw as a child.

3. Marguerite says that the Store is her favorite place to be. What phrases does she use to express its special qualities?

4. Grandmother Henderson tries to raise Marguerite and Bailey to be good children. What are the values she teaches them? How does she make sure they learn these lessons?

5. Marguerite's encounter with Mrs. Bertha Flowers affects her greatly. What does she teach Marguerite that her grandmother does not?

Composition

1. Mrs. Bertha Flowers and Grandmother Henderson were both positive influences on Marguerite's life. Discuss the main differences and the main similarities between the two women. Be sure when you show a characteristic in one person, that you compare it with a similar or different characteristic in the other person.

2. In this story Marguerite describes the Store by comparing it to a surprise package. In another place she describes it as if it were a tired person. Write about a favorite place of yours. Use as many specific details as you can. You also might want to compare your place to some person or object. Use similes or metaphors to make your comparisons.

Vocabulary

When you are reading and come to an unfamiliar word, try to figure out its meaning by using CONTEXT CLUES. They are hints about the meaning of an unknown word that are given by familiar words surrounding it. For example, the word *calamitous* may be unfamiliar to you, but look at the context clues which are given in the sentence below from *I Know Why the Caged Bird Sings:*

"Our parents had decided to put an end to their calamitous marriage, and Father shipped us home to his mother."

If this marriage had been a good and happy one, would the parents have decided to put an end to it? Obviously, the answer is "no." Therefore, the marriage must have been the opposite of "good and happy." Since *calamitous* describes the marriage, this word must mean something like "bad and unhappy."

When you look up *calamitous* in a dictionary, you find that it means "disastrous," or "very unfortunate." That means you were definitely on the right track by defining *calamitous* as "bad and unhappy." For a specific definition, you must rely on a dictionary. But when a general definition will do, context clues—plus a little reasoning on your part—can be very helpful.

On a separate sheet of paper, practice using context clues by writing general meanings for the *italicized* words in the following sentences.

1. If he *prophesied* that the cotton in today's field was going to be sparse and stick to the bolls like glue, every listener would grunt a hearty agreement.

2. Momma said, "Sister, go and change your dress. You going to Sister Flowers's." The *chifforobe* was a maze. What on earth did one put on to go to Mrs. Flowers' house?

3. All adults had to be addressed as Mister, Missus, Miss, Auntie, Cousin, Unk, Uncle, Buhbah, Sister, Brother and a thousand other *appellations*.

4. Negro passengers, who always traveled with loaded lunch boxes, felt sorry for "the poor little motherless darlings" and *plied* us with cold fried chicken and potato salad.

5. *Troubadours* on their ceaseless crawlings through the South leaned across the benches and sang their sad songs while they played juice harps and cigar-box guitars.

Maya Angelou 1928—

Although she was born in America, Maya Angelou considers herself a West African. She was editor of the *African Review* in Ghana and the *Arab Observer* in Egypt. She also lectured extensively in both countries. In addition to being a writer, she is also a singer, dancer, songwriter, conductor, and film director. Angelou's well-known works include her poetry collection, *Just Give Me a Cool Drink of Water 'fore I Diiie;* her autobiography, *I Know Why the Caged Bird Sings;* and her play, *The Clawing Within.* She contends that everyone must encounter defeats, but never be defeated. Speaking about her own experiences, she once said, "One would say of my life—born loser—had to be. I wanted to show that it is a fact, but it is not the truth. . . . In the Black community, however bad it looks, there is a lot of love and so much humor. I wanted to remind Blacks, but once I started writing, I saw it was not just for Black girls, but for young Jewish boys and old Chinese women."

from *I Know Why the Caged Bird Sings*

A Blessing

JAMES WRIGHT

Just off the highway to Rochester, Minnesota,
Twilight bounds softly forth on the grass.
And the eyes of those two Indian ponies
Darken with kindness.
They have come gladly out of the willows   5
To welcome my friend and me.
We step over the barbed wire into the pasture
Where they have been grazing all day, alone.
They ripple tensely, they can hardly contain their happiness
That we have come.   10
They bow shyly as wet swans. They love each other.
There is no loneliness like theirs.
At home once more,

They begin munching the young tufts of spring in the darkness.
I would like to hold the slender one in my arms,   15
For she has walked over to me
And nuzzled my left hand.
She is black and white,
Her mane falls wild on her forehead,
And the light breeze moves me to caress her long ear   20
That is delicate as the skin over a girl's wrist.
Suddenly I realize
That if I stepped out of my body I would break
Into blossom.

Discussion

1. What happens in this poem?

2. Find as many words or phrases in this poem as you can that suggest joy or love.

3. In the last lines of this poem, the narrator says, "That if I stepped out of my body, I would break/Into blossom." What does this line mean in relation to the experience he just had with the ponies?

4. What do you think the title of this poem means?

Vocabulary

An ADVERB is a word used to tell how, when, where, and how much. In the following phrases, each *italicized* word is an adverb:

worked *fast* (how)   looked *around* (where)
leave *immediately* (when)   *very* pleased (how much)

A. In each phrase below, find the adverb and copy it on a separate sheet of paper. Then write a synonym—a word that means almost the same—for each one.

EXAMPLE: walks softly
ANSWER: softly — quietly

1. have come gladly

2. ripple tensely

3. can hardly contain

4. bow shyly

5. mane falls wild

B. The following phrases from "A Blessing" do not contain adverbs. On the same paper, copy each phrase below and add an adverb to it. Then write a synonym for the adverb you chose.

EXAMPLE: twilight comes
ANSWER: twilight comes rapidly — swiftly ·

1. darken with kindness
2. begin munching
3. hold the slender one
4. nuzzled my left hand
5. I realize

James Wright 1927—1980

James Wright was a teacher, lecturer, and poet. His awards include: a Fulbright fellowship, the Bluementhal Award from *Poetry* magazine, and a Pulitzer Prize. He has published several volumes of poetry including: *The Green Wall, Collected Poems,* and *The Branch Will Not Break,* which contains "A Blessing." Commenting on his poetry, Wright once said, "I have written about the things I am deeply concerned with—crickets outside my window, cold and hungry old men, ghosts in the twilight, horses in a field, a red-haired child in her mother's arms, a feeling of desolation in the fall, some cities I've known."

Snakes terrified her. Then why was she on a rattlesnake hunt? Marjorie Rawlings knew this encounter could have fatal results.

Rattlesnake Hunt

MARJORIE KINNAN RAWLINGS

ROSS ALLEN, a young Florida herpetologist,[1] invited me to join him on a hunt in the upper Everglades[2]—for rattlesnakes.

The hunting ground was Big Prairie, south of Arcadia and west of the northern tip of Lake Okeechobee. Big Prairie is a desolate cattle country, half marsh, half pasture, with islands of palm trees and cypresses and oaks. At that time of year the cattlemen and Indians were burning the country, on the theory that the young fresh wire grass that springs up from the roots after a fire is the best cattle forage.[3] Ross planned to hunt his rattlers in the forefront of the fires. They lived in winter, he said, in gopher holes, coming out in the midday warmth to forage, and would move ahead of the flames and be easily taken. We joined forces with a big fellow named Will, his snake-hunting companion of the territory, and set out in early morning, after a long rough drive over deep-rutted roads into the open wilds.

I hope never in my life to be so frightened as I was in those first few hours. I kept on Ross's footsteps, I moved when he moved, sometimes jolting into him when I thought he might leave me behind. He does not use the forked stick of conventional snake hunting, but a steel prong, shaped like an L, at the end of a long stout stick. He hunted casually, calling my attention to the varying vegetation, to hawks overhead, to a pair of rare whooping cranes that flapped over us. In midmorning he stopped short, dropped his stick, and brought up a five-foot rattlesnake draped limply over the steel L. It seemed to me that I should drop in my tracks.

"They're not active at this season," he said quietly. "A snake takes on the temperature of its surroundings. They can't stand too much heat for that reason, and when the weather is cool, as now, they're sluggish."

The sun was bright overhead, the sky a translucent blue, and it seemed to me that it was warm enough for any snake to do as it willed. The sweat poured down my back. Ross dropped the rattler in a crocus sack[4] and Will carried it. By noon, he had caught four. I felt faint and ill. We stopped by a pond and went swimming. The region was flat, the

---

1 **herpetologist:** a person who studies snakes.
2 **Everglades:** a swampy area in southern Florida.
3 **forage** (fôr′ ij): food.

4 **crocus sack:** a large sack, usually made of burlap.

horizon limitless, and as I came out of the cool blue water, I expected to find myself surrounded by a ring of rattlers. There were only Ross and Will, opening the lunch basket. I could not eat. Will went back and drove his truck closer, for Ross expected the hunting to be better in the afternoon. The hunting was much better. When we went back to the truck to deposit two more rattlers into the wire cage, there was a rattlesnake lying under the truck.

Ross said, "Whenever I leave my car or truck with snakes already in it, other rattlers always appear. I don't know whether this is because they scent or sense the presence of other snakes, or whether in this arid area they come to the car for shade in the heat of the day."

The problem was scientific, but I had no interest.

That night Ross and Will and I camped out in the vast spaces of the Everglades' prairies. We got water from an abandoned well and cooked supper under buttonwood bushes by a flowing stream. The campfire blazed cheerfully under the stars and a new moon lifted in the sky. Will told tall tales of the cattlemen and the Indians and we were at peace.

Ross said, "We couldn't have a better night for catching water snakes."

After the rattlers, water snakes seemed innocuous[5] enough. We worked along the edge of the stream and here Ross did not use his L-shaped steel. He reached under rocks and along the edge of the water and brought out harmless reptiles with his hands. I had said nothing to him of my fears, but he understood them. He brought a small dark

snake from under a willow root.

"Wouldn't you like to hold it?" he asked. "People think snakes are cold and clammy, but they aren't. Take it in your hands. You'll see that it is warm."

Again, because I was ashamed, I took the snake in my hands. It was not cold, it was not clammy, and it lay trustingly in my hands, a thing that lived and breathed and had mortality like the rest of us. I felt an upsurgence of spirit.

The next day was magnificent. The air was crystal, the sky was aquamarine, and the far horizon of palms and oaks lay against the sky. I felt a new boldness and followed Ross bravely. He was making the rounds of the gopher holes. The rattlers came out in the midmorning warmth and were never far away. He could tell by their trails whether one had come out or was still in the hole. Sometimes the two men dug the snake out. At times it was down so long and winding a tunnel that the digging was hopeless. Then they blocked the entrance and went on to other holes. In an hour or so they made the original rounds, unblocking the holes. The rattler in every case came out hurriedly, as though anything was preferable to being shut in. All the time Ross talked to me, telling me the scientific facts he had discovered about the habits of the rattlers.

"They pay no attention to a man standing perfectly still," he said, and proved it by letting Will unblock a hole while he stood at the entrance as the snake came out. It was exciting to watch the snake crawl slowly beside and past the man's legs. When it was at a safe distance, he walked within its range of vision, which he had proved to be no higher than a man's knee, and the snake whirled and drew back in an attitude of fighting defense.

---

5 **innocuous** (i nok' yü əs): harmless.

The rattler strikes only for paralyzing and killing its food, and for defense.

"It is a slow and heavy snake," Ross said. "It lies in wait on a small game trail and strikes the rat or rabbit passing by. It waits a few minutes, then follows along the trail, coming to the small animal, now dead or dying. It noses it from all sides, making sure that it is its own kill, and that it is dead and ready for swallowing."

A rattler will lie quietly without revealing itself if a man passes by and it thinks it is not seen. It slips away without fighting if given the chance. Only Ross's sharp eyes sometimes picked out the gray and yellow diamond pattern, camouflaged among the grasses. In the cool of the morning, chilled by the January air, the snakes showed no fight. They could be looped up simply over the steel L and dropped in a sack or up into the wire

cage on the back of Will's truck. As the sun mounted in the sky and warmed the moist Everglades' earth, the snakes were warmed too, and Ross warned that it was time to go more cautiously. Yet having learned that it was we who were the aggressors; that immobility meant complete safety; that the snakes, for all their lightning flash in striking, were inaccurate in their aim, with limited vision; having watched again and again the liquid grace of movement, the beauty of pattern, suddenly I understood that I was drinking in freely the magnificent sweep of the horizon, with no fear of what might be at the moment under my feet. I went off hunting by myself, and though I found no snakes, I should have known what to do.

The sun was dropping low in the west. Masses of white clouds hung above the flat marshy plain and seemed to be tangled in the tops of distant palms and cypresses. The sky turned orange, then saffron. I walked leisurely back toward the truck. In the distance I could see Ross and Will making their way in too. The season was more advanced than at the Creek, two hundred miles to the north, and I noticed that spring flowers were blooming among the lumpy hummocks. I leaned over to pick a white violet. There was a rattlesnake under the violet.

If this had happened the week before, if it had happened the day before, I think I should have lain down and died on top of the rattlesnake, with no need of being struck and poisoned. The snake did not coil, but lifted its head and whirred its rattles lightly. I stepped back slowly and put the violet in a buttonhole. I reached forward and laid the steel L across the snake's neck, just back of the blunt head. I called to Ross: "I've got one."

He strolled toward me.

"Well, pick it up," he said.

I released it and slipped the L under the middle of the thick body.

"Go put it in the box."

He went ahead of me and lifted the top of the wire cage. I made the truck with the rattler, but when I reached up the six feet to drop it in the cage, it slipped off the stick and dropped on Ross's feet. It made no effort to strike.

"Pick it up again," he said. "If you'll pin it down lightly and reach just back of its head with your hand, as you've seen me do, you can drop it in more easily."

I pinned it and leaned over.

"I'm awfully sorry," I said, "but you're pushing me a little too fast."

He grinned. I lifted it on the stick and again as I had it at head height, it slipped off, down Ross's boots and on top of his feet. He stood as still as a stump. I dropped the snake on his feet for the third time. It seemed to me that the most patient of rattlers might in time resent being hauled up and down, and for all the man's quiet certainty that in standing motionless there was no danger, would strike at whatever was nearest, and that would be Ross.

I said, "I'm just not man enough to keep this up any longer," and he laughed and reached down with his smooth quickness and lifted the snake back of the head and dropped it in the cage. It slid in among its mates and settled in a corner. The hunt was over and we drove back over the uneven trail to Will's village and left him and went on to Arcadia and home. Our catch for the two days was thirty-two rattlers.

I said to Ross, "I believe that tomorrow I could have picked up that snake."

Back at the Creek, I felt a new lightness. I had done battle with a great fear, and the victory was mine.

1. How does the author feel and act on the first day of the snake hunt?
2. How does Ross act during the hunt?
3. On the first evening of the hunt, the author discovers something about snakes. What is the discovery? How does this make her feel?
4. What facts about snakes does she learn during her hunting experience? How does this knowledge help her overcome her fear of snakes?
5. At what point in the story does the author overcome her fear of snakes? What does she mean when she says, "I believe that tomorrow I could have picked up that snake."?
6. Compare the author's attitude toward snakes at the beginning of the story with her attitude at the end. What causes this change?

Composition

1. Write a letter to a friend who is afraid of snakes. Explain how Marjorie Rawlings conquered her fear, giving each step she went through. Try to be as understanding of your friend's fear as the men in the story were of Miss Rawlings's.
2. Write a personal account of how you or an imaginary character actually overcame a fear. First tell what that fear was. Then explain what it was like for you when you were afraid—what you did and how you felt. Also describe what stages you went through to overcome the fear. End by telling what you did to prove to yourself that you had finally conquered the fear.

Vocabulary

In "Rattlesnake Hunt," the author describes Big Prairie as "half marsh, half pasture, with islands of *palm* trees." Later the author speaks about holding a snake in the *palm* of her hand. The word *palm* has an entirely different meaning in those two sentences. Any word which has the same spelling and sound as another word—but has a different meaning—is called a MULTIPLE-MEANING WORD.

A. Following are five pairs of sentences. In each pair, one or more multiple-meaning words are in *italics*. On a separate sheet of paper, copy the *italicized* words, and write the meaning each word has in each sentence.

   1. a. A rattler will *lie* quietly without revealing itself if a man passes by.
      b. Don't *lie* to me about where you went!

2. a. He reached under the *rocks* and brought out harmless reptiles.
   b. Sometimes Dad *rocks* the baby to sleep in his arms.
3. a. The snake lived and breathed like the *rest* of us.
   b. Without her eight hours' *rest,* Ann becomes irritable.
4. a. Ross deposited two more rattlers in the *wire* cage.
   b. Some voters sent the President a *wire* about cutting taxes.
5. a. The most patient of rattlers might in time resent being hauled up and down and would *strike* whatever was nearest.
   b. Before the hospital *strike* began, every patient was moved to a place where he or she would receive proper care.

B. Follow the directions for Exercise A. However, some of the multiple-meaning words in these sentences may be unfamiliar to you. If necessary, use a dictionary to find the correct definitions. Be sure to read all the definitions given in the dictionary. Copy only the meaning that fits the sentence.

1. a. Ross told why a snake can't *stand* too much heat.
   b. The governor has taken a firm *stand* on the issues.
2. a. Ross was making the *rounds* of the gopher holes.
   b. The audience gave the singers several *rounds* of applause.
3. a. He told me the scientific facts about the *habits* of rattlesnakes.
   b. After tying up the horses at the stable, the tired riders hung up their *habits* and headed for the showers.
4. a. We got water from an abandoned *well.*
   b. *Well* in advance of the game, the tickets were sold out.

Marjorie Kinnan Rawlings 1896–1953

For several years Marjorie Kinnan Rawlings tried unsuccessfully to write stories she thought magazine editors would buy. In 1928, she gave up all other work, moved to a 72-acre orange grove in Hawthorn, Florida, and concentrated solely on her fiction. Her stories still did not sell. She decided to try one more time, writing for herself rather than for the editors. That effort was successful and marked the beginning of a series of highly praised short stories and novels. *The Yearling,* perhaps her best-known work, won the Pulitzer Prize in 1939.

They were the last of the magnificent wild horses in the area. Was it right to catch them? Donald's encounter with the horses was an experience he would never forget.

The Black Stallion and the Red Mare

GLADYS FRANCIS LEWIS

AT FIRST DONALD lay still. Scarcely a muscle moved. The boulders and the low shrubs screened him from view. Excitement held him motionless. His hands gripped the short grass, and his toes dug into the dry earth. Cautiously he raised himself on his elbows and gazed at the scene below him.

There, in his father's unfenced hay flats, was the outlaw band of wild horses. They were grazing quietly on the rich grass. Some drank from the small hillside stream. Donald tried to count them, but they suddenly began moving about and he could not get beyond twenty. He thought there might be two hundred.

Donald knew a good deal about that band of horses, but he had never had the good luck to see them. They were known over many hundreds of square miles. They had roamed at will over the grain fields, and they had led away many a domestic horse to the wild life. Once in that band, a horse was lost to the farm.

There in the flats was the great black stallion, the hero or the villain of a hundred tales. Over the far-flung prairie and grasslands there was scarcely a boy who had not dreamed of wild rides, with the great body of the stallion beneath him, bearing him through the air with the sharp speed of lightning.

There was the stallion now, moving among the horses with the sureness and ease of a master. As he moved about, teasingly kicking here and nipping there, a restlessness, as of a danger sensed, stirred through the band. The stallion cut to the outside of the group. At a full gallop he snaked around the wide circle, roughly bunching the mares and colts into the smaller circle of an invisible corral.

He was a magnificent creature, huge and proudly built. Donald saw the gloss of the black coat and the great curving muscles of the strong legs, the massive hooves, the powerful arch of the neck, the proud crest of the head. Donald imagined he could see the flash of black, intelligent eyes. Surely a nobler creature never roamed the plains!

Off-wind from the herd, a red mare came

out from the fold of the low hills opposite. She stood motionless a moment, her graceful head held high. Then she nickered.[1] The black stallion drew up short in his herding, nickered eagerly, then bolted off in the direction of the mare. She stood waiting until he had almost reached her; then they galloped back to the herd together.

The shadows crept across the hay flats and the evening stillness settled down. A bird sang sleepily on one note. Donald suddenly became aware of the monotonous song and stirred from his intent watching. He must tell his father and help send news around the countryside. He was still intensely excited as he crept back from the brow of the hill and hurried home. All the time his mind was busy and his heart was bursting.

Donald knew that three hundred years ago the Spaniards had brought horses to Mexico. Descendants of these horses had wandered into the Great Plains. The horses he now was watching were of that Spanish strain. Thousands of them roamed the cattle lands north to the boundary between Canada and the United States. This band now grazed wild over these park lands here in Canada—four hundred and fifty miles north of the boundary.

His father and the farmers for many miles around had determined to round up the horses and make an end of the roving band. As a farmer's son, Donald knew that this was necessary and right. But a certain respect for the band and the fierce loyalty that he felt toward all wild, free creatures made him wish in his heart that they might never be caught, never be broken and tamed. He, who was so full of sympathy for the horses, must be traitor to them!

There had been conflicts in his heart before, but never had there been such a warring of two strong loyalties. He saw himself for the first time as a person of importance because he, Donald Turner, had the power to affect the lives of others. This power, because it could help or harm others, he knew he must use wisely.

When he stood before his father half an hour later, he did not blurt out his news. It was too important for that. But his voice and eyes were tense with excitement. "That band of wild horses is in the hay hollow, west of the homestead quarter," he said. "There must be close to two hundred."

His father was aware of the boy's deep excitement. At Donald's first words he stopped his milking, his hands resting on the rim of the pail as he looked up.

"Good lad, Donald!" he said, quietly enough. "Get your supper and we'll ride to Smith's and Duncan's to start the word around. Tell Mother to pack lunches for tomorrow. We'll start at sunup." He turned to his milking again.

The other men were in the yard shortly after daylight.

Donald afterward wondered how long it would have taken ranch hands to round up the band of horses. These farmers knew horses, but not how to round up large numbers of them as the men of the ranch country knew so well. The farmers learned a good deal in the next two weeks.

Twenty men started out after the band as it thundered out of the hay flats, through the hills, and over the country. The dust rose in clouds as their pounding hooves dug the dry earth. The herd sped before the pursuers with the effortless speed of the wind. The black stallion led or drove his band and kept them

---

1 **nickered:** neighed.

well together. That first day only the young colts were taken.

At sunset the riders unsaddled and staked their horses by a poplar thicket, ate their stale lunches, and lay down to sleep under the stars. Their horses cropped the short grass and drank from the stream. Some slept standing; others lay down.

At dawn the herd was spied moving westward. With the coming of night, they, too, had rested. For a mile or more they now sped along the rim of a knoll, swift as broncos pulled in off the range after a winter out. The black stallion was a hundred feet ahead, running with a tireless, easy swing, his mane and tail streaming and his body stretched level as it cut through the morning mists. Close at his side, but half a length behind him, ran the red mare. The band streamed after.

After that first day's chase and the night under the stars, Donald had ridden back home. Not that he had wanted to go back. He would have given everything that he owned to have gone on with the men. But there were horses and cattle and chores to attend to at home, and there was school.

The roundup continued. Each day saw the capture of more and more horses. As the men doubled back on their course, they began to see that the wild horses traveled in a great circle, coming back again and again over the same ground, stopping at the same watering holes, and feeding in the same rich grass flats. Once this course became clear, fresh riders and mounts in relays were posted along the way, while others drove on from behind. The wild band had still to press on with little chance for rest and feeding. The strain of the pursuit took away their desire for food, but they had a burning thirst, and the black stallion would never let them drink their fill before he drove them on. Fatigue grew on them.

As the roundup continued, the whole countryside stirred with excitement. At every town where there was a grain elevator along the railroad, people repeated the latest news of the chase. On the farms the hay went unmown or unraked, and the plows rested still in the last furrow of the summer fallow. At school the children played roundup at recess. Donald, at his desk, saw the printed pages of his books, but his mind was miles away, running with the now almost exhausted wild horses.

Near the end of the second week of the chase, Donald's father rode into the yard. Donald dropped the wood he was carrying to the house and ran to meet his father.

"Dad, they haven't got the black stallion and the red mare, have they?" Donald could scarcely wait for his father's slow reply.

"No, Donald, lad," he said, "though those two are the only horses still free. They're back in the flats. We'll get them tomorrow."

Donald felt both relief and fear.

In the yellow lamplight of the supper table his father told of the long days of riding, of the farms where he had eaten and rested, and of the adventures of each day.

"That was a gallant band, lad!" he said. "Never shall we see their equal! Those two that are left are a pair of great horses. Most wild horses grow up with little wind or muscle. But these two are sound of wind and their muscles are like steel. Besides that, they have intelligence. They would have been taken long ago if it weren't for that."

No one spoke. Donald felt that his father was on his side, the side of the horses. After a long pause, Mr. Turner continued.

"With his brains and his strength that stallion could have got away in the very beginning. He could have got away a dozen times and would now be free south of the border. But that was his band. He stayed by them, and he tried to get them to safety. This week, when his band had been rounded up, he stuck by that red mare. She is swift, but she can't match his speed. It's curious the way they keep together! He stops and nickers. She nickers in reply and comes close to him, her nose touching his flank. They stand a moment. Then they are away again, she running beside him but not quite neck to neck. Day after day it is the same. They are no ordinary horseflesh, those two, lad!"

There was a lump in Donald's throat. He knew what his father meant. Those horses seemed to stand for something bigger and greater than himself. There were other things that made him feel the same—the first full-throated song of the meadow lark in the spring; ripe, golden fields of wheat with the breeze rippling it in waves; the sun setting over the rim of the world in a blaze of rose and gold; the sun rising again in the quiet east; the smile in the blue depths of his mother's eyes; the still whiteness of the snowbound plains; the story of Columbus dauntlessly sailing off into unknown seas.

These things were part of a hidden, exciting world. The boy belonged to these things in some strange way. He caught only glimpses of that hidden world, but those glimpses were tantalizing. Something deep within him leaped up in joy.

That night Donald dreamed of horses nickering to him, but when he tried to find them, they were no longer there. Then he dreamed that he was riding the great, black stallion, riding over a far-flung range, riding along a hilltop road with the world spread below him on every side. He felt the powerful body of the horse beneath him. He felt the smooth curves of the mighty muscles. Horse and rider seemed as one.

A cold dawn shattered his glorious dream ride. With his father he joined the other horsemen. From the crest of the slope from which Donald had first seen them, the pair of horses was sighted. They were dark, moving shadows in the gray mists of the morning.

They had just finished drinking deep from the stream. Not for two weeks had the men seen the horses drink like that. Thirsty as they were, they had taken but one drink at each water hole. This last morning they were jaded and spent; they had thrown caution to the winds.

At the first suspicion of close danger they stood still, heads and tails erect. Then they dashed toward the protecting hills. There the way forked.

It was then Donald saw happen the strange thing his father had described. At the fork the stallion halted and nickered. The mare answered and came close. She touched his flank with her head. Then they bounded off and disappeared in the path that led northwest to the rougher country where the chase had not led before.

Along the way the horses had been expected to take, grain-fed horses had been stationed. Now these had to move over northwest. But the men were in no hurry today. They were sure of the take before nightfall. The sun was low in the west when two riders spurred their mounts for the close-in. The stallion and the mare were not a hundred yards ahead. They were dead spent. Their glossy coats were flecked with dark foam. Fatigue showed in every line of their bodies. Their gallant spirits could no longer drive their spent bodies. The stallion called to the mare. He heard her answer behind him. He slowed down, turning wildly in every direction. She came up to him; her head drooped on his flank and rested there. In a last wild defiance, the stallion tossed his magnificent head and drew strength for a last mighty effort. Too late!

The smooth coils of a rope tightened around his feet. He was down, down and helpless. He saw the mare fall as the rope slipped over her body and drew tight around her legs. It maddened him. He struggled wildly to be free. The taut rope held. The stallion was conquered. In that last struggle something went out of him. Broken was his body and broken was his spirit. Never again would he roam the plains, proud and free, the monarch of his herd.

Donald saw it all. He felt it all. His hands gripped the pommel of the saddle and his knees pressed hard against his pony's sides. Tears blinded his eyes, and from his throat came the sound of a single sob. It was as if he himself were being broken and tied.

The sun dipped below the rim of the plains. The day was gone; the chase was ended. The men stood about smoking and talking in groups of two's and three's, examining the two roped horses. Donald's father knelt close to the mare, watching her intently. Donald watched him. His father remained quiet for a moment, one knee still resting on the ground, in his hand his unsmoked pipe. Donald waited for his father to speak. At last the words came.

"Boys," he said, without looking up, and with measured words, "do you know this mare is blind—stone blind!"

A week later, Donald and his father stood watching those two horses in the Turner corral. They were not the same spirited creatures, but they were still magnificent horses.

"I figured," his father said, turning to the boy, "that they had won the right to stay together. I've brought them home for you, Donald. They are yours, lad. I know you will be good to them."

1. What conflict does Donald feel inside himself when he first sees the herd of wild horses?
2. On page 49, the author says about Donald, "Those horses seemed to stand for something bigger and greater than himself." What do you think the author means?
3. What early clues does the author provide to suggest that the red mare is blind?
4. How are the stallion and the mare finally captured?
5. Why does the stallion stay with the herd and the red mare when he easily could have escaped by himself?
6. How do you think Donald's observations of the stallion and the mare might affect his own attitudes toward animals and people?
7. You learn only at the end of the story that the red mare is blind. How would the story have been different if this had been stated at the beginning?

Composition

1. Use evidence from this story to support the following statement: "The black stallion was an intelligent and fearless leader of the herd." Begin by briefly restating the situation in the story. Be sure to include the statement above as the basis of your argument. Then in one or more paragraphs, give reasons why the statement is true. In a final paragraph, summarize what you have written.
2. This story was based on a true situation. Write about another incident—true or made up—where animals behave with similar loyalty and devotion toward each other or toward a human. Briefly describe the animals involved and where they are. Then tell about the encounter.

Vocabulary

A PREFIX is a letter or group of letters added to the beginning of a word to change its meaning in some way. In some cases, adding a prefix will completely reverse the meaning of a word. For example, you can reverse the meaning of the word *able* by adding the prefix *un-:*

un- + able = unable (not capable).

Other prefixes can be added to the beginnings of words to reverse their meanings. These include: *in-, im-,* and *dis-.*

A. One of the four prefixes (*un-, in-, im-, dis-*) can be added to reverse the meaning of each of the following words from "The Black Stallion and the Red Mare":

fenced   saddled   visible   appeared
possible   faithful   pleased   proper

On a separate sheet of paper, copy each of the words above. After each one, give the following information: (1) the meaning of the word; (2) the prefix that should be used to reverse its meaning; (3) the new word formed by adding the prefix; and (4) the meaning of the new, prefixed word. Write your answers this way:

fenced (surrounded by a fence) + un = unfenced (not surrounded by a fence)

B. Sometimes the letters *un, in, im,* and *dis* are not prefixes. They are just a part of the regular spelling of words. For example, *imitation* and *discipline* do not contain prefixes.

Make two columns on your paper. In the left-hand column, copy all the words below that use *un-, in-, im-,* and *dis-* as prefixes. In the right-hand column, copy all the remaining words.

disk	indeed	discontented	understand
inexpensive	image	uneven	imperfect
unknown	discuss	impurity	inning
unless	insane	disorganized	imply

Highway: Michigan

THEODORE ROETHKE

Here from the field's edge we survey
The progress of the jaded. Mile
On mile of traffic from the town
Rides by, for at the end of day
The time of workers is their own.   5

They jockey for position on
The strip reserved for passing only.
The drivers from production lines
Hold to advantage dearly won.
They toy with death and traffic fines.   10

Acceleration is their need:
A mania keeps them on the move
Until the toughest nerves are frayed.
They are the prisoners of speed
Who flee in what their hands have made.   15

The pavement smokes when two cars meet
And steel rips through conflicting steel.
We shiver at the siren's blast.
One driver, pinned beneath the seat,
Escapes from the machine at last.   20

Discussion

1. Where is the narrator of this poem?

2. *Jaded* means "tired and worn out by abuse." Who is being called jaded in this poem? Why?

3. The narrator seems to feel that the drivers are not in control of their actions. What lines suggest this?

4. What happens in the last stanza?

5. Do you think the driver who was pinned beneath the seat survives the crash? Explain your answer.

Composition

1. Roethke suggests that Americans have become overly dependent on the automobile. Write a letter to the editor of a newspaper in which you either agree or disagree with his opinion. Begin by stating your position. Support your opinion with facts from current news articles, reference books, or personal experience. End your letter by telling what you think will happen if Americans keep or lose this dependency on the automobile.

2. Set your time machine for the year 2500. First describe the means of transportation that you think will have replaced the car. In a second paragraph tell what normal rush hour traffic will be like then. Try to imagine if people will still have some of the same traffic problems that they do today, or will there be new and different problems? What might they be?

Vocabulary

A word that has more than one definition is called a MULTIPLE-MEANING WORD. To understand which of the meanings is intended by an author, you must look closely at the way the word is used in a sentence. The words which surround the multiple-meaning word, the context clues, will help you decide.

A. The lines below are taken from "Highway: Michigan." Each of them contains a multiple-meaning word in *italics*. On a separate sheet of paper, write the meanings of the *italicized* words as they are used by the author. Then give one other meaning for each word. Use a dictionary if you need help.

EXAMPLE: They *jockey* for position.
ANSWER: author's meaning—make changes by devious means
another meaning—a rider of race horses

1. They jockey for position on
   The *strip* reserved for passing only.
2. They *toy* with death and traffic fines.
3. The pavement smokes when two cars *meet.*
4. We *shiver* at the siren's blast.
5. One driver, *pinned* beneath the seat,
   Escapes from the machine at last.

B. Look up the word *line* in a dictionary. Choose five completely
   different definitions, and write them on your paper. Then write a
   separate sentence for each of the meanings.

Theodore Roethke 1908—1963

As a boy Theodore Roethke worked and played around the
greenhouses of his family's floral business in Saginaw, Michigan. His
attraction to the small features of plants was later seen in his poetry.
He was startled by people who overlooked such natural beauty and
simplicity in favor of complex machinery. Poems like "Highway:
Michigan" reflect this attitude. His career as a poet began in 1941 with
the collection *Open House,* which includes plant imagery of growth
and decay. In 1953, Roethke won the Pulitzer Prize for *The Waking,*
and in 1958, *Words for the Wind* received the Bollingen Prize.

The sperm whale can weigh over ninety tons and can be over eighty feet long. Imagine what a battle could result if the whale had to fight for his life and the life of his mate!

Battle in the Depths

PAUL ANNIXTER

THE DEEP CHURNED. Something was happening far down in the dim, foggy-green depths. Currents and chains of bubbles came rushing to the surface and the upflung waters whipped to foam. Gradually the surface became tinged with a brickish stain that told the story of a battle in these tropic seas.

Now, as if a great fire had been lighted down there, gigantic bubbles rose and broke, the waters boiled. A maelstrom[1] of foam, all creaming and seething, burst to the surface and through it cut a black triangular fin. It disappeared but another followed, and still another.

Then *he* appeared.

At first he seemed but a pearl-wreathed ghost of enormous size, becoming a darkening shadow shape, glaucous,[2] gigantic, and growing as if a mountain or part of the sea bed had risen from the abyss. Up and up he came, an oblong mass like some great blunt-nosed torpedo upended in the swells.

The torpedo shape was merely his head, gigantic, blunt, square-ended, yet mild of aspect as some stupendous pollywog. As he surfaced, a burst of oily vapor spurted from an S-shaped cavity at the top of his head in an upward and forward blast like a jet of steam, that could have been seen by a ship two miles away.

After he blew, yet more head appeared, with little, deep-set eyes placed far back in it, down close to the waterline. Finally, the long, narrow, saw-toothed underjaw was exposed—a flat, twenty-five-foot shaft of bone, hinged like a box and set with fifty enormous, conical teeth that were still chomping on a mass of deep-sea squid, the bait royal of the cachalot[3] clan.

When the whole beast lay on the surface, rising monstrously above the lapping swells, he was a dark, breathing island of whale some eighty or so feet long, and wide in proportion. A bull sperm just reaching his prime, he was already a giant of his giant race. The bulk

---

1 **maelstrom** (māl′ strəm): large whirlpool.
2 **glaucous** (glô′ kəs): gleaming, bluish green.

3 **cachalot** (kash′ə lot): sperm whale.

of him was covered with skin like glistening, dark silk. Behind the head, or "junk," as whalers call it, was a hump, but there was no dorsal[4] fin and the flukes of his tail were set horizontally, not vertically as in fish. An eon or so ago, the cachalot's ancestors had run through the primeval forest on four short legs. Then, like certain other mammals, they had taken to the water for survival during the grim Age of Transition.

He was still chomping on the squid he had fought and vanquished down there in the depths. His nine-inch teeth caught a glint of morning light as he sheared off a few more wriggling arm-tips of the cuttle. The scraps were swiftly snapped up by the mixed company of sharks that ringed him, rushing in and out with a curl of foam. Small as compared with the cachalot, averaging from twelve to twenty feet in length, they comprised the most voracious of sea scavengers, hammerheads, blues, tigers, and the twenty-foot killers known as "gray nurse" to the men of the southern waters. Not content with sharing in his feast these fed also upon their host, lancing in with a twisting turn to snatch chunks of white blubber from the whale's side and to rush off with it in their saw-toothed jaws. As the sharks well knew, the whale had been down deep and was tired and winded. Once he had swallowed his meal and recovered his breath, this would be no place for such as they, but meanwhile these sea jackals would take all possible advantage.

The monster blew again. His spouting continued at regular fourteen-second intervals while his red blood was reoxidized. All that time the sharks nagged him, chop and run. Their ferocity knew no bounds, yet the worst they could do was small in the face of the calm immensity of the giant, the mountainous reservoirs of power and energy in the ninety-odd tons of him. In places his hide alone was a foot and a half thick, with barnacles and shellfish living in the wrinkles. Beneath it were incredible layers of nerveless blubber that swathed him in warmth and protection.

Abruptly, with a rush as of cataracts, the sperm whirled upon himself, flinging his great bulk almost clear of the water. With a crash that shook the sea he struck the surface again, his great jaws clashing shut in the same moment like the dropping of an iron portcullis.[5] His tormentors scattered to all sides, some of them leaping clear of the surface in their speed, revealing their evil mouths and sulphury undersides, only to whip in again when the giant had subsided.

Again and again the twelve-foot flippers of the whale lifted and struck the sea with a smash like the report of a cannon. A hammerhead floated on the surface, broken from end to end. The flipper had caught him squarely, and he lay there, blasted like a ship that had struck a mine.

Finally the tormentors drew off in a dark flotilla[6] and did not sweep in again. For the whale had completely emptied and refilled his lungs and was ready for all comers. As they sped away, the sperm whale swept after them, a furious missile of flesh and blood surrounded by flying white spray as he smashed through the waves, one of the fastest as well as the vastest things alive. Over five miles of sea the chase led, down to a depth of twenty fathoms and up again, twisting, turning, and corkscrewing, and another

---

4 **dorsal**: back.

---

5 **portcullis**: a grate dropped over a gateway.
6 **flotilla** (flō til′ə): a small fleet.

shark, a tiger this time, was chopped almost in two in the whale's jaws as in retribution for their sneak attack.

Then the wrath of the whale wore off, the emberlike gleam faded from his little eyes, and he lay still upon the waters. After a time he turned northward, swimming at a steady ten knots an hour, sounding at intervals to a depth of twelve fathoms where he could get a clearer message through the water wireless. He was answering one of those mysterious calls of sea creatures more wonderful than the migratory sense of birds, a kind of pulse in the waters that told him that others of his kind were congregated a few leagues away. At times he rose on his very tail, twenty feet and more out of the water, the better to sense the situation. About midday he came upon them—a pod[7] of young male sperms like himself, lying like ships off a small island.

There were eleven whales in the pod; and for a couple of days the young bull lay up with them, playing and lazing the time away, diving at intervals to hunt for squid in the depths. For the hunger that drove these monsters was almost beyond conception. Their throats were large enough to swallow two men—it must have been the cachalot that had given rise to the Jonah story[8]— and their stomachs were huge caldrons of

---

7 **pod:** a group of fish, mammals, etc., traveling together.
8 **Jonah story:** Biblical story about a whale that swallowed a man named Jonah.

digestive juices that required endless and constant replenishment.

On the third day when the pod started southward, he, too, went along, a passage that would take them across four degrees of latitude. They traveled at an even ten knots an hour, holding their course as steadily as if a compass were in the brain of each, their flippers churning the sea, their great tails leaving miles of foam behind them.

They swam the sun out of one sky and the moon out of another, only once varying their speed when they came upon a vast school of mullet packed together for nearly a square mile, so that the face of the sea seemed effervescent. Straight through the school they plowed, chomping and gulping as they went, over a hundredweight at every swallow. The mullet were united in migration and did not scatter. When the monsters had passed, the gaps were closed, and the great school passed on into the west, followed by their attendant flock of mewing, screaming sea birds and a swarm of lesser sea jackals.

Some hours later the whale pod passed a school of porpoises. They were hungry again by that time, but left these distant relatives unmolested. The porpoises were warm-blooded mammals like themselves, and whales are not cannibals.

On the fifth day of passage the whales kept sounding several times an hour to feel out the pulse of the sea ahead. From time to time they flung themselves high in the air above the crest of the swells, revolving at the same time so as to peer over the sea with their myopic,[9] little eyes. Each knew now what he sought, the great mother herd from which he

had sprung and which roved up and down the watery bulge of the planet in rhythm with the seasons. Toward day's end the pod sighted whale birds in a cloud, and shortly afterward many white jets of spume showed ahead of them. Sweeping forward in a mist of spray, they saw the calm sea covered with their kind. This was one of the immemorial[10] stopping places of the cachalot, just where the rocks of a submerged mountain offered rubbing places to curry their wrinkled hides, and where, in the valleys below the marine mountain and on its various ledges, octopuses crouched, or walked tip-toe like great spiders.

There were more than a hundred whales in the herd, many unattached females among them, also mothers with calves that gamboled,[11] dived, and nursed as other mammals do ashore. There were young bulls, and aging bulls, and scarred old veterans who took their ease upon the surface swells.

Little notice was taken of the newcomers. The small pod simply hove to and came to rest in the midst of the lazing herd. With this homecoming to the parent group, their heedless young bachelorhood had come to an end. They would now be drawn into the ordered life of the great, moving whale city.

The old schoolmaster of the herd was a monster whose head was covered with the scars of battle and whose great bulk was as full of iron as a blacksmith shop, harpoon shafts and heads from his many encounters with whalers in years past. Those years had brought him much experience and it was to him that they all looked for warning and guidance along the great whale highways of the sea. From the schoolmaster the young

---

9 **myopic**: nearsighted.

10 **immemorial**: ancient.
11 **gamboled**: acted in a frisky, playful manner.

bulls learned the telegraph code of whales, by which they detected one another at great distances and how to warn each other of danger by releasing the *glip*—an acrid oil which ran through the water in long streamers. Nourished by this oil were the whale birds, ever following in the wake of the herd—a species of petrel which fed, rested, and even slept on the backs of the monsters, repaying their hosts by cleaning up the mollusks and crustaceans[12] that the whales could not rub off. They were useful also in giving alarm when whale ships appeared on the horizon, for their sight was far keener than that of the whales.

Keener than any flock of petrels though

---

12 **mollusks and crustaceans** (mol'əsks and krus' tā shənz): in this case, the small shelled creatures which cling to the whale.

was the old schoolmaster in sensing danger from man, the greatest enemy. The young bull knew nothing of men or whalers until the day a ship hove to, half a knot downwind from where he and another young bull were feeding. Small boats put out from her and came nearer. He and his companion were curious about these and surfaced for another look, despite the sting of the *glip* that lay in the wake of the retreating herd. When he surfaced a third time, there was another sharper sting in his side as a harpoon found him. Two such harpoons stood out upon the back of his companion, with taut lines leading from each to the prow of a small boat. He breached sharply in his pain and instinctively sounded.[13] The harpoon line rolled out behind him to its limit, and for a time in an agony of pain, he was towing the small boat and its crew. At last the iron shaft tore loose, and he was free.

Later, as he surfaced he saw his dying companion surrounded by three small boats, with men moving like whale birds on his broad back. He fled with a hard lesson learned.

In the days that followed, the herd traveled slowly southward, following the great chain of whale feeding grounds that were strung from pole to pole and covered all the great ocean deeps. The young bull's wound healed swiftly in the amazing way of sea creatures, but the wariness it had left in him concerning men and ships would be a protection always. He had reached his full maturity and growth that season: eighty-seven and a half English feet, with a girth that was vast in proportion, placing him among the mightiest and most powerful of his race. He had already won the favor of three admiring

young cows who now constituted his self-elected following, the beginning of a family pod, but a spirit of restlessness was still upon him and their favors meant little to him.

It was weeks later that he made a choice of his own among the young females of the herd. She was scarcely half his size, a member of a family pod of five sperms. For a day he swam and fed close to the pod and saw that she was constantly escorted. Sure as he was that she was the answer to his long wanderings, there seemed nothing to do but challenge the scarred master of the pod. But a battle of giants did not ensue. The old one was merely her sire, and willing enough that she take a mate.

She, however, seemed coy and reluctant to leave her family group, though glad of his company. He tagged along. Sometimes they joined in submarine play, diving after each other in long diagonal shafts of silvery light, sounding the rayless depths, looping around and under each other, racing headlong in the dark, rising at last to blow and breathe and rest on the surface. Always there was an urge in him to draw her away toward some sequestered[14] coast where they might live apart for a while. But always she returned to her own pod.

Now the herd had stopped for a time above that mighty chasm known as "The Abyss," which lay to the west of Thursday Island. These great depths went down five miles to the gray-brown mud of the ocean floor, the abysmal ooze consisting of the remains of ages of marine plants, animals, and meteoric dust settled down through centuries from suspension in the sea.

Here in the lightless depths dwelt the giant devilfish or decapod, the monster kraken of

---

13 **sounded:** dived to great depth.

14 **sequestered:** separated; secluded.

Norse legend. *Architeuthis* he was called, great brother to the octopus, the coveted prey of all sperm whales and often their undoing, for victory went not always to the whales.

Here was one of the richest of all whale feeding grounds, and the whole herd became lively and sportive as it spread out in the old familiar waters and began to dive and feed. Even the young female showed a new, venturesome spirit and when she dove to go squid hunting the young bull followed her. A sort of recklessness was upon them both and it was one of the times when they kept going, the female in the lead.

Down and down they plunged to the hundred-fathom depth where the weight of waters pressed like iron bands about them, their great bodies bearing a pressure of thousands of pounds. Only the fact that their brains were wonderfully cushioned in many feet of bone and liquid spermaceti[15] enabled them to function at such a depth. Nothing survived down here, save those creatures whose bodies offset the pressure by being constantly filled with water themselves.

Still farther down they ventured into a realm of deathly cold where not even a ray of green seeped through, and great caverns and gorges yawned between mid-sea mountains. At the half-mile depth the female cut short her dive and began undulating[16] along horizontally, seeking prey, the young bull close behind her. But no squid was about at this level, and presently they sounded again toward the three-thousand-foot level beyond which no warm-blooded mammal may descend and live.

Again they tapered off their dive and went shooting horizontally along the slopes of a submarine mountain. Abruptly, the female, still in the lead, brought up against a forest of bleached, swinging branches. The young bull just behind had a vague impression of her struggling in the mesh of them, like a pollack in a fisherman's net. For the branches were gigantic, living tentacles, waving tree-high—the tentacles of a devilfish. The scent of musk filled the waters.

The whales had run head on into a company of the giant cuttlefish of the seabed. The creatures were lying about everywhere on the mountain slope. The depths were not only lightless but utterly opaque now, for the cuttles had begun squirting out clouds of sepia.[17]

Two mighty tentacles flung themselves around the young bull's head like living *reatas*[18] and pulled taut, crushing his jaw shut. Others leaped snakelike to clutch his tail. The whole underworld rocked, swayed, and tossed as in a windstorm, for all about the monsters were closing in. The very deep was on their side, for the whales had been down long already, and at this depth they were out of their element.

The bull sperm rolled completely over, spinning twice, and backed by his huge weight, burst free. His jaws snapped shut, shearing off one of the pale streamers close to its base. Jetting water from the propulsion sack beneath his head, his attacker shot backward into the depths loosing ink clouds as it went. The bull plunged after, then cut his rush short and swept back at tremendous speed.

A message of dire distress had reached him. The cow sperm, despite her frantic struggles, was being borne deeper down by one of the

---

15 **spermaceti** (spér mə set′ ē): waxy substance in whale oil.
16 **undulating**; moving up and down.

17 **sepia**: a dark brown fluid.
18 *reatas* (rē ä′ təz): Spanish word for lariats or ropes.

huge cuttles. The bull sperm charged at full speed, diving beneath the female, and with his jaws slashing her free from two of the great cables that were dragging her down. But another cuttlefish, the mightiest of them all, had clutched her spiderwise. His bulk, more than twice that of the cow, pulled her irresistibly downward.

Again the bull swept in, cutting through a mighty tentacle. Two others quickly took its place, wrapping around the cow like heavy hawsers[19] from bow to stern. And wherever their sucking disks fastened, the blood oozed forth. The bull sperm seized the attacking cuttle by the side of the head, and with a furious lashing of flukes and tail, strove to draw him upward. The cuttle struggled just as furiously to descend. The sounding of the creature was halted but no more. The mighty tug of war hung at an exact balance, except that the chomping jaws of the whale constantly cut into the boneless body of his foe. The curved beak of the sea devil scored deep gashes in the bull's sides, and the tigerlike claws, that fringed the suction disks on every tentacle, lashed his flanks. But the whale's grip did not slacken and, writhing in its torment, the cuttle finally released the cow and fought for its life.

The bull sperm shook the cuttle in his jaws, dog-fashion; but the instant he ceased the offensive, the devilfish dragged him down as it had the cow. The whale could not remain at this depth much longer and live. Two hours' submersion at ordinary levels was nothing for him, but the pressure of this abyss, plus the strain of battle, had already claimed most of the oxygen in the lungs of the whale pair. Soon they must find relief in the upper waters or die. Perhaps the cuttle sensed this, for his depth pulls were cunning and unceasing.

Abruptly, the young bull gave in as if to go down with the cuttle, descending in a diagonal dive, only to break it and come up again in a long arc with the enemy now uppermost and with an added momentum against which the struggles of the cuttle were powerless. Up and up the battle went now, the devilfish writhing like a tree in a storm, the sperm chewing in and in and shaking the whole, vast bulk of him.

With all his remaining arms the cuttle strove to strangle the bull, to close shut his jaws and stop up his airhole; but a reverse process was on. With every fathom they rose, the power of the cuttlefish weakened, while the whale's increased. And through it all, every instant, the sperm continued to chomp upon the pallid flesh of his foe, feeding even as he fought. The vast mollusk pulsated now with wave upon wave of evil-looking color—purple, red, mud-brown, magenta, and back to brown again.

Up in the belt of shining blue and green the finish was clear. The decapod writhed about to face the foe, but the sperm went on eating his way through the pulsing Medusa-like[20] head, tearing out chunks of flesh as large as washtubs, until it died.

After only partially filling his lungs with air, the young bull plunged into the depths once more, for she had not yet surfaced. He found her helpless once more in the grip of half a dozen strangling tentacles. Only by calling upon that last resource, the mysterious store of oxidized blood carried by whales in the dorsal arteries along their spine, could he

---

19 **hawsers**: large ropes.

20 **Medusa-like**: resembling Medusa, a monster from Greek mythology that had snakes for hair.

summon the strength for further battle. Three times he dove beneath the cow in a ripping charge, his jaws working like the slash of monstrous shears among those twining, living cables, and finally he cut her free.

Together the pair shot surface-ward, racing with death itself, back to the clean, sane world of air and sky and sun. The speed of their ascent was such that their bodies shot clear into the sunlit air and fell back to the surface with a crash that shook the whole watery world. After that they rested long, panting, breathing in enormous quantities of life-giving air. And later when the red sun dipped in the sea, they were still lying there, quite close together and a long way from the herd, feeding on the remains of the king cuttle the male had conquered.

Discussion

1. You have seen that in spite of the whale's strength and size, it still has dangerous enemies. Name some of these enemies. In your opinion, what or who is the whale's worst enemy? Explain by using information from this story.

2. What physical characteristics of the sperm whale most protect it against its enemies?

3. The author presents the whale in this story as a superhero who is victorious over villains. What words can you find in the selection that present sharks as evil villains?

4. For a while it seems possible that the sperm whale and his mate will be killed by the cuttlefish. What are some of the facts or details the author uses to build up this suspense?

5. What two earlier encounters prepare readers for the whale's spectacular victory at the end? How?

Vocabulary

The general meaning of an unknown word can often be gathered from familiar words surrounding that word—or within the word itself. These hints are called context clues. There are many different types of context clues. One of the easiest to recognize is the LANGUAGE CONTEXT CLUE. This kind of clue refers to a short, familiar word contained within a longer word that is unknown. For example:

> Again and again the twelve-foot *flippers* of the whale lifted and struck the sea with a smash like the report of a cannon.

The language context clue is within the word *flippers* itself. Since *flip* means "to toss with a sudden movement," flippers must perform similar actions.

Now look closely at the other types of context clues in the sentence. "Of the whale" tells you that the flippers belong to the whale. "Twelve-foot" tells you that, although large, flippers are not the whale's entire body; that must mean that they are attached to the body. "Lifted and struck the sea" provides a picture of how flippers are used.

By putting these other context clues together with the language context clue itself, you can develop a fairly clear picture of flippers—even if you have never seen them.

Below are sentences from "Battle in the Depths." Use language context clues—along with other context clues—to find a general meaning for each of the *italicized* words below. Write your definitions on a separate sheet of paper.

1. Gradually the surface became tinged with a *brickish* stain that told the story of the battle in these tropic seas.

2. Currents and chains of bubbles came rushing to the surface and the *upflung* waters whipped to foam.

3. The monster blew again. His *spouting* continued at regular fourteen-second intervals while his red blood was reoxidized.

4. Beneath it were incredible layers of *nerveless* blubber that swathed him in warmth and protection.

5. His tormentors scattered to all sides, some of them leaping clear of the surface in their speed, revealing their evil mouths and *sulphury* undersides.

Paul Annixter 1894—

When Paul Annixter was eight years old, he wrote his first work, a ten-page novel on the life of Simon Girty and his Indian friends. It was read only by his grandmother. After leaving school, he traveled the rails, had numerous odd jobs, and worked a timber claim, chopping wood for nearby farmers. Encouraged by friends, he started writing, and he found he could make a living at it. Later he married another writer, Jane Levington Comfort, and together they have written several successful novels and over 500 short stories, many of which concern animals. His most famous work is the novel *Swiftwater*.

ENCOUNTERS

Discussion

1. Five of the selections in this unit showed human beings encountering animals or insects. They were "Leiningen versus the Ants," "A Blessing," "Rattlesnake Hunt," "The Black Stallion and the Red Mare," and "Battle in the Depths." Discuss how some selections showed human beings deliberately setting out to destroy or capture animals or insects. Discuss how one selection showed animals or insects endangering human beings. Discuss how some selections presented human beings as noble and caring toward animals.

2. Why do you think people sometimes behave destructively toward animals? What evidence do you see today that people's attitudes toward animals and their environments are changing?

3. Several of the selections in this unit relate encounters that lead to the improvement or growth of the main character. Which characters showed the most change? Explain the nature or extent of that change.

4. Which characters in this unit were the least changed or affected by their encounters? Explain.

Composition

1. From the selections in this unit, choose the encounter that you found most interesting. First briefly describe the situation and tell who or what was involved. In the second paragraph, tell what you think the main character discovered or learned from this encounter. Relate specific actions from the selection that show how the discovery was made. Then summarize the encounter by describing how the main character might change or did change as a result of the encounter. Finally in your last paragraph, tell what *you* learned from this particular encounter.

2. It is not just famous people or fictional characters who have encounters. All of us have had experiences with nature or other people from time to time. Select an encounter that you feel has made a difference in your life. Write a brief description of this incident. End with a comment about the change the encounter made in your own life.

Scenes from America

SCENES FROM AMERICA

A Song of Greatness

When I hear the old men
Telling of heroes,
Telling of great deeds
Of ancient days—
When I hear that telling,
Then I think within me
I, too, am one of these.

When I hear the people
Praising great ones,
Then I know that I too
Shall be esteemed;
I, too, when my time comes
Shall do mightily.

This poem of the Chippewa Indians tells the story of the American spirit, the subject of this unit. You will read about some of America's heroes and the "great deeds of ancient days." You will meet the people who helped to make America a nation by their mighty accomplishments—the pioneers, the political leaders, the heroes, and the dreamers. You will also look in on the not so famous people of America. You will see them in their homes and at their work. In addition, you will meet vibrant young people who still have their futures to create, who have yet to do "great deeds."

Finally you will see in these brief scenes from America the true miracle of this country. You will see its people and their cities and towns. You will also learn how people from many countries and cultures have come together in America with a common dream of freedom. You will see how this dream can come true so that in America all can "do mightily."

"One, if by land, and two, if by sea." A lone man mounts his horse and rides off into the night to spark the beginning of a new country.

Paul Revere's Ride

HENRY WADSWORTH LONGFELLOW

Listen, my children, and you shall hear
Of the midnight ride of Paul Revere,
On the eighteenth of April, in Seventy-five;
Hardly a man is now alive
Who remembers that famous day and year.   5

He said to his friend, "If the British march
By land or sea from the town tonight,
Hang a lantern aloft in the belfry arch
Of the North Church tower as a signal light—
One, if by land, and two, if by sea;   10
And I on the opposite shore will be,
Ready to ride and spread the alarm
Through every Middlesex village and farm,
For the country folk to be up and to arm."

Then he said, "Good night!" and with muffled oar   15
Silently rowed to the Charlestown shore,
Just as the moon rose over the bay,
Where swinging wide at her moorings lay
The *Somerset,* British man-of-war;
A phantom[1] ship, with each mast and spar   20
Across the moon like a prison bar,
And a huge black hulk, that was magnified
By its own reflection in the tide.

---

1 **phantom** (fan' təm): ghostlike.

Meanwhile, his friend, through alley and street,
Wanders and watches with eager ears,   25
Till in the silence around him he hears
The muster of men at the barrack door,
The sound of arms, and the tramp of feet,
And the measured tread of the grenadiers,
Marching down to their boats on the shore.   30

Then he climbed the tower of the Old North Church,
By the wooden stairs, with stealthy tread,
To the belfry chamber overhead,
And startled the pigeons from their perch
On the somber rafters, that round him made   35
Masses and moving shapes of shade—
By the trembling ladder, steep and tall,
To the highest window in the wall,
Where he paused to listen and look down
A moment on the roofs of the town,   40
And the moonlight flowing over all.

Beneath, in the churchyard, lay the dead,
In their night encampment on the hill,
Wrapped in silence so deep and still
That he could hear, like a sentinel's tread,   45
The watchful night wind, as it went
Creeping along from tent to tent,
And seeming to whisper, "All is well!"
A moment only he feels the spell
Of the place and the hour, and the secret dread   50
Of the lonely belfry and the dead;
For suddenly all his thoughts are bent
On a shadowy something far away,
Where the river widens to meet the bay—
A line of black that bends and floats   55
On the rising tide, like a bridge of boats.

Meanwhile, impatient to mount and ride,
Booted and spurred, with a heavy stride
On the opposite shore walked Paul Revere.
Now he patted his horse's side,   60
Now gazed at the landscape far and near,
Then, impetuous, stamped the earth,
And turned and tightened his saddle girth;

But mostly he watched with eager search
The belfry tower of the Old North Church,   65
As it rose above the graves on the hill,
Lonely and spectral[2] and somber and still.
And lo! as he looks, on the belfry's height
A glimmer, and then a gleam of light!
He springs to the saddle, the bridle he turns,   70
But lingers and gazes, till full on his sight
A second lamp in the belfry burns!

A hurry of hoofs in a village street,
A shape in the moonlight, a bulk in the dark,
And beneath, from the pebbles, in passing, a spark   75
Struck out by a steed flying fearless and fleet:
That was all! And yet, through the gloom and the light,
The fate of a nation was riding that night;
And the spark struck out by that steed, in his flight,
Kindled the land into flame with its heat.   80

He has left the village and mounted the steep,
And beneath him, tranquil and broad and deep,
Is the Mystic, meeting the ocean tides;
And under the alders that skirt its edge,
Now soft on the sand, now loud on the ledge,   85
Is heard the tramp of his steed as he rides.

It was twelve by the village clock,
When he crossed the bridge into Medford town.
He heard the crowing of the cock,
And the barking of the farmer's dog,   90
And felt the damp of the river fog,
That rises after the sun goes down.

It was one by the village clock,
When he galloped into Lexington.
He saw the gilded weathercock   95
Swim in the moonlight as he passed,
And the meetinghouse windows, blank and bare,
Gaze at him with a spectral glare,
As if they already stood aghast
At the bloody work they would look upon.   100

---

2 **spectral:** ghostly.

It was two by the village clock,
When he came to the bridge in Concord town.
He heard the bleating of the flock,
And the twitter of birds among the trees,
And felt the breath of the morning breeze   105
Blowing over the meadows brown.
And one was safe and asleep in his bed
Who at the bridge would be first to fall,
Who that day would be lying dead,
Pierced by a British musket ball.   110

You know the rest. In the books you have read,
How the British Regulars fired and fled—
How the farmers gave them ball for ball,
From behind each fence and farmyard wall,
Chasing the redcoats down the lane,   115
Then crossing the fields to emerge again
Under the trees at the turn of the road,
And only pausing to fire and load.

So through the night rode Paul Revere;
And so through the night went his cry of alarm   120
To every Middlesex village and farm—
A cry of defiance and not of fear,
A voice in the darkness, a knock at the door,
And a word that shall echo forevermore!
For, borne on the nightwind of the Past,   125
Through all our history, to the last,
In the hour of darkness and peril and need,
The people will waken and listen to hear
The hurrying hoofbeats of that steed,
And the midnight message of Paul Revere.   130

Discussion

1. Explain how Paul Revere planned to warn the colonists that the British were coming.
2. What effect is created throughout this poem by the use of such words as *ghosts, phantoms,* and *shadowy things?*
3. What do lines 79–80 mean?
4. The actual description of the ride is in lines 73–110. What are the names of the villages Paul Revere visited? What time did he get to each one? What does the poet say was going to happen in each village?
5. What happens in lines 111–118?
6. What do you think lines 125–130 mean?

Vocabulary

An ANTONYM is a word that means the opposite of another word. For example, *friend* is an antonym for *enemy,* and *huge* is an antonym for *tiny.* Antonyms like these express exactly opposite meanings. Other antonyms, however, express only approximately—or nearly—opposite meanings. For example, *famous* is an approximate antonym for *unknown,* and *noise* is an approximate antonym for *silence.*

A. One word in the right-hand column on the next page is an antonym for a word in the left-hand column. However, the pairs of antonyms are scrambled. On a separate sheet of paper, copy the left-hand column and then beside each word, write its antonym from the right-hand column.

midnight	narrow
alive	under
over	noon
wide	dead

B. The two columns below contain some pairs of exact antonyms and some pairs of approximate antonyms. Follow the directions for Exercise A. If you need help, use a dictionary.

aghast	disappear
borne	slow
emerge	fleshly
fleet	calm
impetuous	safety
peril	bright
somber	thoughtful
spectral	dropped

Henry Wadsworth Longfellow 1807—1882

Longfellow has been called the most popular poet of the 19th century. He was educated privately in America and Europe and was a teacher at Bowdoin College and Harvard. He wrote much, was considered a great poet in his own time, and became rich as a result. Longfellow's greatest power was myth-making. Poems such as "The Village Blacksmith," "The Song of Hiawatha," "Paul Revere's Ride," and "The Courtship of Miles Standish" still remain a part of American mythology. In 1884, Longfellow's statue was placed in the Poets' Corner at Westminster Abbey. He is the only American ever to be honored in this way.

In the 1850s Charles had to return East to find work when the first year's harvest was destroyed by grasshoppers. At seventeen, his wife Caroline was left alone with a small baby in a dugout home, hollowed out of the bank of a creek. She was to remain throughout the winter to protect their farm in South Dakota.

Prairie Winter

ROSE WILDER LANE

THREE DAYS and nights the winds did not cease to howl, and when Caroline opened the door, she could not see the door ledge through swirling snow. How cold it was she could not guess. At the sight of clouds earlier, she had hurriedly crammed every spare inch of the dugout with hay. Twisted hard, it burned with a brief, hot flame. Her palms were soon raw and bleeding from handling the sharp, harsh stuff, but she kept on twisting it. She kept the dugout warm.

In the long dark hours—for she was frugal with kerosene, and only a wavering light came from the drafts and the broken lid of the stove—she began to fight a vague and monstrous dread. It lay beneath her thoughts; she could not grasp it as a whole; she was always aware of it and never able to defeat it. It lay shapeless and dark in the depths of her. From time to time it flung up a question:

What if the baby gets sick?

"He won't be sick!" she retorted. "He's a strong, healthy baby. If he's sick, I'll take care of him. I'd take care of him anyway; there's no doctor in town."

Suppose something has happened to Charles? Suppose he never comes back?

"Be still! I won't listen."

That was like a wolf's howl in the wind. Wolves?

"Nonsense, I have the gun. How could a wolf get through the door?"

When you go out— If a wolf sprang suddenly— What of the baby, alone in the dugout?

"Why am I scaring myself with horrible fancies? Nothing like that will happen."

She could never conquer the shapeless, nameless dread itself. Silenced, it did not leave her. It would begin again.

What if the baby gets sick?

"Oh, stop, stop! I can't stand this!" her spirit cried out in anguish. And she asked herself angrily, "What is the matter with you? Brace up and show a little decent spunk!

It's only a storm; there'll be lots of them before spring." She tried to conquer the shapeless, dark thing by ignoring it.

The wind howled; gray darkness pressed against the paper pane; a little hard snow, dry as sand, was forced through the crack beneath the door.

On the fourth morning, Caroline was awakened by an immense, profound silence. The frosty air stung her nostrils; the blanket was edged with rime from her breath. Snug in the hollow of her body, the baby slept cozily. The window was a vague gray in the dark. She lighted the lamp and started a fire in the cold stove.

She was not perturbed until she tried to open the door. Something outside held it against her confident push. And suddenly a wild terror possessed her. She felt a Thing outside, pressed against the door.

It was only snow. She said to herself that it was only snow. There was no danger; the ledge was narrow. She flung all her strength and weight against the door. The stout planks quivered, and from top to bottom of them ran a sound like a scratch of claws. Then snow fell down the abrupt slope below the ledge, and sunlight pierced Caroline's eyes.

Under the immeasurably vast sky, a limitless expanse of snow refracted the cold glitter of the sun. She drew a deep breath, and with her shovel she attacked the snow. The winds had packed it hard as ice against the door and the creek bank. The path was buried under a slanting drift. Inch by inch, pounding, digging, scraping, lifting, she made a way on which she could safely walk, and that scratch on the measureless waste of trackless snow was a triumph.

A blizzard of such severity so early in October seemed to predict an unusually hard winter. She could not know when the next storm might strike, and her first care was fuel. She dug into the snow-covered stacks by the barn, and tying a rope around big bundles of hay, she dragged them one by one down the path and into the dugout.

Then for three weeks the weather was mild; the snow was melting. There were days when the door stood open and the air was like spring. From above the dugout she could see the town; she could, indeed, see fifty miles beyond it.

In early November the winter settled down. Blizzard followed blizzard out of the northwest. Sometimes there was a clear day between them, sometimes only a few hours. As soon as the winds ceased their howling and the snow thinned so that she could see, she went out with the shovel.

The wind would be steadily blowing, driving a low scud of snow before it. She worked sometimes waist-deep in blown snow so thick that she could not see her feet. The whole world seemed covered with white spray flying under the cold sunshine. Her eyes were bloodshot, and her skin burned red and blistered, and she never came into the dugout without looking to see if her face and ears were frozen.

On the dark days of the blizzards, she twisted hay; she lighted the lamp for cleaning and cooking and washing. And she played with the baby.

Then came the seven days' blizzard. There had been only a few hours of clear weather, but Caroline had worked desperately; she had enough hay for three days, and she had never known a blizzard to last longer. On the third day, she burned the hay sparingly, but she was not alarmed. On the fourth day, she broke up and burned a box, keeping the stove barely warm. On the fifth day, she burned the remaining box. The heavy benches and table were left, and the cradle; but in her folly she had left the ax in the barn.

If she and the baby lay close together under blankets, they could exist for some time in the warmth of their own bodies. If this were to go on forever— It could not, of course. She finally had to give up on the heavy benches, which she could not break up with her hands. It must be the cradle. But she feared to burn it so soon.

During the seventh day, she smashed and frugally burned the cradle. The birds that Charles had carved on it helped to boil tea and potatoes. She mashed a potato in a little hot water and fed it with a spoon to the baby. Then she put out the lamp and lay down with him under all the bedding.

A change in the sound of the wind awakened her. She did not know whether it was night or day, but when she forced the door open, she saw a whiteness of driven snow. A fierce north wind was driving the flakes steadily before it, and Caroline's relief was like a shout of joy. The snow was not swirling; the blizzard was over!

When next she opened the door, the storm had diminished so that she could see vaguely into it. She was able to clear the path, and when she reached its top, she could see dim shapes of barn and haystacks. The wind almost took her off her feet, and when she had a bundle of hay and was dragging it through the soft drifts, she had to fight it as though it were a live thing struggling to get away. After she had filled the dugout with hay, she stretched a rope from the barn to the top of the path so that she could fetch fuel, if necessary, during a blizzard.

Vaguely through the storm she seemed to see a dark patch on the opposite bank of the creek. It troubled her, for she could not imagine what it might be. She shut the door against it hurriedly and gave herself to the marvel of warmth and rest.

In the morning, in a dazzling glitter of sun on snow, she saw across the creek a herd of cattle. Huddled together, heads toward the south and noses drooping to their knees, they stood patiently enduring the cold. In terror she thought of the haystacks. The creek bank hid them from the cattle now, but if the herd moved southeast, across the slough, and saw that food, would all the strength of the wind prevent them from turning and destroying her fuel?

She put on her wraps and took the pistol. Not with pitchfork or ax, she knew, could she keep starving cattle from food. Nor did she dare risk facing the stampede. She could only try to turn it with shots, and failing, take refuge in the barn. If the fuel was lost—

The cattle did not move. It came to her, while she watched, that for a long time they had not moved. She stared at them—gaunt sides and ridged backbones, dropped necks and lax tails, motionless as if carved. Were they dead—frozen? No, breath came white from their nostrils. The thought that they might be dead had brought a vision of meat.

Her courage quailed.[1] There was something monstrous, something that gave her an unreasoning terror, like a breath of the su-

pernatural, in this herd of motionless cattle. Her jaw clenched against the cold; she went slowly, knee-deep in drifts, down the bank and across the frozen creek. Was this too great a risk? Leaving the baby in the dugout and venturing into she knew not what? The cattle did not move. She went within ten yards of them, five, two. They did not even lift their heads.

Over their eyes—thick over their eyes and hollowed temples—were cakes of ice. When she saw this, she understood. Their own breath, steaming upward while they plodded before the storm, had frozen and blinded them.

In a rage of pity, she plunged through the snow to the nearest patiently dying creature, and she wrenched the ice from its eyes. The steer snorted; it flung up its head in terror and ran, staggering. The herd quivered.

Caroline knew what she must do. She thought of the baby, drawing his strength from hers. She held all thought, all feeling, firmly to the baby, and walking to the nearest young steer, she put the pistol to its temple, shut her eyes, and fired. The report crashed through her.

She felt the shudder of all the beasts. When she opened her eyes, they had not moved. The steer lay dead, only a little blood trickling, freezing, from the wound. And perhaps it had been merciful to kill it.

Then, like an inspiration, a revival of all hope, she thought of a cow. A cow! Why not? In the herd there were many cows. Alas, they belonged to somebody. To whom? She did not know; that might never be known; impossible to guess how many miles—hundreds, perhaps—they had been driven by the storm. But they were branded. She could not steal. Yet, if she did not take one of these cows, would it not die? The whole blinded herd

---
1 **quailed** (kwāld): failed.

was helpless and dying. To kill for food was permissible, but to steal? Was she a cattle thief? But a cow—to have a cow! Milk for the baby. To surprise Charles, when he came home, with a cow!

She thought that perhaps there might be a yearling that was not branded. In her excitement, she was almost laughing. Clumsy in boots and coat and shawls, she pushed into the harmless herd. The heifers, she knew, would be in the center. The old bull grumbled in his throat, shaking his blind head, but he did not move; he did not even paw the snow. There was a young heifer, unbranded, almost plump, a clear red all over. Caroline marked it for her own, for their own cow.

This incredible marvel of good fortune filled her with laughing joy. What a triumph, what a joke—to take a cow from the blizzard, to take it from the very midst of a dangerous herd! And to have a cow—after so many calamities, in spite of calamities, to have a cow—this was a vindication of all confidence and hope.

She struggled through the drifts, across the creek, up the bank, to the dugout. She fed the stove with hay; she fed the baby, dressed him warmly, wrapped him in blankets like a cocoon. Then she went to the barn for a rope.

The short winter day gave her not too much time. The sun was overhead before she had succeeded in prodding and tugging the terrified, wild, blinded heifer out of the herd. It clung with desperation to the safety of the herd, and she had still to get across the creek, up the bank and into the barn. Its strength—greater than hers—wore her out. In one frantic lunge and leap it undid the work of half an hour.

It was near sunset before she got the heifer into the barn. She put hay into the manger and tore the ice from the heifer's eyes. With the rope and ax she went back to the herd. She cut the best parts of meat from the half-frozen carcass and tied the pieces together. Then, trembling in her weariness, she went from animal to animal, tearing off the blinding ice. The cattle snorted and plunged; each one staggered a little way and waited, bawling. Slowly the herd drifted before the wind. The sun sank in coldness, the glow faded from the snow, and in the dusk she released the old bull. He lifted his head, bellowed weakly, and plunged, staggering, after the herd.

In the dark they would not see her hay. The wind was blowing toward the town site; let the townspeople deal with the survivors that reached it. Caroline had given the cattle a chance for their lives, and she felt she had earned her cow.

The blizzard that came that night lasted only a day. Caroline lay cozily in bed. The baby gurgled and kicked in exuberance of spirits; a great beef stew simmered on the stove, filling the air with its fragrance. The snowy hay in the manger would suffice the heifer for both food and water. The howling of the blizzard no longer disturbed Caroline.

If only Charles could know that they had a cow! But now she was confident that Charles would come home strong and well; this winter would end; they would be together in the spring.

She had left two haunches of the beef outside the door to freeze on the snow. The blizzard had buried them, and she did not touch that drift when she dug the path again. Snow was still falling thickly enough to fill the air as with a mist, through which she saw the barn and haystacks.

The heifer was still safely tied to the manger. It snorted and plunged, wild-eyed, while she brought in hay and set two pails of snow within its reach. She spoke to it soothingly but did not touch it. In time, it would learn her kindness and be gentle. It had all the marks of a good milch cow.

She closed the barn door and snapped the padlock, feeling a proud sense of property to be taken care of. There was no wind, and all around her she could hear the soft rustle of the falling snow. With the shovel and rope, she went toward the haystack.

Afterward she always said she did not know what made her stop and turn around. By the corner of the barn stood a wolf.

If you went out— If a wolf sprang— What would become of the baby, alone in the dugout? *It's come,* her frozen heart knew.

She had only the shovel.

The wolf's haunches quivered, not quite crouching. The hair stood rough along its back. Fangs showed beneath the curling lip. It was a big, gaunt timber wolf. Its mate could not be far. Its mate was perhaps creeping up somewhere behind her. She dared not turn lest this one spring. Its eyes shone green in the half light. Its mouth opened in a soundless pant. It shifted a paw. Caroline did not move. Swiftly the wolf turned and vanished, a shadow, in the falling snow. The snow at once became a menace, hiding the lurking danger.

Caroline walked steadily through the white blindness toward the dugout. She did not run; she knew that if she ran, her inmost self would yield to shattering terror. As long as the wolf could not be seen anywhere, she was safe; the wolf would not spring unless it could see her. But while she was going down the path in the creek bank, it might spring on her from above. She knew it was following her.

She reached the path and ran. There was no measure in time for the length of that distance from the edge of the prairie to the door's slamming behind her. A long wolf howl rose from the ceiling above her head. Another answered it from the frozen creek below.

That evening she heard snarling and crunching at the door. The wolves had found the fresh meat. They must have been following the cattle, and the carcass of the steer she had killed had kept them near her. She heard a scratch of claws on the door.

She kept the lamp lighted and sat all night watching the paper pane. The window space was too small to let a wolf through easily. If paw or head appeared, she was ready to shoot. The ax was in the dugout, and she decided, rather than to go out in the storm again, to chop up the table and benches and burn them. But she made the hay last two days, and then a sliver of light above the snow, piled against the window, told her that the sun was shining.

Little by little she forced the door open. The pistol was in her hand. She found no trace of the wolves anywhere, and in the barn the heifer was safe. After that, she often heard wolves howling and found their tracks at the door and around the barn. She never left the dugout without the pistol. She was constantly reminded of Charles's warning about wolves—and outlaws. When she stirred the fire, she thought of the smoke ascending from the chimney. For seventy miles around, on clear days, it could be seen that the dugout was inhabited. Claim jumpers would probably not come. But outlaws?

She felt within herself a certainty that at any human threat of danger she would kill. She said to herself that no stranger should enter that dugout—not under any circumstances, not with any fair words. This she determined upon, sure of herself. But she did not yet know herself.

Blizzard followed blizzard, with clear hours or days between. She had lost reckoning of time and was not quite sure whether December had ended and January begun. But each day brought nearer the end of this winter. The baby was healthy, the heifer was safe in the barn, and she was holding out pretty well. More and more often she dreamed of springtime and Charles.

February had come, though she did not know it. Three clear days of terrible cold were ending, near nightfall, in the rising of the blizzard winds. That day Caroline had filled half the barn with hay; the heifer was now so gentle that she could turn it loose with that abundance of feed, and the washtub full of water provided for it if this blizzard lasted a week. The baby slept. The box was full of twisted hay, and the supper dishes were washed. By the faint light of the dying fire, Caroline combed her hair for the night.

A blow struck the door, and all at once the forces of the air gave tongue. Caroline thought how like demon riders they sounded, racing and circling overhead with unearthly, inhuman shriek and scream and wild halloo. A little snow, fine and hard as sand, was driven through the crack beneath the door. She shook her hair back and put up her hands to braid it, and in the gleam of light from the broken stove lid, she saw a joint of the stovepipe suddenly bend. The two ends of pipe slid upon each other; a crack opened between them. Petrified, she heard a human cry, a groaned exclamation.

A man was on top of the dugout. Blind in the storm, he had stumbled against the chimney. No honest man, no lost homesteader. Not for miles around was there an undeserted homestead. All afternoon the blizzard had been threatening; no honest man would have gone far from shelter. Only a rider out of the northwest might have fled before the storm—a rider out of the northwestern refuges of the outlaws. "Wolves and outlaws will be moving back to settled country," Charles had said.

The man had struck the chimney on the eastern side; he was going toward the creek. Only a few steps and he would fall down the creek bank, down into the deep drifts below. He would be gone, lost, buried somewhere by the storm. Only his bones would be found after the snow melted in the spring. "Keep still!" she said to herself. "Don't move. It isn't your business. Don't let him in. Who knows what he is, what he would do? Think of the baby. *What are you doing?*"

Her mouth close to the stovepipe, she shouted, "Stand still! Don't move!" The soot, dislodged from the open joint of the pipe, fell on her face, so quickly had she acted. "You hear me?" she called.

A vague shout replied. He seemed to have fallen or to have wandered a step or two

toward the creek. She knew how the winds were swirling, beating and tugging at him from every side, how the sandlike snow was flaying[2] his face; she saw him blinded, deafened, lost. An outlaw, but human, fighting the storm.

"Lie down! Crawl!" she shouted. "Creek bank ahead! Follow it to the right! The right! Find a rope! You hear?"

His shout was dull through the shriller winds. Then she hesitated. But the barn was

2 **flaying**: cutting open.

padlocked. "There is a path!" she called. "Path! Down! To the left!"

If he shouted again, she did not hear him. She twisted her hair and thrust pins into it, buttoned her basque, and lighted the lamp. She got her pistol and made sure it was loaded. Some instinct, hardly reasonable—for who would harm a baby?—made her lift Charles John, wrap him in a blanket, and lay him on the hay in the woodbox. She felt better with the baby behind her. Then she lifted the bar on the door and, retreating behind the table, she waited.

She had time to regret what she had done and to know that she could not have done otherwise.

The wind suddenly tore open the door. Snow whirled in and cold. The lamp flared smokily, and as she started forward, the man appeared in the white blizzard. He was tall and shapeless in fur coat and cap and earmuffs caked with snow. He was muffled to reddened slits of eyes and snow-matted eyebrows. It was an instant before she knew him and screamed. The wild scream was dizzily circling in her head when his arms closed around her, hard and cold as ice.

"Oh, how—how—how did you get here?" she gasped after a while, unable still to believe it. Her hands kept clutching, clutching up and down the snowy fur, as if her hands were separate things, frantic too, to make sure this was Charles.

"Gosh, I'm freezing you to death! I've got to shut the door," he said.

They were together; everything was all right. She heard the clamor of the storm, all the demons shrieking. But now it was simply a blizzard, simply the winter weather on their farm.

Discussion

1. What were the three main dangers that threatened Caroline and the baby? At what point during the winter were they in the greatest danger? Why? What did Caroline do to save them?

2. What problems did Caroline create for herself?

3. Why was Caroline afraid when she saw the herd of cattle? As it turned out, the cattle were not any threat to her. Why? How did she help the cattle and help herself at the same time?

4. Where did Caroline encounter the wolf? How did she survive this meeting? What had attracted the wolves to her area?

5. When Caroline heard a man on the roof of the dugout, who did she think it was? In spite of her husband's warnings, what did she do? What danger was she in? Why do you think she did what she did?

6. Good luck and Caroline's own resourcefulness both played a part in her survival. Which problems were resolved by luck? Which ones were resolved by Caroline's own efforts?

Vocabulary

A SYNONYM is a word that means exactly the same, or nearly the same, as another word. For example:

cold—chilly   blizzard—snowstorm   dread—fear

An ANTONYM is a word that means exactly the opposite, or nearly the opposite, of another word. For example:

strong—weak   dark—light   winter—summer

A. On a separate sheet of paper, copy the *italicized* words below and write synonyms for them. If you need help, use a dictionary.

1. Caroline learned to be *frugal* with kerosene.
2. The silence around the dugout was immense and *profound*.
3. She was not *perturbed* until she tried to open the door.
4. A blizzard of such *severity* in October predicted a hard winter ahead.
5. The storm *diminished* and she was able to see outside the dugout.

B. In this exercise, copy the *italicized* words and write antonyms for them.

1. The cattle had ridged backbones, dropped necks, and *lax* tails.
2. Caroline's courage eventually *quailed*.
3. The baby's spirits were *exuberant*.
4. *Petrified*, she heard a human cry.
5. The *clamor* of the storm no longer disturbed them.

Rose Wilder Lane 1887—1968

Born in what is now South Dakota, Rose Wilder Lane experienced many of the same problems Caroline did in "Prairie Winter." In fact, for the first seven years of her life, her family suffered crop failures, sickness, and disastrous weather. Finally they moved to the Ozark Mountains in Missouri. Since horse and wagon was the family's only means of transportation, the trip took three months.

It is possible that Rose got her desire to write from her mother, Laura Ingalls Wilder, the author of the "Little House" books.

Thomas Jefferson *1743–1826*

ROSEMARY and STEPHEN VINCENT BENÉT

Thomas Jefferson,
What do you say
Under the gravestone
Hidden away?

"I was a giver, 5
I was a molder,
I was a builder
With a strong shoulder."

Six feet and over,
Large-boned and ruddy, 10
The eyes gray-hazel
But bright with study.

The big hands clever
With pen and fiddle
And ready, ever, 15
For any riddle.

From buying empires
To planting 'taters,
From Declarations[1]
To trick dumb-waiters. 20

"I liked the people,
The sweat and crowd of them,
Trusted them always
And spoke aloud of them.

"I liked all learning 25
And wished to share it
Abroad like pollen
For all who merit.

"I liked fine houses
With Greek pilasters,[2] 30
And built them surely,
My touch a master's.

"I liked queer gadgets
And secret shelves,
And helping nations 35
To rule themselves.

"Jealous of others?
Not always candid?
But huge of vision
And open-handed. 40

"A wild-goose chaser?
Now and again,
Build Monticello,[3]
You little men!

"Design my plow, sirs, 45
They use it still,
Or found my college
At Charlottesville.

---

1 **Declarations:** the Declaration of Independence.

2 **pilasters:** round columns.
3 **Monticello:** Jefferson's home in Virginia.

88   *Scenes from America*

"And still go questing
New things and thinkers,   50
And keep as busy
As twenty tinkers.

"While always guarding
The people's freedom—
You need more hands, sir?   55
I didn't need 'em.

"They call you rascal?
They called me worse.
You'd do grand things, sir,
But lack the purse?   60

"I got no riches.
I died a debtor.
I died free-hearted
And that was better.

"For life was freakish   65
But life was fervent,
And I was always
Life's willing servant.

"Life, life's too weighty?
Too long a haul, sir?   70
I lived past eighty.
I liked it all, sir."

Discussion

1. The use of quotation marks in this poem indicates that it is a conversation. Whom is it between? Where does it take place?

2. What do you think the title of this poem is supposed to represent?

3. What faults did Jefferson readily admit to?

4. How is Jefferson's personality portrayed in this poem? How might this picture of Jefferson be different if he were not describing himself?

Stephen Vincent Benét 1898—1943

Benét was a poet, novelist, dramatist, and short-story writer. He once advised young writers, "Do not use up all your shot on the first chipmunk that crosses your path. Or, when an elephant comes along, you'll have an empty gun." Benét had plenty of literary ammunition and kept using it from his first publication at the age of seventeen until his death. He received many honors and awards for his writings.

*The Europeans who settled along the eastern
coast of America were not the only pioneers. As
this poem points out, in the western part of
America there were the "other pioneers."*

The Other Pioneers

ROBERTO FÉLIX SALAZAR

Now I must write
Of those of mine who rode these plains
Long years before the Saxon and the Irish came.
Of those who plowed the land and built the towns
And gave the towns soft-woven Spanish names.   5
Of those who moved across the Rio Grande
Toward the hiss of Texas snake and Indian yell.
Of men who from the earth made thick-walled homes
And from the earth raised churches to their God.
And of the wives who bore them sons   10
And smiled with knowing joy.

They saw the Texas sun rise golden-red with promised wealth
And saw the Texas sun sink golden yet, with wealth unspent.
"Here," they said. "Here to live and here to love."
"Here is the land for our sons and the sons of our sons."   15
And they sang the songs of ancient Spain
And they made new songs to fit new needs.
They cleared the brush and planted the corn
And saw green stalks turn black from lack of rain.
They roamed the plains behind the herds   20
And stood the Indian's cruel attacks.
There was dust and there was sweat,
And there were tears and the women prayed.

EAST SIDE MAIN PLAZA, SAN ANTONIO, TEXAS *William G. Samuel*

And the years moved on.
Those who were first placed in graves   25
Beside the broad mesquite and the tall nopal.[1]
Gentle mothers left their graces and their arts
And stalwart fathers pride and manly strength.
Salinas, de la Garza, Sánchez, García,
Uribe, González, Martínez, de León: 30
Such were the names of the fathers.
Salinas, de la Garza, Sánchez, García,
Uribe, González, Martínez, de León:
Such are the names of the sons.

---

1 **mesquite** (me skĕt′) . . . **nopal**: a shrub and a cactus
found in the southwestern United States and Mexico.

Discussion

1. Who are the "other pioneers" mentioned in this poem?
2. What problems did these pioneers have?
3. In the last stanza, what does the author say these "other pioneers" left their children?

The Other Pioneers **91**

*The mountain fur trappers of the great
Southwest were independent, brave, and ruthless.
They were adventurers who were out to make a
quick fortune. Unknowingly, however, they also
pointed the way west for other pioneers.*

A Wild Strain

PAUL HORGAN

THE MOUNTAIN SYSTEM of the northern Rio Grande was a vast, secret world. Wandering Indians there made shrines of twig and feather and bone, and went their ways. Close to the high clouds that made their rivers, the inhuman peaks doubled the roar of thunder, or hissed with sheets of rain, or abided in massive silence. Below them lay every variation of park and meadow and lost lake; gashed canyon and rocky roomlike penetralia[1] in the stupendous temples of the high wilderness. Along hidden watercourses and in little cupped lakes lived and worked the family of a small creature destined to be the first cause of great change in the human life of the river during the early 19th century. It was the beaver.

In still pool or mild current the beaver made his house of mud and twig. Its doorway was under water. The occupants dived to enter it and came up beyond into the dry shelter of their lodge that they had built of sticks and mud, where their food was stored and where they were safe from animal predators.[2] The backwater before the den had to be three feet deep, and if this did not exist naturally, the beavers built dams to collect it. They chose a tree by the edge. Sitting upright, they chewed away bark in a belt, eating of it now and then from their paws. Down to bare wood, they gnawed away until the tree was ready to fall. Often it fell into water where it would make a stout beginning for a dam. Working in concert, they brought from nearby woods bundles of stick and bush and, starting out from the bank, began to shore up their barrier. They dived to the bottom of the water and brought up loads of mud. This was plaster. With their broad tails they troweled mud over the laid timbers, layer upon layer, always extending the reach of the dam until it touched the opposite limit of the course or cove where they worked. At times they paused to play, racing each other in the water, diving, and loudly slapping the water with their tails.

When house and dam were finished, it was time to lay up provisions within against

---

1 **penetralia**: the innermost parts of a temple or palace.

2 **predators**: killers.

winter when there would be no green sprouts of willow and cottonwood and fresh grass to eat in season. The beaver clan went foraging, often far inland from their water, in search of bark. The best bark was on the smaller branches high out of reach. The beavers brought down the tree, and then stripped the tender young bark off the branches laid low. They cut the bark into three-foot strips, pulled them to their water, and there floated them to the lodge. They made little signs to guide them as they went—mounds of twig and earth which they impregnated[3] with castorum, a musk secreted[4] by the animal itself, that attracted their sense of smell and reassuringly meant *beaver* and told them where the road lay. Once in the lodge and eating, they were neat and fastidious. They took out through the water doorway all the refuse of a meal and threw it into the current. Drifting away, it lodged down-current out of their way—bits of gnawed stick and knotty branch and hard root.

In the spring came the young. Leaving the mother during gestation, the male went traveling, often far away to other water, where he swam and frolicked, ate tender greens at the bank, and did not return home until the offspring were born. Then he took them in charge, trained them in work, and in the late summer led them out to forage before the sharp frosts and the thickening of their fur against the cold. Everywhere in the secret lakes and along the tributaries and in the quieter passages of the main river this lively cycle was continued by beavers in incalculable thousands, and wherever mountain and water met, evidences of it were scattered and lodged undisturbed—until the last Spanish and the first Mexican years of the Rio Grande.

For by then the beaver's fur was in great demand for the making of men's hats. The hatters of London and Paris, New York, Boston and Philadelphia consumed great cargoes of beaver pelt, and the fur trade moved westward out of St. Louis over the American continent to Astoria and the northern Rockies. While Stephen Austin was completing his organized arrangements with the new government of Mexico to bring new settlers from the east nearer to the lower Rio Grande, the river's upper reaches knew another sort of growing infiltration by men who whether they came alone, or with a few companions, or many, still came without formal approval by the Mexican government, and with no resounding program of colonial loyalty or pious hope.

They came to take beaver in the mountain waters, in spring and autumn up north, or all through the winter in New Mexico if the season was mild. Many of them were French Canadians; the rest were from anywhere in the United States, though mostly from the frontier settlements. They outfitted themselves at St. Louis, and remembering what was commonly known out of Pike's[5] reports, crossed the plains and entered the mountains by the hundreds in the 1820s. Among their number were men who made the first trails beyond the prairies, that led overland as early as 1826, to the Pacific. Jedediah Smith, Charles Beaubien, the Roubidoux brothers, Céran St. Vrain, Bill Williams, the youthful runaway Kit Carson for whose return a reward of one cent was posted by the employer to whom he was apprenticed—such

---

3 **impregnated**: soaked.
4 **musk secreted** (si krēt′ ed): perfume substance given out.

5 **Pike's**: a reference to Z. M. Pike (1779—1813), an American general and explorer.

men went to the mountains after beaver skins to sell for a few dollars a pound, and all unwittingly showed the way across the continent.

The movement had already had its pioneer in James Pursley, the Kentuckian, who had been detained at Santa Fe in 1805 under the Spanish governor. Others entering New Mexico from the plains were arrested, to be marched down the Rio Grande to El Paso and the prisons of Chihuahua in 1812, after confiscation of their goods, and were not released until the freeing of Mexico in 1821. Another party of trappers was taken by the provincial Spanish government in 1817, jailed in irons for forty-eight days at Santa Fe, and was finally released after being stripped of thirty thousand dollars' worth of furs and supplies. Such actions by the government were meant to protect the trapping industry already worked on a small scale by the Mexicans of the valley. Regulations declared that only permanent residents might hunt beaver. They were required to buy a hunting license, their number in any party was carefully fixed and recorded, and so were the length of time to be spent in the hunt and the weapons to be used—traps, firearms, or snares. If the early American trappers could not buy official licenses, they soon found a way to get around the law. "The North Americans began to corrupt the New Mexicans," noted a Santa Fe lawyer, "by purchasing their licenses from them," and so risked arrest.

But still the trappers came, and against other hazards. The greatest of these were the roving Indians on the prairies and the eastern upsweeps of the Rocky Mountains. For an Indian hunter could read the menace that came with the white hunter; and he moved with every savagery to defend his hunting grounds. The trapper retaliated. He fought the Indian with Indian ways . . . and pressed westward. He fought distance, hunger, and thirst, and if he was unwary enough to be bitten by a rattlesnake, he cauterized[6] the wound by burning a thick pinch of gunpowder in it. Once in the mountains he met his second greatest adversary in great numbers. This was the great grizzly bear, who was curious, fearless and gifted with a massive ursine[7] intelligence. With lumbering speed the grizzlies could travel forty miles between dawn and dark through mountains. It was not unusual for trappers to kill five or six in a day, or to see fifty or sixty, and one hunter declared that one day he saw two hundred and twenty of them. The grizzly towered above a man. His forepaws were eight or nine inches wide, and his claws six inches long. He weighed from fifteen to eighteen hundred pounds. His embrace was certain death. So steadily did he smell and find the trappers that in a few decades by their guns his kind was made almost extinct.

The earthen village of Ranchos de Taos near the Rio Grande was the northern town nearest the beaver waters of the mountains, and there came the mountain men to organize their supplies for the trapping seasons. They found that some men of the Ranchos de Taos already, though to a limited degree, followed the trapper's life. Seeing how swarthy they were, the newcomers thought they must be of mixed Negro and Indian blood. It was astonishing how primitive were the ways of life in Taos—the farmers used only oxen in cultivating their fields, and a miserable plow made of a Y-shaped branch

---

6 **cauterized**: burned as a cure to prevent infection.
7 **ursine** (ėr′ sīn): bearlike.

Courtesy of the Buffalo Bill Historical Center, Cody, Wyoming

THE LOST GREENHORN *Alfred Jacob Miller* (detail)

from a tree, with an iron head to its end that turned the earth. There were no sawmills; no mechanical ingenuities to speed up work; and—what was oddest to the squinting and raring trappers from the East—the people seemed to have no desire for such means to change their slow, simple ways.

The mountain men encountered at Taos their first experience of the Mexican government. Taos was the seat of the northernmost customs house of Mexico. As the trappers brought little to declare in goods for sale, they were evidently allowed to go about their preparations for departure into the mountains. They bought what flour and produce they could, and recruited an occasional Taoseño[8] to join their parties, and

made ready their equipment. In the far northern Rockies the trapping parties were often large, numbering from fifty to a hundred men. Most of these were camp personnel who maintained a base for the trappers and hunters who went forward into the wilderness. The "Frenchmen" from Canada sometimes kept Indian wives, and established in the mountains a semipermanent household with rude domestic amenities. Other parties were smaller, and instead of working for the great fur companies as contract employees, went their ways alone, as "free" trappers. Those who descended to the Rio Grande's northern reaches were more often than not in small units of a dozen, or three or four, or even a single man, who meant to take their furs and sell them to the highest bidder at the season's end. But all the trappers

---

8 **Taoseño** (tä ōsen′ yō): native of Taos, New Mexico.

shared aspects of costume, equipment and even character, many of which grew from the tradition of the forest frontiersman of the late 18th century.

The mountain man was almost Indian-colored from exposure to the weather. His hair hung upon his shoulders. He was bearded. Next to his skin he wore a red flannel loincloth. His outer clothes were of buckskin, fringed at all the seams. The jacket sometimes reached to the knee over tight, wrinkled leggings. His feet were covered by moccasins made of deer or buffalo leather. Around his waist was a leather belt into which he thrust his flintlock pistols, his knife for skinning or scalping, and his shingling hatchet. Over one shoulder hung his bullet pouch, and over the other his powder horn. To their baldrics[9] were attached a bullet mold, ball screw, wiper and an awl for working leather. When he moved he shimmered with fringe and rang and clacked with accouterments[10] of metal and wood. The most important of these were his traps, of which he carried five or six, and his firearm with its slender separate crutch of hardwood. It was always a rifle—never a shotgun, which he scorned as an effete[11] fowling piece. Made in the gun works of the brothers Jacob and Samuel Hawken, of St. Louis, the rifle had two locks for which he kept about him a hundred flints, twenty-five pounds of powder and several pounds of lead. The barrel, thirty-six inches long, was made by hand of soft iron. The recoil of its blast shocked into a hardwood stock beautifully turned and slender. Peering vividly out from under his low-crowned hat of rough wool,

he was an American original, as hard as the hardest thing that could happen to him.

Alone, or with a companion or a small party, he packed his supplies on two horses and, riding a third, left Taos for the mountains in the autumn. He was wary of roaming Indians, dangerous animals—and other trapper parties. For nobody could stake a claim on hunting country, and every trapper party competed against each other. He did his best to keep his movement and direction secret, to throw others off the trail, and find the wildest country where he would be most free from rivalry. Following the groins of the foothills, the mountain men came among high slopes and rocky screens. If two worked as a pair, they sought for a concealed place where they could make camp and tether their horses near beaver water. There they built a shelter, and if their goal was a mountain lake, or a slow passage of stream, they set to work hacking out a cottonwood canoe. In natural forest paths they looked for the little musky mounds that marked beaver trails. They searched currents for the drift of gnawed beaver sticks. Every such sign took them closer to their prey. When they were sure they had found its little world, at evening under the pure suspended light of mountain skies they silently coasted along the shores of quiet water to set their traps.

They laid each trap two or three inches underwater on the slope of the shore, and, a little removed, they fixed a pole in deep mud and chained the trap to it. They stripped a twig of its bark and dipped one end into a supply of castorum, the beaver's own secretion that would be his bait. They fastened the twig between the open jaws of the trap, leaving the musky end four inches above water. The beaver in the nighttime was drawn to it by scent. He raised his muzzle to

9 **baldrics**: belts.
10 **accouterments** (ə kü′ tər mənts): equipment.
11 **effete** (i fēt′): ineffective.

inhale, his hindquarters went lower in the water, and the trap seized him. He threw himself into deeper water; but the trap held him, and the pole held the trap, and presently he sank to drown. In the high, still daybreak, the trappers coasted by their traps again in the canoe, and took up their catch.

Working a rocky stream from the bank, the trappers lodged the trap and its chained pole in the current, where the beaver found the scent. In his struggles he might drag the trap and pole to the shore, where his burden became entangled in "thickets of brook willows," and held him till found. Sometimes he struggled to deeper midstream water, where the pole floated as a marker; and then the trappers putting off their buckskins, that if saturated would dry slowly and then be hard as wood, went naked and shivering into the cold mountain stream to swim for their take. And some parties rafted down the whole length of the river in New Mexico, all the way to El Paso. Their method astonished the New Mexicans, to whom it seemed suspect because it was new. Was it proper to use a new kind of trap and float noiselessly to a beaver site, taking their catch by surprise, and spend the night in midstream with the raft moored to trees on each bank to be out of reach of wild animals? And at the end of the journey, to sell the timbers of the raft for a good price at El Paso where wood was so scarce, take up the catch and vanish overland eastward without reporting to the government? The New Mexicans frowned at such ingenuity, energy and novelty.

When in the mountains they had exhausted a beaver site, the trappers moved on to another. With their traps over their shoulders they forded streams amidst floating ice; or with their traps hanging down their backs, they scaled and descended the hard ridges between watercourses where the harder the country, the better the chance that no others had come there before them. The trap weighed about five pounds, and its chain was about five feet long. A full-grown beaver weighed between thirty and forty pounds. The catch was an awkward burden to carry back to camp for skinning. Removing the pelt from the animal, the trappers stretched it on a frame of sprung willow withes to dry. The flesh they cooked by hanging it before a fire from a thong. The carcass turned by its own weight, roasting evenly. The broad, flat tail they liked best of all. They cut it off, skinned it, toasted it at the end of a stick, and ate it with relish, as a relief from the usual hunter's diet of deer, elk, antelope, bear, lynx, or buffalo meat, or buffalo marrow-bones, or buffalo blood drunk spurting and warm from the throat of a newly killed specimen.

All through the winter-fast months the mountain men worked, obedient to animal laws and themselves almost animal in their isolation, freedom and harmony with the wilderness. Their peltries were cached[12] and the piles grew, in the end to be baled with rawhide thongs. A trapper took in a good season about four hundred pounds of beaver skins. Sometimes his cache was invaded and destroyed by prowling animals, or stolen by mountain Indians; and then his months of hardship went for nothing. But if he kept his pile, he was ready to come out of the boxed mountains whose cool winds brushing all day over high-tilted meadows carried the scent of wild flowers down the open slopes where he descended with his haul. At five dollars a pound, it would bring him two thousand dollars in the market.

---

12 **peltries were cached:** skins were hidden.

But once again in Taos, he might then meet trouble with the Mexican authorities. Now that he had his cargo, they showed an interest in him. If he was unlucky, they questioned him, examined his bales, and invoking[13] regulations that nobody mentioned when he started out months before, confiscated his whole catch. If he resisted he was taken to Santa Fe and jailed, with official talk about the Mexican decree of 1824 that prohibited trapping by foreigners in Mexican territory. Since there were no public warehouses, hunters could only store their catches in towns by making deals with local citizens for storage space on private premises. If a Mexican citizen gave protection to a foreign trapper, he was in danger from his own government. At Peña Blanca on the Rio Grande in 1827, one Luís María Cabeza de Vaca hid in his house the "contraband" of beaver skins left there for safe keeping by a trapper named Young. From Santa Fe a corporal and eight soldiers of the presidial company came to seize it. Cabeza de Vaca resisted them, firing upon them in protection of his home. The soldiers returned the fire and killed him. The official report of the affair stated that "the deceased died while defending a violation of the . . . rights of the Nation," and asked exoneration[14] for the corporal and his squad.

But local officials might be bribed, and a license trumped up, and the catch restored to the trapper. In any case, after his mountain months, he was ready to burst his bonds of solitude, and he did so with raw delight. All his general passion and violence, that his mountain work required him to suppress while moving lithe and crafty after watchful creatures, he now broke free in the clay village where he returned among men and women. He had a frosty look of filth over him. His hair was knotted and his beard was a catch-all for the refuse of months. His clothes reeked like his body. His mouth was dry with one kind of thirst. If the one tavern in the town was full, he went to a house and asked for a corner of the packed mud floor where he could throw his gear, and was granted it. The family knew what he came to seek with his comrades. The women took kettles out of doors and built fires around them to heat water. When it was hot, they brought it in and found him waiting in his crusted skin sitting in a wooden tub. The women poured the water over him. He thrashed. He was as hairy as an animal. The water hit him and he gave the recognized cry of the mountain man—"Wagh!"—a grunt, a warning, and a boast. Bathing as violently as he did all other acts, he began again to know forgotten satisfactions. As he emerged with wet light running on his skin, white everywhere but on face and hands whose weather would not wash off, he was a new man. . . .

Presently he traveled to a trading post on the prairies, or to St. Louis, to sell his catch. In the frontier cities of the United States he was a prodigal[15] spender, uneasy in their relatively ordered society, loose as it was compared to life in older and more easterly places. When the season rolled around again, he was off again to his lost lakes and rivers where obscurely content he felt most like the self he imagined until it came true.

For over three decades the trapping trade flourished. At its height the animal shipment of beaver skins from Abiquiu on the Chama

---

13 **invoking:** put into effect.
14 **exoneration** (eg zon'ə rā' shən): release from blame.

15 **prodigal** (prod'ə gəl): wasteful.

and Taos on the Rio Grande was worth two hundred thousand dollars. But in the 1830s the market for beaver began to break, for the China trade out of England and New England was growing, and the clipper ships were bringing silk in great quantities to the manufacturing cities of the world. Fashion changed. Silk was offered for hats instead of fur; and the change brought the decline and finally the almost virtual abolishment of the Rocky Mountain fur trade. The trapper was cast adrift to find new work. He could abide it only in the land of his hardy prowess, and there he found it, whether he joined the overland commercial caravans as a wagon hand, or the American Army's later surveying expeditions as a guide, or amazingly settled on river land as a farmer. He knew the craft of the wilderness and he made its first trails for the westering white man. Some of the earliest venturers in the Mexico trade were trappers; and as the trade continued to grow and establish its bases ever farther west, the trappers met it with their wares; and what had been a memorized path became a visible road; and along it moved another of the unofficial invasions of the Mexican Rio Grande that could only end by changing nations. The first sustained effort toward that end was made by the individual trapper. His greatest power to achieve it lay in his individualism. Where the Mexican was hedged by governmental authority, the trapper made his own. Where the Mexican was formal, he was wild. . . . The invasion, unorganized as it was, commercial in purpose, wild and free in its individuals, seemed to express some secret personal motive beyond the material. The trappers forecast a new, a wild, strain of human society to come to the northern river.

Discussion

1. Describe the appearance of the men who trapped beaver in the northern Rio Grande area. What kind of men were they? Where did they come from? Why did they trap beaver?

2. Describe the trappers' method of catching beaver. Why were the people living in New Mexico upset by this method?

3. Why did beaver trapping finally stop? What did the trappers do then?

4. What was the value of these trappers to the later development of western America? In what way were they a "wild strain"?

Composition

1. Imagine you are living in Taos, New Mexico, during the height of the fur trapping season. Your parents have rented a room to a fur trapper. In the course of his stay, he tells you about his life and work in the mountains. Write a letter to a friend back East describing him. First tell what he looks like. Then tell how he traps

the beaver and how he survives living in the mountains. End with your opinion of a trapper's life.

2. On page 96, there is a description of a fur trapper in his working clothes. It describes many men who followed this occupation, not just one man. Select some occupation that uses special clothing and equipment and describe a worker—either a man or a woman—in a similar way. You could, for example, describe a farmer, a construction worker, a police officer, a teacher, a salesclerk, a nurse, or a person in business. Using the example on page 96 as a model, first describe the person's face and head, then the clothing, and finally the equipment. End your portrait of this American worker with a phrase that would be a compliment to his or her occupation. Notice how this author closes with, "He was an American original. . . ."

Paul Horgan 1903—

Paul Horgan was born in Buffalo, New York, but when he was eleven, his parents moved to New Mexico where he spent much of his life. He attended the New Mexico Military Institute for three years and later returned there as a staff member. During World War II, he was a Lt. Colonel in the United States Army and later served on the general staff of the Department of the Army. Horgan's writing has been praised for its historical accuracy and literary value. His book *The Fault of Angels* won the Harper Prize Novel Award in 1933, and in 1955, *Great River: The Rio Grande in North American History* was awarded both the Pulitzer Prize and the Bancroft Prize of Columbia University. Horgan has also written plays for television and an adaptation of his novel, *Things As They Are,* was filmed in 1970.

Of all of the legendary pioneers who settled the West, Johnny Appleseed was surely the most unusual. He owned no land, raised no family, made no money. Yet, his famous trees continue to enrich America today.

Johnny Appleseed: A Pioneer Hero

W. D. HALEY

THE "FAR WEST" is rapidly becoming only a traditional designation:[1] railroads have destroyed the romance of frontier life, or have surrounded it with so many appliances of civilization that the pioneer character is rapidly becoming mythical. The men and women who obtain their groceries and dry goods from New York by rail in a few hours have nothing in common with those who, fifty years ago, "packed" salt a hundred miles to make their mush palatable, and could only exchange corn and wheat for molasses and calico by making long and perilous voyages in flat boats down the Ohio and Mississippi rivers to New Orleans.

The first reliable trace of our modest hero finds him in the Territory of Ohio, in 1801, with a horseload of apple seeds, which he planted in various places on and about the borders of Licking Creek, the first orchard thus originated by him being on the farm of Isaac Stadden, in what is now known as Licking County, in the state of Ohio. During

the five succeeding years we have no authentic account of his movements until we reach a pleasant spring day in 1806, when a pioneer settler in Jefferson County, Ohio, noticed a peculiar craft, with a remarkable occupant and a curious cargo, slowly dropping down with the current of the Ohio River. It was "Johnny Appleseed," by which name Jonathan Chapman was afterward known in every log cabin from the Ohio River to the Northern lakes, and westward to the prairies of what is now the State of Indiana. With two canoes lashed together he was transporting a load of apple seeds to the Western frontier, for the purpose of creating orchards on the farthest verge of white settlements. A long and toilsome voyage it was, and must have occupied a great deal of time, as the lonely traveler stopped at every inviting spot to plant the seeds and make his infant nurseries. These are the first well authenticated facts in the history of Jonathan Chapman, whose birth, there is good reason for believing, occurred in Boston, Massachusetts, in 1775. According to this, which was his own

---

1 **designation**: name.

statement in one of his less modest moods, he was, at the time of his appearance on Licking Creek, twenty-six years of age. His whole after-life was devoted to the work of planting apple seeds in remote places. The seeds he gathered from the cider presses of Western Pennsylvania; but his canoe voyage in 1806 appears to have been the only occasion upon which he adopted that method of transporting them, as all his subsequent journeys were made on foot.

In personal appearance Chapman was a small, wiry man, full of restless activity; he had long dark hair, a scanty beard that was never shaved, and keen black eyes that sparkled with a peculiar brightness. His dress was of the oddest description. Generally, even in the coldest weather, he went barefooted, but sometimes, for his long journeys, he would make himself a rude pair of sandals; at other times he would wear any cast-off foot covering he chanced to find—a boot on one foot and an old brogan or a moccasin on the other.

It appears to have been a matter of conscience with him never to purchase shoes, although he was rarely without money enough to do so. On one occasion, in an unusually cold November, while he was traveling barefooted through mud and snow, a settler, who happened to possess a pair of shoes that were too small for his own use, forced their acceptance upon Johnny, declaring that it was sinful for a human being to travel with naked feet in such weather. A few days afterward the donor was in the village that has since become the thriving city of Mansfield, and met his beneficiary contentedly plodding along with his feet bare and half frozen. With some degree of anger he inquired for the cause of such foolish conduct, and received for reply that Johnny had over-

taken a poor, barefooted family moving Westward, and as they appeared to be in much greater need of clothing than he was, he had given them the shoes.

Johnny's dress was generally composed of cast-off clothing, that he had taken in payment for apple trees; and as the pioneers were far less extravagant than their descendants in such matters, the homespun and buckskin garments that they discarded would not be very elegant or serviceable. In his later years, however, he seems to have thought that even this kind of second-hand raiment was too luxurious, as his principal garment was made of a coffee sack, in which he cut holes for his head and arms to pass through, and pronounced it "a very serviceable cloak, and as good clothing as any man need wear."

In the matter of headgear his taste was equally unique; his first experiment was with a tin vessel that served to cook his mush, but this was open to the objection that it did not protect his eyes from the beams of the sun; so he constructed a hat of pasteboard with an immense peak in front, and having thus secured an article that combined usefulness with economy, it became his permanent fashion.

Thus strangely clad, he was perpetually wandering through forests and morasses,[2] and suddenly appearing in white settlements and Indian villages; but there must have been some rare force of gentle goodness dwelling in his looks and breathing in his words, for it is the testimony of all who knew him that, notwithstanding his ridiculous attire, he was always treated with the greatest respect by the simplest frontiersman, and, what is a better test, the boys of the settlements forbore to jeer at him. With grown-up people and

2 **morasses** (me ras′ es): marshes and swamps.

boys he was usually shy, but showed great affection for little girls, always having pieces of ribbon and gay calico to give to his little favorites. When he consented to eat with any family, he would never sit down to the table until he was assured that there was an ample supply for the children; and his sympathy for their youthful troubles and his kindness toward them made him friends among all the juveniles of the borders.

The Indians also treated Johnny with the greatest kindness. He was regarded as a "great medicine man," on account of his strange appearance, eccentric actions, and, especially, the fortitude with which he could endure pain, in proof of which he would often thrust pins and needles into his flesh. His nervous sensibilities really seem to have been less acute than those of ordinary people, for his method of treating the cuts and sores that were the consequences of his barefooted wanderings through briers and thorns was to sear the wound with a red-hot iron, and then cure the burn. . . .

It was his custom, when he had been welcomed to some hospitable log house after a weary day of journeying, to lie down on the split-log floor, and, after inquiring if his auditors would hear "some news right fresh from heaven," produce his few tattered books, among which would be a New Testament, and read and expound until his uncultivated hearers would catch the spirit and glow of his enthusiasm, while they scarcely comprehended his language.

A lady who knew him in his later years writes in the following terms of one of these domiciliary[3] readings of poor, self-sacrificing Johnny Appleseed: "We can hear him read now, just as he did that summer day, when we were busy quilting upstairs, and he lay near the door, his voice rising denunciatory and thrilling—strong and loud as the roar of wind and waves, then soft and soothing as the balmy airs that quivered the morning glory leaves about his gray beard. His was a strange eloquence at times, and he was undoubtedly a man of genius."

Next to his advocacy of his religious ideas, his enthusiasm for the cultivation of apple trees in what he termed "the only proper way"—that is, from the seed—was the absorbing object of his life. Upon this, as upon religion, he was eloquent in his appeals. He would describe the growing and ripening fruit as such a rare and beautiful gift of the Almighty with words that became pictures, until his hearers could almost see its manifold forms of beauty present before them. To his eloquence on this subject, as well as to his actual labors in planting nurseries, the country over which he traveled for so many years is largely indebted for its numerous orchards. But he denounced as absolute wickedness all devices of pruning and grafting, and would speak of the act of cutting a tree as if it were a cruelty inflicted upon a feeling being.

Whenever Johnny saw an animal abused, or heard of it, he would purchase it and give it to some more humane settler, on condition that it should be kindly treated and properly cared for. It frequently happened that the long journey into the wilderness would cause the new settlers to be encumbered with lame and broken-down horses, that were turned loose to die. In the autumn Johnny would make a diligent search for all such animals, and, gathering them up, he would bargain for their food and shelter until the next spring, when he would lead them away to some good pasture for the summer. If they recovered so as to be capable of working, he would never sell them, but would lend or give them away, stipulating for their good usage. His conception of the absolute sin was the inflicting of pain or death upon any creature. The only occasion on which he destroyed a venomous reptile was a source of long regret, to which he could never refer without sadness.

Johnny had elected a suitable place for planting apple seeds on a small prairie, and in order to prepare the ground he was mowing the long grass, when he was bitten by a rattlesnake. In describing the event, he sighed heavily and said, "Poor fellow, he only just touched me, when I, in the heat of my

---

3 domiciliary (dom′ə sil′ ē er′ ē): home.

ungodly passion, put the heel of my scythe in him and went away. Some time afterward I went back, and there lay the poor fellow dead."

In 1838—thirty-seven years after his appearance on Licking Creek—Johnny noticed that civilization, wealth, and population were pressing into the wilderness of Ohio. Hitherto he had easily kept just in advance of the wave of settlement; but now towns and churches were making their appearance, and even, at long intervals, the stage driver's horn broke the silence of the grand old forests, and he felt that his work was done in the region in which he had labored so long. He visited every house, and took a solemn farewell of all families.

During the succeeding nine years Johnny Appleseed pursued his eccentric avocation on the western border of Ohio and in Indiana. In the summer of 1847, when his labors had literally borne fruit over a hundred thousand square miles of territory, at the close of a warm day, after traveling twenty miles, he entered the house of a settler in Allen County, Indiana, and was, as usual, warmly welcomed. He declined to eat with the family, but accepted some bread and milk, which he partook of sitting on the doorstep and gazing on the setting sun.

Later in the evening he delivered his "news right fresh from heaven" by reading the Beatitudes. Declining other accommodation, he slept, as usual, on the floor, and in the early morning he was found with his features all aglow, and his body so near death that he could not talk. The physician, who was hastily summoned, pronounced him dying, but added that he had never seen a man in so placid[4] a state at the approach of death. At seventy-two years of age, forty-six of which had been devoted to his self-imposed mission, he ripened into death as naturally and beautifully as the seeds of his own planting had grown into fiber and bud and blossom and the matured fruit.

Thus died one of the memorable men of pioneer times, who never inflicted pain or knew an enemy—a man of strange habits, in whom there dwelt a comprehensive love that reached with one hand downward to the lowest forms of life, and with the other upward to the very throne of God. A laboring, self-denying benefactor of his race, homeless, solitary, and ragged, he trod the thorny earth with bare and bleeding feet, intent only upon making the wilderness fruitful.

---

4 **placid** (plas' id): peaceful.

Discussion

1. When and where did Johnny Appleseed plant his apple orchards?
2. What did Johnny Appleseed look like? Why did he dress so strangely?
3. How did the people treat Johnny Appleseed?
4. What acts of kindness was he remembered for?

Composition

1. Johnny Appleseed could be viewed in at least two ways. He was either a harmless but strange man who only wanted to plant trees, or he might have been the first of the modern environmentalists. Write your opinion of him. Be sure to include specific examples from the story to support your opinion.

2. Suppose there was a Johnny Appleseed Golden Award given each year to the person who has made the most unselfish contribution to society. Whom would you nominate for the award? Give as many reasons as possible that explain why this person should receive the award. (You may nominate someone famous or someone whom you know personally.)

Vocabulary

Imagine that you are taking a test on "Johnny Appleseed." You come to this question: *Tell how Johnny Appleseed became known as a benefactor.* Unless you know what a *benefactor* is, you cannot answer the question correctly. That's why you should always look up the meaning of an unfamiliar word in a DICTIONARY.

The sentences below are worded like test questions. They contain some words you probably do not know. On a separate sheet of paper, restate each question. To do this, look up the meanings of all unfamiliar, *italicized* words in a dictionary. Then replace them with synonyms or groups of words that explain their meanings. For example, the sentence above using *benefactor* could be restated as: *Tell how Johnny Appleseed became known as a person who helps others.*

1. Describe Johnny Appleseed's *attire*.
2. Why did pioneer boys *forbear* to *jeer* at Johnny Appleseed and his *raiment?*
3. How did Johnny Appleseed show the *fortitude* that the Indians admired?
4. What *advocacy* of Johnny Appleseed's was of even greater importance to him than the *avocation* that made his name *memorable?*
5. By the time of Johnny Appleseed's *placid* death at age seventy-two, why was it appropriate to say that "his love was *comprehensive*"?

To match the enormous expanse of the land, the Old West was filled with legends of superdeeds done by superheroes. The mightiest superhero of all, though, was Paul Bunyan.

Paul Bunyan of the North Woods

CARL SANDBURG

Who made Paul Bunyan, who gave him birth as a myth, who joked him into life as the Master Lumberjack, who fashioned him forth as an apparition[1] easing the hours of men amid axes and trees, saws and lumber? The people, the bookless people, they made Paul and had him alive long before he got into the books for those who read. He grew up in shanties,[2] around the hot stoves of winter, among socks and mittens drying, in the smell of tobacco smoke and the roar of laughter mocking the outside weather. And some of Paul came overseas in wooden bunks below decks in sailing vessels. And some of Paul is old as the hills, young as the alphabet.

The Pacific Ocean froze over in the winter of the Blue Snow and Paul Bunyan had long teams of oxen hauling regular white snow over from China. This was the winter Paul gave a party to the Seven Axmen. Paul fixed a granite floor sunk two hundred feet deep for them to dance on. Still, it tipped and tilted as the dance went on. And because the Seven Axmen refused to take off their hobnailed boots, the sparks from the nails of their dancing feet lit up the place so that Paul didn't light the kerosene lamps. No women being on the Big Onion river at that time the Seven Axmen had to dance with each other, the one left over in each set taking Paul as a partner. The commotion of the dancing that night brought on an earthquake and the Big Onion river moved over three counties to the east.

One year when it rained from St. Patrick's Day till the Fourth of July, Paul Bunyan got disgusted because his celebration on the Fourth was spoiled. He dived into Lake Superior and swam to where a solid pillar of water was coming down. He dived under this pillar, swam up into it and climbed with powerful swimming strokes, was gone about an hour, came splashing down, and as the rain stopped, he explained, "I turned the dam thing off." This is told in the Big North Woods and on the Great Lakes, with many particulars.

---

1 **apparition** (ap′ə rish′ ən): ghost.
2 **shanties**: small shacks.

Two mosquitoes lighted on one of Paul Bunyan's oxen, killed it, ate it, cleaned the bones, and sat on a grub shanty picking their teeth as Paul came along. Paul sent to Australia for two special bumblebees to kill these mosquitoes. But the bees and the mosquitoes intermarried; their children had stingers on both ends. And things kept getting worse till Paul brought a big boat-load of sorghum[3] up from Louisiana and while all the bee-mosquitoes were eating at the sweet sorghum he floated them down to the Gulf of Mexico. They got so fat that it was easy to drown them all between New Orleans and Galveston.

Paul logged on the Little Gimlet in Oregon one winter. The cookstove at that camp covered an acre of ground. They fastened the side of a hog on each snowshoe and four men used to skate on the griddle while the cook flipped the pancakes. The eating table was three miles long, elevators carried the cakes to the ends of the table where boys on bicycles rode back and forth on a path down the center of the table dropping the cakes where called for.

Benny, the Little Blue Ox of Paul Bunyan, grew two feet every time Paul looked at him, when a youngster. The barn was gone one morning and they found it on Benny's back; he grew out of it in one night. One night he kept pawing and bellowing for more pancakes, till there were two hundred men at the cook-shanty stove trying to keep him fed. About breakfast time Benny broke loose, tore down the cook-shanty, ate all the pan-cakes piled up for the loggers' breakfast. And after that Benny made his mistake; he ate the red-hot stove, and that finished him. This is only one of the hot-stove stories told in the North Woods.

---

3 **sorghum** (sôr' gəm): a sweet grain.

Discussion

1. Who are the "bookless" people who created Paul Bunyan? Why was he created?

2. What is meant by ". . . some of Paul is old as the hills, young as the alphabet"?

3. What do these stories reveal about the character and abilities of Paul Bunyan? Find examples to support your statements. Do you think these qualities have anything to do with the real life of a logger? Explain your answer.

Composition

1. Writers often use exaggeration to create humor. Explain how this statement applies to this tale. First tell about the best example of exaggeration in this Paul Bunyan tale. Then explain how the exaggeration made the situation humorous.

2. Create a "Paul Bunyan" type of character of your own. First describe your superhero. Then write a tall tale of a single incident which would be funny because of the extreme exaggeration. Your character might be, for example, the greatest baseball player, the greatest musician, the greatest teacher, or the greatest parent.

Carl Sandburg 1878—1967

In many ways Carl Sandburg represented the frontier spirit. Like his predecessor, Mark Twain, he was largely a self-taught writer. Experience was his teacher as demonstrated by the many odd jobs he held while establishing himself as a writer. He was a milk delivery boy, barber shop porter, truck operator, house painter, motion picture editor, political organizer, reporter, lecturer, and folk singer. Once a well-known poet criticized Sandburg by saying that he was "a lumberjack who taught himself all he knows." Ironically, lumberjacking was one of the few occupations Sandburg had never tried.

from Pioneers in Protest

LERONE BENNETT, JR.

BLACK AS THE NIGHT, and as bold, she slipped across the Mason-Dixon line and headed for a rendezvous point in the old slave South. With revolver cocked, she moved unerringly across the fields and through the forests, flitting from tree to tree and from ditch to ditch.

From time to time, she froze in her tracks, forewarned by a personal radar that never failed. A broken twig, the neigh of a horse, a cough, a sneeze: these said danger ahead. And so she halted, listening, waiting, her body tensed for attack. She was a gentle woman, but she was Black and she could ill afford sentimentality. There was a price on her head, some forty thousand dollars, and the slightest mistake would mean death. Slave patrols, guards, planters—eyes—were everywhere, and all were on the lookout for fugitive slaves in general and one woman in particular. No matter. The short Black woman was without nerves and she had no peer, male or female, in her chosen trade: organizing and managing slave escapes. She had been this way many times before and she had brought out hundreds of slaves. Now she was at it again, slipping through Pennsylvania, Delaware, and Maryland.

On and on she went, deeper and deeper into the slave South, traveling by night and hiding by day, moving closer and closer to a rendezvous point on the Eastern Shore of Maryland near Cambridge. There, a group of slaves, forewarned by a code letter to a sympathetic free Negro, waited with terror and with hope. Harriet Tubman materialized from nowhere, rapping her code on a chosen door in the slave quarters or standing deep in the woods and singing, for a tantalizing moment, a few bars of a Spiritual code:

I'll meet you in the morning
   Safe in the Promised Land,
On the other side of Jordan,
   Bound for the Promised Land.

Waiting ears, hearing the code knock or the code song, perked up and word raced through the cabins of the initiated: "Moses[1] is here." After certain preparations, "the woman," as she was called, led a group of slaves through Maryland, Delaware, Pennsylvania, and New York into the Promised Land of Canada. Nineteen times she made this dangerous round trip; nineteen times, single-handed, she baited the collective might of the slave power—and nineteen times she won. . . .

The great slave rebel, whose name struck terror in the hearts of Eastern Shore planters, was born a slave and lived the life of a slave. She was born in 1820 or 1821 in Bucktown near Cambridge on the Eastern Shore, one of the eleven children of Harriet Green and Benjamin Ross. As a child, she was called both Harriet and Araminta. But she was never really a child. For at the age of five, she was working full-time, cleaning white people's houses during the day and tending their babies at night. When she fell asleep, she was whipped mercilessly.

"I grew up," she said later, "like a neglected weed—ignorant of liberty, having no experience of it. I was not happy or contented: every time I saw a white man I was afraid of being carried away. I had two sisters carried away in a chain gang—one of them left two children. We were always uneasy. . . . I think slavery is the next thing to hell. If a person would send another into bondage he would, it appears to me, be bad enough to send him to hell if he could."

Harriet was a rebellious child. It would not be too much of an exaggeration to say that she was born a rebel. Fighting back with whatever she could lay hands on, she survived; and, having survived, she set her sights higher. By the time Harriet reached her teens, her master, despairing of ever making her a house servant, put her out to field where she plowed, drove oxen, and cut wood. She remembered later with pride that she "could lift huge barrels of produce and draw a loaded stone boat like an ox."

All this time, young Harriet was gathering fury against the slave system. She was, by all accounts, the despair of white overseers, who could not break her rebellious will. On one occasion, a male slave abandoned his post and went to town. The slave was closely followed by the overseer, who was closely followed by Harriet. The overseer cornered the slave in a store and called on Harriet for aid. The young slave girl, who was only thirteen, ignored the order and went to the aid of the slave. When the slave dashed through the door, Harriet stepped between him and the overseer. The overseer, enraged, picked up a two-pound weight and flung it at the escaping slave. The weight struck Harriet, tearing a hole in her skull.

---

1 **Moses:** the man who led enslaved Israelites out of Egypt.

For several weeks, Harriet hovered between life and death. Then, slowly, she began to recover. It was discovered that the blow had pushed a portion of her skull against her brain. Ever afterwards, she suffered from what was called a "stupor" or "sleeping sickness." Four or five times a day, she would suddenly fall asleep. After a short spell, she would regain consciousness and continue the conversation or her work at the precise point where she left off. Because of this ailment, white people in the neighborhood, and some slaves, assumed that Harriet was "half-witted"—an assumption the wily Harriet encouraged.

During her lengthy convalescence . . . Harriet began to consider seriously the possibilities of escape. The constantly recurring idea of escape struck such deep roots in her mind that she dreamed repeatedly of a "line" across which there was freedom and human dignity. After her marriage to John Tubman, a free Black man, the dreams increased in frequency and intensity. When Harriet learned that her new master planned to sell her and two of her brothers, she decided to run away. She tried to persuade her brothers to accompany her, but they refused. So she set out alone in the summer of 1849, traveling at night through Maryland and Delaware and finally reaching Philadelphia. She went with a threat in her heart. "For," she said, "I had reasoned this out in my mind; there was one of two things I had a *right* to, liberty or death; if I could not have one, I would have the other, for no man should take me alive. . . ."

When she crossed the "line" between slavery and freedom, she was overwhelmed by a sense of fulfillment. "I looked at my hands," she said, "to see if I was the same person now I was free. There was such a glory over everything; the sun came like gold through the trees, and over the fields. . . ."

But there was a shadow in Harriet's Eden.[2] She perceived suddenly with startling clarity that she could never be free until her people were free. " I knew of a man," she said, "who was sent to State Prison for twenty-five years. All these years he was always thinking of his home, and counting by years, months, and days, the time till he should be free, and see his family and friends once more. The years roll on, the time of imprisonment is over, the man is free. He leaves the prison gates; he makes his way to his old home, but his old home is not there. The house in which he had dwelt in his childhood had been torn down, and a new one had been put in its place; his family was gone, their very name was forgotten, there was no one to take him by the hand to welcome him back to life."

"So it was with me," Harriet added. "I had crossed the line of which I had so long been dreaming. I was free, but there was no one to welcome me to the land of freedom. I was a stranger in a strange land, and my home after all was down in the old cabin quarter, with the old folks and my brothers and sisters. But to this solemn resolution I came; I was free, and they should be free also; I would make a home for them in the North, and the Lord helping me, I would bring them all here. . . ."

So resolving, Harriet Tubman dedicated herself to work unceasingly for the complete emancipation of her people. In Philadelphia and other Northern cities, she worked day and night as a domestic. When she had accumulated enough money to finance a slave escape, she would return to the South and lead out a group of slaves. The first trip

2 **Eden:** here, a perfect place.

occurred shortly after her escape. In December, 1850, she returned to Maryland and spirited out her sister and two children. Four months later, she returned and guided her brother and two other slaves to freedom. Returning to the South in the fall of 1851 for her husband, she discovered he had married again. This was a shattering blow, but Harriet had no time to grieve over personal problems. Abandoning her original plan, putting John Tubman behind her, she organized a group of slaves and carried them to Canada. Thereafter, she made a series of forays into the South, bringing out relatives, friends, and anyone else who wanted to go.

To understand what Harriet was about, to understand the magnitude of her accomplishments, it is necessary to understand the system she was challenging. The slave South was a totalitarian system.[3] Every instrument of power in the South was bent to the detection and destruction of slaves like Harriet Tubman. To penetrate the defenses of this system, to guide hundreds of slaves of all ages and physical conditions through thousands of miles of closely guarded territory required tactical ability approaching genius.

Harriet approached her task with thoroughness and dispatch. Between trips, she accumulated money by working as a cook, maid, laborer. Since she could neither read nor write, she employed Northern confederates to write coded letters to free Negroes or sympathetic whites in the area she planned to visit. A free Negro in Cambridge, for example, received the following letter before a Harriet Tubman strike. "Read my letter to the old folks, and give my love to them, and tell my brothers to be always watching unto prayer, and when the good old ship of Zion comes along, to be ready to step aboard."

After contacting the slaves, Harriet accumulated the tools of her trade: a revolver and fresh ammunition, fake passes for slaves of varying description, and paregoric to drug babies. With these and other "tools" hidden on her person, she slipped across the Mason-Dixon line and made her way to selected plantations where slaves were informed of her presence by code songs, prayers, or some other strategem. Selected slaves were then apprised of the rendezvous area and the time of departure. General Tubman, as she was called, was very strict about time. She waited for no one—not even a brother who was delayed on one trip by the imminent arrival of a new baby in his family.

Once the slaves were assembled, Harriet sized them up, searching them closely with her eyes. Satisfied, she placed the group under strict military discipline. During the trip, she was in absolute and total control and no one could question her orders. William Still, the Black rebel who operated the key Philadelphia station of the Underground Railroad, said she "had a very short and pointed rule of law of her own which implied death to anyone who talked of giving out and going back." Once a slave committed himself to a Tubman escape, he was committed to freedom or death. On several occasions, slaves collapsed and said they were tired, sick, scared. Harriet always cocked her revolver and said: "You go on or die. Dead people tell no tales." Faced with a determined Harriet Tubman, slaves always found new strength and determination. During ten years of guerrilla action, the great commando leader never lost a slave through capture or return.

Harriet almost always began her escapes on Saturday night. Since it was impossible to

---

3 **totalitarian system**: a political system in which the government has total control over the people.

advertise for runaway slaves on Sunday, this gave her a twenty-four-hour start on pursuers. She also made a practice of escaping in the carriages of masters, covering the slaves with vegetables or baggage and driving all night Saturday and all day Sunday before abandoning the appropriated vehicle. This stratagem served two purposes. It rapidly moved escapees from the immediate neighborhood, and it befuddled guards and planters who assumed usually that a slave boldly driving a carriage was on an errand for his master.

After abandoning the carriage, Harriet and her charges made their way north by following the North Star or feeling the moss on the sides of trees. Harriet tried usually to keep her groups together, but she sometimes dispersed them, sending twos or threes through hostile towns. On occasions, she dressed men in women's clothes and vice versa.

In an emergency, the guerrilla leader acted swiftly, even ruthlessly. On one night, she escaped capture by hiding her charges in a manure pile and sticking straws in their mouths so they could breathe. On another trip, she eluded pursuers by buying tickets and putting the slaves on a train *heading south*. No one, of course, expected fugitive slaves to be on a southbound train.

The great slave rebel was helped enormously in her extraordinary career by a natural talent for acting. Indeed, Thomas Wentworth Higginson, the antislavery preacher, believed she was one of the greatest actresses and comediennes of the age. "One of her most masterly accomplishments," he said, "was the impression of a decrepit old woman. On one of her expeditions . . . she had the incredible nerve to enter a village where lived one of her former masters. This was necessary for the carrying out of her plans for

the trip. Her only disguise was a bodily assumption of age. To reinforce this, her subtle foresight prompted her to buy some live chickens, which she carried suspended by the legs from a cord. As she turned a corner, she saw coming toward her none other than her old master. Lest he might see through her impersonation and to make an excuse for flight, she loosed the cord that held the fowls, and, amid the laughter of the bystanders, gave chase to them as they flew squawking over a nearby fence."

No less effective was the use Harriet made of melody. She was proud of her singing voice and she used it repeatedly in managing slave escapes. Alice Stone Blackwell, the feminist leader, said: "If I remember correctly, Harriet Tubman told me that when she was convoying parties of fugitives, she used to guide them by the songs that she sang as she walked along the roads. . . . It was when her parties of fugitives were in hiding, that she directed them by her songs as to whether they might show themselves, or must continue to lie low. . . . No one would notice what was sung by an old colored woman, as she trudged along the road."

What made the Tubman exploits so extraordinary was the fact that she could not read or write. This led, on occasion, to hair-raising encounters. The story is told of the time she fell asleep on a train beneath a "wanted" poster bearing her likeness. Awakening and hearing several white men discussing her and the poster, Harriet grabbed a book and began to "read," praying fervently that she was not holding the book upside down. The white men lost interest for the poster said clearly that the "dangerous" wanted woman could neither read nor write.

A cool customer, Harriet Tubman—cool, determined and bold, never wanting for the

Philbrook Art Center

SLAVES ESCAPING THROUGH THE SWAMP *Thomas Moran*

right gesture or the right retort. Her steadiness stemmed from a total and absolute faith in God. She talked to God every day, believed He was always with her and would never let her down.

On one expedition, Harriet's personal radar told her there was danger, great danger, ahead. She discussed the matter with God, saying: "You been wid me in six troubles, Lord, be wid me in the seventh." What happened next was related by Thomas Garrett, who heard it from Harriet Tubman's lips. "She said that God told her to stop, which she did; and then she asked Him what

she must do. He told her to leave the road, and turn to the left; she obeyed, and soon came to a small stream of tidewater; there was no boat; no bridge; she again inquired of her Guide what she was to do. She was told to go through. It was cold, in the month of March; but having confidence in her Guide, she went in; the water came up to her armpits; the men refused to follow till they saw her safe on the opposite shore. They then followed, and, if I mistake not, she had soon to wade a second stream, soon after which she came to a cabin of colored people, who took them all in, put them to bed, and dried their

from *Pioneers in Protest* 115

clothes, ready to proceed next night on the journey. . . . The strange part of the story was that the masters of these men had put up the previous day, at the railroad station near where she left, an advertisement offering a large reward for their apprehension."

During the first phase of the Civil War, Harriet Tubman continued her guerrilla strikes, leading slaves to federal lines in Maryland and other states. In May, 1862, she was sent by Governor Andrews of Massachusetts to Port Royal, South Carolina, which was then under the control of federal troops. She served in the Port Royal area as a liaison[4] person between federal troops and freedmen and as a nurse in camp hospitals.

Even more important perhaps was her work as a Union Army spy, scout, commando. At the request of Union officers, she organized an intelligence service, recruiting several former slaves from surrounding areas. She later accompanied Colonel James Montgomery on several raids in South Carolina and Georgia. Indeed, there is a great deal of evidence which indicates that Harriet, not Montgomery, was the commander of Montgomery's most famous exploit, the June 2, 1863, raid up South Carolina's Combahee River. Harriet's role in this raid was clearly indicated by a dispatch which appeared on the front page of the *Commonwealth*, a Boston newspaper, on July 10, 1863:

HARRIET TUBMAN

Col. Montgomery and his gallant band of 300 black soldiers, under the guidance of a black woman, dashed into the enemy's country, struck a bold and effective blow, destroying millions of dollars worth of commissary stores, cotton, and lordly dwellings, and striking terror into the heart of rebeldom, brought off near 800 slaves and thousands of dollars worth of property, without losing a man or receiving a scratch. . . .

Since the rebellion the black woman has devoted herself to her great work of delivering the bondman, with an energy and sagacity[5] that cannot be exceeded. Many and many times she had penetrated the enemy's lines and discovered their situation and condition, and escaped without injury, but not without extreme hazard.

At war's end, Harriet returned to her home in Auburn and began a thirty-seven-year effort to get government compensation for three years of war services. She wanted the money not for herself but to found schools and rest homes for the freedmen and their children. Although high-ranking officers and officials furnished depositions and affidavits on her war services, the federal government never fully paid the claim.

It was, in part, to buttress Harriet's claims that Sarah H. Bradford wrote a book on her life in 1886. Harriet and the author requested commendations from several prominent Americans, including Frederick Douglass, who answered: "You ask for what you do not need when you call upon me for a word of commendation. I need such words from you more than you can need them from me, especially where your superior labors and devotions to the cause of the lately enslaved of our land are known as I know them. The difference between us is very marked. Most that I have done and suffered in the service of our cause has been in public, and I have received encouragement at every step of the way. You, on the other hand, have labored in

---

4 **liaison** (lē′ ā zon′): one who establishes and maintains understanding between two groups.

5 **sagacity** (sə gas′ə tē): wisdom.

a private way. I have wrought in the day—you in the night. I have had the applause of the crowd and the satisfaction that comes of being approved by the multitude, while the most that you have done has been witnessed by a few trembling, scared, and foot-sore bondsmen and women, whom you have led out of the house of bondage, and whose heartfelt *'God bless you'* has been your only reward. The midnight sky and the silent stars have been the witnesses of your devotion to freedom and of your heroism." . . .

The book Douglass commended brought Harriet Tubman a thousand dollars which she contributed to Black schools in the South. Harriet also maintained open house in her home in Auburn, giving all she had to the poor, the needy, and the infirm.

During this period, she married a young Union Army veteran she had met in the Port Royal area. Her new husband, Nelson Davis, was in poor health and he soon died. After his death, the government gave Harriet a widow's pension of eight dollars a month. The pension was later increased to twenty dollars a month. . . .

As the years passed, turning the fork of the fateful twentieth century, Harriet Tubman girded herself for one last effort on behalf of her lifelong dream, a "John Brown Home" for indigent[6] Black people. By peddling fruit and by begging, she accumulated enough money to buy land and lay the foundations for the home. She later deeded the property and her home to the African Methodist Episcopal Zion Church.

As 1913 approached, Harriet turned her face toward the other world. She went to her favorite AME Zion Church for the last time and told the parishioners that the end was near. "I am nearing the end of my journey," she said. "I can hear them bells a-ringing, I can hear the angels singing, I can see the hosts a-marching. I hear somebody say: 'There is one crown left and that is for Old Aunt Harriet and she shall not lose her reward.'"

On March 10, 1913, in the fiftieth year of Emancipation, Harriet Tubman claimed her crown. She was buried with military rites and the next year the city of Auburn closed down in an unprecedented one-day memorial to the rebel and Union spy.

---

6 **indigent** (in' də jənt): needy.

Discussion

1. Explain the personal danger Harriet Tubman risked each time she led slaves to free territory.

2. What were Harriet Tubman's rules for any slave she helped escape? Why were these rules necessary?

3. What was the Underground Railroad?

4. Since the risk of capture was so great, Harriet Tubman had to be very clever. What methods did she use to let the slaves know she was ready to go? What things did she do to keep the people safe during their trip?

5. How did Harriet Tubman serve the Union Army during the Civil War?

6. How did she continue to serve Black people after the war?

Vocabulary

Because of the way she led slaves to freedom, Harriet Tubman was compared to an army general. She succeeded in her work by demanding strict, military-style discipline. Therefore, this selection from *Pioneers in Protest* uses many military terms.

You can find the ORIGINS, or sources, of these and other terms simply by looking in a dictionary. Here is a typical dictionary entry:

mil i tar y (mil'ə ter' ē), *adj.* of or for soldiers; done by soldiers; [<Latin *militaris* < *militem* soldier]

The word's origin is given in brackets [ ], usually after—although sometimes before—the definition. If the origin of the word *military* were completely written out, it would read like this:

Military came into English from the Latin word *militaris,* which came from the Latin word *militem* which means "soldier."

Often the relationship between the modern meaning of a word and its origin is simple and clear, as in the case of *military.* Sometimes, however, you must use reasoning and imagination to see how the modern meaning of a word connects with the word's origin. For example:

colo nel (kėr' nl), *n.* a commissioned officer in the army, air force or Marine Corps ranking next above a lieutenant colonel and next below a brigadier general. [<Middle French *coronel,* colonel < Italian *colonello* commander of a regiment < *colonna* military column < Latin *columna* column]

Careful thought could help you figure out that *officers* who led *columns* of soldiers could gradually come to be called *colonels.*

Here are some of the other military terms used in the selection from *Pioneers in Protest:*

crusade   liaison   rebel   patrol   recruit

On a separate sheet of paper, follow these steps in tracing the origins of the five words above: (1) Copy each word. (2) Find the meaning of the word in a dictionary. (3) If more than one definition is given, choose the one that relates to war or soldiers and copy that.

(4) Then explain briefly the origin of the word. Write your answers this way:

guerrilla—
definition: a fighter who does not belong to an official military unit
origin: guerrilla comes from the Spanish word *guerrilla* which is a form of *guerra,* meaning "war."

Lerone Bennett, Jr. 1928——

Lerone Bennett, Jr., has had a long and impressive literary career. He was a reporter and city editor for the *Atlanta Daily World,* associate editor for *Jet* magazine, and both associate and chief editor for *Ebony* magazine. He has written numerous articles, short stories, and poems. He is best known for his biographies and other nonfiction works such as *Pioneers in Protest.* When he was once asked about his writing, he replied, "Almost by accident, you see, I got involved in doing this series of nonfiction projects. It's been gratifying, and I could get lost in the 1860s and 1870s. It's like a mystery story trying to put the facts together from old musty books. I've had the good fortune to be of some small help to a great many kids—Black and white—who have not been exposed to a lot of material regarding our common past."

Abraham Lincoln died for the cause of freedom. But what was he like when he was alive? How did his mother see him? How did the people of America see him?

Nancy Hanks

ROSEMARY and STEPHEN VINCENT BENÉT

If Nancy Hanks
Came back as a ghost,
Seeking news
Of what she loved most,
She'd ask first   5
"Where's my son?
What's happened to Abe?
What's he done?

"Poor little Abe,
Left all alone   10
Except for Tom,
Who's a rolling stone;
He was only nine
The year I died.
I remember still   15
How hard he cried.

"Scraping along
In a little shack,
With hardly a shirt
To cover his back,   20
And a prairie wind
To blow him down,
Or pinching times
If he went to town.

"You wouldn't know   25
About my son?
Did he grow tall?
Did he have fun?
Did he learn to read?
Did he get to town?   30
Do you know his name?
Did he get on?"

O Captain! My Captain!

WALT WHITMAN

O Captain! my Captain! our fearful trip is done,
The ship has weathered every rack, the prize we sought is won,
The port is near, the bells I hear, the people all exulting,
While follow eyes the steady keel, the vessel grim and daring;
   But O heart! heart! heart!   5
     O the bleeding drops of red,
        Where on the deck my Captain lies,
           Fallen cold and dead.

O Captain! my Captain! rise up and hear the bells;
Rise up—for you the flag is flung—for you the bugle trills,   10
For you bouquets and ribboned wreaths—for you the shores a-crowding,
For you they call, the swaying mass, their eager faces turning;
    Here Captain! dear father!
        The arm beneath your head!
            It is some dream that on the deck,   15
                You've fallen cold and dead.

My Captain does not answer, his lips are pale and still.
My father does not feel my arm, he has no pulse nor will,
The ship is anchored safe and sound, its voyage closed and done,
From fearful trip the victor ship comes in with object won: 20
    Exult O shores, and ring O bells!
        But I with mournful tread,
            Walk the deck my Captain lies,
                Fallen cold and dead.

Discussion

1. How does Nancy Hanks remember her son, Abraham Lincoln?

2. What questions does she ask about her son?

3. In light of Lincoln's life, why are the questions Nancy Hanks asks in the last stanza so unusual?

4. In "O Captain! My Captain!" the poet compares the government of the United States to the "Ship of State." Who, then, is the fallen or dead captain of the "ship"?

5. What is meant by the words: "O Captain! my Captain! our fearful trip is done . . . the prize we sought is won, the port is near . . ."?

6. The poet of "O Captain! My Captain!" contrasts two emotions throughout the poem—joy and sadness. For example, in the first stanza the ship is coming into port and the people are all cheering; the bells are ringing. These are all joyful actions. This joy is contrasted with the absolute stillness of the picture of a dead captain "bleeding drops of red." Select words from the other two stanzas that show the contrast of each emotion.

7. Which of the two poems expresses the strongest emotion? Why?

Vocabulary

Sometimes authors use words that you don't know. Before you go to a dictionary, however, look at the words surrounding an unfamiliar word. They may help you figure out the meaning. These words surrounding an unknown word are called context clues.

There are many different kinds of context clues. Among them is the EXPERIENCE CONTEXT CLUE. Authors might surround an unfamiliar word, for example, with descriptions that remind you of your own experiences. In this way they give you experience context clues to help you understand the meanings of words you have not yet learned.

This example is condensed from a Walt Whitman poem:

Up through the darkness,
While clouds lower fast down the sky,
Amid a transparent clear belt of *ether*,
The lord-star Jupiter ascends.

In this poem *ether* obviously does not mean the gas that is used to put patients to sleep during an operation. Either directly or through pictures, you have witnessed the rising of stars and planets. What do they rise through? The context clues—*darkness, cloud, ascends,* and especially the word *sky*—all refer to things you have experienced. You also notice another experience context clue: Jupiter is rising in "a transparent clear belt." If you check *ether* in a dictionary, you will find a definition similar to this: "clear upper regions of atmosphere or space." In this way experience context clues—along with your own power of reasoning—can often bring you very close to the correct definition of an unknown word.

A. Use experience context clues to figure out the meanings of the *italicized* words in the lines below from "O Captain! My Captain!" On a separate sheet of paper, write both the *italicized* words and the definitions you figure out. Write your answers this way:

ether—sky

1. But I with mournful *tread*,
   Walk the deck my Captain lies,
   Fallen cold and dead.
2. Rise up—for you the flag is flung—for you the bugle *trills*.
3. The port is near, the bells I hear, the people all *exulting*.
4. The ship has *weathered* every (storm), the prize we sought is won.
5. For you they call, the swaying *mass*, their eager faces turning.

B. Now use a dictionary to check your definitions. After each of your answers for Exercise A, copy the dictionary definition. When the dictionary contains more than one definition, choose the one that best applies to the line in the poem. Write your answers this way:

ether—sky "clear upper regions of atmosphere"

Rosemary Carr Benét 1900—1962

Rosemary Carr Benét was born in Chicago and graduated Phi Beta Kappa from the University of Chicago. She then attended school in Paris and wrote for various publications. In 1921, she married Stephen Vincent Benét. After a two-year stay in Paris, they returned to New York and together wrote *A Book of Americans*. This collection of poems is about famous pilgrims, pioneers, and Presidents. Benét also wrote articles for various magazines and was a member of the Book-of-the-Month Club editorial staff.

Walt Whitman 1819—1892

Walt Whitman was one of the first poets to speak for America, not as an extension of Europe but as a new land. Because he realized American ideas and attitudes were different, he was constantly seeking a new poetic form to fit his new poetic content. For example, he rarely used rhyme. His most famous work, *Leaves of Grass*, first appeared in 1855. Although it was not a popular success, it was probably the most influential book of poetry in American literature.

During the Civil War, Whitman worked as a volunteer nurse in army hospitals in Washington, D. C. To Whitman the union had a mystic significance from which grew his hopes for the future. He was one of Lincoln's earliest admirers and supporters. Although he considered Lincoln a "brother in spirit," no proof exists that the two ever met.

On November 22, 1963, John Fitzgerald Kennedy, the 35th President of the United States, was assassinated as he rode in a motorcade through the streets of Dallas, Texas. The entire nation was shocked when it heard the news of this tragic event.

On the Death of the President

November 22, 1963

ANN STANFORD

In a current of eagles and parks and green,
In a blue ripple of shouts, in the hearty sun,
The day moves with autumn and feasting,
Cheers, and the rustle of crowds, and the held faces.

Stretched beyond the green savannahs[1] of our knowing   5
Deep in marshes and trees, in scrub oak, the deer
Stands flicking his shoulders, dappled in shade.
The dogs scare up the autumn colors of partridge.

The world centers on noon,[2] the White Mountains have passed it,
The Rockies still hold morning's sun on the early snow.   10
In the Cascades the spruces cast their shadows westward.
The country gathers toward noon in the midst of the country.

Into the forest of our knowing, across the marked paths,
Over the billow of flags and the hails and the shot,
Beneath the crowd's crumpled breath,   15
Hunted and fallen, the fated and noontime meet.

---

1 **savannahs** (sə van′ əs): areas of level land covered with low growing vegetation.
2 **noon**: President Kennedy was shot in Dallas, Texas, at 12:30 P.M.

Noon turns suddenly black, and the sigh falls over
The sun like the shadow of all the mists of breath,
Like a prayer tears fall among the avenues,
The noon's huge sun wrapped in the mists of mourning.   20

Through the long afternoon a coffin rides the skies
Death flies above, the air weeps at his passing,
Awake we dream our woe, the day curves on,
Earthbound, we walk through autumn bells and harvests.

In afternoon's fields we gather, we gather in folds   25
And all the flowers are garnered and gathered
In the mountains, in the fields and towns, under the pine trees:
Goldenrod, firethorn, buckwheat, red-leaved sumac.

Into the soft-leaved evening we wait and the flight is ended.
End and beginning and end, forever and ever.   30
The dead and the living
Enter the darkening field—and each to his fortune.

While the dark with its loss falls over the capital
And seeps over the Potomac into the fields of Arlington
And spreads over West Virginia and the Appalachians   35
And drops over the great plains of the Mississippi
Engulfs the Bad Lands and the Black Hills
And creeps slowly up over Sante Fé and the Sangre de Cristo
Over the Wind River and the Great Basin and the Mojave
And high, high over the Sierra Nevada—without a star—   40
And drifts down over the calm Pacific.

Discussion

1. What does the first stanza describe? What is the mood?

2. The second stanza shows a peaceful scene in nature: "The deer flicking his shoulders," and the dogs chasing partridges. These events take place far away from the Dallas streets. Contrast this scene with the events that followed.

3. Why are the words "noon" and "midst of the country" emphasized in the third stanza?

4. What is the mood in stanza five? What words describe this mood?

5. In stanza seven, what do the people do when the body of the President is flown from Dallas to Washington?

6. In the last stanza, the darkness of the night covers the East. Then it moves across the time zones to the Pacific. What does the phrase "without a star" refer to?

Ann Stanford 1916—

Ann Stanford's poetry is only a part of her literary career. She is an English professor and has also been a journalism consultant and a poetry critic. She received the Commonwealth Club of California Silver Award in poetry and the University of Redlands Browning Prize in 1959 for her collection, *Magellan.* In addition, she received the Borestone Mountain Poetry Award for "Pandora," and the Shelley Memorial Award in 1969. Commenting on her poetry, she once said, "I try to set down the inner experiences of human beings, especially their relationships to time and the world."

How do you prove to your parents that you are old enough to take care of yourself? This is a particularly difficult question to answer if you are a Chinese daughter.

A Measure of Freedom

JADE SNOW WONG

SO, WITHOUT much enthusiasm, Jade Snow decided upon junior college. Now it was necessary to inform Mama and Daddy. She chose an evening when the family was at dinner. All of them were in their customary places, and Daddy, typically, was in conversation with Older Brother about the factory:

"Blessing, when do you think Lot Number fifty-one twenty-six will be finished? I want to ask for a check from our jobber so that I can have enough cash for next week's payroll."

To which Older Brother replied, "As soon as Mama is through with the seams in Mrs. Lee's and Mrs. Choy's bundles, the women can finish the hems. Another day, probably."

Mama had not been consulted; therefore, she made no comment. Silence descended as the Wongs continued their meal, observing the well-learned precept that talk was not permissible while eating.

Jade Snow considered whether to break the silence. Three times she thought over what she had to say, and still found it worth saying. This also was according to family precept.

"Daddy," she said. "I have made up my mind to enter junior college here in San Francisco. I will find a steady job to pay my expenses, and by working in the summers I'll try to save enough money to take me through my last two years at the university."

Then she waited. Everyone went on eating. No one said a word. Apparently no one was interested enough to be curious. But at least no one objected. It was settled.

Junior college was at first disappointing in more ways than one. There was none of the glamor usually associated with college because the institution was so young that it had not yet acquired buildings of its own. Classes were held all over the city, wherever accommodations were available. The first days were very confusing to Jade Snow, especially when she discovered that she must immediately decide upon a college major.

While waiting to register, she thumbed through the catalogue in search of a clue. English . . . mathematics . . . chemistry.

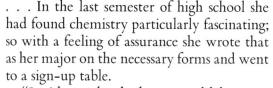

. . . In the last semester of high school she had found chemistry particularly fascinating; so with a feeling of assurance she wrote that as her major on the necessary forms and went to a sign-up table.

"I wish to take the lecture and laboratory classes for Chemistry 1A," she informed the gray-haired man who presided there.

He looked at her, a trifle impatiently, she thought.

"Why?"

"Because I like it." To herself she sounded reasonable.

"But you are no longer in high school. Chemistry here is a difficult subject on a university level, planned for those who are majoring in medicine, engineering, or the serious sciences."

Jade Snow set her chin stubbornly. "I still want to take Chemistry 1A."

Sharply he questioned: "What courses in mathematics have you had? What were your grades?"

Finally Jade Snow's annoyance rose to the surface. "Straight A's. But why must you ask?

Do you think I would want to take a course I couldn't pass? Why don't you sign me up and let the instructor be the judge of my ability?"

"Very well," he replied stiffly. "I'll accept you in the class. And for your information, young lady, I am the instructor!"

With this inauspicious start, Jade Snow began her college career.

To take care of finances, she now needed to look for work. Through a friend she learned that a Mrs. Simpson needed someone to help with household work. "Can you cook?" was Mrs. Simpson's first question.

Jade Snow considered a moment before

answering. Certainly she could cook Chinese food, and she remembered a common Chinese saying, "A Chinese can cook foreign food as well as, if not better than, the foreigners, but a foreigner cannot cook Chinese food fit for the Chinese." On this reasoning it seemed safe to say "Yes."

After some further discussion Jade Snow was hired. Cooking, she discovered, included everything from pastries, puddings, meats, steaks, and vegetables, to sandwiches. In addition, she served the meals, washed dishes, kept the house clean, did the light laundry and ironing for Mr. and Mrs. Simpson and their career daughter—and always appeared in uniform, which she thoroughly disliked. In return she received twenty dollars a month. At night, she did her studying at home, and sometimes after a hard day she was so tired that the walk from the Simpson flat to the streetcar on Chestnut Street was a blessed respite, a time to relax and admire the moon if she could find it, and to gather fresh energy for whatever lay ahead.

Desserts, quite ignored in a Chinese household, were of first importance in the Simpson household. One particular Saturday, Jade Snow was told to bake a special meringue sponge cake with a fancy fruit filling of whipped cream and peeled and seeded grapes. Following a very special recipe of Mrs. Simpson's, she mixed it for the first time and preheated the oven. Mrs. Simpson came into the kitchen, checked and approved the prepared cake batter, and said that she would judge when it was done. Meantime she and her husband and their guests lounged happily in the garden.

Almost an hour passed. The meringue was baking in a slow oven. The recipe said not to open the door, as the cake might fall. An hour and a quarter passed, and the pastry smelled sweetly delicate. Yet Mrs. Simpson did not come. Jade Snow wondered whether or not to call her. But she remembered that her employer disliked being disturbed when entertaining officials of her husband's company.

After an hour and forty-five minutes the cake no longer smelled delicate. Jade Snow was worn out! What could she do? At last, there was a rush of high-heeled footsteps; swish went the kitchen door, and Mrs. Simpson burst in, flushed from the sun or excitement.

"I must look at that meringue cake," she burst out.

The oven door was pulled open, and Jade Snow peered in anxiously over her employer's shoulder. Too late! It had fallen and become a tough, brown mass. Jade Snow was dumb with a crushed heart, inspecting the flattened pancake, mentally reviewing all the processes of whipping, measuring, and sifting that she had gone through for hours to achieve this unpalatable result.

Mrs. Simpson crisply broke through to her anguish, "Well, there's nothing to be done but for you to make another."

That afternoon was a torturous nightmare and a fever of activity—to manage another meringue cake, to get rolls mixed, salad greens cleaned and crisped, vegetables cut, meat broiled, the table set, and all of the other details of a "company" dinner attended to. By the time she was at last washing the dishes and tidying the dining room, she felt strangely vague. She hadn't taken time to eat her dinner; she was too tired anyway. How she wished that she had been asked to cook a Chinese dinner instead of this interminable American meal, especially that cake!

Of her college courses, Latin was the easiest. This was a surprise, for everyone had told her of its horrors. It was much more logical than French, almost mathematical in its orderliness and precision, and actually a snap after nine years of Chinese.

Chemistry, true to the instructor's promise, was difficult, although the classes were anything but dull. It turned out that he was a very nice person with a keen sense of humor and a gift for enlivening his lectures with stories of his own college days. There were only two girls in a class of more than fifty men—a tense blonde girl from Germany, who always ranked first; and Jade Snow, who usually took second place.

But if Latin was the easiest course and chemistry the most difficult, sociology was the most stimulating. Jade Snow had chosen it without thought, simply to meet a requirement; but that casual decision completely revolutionized her thinking, shattering her Wong-constructed conception of the order of things. This was the way it happened:

After several uneventful weeks during which the class explored the historical origins of the family and examined such terms as *norms, mores, folkways*,[1] there came a day when the instructor stood before them to discuss the relationship of parents and children. It was a day like many others, with the students listening in varying attitudes of interest or indifference. The instructor was speaking casually of ideas to be accepted as standard. Then suddenly upon Jade Snow's astounded ears there fell this statement:

"There was a period in our American history when parents had children for economic reasons, to put them to work as soon as possible, especially to have them help on the

farm. But now we no longer regard children in this way. Today we recognize that children are individuals, and that parents can no longer demand their unquestioning obedience. Parents should do their best to understand their children, because young people also have their rights."

The instructor went on talking, but Jade Snow heard no more, for her mind was echoing and re-echoing this startling thought. "Parents can no longer demand unquestioning obedience from their children. They should do their best to understand. Children also have their rights." For the rest of the day, while she was doing her chores at the Simpsons', while she was standing in the streetcar going home, she was busy translating the idea into terms of her own experience.

"My parents demand unquestioning obedience. Older Brother demands unquestioning obedience. By what right? I am an individual besides being a Chinese daughter. I have rights too."

Could it be that Daddy and Mama, although they were living in San Francisco in the year 1938, actually had not left the Chinese world of thirty years ago? Could it be that they were forgetting that Jade Snow would soon become a woman in a new America, not a woman in old China? In short, was it possible that Daddy and Mama could be wrong?

For days Jade Snow gave thought to little but her devastating discovery that her parents might be subject to error. As it was her habit always to act after reaching a conclusion, she wondered what to do about it. Should she tell Daddy and Mama that they needed to change their ways? One moment she thought she should; the next she thought not. At last she decided to overcome her fear in the

---

1 *norms, mores, folkways:* the traditional ways people observe in their daily living.

interests of education and better understanding. She would at least try to open their minds to modern truths. If she succeeded, good! If not, she was prepared to suffer the consequences.

In this spirit of patient martyrdom she waited for an opportunity to speak.

It came, surprisingly, one Saturday. Ordinarily that was a busy day at the Simpsons', a time for entertaining, so that Jade Snow was not free until too late to go anywhere, even had she had a place to go. But on this particular Saturday the Simpsons were away for the weekend, and by three in the afternoon Jade Snow was ready to leave the apartment with unplanned hours ahead of her. She didn't want to spend these rare hours of freedom in any usual way. And she didn't want to spend them alone.

"Shall I call Joe?"[2] she wondered. She had never telephoned to a boy before, and she debated whether it would be too forward. But she felt too happy and carefree to worry much, and she was confident that Joe would not misunderstand.

Even before reporting to Mama that she was home, she ran downstairs to the telephone booth and gave the operator Joe's number. His mother answered and then went to call him while Jade Snow waited in embarrassment.

"Joe." She was suddenly tongue-tied. "Joe, I'm already home."

That wasn't at all what she wanted to say. What did she want to say?

"Hello! Hello!" Joe boomed back. "What's the matter with you? Are you all right?"

"Oh, yes, I'm fine. Only, only . . . well, I'm through working for the day." That was

really all she had to say, but now it sounded rather pointless.

"Isn't that wonderful? It must have been unexpected." That was what was nice and different about Joe. He always seemed to know without a lot of words. But because his teasing was never far behind his understanding, he added quickly, "I suppose you're going to study and go to bed early."

Jade Snow was still not used to teasing and didn't know how to take it. With an effort she swallowed her shyness and disappointment. "I thought we might go for a walk . . . that is, if you have nothing else to do . . . if you would care to . . . if . . ."

Joe laughed. "I'll go you one better. Suppose I take you to a movie. I'll even get all dressed up for you, and you get dressed up too."

Jade Snow was delighted. Her first movie with Joe! What a wonderful day. In happy anticipation she put on her long silk stockings, lipstick, and the nearest thing to a suit she owned—a hand-me-down jacket and a brown skirt she had made herself. Then with a bright ribbon tying back her long black hair she was ready.

Daddy didn't miss a detail of the preparations as she dashed from room to room. He waited until she was finished before he demanded, "Jade Snow, where are you going?"

"I am going out into the street," she answered.

"Did you ask my permission to go out into the street?"

"No, Daddy."

"Do you have your mother's permission to go out into the street?"

"No, Daddy."

A sudden silence from the kitchen indicated that Mama was listening.

---

2 **Joe:** friend of Jade Snow's.

Daddy went on: "Where and when did you learn to be so daring as to leave this house without permission of your parents? You did not learn it under my roof."

It was all very familiar. Jade Snow waited, knowing that Daddy had not finished. In a moment he came to the point.

"And with whom are you going out into the street?"

It took all the courage Jade Snow could muster, remembering her new thinking, to say nothing. It was certain that if she told Daddy that she was going out with a boy whom he did not know, without a chaperone, he would be convinced that she would lose her maidenly purity before the evening was over.

"Very well," Daddy said sharply. "If you will not tell me, I forbid you to go! You are now too old to whip."

That was the moment.

Suppressing all anger, and in a manner that would have done credit to her sociology instructor addressing his freshman class, Jade Snow carefully turned on her mentally rehearsed speech.

"That is something you should think more about. Yes, I am too old to whip. I am too old to be treated as a child. I can now think for myself, and you and Mama should not demand unquestioning obedience from me. You should understand me. There was a time in America when parents raised children to make them work, but now the foreigners regard them as individuals with rights of their own. I have worked too, but now I am an individual besides being your fifth daughter."

It was almost certain that Daddy blinked, but after the briefest pause he gathered himself together.

"Where," he demanded, "did you learn such an unfilial[3] theory?"

Mama had come quietly into the room and slipped into a chair to listen.

"From my teacher," Jade Snow answered triumphantly, "who you taught me is supreme after you, and whose judgment I am not to question."

Daddy was feeling pushed. Thoroughly aroused, he shouted: "A little learning has gone to your head! How can you permit a foreigner's theory to put aside the practical experience of the Chinese, who for thousands of years have preserved a most superior family pattern? Confucius[4] had already presented an organized philosophy of manners and conduct when the foreigners were unappreciatively persecuting Christ. Who brought you up? Who clothed you, fed you, sheltered you, nursed you? Do you think you were born aged sixteen? You owe honor to us before you satisfy your personal whims."

Daddy thundered on, while Jade Snow kept silent.

"What would happen to the order of this household if each of you children started to behave like individuals? Would we have one peaceful moment if your personal desires came before your duty? How could we maintain our self-respect if we, your parents, did not know where you were at night and with whom you were keeping company?"

With difficulty Jade Snow kept herself from being swayed by fear and the old familiar arguments. "You can be bad in the daytime as well as at night," she said defensively. "What could happen after eleven that couldn't happen before?"

Daddy was growing excited. "Do I have to justify my judgment to you? I do not want a

---

3 **unfilial**: not respectful of parents.
4 **Confucius**: (551—479 B.C.) a Chinese philosopher.

daughter of mine to be known as one who walks the streets at night. Have you no thought for our reputations if not for your own? If you start going out with boys, no good man will want to ask you to be his wife. You just do not know as well as we do what is good for you."

Mama fanned Daddy's wrath, "Never having been a mother, you cannot know how much grief it is to bring up a daughter." . . .

"Oh, Mama!" Jade Snow retorted. "This is America, not China. Don't you think I have any judgment? How can you think I would go out with just any man?"

"Men!" Daddy roared. "You don't know a thing about them. I tell you, you can't trust any of them."

Now it was Jade Snow who felt pushed.

She delivered the balance of her declaration of independence: "Both of you should understand that I am growing up to be a woman in a society greatly different from the one you knew in China. You expect me to work my way through college—which would not have been possible in China. You expect me to exercise judgment in choosing my employers and my jobs and in spending my own money in the American world. Then why can't I choose my friends? Of course independence is not safe. But safety isn't the only consideration. You must give me the freedom to find some answers for myself."

Mama found her tongue first. "You think you are too good for us because you have a little foreign book knowledge."

"You will learn the error of your ways after it is too late," Daddy added darkly.

By this Jade Snow knew that her parents had conceded defeat. Hoping to soften the blow, she tried to explain: "If I am to earn my living, I must learn how to get along with many kinds of people, with foreigners as well as Chinese. I intend to start finding out about them now. You must have confidence that I shall remain true to the spirit of your teachings. I shall bring back to you the new knowledge of whatever I learn."

Daddy and Mama did not accept this offer graciously. "It is as useless for you to tell me such ideas as 'The wind blows across a deaf ear.' You have lost your sense of balance," Daddy told her bluntly. "You are shameless. Your skin is yellow. Your features are forever Chinese. We are content with our proven ways. Do not try to force foreign ideas into my home. Go. You will one day tell us sorrowfully that you have been mistaken."

After that there was no further discussion of the matter. Jade Snow came and went without any questions being asked. In spite of her parents' dark predictions, her new freedom in the choice of companions did not result in a rush of undesirables. As a matter of fact, the boys she met at school were more concerned with copying her lecture notes than with anything else. . . .

But while the open rebellion gave Jade Snow a measure of freedom she had not had before, and an outer show of assurance, she was deeply troubled within. It had been simple to have Daddy and Mama tell her what was right and wrong; it was not simple to decide for herself. No matter how critical she was of them, she could not discard all they stood for and accept as a substitute the philosophy of the foreigners. It took very little thought to discover that the foreign philosophy also was subject to criticism, and that for her there had to be a middle way.

In particular, she could not reject the fatalism that was at the core of all Chinese thinking and behavior, the belief that the broad pattern of an individual's life was ordained by fate, although within that pattern he was capable of perfecting himself and accumulating a desirable store of good will. Should the individual not benefit by his good works, still the rewards would pass on to his children or his children's children. Epitomized by the proverbs: "I save your life, for your grandson might save mine" and "Heaven does not forget to follow the path a good man walks," this was a fundamental philosophy of Chinese life which Jade Snow found fully as acceptable as some of the so-called scientific reasoning expounded in the sociology class, where heredity and environment were assigned all the responsibility for personal success or failure.

There was good to be gained from both concepts if she could extract and retain her own personally applicable combination. She studied her neighbor in class, Stella Green, for clues. Stella had grown up reading Robert Louis Stevenson, learning to swim and play tennis, developing a taste for roast beef, mashed potatoes, sweets, aspirin tablets, and soda pop, and she looked upon her mother and father as friends. But it was very unlikely that she knew where her great-grandfather was born, or whether or not she was related to another strange Green she might chance to meet. Jade Snow had grown up reading Confucius, learning to embroider and cook rice, developing a taste for steamed fish and bean sprouts, tea, and herbs, and she thought of her parents as people to be obeyed. She not only knew where her ancestors were born but where they were buried, and how many chickens and roast pigs should be brought annually to their graves to feast their spirits. She knew all of the branches of the Wong family, the relation of each to the other, and understood why Daddy must help support the distant cousins in China who bore the sole responsibility of carrying on the family heritage by periodic visits to the burial grounds in Fragrant Mountains. She knew that one could purchase in a Chinese stationery store the printed record of her family tree relating their Wong line and other Wong lines back to the original Wong ancestors. In such a scheme the individual counted for little, weighed against the family, and after sixteen years it was not easy to sever roots.

There were, alas, no books or advisers to guide Jade Snow in her search for balance between the pull from two cultures. If she chose neither to reject nor accept *in toto*,[5] she must sift both and make her decisions alone. It would not be an easy search. But pride and determination, which Daddy had given her, prevented any thought of turning back.

---

5 *in toto:* completely.

Discussion

1. How does Jade Snow tell her parents that she wants to go to college? What is she afraid they will say? What is the outcome?
2. How does Jade Snow's sociology class influence her attitude toward her parents? What arguments does she offer her parents?
3. What is the outcome of the conflict between Jade Snow and her parents?
4. In spite of Jade Snow's new "American" ideas, she still appreciates much of her Chinese heritage. What specific aspects of her heritage does she hold on to?

Vocabulary

The context clues of an unknown word are the familiar words that surround it. One kind of context clue is the RESTATEMENT CONTEXT CLUE. It is the one in which an author includes either a synonym or a definition that tells the meaning of an unfamiliar word. For example:

Jade Snow always followed the *precept*, or rule, that people should not talk while eating.

Following immediately after the word *precept* is the synonym *rule*. It provides an unmistakable context clue to the meaning of the unknown word. However, not all restatement context clues are quite so obvious. For example:

The *precept* that people should not talk while eating was one rule Jade Snow always followed.

In this case, the words *precept* and *rule* are not next to each other. Nevertheless, their relationship within the sentence still makes it clear that both words refer to the same thing.

Each of the following sentences about Jade Snow contains an *italicized* word. Copy these words on a separate sheet of paper. After each word, write a restatement context clue that tells that word's general meaning.

1. Jade Snow's attitude was *epitomized,* or summarized, by an old Chinese proverb: "I save your life, for your grandson might save mine."

2. After sixteen years, it was not easy for Jade Snow to *sever* roots, to cut herself off from the idea that the individual counts for little, weighed against the family.

3. The walk to the streetcar was a blessed *respite,* a time to relax and admire the moon if she could find it.

4. As she looked at the flattened cake, Jade Snow's heart filled with pain; but her *anguish* was soon broken through by Mrs. Simpson.

5. She could not reject the *fatalism* that was at the core of Chinese thinking, the belief that an individual's life is arranged in advance by fate.

Jade Snow Wong 1922—

Jade Snow Wong, a second-generation Chinese-American, got her middle name because she was born during a rare snowfall in San Francisco. She graduated from Mills College, worked for the navy during World War II, and later began making ceramics in San Francisco. Her book, *Fifth Chinese Daughter,* tells the story of an independent-minded girl who grew up in a traditional Chinese home where the main duty of the parents is to shape the child. The book, which was published in 1950, has been sold to over a quarter million Americans and translated into many foreign languages. Her second book, *No Chinese Stranger,* is a memoir which relates the life of a Chinese-American to the traditions of mainland China.

Each city has its own magic—its own appeal. It could be the excitement and beauty of a big city or the quiet security of a small town. But even more important than any of these things, each town and city becomes home to the people who live there.

in the inner city

LUCILLE CLIFTON

in the inner city
or
like we call it
home
we think a lot about uptown   5
and the silent nights
and the houses straight as
dead men
and the pastel lights
and we hang on to our no place   10
happy to be alive
and in the inner city
or
like we call it
home   15

SUNNY SIDE OF THE STREET *Philip Evergood*

Sunset: St. Louis

SARA TEASDALE

Hushed in the smoky haze of summer sunset,
When I came home again from far-off places,
How many times I saw my western city
   Dream by her river.

Then for an hour the water wore a mantle   5
Of tawny gold and mauve[1] and misted turquoise
Under the tall and darkened arches bearing
   Gray, high-flung bridges.

Against the sunset, water-towers and steeples
Flickered with fire up the slope to westward,   10
And old warehouses poured their purple shadows
   Across the levee.[2]

High over them the black train swept with thunder,
Cleaving[3] the city, leaving far beneath it
Wharf-boats moored beside the old side-wheelers   15
   Resting in twilight.

---

1 **mauve** (mōv): a pale bluish-purple.
2 **levee** (lev′ ē): a river embankment to prevent floods.
3 **cleaving** (klēv′ ing): dividing in two.

Midwest Town

RUTH DELONG PETERSON

Farther east it wouldn't be on the map—
    Too small—but here it rates a dot and name.
In Europe it would wear a castle cap
    Or have a cathedral rising like a flame.

But here it stands where the section roadways meet,   5
    Its houses dignified with trees and lawn;
The stores hold tête-à-tête[1] across Main Street;
    The red brick school, a church—the town is gone.

America is not all traffic lights
    And beehive homes and shops and factories;   10
No, there are wide green days and starry nights,
    And a great pulse beating strong in towns like these.

---

1 **tête-à-tête** (tāt′ə tāt′): a private conversation.

STONE CITY, IOWA *Grant Wood*

Joslyn Art Museum, Omaha, Nebraska

Discussion

1. In the poem "in the inner city," the poet contrasts "uptown" with "inner city." What does "uptown" look like? Why isn't it an appealing place?
2. In "in the inner city," what does the poet say is good about the inner city?
3. In "Sunset: St. Louis," the poet describes St. Louis as if it were a color snapshot. What is captured in this picture?
4. In "Midwest Town," what does the poet feel small towns have to offer? Answer in your own words.
5. How do the landscapes in "Sunset: St. Louis" and "Midwest Town" differ?
6. What common feeling do all three poets share about their own particular hometowns?

Composition

1. These three poems were written by poets who feel very positive about their hometowns. Using evidence from one poem, explain how you know its author prefers her hometown to any other.
2. Pretend your town is a person. Write a description of what it would look like. Would it, for example, look more like an energetic disc jockey or a sensitive violin player? After you have described its physical appearance, write about your town's personality. Give it as many human features and characteristics as you can.

Vocabulary

To describe their experiences more fully, authors often use DESCRIPTIVE WORDS that appeal to the senses. Words that name colors are especially effective. In "Sunset: St. Louis," the poet, Sara Teasdale, creates a clear mental picture for readers by using many colors in the scene she describes.

A. In a single column on the left-hand side of a separate sheet of paper, copy from the poem all the color descriptive words that Sara Teasdale uses to describe the sunset colors. Beside each unusual term, such as *tawny*, write a short definition of the color to which it refers. Use a dictionary if you need help.

B. Reread Ruth Peterson's "Midwest Town" and Lucille Clifton's "in the inner city." List descriptive words and phrases from both poems. Tell to which sense each word or phrase appeals.

Lucille Clifton 1936—

Lucille Clifton's poems are usually short and pointed, demonstrating both dignity and poise. There is celebration and affirmation of Black life in her works. She once commented, "I am a Black woman poet, and I sound like one." Mrs. Clifton was born in Depew, New York, and educated at Howard University. She once was a visiting writer at Columbia University and a poet-in-resident at Coppin State College in Baltimore. In 1969, she received the YM-YWCA Poetry Center Discovery Award and a National Endowment for the Arts grant. Her poetry collections include: *Good Times, Good News about the Earth,* and *An Ordinary Woman.*

Sara Teasdale 1884–1933

Sara Teasdale was a delicate and neurotic child. Her elderly, overprotective parents provided her with an education at home and at private schools. When she finished her schooling, she traveled extensively throughout the United States, Europe, and the Near East. During her unhappy marriage, she became more and more withdrawn. She later moved to New York where she lived in seclusion.

Teasdale's poetry has been admired for its simplicity, feeling, and perfection of form. Her collections include: *Rivers to the Sea, Flame and Shadow, Dark of the Moon, Strange Victories,* and *Love Songs,* which received a special Pulitzer Prize in 1918. She once said of her own work, "I try to say what moves me. I never care to surprise my reader."

He was an orphan in a strange new country. Everything was so different. Where were the locks? The fences? The police?

Stephen's First Week

EVA KNOX EVANS

S TEPHEN LESVEDIN was in America. At last he was here—a place dreamed of for almost as long as he remembered. The American soldiers stationed in the little South Austrian town had teased him about coming. Now he was here.

That fact was the only unconfused thing in Stephen's life at the moment. Everything else was a merry-go-round, a kaleidoscope[1] of confusion. The talk went on around him—talk he could understand if only he could have time to figure it out. But it went so fast and switched so often and was always being interrupted with laughter and fussing and teasing and frowns. While he was making sure he understood the comment Madame had made, the little one, Ellie, had spilled her milk, and Lucy was jumping and fussing, and the father was laughing, and Ricky was talking about hunting. All at once the talk exploded around him.

The food was confusing, too. At first, it was just a miracle, a three-times-a-day wonder. Two eggs for breakfast the first morning, and surely that was only because he was new. But after a week there had always been two eggs every morning for breakfast for every member of the family. Twelve eggs every day! Surely they would sometimes run out. And the sweets! And the full-flavored bread! And the great slabs of butter to go on the bread.

Stephen had made so many funny mistakes that first week, all because he could not seem to get it into his head that there was so much plenty. The soap, for instance. He chuckled to himself as he thought about it.

A big cake of it lay in a little dish above the kitchen sink. It was queer to see such a big cake lying there so openly, and all of the family seemed to use it. But Stephen did not dare. He scrubbed his hands and face the best way he could with warm water from the kettle on the stove. On the third day, however, he came for his midday dinner after cleaning the pigpens, and no matter how much water he used, he could not get the odor of the pigs from his hands. He washed them and smelled them, washed them and smelled them.

Mrs. Halstead was busy at the stove.

---

1 **kaleidoscope** (kə lī′ də skōp): Here it means fast-changing events.

Would it be impolite to ask to use the soap? Wouldn't it be more impolite to sit down at the table with his smelly hands? Stephen did not know what to do and stood, hesitant, beside the sink.

"What is it, Stephen?" Mrs. Halstead looked up from her frying pan.

"Is it permitted that I use a little of the soap?" he asked. "I know it is scarce, but . . ."

Instead of answering, Mrs. Halstead sat down on one of the kitchen chairs and laughed and laughed.

"Oh, Stephen," she said finally, "we have wondered and wondered. I was afraid to ask you because I didn't want you to feel that we didn't think you were clean enough. But I couldn't understand why you didn't when it was right in front of your eyes."

"But there is so little soap." Stephen was still puzzled. "I did not think it polite to use it unless—"

"Oh, my goodness, I didn't understand." Mrs. Halstead opened the pantry door. "Look!" she said, pointing to one of the shelves.

Stephen stood speechless before the shelf. There were rows of yellow soap and stacks of blue-wrapped soap and boxes of soap powder lined up along the shelf.

"That's one thing we have plenty of," laughed Mrs. Halstead. "I make some of it, and we can buy all we want. So you use it every time you feel like it."

Stephen took the cake of soap lovingly in his hands. He laughed aloud as the foamy suds oozed out between his fingers and plopped down into the sink. Here was soap he could use whenever he felt like it!

There was the wonder of the farm! In the times when Tim had told him about his home, and after, when he had dreamed of

coming and doing the work Tim had expected to do, he had pictured something very different—a small plot of land, and himself bent over the plow, or hitched to it while the father furrowed the neat rows. Tim had never spoken of horses on his farm, so surely this would be the way it was done. He could never have imagined in his wildest dreams the roaring tractor that plowed a field as easily as driving an automobile over it.

There were the milk cows and the cackling chickens and the great fat hogs in the pens. There was the tractor in the barn, and the truck in the garage, and rooms for sleeping so that each had his own. And yet this family was not rich. Stephen was sure they did not behave as rich people should. There were no servants to wait on them; the mother did all the work. There was not even a gleaming white bathroom like the ones he had seen in the magazines.

Over and over, Stephen would lie in his little room off the living room and shake his head and wonder.

Through the open door of the closet he could see his clothes hanging. The wonder of it, to have so many clothes—new clothes, too, and bought with his own money. For the father had told him he would pay him for his work on the farm and had given him his month's pay before he had done the work.

While Ricky and Lucy studied around the big table in the kitchen, he and Madame had looked through the thick catalogue with more things pictured in it than he could ever buy in the biggest store in Austria. And she had helped him pick out the clothes: bright plaid shirts and heavy pants, high-laced boots and a sheepskin-lined coat. The order had been sent to Boston, and in a few days there was the postman bringing the big packages.

He could not get enough of looking at his

new clothes or the feel of the good cloth under his hands and the knowledge that no one had ever worn them before.

Tim had tried to tell him everything about his home, but there was so much he hadn't said, Stephen realized now. And of course, Tim had expected to be here, too.

Stephen stretched out in his clean bed in Tim's home and remembered again the bright ordinary day that Tim had waved him good-by from the door of the plane, off on a safe routine trip that had ended in a wrecked plane and a crumpled body and a dark time. He had tried to run away in his black despair, away from everything that reminded him of Tim. But the other G.I.'s had found him and brought him back, and gradually he had gotten used to the idea that Tim was gone.

Now he was here with Tim's family. After begging in the streets and belonging no-where, after two years with the American soldiers and watching his friends there leave for home one by one, and then the time in the Displaced Persons' camp, where there was kindness and care but no closeness and affection, here he was with Tim's family. He hoped with an awful longing that they could be his family, too.

The most confusing time was his first trip to town—the Saturday trip to town. Every-one was going.

"Come, Stephen," Madame had called. "Ready?"

And they were all there in the truck— Madame and the little one in the front cab and Lucy and Ricky on the floor in the back. Mr. Halstead was coming from the barn ready to drive.

"I stay," suggested Stephen. "I stay to guard the place."

"Silly!" laughed Lucy. "We don't need a guard."

"But the cows," protested Stephen. "The cows someone may steal, and the big tractor and the pig—"

"No," said the father firmly. "We never worry about that. Nothing will be stolen. Just slam the kitchen door and come."

Stephen leaped lightly into the back of the truck and sat down on the floor, leaning back against the sides, his legs stretched out before him. Oh, what a picnic life! Oh, what free-dom!

The town was confusing. Stephen had not had a chance to look at it when he had arrived so unexpectedly the Saturday before. Then he was intent only on getting to the place he was supposed to go. The kind lady who had helped him in Boston and put him on the right train had told him he must go directly to the farm, and that he had done.

Now, he looked at the town. With Ellie's hand in his, he stood along the edge of the sidewalk and looked at the town—the people walking along the Saturday streets, stopping and talking together, joking and slapping their knees; the rosy, round faces of the children skipping along in front of their parents; the store windows full of food and clothes and bicycles and electric clocks.

He could not get enough of looking at the store windows. Ellie, bored with standing still, would jerk on his hand, but always he came back to them, always to see something he had never seen before. The shiny pans for cooking and the bright china, boxes of pencils and enough paper to write three books, matches—more matches than he had ever seen before—and the little glass ash trays and electric lamps. It would be so easy for dis-honest persons to break the glass, he thought, and take what they wanted. But there were no guards at the windows; he did not see a single policeman.

At first, he hovered near the parked truck. Lucy and Mrs. Halstead went darting into stores and came darting out again with wrapped parcels and bags, which they threw into the back of the truck. Ricky and Father came staggering out of the feed store, and Stephen rushed to help them dump those sacks in, too.

"This I will guard," thought Stephen.

But Mrs. Halstead said, "Why don't you and Ellie take a little walk? You can see the houses and the schools and the bank."

"But the truck with its load," Stephen protested. "I guard it."

"Silly!" laughed Lucy again. "If you want to guard something, guard Ellie. She needs it; the truck doesn't."

"Meet us in about half an hour at the drugstore," said Mrs. Halstead. "We'll all meet there."

"At the store where the medicines are sold?" asked Stephen.

"It's right on the corner there," said Lucy, pointing, and away she went down the street in the other direction.

Ellie and Stephen started up the street. Ellie held tight to his hand as they pushed through the crowds around the store fronts. They did not notice that the talking stopped as soon as Stephen appeared. They did not sense the nudging after they had passed nor hear the comments.

"That's the foreign boy Lem Halstead's taken."

"Fool idea, I'd say."

"Make good workers, I've heard tell."

"I don't hold with foreigners. Can't never tell what they're thinkin'."

Stephen and Ellie, the stores behind them, walked along the golden-shaded streets lined with houses on either side. The houses looked incomplete and exposed to Stephen, and at first he did not know why. For they were neat and painted, with curtains at the windows and flowering shrubs against the porches. As he looked down the long street, the houses seemed to belong together; there was nothing to separate them except an occasional concrete drive.

"No fences!" he thought suddenly. There were the green lawns and flower beds, and no fences to keep people away.

"That's where Ricky and Lucy go." Ellie interrupted his thoughts to point out the school.

There was the big red building set far back from the street and a baseball diamond off to one side. He stood still to look at the vacant building and wondered what it would be like to go to a school like that.

Ellie suddenly let go of his hand and darted forward away from him. He quickened his pace to keep up when, with a quick skip, she turned, ran over a grassy yard, and disappeared behind a house.

Stephen, startled, didn't stop to think of anything except that Ellie might get lost. And then what could he tell Madame? He raced as hard as he could across the yard and behind the house, too. But Ellie hadn't waited. She had crossed one yard and was standing under an oak tree in the adjacent garden, staring intently into the branches.

"A squirrel!" she yelled. "Come look at the wild squirrel!"

"A wild animal," thought Stephen. "The little one must be protected." He dashed to the tree to grab Ellie away from danger, just as the squirrel ran circle-wise down the trunk of the tree.

"Oh, ho!" laughed Stephen. "This wild animal I know. I did not know its English name!"

And Ellie joined in the laughter although she did not know the joke.

A door slammed them into silence. Stephen looked up startled to see a man standing on the back porch, a stout cane in his hand. He stood tall and straight, and his bristling white mustache and cold blue eyes made his look as severe as a Tartar.[2]

"Who's there?" he called.

"I . . . I . . ." stammered Stephen. How could he explain to this cold man why he was trespassing? "The little one . . ." he began.

But the man was coming slowly toward them, cane lifted. Stephen wanted to run, but he knew it would make no difference. He pushed Ellie behind him and stood his

ground, red-faced and frightened. Now, on this, his first trip to an American town, he would be arrested and put in the jail for being where he had no business to be.

The man stood in front of him; surely the cane would land any minute across Stephen's head. The cold blue eyes stared at him, at Ellie.

"Why!" he exclaimed suddenly, and there was a smile in his voice. "That's Lem Halstead's littlest! You the foreign boy come to live here?"

"Yes, sir," said Stephen, giving his little formal bow. "I'm sorry, sir . . ." he stammered.

"Never knew foreigners grew so big," said the man. "Glad to've seen you. Come back any time."

Ellie's hand tight in his, Stephen quickly

---

2 **Tartar:** Here it means a cruel person.

retreated across the grass and to the sidewalk again. They hurried up the street to meet the family. And in Stephen's heart there beat a little song of wonder: No fences! No fences to guard the houses! No fences for keeping people out!

Stephen told Lucy and Ricky all about it on the way home in the back of the truck.

"That's Chet Hoyt," said Ricky. "He's not mean. He's going blind, and he can't see you until he's right on top of you."

"And together with Ellie," Stephen went on with his story, "we hurry to meet you at the medicine store."

"Drugstore," corrected Lucy.

"Drugstore," Stephen repeated. "I look in one door, and there are people eating. Drinking coffee, eating the sandwiches and ice cream. This is a restaurant—not, how do you say? a drugstore. So there is another door a little way away in the same building. That must be it! I look in there, and can you imagine? There are books! Rows of books and magazines. So, a bookstore. Where is this drugstore?" Stephen raised his shoulders helplessly to show how he had felt. "Then we walk around the corner, and it is still the same building, to look in the window. And can you imagine? In this window there are the toys for children to play!"

"But that's a drugstore," protested Ricky. "Anyone knows that."

"Beyond the window," Stephen went on, "there was your mother, and I know it is right to go inside."

"But medicines are sold there," Lucy defended the store.

"I then saw," said Stephen. "The medicines were in a little glass cage at the back of the store."

He thought a minute and smiled to himself.

"This drugstore I like," he said aloud. "The bad-tasting medicines hidden behind the toys for play and the books to read and the good-tasting food."

Discussion

1. How did Stephen get to come to America?
2. Why doesn't he want to use the soap in his American home?
3. Why doesn't Stephen want to go into town with the Halstead family? What worries him while he is in town? What do these worries reveal about his earlier life?

Vocabulary

A SUFFIX is a letter or group of letters added to the end of a word to change the word in some way. One of the most common suffixes is -*ing*. This suffix is most often added to verbs (action words). It changes the verbs so that they will mean "an act in progress." For example:

Stephen and Ellie were look*ing* at the squirrel.
The owner of the house was com*ing* toward them.

There are also two other uses for the -*ing* suffix:

1. By adding -*ing* to a verb, you can change it into a *noun* (naming word). For example:

Shopp*ing* was a regular Saturday activity for the Halstead family.
The Halsteads enjoyed driv*ing* into town in the truck.

2. By adding -*ing* to a verb, you can also change it into an *adjective* (describer of nouns). For example:

Stephen lay in his bed off the liv*ing* room and wondered.
There was no gleam*ing* bathroom like the ones in magazines.

These two special uses of verbs + -*ing* have their own names. When a verb + -*ing* is used as a noun, it is called a GERUND. When a verb + -*ing* is used as an adjective, it is called a PARTICIPLE.

On a separate sheet of paper, copy the verb + -*ing* from each of the following sentences. Then according to how the word is used in the sentence, write whether it is a gerund or a participle. If you need help telling the difference, review the examples above.

1. Stephen could never have imagined this roaring tractor.
2. There were milk cows and cackling hens.
3. The most confusing time was his first trip to town.
4. Looking into store windows fascinated Stephen.
5. He saw shiny pans for cooking.
6. The man's bristling mustache and cold eyes made him look severe.
7. Ellie and Stephen did not notice that the talking stopped.

Eva Knox Evans 1905——

Eva Knox Evans is forever taking notes on how people talk and act. She scribbles down ideas and sentences whenever she reads. Then sometimes she uses these notes in her writing. Evans once said, "I always keep thinking, 'Someday, someday, I may write a truly good book'." She already has. Since the publication of *Ariminta* in 1935, she has written numerous stories for young people including: *Home Is a Very Special Place, People Are Important, Sleepy Time,* and *The Snow Book.*

New Mexican Mountain

ROBINSON JEFFERS

I watch the Indians dancing to help the young corn at Taos
    pueblo.[1] The old men squat in a ring
And make the song, the young women with fat bare arms, and
    a few shame-faced young men, shuffle the dance.

The lean-muscled young men are naked to the narrow loins,   5
    their breasts and backs daubed with white clay,
Two eagle-feathers plume the black heads. They dance with
    reluctance, they are growing civilized; the old men
    persuade them.

Only the drum is confident, it thinks the world has not
    changed; the beating heart, the simplest of rhythms,   10
It thinks the world has not changed at all; it is only a
    dreamer, a brainless heart, the drum has no eyes.

These tourists have eyes, the hundred watching the dance,
    white Americans, hungrily too, with reverence, not
    laughter;
Pilgrims from civilization, anxiously seeking beauty,   15
    religion, poetry; pilgrims from the vacuum.[2]

People from cities, anxious to be human again. Poor show
    how they suck you empty! The Indians are emptied,
And certainly there was never religion enough, nor beauty
    not poetry here . . . to fill Americans.   20

---

1 **pueblo** (pweb′ lō): Spanish for city. Here it refers to the
Indian village in ancient Taos.
2 **vacuum** (vak′ yüm): total emptiness.

Only the drum is confident, it thinks the world has not
    changed. Apparently only myself and the strong
Tribal drum, and the rockhead of Taos mountain, remember
    that civilization is a transient[3] sickness.

---

3 **transient** (tran′ shənt): passing.

Discussion

1. Where is the narrator of this poem? What is he watching?
2. What are the attitudes of the young dancers? Why do they feel that way?
3. Why are the white people watching the dance so respectfully?
4. The drum in this poem represents the age-old knowledge and traditions of the Native Americans. What is the feeling of the drum?
5. How are the Taos mountain and the drum alike?

Robinson Jeffers 1887—1962

Robinson Jeffers had a varied and extensive education. His father was a theology teacher who trained him thoroughly in the classics. He graduated from Occidental College and did further study at the University of Zurich in Switzerland. He then returned to the United States and studied medicine and forestry. After this broad education, he decided to devote himself to poetry, which became his all-absorbing interest. His first two books received little acclaim, but his third book, *Taniar and Other Poems,* brought him fame. This book revealed the unique style and ideas which he later developed in his other books: *Cawdor, Thurso's Landing,* and *Be Angry at the Sun.* Poems such as "New Mexican Mountain" demonstrate Jeffers' idea of the frantic nature of human life and the "self-conscious" condition which causes a civilization to decline.

Zuni Prayer

My fathers,
Our sun father,
Our mothers,
Dawn
As you arise and come out to your sacred place,   5
I pass you on your road.
The source of our flesh,
White corn,
Prayer meal,
Shell,   10
Pollen,
I offer to you.
Our sun father,
To you I offer prayer meal.
To you we offer it.   15
To you we offer pollen.
According to the words of my prayer
Even so may it be.
There shall be no deviation.
Sincerely   20
From my heart I send forth my prayers.
To you prayer meal,
Shall I offer.
Pollen I offer.
According to the words of my prayer.   25

Even so may it be.
Now this day,
My ancestors,
You have attained the far-off place of waters.

This day,   30
Carrying plume[1] wands,
Plume wands which I have prepared for your use,
I pass you on your roads.
I offer you plume wands.
When you have taken my plume wands,   35
All your good fortune whereof you are possessed
You will grant to me.
And furthermore
You, my mother,
Verily, in the daylight   40
With thoughts embracing,
We passed our days.
Now you have attained the far-off place of waters.
I give you plume wands,
Plume wands which I have prepared for your use. 45
Drawing your plume wands to you,
And sharing my plume wands.

All of your good fortune whatsoever
May you grant to us.
Preserving us along a safe road,   50
May our roads be fulfilled.

---

1 **plume:** feather.

Discussion

1. To whom is this prayer being addressed?

2. What do the Zuni offer the sun father in their prayer? How many times is the gift offered?

3. What do the Zuni offer their ancestors and mother? What is asked for in return?

4. What do you think is the meaning of the last line: "May our roads be fullfilled."?

5. Zuni do not ask their gods to grant them their prayers. Instead, Zuni bargain with them. Explain what is being bargained in this prayer.

On August 28, 1963, 200,000 people gathered in front of the Lincoln Memorial in Washington, D.C., in support of civil rights. The highlight of the day was a speech by Martin Luther King, Jr.

I Have a Dream . . .

DR. MARTIN LUTHER KING, JR.
as reported by JAMES RESTON

WASHINGTON, Aug. 28—Abraham Lincoln, who presided in his stone temple[1] today above the children of the slaves he emancipated, may have used just the right words to sum up the general reaction to the Negroes' massive march on Washington. "I think," he wrote to Gov. Andrew G. Curtin of Pennsylvania in 1861, "the necessity of being ready increases. Look to it." Washington may not have changed a vote today, but it is a little more conscious tonight of the necessity of being ready for freedom. It may not "look to it" at once, since it is looking to so many things, but, it will be a long time before it forgets the melodious and melancholy voice of the Rev. Dr. Martin Luther King, Jr., crying out his dreams to the multitude.

It was Dr. King who, near the end of the day, touched the vast audience. Until then the pilgrimage was merely a great spectacle. Only those marchers from the embattled towns in the Old Confederacy had anything like the old crusading zeal. For many the day seemed an adventure, a long outing in the late summer sun—part liberation from home, part Sunday School picnic, part political convention, and part fish-fry.

But Dr. King brought them alive in the late afternoon with a peroration[2] that was an anguished echo from all the old American reformers. Roger Williams calling for religious liberty, Sam Adams calling for political liberty, old man Thoreau denouncing coercion,[3] William Lloyd Garrison demanding emancipation, and Eugene V. Debs crying for economic equality—Dr. King echoed them all.

"I have a dream," he cried again and again. And each time the dream was a promise out of our ancient articles of faith; phrases from the Constitution, lines from the great anthem of the nation, guarantees from the Bill of

---

1 **temple:** the Lincoln Memorial.

2 **peroration:** conclusion of a speech.
3 **coercion:** forcing someone to do something against his or her will.

Rights, all ending with a vision that they might one day all come true.

Dr. King touched all the themes of the day, only better than anybody else. He was full of the symbolism of Lincoln and Gandhi,[4] and the cadences[5] of the Bible. He was both militant and sad, and he sent the crowd away feeling that the long journey had been worthwhile.

This demonstration impressed political Washington because it combined a number of things no politician can ignore. It had the force of numbers. It had the melodies of both the church and the theater. And it was able to invoke the principles of the founding fathers to rebuke the inequalities and hypocrisies of modern American life.

---

4 **Gandhi**: Mahatma Gandhi, a Hindu religious leader who led India in a passive resistance against the British.
5 **cadences**: rhythms.

There was a paradox in the day's performance. The Negro leaders demanded equality "now," while insisting that this was only the "beginning" of the struggle. Yet it was clear that the "now," which appeared on almost every placard on Constitution Avenue, was merely an opening demand, while the exhortation to increase the struggle was what was really on the leaders' minds.

It is a question whether this rally raised too many hopes among the Negroes or inspired the Negroes here to work harder for equality when they got back home. Most observers here think the latter is true, even though all the talk of "Freedom NOW" and instant integration is bound to lead to some disappointment.

The meetings between the Negro leaders on the one hand and President Kennedy and the Congressional leaders on the other also went well and probably helped the Negro cause. The Negro leaders were careful not to seem to be putting improper pressure on Congress. They made no specific requests or threats, but they argued their case in small groups and kept the crowd off Capitol Hill.

Whether this will win any new votes for the civil rights and economic legislation will probably depend on the overall effect of the day's events on the television audience.

Above all, they got over Lincoln's point that "the necessity of being ready increases." For they left no doubt that this was not the climax of their campaign for equality but merely the beginning; that they were going to stay in the streets until they could get equality in the schools, restaurants, houses and employment agencies of the nation, and that, as they demonstrated here today, they had found an effective way to demonstrate for changes in the laws without breaking the law themselves.

Now is the time to make real the promises of democracy. Now is the time to rise from the dark and desolate valley of segregation to the sunlit path of racial justice. Now is the time to lift our nation from the quicksands of racial injustice to the solid rock of brotherhood. Now is the time to make justice a reality for all of God's children.

There will neither be rest nor tranquility in America until the Negro is granted his citizenship rights. The whirlwinds of revolt will continue to shake the foundations of our nation until the bright day of justice emerges.

And that is something that I must say to my people who stand on the threshold which leads to the palace of justice. In the process of gaining our rightful place, we must not be guilty of wrongful deeds.

Again and again, we must rise to the majestic heights of meeting physical force with soul force. The marvelous new militancy which has engulfed the Negro community must not lead us to a distrust of all white people, for many of our white brothers as evidenced by their presence here today have come to realize that their destiny is tied up with our destiny.

There are those who are asking the devotees of civil rights, "When will you be satisfied?" We can never be satisfied as long as the Negro is the victim of the unspeakable horrors of police brutality. We can never be satisfied as long as our bodies, heavy with the fatigue of travel, cannot gain lodging in the motels of the highways and the hotels of the cities.

We can never be satisfied as long as our children are stripped of their selfhood and robbed of their dignity by signs saying "for whites only." We cannot be satisfied as long

as the Negro in Mississippi cannot vote and the Negro in New York believes he has nothing for which to vote.

No, we are not satisfied and we will not be satisfied until justice rolls down like water and righteousness like a mighty stream.

Now, I am not unmindful that some of you have come here out of great trials and tribulations. Some of you have come fresh from narrow jail cells.

Continue to work with the faith that honor in suffering is redemptive.[6] Go back to Mississippi, go back to Alabama, go back to South Carolina, go back to Georgia, go back to Louisiana, go back to the slums and ghettos of our Northern cities, knowing that somehow this situation can and will be changed. Let us not wallow in the valley of despair.

Now, I say to you today, my friends, so even though we face the difficulties of today and tomorrow, I still have a dream. It is a dream deeply rooted in the American dream. I have a dream that one day this nation will rise up and live out the true meaning of its creed: "We hold these truths to be self-evident, that all men are created equal."

I have a dream that one day on the red hills of Georgia the sons of former slaves and the sons of former slaveowners will be able to sit down together at the table of brotherhood.

I have a dream that one day even the state of Mississippi, a state sweltering with the people's injustice, sweltering with the heat of oppression, will be transformed into an oasis of freedom and justice.

I have a dream that my four little children will one day live in a nation where they will not be judged by the color of their skin, but by the content of their character.

This is our hope. This is the faith that I go back to the South with—with this faith we will be able to hew out of the mountain of despair a stone of hope.

---

6 **redemptive:** rewarding.

1. When was the newspaper article preceding the speech written? What information does it provide?

2. As the newspaper article indicates, this speech was a high point in the civil rights movement. Why do you think the Lincoln Memorial was selected as the site for the rally?

3. What were Martin Luther King's feelings about force and violence?

4. What do you think Martin Luther King meant when he said, "We can never be satisfied . . ."?

5. In his speech Martin Luther King repeated certain phrases. For example, "Now is . . ." is repeated four times. Find three other expressions which are repeated several times. What is the effect of these repetitions in his speech?

6. In your words, what was Martin Luther King's dream for America?

7. Which phrases from Martin Luther King's speech are similes or metaphors?

Vocabulary

Context clues are hints about the meaning of an unknown word found in the familiar words which surround it. There are many different kinds of context clues. One of them is the CONTRAST CONTEXT CLUE. It is a familiar word that means the opposite of the word which is unknown. For example:

Luisa wanted to buy a real diamond, but the jeweler sold her a *bogus* one.

The word *but* alerts you to the fact that *bogus* must be the opposite of *real.* An antonym (opposite-meaning word) of *real* is *false,* and that is exactly what *bogus* means. Here is another example:

Although Lee is fat, his brother is *gaunt.*

The word *although* hints that this sentence contains an opposite. *Thin* is an antonym for *fat,* and *thin* is what *gaunt* means.

A. Practice using contrast context clues in the following sentences from "I Have a Dream." On a separate sheet of paper, write a general definition for each *italicized* word. Beside it, write the contrast context clue which is given for that word.

1. Now is the time to lift our nation from the *quicksands* of racial injustice to the solid rock of brotherhood.

2. In the process of gaining our rightful place, we must not be guilty of *wrongful* deeds.

3. Again and again, we must rise to the majestic heights of meeting physical force with *soul* force.

4. With this faith, we will be able to hew out of the mountain of *despair* a stone of hope.

B. On the same paper, write general definitions for the *italicized* words in the following sentences. In these examples, the contrast context clues are not as clearly stated as the examples in Exercise A.

1. Benefits and privileges which until now have seemed *irretrievably* lost to us will some day be regained.

2. Where only *despondency* exists today, there will be promise of a happier world tomorrow.

3. No individual will be denied opportunities to gain an education, to hold a job, or to live in the neighborhood of his or her choice; instead, all citizens will be treated with complete *impartiality*.

4. Rather than let our spirits be broken by insult and cruelty, we will remain *indomitable*.

Martin Luther King, Jr. 1929–1968

Martin Luther King was fourteen years old when he first experienced racial prejudice. He and Mrs. Bradley, his teacher, were returning home from Atlanta after a speech contest. Commenting on the incident, King once said, "At a small town along the way, some white passengers boarded the bus, and the white driver ordered us to get up and give the whites our seats. We didn't move quickly enough to suit him, so he began cursing us. I intended to stay right in that seat, but Mrs. Bradley finally urged me up, saying we had to obey the law. And so we stood up in the aisle for the 90 minutes to Atlanta. It was the angriest I have ever been in my life."

Although King was angered by racial prejudice, he always insisted on change through nonviolent means. His belief and practice of nonviolence won him acclaim as a social reformer, theologian, and teacher. He received many honors and awards, including: the *Time* Man of the Year in 1963, the Nobel Prize for Peace in 1964, and the Nehru Award for International Understanding in 1968.

In the 1940s and 50s, it made no difference how intelligent you were . . . if you were Black and a woman! But Shirley Chisholm fought back and became the first Black woman to hold a seat in the United States Congress. Here she tells how she got started on that political road.

Shirley Chisholm: College Years

SHIRLEY CHISHOLM

I F I HAD GONE to Vassar, the rest of my life might have been different. Would I have become one of the pseudo-white upper-middle-class black women professionals, or a doctor's wife with furs, limousines, clubs, and airs? I can't believe that would have happened, but one never knows. At any rate, Brooklyn College changed my life. I was still naïve about most things when I entered college, not quite eighteen. My fiercely protective parents had given me a sheltered upbringing that was incredible, considering the time and place in which I grew up. In school, my intelligence had put me in a special category. In college, I began to bump up against more of the world.

One needed an 89 percent average to enter Brooklyn College then, so there were only about sixty black students in the day school. Brooklyn was the largest of the five city-run colleges, and its campus was supposed to be especially for bright lower-class, poorer students. Tuition was free; it was a "subway campus," and one would have expected more black students. The trouble was, of course,

that the grade and high schools they attended—then as now—did not do enough to overcome the handicaps of their background. So 98 percent of the students at the city colleges were white.

Brooklyn College was alive with activity. Bulletin boards and walls were full of posters for meetings, clubs, and programs. There were more organizations and extracurricular activities than anyone could count. Many of them were politically oriented and most of these were ultraprogressive. Brooklyn's president, Dr. Harry Gideonse, was always under attack from some office seeker who claimed that the faculty was riddled with Reds. It wasn't, of course, but for those days it was radical.

I had already decided to become a teacher. There was no other road open to a young black woman. Law, medicine, even nursing were too expensive, and few schools would admit black men, much less a woman. Social work was not yet open to blacks in the early 1940s. If I had other ideas about what I might do, I dismissed them. My youth may have been sheltered from boys and some other realities, but I was black, and nobody needed to draw me a diagram. No matter how well I prepared myself, society wasn't going to give me a chance to do much of anything else. (My sister Muriel, who entered Brooklyn College a few years later, majored in physics and graduated magna cum laude.[1] She was unable to find a job, even as a laboratory technician.) I knew it would have to be teaching for me; but I took no education courses, for some reason. I majored in sociology and minored in Spanish.

There was one all-black student group, the Harriet Tubman[2] Society. Some upperclassmen had started it, about a year before I joined it in my sophomore year. There I first heard people other than my father talk about white oppression, black racial consciousness, and black pride. The black students kept to their own tables in the cafeteria. We talked.

No one said "rap" then, but that's what we did. I had some things to contribute, more out of my reading than my experience. I knew about Harriet Tubman and Frederick Douglass, W. E. B. Du Bois and George W. Carver, and I had managed to find some books in the public library about our African heritage that few people then studied or talked about; I knew about the Ashanti[3] kingdoms, for instance. Some of the Tubman Society speakers warned of the future: "The day is going to come when blacks and whites will be at each other's throats in their own communities." We found that hard to believe then, although the 1943 Detroit riots had happened to serve as a portent.[4]

Other experiences sharpened my feeling for how racism was woven through American life. I belonged to the Political Science Society, which naturally thought itself progressive. Some of its speakers, I became aware, looked at my people as another breed, less human than they. Politicians came to talk and gave us such liberal sentiments as, "We've got to help the Negro because the Negro is limited," or, "Of course, the Negro people have always been the laborers and will continue to be. So we've got to make it more comfortable for them." Few white speakers would dare to say such things even to all-white audiences now. They were more innocent about prejudice twenty years ago.

For a long time I watched such white people closely, listened to them, and observed silently the treatment blacks were given in social and political situations. It grew on me that we, black men especially, were expected to be subservient even in groups where ostensibly everyone was equal. Blacks played

---

1 **magna cum laude**: with great honor.
2 **Harriet Tubman**: a Black woman who was responsible for the escape of many slaves through the underground railroad.

3 **Ashanti**: West African people of Ghana.
4 **portent**: a sign of things to come in the future.

by those rules; if a white man walked in, they came subtly to attention. But I could see their fear, helplessness, and discomfort.

When I looked at the white people who were doing this, consciously or not, it made me angry because so many of them were baser, less intelligent, less talented than the people they were lording it over. But the whites were in control. We could do nothing about it. We had no power. That was the way society was. I perceived that this was the way it was meant to be: things were organized to keep those who were on top up there. The country was racist all the way through.

More and more people, white and black, began to tell me things like, "Shirley, you have potential. You should do something with your life." I felt they were right. There must be a role for me to play, but what? As a teacher, perhaps I could use the talents people were telling me about and which I felt were there to do something that would be of service to society—especially to children. I volunteered to work in an Urban League settlement house, teaching art classes and sewing, and writing and producing skits and plays, which I loved. I decided to devote my life to children. But the resolve was also there (I did not realize yet how fierce it had grown) to do something about the way whites treated my people. Political action was hardly even a fantasy for me at that time. But I decided that if I ever had a chance, somehow I would tell the world how things were as I saw them.

A blind political science professor, Louis Warsoff, became interested in me, and we had long talks. I called him "Proffy," affectionately. He was one of the first white men whom I ever really knew and trusted. Our white neighbors and my father's co-workers had never been friends; they did not visit us

and we did not visit them, and our interrelations were always a little strained even when they were at their best. From Professor Warsoff I learned that white people were not really different from me. I loved formal debating particularly, and once after I starred in a match he told me, "You ought to go into politics." I was astonished at his naïveté.[5]

"Proffy," I said, "you forget two things. I'm black—and I'm a woman."

"You really have deep feelings about that, haven't you?" he countered. The conversation stuck in my mind. I realized that I did have deep feelings, on both scores.

Women were not even elected to campus offices then. Twice when girls ran for president of the Student Council (they were white, of course) I threw myself into the campaigns. I painted posters, helped write slogans and speeches, helped organize rallies and spoke at them myself. The white girls did not win.

Black students were not welcome in social clubs, so some friends and I formed a sorority-like black women students' society that I named Ipothia, which stood for "in pursuit of the highest in all." We were tired of trying to get into white groups, and decided, "Who needs them?" Ipothia grew to about twenty-six members. It is gone now; white groups started taking in black students, and the need for Ipothia passed.

I was still living at home, still going to church three times on Sundays, and still forbidden to date. I spent hours in the college library, and made no new, close friends in school. Naturally, the boys considered me a bookworm. It didn't bother me too much. They were surprised, though, when I showed

---

5 **naïveté** (nä ē′ və tā′): lacking worldly wisdom or knowledge.

up at parties and they discovered that I could dance, and loved to. No one ever had to teach me how; I just naturally danced. "That Shirley St. Hill can really move on the floor," I heard one boy say. But still the word was "Stay away from her—she's too intellectual, always talking about some big, serious thing."

During college I joined the Brooklyn chapter of the NAACP,[6] but I was not too active. It was primarily interested in economic issues such as discrimination in hiring, working conditions, pay, promotion. I had begun what was to be a twenty-year-long round of involvement with one community service organization after another, most of which I would eventually drop. I worked for the Urban League, I worked in hospitals, reading to old people and organizing programs to entertain them. I am still active in a few of these groups, like the Brooklyn Home for the Aged. As for the rest, after I give an organization a fair chance to show that it is really out to do something, if it doesn't, I get angry. In the last twenty years I have sat through more meetings and discussions than I ever want to remember and have seen very little get done. Even as an undergraduate, I was beginning to feel how useless it was for blacks to sit and talk with "the leading people" in the community, on biracial committees. It had begun to be clear that as long as we kept talking, nothing much was going to happen, and that this was what the "leading people" really wanted.

During 1945 we moved for the last time, when my father bought a house, a solid three-story one on Prospect Place. It cost him $10,000, all of it painfully saved from his wages at the bag factory, where he worked until his death. My mother and two of my sisters still live there; Selma, who is unmarried, lives on the second floor, and Odessa has her own apartment with her husband and her two children. Buying a house had always been my parents' second great goal; an education for their children was the only thing that mattered more to them. Now they had provided for both, which was a really remarkable achievement for parents of four children, who started with nothing and lived through the depression on a laborer's and a domestic's pay.

When I graduated in 1946, cum laude, I was nearly twenty-two but I looked sixteen or seventeen; I weighed about ninety pounds. It made job hunting hard. School after school turned me down, even as a teacher's aide; I didn't look old enough to teach, and most of my interviewers told me so. Day after day I stomped the streets. Finally I blew up at one nursery school director. "At least you could try me!" I exploded. "Put me on as a probationer![7] Give me a chance to show you! Give me a chance to find out whether I can do the job . . . don't judge me by my size." Mrs. Eula Hodges, director of the Mt. Calvary Child Care Center in Harlem, was persuaded. I worked there for seven years.

Even before I had finished my probation and become a full-fledged teacher's aide, I was sure that this was going to be my life-work. So, to be as well prepared as possible, I enrolled in Columbia University to work evenings for a master's degree in early childhood education. It was about then that I had my own early education in politics, in the toughest and most instructive school possible, New York City's old-time clubhouses.

---

6 **NAACP:** National Association for the Advancement of Colored People.

7 **probationer:** one who is tested during a trial period.

1. What did Shirley Chisholm train for in college? Why did she make that choice?
2. How did belonging to the Harriet Tubman Society at Brooklyn College influence Shirley Chisholm's thinking?
3. What other organization did she belong to in college? What prejudices did visiting political speakers express? Why did these attitudes cause her so much frustration?
4. What experience made Shirley Chisholm decide to devote her life to children? Why did she make this decision?
5. Who encouraged her to get involved in politics? Why did she join the Brooklyn chapter of the NAACP?
6. What problems did she have finding her first teaching job?

Shirley Chisholm 1924—

Shirley Chisholm's rise from neighborhood worker to "the first Black woman ever elected to Congress" was certainly no accident. Her political attitudes are the same as the title of her book, *Unbought and Unbossed*. She has never deviated from her pursuit of obtaining better educational opportunities for minority groups, programs for the poor and disadvantaged, and equality for ethnic minorities and women. Commenting on how she would like people to remember her, she once said, "I'd like them to say that Shirley Chisholm had guts. That's how I'd like to be remembered."

In this unit you have read about brave pioneers settling the wilderness. You have also read about brilliant leaders shaping the future of this country. But all of these accomplishments seem small beside the miracle of Helen Keller.

How I Learned to Speak

HELEN KELLER

THE MOST IMPORTANT DAY I remember in all my life is the one on which my teacher, Anne Mansfield Sullivan, came to me. I am filled with wonder when I consider the immeasurable contrasts between the two lives which it connects. It was the third of March, 1887, three months before I was seven years old.

On the afternoon of that eventful day, I stood on the porch, dumb, expectant. I guessed vaguely from my mother's signs and from the hurrying to and fro in the house that something unusual was about to happen, so I went to the door and waited on the steps. The afternoon penetrated the mass of honeysuckle that covered the porch and fell on my upturned face. My fingers lingered almost unconsciously on the familiar leaves and blossoms which had just come forth to greet the sweet southern spring. I did not know what the future held of marvel or surprise for me. Anger and bitterness had preyed upon me continually for weeks and a deep languor[1] had succeeded this passionate struggle.

---

1 **languor:** a state of inactivity or indifference.

Have you ever been at sea in a dense fog, when it seemed as if a tangible white darkness shut you in, and the great ship, tense and anxious, groped her way toward the shore with plummet and sounding-line,[2] and you waited with beating heart for something to happen? I was like that ship before my education began, only I was without compass or sounding-line, and had no way of knowing how near the harbor was. "Light! give me light!" was the wordless cry of my soul, and the light of love shone on me in that very hour.

I felt approaching footsteps. I stretched out my hand as I supposed to my mother. Some-one took it, and I was caught up and held close in the arms of her who had come to reveal all things to me, and, more than all things else, to love me.

The morning after my teacher came, she led me into her room and gave me a doll. The little blind children at the Perkins Institution[3] had sent it and Laura Bridgman[4] had dressed it, but I did not know this until afterward. When I had played with it a little while, Miss Sullivan slowly spelled into my hand the word "d-o-l-l." I was at once interested in this finger play and tried to imitate it. When I finally succeeded in making the letters correctly, I was flushed with childish pleasure and pride. Running downstairs to my mother, I held up my hand and made the letters for doll. I did not know that I was spelling a word or even that words existed; I was simply making my fingers go in monkeylike imitation. In the days that

followed I learned to spell in this uncomprehending way a great many words, among them *pin, hat, cup* and a few verbs like *sit, stand,* and *walk.* But my teacher had been with me several weeks before I understood that everything has a name.

One day, while I was playing with my new doll, Miss Sullivan put my big rag doll into my lap also, spelled "d-o-l-l" and tried to make me understand that "d-o-l-l" applied to both. Earlier in the day we had had a tussle over the words "m-u-g" and "w-a-t-e-r." Miss Sullivan had tried to impress it upon me that "m-u-g" is *mug* and that "w-a-t-e-r" is *water,* but I persisted in confounding the two. In despair she had dropped the subject for the time, only to renew it at the first opportunity. I became impatient at her repeated attempts and, seizing the new doll, I dashed it upon the floor. I was keenly delighted when I felt the fragments of the broken doll at my feet. Neither sorrow nor regret followed my passionate outburst. I had not loved the doll. In the still, dark world in which I lived there was no strong sentiment or tenderness. I felt my teacher sweep the fragments to one side of the hearth, and I had a sense of satisfaction that the cause of my discomfort was removed. She brought me my hat, and I knew I was going out into the warm sunshine. This thought, if a wordless sensation may be called a thought, made me hop and skip with pleasure.

We walked down the path to the well house, attracted by the fragrance of the honeysuckle with which it was covered. Some-one was drawing water and my teacher placed my hand under the spout. As the cool stream gushed over one hand, she spelled into the other the word *water,* first slowly, then rapidly. I stood still, my whole attention fixed upon the motions of her fingers.

---

2 **sounding-line:** a wire or cord with a weight (plummet) on it, used to measure water depth.
3 **Perkins Institution:** a school for the blind near Boston, Massachusetts.
4 **Laura Bridgman:** the first blind deaf-mute to be successfully educated.

Suddenly I felt a misty consciousness as of something forgotten—a thrill of returning thought; and somehow the mystery of language was revealed to me. I knew then that "w-a-t-e-r" meant the wonderful cool something that was flowing over my hand. That living word awakened my soul, gave it light, hope, joy, set it free! There were barriers still, it is true, but barriers that could in time be swept away.

I left the well house eager to learn. Everything had a name, and each name gave birth to a new thought. As we returned to the house, every object which I touched seemed to quiver with life. That was because I saw everything with the strange, new sight that had come to me. On entering the door, I remembered the doll I had broken. I felt my way to the hearth and picked up the pieces. I tried vainly to put them together. Then my eyes filled with tears, for I realized what I had done, and for the first time I felt repentance and sorrow.

I learned a great many new words that day. I do not remember what they all were; but I do know that *mother, father, sister, teacher* were among them—words that were to make the world blossom for me, "like Aaron's rod, with flowers." It would have been difficult to find a happier child than I was as I lay in my crib at the close of that eventful day and lived over the joys it had brought me, and for the first time longed for a new day to come. . . .

I had now the key to all language, and I was eager to learn to use it. Children who hear acquire language without any particular effort; the words that fall from others' lips they catch on the wing, as it were, delightedly, while the little deaf child must trap them by a slow and often painful process. But whatever the process, the result is wonderful. Gradually from naming an object, we advance step by step until we have traversed the vast distance between our first stammered syllable and the sweep of thought in a line of Shakespeare.

At first, when my teacher told me about a new thing, I asked very few questions. My ideas were vague, and my vocabulary was inadequate; but as my knowledge of things grew, and I learned more and more words, my field of inquiry broadened, and I would return again and again to the same subject, eager for further information. Sometimes a new word revived an image that some earlier experience had engraved on my brain.

I remember the morning that I first asked the meaning of the word *love*. This was before I knew many words. I had found a few early violets in the garden and brought them to my teacher. She tried to kiss me, but at that time I did not like to have anyone kiss me except my mother. Miss Sullivan put her arm gently round me and spelled into my hand, "I love Helen."

"What is love?" I asked.

She drew me closer to her and said, "It is here," pointing to my heart, whose beats I was conscious of for the first time. Her words puzzled me very much because I did not then understand anything unless I touched it.

I smelt the violets in her hand and asked, half in words, half in signs, a question which meant, "Is love the sweetness of flowers?"

"No," said my teacher.

Again I thought. The warm sun was shining on us.

"Is this not love?" I asked, pointing in the direction from which the heat came. "Is this not love?"

It seemed to me that there could be nothing more beautiful than the sun, whose warmth makes all things grow. But Miss Sullivan shook her head, and I was greatly puzzled and disappointed. I thought it strange that my teacher could not show me love.

A day or two afterward I was stringing beads of different sizes in symmetrical groups—two large beads, three small ones, and so on. I had made many mistakes, and Miss Sullivan had pointed them out again and again with gentle patience. Finally I noticed a very obvious error in the sequence and for an instant I concentrated my attention on the lesson and tried to think how I should have arranged the beads. Miss Sullivan touched my forehead and spelled with decided emphasis, "Think."

In a flash I knew that that word was the

name of the process that was going on in my head. This was my first conscious perception of an abstract idea.

For a long time I was still—I was not thinking of the beads in my lap, but trying to find a meaning for "love" in the light of this new idea. The sun had been under a cloud all day, and there had been brief showers; but suddenly the sun broke forth in all its southern splendor.

Again I asked my teacher, "Is this not love?"

"Love is something like the clouds that were in the sky before the sun came out," she replied. Then in simpler words than these, which at that time I could not have understood, she explained, "You cannot touch the clouds, you know; but you feel the rain and know how glad the flowers and the thirsty earth are to have it after a hot day. You cannot touch love either, but you feel the sweetness that it pours into everything. Without love you would not be happy or want to play."

The beautiful truth burst upon my mind—I felt that there were invisible lines stretched between my spirit and the spirits of others.

From the beginning of my education Miss Sullivan made it a practice to speak to me as she would speak to any hearing child; the only difference was that she spelled the sentences into my hand instead of speaking them. If I did not know the words and idioms necessary to express my thoughts, she supplied them, even suggesting conversation when I was unable to keep up my end of the dialogue.

This process was continued for several years; for the deaf child does not learn in a month, or even in two or three years, the numberless idioms and expressions used in the simplest daily intercourse. The little hearing child learns these from constant repetition and imitation. The conversation he hears in his home stimulates his mind and suggests topics and calls forth the spontaneous expression of his own thoughts. This natural exchange of ideas is denied to the deaf child. My teacher, realizing this, determined to supply the kinds of stimulus I lacked. This she did by repeating to me as far as possible, verbatim, what she heard, and by showing me how I could take part in the conversation. But it was a long time before I ventured to take the initiative, and still longer before I could find something appropriate to say at the right time.

The deaf and the blind find it very difficult to acquire the amenities of conversation. How much more this difficulty must be augmented[5] in the case of those who are both deaf and blind! They cannot distinguish the tone of the voice or, without assistance, go up and down the gamut of tones that give significance to words; nor can they watch the expression of the speaker's face, and a look is often the very soul of what one says. . . .

It was in the spring of 1890 that I learned to speak. The impulse to utter audible sounds had always been strong within me. I used to make noises, keeping one hand on my throat while the other hand felt the movements of my lips. I was pleased with anything that made a noise, and I liked to feel the cat purr and the dog bark. I also liked to keep my hand on a singer's throat, or on a piano when it was being played. Before I lost my sight and hearing, I was fast learning to talk, but after my illness it was found that I had ceased to speak because I could not hear. I used to sit in my mother's lap all day long and keep my

---

5 augmented: increased.

hands on her face because it amused me to feel the motions of her lips; and I moved my lips, too, although I had forgotten what talking was. My friends say that I laughed and cried naturally, and for awhile I made many sounds and word-elements, not because they were a means of communication, but because the need of exercising my vocal organs was imperative. There was, however, one word, the meaning of which I still remembered, *water*. I pronounced it "wa-wa." Even this became less and less intelligible until the time when Miss Sullivan began to teach me. I stopped using it only after I had learned to spell the word on my fingers.

I had known for a long time that the people about me used a method of communication different from mine; and even before I knew that a deaf child could be taught to speak, I was conscious of dissatisfaction with the means of communication I already possessed. One who is entirely dependent upon the manual alphabet has always a sense of restraint, or narrowness. This feeling began to agitate me with a vexing, forward-reaching sense of a lack that should be filled. My thoughts would often rise and beat up like birds against the wind, and I persisted in using my lips and voice. Friends tried to discourage this tendency, fearing lest it would lead to disappointment. But I persisted, and an accident soon occurred which resulted in the breaking down of this great barrier—I heard the story of Ragnhild Kaata.

In 1890, Mrs. Lamson, who had been one of Laura Bridgman's teachers, and who had just returned from a visit to Norway and Sweden, came to see me and told me of Ragnhild Kaata, a deaf and blind girl in Norway who had actually been taught to speak. Mrs. Lamson had scarcely finished telling me about this girl's success before I was

on fire with eagerness. I resolved that I, too, would learn to speak. I would not rest satisfied until my teacher took me, for advice and assistance, to Miss Sarah Fuller, principal of the Horace Mann School. This lovely, sweet-natured lady offered to teach me herself, and we began the twenty-sixth of March, 1890.

Miss Fuller's method was this: she passed my hand lightly over her face, and let me feel the position of her tongue and lips when she made a sound. I was eager to imitate every motion and in an hour had learned six elements of speech: M, P, A, S, T, I. Miss Fuller gave me eleven lessons in all. I shall never forget the surprise and delight I felt when I uttered my first connected sentence, "It is warm." True, they were broken and stammering syllables, but they were human speech. My soul, conscious of new strength, came out of bondage and was reaching through those broken symbols of speech to all knowledge and all faith.

No deaf child who has earnestly tried to speak the words which he has never heard—to come out of the prison of silence, where no tone of love, no song of bird, no strain of music ever pierces the stillness—can forget the thrill of surprise, the joy of discovery which came over him when he uttered his first word. Only such a one can appreciate the eagerness with which I talked to my toys, to stones, trees, birds and dumb animals, or the delight I felt when at my call, Mildred[6] ran to me or my dogs obeyed my commands. It is an unspeakable boon to me to be able to speak in winged words that need no interpretation. As I talked, happy thoughts fluttered up out of my words that might perhaps have struggled in vain to escape my fingers.

But it must not be supposed that I could

---

6 **Mildred:** Helen Keller's younger sister.

really talk in this short time. I had learned only the elements of speech. Miss Fuller and Miss Sullivan could understand me, but most people would not have understood one word in a hundred. Nor is it true that, after I had learned these elements, I did the rest of the work myself. But for Miss Sullivan's genius, untiring perseverance and devotion, I could not have progressed as far as I have toward natural speech. In the first place, I labored night and day before I could be understood even by my most intimate friends; in the second place, I needed Miss Sullivan's assistance constantly in my efforts to articulate each sound clearly and to combine all sounds in a thousand ways. Even now she calls my attention daily to mispronounced words.

All teachers of the deaf know what this means, and only they can at all appreciate the peculiar difficulties with which I had to contend. In reading my teacher's lips, I was wholly dependent on my fingers; I had to use the sense of touch in catching the vibrations of the throat, the movements of the mouth and the expression of the face; and often this sense was at fault. In such cases I was forced to repeat the words or sentences, sometimes for hours, until I felt the proper ring in my own voice. My work was practice, practice, practice. Discouragement and weariness cast me down frequently; but the next moment the thought that I should soon be at home and show my loved ones what I had accomplished, spurred me on, and I eagerly looked forward to their pleasure in my achievement.

"My little sister will understand me now," was a thought stronger than all obstacles. I used to repeat ecstatically, "I am not dumb now." I could not be despondent while I anticipated the delight of talking to my mother and reading her responses from her lips. It astonished me to find how much easier it is to talk than to spell with the fingers, and I discarded the manual alphabet as a medium of communication on my part; but Miss Sullivan and a few friends still use it in speaking to me, for it is more convenient and more rapid than lip reading.

Just here, perhaps, I had better explain our use of the manual alphabet, which seems to puzzle people who do not know us. One who reads or talks to me spells with his hand, using the single-hand manual alphabet generally employed by the deaf. I place my hand on the hand of the speaker so lightly as not to impede its movements. The position of the hand is as easy to feel as it is to see. I do not feel each letter any more than you see each letter separately when you read. Constant practice makes the fingers very flexible, and some of my friends spell rapidly—about as fast as an expert writes on a typewriter. The mere spelling is, of course, no more a conscious act than it is in writing.

When I had made speech my own, I could not wait to go home. At last the happiest of happy moments arrived. I made my homeward journey, talking constantly to Miss Sullivan, not for the sake of talking, but determined to improve to the last minute. Almost before I knew it, the train stopped at the Tuscumbia station, and there on the platform stood the whole family. My eyes fill with tears now as I think how my mother pressed me close to her, speechless and trembling with delight, taking in every syllable that I spoke, while little Mildred seized my free hand and kissed it and danced, and my father expressed his pride and affection in a big silence. It was as if Isaiah's prophecy had been fulfilled in me, "The mountains and the hills shall break forth before you into singing, and all the trees of the field shall clap their hands!"

Discussion

1. What was Helen's life like before she learned language?
2. How did Anne Sullivan teach her language?
3. Why were words for abstract ideas such as *love* very difficult for Helen to learn?
4. How did she learn to talk?
5. Why was it so important to Helen that she learn to talk?

Composition

1. Pretend you are Anne Sullivan. It is the day you took Helen Keller out to the well. For the first time she understood the meaning of *water*. Write in your diary the events of that experience. First tell exactly what happened. Then tell how Helen reacted when she understood. Finally tell your reaction to this first step in Helen's learning to speak.

2. Helen Keller learned to see the entire world without the senses of sight and hearing. She relied primarily on her sense of touch to understand what was happening around her. Try an experiment. Use a blindfold and earplugs to shut out both of these senses. Then have a friend lead you to a strange place such as an unfamiliar classroom, a neighborhood store, or a friend's house. Try to learn as much about the place as you can by relying only on your senses of touch and smell. Afterwards write a description of your experience. End by stating some of the problems you had being handicapped in this way.

Helen Keller 1880—1968

A famous author once suggested that Helen Keller could have taken this sentence as the motto of her life: "Life is too short to be little." Mark Twain called her the most marvelous woman since Joan of Arc. Both statements are probably accurate. This deaf and blind woman not only learned to communicate with the rest of the world, but she went on to graduate with honors from Radcliffe. She also wrote numerous books, including *Story of My Life*. Her teacher, Anne Sullivan, remained her constant companion and friend until her death in 1936.

Discussion

1. In this unit you read about real people who led the way toward the development of this country. In your opinion, which four people made the most important contributions to America? Briefly describe their contributions.

2. This unit contains several selections in which different cultures met in America. What were some of the conflicts that resulted? What solutions to these conflicts were presented?

3. In the selection from *Pioneers in Protest*, you learned that Harriet Tubman risked her life to free hundreds of slaves. How did Abraham Lincoln and Martin Luther King, Jr., each carry on her work?

4. Thomas Jefferson gave hope to a new nation when he wrote the Declaration of Independence. How do you think Helen Keller's life was also a type of declaration of independence?

Composition

1. From this unit choose one character whom you think is the best example of what a good American is or should be. Write a description of this person. Begin by identifying the character. Tell about the person's appearance, and then tell what kind of person you believe the character was or is. As evidence, use examples of what the character said or did in the story. End by telling why you think this person is a good example of an American.

2. This unit focused on a few scenes from America. In order to make a more complete picture, select a poem, story, article, movie, or picture that represents one of your favorite scenes of America. Write an explanation of what your scene tells about America and why it is a favorite of yours. If you wish, you may write your own story or poem.

3

LEVELS NO. 452 *Vasily Kandinsky* 1929 Collection, the Solomon R. Guggenheim Museum

Plot

PLOT

Imagine that you have just finished reading a story about a boy who risked his life to save his horse. You're curious. Is this a true story? It might be, but more likely it was made up by the author. If it were made up—if it had imaginary characters, events, or setting—it would be called FICTION.

The type of fiction you will read in this unit is the SHORT STORY, and a short story is exactly what it says it is—short. It usually can be read in one sitting. Also, since it is short, it normally involves only a few characters and events. Usually there will be only one main character who is involved in most of the important action.

All short stories, of course, have a plot to keep readers interested. Most writers follow one basic plot pattern to relate the events of their stories. First they let readers know something about the main conflict of the story. The conflict places the main character against an opposing force. Next, authors reveal some of the problems that prevent the main character from resolving the conflict. Suspense continues to build until the climax or turning point of the story. That is the moment when readers finally learn if the main character will win or lose the struggle. Short story writers usually end their stories soon after the climax. The conclusion of the story just ties up the loose ends.

As you can see, making up a story that captures and holds a reader's attention is not easy. But even though the writer is like a magician in creating the illusion of reality, you—the reader—must also do your share. You must be able to put the pieces of the story together in your mind to make the plot come alive.

As you read the stories in this unit, get involved in a game of wits with the authors to see if you can figure out the solution to the main character's problem. You will have the opportunity, for example, to solve one of Sherlock Holmes's most intriguing cases, to adjust to life on another planet, and to escape from prison using only your wits.

Sherlock Holmes is at it again—here is one of his most unusual cases. It involves two men—one with red hair and one with an acid scar on his face.

The Redheaded League

SIR ARTHUR CONAN DOYLE

I HAD CALLED upon my friend, Mr. Sherlock Holmes, one day in the autumn of last year and found him in deep conversation with a very stout, florid-faced, elderly gentleman with fiery red hair. With an apology for my intrusion, I was about to withdraw when Holmes pulled me abruptly into the room and closed the door behind me.

"You could not possibly have come at a better time, my dear Watson," he said cordially.

"I was afraid that you were engaged."

"So I am. Very much so."

"Then I can wait in the next room."

"Not at all. This gentleman, Mr. Wilson, has been my partner and helper in many of my most successful cases, and I have no doubt that he will be of the utmost use to me in yours also."

The stout gentleman half rose from his chair and gave a bob of greeting, with a quick little questioning glance from his small, fat-encircled eyes.

"Try the settee," said Holmes, relapsing into his armchair and putting his finger tips together, as was his custom when in judicial moods. "I know, my dear Watson, that you share my love of all that is bizarre and outside the conventions and humdrum routine of everyday life. You have shown your relish for it by the enthusiasm which has prompted you to chronicle,[1] and, if you will excuse my saying so, somewhat to embellish so many of my own little adventures."

"Your cases have, indeed, been of the greatest interest to me," I observed.

"You will remember that I remarked the other day, just before we went into the very simple problem presented by Miss Mary Sutherland, that for strange effects and extraordinary combinations we must go to life itself, which is always far more daring than any effort of the imagination."

"A proposition which I took the liberty of doubting."

"You did, Doctor, but nonetheless you must come round to my view, for otherwise I shall keep on piling fact upon fact on you until your reason breaks down under them and acknowledges me to be right. Now, Mr. Jabez Wilson here has been good enough to

---

1 chronicle (kron′ə kəl): record.

call upon me this morning, and to begin a narrative which promises to be one of the most singular which I have listened to for some time. You have heard me remark that the strangest and most unique things are very often connected not with the larger but with the smaller crimes, and occasionally, indeed, where there is room for doubt whether any positive crime has been committed. As far as I have heard, it is impossible for me to say whether the present case is an instance of crime or not, but the course of events is certainly among the most singular that I have ever listened to. Perhaps, Mr. Wilson, you would have the great kindness to recommence your narrative. I ask you not merely because my friend Dr. Watson has not heard the opening part but also because the peculiar nature of the story makes me anxious to have every possible detail from your lips. As a rule, when I have heard some slight indication of the course of events, I am able to guide myself by the thousands of other similar cases which occur to my memory. In the present instance I am forced to admit that the facts are, to the best of my belief, unique."

The portly client puffed out his chest with an appearance of some little pride and pulled a dirty and wrinkled newspaper from the inside pocket of his greatcoat. As he glanced down the advertisement column, with his head thrust forward and the paper flattened out upon his knee, I took a good look at the man and endeavored, after the fashion of my companion, to read the indications which might be presented by his dress or appearance.

I did not gain very much, however, by my inspection. Our visitor bore every mark of being an average commonplace British tradesman, obese, pompous, and slow. He wore rather baggy gray shepherd's check trousers, a not over-clean black frock coat, unbuttoned in the front, and a drab waistcoat with a heavy brassy Albert chain and a square pierced bit of metal dangling down as an ornament. A frayed top hat and a faded brown overcoat with a wrinkled velvet collar lay upon a chair beside him. Altogether, look as I would, there was nothing remarkable about the man save his blazing red head and the expression of extreme chagrin and discontent upon his features.

Sherlock Holmes's quick eye took in my occupation, and he shook his head with a smile as he noticed my questioning glances. "Beyond the obvious facts that he has at some time done manual labor, that he takes snuff, that he is a Freemason,[2] that he has been in China, and that he has done a considerable amount of writing lately, I can deduce nothing else."

Mr. Jabez Wilson started up in his chair, with his forefinger upon the paper, but his eyes upon my companion.

"How, in the name of good fortune, did you know all that, Mr. Holmes?" he asked. "How did you know, for example, that I did manual labor? It's as true as gospel, for I began as a ship's carpenter."

"Your hands, my dear sir. Your right hand is quite a size larger than your left. You have worked with it, and the muscles are more developed."

"Well, the snuff, then, and the Freemasonry?"

"I won't insult your intelligence by telling you how I read that, especially as, rather against the strict rules of your order, you use an arc-and-compass breastpin."

"Ah, of course, I forgot that. But the writing?"

---

2 **Freemason:** a member of a secret society.

"What else can be indicated by that right cuff so very shiny for five inches, and the left one with the smooth patch near the elbow where you rest it upon the desk?"

"Well, but China?"

"The fish that you have tattooed immediately above your right wrist could only have been done in China. I have made a small study of tattoo marks and have even contributed to the literature of the subject. That trick of staining the fish's scales of a delicate pink is quite peculiar to China. When, in addition, I see a Chinese coin hanging from your watch chain, the matter becomes even more simple."

Mr. Jabez Wilson laughed heavily. "Well, I never!" said he. "I thought at first that you had done something clever, but I see that there was nothing in it, after all."

"I begin to think, Watson," said Holmes,

"that I make a mistake in explaining. '*Omne ignotum pro magnifico,*'[3] you know, and my poor little reputation, such as it is, will suffer shipwreck if I am so candid. Can you not find the advertisement, Mr. Wilson?"

"Yes, I have got it now," he answered with his thick red finger planted halfway down the column. "Here it is. This is what began it all. You just read it for yourself, sir."

I took the paper from him and read as follows:

TO THE REDHEADED LEAGUE:

On account of the bequest[4] of the late Ezekiah Hopkins, of Lebanon, Pennsylvania, U.S.A., there is now another vacancy open which entitles a member of the League to a salary of £4 a week for purely nominal services. All redheaded men who are sound in body and mind, and above the age of twenty-one years, are eligible. Apply in person on Monday, at eleven o'clock, to Duncan Ross, at the offices of the League, 7 Pope's Court, Fleet Street.

"What on earth does this mean?" I ejaculated after I had twice read over the extraordinary announcement.

Holmes chuckled and wriggled in his chair, as was his habit when in high spirits. "It is a little off the beaten track, isn't it?" said he. "And now, Mr. Wilson, off you go at scratch and tell us all about yourself, your household, and the effect which this advertisement had upon your fortunes. You will first make a note, Doctor, of the paper and the date."

"It is *The Morning Chronicle* of April 27, 1890. Just two months ago."

"Very good. Now, Mr. Wilson?"

"Well, it is just as I have been telling you,

Mr. Sherlock Holmes," said Jabez Wilson, mopping his forehead; "I have a small pawnbroker's business at Coburg Square, near the City. It's not a very large affair, and of late years it has not done more than just give me a living. I used to be able to keep two assistants, but now I only keep one; and I would have a job to pay him but that he is willing to come for half wages so as to learn the business."

"What is the name of this obliging youth?" asked Sherlock Holmes.

"His name is Vincent Spaulding, and he's not such a youth, either. It's hard to say his age. I should not wish a smarter assistant, Mr. Holmes; and I know very well that he could better himself and earn twice what I am able to give him. But, after all, if he is satisfied, why should I put ideas into his head?"

"Why, indeed? You seem most fortunate in having an employee who comes under the full market price. It is not a common experience among employers in this age. I don't know that your assistant is not as remarkable as your advertisement."

"Oh, he has his faults, too," said Mr. Wilson. "Never was such a fellow for photography. Snapping away with a camera when he ought to be improving his mind, and then diving down into the cellar like a rabbit into its hole to develop his pictures. That is his main fault, but on the whole he's a good worker. There's no vice in him."

"He is still with you, I presume?"

"Yes, sir. He and a girl of fourteen, who does a bit of simple cooking and keeps the place clean—that's all I have in the house, for I am a widower and never had any family. We live very quietly, sir, the three of us; and we keep a roof over our heads and pay our debts, if we do nothing more.

"The first thing that put us out was the advertisement. Spaulding, he came down

---

3 *Omne . . . magnifico:* "Whatever is unknown is magnified."
4 **bequest:** will; something given away after death.

into the office just this day eight weeks, with this very paper in his hand, and he says:

"'I wish to the Lord, Mr. Wilson, that I was a redheaded man.'

"'Why's, that?' I asks.

"'Why,' says he, 'here's another vacancy on the League of Redheaded Men. It's worth quite a little fortune to any man who gets it, and I understand that there are more vacancies than there are men, so that the trustees are at their wits' end what to do with the money. If my hair would only change color, here's a nice little crib all ready for me to step into.'

"'Why, what is it, then?' I asked. You see, Mr. Holmes, I am a very stay-at-home man, and as my business came to me instead of my having to go to it, I was often weeks on end without putting my foot over the doormat. In that way I didn't know much of what was going on outside, and I was always glad of a bit of news.

"'Have you never heard of the League of the Redheaded Men?' he asked with his eyes open.

"'Never.'

"'Why, I wonder at that, for you are eligible yourself for one of the vacancies.'

"'And what are they worth?' I asked.

"'Oh, merely a couple of hundred a year, but the work is slight, and it need not interfere very much with one's other occupations.'

"Well, you can easily think that that made me prick up my ears, for the business has not been over-good for some years, and an extra couple of hundred would have been very handy.

"'Tell me all about it,' said I.

"'Well,' said he, showing me the advertisement, 'you can see for yourself that the League has a vacancy, and there is the address where you should apply for particulars. As far as I can make out, the League was founded by American millionaire, Ezekiah Hopkins, who was very peculiar in his ways. He was himself redheaded, and he had a great sympathy for all redheaded men; so when he died, it was found that he had left his enormous fortune in the hands of trustees, with instructions to apply the interest to the providing of easy berths to men whose hair is of that color. From all I hear, it is splendid pay and very little to do.'

"'But,' said I, 'there would be millions of redheaded men who would apply.'

"'Not so many as you might think,' he answered. 'You see it is really confined to Londoners and to grown men. This American had started from London when he was young, and he wanted to do the old town a good turn. Then, again, I have heard it is no use your applying if your hair is light red, or dark red, or anything but real bright, blazing, fiery red. Now, if you cared to apply, Mr. Wilson, you would just walk in; but perhaps it would hardly be worth your while to put yourself out of the way for the sake of a few hundred pounds.'

"Now, it is a fact, gentlemen, as you may see for yourselves, that my hair is of a very full and rich tint, so that it seemed to me that if there was to be any competition in the matter I stood as good a chance as any man that I had ever met. Vincent Spaulding seemed to know so much about it that I thought he might prove useful, so I just ordered him to put up the shutters for the day and to come right away with me. He was very willing to have a holiday, so we shut the business up and started off for the address that was given us in the advertisement.

"I never hope to see such a sight as that again, Mr. Holmes. From north, south, east, and west every man who had a shade of red in his hair had tramped into the city to answer the advertisement. Fleet Street was choked with redheaded folk, and Pope's Court looked like a coster's[5] orange barrow. I should not have thought there were so many in the whole country as were brought together by that single advertisement. Every shade of color they were—straw, lemon, orange, brick, Irish setter, liver, clay; but, as Spaulding said, there were not many who had the real vivid flame-colored tint. When I saw how many were waiting, I would have given up in despair; but Spaulding would not hear of it. How he did it I could not imagine, but he pushed and pulled and butted until he got me through the crowd, and right up to the steps which led to the office. There was a double stream upon the stair, some going up in hope, and some coming back dejected; but we wedged in as well as we could and soon found ourselves in the office."

"Your experience has been a most entertaining one," remarked Holmes as his client paused and refreshed his memory with a huge pinch of snuff. "Pray continue your very interesting statement."

"There was nothing in the office but a couple of wooden chairs and a deal table, behind which sat a small man with a head that was even redder than mine. He said a few words to each candidate as he came up, and then he always managed to find some fault in them which would disqualify them. Getting a vacancy did not seem to be such a very easy matter, after all. However, when our turn came, the little man was much more favorable to me than to any of the others, and he closed the door as we entered, so that he might have a private word with us.

---

5 **coster:** seller.

"'This is Mr. Jabez Wilson,' said my assistant, 'and he is willing to fill a vacancy in the League.'

"'And he is admirably suited for it,' the other answered. 'He has every requirement. I cannot recall when I have seen anything so fine.' He took a step backward, cocked his head on one side, and gazed at my hair until I felt quite bashful. Then suddenly he plunged forward, wrung my hand, and congratulated me warmly on my success.

"'It would be injustice to hesitate,' said he. 'You will, however, I am sure, excuse me for taking an obvious precaution.' With that he seized my hair in both his hands, and tugged until I yelled with the pain. 'There is water in your eyes,' said he as he released me. 'I perceive that all is as it should be. But we have to be careful, for we have twice been deceived by wigs and once by paint. I could tell you tales of cobbler's wax which would disgust you with human nature.' He stepped over to the window and shouted through it at the top of his voice that the vacancy was filled. A groan of disappointment came up from below, and the folk all trooped away in different directions until there was not a redhead to be seen except my own and that of the manager.

"'My name,' said he, 'is Mr. Duncan Ross, and I am myself one of the pensioners upon the fund left by our noble benefactor. Are you a married man, Mr. Wilson? Have you a family?'

"I answered that I had not.

"His face fell immediately.

"'Dear me!' he said gravely, 'that is very serious indeed! I am sorry to hear you say that. The fund was, of course, for the propagation and spread of the redheads as well as for their maintenance. It is exceedingly unfortunate that you should be a bachelor.'

"My face lengthened at this, Mr. Holmes, for I thought that I was not to have the vacancy after all; but after thinking it over a few minutes, he said that it would be all right.

"'In the case of another,' said he, 'the objection might be fatal, but we must stretch a point in favor of a man with such a head of hair as yours. When shall you be able to enter upon your new duties?'

"'Well, it is a little awkward, for I have a business already,' said I.

"'Oh, never mind about that, Mr. Wilson!' said Vincent Spaulding. 'I should be able to look after that for you.'

"'What would be the hours?' I asked.

"'Ten to two.'

"Now a pawnbroker's business is mostly done on an evening, Mr. Holmes, especially Thursday and Friday evening, which is just before payday; so it would suit me very well to earn a little in the mornings. Besides, I knew that my assistant was a good man, and that he would see to anything that turned up.

"'That would suit me very well,' said I. 'And the pay?'

"'Is £4 a week.'

"'And the work?'

"'Is purely nominal.'

"'What do you call purely nominal?'

"'Well, you have to be in the office, or at least in the building, the whole time. If you leave, you forfeit your whole position forever. The will is very clear upon that point. You don't comply with the conditions if you budge from the office during that time.'

"'It's only four hours a day, and I should not think of leaving,' said I.

"'No excuse will avail,' said Mr. Duncan Ross; 'neither sickness nor business nor anything else. There you must stay, or you lose your billet.'[6]

---

6 **billet:** job; position.

"'And the work?'

"'Is to copy out the *Encyclopedia Britannica*. There is the first volume of it in that press. You must find your own ink, pens, and blotting paper, but we provide this table and chair. Will you be ready tomorrow?'

"'Certainly,' I answered.

"'Then, good-by, Mr. Jabez Wilson, and let me congratulate you once more on the important position which you have been fortunate enough to gain.' He bowed me out of the room, and I went home with my assistant, hardly knowing what to say or do, I was so pleased at my own good fortune.

"Well, I thought over the matter all day, and by evening I was in low spirits again; for I had quite persuaded myself that the whole affair must be some great hoax or fraud, though what its object might be I could not imagine. It seemed altogether past belief that anyone could make such a will, or that they would pay such a sum for doing anything so simple as copying out the *Encyclopedia Britannica*. Vincent Spaulding did what he could to cheer me up, but by bedtime I had reasoned myself out of the whole thing. However, in the morning I determined to have a look at it anyhow, so I bought a penny bottle of ink, and with a quill pen, and seven sheets of foolscap paper, I started off for Pope's Court.

"Well, to my surprise and delight, everything was right as possible. The table was set out ready for me, and Mr. Duncan Ross was there to see that I got fairly to work. He started me off upon the letter *A*, and then he left me; but he would drop in from time to time to see that all was right with me. At two o'clock he bade me good day, complimented me upon the amount that I had written, and locked the door of the office after me.

"This went on day after day, Mr. Holmes, and on Saturday the manager came in and planked down four golden sovereigns for my week's work. It was the same next week, and the same the week after. Every morning I was there at ten, and every afternoon I left at two. By degrees Mr. Duncan Ross took to coming in only once of a morning, and then, after a time, he did not come at all. Still, of course, I never dared to leave the room for an instant, for I was not sure when he might come, and the billet was such a good one, and suited me so well, that I would not risk the loss of it.

"Eight weeks passed away like this, and I had written about Abbots and Archery and Armor and Architecture and Attics, and hoped with diligence that I might get on to the *B*'s before very long. It cost me something in foolscap, and I had pretty nearly filled a shelf with my writings. And then suddenly the whole business came to an end."

"To an end?"

"Yes, sir. And no later than this morning. I went to my work as usual at ten o'clock, but the door was shut and locked, with a little square of cardboard hammered on to the middle of the panel with a tack. Here it is, and you can read for yourself."

He held up a piece of white cardboard about the size of a sheet of note paper. It read in this fashion:

THE REDHEADED LEAGUE

IS

DISSOLVED

October 9, 1890.

Sherlock Holmes and I surveyed this curt announcement and the rueful face behind it, until the comical side of the affair so completely overtopped every other consideration that we both burst out into a roar of laughter.

"I cannot see that there is anything very

funny," cried our client, flushing up to the roots of his flaming head. "If you can do nothing better than laugh at me, I can go elsewhere."

"No, no," cried Holmes, shoving him back into the chair from which he had half risen. "I really wouldn't miss your case for the world. It is most refreshingly unusual. But there is, if you will excuse my saying so, something just a little funny about it. Pray what steps did you take when you found the card upon the door?"

"I was staggered, sir. I did not know what to do. Then I called at the offices round, but none of them seemed to know anything about it. Finally, I went to the landlord, who is an accountant living on the ground floor, and I asked him if he could tell me what had become of the Redheaded League. He said that he had never heard of any such body. Then I asked him who Mr. Duncan Ross was. He answered that the name was new to him.

"'Well,' said I, 'the gentleman at No. 4.'

"'What, the redheaded man?'

"'Yes.'

"'Oh,' said he, 'his name was William Morris. He was a solicitor[7] and was using my room as a temporary convenience until his new premises were ready. He moved out yesterday.'

"'Where could I find him?'

"'Oh, at his new office. He did tell me the address. Yes, 17 King Edward Street, near St. Paul's.'

"I started off, Mr. Holmes, but when I got to that address, it was a manufactory of artificial kneecaps, and no one in it had ever heard of either Mr. William Morris or Mr. Duncan Ross."

"And what did you do then?" asked Holmes.

"I went home to Saxe-Coburg Square, and I asked the advice of my assistant. But he could not help me in any way. He could only say that if I waited, I should hear by post. But that was not quite good enough, Mr. Holmes. I did not wish to lose such a place without a struggle, so as I had heard that you were good enough to give advice to poor folk who were in need of it, I came right away to you."

"And you did very wisely," said Holmes. "Your case is an exceedingly remarkable one, and I shall be happy to look into it. From what you have told me, I think that it is possible that graver issues hang from it than might at first sight appear."

"Grave enough!" said Mr. Jabez Wilson. "Why, I have lost four pound a week."

"As far as you are personally concerned," remarked Holmes, "I do not see that you have any grievance against this extraordinary league. On the contrary, you are, as I understand, richer by some £30, to say nothing of the minute knowledge which you have gained on every subject which comes under the letter A. You have lost nothing by them."

"No, sir. But I want to find out about them, and who they are, and what their object was in playing this prank—if it was a prank—upon me. It was a pretty expensive joke for them, for it cost them two and thirty pounds."

"We shall endeavor to clear up these points for you. And, first, one or two questions, Mr. Wilson. This assistant of yours who first called your attention to the advertisement—how long had he been with you?"

"About a month then."

"How did he come?"

"In answer to an advertisement."

"Was he the only applicant?"

---

7 **solicitor** (sə lis′ə tər): lawyer.

"No, I had a dozen."

"Why did you pick him?"

"Because he was handy and would come cheap."

"At half wages, in fact."

"Yes."

"What is he like, this Vincent Spaulding?"

"Small, stout-built, very quick in his ways, no hair on his face, though he's not short of thirty. Has a white splash of acid upon his forehead."

Holmes sat up in his chair in considerable excitement. "I thought as much," said he. "Have you ever observed that his ears are pierced for earrings?"

"Yes, sir. He told me that a gypsy had done it for him when he was a lad."

"Hum!" said Holmes, sinking back in deep thought. "He is still with you?"

"Oh, yes, sir; I have only just left him."

"And has your business been attended to in your absence?"

"Nothing to complain of, sir. There's never very much to do of a morning."

"That will do, Mr. Wilson. I shall be happy to give you an opinion upon the subject in the course of a day or two. Today is Saturday, and I hope that by Monday we may come to a conclusion."

"Well, Watson," said Holmes when our visitor had left us, "what do you make of it all?"

"I make nothing of it," I answered frankly. "It is a most mysterious business."

"As a rule," said Holmes, "the more bizarre a thing is, the less mysterious it proves to be. It is your commonplace, featureless crimes which are really puzzling, just as a commonplace face is the most difficult to identify. But I must be prompt over this matter."

"What are you going to do, then?" I asked.

"To smoke," he answered. It is quite a three-pipe problem, and I beg that you won't speak to me for fifty minutes." He curled himself up in his chair, with his thin knees drawn up to his hawklike nose, and there he sat with this eyes closed and his black clay pipe thrusting out like the bill of some strange bird. I had come to the conclusion that he had dropped asleep, and indeed was nodding myself, when he suddenly sprang out of his chair with the gesture of a man who has made up his mind and put his pipe down upon the mantlepiece.

"Sarasate[8] plays at the St. James's Hall this afternoon," he remarked. "What do you think, Watson? Could your patients spare you for a few hours?"

"I have nothing to do today. My practice is never very absorbing."

"Then put on your hat and come. I am going through the City first, and we can have some lunch on the way. I observe that there is a good deal of German music on the program which is rather more to my taste than Italian or French. It is introspective, and I want to introspect. Come along!"

We traveled by the Underground as far as Aldersgate; and a short walk took us to Saxe-Coburg Square, the scene of the singular story which we had listened to in the morning. It was a poky, little, shabby-genteel place, where four lines of dingy two-storied brick houses looked out into a small railed-in enclosure, where a lawn of weedy grass and a few clumps of faded laurel bushes made a hard fight against a smoke-laden and uncongenial atmosphere. Three gilt balls and a brown board with "Jabez Wilson" in white letters upon a corner house, announced the place where our redheaded client carried on

---

8 **Sarasate:** a concert violinist.

his business. Sherlock Holmes stopped in front of it with his head on one side and looked it all over, with his eyes shining brightly between puckered lids. Then he walked slowly up the street and then down again to the corner, still looking keenly at the houses. Finally he returned to the pawn-broker's, and, having thumped vigorously upon the pavement with his stick two or three times, he went up to the door and knocked. It was instantly opened by a bright-looking, clean-shaven young fellow, who asked him to step in.

"Thank you," said Holmes, "I only wished to ask you how you would go from here to the Strand."

"Third right, fourth left," answered the assistant promptly, closing the door.

"Smart fellow, that," observed Holmes as we walked away. "He is, in my judgment, the fourth smartest man in London, and for daring I am not sure that he has not a claim to be third. I have known something of him before."

"Evidently," said I, "Mr. Wilson's assistant counts for a good deal in this mystery of the Redheaded League. I am sure that you in-quired your way merely in order that you might see him."

"Not him."

"What then?"

"The knees of his trousers."

"And what did you see?"

"What I expected to see."

"Why did you beat the pavement?"

"My dear doctor, this is a time for obser-vation, not for talk. We are spies in an enemy's country. We know something of Saxe-Coburg Square. Let us now explore the parts which lie behind it."

The road in which we found ourselves as we turned round the corner from the retired Saxe-Coburg Square presented as great a contrast to it as the front of a picture does to the back. It was one of the main arteries which conveyed the traffic of the City to the north and west. The roadway was blocked with the immense stream of commerce, flowing in a double tide inward and outward, while the footpaths were black with the hurrying swarm of pedestrians. It was diffi-cult to realize as we looked at the line of fine shops and stately business premises that they really abutted on the other side upon the faded and stagnant square which we had just quitted.

"Let me see," said Holmes, standing at the

corner and glancing along the line, "I should like just to remember the order of the houses here. It is a hobby of mine to have an exact knowledge of London. There is Mortimer's, the tobacconist, the little newspaper shop, the Coburg branch of the City and Suburban Bank, the Vegetarian Restaurant, and McFarlane's carriage-building depot. That carries us right on to the other block. And now, Doctor, we've done our work, so it's time we had some play. A sandwich and a cup of coffee, and then off to violinland, where all is sweetness and delicacy and harmony, and there are no redheaded clients to vex us with their conundrums."[9]

My friend was an enthusiastic musician, being himself not only a very capable performer but a composer of no ordinary merit. All the afternoon he sat in the stalls wrapped in the most perfect happiness, gently waving his long, thin fingers in time to the music, while his gently smiling face and his languid, dreamy eyes were as unlike those of Holmes, the sleuth-hound, Holmes the relentless, keen-witted, ready-handed criminal agent, as it was possible to conceive. In his singular character the dual nature alternately asserted itself, and his extreme exactness and astuteness represented, as I have often thought, the reaction against the poetic and contemplative mood which occasionally predominated in him. The swing of his nature took him from extreme languor to devouring energy; and, as I knew well, he was never so truly formidable as when, for days on end, he had been lounging in his armchair amid his improvisations and his black-letter editions. Then it was that the lust of the chase would suddenly come upon him, and that his brilliant reasoning power would rise to the level of

---

9 conundrums (kə nun' drəms): riddles.

intuition, until those who were unacquainted with his methods would look askance at him as on a man whose knowledge was not that of other mortals. When I saw him that afternoon so enwrapped in the music at St. James's Hall, I felt that an evil time might be coming upon those whom he had set himself to hunt down.

"You want to go home, no doubt, Doctor," he remarked as we emerged.

"Yes, it would be as well."

"And I have some business to do which will take some hours. This business at Coburg Square is serious."

"Why serious?"

"A considerable crime is in contemplation. I have every reason to believe that we shall be in time to stop it. But today being Saturday rather complicates matters. I shall want your help tonight."

"At what time?"

"Ten will be early enough."

"I shall be at Baker Street at ten."

"Very well. And, I say, Doctor, there may be some little danger, so kindly put your army revolver in your pocket." He waved his hand, turned on his heel, and disappeared in an instant among the crowd.

I trust that I am not more dense than my neighbors, but I was always oppressed with a sense of my own stupidity in my dealings with Sherlock Holmes. Here I had heard what he had heard, I had seen what he had seen, and yet from his words it was evident that he saw clearly not only what had happened but what was about to happen, while to me the whole business was still confused and grotesque. As I drove home to my house in Kensington, I thought over it all, from the extraordinary story of the redheaded copier of the encyclopedia down to the visit to Saxe-Coburg Square, and the ominous words with which he had parted from me. What was this nocturnal expedition, and why should I go armed? Where were we going, and what were we to do? I had the hint from Holmes that this smooth-faced pawnbroker's assistant was a formidable man—a man who might play a deep game. I tried to puzzle it out, but gave it up in despair and set the matter aside until night should bring an explanation.

It was a quarter past nine when I started from home and made my way across the Park, and so through Oxford Street to Baker Street. Two hansoms[10] were standing at the door, and as I entered the passage, I heard the sound of voices from above. On entering his room, I found Holmes in animated conversation with two men, one of whom I recognized as Peter Jones, the official police agent, while the other was a long, thin, sad-faced man, with a very shiny hat and oppressively respectable frock coat.

"Ha! our party is complete," said Holmes, buttoning up his pea jacket and taking his heavy hunting crop from the rack. "Watson, I think you know Mr. Jones, of Scotland Yard? Let me introduce you to Mr. Merryweather, who is to be our companion in tonight's adventure."

"We're hunting in couples again, Doctor, you see," said Jones in his consequential way. "Our friend here is a wonderful man for starting a chase. All he wants is an old dog to help him to do the running down."

"I hope a wild goose may not prove to be the end of our chase," observed Mr. Merryweather gloomily.

"You may place considerable confidence in Mr. Holmes, sir," said the police agent loftily. "He has his own little methods, which are, if he won't mind my saying so, just a little too theoretical and fantastic, but he has the makings of a detective in him. It is not too much to say that once or twice, as in that business of the Sholto murder and the Agra treasure, he has been more nearly correct than the official force."

"Oh, if you say so, Mr. Jones, it is all right," said the stranger with deference. "Still, I confess that I miss my rubber.[11] It is the first Saturday night for seven-and-twenty years that I have not had my rubber."

"I think you will find," said Sherlock Holmes, "that you will play for a higher stake tonight than you have ever done yet, and that the play will be more exciting. For you, Mr. Merryweather, the stake will be some £30,000; and for you, Jones, it will be the man upon whom you wish to lay your hands."

"John Clay, the murderer, thief, smasher, and forger. He's a young man, Mr. Merryweather, but he is at the head of his profession, and I would rather have my bracelets on him than on any criminal in London. He's a remarkable man, is young John Clay. His grandfather was a royal duke, and he himself has been to Eton and Oxford. His brain is as cunning as his fingers, and though we meet signs of him at every turn, we never know where to find the man himself. He'll crack a crib in Scotland one week, and be raising money to build an orphanage in Cornwall the next. I've been on his track for years and have never set eyes on him yet."

"I hope that I may have the pleasure of introducing you tonight. I've had one or two little turns also with Mr. John Clay, and I agree with you that he is at the head of his

---

10 **hansoms:** horse-drawn, two-wheeled carriages.

11 **rubber:** a round of whist, a card game.

profession. It is past ten, however, and quite time that we started. If you two will take the first hansom, Watson and I will follow in the second."

Sherlock Holmes was not very communicative during the long drive and lay back in the cab humming the tunes which he had heard in the afternoon. We rattled through an endless labyrinth of gaslit streets until we emerged into Farrington Street.

"We are close there now," my friend remarked. "This fellow Merryweather is a bank director and personally interested in the matter. I thought it as well to have Jones with us also. He is not a bad fellow, though an absolute imbecile in his profession. He has one positive virtue. He is as brave as a bulldog and as tenacious as a lobster if he gets his claws upon anyone. Here we are, and they are waiting for us."

We had reached the same crowded thoroughfare in which we had found ourselves in the morning. Our cabs were dismissed, and, following the guidance of Mr. Merryweather, we passed down a narrow passage and through a side door, which he opened for us. Within there was a small corridor, which ended in a very massive iron gate. This also was opened, and led down a flight of winding stone steps, which terminated at another formidable gate. Mr. Merryweather stopped to light a lantern, and then conducted us down a dark, earth-smelling passage, and so, after opening a third door, into a huge vault or cellar, which was piled all round with crates and massive boxes.

"You are not very vulnerable from above," Holmes remarked as he held up the lantern and gazed about him.

"Nor from below," said Mr. Merryweather, striking his stick upon the flags which lined the floor. "Why, dear me, it sounds quite hollow!" he remarked, looking up in surprise.

"I must really ask you to be a little more quiet!" said Holmes severely. "You have already imperiled the whole success of our expedition. Might I beg that you would have the goodness to sit down upon one of those boxes and not to interfere?"

The solemn Mr. Merryweather perched himself upon a crate, with a very injured expression upon his face, while Holmes fell upon his knees upon the floor and, with the lantern and a magnifying lens, began to examine minutely the cracks between the stones. A few seconds sufficed to satisfy him, for he sprang to his feet again and put his glass in his pocket.

"We have at least an hour before us," he remarked, "for they can hardly take any steps until the good pawnbroker is safely in bed. Then they will not lose a minute, for the sooner they do their work, the longer time they will have for their escape. We are at present, Doctor—as no doubt you have divined—in the cellar of the City branch of one of the principal London banks. Mr. Merryweather is the chairman of directors, and he will explain to you that there are reasons why the more daring criminals of London should take a considerable interest in this cellar at present."

"It is our French gold," whispered the director. "We have had several warnings that an attempt might be made upon it."

"Your French gold?"

"Yes. We had occasion some months ago to strengthen our resources and borrowed for that purpose 30,000 napoleons from the Bank of France. It has become known that we have never had occasion to unpack the money, and that it is still lying in our cellar. The crate upon which I sit contains 2,000 napoleons packed between layers of lead foil. Our reserve of bullion is much larger at present than is usually kept in a single branch office, and the directors have had misgivings upon the subject."

"Which were very well justified," observed Holmes. "And now it is time that we arranged our little plans. I expect that within an hour matters will come to a head. In the meantime, Mr. Merryweather, we must put the screen over that dark lantern."

"And sit in the dark?"

"I am afraid so. I had brought a pack of cards in my pocket, and I thought that, as we were a *partie carrée*,[12] you might have your rubber after all. But I see that the enemy's preparations have gone so far that we cannot risk the presence of a light. And, first of all, we must choose our positions. These are daring men, and though we shall take them at a disadvantage, they may do us some harm unless we are careful. I shall stand behind this crate, and do you conceal yourselves behind those. Then, when I flash a light upon them, close in swiftly. If they fire, Watson, have no compunction about shooting them down."

I placed my revolver, cocked, upon the top of the wooden case behind which I crouched. Holmes shot the slide across the front of his lantern and left us in pitch darkness—such an absolute darkness as I have never before experienced. The smell of hot metal remained to assure us that the light was still there, ready to flash out at a moment's notice. To me, with my nerves worked up to a pitch of expectancy, there was something depressing and subduing in the sudden gloom and in the cold, dank air of the vault.

"They have but one retreat," whispered Holmes. "That is back through the house into Saxe-Coburg Square. I hope that you have done what I asked you, Jones?"

"I have an inspector and two officers waiting at the front door."

"Then we have stopped all the holes. And now we must be silent and wait."

What a time it seemed! From comparing notes afterwards it was but an hour and a quarter, yet it appeared to me that the night must have almost gone, and the dawn be breaking above us. My limbs were weary and stiff, for I feared to change my position; yet my nerves were worked up to the highest pitch of tension, and my hearing was so acute that I could not only hear the gentle breathing of my companions, but I could distinguish the deeper, heavier inbreath of the bulky Jones from the thin, sighing note of the bank director. From my position I could look over the case in the direction of the floor. Suddenly my eyes caught the glint of a light.

At first it was but a lurid spark upon the stone pavement. Then it lengthened out until it became a yellow line, and then, without any warning or sound, a gash seemed to open and a hand appeared; a white, almost womanly hand, which felt about in the center of the little area of light. For a minute or more the hand, with its writhing fingers, protruded out of the floor. Then it was withdrawn as suddenly as it appeared, and all was dark again save the single lurid spark which marked a chink between the stones.

Its disappearance, however, was but momentary. With a rending, tearing sound, one of the broad, white stones turned over upon its side and left a square, gaping hole, through which streamed the light of a lantern. Over the edge there peeped a clean-cut, boyish face, which looked keenly about it, and then, with a hand on either side of the aperture, drew itself shoulder-high and waist-high,

12 *partie carrée:* foursome.

until one knee rested upon the edge. In another instant he stood at the side of the hole and was hauling after him a companion, lithe and small like himself, with a pale face and a shock of very red hair.

"It's all clear," he whispered. "Have you the chisel and the bags? Great Scott! Jump, Archie, jump, and I'll swing for it!"

Sherlock Holmes had sprung out and seized the intruder by the collar. The other dived down the hole, and I heard the sound of rending cloth as Jones clutched at his skirts. The light flashed upon the barrel of a revolver, but Holmes's hunting crop came down on the man's wrist, and the pistol clinked upon the stone floor.

"It's no use, John Clay," said Holmes blandly. "You have no chance at all."

"So I see," the other answered with the utmost coolness. "I fancy that my pal is all right, though I see you have got his coattails."

"There are three men waiting for him at the door," said Holmes.

"Oh, indeed! You seem to have done the thing very completely. I must compliment you!"

"And I you," Holmes answered. "Your redheaded idea was very new and effective."

"You'll see your pal again presently," said Jones. "He's quicker at climbing down holes than I am. Just hold out while I fix the derbies."[13]

"I beg that you will not touch me with your filthy hands," remarked our prisoner as the handcuffs clattered upon his wrists. "You may not be aware that I have royal blood in

_____

13 **derbies**: handcuffs.

my veins. Have the goodness, also, when you address me always to say 'sir' and 'please.'"

"All right," said Jones with a stare and a snigger. "Well, would you please, sir, march upstairs, where we can get a cab to carry your Highness to the police station?"

"That is better," said John Clay serenely. He made a sweeping bow to the three of us and walked quietly off in the custody of the detective.

"Really, Mr. Holmes," said Mr. Merryweather as we followed them from the cellar, "I do not know how the bank can thank you or repay you. There is no doubt that you have detected and defeated in the most complete manner one of the most determined attempts at bank robbery that has ever come within my experience."

"I have had one or two little scores of my own to settle with Mr. John Clay," said Holmes. "I have been at some small expense over this matter, which I shall expect the bank to refund, but beyond that I am amply repaid by having had an experience which is in many ways unique, and by hearing the very remarkable narrative of the Redheaded League."

"You see, Watson," he explained in the early hours of the morning as we sat over a glass of whisky and soda in Baker Street, "it was perfectly obvious from the first that the only possible object of this rather fantastic business of the advertisement of the League, and the copying of the encyclopedia, must be to get this not over-bright pawnbroker out of the way for a number of hours every day. It was a curious way of managing it, but, really, it would be difficult to suggest a better. The method was no doubt suggested to Clay's ingenious mind by the color of his accomplice's hair. The £4 a week was a lure which must draw him, and what was it to them,

who were playing for thousands? They put in the advertisement, one rogue has the temporary office, the other rogue incites the man to apply for it, and together they manage to secure his absence every morning in the week. From the time that I heard of the assistant having come for half wages, it was obvious to me that he had some strong motive for securing the situation."

"But how could you guess what the motive was?"

"Had there been women in the house, I should have suspected a mere vulgar intrigue. That, however, was out of the question. The man's business was a small one, and there was nothing in his house which could account for such elaborate preparations, and such an expenditure as they were at. It must, then, be something out of the house. What could it be? I thought of the assistant's fondness for photography and his trick of vanishing into the cellar. The cellar! There was the end of this tangled clue. Then I made inquiries as to this mysterious assistant and found that I had to deal with one of the coolest and most daring criminals in London. He was doing something in the cellar—something which took many hours a day for months on end. What could it be, once more? I could think of nothing save that he was running a tunnel to some other building.

"So far I had got when we went to visit the scene of action. I surprised you by beating upon the pavement with my stick. I was ascertaining whether the cellar stretched out in front or behind. It was not in front. Then I rang the bell, and, as I hoped, the assistant answered it. We have had some skirmishes, but we had never set eyes upon each other before. I hardly looked at his face. His knees were what I wished to see. You must yourself have remarked how worn, wrinkled, and stained they were. They spoke of those hours of burrowing. The only remaining point was what they were burrowing for. I walked 'round the corner, saw the City and Suburban Bank abutted on our friend's premises, and felt that I had solved my problem. When you drove home after the concert, I called upon Scotland Yard and upon the chairman of the bank directors, with the result that you have seen."

"And how could you tell that they would make their attempt tonight?" I asked.

"Well, when they closed their League offices that was a sign that they cared no longer about Mr. Jabez Wilson's presence—in other words, that they had completed their tunnel. But it was essential that they should use it soon, as it might be discovered, or the bullion might be removed. Saturday would suit them better than any other day, as it would give them two days for their escape.

For all these reasons I expected them to come tonight."

"You reasoned it out beautifully," I exclaimed in unfeigned admiration. "It is so long a chain, and yet every link rings true."

"It saved me from ennui,"[14] he answered, yawning. "Alas! I already feel it closing in upon me. My life is spent in one long effort to escape from the commonplaces of existence. These little problems help me to do so."

"And you are a benefactor of the race," said I.

He shrugged his shoulders. "Well, perhaps, after all, it is of some little use," he remarked. "'L'homme c'est rien—l'oeuvre c'est tout,'[15] as Gustave Flaubert wrote to George Sand."[16]

---

14 ennui (än' wē): boredom.
15 l'homme . . . tout: "Man is nothing; his work everything."
16 Gustave Flaubert . . . George Sand: Both were 19th century French writers.

Discussion

1. After observing Jabez Wilson's physical appearance for a few minutes, what does Sherlock Holmes learn about him?

2. What does Wilson want Holmes to do for him?

3. When Holmes questions Wilson about his employee, Vincent Spaulding, what does he find out?

4. What things were suspicious about Wilson's introduction to the Redheaded League?

5. When were you absolutely sure that Holmes had solved the mystery of the Redheaded League? When is the nature of the crime disclosed to Dr. Watson?

6. When do the reader and Dr. Watson receive a full explanation of how Holmes figured out the mystery?

7. Why do you think Dr. Watson is a necessary character in this story?

What makes a story interesting? Among the most important things are the opposing forces in a story. For example, a man is cornered in an alley facing a thief. Or, a girl wants to join the basketball team, but the coach does not like her. In other words, the main character faces some enemy or opposing force. The problem, then, is how will the main character overcome or defeat the enemy. This struggle is called the CONFLICT.

Although the main character may be fighting some force in nature such as cold, heat, or a dangerous animal, usually the conflict is with another person. In detective stories, for example, the main character often uses brains and bravery to catch the criminal.

1. The major conflict of "The Redheaded League" is between which characters?
2. When does the reader first learn about the conflict?
3. What does Holmes do to make sure he will win the conflict?
4. How is the conflict finally resolved?

Composition

1. Draw a word picture of Sherlock Holmes. Although this story does not tell you much about his physical appearance, it does tell you a lot about his personality. Begin by telling about his great abilities as a detective. Then tell about his other side—the personal man. Be sure to use examples of what he says and does from the story to support your statements. Summarize your description by telling why you feel most people think of Sherlock Holmes as a real person, rather than a fictional character.

2. You are walking over a bridge in California when you see a woman's coat and purse on the walkway. The coat, which is carefully folded, is made of heavy material. It has a large fur collar, but the cuffs of the sleeves are worn. The torn lining of the coat has been mended in several places. The large black leather purse contains a silver dollar and assorted change, but the card case is bare. There is no driver's license, social security card, or any credit card. However, there are several other items: a ticket stub from the Greyhound Bus Lines, a small packet of tissues, a can opener, a pocket knife, a deck of cards, and an unopened package of crackers. Based on this evidence, write about the owner of the coat and purse. As much as you can, include references to age, occupation, interests, and personality. Also include your theory about what happened to the owner. Be sure to explain your reasons for coming to such a conclusion.

Some stories contain words that are unfamiliar to you. When you come across such a story, it is often helpful to PARAPHRASE the parts of the story that give you trouble. To paraphrase means to restate something in familiar words—without changing the meaning. Following is a paraphrase of a sentence from "The Redheaded League":

ORIGINAL VERSION: "The portly client puffed out his chest with an appearance of some little pride and pulled a wrinkled and dirty newspaper from his greatcoat pocket."

PARAPHRASE: "The fat man pushed out his chest rather proudly and pulled a wrinkled and dirty newspaper from his overcoat pocket."

To write a paraphrase, find synonyms for unfamiliar words in a dictionary. Sometimes a whole phrase can even be replaced with just one or two words.

On a separate sheet of paper, write paraphrases of the passages below. If you need help, use a dictionary.

1. You have shown your relish for it by the enthusiasm which has prompted you to chronicle, and if you will excuse my saying so, somewhat to embellish so many of my own little adventures.

2. On account of the bequest of the late Ezekiah Hopkins, of Lebanon, Pennsylvania, U.S.A., there is now another vacancy open which entitles a member of the League to a salary of £4 a week for purely nominal services.

Sir Arthur Conan Doyle 1859–1930

Sir Arthur Conan Doyle was born in Edinburgh, Scotland, where he studied medicine and qualified as a doctor. When his practice did not go well, he began to write detective stories. Doyle modeled Sherlock Holmes after Joseph Bell, a doctor he had studied under. Bell had constantly figured out all sorts of things about people from their looks and habits. Doyle once killed Holmes in a story, but he was persuaded by public opinion to bring him back to life. Eventually over fifty Holmes stories were published in five volumes. Doyle also published two Holmes novels, *The Hound of the Baskervilles* and *The Valley of Fear*.

*A young girl must face life with a new
stepmother in a new town where she has no
friends. How can she deal with her terrible
loneliness? Where can she turn?*

The Long Way Around

JEAN McCORD

I HADN'T SPOKEN to my stepmother in three days. I was absorbed by an inner grief and anger because she had given away my mother's dresses to the Salvation Army.

I could still feel my mother around the house. Sometimes I'd come bursting in from school with some important piece of news that I wanted to share immediately, and coming through the door, I'd shout, "Mother, I'm home. Where are you?" and instantly, before the echo had died, I'd remember, too late.

My stepmother had answered once, the first time, coming out from her bedroom with a smile on her face, thinking I was calling her, saying "Yes, Patty, what is it?" But my face was set in a frozen scowl, and I was standing there rigid, unyielding and furious at myself for such a mistake. She understood and turning away without pressing me any further, she went back into her room and closed her door.

My mother had died two years before when I was twelve, and even though I knew better, sometimes in the middle of the night,

I'd awake in a terrible fear and to comfort myself back to sleep I'd whisper into the pillow, "She's only gone away on a trip. And she'll be back." In the morning I had to face my own lie.

My father had married again last year and though my two little brothers, Jason and Scott, called this new woman "Mother," my father had told me I didn't have to do so. I called her *Alice* even though sometimes it felt strange to call a grown woman by her first name. This Alice wasn't anything at all like my own mother. For one thing, she couldn't cook. My mother had been the best cook in the whole neighborhood. Even the other mothers around us used to say that and would come over for coffee and butter scones and things that my mother would just whip up on a moment's notice. This Alice . . . well, sometimes our whole supper ended up in the garbage can, and my father would take us out to a restaurant. I thought it was pretty stupid and expensive, but of course Jason and Scott loved it.

To make things even worse, so it seemed to me, my father had taken a new job, and we had moved away from the town and the neighborhood where I'd spent my whole life with kids I knew and had grown up with and gone to school with and graduated with.

Now I was in junior high with a whole new batch of kids and I didn't like any of them. They didn't like me, either. I kept my distance and when school was over, I walked home alone, carrying my books with my head down and hurrying by the groups of girls laughing and giggling over some private joke. I could feel them looking at my back and the talk always hushed a little until I was by, then they'd break out into silly, stifled snickers when I was down the street a ways.

Actually I hated them all. I hated the teachers and the new school and my new stepmother and my father who seemed a new person too. Even my little brothers seemed to deserve a good slap for the way they had forgotten and called this Alice "Mother" as if they had never had a mother of their own.

The only one who hadn't changed, who was still the way he had always been, was Rufus, our old Samoyed. Rufus is as old as I am, and in his way he understood. After my mother died, he'd lain on his braided rag rug and refused to move for over two weeks. He wouldn't eat because he was used to my mother fixing him up a strange mixture of dog food with raw egg and bacon drippings, and nobody else seemed to know just how to do it. Finally I tried and after a while he ate while looking at me from the corner of his eyes and seeming to apologize for it. I sat down beside him and cried into his neck, and he stopped eating long enough to lick my face which only made me cry harder.

Now the only reason I had for getting up in the morning was to greet Rufus and give him an egg. After school the only reason I came home was to take Rufus for a walk and together we had covered most of this new town. The only trouble was that the town stayed new. Somehow no matter how often we walked down the same streets, the houses always seemed strange. Rufus would plod along at my side, his head just at the reach of my hand. He stumbled once in a while over a curb, but that was because his eyesight wasn't too good any more. My own eyesight seemed slightly affected too because there was a gray film between me and everything I looked at.

We walked all over town after school, my feet just leading the two of us. Finally I knew we had tromped over every square inch of all the streets, but still nothing looked familiar. Sometimes returning home, I wouldn't even know we had reached the end of the walk until Rufus turned off the sidewalk and went up our front steps.

One Saturday morning I woke up very early. This was about a month ago, I think, or maybe two months. I had lain awake a long time that night watching the shadow patterns change on the ceiling when the wind tossed the big snowball bush outside my window. It seemed like the night was trying to tell me something, but I couldn't quite make out what it was. Out in the kitchen I could hear that Rufus was awake too; because every time he left his rug and walked across the floor, his toenails clicked on the linoleum. He seemed to be pacing the floor as if he wanted to go out into the night. Maybe he sensed something waiting out there for him. If my mother had been here, she'd know . . . she would have known. . . .

Somewhere there in the middle of the night, I must have made up my mind what I was going to do. When the dawn came, I just rose and dressed and without even consciously thinking about it, I packed my small overnight case, putting in my parents' wedding picture which I had retrieved from a trunk in the attic, all the socks I had, two books from the library which were due in three days, one book of my own, and a little stuffed felt doll which I had given to Jason and then taken back from him. I rolled up my printed-rose quilt and tied it in several places with my belts. Then in blue jeans and a ski jacket I tiptoed out to the kitchen with my belongings and looked down at Rufus who thumped his tail hard against the floor and got up. He stood with his chin over his dish waiting for me to break his egg into it. I saw then that I couldn't leave him behind so while he slurped his egg I rolled his rug around the outside of my quilt. Now it was a big sloppy bundle but I didn't care.

Just as I was easing open the kitchen door I remembered I had no money, so I had to carefully put everything down and return to my bedroom. I had had a dollar put away for a long time because there was nothing I wanted to spend it on. Outside in the snowball bush the birds were beginning to cheep and call with a tremendous clatter. They were so noisy I wondered how anyone could sleep through that, and I knew I had to get away quickly.

Rufus was waiting with his head leaning against the kitchen door. He knew we were going for a walk. I wanted to take his dish, but didn't see how I could carry everything. We'd manage somehow. I stepped out into the cool grayness with those birds still clattering and the eastern sky beginning to flag out in streaks of red. It was going to be a warm day, and I knew I wouldn't need the ski jacket. Still, I thought . . . at night. . . .

Rufus and I headed toward what I hoped was south. This was vaguely the direction where our old town and old friends were.

I had looked at it often enough on the map, but I wasn't sure of just what road to go along. And besides I wanted to stay off the roads. I could picture my father driving along looking for us soon enough, right about breakfast time, I thought, when they would first miss me. But they wouldn't know anything for sure, I told myself, until I remembered I was carrying Rufus' rug.

"That was very stupid of you," I told Rufus severely, "to let me take your old rug when you knew it would give us away."

I walked a few swift steps ahead of him.

"Just for that, I ought to make you go back alone. Without me. Serve you right."

I was very angry. Rufus was hanging his head. The tone of my voice told him he'd done something really bad, but I finally had to forgive him. After all, it had been my own idea.

We used the road only far enough to get us out of town, then I decided we'd better strike across country even though it would be harder traveling, and we would have to climb a lot of fences. It would be safer that way. I soon found out I was right about one thing; it was a lot harder going. We walked through pastures where the ground was spongy and wet and my shoes became water-logged. We fought our way through brush that kept trying to tear my bundles away from me, and by this time, they really felt heavy. I gave Rufus a sour look, wishing he could carry his own rug at least. We puffed up hills that gave me a stitch in the side, and I noticed that Rufus wasn't holding up too well. He was panting and beginning to lag behind.

By the time the sun was high, I was starving to death. Rufus, at least, had eaten an egg for breakfast, but I hadn't had a bite. And of course by now, I had lost my sense of direction completely. I had no idea which way was south although I had been keeping my eyes open looking for the moss that is supposed to grow on the north side of trees. I hadn't found any.

Every once in a while we would come close to a farmhouse and there was always trouble. Farmers must keep the meanest dogs in the world. At each place a big shrieking dog would come bounding out at us, and try to pick a fight with Rufus just because we were walking nearby. Rufus would say, "Urrgghh," and show all his teeth with his black lips drawn so far back he looked like a snarling wolf and the farm dogs would back off towards home, but never shut up. I was afraid the farmers might call the police, so we would hurry on.

It was a long time before I saw a country road which I figured was safe enough to walk on. In a couple of miles we came up to a crossroads and a store with one red gas pump squatting to one side and looking like it never had any customers.

I dropped my bundles outside and went into darkness and unfamiliar smells and there was this old farmer-type man dressed in striped overalls sitting on a sack of something. I didn't know what I wanted to buy, but anything would do. He had a small candy counter, so I brought three chocolate bars. I decided that canned dog food would keep the best for Rufus, so I got seven cans which took all the rest of my money.

"Stranger round here, aren't you, Miss?" the storekeeper said.

I mumbled something and waved backwards, because my mouth was full of stale-tasting candy. He put the cans in a sack and I left, but he followed me to the door and watched very slyly as I had to pick up my suitcase and rolled quilt which left me no way to carry the dog food. I struggled to force it under my arm, but the sack broke and the cans rolled all over the ground. In desperation I knelt and shoved them into my suitcase and Rufus and I marched down the road with the striped overalls watching us all the way.

I could just almost hear him on the telephone, if he had such a thing, saying, "Sheriff, there's a strange gal going down the road with a big old dog and a suitcase full of dog food. Looks mighty suspicious to me." So there was no choice; we had to leave the road and go back to the pastures and farmhouses.

In the middle of the day I knew I couldn't carry that terribly heavy suitcase any further, so I said to Rufus, "You are going to carry some of your own food inside of you."

We sat down in the shade of some bushes, and I opened the suitcase to get out a couple of the cans. Then I broke into tears from sheer rage. I had forgotten to bring along a can opener.

I cried a long time while Rufus looked at me sadly, laying his heavy head on my knee, and banging his tail, which was full of burrs and briars, against the stony ground.

My vaguely formed idea when we first started out was that we'd make our way back to our old town and maybe one of the old neighbors or even my favorite teacher, Miss Virginia Townsend, would take us in and keep us both if I worked for our board and room. Now I saw clearly that we weren't

going to make it. It was over two hundred miles back there, and without even a can opener, well. . . .

We rested for an hour or so while I talked it over with Rufus who was a good listener and always agreed with me.

"You knew it was a long ways when you started out with me, didn't you?"

He thumped his tail once. I guess he was too tired to argue.

"I always understood that dogs knew their own way back to their old homes. Why didn't you lead?"

He looked away down the hill as if he was searching for the right direction.

"If we go back, you know what it means, don't you? They'll all be against us, and you'll certainly have to mind your P's and Q's from here on in!"

He hung his head in shame, but how can you ask a fourteen-year-old dog to walk two hundred miles when he was all worn out from doing about ten?

We stood up and looked out over a valley that faded into a blue haze in the far distance. I picked up the luggage, and we went back down the hill toward the country store. By the time we got there Rufus was limping.

I went into that dim interior again, and the man was back on his sack, just resting and waiting with his legs crossed.

"Thought you'd be back," he said with a snort of choked laughter.

"Could I please use your telephone?" I asked with great dignity.

"In the back there. Ask the Missus." He jerked his head.

I had to go into their living quarters. It seems they lived right there surrounded by all those groceries and hardware and chicken feed and medicine for cows and horses. His Missus was a pleasant, stumpy woman with square glasses, and after I'd called home, she gave me a glass of lemonade. I had to ask her where we were, and she took the telephone to give my father directions. He was really boiling mad and hollered over the phone at me, "Swanson's Corner! Where is that?"

I went outside to call Rufus, and she let him come into the kitchen for a drink of cold water. While we waited for my father, I tried to think how to explain all those cans of dog food and the quilt and Rufus' rug, but there didn't seem to be any way. When my father drove up we climbed in and rode all the way home in guilty silence. My stepmother, Alice, must have told him not to say a word.

When we got home my little brothers looked at me fearfully and my father said with a glint in his eye, "Go to your room and stay there. I'll deal with you later."

Nothing more ever came of it which surprised me no end because I waited all week for punishment.

So now it was a month later, or maybe more.

I still kept to myself at school and if a person talked to me, I just turned away because I had nothing to say to any of them.

On the 5th of November it was my birthday. I woke up with poison in my heart and an ache in my throat that I had to keep swallowing because I was remembering my twelfth birthday when my mother had made a dress for me and also bought me *Tales of Robin Hood* which I don't read anymore, but it was the book I had taken with me when Rufus and I ran away.

Breakfast seemed strangely quiet, all the more so because nobody said a thing, not even "Happy Birthday." I knew they had forgotten.

At school, like always, I answered if I was called on, but not otherwise. I ate my lunch by myself and passed most of the day think-ing of how many birthdays I would have to live through before Rufus and I could leave again for good. About four more, I decided, then knew with a deep sorrow that Rufus wouldn't last to be eighteen.

When school was out, I turned in the wrong direction from home and headed for a park up on a high bluff. It was pleasant and empty. The trees were dropping their leaves in little piles and a couple of squirrels chased each other around tree trunks like they were on a merry-go-round. I wanted to stay there forever. I wanted the leaves to cover me like little Hansel and Gretel when they were lost in the woods. I wondered if they had had a stepmother who drove them off, and then I said aloud, "No, that isn't fair. You know it isn't Alice's fault. I don't know whose fault it is for feeling so left out of things."

I looked again at the fallen leaves and thought that my family was like the strong tree that would survive the winter, but I was probably one of the lost leaves.

"I didn't expect them to give me any presents," I kicked at the leaves. I propped my chin on my knees and sat for a long time, thinking, and because it was getting late, I read my next day's history lesson. Finally it was too hard to read, and looking up, I saw it was almost dark and it was a long way home.

I walked home like I always walked, neither slow nor hurrying. It was just too bad if I was late for supper. I didn't want any anyhow.

When I opened the door the house felt strange. My father was sitting in the front room behind his paper which he put aside for a moment, looked at me and said, "Humph!"

Jason came dancing up to me and grabbed me by the hand, pulling me into the dining room.

"Where you been, Patty?" he said. "Everybody waited and waited."

Rufus rushed out from the kitchen to greet me as always, but he was wearing a silly little paper hat tied under his chin. I stood in the brightly lighted room and looked around confused. There had obviously been a party. Used paper plates lay all over and the remains of a big frosted cake were crumpled in the center of the table which had a good linen cloth on it. A pile of wrapped presents lay on the sideboard. In the kitchen I could hear Scott chattering to Alice like a little parakeet and Jason, still clutching my hand, was trying to tell me something.

"All your classmates, Patty," he was saying. "All of them. When you dint come home, we had to have the party without you. Your presents are here."

He tried to drag me towards them, but I shucked him off and rushed to my room.

I was pretty shamefaced when Alice came in to see if I wanted supper. She sat beside me on the bed and patted me on the back.

"It was my fault," she said. "I shouldn't have tried to surprise you. Anyway, come on out and feed Rufus. I think he's going to be sick from all that cake he was given."

So that's how matters stand now.

Nothing is going to change very much. I don't feel quite so mad at the whole world, and I notice my actions toward Alice are a lot friendlier. It doesn't bother me any when the boys call her "Mother." Maybe, sometime, a long time from now, I might start calling her that myself. Maybe, by spring or so, I might start growing myself back on that family tree.

Discussion

1. Why is Patty so upset with her stepmother? Do you think her stepmother has done anything to deserve Patty's anger? How is she trying to win Patty's acceptance?

2. What problems does Patty have when she runs away?

3. Does Patty ever come to understand and appreciate her stepmother? When does she see that her stepmother is not to blame for her unhappiness?

4. Patty makes her life more miserable by some of her *own* actions. What does she do?

5. Who solves Patty's problems? Explain your answer.

6. What does Patty mean when she says at the end of the story, "Maybe, by spring or so, I might start growing myself back on that family tree."?

Vocabulary

A HOMONYM is a word that sounds the same as another word but has a different meaning and often is spelled differently. For example:

would—wood   grown—groan   tail—tale   one—won

A. Each of the following sentences from "The Long Way Around" contains an *italicized* word. On a separate sheet of paper, list the *italicized* words, and write a homonym for each one. Then write original sentences which use the homonyms correctly.

> EXAMPLE: *So* that's how matters stand now.
> ANSWER: so—sew Can you *sew* on this button?

1. I could almost *hear* him on the telephone.
2. "Could I please use *your* telephone?" I asked.
3. My stepmother Alice must have told him not *to* say a word.
4. I was standing *there* rigid, unyielding and furious at myself for such a mistake.
5. We had moved away from the town and the neighborhood where I'd spent my *whole* life with kids I knew.

B. In each sentence above, there are other words—besides the ones in *italics*—that have one or more homonyms. On the same paper, make a list of these words and give their homonyms.

Jean McCord 1924—

Jean McCord was born in Hayward, Wisconsin, and attended the College of Saint Scholastica and the University of California. One of her 45 different occupations included working in the Women's Army Corps. Her works include *Deep Where the Octopi Lie* and *Bitter Is the Hawk's Path*. Her stories have also appeared in *Best American Short Stories* and *Seventeen* magazine.

All Summer in a Day

RAY BRADBURY

"Ready?"

"Ready."

"Now?"

"Soon."

"Do the scientists really know? Will it happen today, will it?"

"Look, look; see for yourself!"

The children pressed to each other like so many roses, so many weeds, intermixed, peering out for a look at the hidden sun.

It rained.

It had been raining for seven years; thousands upon thousands of days compounded and filled from one end to the other with rain, with the drum and gush of water, with the sweet crystal fall of showers and the concussion of storms so heavy they were tidal waves come over the islands. A thousand forests had been crushed under the rain and grown up a thousand times to be crushed again. And this was the way life was forever on the planet Venus, and this was the schoolroom of the children of the rocket men and women who had come to a raining world to set up civilization and live out their lives.

"It's stopping, it's stopping!"

"Yes, yes!"

Margot stood apart from them, from these children who could never remember a time when there wasn't rain and rain and rain. They were all nine years old, and if there had been a day, even years ago, when the sun came out for an hour and showed its face to the stunned world, they could not recall. Sometimes, at night, she heard them stir, in remembrance, and she knew they were dreaming and remembering gold or a yellow crayon or a coin large enough to buy the world with. She knew they thought they remembered a warmness, like a blushing in the face, in the body, in the arms and legs and trembling hands. But then they always awoke to the tatting drum, the endless shaking down of clear bead necklaces upon the roof, the walk, the gardens, the forests, and their dreams were gone.

All day yesterday they had read in class about the sun. About how like a lemon it was, and how hot. And they had written small stories or essays or poems about it:

I think the sun is a flower,
That blooms for just one hour.

That was Margot's poem, read in a quiet

voice in the still classroom while the rain was falling outside.

"Aw, you didn't write that!" protested one of the boys.

"I did," said Margot. "I *did*."

"William!" said the teacher.

But that was yesterday. Now the rain was slackening, and the children were crushed in the great thick windows.

"Where's teacher?"

"She'll be back."

"She'd better hurry, we'll miss it!"

They turned on themselves, like a feverish wheel, all tumbling spokes.

Margot stood alone. She was a very frail girl who looked as if she had been lost in the rain for years and the rain had washed out the blue from her eyes and the red from her mouth and the yellow from her hair. She was an old photograph dusted from an album, whitened away, and if she spoke at all her voice would be a ghost. Now she stood, separate, staring at the rain and the loud wet world beyond the huge glass.

"What're *you* looking at?" said William.

Margot said nothing.

"Speak when you're spoken to." He gave her a shove. But she did not move; rather she let herself be moved only by him and nothing else.

They edged away from her, they would not look at her. She felt them go away. And this was because she would play no games with them in the echoing tunnels of the underground city. If they tagged her and ran, she stood blinking after them and did not follow. When the class sang songs about happiness and life and games her lips barely moved. Only when they sang about the sun and the summer did her lips move as she watched the drenched windows.

And then, of course, the biggest crime of all was that she had come here only five years ago from Earth, and she remembered the sun and the way the sun was and the sky was when she was four in Ohio. And they, they had been on Venus all their lives, and they had been only two years old when last the sun came out and had long since forgotten the color and heat of it and the way it really was. But Margot remembered.

"It's like a penny," she said once, eyes closed.

"No it's not!" the children cried.

"It's like a fire," she said, "in the stove."

"You're lying, you don't remember!" cried the children.

But she remembered and stood quietly apart from all of them and watched the patterning windows. And once, a month ago, she had refused to shower in the school shower rooms, and clutched her hands to her ears and over her head, screaming the water mustn't touch her head. So after that, dimly, dimly, she sensed it, she was different and they knew her difference and kept away.

There was talk that her father and mother were taking her back to Earth next year; it seemed vital to her that they do so, though it would mean the loss of thousands of dollars to her family. And so, the children hated her for all these reasons of big and little consequence. They hated her pale snow face, her waiting silence, her thinness, and possible future.

"Get away!" The boy gave her another push. "What're you waiting for?"

Then, for the first time, she turned and looked at him. And what she was waiting for was in her eyes.

"Well, don't wait around here!" cried the boy savagely. "You won't see nothing!"

Her lips moved.

"Nothing!" he cried. "It was all a joke,

wasn't it?" He turned to the other children. "Nothing's happening today. *Is* it?"

They all blinked at him and then, understanding, laughed and shook their heads. "Nothing, nothing!"

"Oh, but," Margot whispered, her eyes helpless. "But this is the day, the scientists predict, they say, they *know* the sun. . . ."

"All a joke!" said the boy, and seized her roughly. "Hey, everyone, let's put her in a closet before teacher comes!"

"No," said Margot, falling back.

They surged about her, caught her up and bore her, protesting, and then pleading, and then crying, back into a tunnel, a room, a closet, where they slammed and locked the door. They stood looking at the door and saw it tremble from her beating and throwing herself against it. They heard her muffled cries. Then, smiling, they turned and went out and back down the tunnel, just as the teacher arrived.

"Ready, children?" She glanced at her watch.

"Yes!" said everyone.

"Are we all here?"

"Yes!"

The rain slackened still more.

They crowded to the huge door.

The rain stopped.

It was as if, in the midst of a film concerning an avalanche, a tornado, a hurricane, a volcanic eruption, something had, first, gone wrong with the sound apparatus, thus muffling and finally cutting off all noise, all of the blasts and repercussions and thunders, and then, second, ripped the film from the projector and inserted in its place a peaceful tropical slide which did not move or tremor. The world ground to a standstill. The silence was so immense and unbelievable that you felt your ears had been stuffed or you had lost

your hearing altogether. The children put their hands to their ears. They stood apart. The door slid back and the smell of the silent, waiting world came in to them.

The sun came out.

It was the color of flaming bronze and it was very large. And the sky around it was a blazing blue tile color. And the jungle burned with sunlight as the children, released from their spell, rushed out, yelling, into the springtime.

"Now, don't go too far," called the teacher after them. "You've only two hours, you know. You wouldn't want to get caught out!"

But they were running and turning their faces up to the sky and feeling the sun on their cheeks like a warm iron; they were taking off their jackets and letting the sun burn their arms.

"Oh, it's better than the sun lamps, isn't it?"

"Much, much better!"

They stopped running and stood in the great jungle that covered Venus, that grew and never stopped growing, tumultuously, even as you watched it. It was a nest of octopi, clustering up great arms of fleshlike weed, wavering, flowering in this brief spring. It was the color of rubber and ash, this jungle, from the many years without sun. It was the color of stones and white cheeses and ink, and it was the color of the moon.

The children lay out, laughing, on the jungle mattress, and heard it sigh and squeak under them, resilient and alive. They ran among the trees, they slipped and fell, they pushed each other, they played hide-and-seek and tag, but most of all they squinted at the sun until tears ran down their faces. They put their hands up to that yellowness and that amazing blueness and they breathed of

SUNRISE IV *Arthur Dove*

the fresh, fresh air and listened and listened to the silence which suspended them in a blessed sea of no sound and no motion. They looked at everything and savored everything. Then, wildly, like animals escaped from their caves, they ran and ran in shouting circles. They ran for an hour and did not stop running.

And then—

In the midst of their running one of the girls wailed.

Everyone stopped.

The girl, standing in the open, held out her hand.

"Oh, look, look," she said trembling.

They came slowly to look at her opened palm.

In the center of it, cupped and huge, was a single raindrop.

She began to cry, looking at it.

They glanced quietly at the sky.

"Oh. Oh."

A few cold drops fell on their noses and their cheeks and their mouths. The sun faded behind a stir of mist. A wind blew cool around them. They turned and started to walk back toward the underground house, their hands at their sides, their smiles vanishing away.

A boom of thunder startled them and like leaves before a new hurricane, they tumbled upon each other and ran. Lightning struck ten miles away, five miles away, a mile, a half mile. The sky darkened into midnight in a flash.

They stood in the doorway of the underground for a moment until it was raining hard. Then they closed the door and heard the gigantic sound of the rain falling in tons and avalanches, everywhere and forever.

"Will it be seven more years?"

"Yes. Seven."

Then one of them gave a little cry.

"Margot!"

"What?"

"She's still in the closet where we locked her."

"Margot."

They stood as if someone had driven them, like so many stakes, into the floor. They looked at each other and then looked away. They glanced out at the world that was raining now and raining and raining steadily. They could not meet each other's glances. Their faces were solemn and pale. They looked at their hands and feet, their faces down.

"Margot."

One of the girls said, "Well . . . ?"

No one moved.

"Go on," whispered the girl.

They walked slowly down the hall in the sound of the cold rain. They turned through the doorway to the room in the sound of the storm and thunder, lightning on their faces, blue and terrible. They walked over to the closet door slowly and stood by it.

Behind the closet door was only silence.

They unlocked the door, even more slowly, and let Margot out.

Discussion

1. What do you think are the children's reasons for disliking Margot?

2. What do you think the author means when he compares Margot to "an old photograph, dusted from an album"?

3. How do the children spend their short time in the sun? Find examples from the story.

4. How do the children feel after the sun has gone and they remember to let Margot out of the closet? Find specific examples to prove your answer.

5. Where does this story take place? What does the outside look like? What sound is heard most? What color is most evident?

6. How does the constant rain affect the people's lives?

7. Explain why this story depends completely on its setting.

Composition

1. Write a conversation between two of Margot's classmates. (Be sure to give them names.) They should be talking about how they feel about their part in locking up Margot while the sun was out. First have them go over the reasons why it happened. Then have them discuss how they think she must have felt. Finally have them say how they feel about what they did.

2. Project yourself into the future and write a description of an underground city on Venus. (As a guide, you first might want to draw a picture to get it clearly in your mind.) Stress the main characteristics of the town: the buildings, homes, transportation, and recreational areas. Include as many details as possible. End by stating any advantages or disadvantages this city would have when compared to a city on earth today.

Vocabulary

"I know what I want to say, but I can't think of the right word." If that is ever your problem, you can get help from a THESAURUS. It is a book which provides lists of synonyms and antonyms. It groups them under general headings such as "rain," "walk," or "sweet." Then the synonyms and antonyms are grouped under subheadings by parts of speech. For example, below is a shortened version of what you would find under "rain" in the 1977 edition of *Roget's Thesaurus* (Thomas Y. Crowell Co., Section 394):

rain
(1) N. rainfall, precipitation, moisture, wet; flurry, patter, pitter-patter, splatter; rainstorm, cloudburst, downpour, driving—, pouring—, drenching—; rainy season, monsoon; mizzle, drizzle, etc. thunderstorm, thundersquall; drencher, soaker, deluge, mist, misty, rain, scotch mist.
(2) V. precipitate, fall; weep; shower, shower down; sprinkle, spatter, patter, pitter-patter; drizzle, mizzle; pour, stream, pelt, drum; rain —buckets, —in torrents, —cats and dogs, —pitchforks; come down in sheets; pour, sprinkle.
(3) ADJ. rainy, showery; drizzly, drippy; steaming, pluvial, pluviose.

On a separate sheet of paper, answer the following questions about this thesaurus entry and about thesaurus entries in general.

1. Why shouldn't you look for definitions of words in a thesaurus?
2. What do the following abbreviations stand for: N., V., and ADJ.?
3. Under what three main subheadings are the words in a thesaurus entry arranged?

4. Assume that you want help in naming some different kinds of rainfall.
   a. Under which subheading should you look?
   b. List three words or terms given under that subheading in this entry.
5. Under what subheading would you look for words that would show what rain does?
6. Imagine that you are describing a rainy day. Copy three words you might use in your description.
7. In section (1), what does each dash (–) stand for in this series: "driving–, pouring–, drenching–"?
8. In section (2), what does each dash stand for in this series: "–buckets, –in torrents, –cats and dogs, –pitchforks"?

Ray Bradbury 1920—

Ray Bradbury started his writing career in high school where he founded and printed a quarterly called *Futuria Fantasia*. After high school he worked for a year with a theater group and then sold newspapers in downtown Los Angeles to finance his writing. He sold his first short story on his twenty-first birthday.

Despite his futuristic mind and familiarity with outer space, Bradbury has never learned to drive a car and has never flown in an airplane. He bicycles on many of his business errands. His short story collections include: *The Martian Chronicles, Dark Carnival,* and *The Illustrated Man.* His novels include: *Fahrenheit 451* and *Something Wicked This Way Comes.*

People who live in Communist countries do not travel freely back and forth across their borders. Spies are everywhere to catch those who try. Was there a spy on this night train bound for the Czechoslovakian border?

Stranger on the Night Train

MARY HOCKING

"A BEAUTIFUL WOMAN should never travel alone." My mind, which had been occupied with pleasant thoughts of my home in England, came spinning back to the present. I like to think, in my better moments, that I am attractive; but I know I am not beautiful. Nevertheless, the remark produced a pleasant glow until I realized that it was addressed to the woman sitting opposite to me.

Hers was the intense, troubled kind of beauty which stirs the imagination. Beneath strongly marked brows her eyes were dark and fathomless; the firm straight mouth was almost severe; yet despite her impassivity, you felt that passion smoldered beneath the still, white surface of her face.

We had traveled all the way from Prague[1] together—she, the American, and I—and yet we had not spoken to one another. We each had our own thoughts as the train hurtled through the night, carrying us toward the Czechoslovakian border where the Iron Curtain would part and let us through.

---

1 **Prague:** the capital of Czechoslovakia.

Now a fourth passenger, who had joined us at the last stop, had broken the spell. "A beautiful woman should never travel alone." he repeated. The remark he had made was probably one of his routine phrases. He was tall, white-haired, with elegant features, and there emanated from him a smell compounded of Eau de Cologne, garlic, and brandy. He was accustomed to success.

I do not believe that she deliberately ignored him; she simply did not hear him. But he took her silence as a rebuff.

He got to his feet with heavy dignity, made her a stiff little bow, and intimated that he knew when he was not wanted. As he went out, she turned her head away from the window and looked after him in surprise, blinking a little, as though the light in the compartment dazzled her after the darkness outside. She looked at me inquiringly.

I explained the incident to her. It is my experience that a woman soon learns to accept tributes to her beauty, and I was surprised to see that she was disconcerted. The diamond was not polished. She turned away and looked out of the window again.

The American said to me, "Been here long?"

"Two years at the British Embassy in Prague."

He smiled. "Two years too long, I guess." He had a nice smile, slow, and it deepened the lines around his eyes and mouth. He was the kind of American built in the Lincoln tradition, tall and shambling and deceptively helpless looking.

"I am with Ocean Press and I've been around Prague quite a bit. Strange I never met you." But he was not angling for a closer acquaintance. He was completely taken up with the woman opposite me. Ever since she had come into the compartment he had been watching her, discreetly, as though she were some kind of goddess.

"Do you know Texas?" It was a deep voice, more thrilling than any voice I remember since Garbo.[2] We both turned toward her. She went on, hesitantly, as though she was unused to speaking to strangers: "My brother is in Texas."

2 **Garbo**: Greta Garbo, a film actress known for her deep, throaty voice.

The American said, with a look that was almost anguished, "I'm afraid I don't know Texas. I'm from Maine." He paused, and then, eager to make amends, added, "They tell me it's a wonderful place—Texas."

On an impulse, I asked her, "Are you going there?"

After a pause, she said, "I am going just to Nuremberg, in Germany." Her face had become inscrutable again. She turned back to the window. I wondered whether she was German, or perhaps Viennese. At that time, I dismissed the idea of her being a Czech, since traveling is not their usual pastime.

The American and I chatted together but from time to time we found ourselves glancing at her. She was dressed in a plain black suit; it was not very well cut and the material was poor; the whole effect was one of decent poverty. Yet she wore a pearl brooch which looked good, and on her finger there was a ring with a stone which I thought was a ruby. The stone glowed against her white skin.

The train raced through the night. We did not try to sleep; the frontier was too near. She stared out into the darkness. Once the American said, "Where are we, I wonder?" and she answered immediately, "Near the village of Senka." There was no moon. She must have been visualizing the landscape in her mind. That . . . or she did this journey often.

I took down my case and unwrapped my sandwiches; the food on the trains was usually very poor. The American had one of those magnificent packed meals. He gave me a leg of chicken and a bag of nuts; he offered her food, too, but she said that she was not hungry. Just when I was wishing I had brought some coffee, he produced a thermos flask.

Suddenly, as he held the flask in his hands,

he said, "I guess it doesn't matter, telling you." As he spoke he was fingering the casing down the side; there was a faint click and the flask opened at the bottom. He drew out an object wrapped in tissue paper. He folded the tissue paper back and laid something, very gently, on the palm of his hand for me to see.

As long as I live, I shall remember it: the little ivory madonna.[3] The unknown craftsman whose hand had formed it, many hundreds of years ago, had put all he knew of love and tenderness into every tiny detail, from the sweet tranquillity of the face to the gentle folds of the robe falling to the tiny feet.

A shadow fell across it, and I saw the woman standing there, her hand outstretched. He gave it to her without a word. She held it in the palm of her hand, and her smile was like the sun on an Easter morning. I think, as he watched her then, that he wanted to give the madonna to her.

When she handed it back, she said, "They do not like these things to go out of the country. With them, it is a question of pride—the beauty does not matter."

"The man who owned it sold it to me, fair and square." He smiled wryly, and added, "For more than I could afford."

She sat down beside him. "You collect?" she asked.

He looked at the little ivory figure. "No. I don't really know anything about these things. It sounds silly, I guess, but I think it was just that it seemed . . . almost real. I felt I had to take it away, out of this country."

Her face was in the shadow, but I thought there was an odd note in her voice as she asked, "Was it worth so much, to do that?"

He nodded. "Yes, it was. Perhaps it's just a

3 **madonna:** a small statue of the Virgin Mary.

meaningless gesture. But I got so . . . so angry, living there; I needed to make a gesture."

He picked up the tissue paper. She stayed his hand, and she looked down at the madonna for a long time.

When he placed it back in its hiding place, she asked: "How does it work, this spring?" I remember at the time I thought it was odd that she should take so much interest in the mechanism.

The journey was nearly over. We drew into the frontier station, and I leaned out of the window. There was a small platform and beyond it I could see a winding road, and across the road there was a barrier; beyond the barrier the road rambled on, westward.

Ours was the end carriage and we had to wait a long time. The customs officials came at last, accompanied by a uniformed guard. They had flat, peasants' faces, with hard eyes that were untrusting and unintelligent. They looked at the American's passport and checked his luggage, and they were turning toward me when she spoke. She spoke in a sharp, commanding voice, in a language I knew well. I stared at her face. It was like a stone. They took the thermos flask and she showed them the spring; they lifted out the little ivory madonna, and she told them about it, just in case they did not realize its value. The American went away with them.

She sat silently, with her long, thin hands quite still on her lap. I wanted to shout at her, to ask her how often she did the journey and if they paid her well. But what was the point? I shut my case and put my things away; they would not trouble with me now.

In a quarter of an hour the American came back. She turned her eyes away and got up and left the compartment. Shortly afterward we crossed the frontier. I wondered whether she changed trains at the German frontier station, or whether she went right on to Nuremberg and started again there.

The American was sitting looking out of the window; his face was blank and he looked much older.

I said, "They took it away, of course?"

He nodded.

"They won't—"

He said sharply, "They won't give me the money back. I don't care about the money anyway." It seemed that it was not the madonna that he cared about either, for he went on, unsteadily, "God! How I hate them and their filthy regime! What do they do to people, to turn a woman like that into a spy?" He put his hand across his eyes, and I saw that he was crying.

I went along to the dining car for a late meal. Not that I was hungry. The German customs came while I was there, but they only wanted to see my passport.

I was drinking my coffee when her shadow fell across the table. I looked up, and she was standing there, hand outstretched, just as she had stood when he handed her the madonna.

This time, though, the brooch and the ring were lying on the palm of her hand.

She said, "Will you give them to the American, please, when the train has left Nuremberg? They are all I have, and they are worth much money."

Behind her I saw German officials hovering, their faces very serious. As I stared in astonishment, she went on:

"It was necessary to create a diversion.[4] That was always my only hope when I finally found courage to get on this train. You see, I had no papers to leave the country. When you have nothing to lose, you will risk anything."

"But what will happen to you?" I said.

"I shall ask for political asylum.[5] I have friends in Nuremberg who will fight for me." One of the German guards beckoned to her.

As she turned to go, she said, "Tell the American: I needed to leave the country, more than the little madonna."

---

4 **diversion** (də vér′ zhən): a distraction.
5 **asylum** (ə sī′ ləm): a safe place.

Discussion

1. Why does the woman behave so mysteriously during the train ride?

2. What is the surprise ending to this story?

3. Throughout the story, what puzzling details about the woman suggest that she is a spy? What is the real explanation of these details?

4. Even though the woman has no papers, how does she get safely across the Czechoslovakian border?

5. Throughout most of the story, the woman appears to be mysterious, cold, and unkind. However, how does the end of the story reveal her true personality? Explain.

Songs have different beats or rhythms. Some are fast and lively, while others are slow and less vigorous. Stories also have their own beat or rhythm. It is called PACE. A fast pace might occur when there is much action. A slow pace might occur when the author is describing characters or setting. Just as in music, the pace can change from page to page. A change of pace gives variety and helps maintain readers' interest. While a fast pace makes a part of a story exciting, a slow pace provides important details that are needed to understand and enjoy the story.

1. Find sections from "Stranger on the Night Train" that have a very fast pace.

2. Find other sections where the pace is considerably slower.

3. Examine one of the slower paced events. Explain how the additional information helps the reader understand and enjoy the story more.

Composition

1. This story would make a suspenseful movie. If you were the director of this film, what major events would you want to include? Write a brief description of each one. Include which characters are involved in that particular event and tell briefly what takes place.

2. Write a final scene to this story. Tell what might have happened when the narrator gave the American the woman's jewelry and explained what really happened. How would the American react? What do you think he would do with the jewelry?

Mary Hocking 1921—

While working for the British government for 24 years, Mary Hocking wrote in her spare time. Then in 1970, she quit to write full time. Her books include: *The Sparrow*, *A Time of War*, and *Daniel Come to Judgement*.

They had a simple kidnapping plan—too simple as it turned out. They were not prepared for the unexpected. They certainly were not prepared for Red Chief!

The Ransom of Red Chief

O. HENRY

IT LOOKED LIKE A GOOD THING: but wait till I tell you. We were down South, in Alabama—Bill Driscoll and myself—when this kidnapping idea struck us. It was, as Bill afterward expressed it, "during a moment of temporary mental apparition";[1] but we didn't find that out till later.

There was a town down there, as flat as a flannel cake, and called Summit, of course. It contained inhabitants of as undeleterious[2] and self-satisfied a class of peasantry as ever clustered around a Maypole.

Bill and me had a joint capital of about six hundred dollars, and we needed just two thousand more to pull off a fraudulent town-lot scheme in Western Illinois with. We talked it over on the front steps of the hotel. Philoprogenitoveness,[3] says we, is strong in semirural communities; therefore, and for other reasons, a kidnapping project ought to do better there than in the radius of newspapers that send reporters out in plain clothes to stir up talk about such things. We knew that Summit couldn't get after us with anything stronger than constables and, maybe, some lackadaisical bloodhounds and a diatribe or two in the *Weekly Farmers' Budget.* So, it looked good.

We selected for our victim the only child of a prominent citizen named Ebenezer Dorset. The father was respectable and tight, a mortgage fancier and a stern, upright collection-plate passer and forecloser. The kid was a boy of ten, with bas-relief freckles, and hair the color of the cover of the magazine you buy at the newsstand when you want to catch a train. Bill and me figured that Ebenezer would melt down for a ransom of two thousand dollars to a cent. But wait till I tell you.

About two miles from Summit was a little mountain, covered with a dense cedar brake. On the rear elevation of this mountain was a cave. There we stored provisions.

One evening after sundown, we drove in a buggy past old Dorset's house. The kid was in the street, throwing rocks at a kitten on the opposite fence.

"Hey, little boy!" says Bill, "would you

---

1 **apparition**: Here Bill means "abberation," a disorder of the mind.
2 **undeleterious**: not harmful.
3 **Philoprogenitoveness**: Here Sam means "philoprogenitiveness," love for offspring.

like to have a bag of candy and a nice ride?"

The boy catches Bill neatly in the eye with a piece of brick.

"That will cost the old man an extra five hundred dollars," says Bill, climbing over the wheel.

That boy put up a fight like a welterweight cinnamon bear; but, at last, we got him down in the bottom of the buggy and drove away. We took him up to the cave, and I hitched the horse in the cedar brake. After dark I drove the buggy to the little village, three miles away, where we had hired it, and walked back to the mountain.

Bill was pasting court plaster over the scratches and bruises on his features. There was a fire burning behind the big rock at the entrance of the cave, and the boy was watching a pot of boiling coffee, with two buzzard tail-feathers stuck in his red hair. He points a stick at me when I come up, and says:

"Ha! cursed paleface, do you dare to enter the camp of Red Chief, the terror of the plains?"

"He's all right now," says Bill, rolling up his trousers and examining some bruises on his shins. "We're playing Indian. We're making Buffalo Bill's show look like magic-lantern views of Palestine in the town hall. I'm Old Hank, the Trapper, Red Chief's captive, and I'm to be scalped at daybreak. By Geronimo! that kid can kick hard."

Yes, sir, that boy seemed to be having the time of his life. The fun of camping out in a cave had made him forget that he was a captive himself. He immediately christened me Snake-eye, the Spy, and announced that, when his braves returned from the warpath, I was to be broiled at the stake at the rising of the sun.

Then we had supper; and he filled his mouth full of bacon and bread and gravy, and began to talk. He made a during-dinner speech something like this:

"I like this fine. I never camped out before; but I had a pet 'possum once, and I was nine last birthday. I hate to go to school. Rats ate up sixteen of Jimmy Talbot's aunt's speckled hen's eggs. Are there any real Indians in these woods? I want some more gravy. Does the

221

trees moving make the wind blow? We had five puppies. What makes your nose so red, Hank? My father has lots of money. Are the stars hot? I whipped Ed Walker twice, Saturday. I don't like girls. You dassent catch toads unless with a string. Do oxen make any noise? Why are oranges round? Have you got beds to sleep on in this cave? Amos Murray has got six toes. A parrot can talk, but a monkey or a fish can't. How many does it take to make twelve?"

Every few minutes he would remember that he was a pesky redskin, and pick up his stick rifle and tiptoe to the mouth of the cave to rubber for the scouts of the hated paleface. Now and then he would let out a war whoop that made Old Hank, the Trapper, shiver. That boy had Bill terrorized from the start.

"Red Chief," says I to the kid, "would you like to go home?"

"Aw, what for?" says he. "I don't have any fun at home. I hate to go to school. I like to camp out. You won't take me back home again, Snake-eye, will you?"

"Not right away," says I. "We'll stay here in the cave awhile."

"All right!" says he. "That'll be fine. I never had such fun in all my life."

We went to bed about eleven o'clock. We spread down some wide blankets and quilts and put Red Chief between us. We weren't afraid he'd run away. He kept us awake for three hours, jumping up and reaching for his rifle and screeching: "Hist! pard," in mine and Bill's ears, as the fancied crackle of a twig or the rustle of a leaf revealed to his young imagination the stealthy approach of the outlaw band. At last, I fell into a troubled sleep, and dreamed that I had been kidnapped and chained to a tree by a ferocious pirate with red hair.

Just at daybreak, I was awakened by a series of awful screams from Bill. They weren't yells, or howls, or shouts, or whoops, or yawps, such as you'd expect from a manly set of vocal organs—they were simply indecent, terrifying, humiliating screams, such as people emit when they see ghosts or caterpillars. It's an awful thing to hear a strong, desperate, fat man scream incontinently in a cave at daybreak.

I jumped up to see what the matter was. Red Chief was sitting on Bill's chest, with one hand twined in Bill's hair. In the other he had the sharp case knife we used for slicing bacon; and he was industriously and realistically trying to take Bill's scalp, according to the sentence that had been pronounced upon him the evening before.

I got the knife away from the kid and made him lie down again. But, from that moment, Bill's spirit was broken. He laid down on his side of the bed, but he never closed an eye again in sleep as long as that boy was with us. I dozed off for a while, but along toward sunup I remembered that Red Chief had said I was to be burned at the stake at the rising of the sun. I wasn't nervous or afraid; but I sat up and lit my pipe and leaned against a rock.

"What you getting up so soon for, Sam?" asked Bill.

"Me?" says I. "Oh, I got a kind of pain in my shoulder. I thought sitting up would rest it."

"You're a liar!" says Bill. "You're afraid. You was to be burned at sunrise, and you was afraid he'd do it. And he would, too, if he could find a match. Ain't it awful, Sam? Do you think anybody will pay out money to get a little imp like that back home?"

"Sure," said I. "A rowdy kid like that is just the kind that parents dote on. Now, you and the Chief get up and cook breakfast, while I go up on the top of this mountain and reconnoiter."[4]

I went up on the peak of the little mountain and ran my eye over the contiguous vicinity. Over toward Summit I expected to see the sturdy yeomanry of the village armed with scythes and pitchforks beating the countryside for the dastardly kidnappers. But what I saw was a peaceful landscape dotted with one man plowing with a dun mule. Nobody was dragging the creek; no couriers

---

4 **reconnoiter** (rek'ə noi' tər): to examine or survey a situation.

dashed hither and yon, bringing tidings of no news to the distracted parents. There was a sylvan attitude of somnolent sleepiness pervading that section of the external outward surface of Alabama that lay exposed to my view. "Perhaps," says I to myself, "it has not yet been discovered that the wolves have borne away the tender lambkin from the fold. Heaven help the wolves!" says I, and I went down the mountain to breakfast.

When I got to the cave I found Bill backed up against the side of it, breathing hard, and the boy threatening to smash him with a rock half as big as a coconut.

"He put a red-hot boiled potato down my back," explained Bill, "and then mashed it with his foot; and I boxed his ears. Have you got a gun about you, Sam?"

I took the rock away from the boy and kind of patched up the argument. "I'll fix you," says the kid to Bill. "No man ever yet struck the Red Chief but he got paid for it. You better beware!"

After breakfast the kid takes a piece of leather with strings wrapped around it out of his pocket and goes outside the cave unwinding it.

"What's he up to now?" says Bill, anxiously. "You don't think he'll run away, do you, Sam?"

"No fear of it," says I. "He don't seem to be much of a homebody. But we've got to fix up some plan about the ransom. There don't seem to be much excitement around Summit on account of his disappearance; but maybe they haven't realized yet that he's gone. His folks may think he's spending the night with Aunt Jane or one of the neighbors. Anyhow, he'll be missed today. Tonight we must get a message to his father demanding the two thousand dollars for his return."

Just then we heard a kind of war whoop, such as David might have emitted when he knocked out the champion Goliath. It was a sling that Red Chief had pulled out of his pocket, and he was whirling it around his head.

I dodged, and heard a heavy thud and a kind of a sigh from Bill, like a horse gives out when you take his saddle off. A rock the size of an egg had caught Bill just behind his left ear. He loosened himself all over and fell in the fire across the frying pan of hot water for washing the dishes. I dragged him out and poured cold water on his head for half an hour.

By and by, Bill sits up and feels behind his ear and says: "Sam, do you know who my favorite Biblical character is?"

"Take it easy," says I. "You'll come to your senses presently."

"King Herod,"[5] says he. "You won't go away and leave me here alone, will you, Sam?"

I went out and caught that boy and shook him until his freckles rattled.

"If you don't behave," says I, "I'll take you straight home. Now, are you going to be good, or not?"

"I was only funning," says he, sullenly. "I didn't mean to hurt Old Hank. But what did he hit me for? I'll behave, Snake-eye, if you won't send me home, and if you'll let me play the Black Scout today."

"I don't know the game," says I. "That's for you and Mr. Bill to decide. He's your playmate for the day. I'm going away for a while, on business. Now, you come in and make friends with him and say you are sorry for hurting him, or home you go, at once."

I made him and Bill shake hands, and then

---

5 **King Herod:** an ancient king of Judea who ordered all the infants in Bethlehem killed.

I took Bill aside and told him I was going to Poplar Grove, a little village three miles from the cave, and find out what I could about how the kidnapping had been regarded in Summit. Also, I thought it best to send a peremptory letter to old man Dorset that day, demanding the ransom and dictating how it should be paid.

"You know, Sam," says Bill, "I've stood by you without batting an eye in earthquakes, fire and flood—in poker games, dynamite outrages, police raids, train robberies, and cyclones. I never lost my nerve yet till we kidnapped that two-legged skyrocket of a kid. He's got me going. You won't leave me long with him, will you, Sam?"

"I'll be back some time this afternoon," says I. "You must keep the boy amused and quiet till I return. And now we'll write the letter to old Dorset."

Bill and I got paper and pencil and worked on the letter while Red Chief, with a blanket wrapped around him, strutted up and down, guarding the mouth of the cave. Bill begged me tearfully to make the ransom fifteen hundred dollars instead of two thousand. "I ain't attempting," says he, "to decry the celebrated moral aspect of parental affection, but we're dealing with humans, and it ain't human for anybody to give up two thousand dollars for that forty-pound chunk of freckled wildcat. I'm willing to take a chance at fifteen hundred dollars. You can charge the difference up to me."

So, to relieve Bill, I acceded, and we collaborated a letter that ran this way:

Ebenezer Dorset, Esq.:

We have your boy concealed in a place far from Summit. It is useless for you or the most skillful detectives to attempt to find him. Absolutely, the only terms on which you can have him restored to you are these: We demand fifteen hundred dollars in large bills for his return; the money to be left at midnight tonight at the same spot and in the same box as your reply—as hereinafter described. If you agree to these terms, send your answer in writing by a solitary messenger tonight at half past eight o'clock. After crossing Owl Creek on the road to Poplar Grove, there are three large trees about a hundred yards apart, close to the fence of the wheat field on the right-hand side. At the bottom of the fence post, opposite the third tree, will be found a small pasteboard box.

The messenger will place the answer in this box and return immediately to Summit.

If you attempt any treachery or fail to comply with our demand as stated, you will never see your boy again.

If you pay the money as demanded, he will be returned to you safe and well within three hours. These terms are final, and if you do not accede to them no further communication will be attempted.

Two Desperate Men

I addressed this letter to Dorset, and put it in my pocket. As I was about to start, the kid comes up to me and says:

"Aw, Snake-eye, you said I could play the Black Scout while you was gone."

"Play it, of course," says I. "Mr. Bill will play with you. What kind of a game is it?"

"I'm the Black Scout," says Red Chief, "and I have to ride to the stockade to warn the settlers that the Indians are coming. I'm tired of playing Indian myself. I want to be the Black Scout."

"All right," says I. "It sounds harmless to me. I guess Mr. Bill will help you foil the pesky savages."

"What am I to do?" asks Bill, looking at the kid suspiciously.

"You are the hoss," says Black Scout. "Get down on your hands and knees. How can I ride to the stockade without a hoss?"

"You'd better keep him interested," said I, "till we get the scheme going. Loosen up."

Bill gets down on his all fours, and a look comes in his eye like a rabbit's when you catch it in a trap.

"How far is it to the stockade, kid?" he asks, in a husky manner of voice.

"Ninety miles," says the Black Scout. "And you have to hump yourself to get there on time. Whoa, now!"

The Black Scout jumps on Bill's back and digs his heels in his sides.

"For Heaven's sake," says Bill, "hurry back, Sam, as soon as you can. I wish we hadn't made the ransom more than a thousand. Say, you quit kicking me or I'll get up and warm you good."

I walked over to Poplar Grove and sat around the post office and store, talking with the chawbacons that came in to trade. One whiskerando says that he hears Summit is all upset on account of Elder Ebenezer Dorset's boy having been lost or stolen. That was all I wanted to know. I bought some smoking tobacco, referred casually to the price of black-eyed peas, posted my letter surreptitiously, and came away. The postmaster said the mail carrier would come by in an hour to take the mail to Summit.

When I got back to the cave Bill and the boy were not to be found. I explored the vicinity of the cave, and risked a yodel or two, but there was no response.

So I lighted my pipe and sat down on a mossy bank to await developments.

In about half an hour I heard the bushes rustle, and Bill wobbled out into the little glade in front of the cave. Behind him was the kid, stepping softly like a scout, with a broad grin on his face. Bill stopped, took off his hat, and wiped his face with a red hand-kerchief. The kid stopped about eight feet behind him.

"Sam," says Bill, "I suppose you'll think I'm a renegade, but I couldn't help it. I'm a grown person with masculine proclivities and habits of self-defense, but there is a time when all systems of egotism and predominance fail. The boy is gone. I sent him home. All is off. There was martyrs in old times," goes on Bill, "that suffered death rather than give up the particular graft they enjoyed. None of 'em ever was subjugated to such supernatural tortures as I have been. I tried to be faithful to our articles of depredation;[6] but there came a limit."

"What's the trouble, Bill?" I asks him.

"I was rode," says Bill, "the ninety miles to the stockade, not barring an inch. Then, when the settlers was rescued, I was given oats. Sand ain't a palatable substitute. And then, for an hour I had to try to explain to him why there was nothin' in holes, how a road can run both ways, and what makes the grass green. I tell you, Sam, a human can only stand so much. I takes him by the neck of his clothes and drags him down the mountain. On the way he kicks my legs black-and-blue from the knees down; and I've got to have two or three bites on my thumb and hand cauterized.[7]

"But he's gone"—continued Bill—"gone home. I showed him the road to Summit and kicked him about eight feet nearer there at one kick. I'm sorry we lose the ransom; but it was either that or Bill Driscoll to the madhouse."

Bill is puffing and blowing, but there is a look of ineffable peace and growing content on his rose-pink features.

---

6 **depredation:** act of plundering; robbery; ravaging.

7 **cauterize** (kô′ tə rīz′): burn to prevent bleeding or infection.

"Bill," says I, "there isn't any heart disease in your family, is there?"

"No," says Bill, "nothing chronic except malaria and accidents. Why?"

"Then you might turn around," says I, "and have a look behind you."

Bill turns and sees the boy, and loses his complexion and sits down plump on the ground and begins to pluck aimlessly at grass and little sticks. For an hour I was afraid of his mind. And then I told him that my scheme was to put the whole job through immediately and that we would get the ransom and be off with it by midnight if old Dorset fell in with our proposition. So Bill braced up enough to give the kid a weak sort of a smile and a promise to play the Russian in a

Japanese war with him as soon as he felt a little better.

I had a scheme for collecting that ransom without danger of being caught by counterplots that ought to commend itself to professional kidnappers. The tree under which the answer was to be left—and the money later on—was close to the road fence with big, bare fields on all sides. If a gang of constables should be watching for anyone to come for the note, they could see him a long way off crossing the fields or in the road. But no, sirree! At half-past eight I was up in that tree as well hidden as a tree toad, waiting for the messenger to arrive.

Exactly on time, a half-grown boy rides up the road on a bicycle, locates the pasteboard box at the foot of the fence post, slips a folded piece of paper into it, and pedals away again back toward Summit.

I waited an hour and then concluded the thing was square. I slid down the tree, got the note, slipped along the fence till I struck the woods, and was back at the cave in another half an hour. I opened the note, got near the lantern, and read it to Bill. It was written with a pen in a crabbed hand, and the sum and substance of it was this:

Two Desperate Men.

Gentlemen: I received your letter today by post, in regard to the ransom you ask for the return of my son. I think you are a little high in your demands, and I hereby make you a counterproposition, which I am inclined to believe you will accept. You bring Johnny home and pay me two hundred and fifty dollars in cash, and I agree to take him off your hands. You had better come at night, for the neighbors believe he is lost, and I couldn't be responsible for what they would do to anybody they saw bringing him back. Very respectfully,

Ebenezer Dorset

"Great Pirates of Penzance," says I; "of all the impudent——"

But I glanced at Bill, and hesitated. He had the most appealing look in his eyes I ever saw on the face of a dumb or a talking brute.

"Sam," says he, "what's two hundred and fifty dollars, after all? We've got the money. One more night of this kid will send me to a bed in Bedlam.[8] Besides being a thorough gentleman, I think Mr. Dorset is a spendthrift for making us such a liberal offer. You ain't going to let the chance go, are you?"

"Tell you the truth, Bill," says I, "this little he ewe lamb has somewhat got on my nerves too. We'll take him home, pay the ransom, and make our getaway."

We took him home that night. We got him to go by telling him that his father had bought a silver-mounted rifle and a pair of moccasins for him, and we were to hunt bears the next day.

It was just twelve o'clock when we knocked at Ebenezer's front door. Just at the moment when I should have been abstracting the fifteen hundred dollars from the box under the tree, according to the original proposition, Bill was counting out two hundred and fifty dollars into Dorset's hand.

When the kid found out we were going to leave him at home he started up a howl like a calliope[9] and fastened himself as tight as a leech to Bill's leg. His father peeled him away gradually, like a porous plaster.

"How long can you hold him?" asks Bill.

"I'm not as strong as I used to be," says old Dorset, "but I think I can promise you ten minutes."

---

8 **Bedlam:** an insane asylum.
9 **calliope** (kə lī′ə pē): a loud instrument similar to a pipe organ which is used in circus parades.

"Enough," says Bill. "In ten minutes I shall cross the Central, Southern, and Middle Western States, and be legging it trippingly for the Canadian border."

And, as dark as it was, and as fat as Bill was, and as good a runner as I am, he was a good mile and a half out of Summit before I could catch up with him.

Discussion

1. What things do Bill and Sam look for in selecting their kidnap victim?
2. What goes wrong with their plan?
3. What things does Red Chief do that drive Bill and Sam crazy and make them think about giving up their ransom plan?
4. What details and events make this story light-hearted and humorous?
5. Why is the title, "The Ransom of Red Chief," a better choice for this story than "The Kidnapping of Red Chief"?

O. Henry (William Sidney Porter) 1862–1910

At eighteen, after working for three years in his uncle's drugstore in North Carolina, William Porter went to Texas. There he worked as a ranch hand, a bank clerk, and a newspaper reporter. He also published his own humorous weekly, *The Rolling Stone*. During this time he was indicted for embezzling funds from the bank, and he fled to Central America. He later returned to the United States to see his dying wife. He was tried, convicted, and sent to prison. During his three-and-a-half-year sentence, he served as the prison pharmacist and began writing short stories under pseudonyms. He finally chose the name O. Henry. After his release, Porter went to New York and wrote several short story collections; the best known are *Cabbages and Kings*, *The Four Million*, and *The Trimoned Lamp*.

Running out of food could mean death to a trapper in the cold, snow-covered wilderness. What should be done, then, to someone who steals his food?

Without Words

ELLIOTT MERRICK

HE CAME OVER A KNOLL and stopped, head back, his rifle in one mitten, his ax in the other. Below him spread the river, ice-locked between the hills. A mile across, the birch bluffs were turning blue in the twilight.

He was not given to poetic fancies, but it touched him always, coming out to the river after days and nights in the spruces to the west, following brooks and isolated chains of lakes that didn't lead anywhere, plowing through willow tangles and up and down the wooded hills. It gave him a feeling of spaciousness, like stepping out of doors to see the broad river again, sweeping out of sight between the hills.

That country behind him, his east trap line where he had been for ten days, was just a cut-up jumble of wilderness, lost, nameless, known only to himself. But the river was the river. This was the road to home, this was the known thread that joined him to other men.

This water that was flowing under the ice would slide past the village sometime, in a month maybe. "It'll get there 'fore I do, anyways," he said aloud. It was nine weeks now since the day the crowd had waved from the wharf, and the double-barrel shotguns split the air in the old-time farewell, "Boomboom". . . and a pause to load . . . "Boom," saying "Good-bye. . . . Luck"; nine weeks since the trappers fired their one answering shot, "Luck." It gave a fellow something to remember way off here where you didn't hear anything much except your own voice.

It would be pretty near three months yet before he'd be home and maybe see Luce, he was thinking as he scrambled down the bank and legged it along the ice for the house. *This* cabin had a window, and a door with hinges, a good tight roof of birch bark, and within, such luxuries as a sleeping bag, which his tiny log tilts back in the woods had not.

It was nearly dark when he got there, but not too dark to see in the cove the print of strange snowshoes. And by the point where the current flowed fast and the ice was thin, somebody had been chopping a waterhole. "Hello!" he called to the cabin.

From the ridge that rose up behind the cabin came a silvery, mocking "hello," and faintly, seconds later, a distant hello from across the river, the echo of the echo. Jan crossed the cove, bent double, studying the tracks. There were three of them, a big pair of snowshoes and two smaller pairs. The smaller snowshoes had been dragging in a stick of firewood from alongshore—the women.

Jan threw off his bag and hurried into the cabin. Nobody made snowshoes of that pattern but Mathieu Susaka-shish, the Seven Islands Indian. Nobody but Mathieu knew this cabin was here. He and his wife and daughter had come last year and begged a little tea and sugar. Now they were here again with their Indian idea that food belongs to anybody who is hungry. The dirty dogs! Where three fifty-pound bags of flour had been hanging, only two hung now. They had dripped candle grease onto his bunk and left his big meat kettle unwashed. He dove under the bunk and pulled out his food boxes. They'd made off with some of his split peas and a few of his beans, a handful of candles too. They had sliced a big chunk of salt pork neatly down the middle.

In a frenzy of rage he ripped open his fur bag. Every skin was there, and in addition, a black and shining otter skin lay crosswise on his bundles of mink and marten, fox and ermine. He held it up and blew the hair and felt its thickness and its length, stroking its blue-black luster. It was a prize. It would bring forty dollars, perhaps. But the sight of it made him angrier than before.

"So!" he muttered. "Mathieu thinks one miserable skin of fur pays me for my grub, eh?" He lit a candle, and his hand was trembling with rage. From now on he'd be half-hungry all the time, and hunting meat when he ought to be tending the trap line. This was his whole year's earnings, these five

months in the bush. And Mathieu thought he could steal the grub that made it possible, did he? He thought he could come every year and fit himself out, likely.

Jan took his rifle and emptied the magazine. It was only one bag of flour—but still, there were men way off here in the country who'd died for lack of a cupful, yes, a spoonful. Slowly he reloaded with the soft-nosed cartridges he had always kept for caribou, heretofore. Would he ever tell anybody, Luce for instance, would he ever be able to forget that somewhere back in the ridges, by some secret little lake that no one knew, he had shot three Indians and stuffed them through the ice? Didn't the Bible say, an eye for an eye and a tooth for a tooth?

Jan had already walked twenty miles today. And he was tired with the piled-up weariness of weeks and weeks of that, traveling, traveling to cover and re-cover his two hundred miles of fur paths. With a sigh he set to work; wood to chop, water from the river, a partridge to be stewed and ten cakes of bannock bread to bake in the frying pan. While the bread was baking he skinned two mink, a marten, four weasels, humming as he did so a song that he was very fond of:

"Oh, we've sailed the seven seas from
    pole to pole,
And we've conquered stormy gale
    and stinging foam,
And we've seen the strangest sights
    of far-off lands,
But the best is to see the cheery
    lights of home."

It called up visions of a light in the window, if he should ever have a real home, if, perhaps, Luce did not go away at all.

It was too bad he couldn't just shoot Mathieu, but it would be no use to leave the women to wander around and starve. At the

thought of actually squeezing the trigger and seeing them drop, he shuddered.

It was nearly midnight when he stoked up the stove and rolled in on the bunk for the last good sleep he expected to know for a while. At five o'clock, in the starlight, he was out on the river shore with a candle lantern made of a baking powder can, examining tracks. The polished, shallow trench that their two toboggans had left was so plain a child could have followed it. Mathieu was ahead, taking long steps, hurrying. The two women were behind, hauling their toboggan in double harness, tandem fashion. One of them fell and left the print of her knee going down the bank. Jan smiled as though he had seen it and heard her mutter.

He followed their track across the river to the top of a draw between two bare hills. There in the sunrise he turned and looked back at the ice, sparkling with frost in the soft golden light, spotted with long blue shadows of the hills. As he plunged downhill into the thick country to the north he had an ominous feeling that he was leaving something. Maybe Mathieu would ambush him; it would be an easy thing to do on a track like this. Would Mathieu guess that he was being tracked?

Jan studied the track, unconsciously noting every detail. Here in this book of the snow he might perhaps read Mathieu's thoughts, even a warning of an ambush. Ah, but Indians were smart in the woods. Did he really think he could outtrack an Indian hunter?

"I can have a try," he whispered to himself.

Two mornings ago, he decided it was, that they had passed through here under the firs, across that little brook. Two days were not much of a start for them. They had sleds and he had none. Mathieu had to break trail, while he had their hard frozen track to walk on. They had all their winter gear, their blankets and kettles, their tin stove and tent, traps, trout nets probably. He had nothing but the gamebag on his back, nine cakes of bread, tea and sugar, his rifle and ax, a single blanket. The chances were he could travel twice as fast as they.

He passed their first fire, where they had stopped to boil tea and thrown the leaves on the embers. The tea leaves were frozen stiff.

All day he swung on, parting the boughs where the spruces were thick, slipping through them as effortlessly as a weasel, trotting down all the hills with a tireless shuffle, trotting again where the way was level and open. Once he stopped for ten minutes to sit on a log and munch dry bread, then lit his pipe and swung on. It was frosty, and the edges of his fur cap grew white with his breathing.

Before sunset he had long passed their first night's camp. Through the semidarkness of early twilight he pressed on, following the hardness of their track more by touch than by sight. In the starlight he made his fire and boiled tea in a ravine by a brook. Here and there a tree snapped with the frost. The brook murmured under the ice. On the western hill a horn owl was hooting.

Every hour he woke with the cold, threw on more wood, turned over and slept again. Once, around three o'clock, he woke and

could not sleep. He sat hunched in the blanket looking into the fire thinking what a fool he was. He should be on the trap line, not here. He had not come up the river so far away to waste time chasing Indians around the hills. Already he was hungry and wished he had brought more food.

The wind had risen and was blowing hard. That was bad. He could not feel it here, but the treetops were rocking, and branches now and then rubbed together and spoke with weird, childlike voices.

By half past four he had boiled tea and eaten, and was picking his way along the track again. He should have rested another hour, he knew. But he could not rest, though he was tired. He wanted to get it over with. Probably they would not bleed much, it was so cold.

The Indians were still heading northwest. Likely they were bound for the headwaters of streams that flowed into Hudson's Bay. Mathieu would feel safe there. And he would be too. It was much farther than Jan could track him with only three days' grub in the bag.

In the morning he passed their second night's camp. By noontime he had come to the edge of a big, oval marsh that was about six miles wide at its narrowest. On its barren floor were occasional clumps of dead sticks, juniper and fir, no higher than a man's head, the firs rotten and falling, the junipers gaunt and wind-carved. Compared to its bleak, dead savagery the greenwoods' borders seemed sociable and friendly and snug. As the merciless northwest wind had stunted and killed the trees, so it could shrivel and kill a man if it caught him out there in a blizzard.

The trail was dim and wind-scoured on the marsh. A mile out and there was nothing but the dully shining spots the sleds had polished; two miles out and Mathieu was veering off to the east, deviating for the first time from his northwest course.

The marks petered out entirely, heading at the last straight east. Jan stopped and rubbed his forehead. "Mathieu, you're a cute fox, eh?"

If Mathieu was heading northwest the blue notch was the obvious way for him. Then why, in the middle of the marsh, did he swing off for the steep ridges?

Jan trotted about in a circle, slapping his mittens together and pounding the toes that were aching in his moccasins. The drifting snow slid by like sand, rising in little eddies as the wind rose.

He stopped and stood with his back to the wind, leaning against it. "Now look. Mathieu wants to go through the blue notch, but it's too plain. He knows I'd pick up his track there first thing. So he cuts off in the middle of the marsh, thinkin' there'll be no sign of it when I gets yere, and he makes a big half a circle. When I gets to the blue draw I can't find ere a sign of him, and I don't know where he's gone.

"I don't, eh? Well, I know he's got to strike the valley of that notch-stream some-wheres. Him and his women haulin' sleds can't get along in the hills no faster than a fox with a trap on his foot."

Jan picked up his gamebag and trotted off toward the now-invisible notch. If he'd guessed right, all right; if he's guessed wrong, all right too. What odds! He was hungry. In all this time he hadn't seen a partridge, though he'd seen plenty of feathers where that devil Mathieu'd shot all there was.

He began to sing a song to rival the sweep of the strong wind. In the wind it was good to sing, the wind drowned sound, sang a song of its own, saved a man from feeling that miles of quiet woods were listening. He roared in strong baritone:

"Oh, we've sailed the seven seas from pole to pole,
And we've conquered stormy gale and stinging foam,
And we've seen the strangest sights of far-off lands,
But the be-e-e-est is to see the chee-eery lights of ho-o-me."

The drift had obscured the shores now and he was as though alone in the middle of a white sea, snow above, below and on all sides. But he did not think of it. The wind was compass enough for him and had been since boyhood.

He clasped his gun and ax in the crook of one elbow, put his curled mitts up around his mouth and imitated a mouth organ, hunching his shoulders and swinging his body, dancing on his snowshoes in the gale. When he got home and the fiddle was squeaking in the schoolhouse and old Si Willets was callin' out the figures, oh he'd swing his girl like this—and he whirled around with his gun and ax, holding them high in the air and shaking them.

"You! you got no more sense than a porcupine," he said.

At dusk, miles beyond the blue notch he picked up the Indians' track again. He glowed with the warmth of a hunter's pride, his nostrils quivered and his jaw clenched. How they had traveled. But he had them now. They'd never get away, they were doomed, unless it snowed.

A mile farther on they had camped, and there he camped too. A few split chunks of wood that they hadn't burned he used. There was still a faint warmth in the depths of their ashes. But something in the low branches of a spruce made him pause. Lashed there, rolled up in a hairy caribou skin were a big trout net and a heavyish iron Dutch oven. So, they were lightening loads were they? They knew they were being tracked then. How did they know?

Jan sat on the fire brush of their tent site and thought about it. They didn't know, they couldn't know. Mathieu was just playing safe, that was all, announcing, if he should be followed, that he was still a-drivin' 'er for all he was worth, bluffing a pursuer, trying to say, "I know I am being followed"—just in case he should be followed. Mathieu would go on for a week, get his women set in a good camp, then circle back, hunting, setting traps in likely places, looking for beaver houses, back to this very tree. Here he'd pick up his stuff, have a look around, and mosey along westward.

"That's what you think, Mathieu."

That night he ate another half a bannock, only half when he could easily have eaten three whole ones. What a fool he was to have traveled so light. If by some mischance he didn't catch them now, he'd be stranded off here with nothing to eat.

Rolled in his blanket and their caribou robe he had the best sleep yet. It was risky. He had his gun beside him. For why couldn't Mathieu come back tonight as well as in a week? All about was the ring of darkness. Here was the firelight. What a perfect mark to shoot at. Yes, but Mathieu wouldn't shoot him. Why, Mathieu's father used to camp on the shore at Turner's Harbor years ago. Mathieu's cousin used to wrestle with Jan by the hour, and Mathieu himself had been in the foot races they ran on the beach summer afternoons long ago by the blue cool bay. Mathieu knew him all to pieces, even if they didn't meet but once in years and years way off in the country. Mathieu'd steal a little

grub, but Mathieu'd never shoot him.

He sat looking into the fire. "Mathieu wouldn't shoot you," he said, "but you'd shoot Mathieu. You wouldn't steal Mathieu's grub, but he'd steal yours." He rocked his head in his hands, bewildered and hating this mental tangle. Life was simple. You went up the river in winter, and you were home by the bay in summer. You had good luck furring, or you didn't. You were hungry once in a while, and you froze your chin, or a cheek or a toe odd times, but what was that? You fell through the thin ice, or you didn't. You lived or you died, and that was all there was to it.

Yes, but it wasn't so simple when people stole your grub. Oh, if only Mathieu hadn't taken a whole bag of flour, he would be so glad for Mathieu. He settled it this way: if Mathieu wants to come along and shoot me tonight, let him, that's good luck for Mathieu; but if Mathieu doesn't, maybe Mathieu will get shot himself tomorrow night.

The stars paled and the east grayed the same as on other mornings. Jan did not set out until there was a little light. It would be so easy for Mathieu to wait hidden by the track.

He walked with his cap on the side, exposing one ear, and when that ear began to freeze he tilted the cap and uncovered the other. Every mile he stopped and listened, mouth open, holding his breath. Late in the forenoon he came to a small valley thick with willows and boulders. As he examined it he was conscious from the corner of his eye that a tuft of snow was slipping down the face of a gray boulder on his left. Was somebody behind there? He turned and ran, dodging through the trees. Skirting the end of the willows he stealthily approached the trail farther on. No, no one had been there. It must have been a willow twig brushing the rock in the breeze. Here were the three prints, just the three prints, Mathieu's almost indistinguishable under the women's and the sled's. The women had given up hauling the tandem. They took turns single, and when they changed places Mathieu didn't wait for them. They had to run a little to catch up, poor things. Luce could never have hauled like that.

As he tramped he got to thinking of the otter skin Mathieu had left. It was funny the way Indian hunters would take food. They'd been hunting for so many ages they thought a bag of flour, like a caribou, was for anybody who needed it. But they wouldn't steal fur. It would be better if they *did* steal fur and left the grub alone. They could pack food into this height-of-land country as well as anybody else if they wanted to. They let the trappers wear themselves to skin and bone struggling up the river in canoes loaded to the gunnels, risking their lives for it in the white rapids, lugging their loads up The Great Bank, a mile long and steeper than the bridge of Satan's own nose, breaking their backs for it across twelve miles of swamps and brooks and slippery rocks on the Grand Portage where the tumplines[1] pulled their hair out by the roots and they carried till their eyes turned black and their trembling knees sagged under them. And then—then the Indians came along and helped themselves as though flour were worth no more up here than down on the bay shore.

"They won't help themselves to my grub," said Jan grimly. "Some day I'll come back to my house maybe, and find it cleaned right out. And then what about me, livin' on jays' legs and moss till I fall in the snow and die?"

The sky was growing deeper gray, darkness coming early. The air was chill with a suspicion of dampness. Come a big batch of snow to cover their track and make the walkin' back heavy, right to the knees, no food, he'd be in a fine fix, wouldn't he? He smelled the wind and it smelled like snow. Before dark it began to fall, and at dark he still had not caught them. Must be gettin' weak, he thought ruefully. He'd set some rabbit snares tonight. Or maybe he'd get a partridge. And maybe he wouldn't.

He stood on the shore of a little lake and leaned against a tree, uncertain. What with the new snow and the dark, there was only the barest sign of the track now. By morning it would be gone. What was that sharp smell?

He threw back his head and sniffed. Wood smoke! He had caught them. Let the snow pelt down. Let it snow six feet in the night, he had caught them and they couldn't get away.

Strange, though, that they should camp before the snow got thick. An hour more and they would have been safe. Well, Mathieu had made his last mistake this time.

Over a knoll in a thick clump of firs he built a small fire to boil the kettle. He was ravenous, and weary to the bone. They were camped, they would keep till he got ready for them. And they couldn't smell his smoke with the wind this way.

He ate the last of his bannock, drank four cups of tea and smoked his pipe to the last dregs. Then he left his bag and ax, took his rifle and stole out across the dark lake. It was black as ink, and the new snow was like cotton wool to muffle his steps. Just back from the far shore he saw their dome-shaped *meetchwop*[2] glimmering. They were burn-

1 **tumplines** (tump′ lĭns): head straps to support a load carried on the back.

2 *meetchwop:* a tent-like shelter.

ing a candle in there, one of his own probably.

He crept up closer, on his belly, foot by
foot. The two sleds were stuck up against a
tree, there was the chopping block, the ax,
the chips. Snowshoes were hanging from a
limb, the two small pairs. The women inside
were baking bread. He could hear the frying
pan scrape on the tin stove. They were
talking in their soft musical voices, more like
a brook under the ice than like human talk.
But he could not bring himself to walk into
the tent and shoot the women in cold blood.
Better get Mathieu first. But where was
Mathieu? Behind that black tree there with
his rifle cocked?

Jan lay silent, scarcely breathing, ears
stretched for the slightest sound. But there
were only the wind and the falling snow and
the women's voices and the scraping pan.

Fifteen minutes, half an hour, he lay thus.

He was freezing, he couldn't lie there all
night. Inch by inch he crawled away. Silent as
a shadow he went back across the lake. There
was danger everywhere now, every time he
moved a muscle. He could feel it all around
him, feel a prickling in his scalp and a supernatural certainty that as he was stalking
Mathieu, Mathieu was stalking him. Cautiously, with long waits, he approached his
camp. The fire was out. His fingers touched
the gamebag and drew back. Something was
there, something that shouldn't be! *Something
was wrong*. Chills went up and down his
spine. He whirled toward a deeper patch of
shadow, knowing with the certainty of panic
that gunfire would belch from that shadow
and blind him. His eyes roamed round in his
head in the darkness and he waited, turned to
stone.

There was no sound. Nothing but the soft
hiss of the snowflakes drifting down.

Then he smelled it. Bread, new-baked
bread, sweet as life to his nostrils. He drew off
his mitten and touched the gamebag again.
His finger counted them—seven crusty bannock cakes, still warm.

"Mathieu," he whispered to the engulfing
darkness. There was no answer. He struck a
match and looked at the cakes. He bit one,
and shook his head, ashamed. All his muscles
sagged, and he slumped into the snow as
though it were a bed.

Everything was different now. Noisily he
crashed down a big tree for his night's fire. He
was sticking up a lean-to by the fireplace,
chilled by the night's cold, not by the cold
horror of that other unthinkable job. He'd
rather Mathieu plugged him full of holes
than to take a sight on Mathieu. It was like
waking up from a nightmare. He had half a
mind to go across the lake now and ask
Mathieu's women to sew up the tear in his
britches and have a good sleep in the Indian's
warm tent. How they'd giggle and talk, with
their black eyes!

But he was too ashamed. Mathieu was a
better man than he was, that was all; more
forgiving, smarter in the woods. "I wouldn't
forgive him for taking a bag of flour, but he
forgives me for tryin' to kill him. All the time
the snow's comin' down and he only had to
go on a little piece farther tonight to lose me
altogether. He knows that and he knows I
was going to shoot him. But he takes a chance
and sneaks back to feed me, me that's chasin'
him to kill him. Mathieu don't want I should
starve goin' back to the river. Mathieu—he
don't want us to part unfriendly."

It beat all. If ever he told this to Luce, she'd
say he was the head liar of all the liars on the
whole river.

He finished one of the fragrant, tender
bread cakes and lay down with his back to

the fire. It was a long time since he'd felt so happy. Wonderful strange too, how much he and Mathieu had said to each other without words, way off here, never meeting, eating each other's grub.

Toward morning the snow stopped. Just after sunrise the Indian family broke camp and climbed the hill up from the shore. Jan, watching from the opposite hill across the lake, saw them silhouetted, three dark figures on the bare ridge. He pointed his gun at a treetop and let go greeting. Boom-boom. . . . Boom. He saw the two women, startled, duck behind their sled.

But Mathieu stood erect against the brightening sky. He raised his rifle and fired one answering shot.

So they stood for a moment, on opposite hills, with upraised hand. *Good-bye. Luck.*

Discussion

1. When Jan arrives at his base cabin, how does he know someone has been there? Who does he think it was? Why?

2. According to Jan, what is the difference between Mathieu's idea of sharing food and his? How is Jan's punishment for stealing food different from Mathieu's?

3. What signs do Mathieu and his family leave that enable Jan to track them successfully?

4. What does Jan learn about Mathieu's plans by studying the toboggan tracks and the caribou skin?

5. Why does Jan think Mathieu might ambush him? What, in fact, does Mathieu actually do? Why does Mathieu stay hidden?

6. Why is "Without Words" a good title for this story?

Writer's Craft

Who is telling this story? That is a good question to ask yourself as you begin to read any story. Most stories are told through the eyes of only one person. In some cases the author uses *I*. The person who tells the story is either a main character, a participant in the action, or an observer. That is called first person point of view. For example, the following lines from "The Long Way Around" are written in the first person—from Patty's point of view.

> "I walked home like I always walked, neither slow nor hurrying. It was just too bad if I was late for supper. I didn't want any anyhow."

There is another way in which an author can tell a story from one person's point of view. That is called THIRD PERSON LIMITED. Even though *I* is replaced by *he* or *she,* the reader still only sees what is happening from one character's point of view. The author can reveal only what that *one* character sees, hears, thinks, or feels.

1. Through whose eyes and mind does the reader view the action in this story? How does this limit what the author can reveal?
2. Select passages that show what Jan sees, thinks, and feels.
3. Select passages from "Without Words" that are written in the third person limited. Then show how you would change them to first person point of view.
4. Suppose the author of this story had chosen *not* to use the third person limited point of view. Instead, he had decided to tell the story from an omniscient point of view in which the author can reveal what *all* the characters think and feel. How would this story be changed? What difference would this make to the readers?

Composition

1. Imagine that you are Jan. You have just returned home to your wife. Tell her about your tracking Mathieu. Since she will consider you "the head liar of the liars on the whole river," you must persuade her that it really happened. To do this, include as many of the facts as you can. Begin by giving your reasons for tracking Mathieu. Then tell her what you learned about Mathieu from his tracks. Finally explain what happened the day he left the bread for you.
2. Rewrite the last scene where Mathieu leaves the bread for Jan, but retell the scene through Mathieu's eyes. Keep in mind that he is probably afraid that Jan will shoot him if he is discovered. When referring to Mathieu, use the pronouns *he* or *him* or use his name. Be sure to include *only* what Mathieu would see, think, or feel.

Vocabulary

Many words in the English language have more than one meaning. For example, *light* can mean "brightness," "pale in color," or "low in weight." Any word which has more than one definition is called a MULTIPLE-MEANING WORD.

Context clues, hints about a word's meaning found in surrounding words, can help a reader understand which definition of a multiple-meaning word is intended in a particular sentence. For example, the differences between the above three definitions of *light* become clear from the contexts of these sentences.

They were blinded by the *light*.
She wore a *light* blue shirt.
The bundle he carried was *light*.

A. Each sentence below contains one multiple-meaning word in *italics*. On a separate sheet of paper, copy these words, and write short definitions for them based on how they are used in each sentence. Then for each word, write a different definition, and use that meaning in a sentence of your own.

EXAMPLE: All about was a *ring* of darkness.
ANSWER: ring: a circle—sound a bell
          We wished the bell would *ring.*

1. Here was the firelight. What a perfect *mark* to shoot at!
2. Jan took his rifle and emptied the *magazine.*
3. This was his whole year's earnings, these five months in the *bush.*
4. A mile across, the birch *bluffs* were turning blue in the twilight.
5. The *drift* had obscured the shores now and he was as though alone in the middle of a white sea, snow above, below and on all sides.

B. The word *bank* is one of the multiple-meaning words used in "Without Words." Look it up in a dictionary. Write five different definitions on your paper. Then for each definition, write a sentence which uses the word *bank* in a different way.

Elliott Merrick 1905 —

After graduating from Yale, Elliott Merrick worked as a cub reporter in New Jersey and did publicity and advertising writing in New York. Then in 1929, he went to Canada to work for the Grenfell Mission. During that period he obtained much of the material for his books while traveling with trappers on the rivers and interior lakes. Later he and his wife, who was a nurse at the mission, moved to Vermont where he taught English at the University of Vermont. During World War II, he wrote for the Office of War Information. From these experiences he got material for *Green Mountain Farm,* a story of a Vermont farm family, and *Passing By,* a novel concerning the crews of merchant ships during World War II.

Imagine a world where wishes come true. But, what if someone else were making those wishes for you?

All You've Ever Wanted

JOAN AIKEN

MATILDA, YOU WILL AGREE, was a most unfortunate child. Not only had she three names each worse than the others—Matilda, Eliza, and Agatha—but her father and mother died shortly after she was born, and she was brought up exclusively by her six aunts. These were all energetic women, and so on Monday Matilda was taught algebra and arithmetic by her Aunt Aggie, on Tuesday biology by her Aunt Beattie, on Wednesday classics by her Aunt Cissie, on Thursday dancing and deportment by her Aunt Dorrie, on Friday essentials by her Aunt Effie, and on Saturday French by her Aunt Florrie. Friday was the most alarming day, as Matilda never knew beforehand what Aunt Effie would decide on as the day's essentials—sometimes it was cooking, or revolver practice, or washing, or boilermaking ("For you never know what a girl may need nowadays," as Aunt Effie rightly observed).

So that by Sunday, Matilda was often worn out, and thanked her stars that her seventh aunt, Gertie, had left for foreign parts many years before, and never threatened to come back to teach her geology or grammar on the only day when she was able to do as she liked.

However, poor Matilda was not entirely free from her Aunt Gertie, for on her seventh birthday, and each one after it, she received a little poem wishing her well, written on pink paper, decorated with silver flowers, and signed "Gertrude Isabel Jones, to her niece, with much affection." And the terrible disadvantage of the poems, pretty though they were, was that the wishes in them invariably came true. For instance, the one on her eighth birthday read:

> *Now you're eight Matilda dear*
> *May shining gifts your place adorn*
> *And each day through the coming year*
> *Awake you with a rosy morn.*

The shining gifts were all very well—they consisted of a torch,[1] a luminous watch, pins, needles, a steel soapbox, and a useful little silver brooch which said "Matilda" in case she ever forgot her name—but the rosy morns

---

1 **torch:** flashlight.

were a great mistake. As you know, a red sky in the morning is the shepherd's warning, and the fatal results of Aunt Gertie's well-meaning verse were that it rained every day for the entire year.

Another one read:

Each morning make another friend
Who'll be with you till light doth end.
Cheery and frolicsome and gay,
To pass the sunny hours away.

For the rest of her life Matilda was overwhelmed by the number of friends she made in the course of that year—three hundred and sixty-five of them. Every morning she found another of them, anxious to cheer her and frolic with her, and the aunts complained that her lessons were being constantly interrupted. The worst of it was that she did not really like all the friends—some of them were so very cheery and frolicsome, and insisted on pillow fights when she had a toothache, or sometimes twenty-one of them would get together and make her play hockey, which she hated. She was not even consoled by the fact that all her hours were sunny, because she was so busy in passing them away that she had no time to enjoy them.

Long miles and weary though you stray
Your friends are never far away,
And every day though you may roam,
Yet night will find you back at home.

was another inconvenient wish. Matilda found herself forced to go for long, tiresome walks in all weathers, and it was no comfort to know that her friends were never far away, for although they often passed her on bicycles or in cars, they never gave her lifts.

However, as she grew older, the poems became less troublesome, and she began to enjoy bluebirds twittering in the garden, and

endless vases of roses on her windowsill. Nobody knew where Aunt Gertie lived, and she never put in an address with her birthday greetings. It was therefore impossible to write and thank her for her varied good wishes, or hint that they might have been more carefully worded. But Matilda looked forward to meeting her one day, and thought that she must be a most interesting person.

"You never knew what Gertrude would be up to next," said Aunt Cissie. "She was a thoughtless girl, and got into endless scrapes, but I will say for her, she was very good-hearted."

When Matilda was nineteen she took a job in the Ministry of Alarm and Despondency, a very cheerful place where, instead of typewriter ribbon, they used red tape, and there was a large laundry basket near the main entrance labeled The Usual Channels, where all the letters were put which people did not want to answer themselves. Once every three months the letters were re-sorted and dealt out afresh to different people.

Matilda got on very well here and was perfectly happy. She went to see her six aunts on Sundays, and had almost forgotten the seventh by the time that her twentieth birthday had arrived. Her aunt, however, had not forgotten her.

On the morning of her birthday Matilda woke very late, and had to rush off to work, cramming her letters unopened into her pocket, to be read later on in the morning. She had no time to read them until ten minutes to eleven, but that, she told herself, was as it should be, since, as she had been born at eleven in the morning, her birthday did not really begin until then.

Most of the letters were from her three hundred and sixty-five friends, but the usual pink and silver envelope was there, and she

opened it with the usual feeling of slight uncertainty.

May all your leisure hours be blest
Your work prove full of interest,
Your life hold many happy hours
And all your way be strewn with flowers,

said the pink and silver slip in her fingers. "From your affectionate Aunt Gertrude."

Matilda was still pondering this when a gong sounded in the passage outside. This was the signal for everyone to leave their work and dash down the passage to a trolley which sold them buns and coffee. Matilda left her letters and dashed with the rest. Sipping her coffee and gossiping with her friends, she had forgotten the poem, when the voice of the Minister of Alarm and Despondency himself came down the corridor.

"What is all this? What does this mean?" he was saying.

The group around the trolley turned to see what he was talking about. And then Matilda flushed scarlet and spilled some of her coffee on the floor. For all along the respectable brown carpeting of the passage were growing flowers in the most riotous profusion—daisies, campanulas, crocuses, mimosas, foxgloves, tulips, and lotuses. In some places the passage looked more like a jungle than anything else. Out of this jungle the little red-faced figure of the Minister fought its way.

"Who did it?" he said. But nobody answered.

Matilda went quietly away from the chattering group and pushed through the vegetation to her room, leaving a trail of buttercups and rhododendrons across the floor to her desk.

"I can't keep this quiet," she thought desperately. And she was quite right. Mr. Willoughby, who presided over the General Gloom Division, noticed almost immediately that when his secretary came into his room, there was something unusual about her.

"Miss Jones," he said, "I don't like to be personal, but have you noticed that wherever you go, you leave a trail of mixed flowers?"

Poor Matilda burst into tears.

"I know, I don't know *what* I shall do about it," she sobbed.

Mr. Willoughby was not used to secretaries who burst into tears, let alone ones who left lobelias, primroses, and the rarer forms of cactus behind them when they entered the room.

"It's very pretty," he said, "but not very practical. Already it's almost impossible to get along the passage, and I shudder to think what this room will be like when these have grown a bit higher. I really don't think you can go on with it, Miss Jones."

"You don't think I do it on purpose, do

you?" said Matilda, sniffing into her hand-kerchief. "I can't stop it. They just keep on coming."

"In that case, I am afraid," replied Mr. Willoughby, "that you will not be able to keep on coming. We really cannot have the Ministry overgrown in this way. I shall be very sorry to lose you, Miss Jones. You have been most efficient. What caused this unfortunate disability, may I ask?"

"It's a kind of spell," Matilda said, shaking the damp out of her handkerchief onto a fine polyanthus.

"But my dear girl," Mr. Willoughby exclaimed testily, "you have a National Magic Insurance Card, haven't you? Good heavens—why don't you go to the public magician?"

"I never thought of that," she confessed. "I'll go at lunchtime."

Fortunately for Matilda the public magician's office lay just across the square from where she worked, so that she did not cause too much disturbance, though the Borough Council could never account for the rare and exotic flowers which suddenly sprang up in the middle of their dusty lawns.

The public magician received her briskly, examined her with an occultiscope, and asked her to state particulars of her trouble.

"It's a spell," said Matilda, looking down at a pink Christmas rose growing unseasonably beside her chair.

"In that case we can soon help you. Fill in that form, *if* you please." He pushed a printed slip at her from across the table.

It said: "To be filled in by persons suffering from spells, incantations, philters, Evil Eye, etc."

Matilda filled in name and address of patient, nature of spell, and date, but when she came to name and address of person by whom spell was cast, she paused.

"I don't know her address," she said.

"Then I'm afraid you'll have to find it. Can't do anything without an address," the public magician replied.

Matilda went out into the street very disheartened. The public magician could do nothing better than advise her to put an advertisement into the *Times* and *International Sorcerers' Bulletin,* which she accordingly did:

AUNT GERTRUDE *please communicate. Matilda much distressed by last poem.*

While she was in the post office sending off her advertisements (and causing a good deal of confusion by the number of forget-me-nots she left about), she wrote and posted her resignation to Mr. Willoughby, and then went sadly to the nearest underground station.

"Ain'tcher left something behind?" a man said to her at the top of the escalator. She looked back at the trail of daffodils across the station entrance and hurried anxiously down the stairs. As she ran around a corner at the bottom, angry shouts told her that blooming lilies had interfered with the works and the escalator had stopped.

She tried to hide in the gloom at the far end of the platform, but a furious station official found her.

"Wotcher mean by it?" he said, shaking her elbow. "It'll take three days to put the station right, and look at my platform!"

The stone slabs were split and pushed aside by vast peonies, which kept growing, and threatened to block the line.

"It isn't my fault—really it isn't," poor Matilda stammered.

"The company can sue you for this, you know," he began, when a train came in.

Pushing past him, she squeezed into the nearest door.

She began to thank her stars for the escape, but it was too soon. A powerful and penetrating smell of onions rose around her feet where the white flowers of wild garlic had sprung.

When Aunt Gertie finally read the advertisement in a ten-months'-old copy of the *International Sorcerers' Bulletin*, she packed her luggage and took the next airplane back to England. For she was still just as Aunt Cissie had described her—thoughtless, but very good-hearted.

"Where is the poor child?" she asked Aunt Aggie.

"I should say she was poor," her sister replied tartly. "It's a pity you didn't come home before, instead of making her life a misery for twelve years. You'll find her out in the summerhouse."

Matilda had been living out there ever since she left the Ministry of Alarm and Despondency, because her aunts kindly but firmly, and quite reasonably, said that they could not have the house filled with vegetation.

She had an ax, with which she cut down the worst growths every evening, and for the rest of the time she kept as still as she could, and earned some money by doing odd jobs of typing and sewing.

"My poor dear child," Aunt Gertie said breathlessly, "I had no idea that my little verses would have this sort of effect. Whatever shall we do?"

"Please do something," Matilda implored her, sniffing. This time it was not tears, but a cold she had caught from living in perpetual drafts.

"My dear, there isn't anything I can do. It's bound to last till the end of the year—that sort of spell is completely unalterable."

"Well, at least can you stop sending me the verses?" asked Matilda. "I don't want to sound ungrateful."

"Even that I can't do," her aunt said gloomily. "It's a banker's order at the Magician's Bank. One a year from seven to twenty-one. Oh dear, and I thought it would be such *fun* for you. At least you only have one more, though."

"Yes, but heaven knows what that'll be." Matilda sneezed despondently and put another sheet of paper into her typewriter. There seemed to be nothing to do but wait. However, they did decide that it might be a good thing to go and see the public magician on the morning of Matilda's twenty-first birthday.

Aunt Gertie paid the taxi driver and tipped him heavily not to grumble about the mass of delphiniums sprouting out of the mat of his cab.

"Good heavens, if it isn't Gertrude Jones!" the public magician exclaimed. "Haven't seen you since we were at college together.

How are you? Same old irresponsible Gertie? Remember that hospital you endowed with endless beds and the trouble it caused? And the row with the cigarette manufacturers over the extra million boxes of cigarettes for the soldiers?"

When the situation was explained to him he laughed heartily.

"Just like you, Gertie. Well-meaning isn't the word."

At eleven promptly, Matilda opened her pink envelope.

Matilda, now you're twenty-one,
May you have every sort of fun;
May you have all you've ever wanted,
And every future wish be granted.

"Every future wish be granted—then I wish Aunt Gertie would lose her power of wishing," cried Matilda; and immediately Aunt Gertie did.

But as Aunt Gertie with her usual thoughtlessness had said, "May you have all you've *ever* wanted," Matilda had quite a lot of rather inconvenient things to dispose of, including a lion cub and a baby hippopotamus.

Discussion

1. What is so unusual about Aunt Gertrude's birthday wishes?

2. Describe Aunt Gertrude's good and bad personality traits. How do you learn about these traits?

3. Plots are constructed by close-linking events. One thing will cause another to happen. For example, because Mr. Morris forgot to pay his electric bill, all the lights in his house went out one night. In this story Aunt Gertrude's wishes cause changes in Matilda's life. Name the wishes and then tell what results because of them.

4. What does the title of this story mean?

5. What lesson or moral about wishes could you draw from this story?

Close your eyes and imagine a world where there is no war, no one is hungry, and people have all the money they want. Impossible? Of course it is, but many stories and books are written about impossible places, people, and situations. This kind of literature is called FANTASY. Below are some general guidelines to fantasies:

—The impossible sounds true.
—Magic happens. Spells can be cast.
—Creatures and animals can talk, think, and feel like human beings.
—People can change sizes and bodies.
—Imaginary people do things in the real world. Real people sometimes visit imaginary worlds.
—Ghosts and spirits can appear.

1. Authors seldom tell readers that they are about to read a fantasy, but they do give clues. What are some clues that "All You've Ever Wanted" is a fantasy?
2. Some fantasies are written seriously. For example, authors may tell what they actually think the future will be like. This story, however, is meant to entertain more than it is meant to be taken seriously. Find some examples which prove its humorous nature.

Joan Aiken 1924—

Joan Aiken was born to American parents in England, but she never became a United States citizen because her parents failed to register her with the United States embassy. She later married a British journalist who became ill and died of lung cancer. She then supported herself and her two small children by writing. Her children's books include: *All You've Ever Wanted, Black Hearts in Batter Sea, Night Birds on Nantucket,* and *Nightfall.* The three latter works were Junior Literary Guild selections. Aiken has also written a number of adult stories. She once said that she makes very little distinction between writing for children and for adults. She just enjoys writing.

It was a maximum security prison, but he said he could escape from it within a week. Was he crazy, or could he really do it?

The Problem of Cell 13

JACQUES FUTRELLE

PRACTICALLY ALL those letters remaining in the alphabet after Augustus S. F. X. Van Dusen was named were afterward acquired by that gentleman in the course of a brilliant scientific career, and, being honorably acquired, were tacked on to the other end. His name, therefore, taken with all that belonged to it, was a wonderfully imposing structure. He was a Ph.D., an LL.D., an F.R.S., an M.D., and an M.D.S.[1] He was also some other things—just what he himself couldn't say—through recognition of his ability by various foreign educational and scientific institutions.

In appearance he was no less striking than in nomenclature.[2] He was slender with the droop of the student in his thin shoulders and the pallor of a close, sedentary life on his clean-shaven face. His eyes wore a perpetual, forbidding squint—the squint of a man who studies little things—and when they could be seen at all through his thick spectacles, were mere slits of watery blue. But above his eyes was his most striking feature. This was a tall, broad brow, almost abnormal in height and width, crowned by a heavy shock of bushy, yellow hair. All these things conspired to give him a peculiar, almost grotesque, personality.

Professor Van Dusen was remotely German. For generations his ancestors had been noted in the sciences; he was the logical result, the master mind. First and above all he was a logician. At least thirty-five years of the half century or so of his existence had been devoted exclusively to proving that two and two always equal four, except in unusual cases, where they equal three or five, as the case may be. He stood broadly on the general proposition that all things that start must go somewhere, and was able to bring the concentrated mental force of his forefathers to bear on a given problem. Incidentally it may be remarked that Professor Van Dusen wore a No. 8 hat.

The world at large had heard vaguely of Professor Van Dusen as The Thinking Machine. It was a newspaper catch-phrase applied to him at the time of a remarkable exhibition at chess; he had demonstrated then that a stranger to the game might, by the force of inevitable logic, defeat a champion who had devoted a lifetime to its study. The Thinking Machine! Perhaps that more nearly described him than all his honorary

---

1 **Ph.D . . . M.D.S.:** advanced educational degrees.
2 **nomenclature** (nō′ mən klā′ chər): name.

initials, for he spent week after week, month after month, in the seclusion of his small laboratory from which had gone forth thoughts that staggered scientific associates and deeply stirred the world at large.

It was only occasionally that The Thinking Machine had visitors, and these were usually men who, themselves high in the sciences, dropped in to argue a point and perhaps convince themselves. Two of these men, Dr. Charles Ransome and Alfred Fielding, called one evening to discuss some theory which is not of consequence here.

"Such a thing is impossible," declared Dr. Ransome emphatically, in the course of the conversation.

"Nothing is impossible," declared The Thinking Machine with equal emphasis. He always spoke petulantly. "The mind is master of all things. When science fully recognizes that fact a great advance will have been made."

"How about the airship?" asked Dr. Ransome.

"That's not impossible at all," asserted The Thinking Machine. "It will be invented some time. I'd do it myself, but I'm busy."

Dr. Ransome laughed tolerantly.

"I've heard you say such things before," he said. "But they mean nothing. Mind may be master of matter, but it hasn't yet found a way to apply itself. There are some things that can't be *thought* out of existence, or rather which would not yield to any amount of thinking."

"What, for instance?" demanded The Thinking Machine.

Dr. Ransome was thoughtful for a moment as he smoked.

"Well, say prison walls," he replied. "No man can *think* himself out of a cell. If he could, there would be no prisoners."

"A man can so apply his brain and ingenuity that he can leave a cell, which is the same thing," snapped The Thinking Machine.

Dr. Ransome was slightly amused.

"Let's suppose a case," he said, after a moment. "Take a cell where prisoners under sentence of death are confined—men who are desperate and, maddened by fear, would take any chance to escape—suppose you were locked in such a cell. Could you escape?"

"Certainly," declared The Thinking Machine.

"Of course," said Mr. Fielding, who entered the conversation for the first time, "you might wreck the cell with an explosive—but inside, a prisoner, you couldn't have that."

"There would be nothing of that kind," said The Thinking Machine. "You might treat me precisely as you treated prisoners under sentence of death, and I would leave the cell."

"Not unless you entered it with tools prepared to get out," said Dr. Ransome.

The Thinking Machine was visibly annoyed and his blue eyes snapped.

"Lock me in any cell in any prison anywhere at any time, wearing only what is necessary, and I'll escape in a week," he declared, sharply.

Dr. Ransome sat up straight in the chair, interested. Mr. Fielding lighted a new cigar.

"You mean you could actually *think* yourself out?" asked Dr. Ransome.

"I would get out," was the response.

"Are you serious?"

"Certainly I am serious."

Dr. Ransome and Mr. Fielding were silent for a long time.

"Would you be willing to try it?" asked Mr. Fielding, finally.

"Certainly," said Professor Van Dusen,

and there was a trace of irony in his voice. "I have done more asinine things than that to convince other men of less important truths."

The tone was offensive and there was an undercurrent strongly resembling anger on both sides. Of course it was an absurd thing, but Professor Van Dusen reiterated his willingness to undertake the escape and it was decided upon.

"To begin now," added Dr. Ransome.

"I'd prefer that it begin tomorrow," said The Thinking Machine, "because—"

"No, now," said Mr. Fielding, flatly. "You are arrested, figuratively, of course, without any warning locked in a cell with no chance to communicate with friends, and left there with identically the same care and attention that would be given to a man under sentence of death. Are you willing?"

"All right, now, then," said The Thinking Machine, and he arose.

"Say, the death cell in Chisholm Prison."

"The death cell in Chisholm Prison."

"And what will you wear?"

"As little as possible," said The Thinking Machine. "Shoes, stockings, trousers and a shirt."

"You will permit yourself to be searched, of course?"

"I am to be treated precisely as all prisoners are treated," said The Thinking Machine. "No more attention and no less."

There were some preliminaries to be arranged in the matter of obtaining permission for the test, but all three were influential men and everything was done satisfactorily by telephone, albeit the prison commissioners, to whom the experiment was explained on purely scientific grounds, were sadly bewildered. Professor Van Dusen would be the most distinguished prisoner they had ever entertained.

When The Thinking Machine had donned those things which he was to wear during his incarceration[3] he called the little old women who was his housekeeper, cook and maidservant all in one.

"Martha," he said, "it is now twenty-seven minutes past nine o'clock. I am going away. One week from tonight, at half past nine, these gentlemen and one, possibly two, others will take supper with me here. Remember Dr. Ransome is very fond of artichokes."

The three men were driven to Chisholm Prison, where the warden was awaiting them, having been informed of the matter by telephone. He understood merely that the eminent Professor Van Dusen was to be his prisoner, if he could keep him, for one week; that he had committed no crime, but that he was to be treated as all other prisoners were treated.

"Search him," instructed Dr. Ransome.

The Thinking Machine was searched. Nothing was found on him; the pockets of the trousers were empty; the white, stiff-bosomed shirt had no pocket. The shoes and stockings were removed, examined, then replaced. As he watched all these preliminaries, and noted the pitiful, childlike physical weakness of the man—the colorless face, and the thin, white hands—Dr. Ransome almost regretted his part in the affair.

"Are you sure you want to do this?" he asked.

"Would you be convinced if I did not?" inquired The Thinking Machine in turn.

"No."

"All right. I'll do it."

What sympathy Dr. Ransome had was

---

3 incarceration (in kär′ sə rā′ shən): imprisonment.

dissipated by the tone. It nettled him, and he resolved to see the experiment to the end; it would be a stinging reproof to egotism.[4]

"It will be impossible for him to communicate with anyone outside?" he asked.

"Absolutely impossible," replied the warden. "He will not be permitted writing materials of any sort."

"And your jailers, would they deliver a message from him?"

"Not one word, directly or indirectly," said the warden. "You may rest assured of that. They will report anything he might say or turn over to me anything he might give them."

"That seems entirely satisfactory," said Mr. Fielding, who was frankly interested in the problem.

"Of course, in the event he fails," said Dr. Ransome, "and asks for his liberty, you understand you are to set him free?"

"I understand," replied the warden.

The Thinking Machine stood listening, but had nothing to say until this was all ended, then:

"I should like to make three small requests. You may grant them or not, as you wish."

"No special favors, now," warned Mr. Fielding.

"I am asking none," was the stiff response. "I should like to have some tooth powder—buy it yourself to see that it is tooth powder—and I should like to have one five-dollar and two ten-dollar bills."

Dr. Ransome, Mr. Fielding and the warden exchanged astonished glances. They were not surprised at the request for tooth powder, but were at the request for money.

4 **What sympathy** . . . **egotism:** Van Dusen's arrogance irritated Dr. Ransome. He almost wished that Van Dusen would fail so he would not be so proud and boastful anymore.

"Is there any man with whom our friend would come in contact that he could bribe with twenty-five dollars?"

"Not for twenty-five hundred dollars," was the positive reply.

"Well, let him have them," said Mr. Fielding. "I think they are harmless enough."

"And what is the third request?" asked Dr. Ransome.

"I should like to have my shoes polished."

Again the astonished glances were exchanged. This last request was the height of absurdity, so they agreed to it. These things all being attended to, The Thinking Machine was led back into the prison from which he had undertaken to escape.

"Here is Cell 13," said the warden, stopping three doors down the steel corridor. "This is where we keep condemned murderers. No one can leave it without my permission; and no one in it can communicate with the outside. I'll stake my reputation on that. It's only three doors back of my office and I can readily hear any unusual noise."

"Will this cell do, gentlemen?" asked The Thinking Machine. There was a touch of irony in his voice.

"Admirably," was the reply.

The heavy steel door was thrown open, there was a great scurrying and scampering of tiny feet, and The Thinking Machine passed into the gloom of the cell. Then the door was closed and double-locked by the warden.

"What is that noise in there?" asked Dr. Ransome, through the bars.

"Rats—dozens of them," replied The Thinking Machine, tersely.

The three men, with final good nights, were turning away when The Thinking Machine called:

"What time is it exactly, Warden?"

"Eleven seventeen," replied the warden.

"Thanks. I will join you gentlemen in your office at half past eight o'clock one week from tonight," said The Thinking Machine.

"And if you do not?"

"There is no 'if' about it."

Chisholm Prison was a great, spreading structure of granite, four stories in all, which stood in the center of acres of open space. It was surrounded by a wall of solid masonry eighteen feet high, and so smoothly finished inside and out as to offer no foothold to a climber, no matter how expert. Atop of this fence, as a further precaution, was a five-foot fence of steel rods, each terminating in a keen point. This fence in itself marked an absolute deadline between freedom and imprisonment, for, even if a man escaped from his cell, it would seem impossible for him to pass the wall.

The yard, which on all sides of the prison building was twenty-five feet wide, that being the distance from the building to the wall, was by day an exercise ground for those prisoners to whom was granted the boon of occasional semi-liberty. But that was not for those in Cell 13. At all times of the day there were armed guards in the yard, four of them, one patrolling each side of the prison building.

By night the yard was almost as brilliantly lighted as by day. On each of the four sides was a great arc light which rose above the prison wall and gave to the guards a clear sight. The lights, too, brightly illuminated the spiked top of the wall. The wires which fed the arc lights ran up the side of the prison building on insulators and from the top story led out to the poles supporting the arc lights.

All these things were seen and comprehended by The Thinking Machine, who was only enabled to see out his closely barred cell window by standing on his bed. This was on the morning following the incarceration. He gathered, too, that the river lay over there beyond the wall somewhere, because he heard faintly the pulsation of a motor boat and high up in the air saw a river bird. From that same direction came the shouts of boys at play and the occasional crack of a batted ball. He knew then that between the prison wall and the river was an open space, a playground.

Chisholm Prison was regarded as absolutely safe. No man had ever escaped from it. The Thinking Machine, from his perch on the bed, seeing what he saw, could readily understand why. The walls of the cell, though built he judged twenty years before, were perfectly solid, and the window bars of new iron had not a shadow of rust on them. The window itself, even with the bars out, would be a difficult mode of egress[5] because it was small.

Yet, seeing these things, The Thinking

Machine was not discouraged. Instead, he thoughtfully squinted at the great arc light—there was bright sunlight now—and traced with his eyes the wire which led from it to the building. That electric wire, he reasoned, must come down the side of the building not a great distance from his cell. That might be worth knowing.

Cell 13 was on the same floor with the offices of the prison—that is, not in the basement, nor yet upstairs. There were only four steps up to the office door, therefore the level of the floor must be only three or four feet above the ground. He couldn't see the ground directly beneath his window, but he could see it further out toward the wall. It would be an easy drop from the window. Well and good.

Then The Thinking Machine fell to remembering how he had come to the cell. First, there was the outside guard's booth, a part of the wall. There were two heavily barred gates there, both of steel. At this gate was one man always on guard. He admitted persons to the prison after much clanking of keys and locks, and let them out when ordered to do so. The warden's office was in the prison building, and in order to reach that official from the prison yard one had to pass a gate of solid steel with only a peephole in it. Then coming from that inner office to Cell 13, where he was now, one must pass a heavy wooden door and two steel doors into the corridors of the prison; and always there was the double-locked door of Cell 13 to reckon with.

There were then, The Thinking Machine recalled, seven doors to be overcome before one could pass from Cell 13 into the outer world, a free man. But against this was the fact that he was rarely interrupted. A jailer appeared at his cell door at six in the morning

5 **egress** (ē′ gres): exit.

with a breakfast of prison fare; he would come again at noon, and again at six in the afternoon. At nine o'clock at night would come the inspection tour. That would be all.

"It's admirably arranged, this prison system," was the mental tribute paid by The Thinking Machine. "I'll have to study it a little when I get out. I had no idea there was such great care exercised in the prisons."

There was nothing, positively nothing, in his cell, except his iron bed, so firmly put together that no man could tear it to pieces save with sledges or a file. He had neither of these. There was not even a chair, or a small table, or a bit of tin or crockery. Nothing! The jailer stood by when he ate, then took away the wooden spoon and bowl which he had used.

One by one these things sank into the brain of The Thinking Machine. When the last possibility had been considered he began an examination of his cell. From the roof, down the walls on all sides, he examined the stones and the cement between them. He stamped over the floor carefully time after time, but it was cement, perfectly solid. After the examination he sat on the edge of the iron bed and was lost in thought for a long time. For Professor Augustus S. F. X. Van Dusen, The Thinking Machine, had something to think about.

He was disturbed by a rat, which ran across his foot, then scampered away into a dark corner of the cell, frightened at its own daring. After a while The Thinking Machine, squinting steadily into the darkness of the corner where the rat had gone, was able to make out in the gloom many little beady eyes staring at him. He counted six pair, and there were perhaps others; he didn't see very well. Then The Thinking Machine, from his seat on the bed, noticed for the first time the bottom of his cell door. There was an opening there of two inches between the steel bar and the floor. Still looking steadily at this opening, The Thinking Machine backed suddenly into the corner where he had seen the beady eyes. There was a great scampering of tiny feet, several squeaks of frightened rodents, and then silence.

None of the rats had gone out the door, yet there were none in the cell. Therefore there must be another way out of the cell, however small. The Thinking Machine, on hands and knees, started a search for this spot, feeling in the darkness with his long, slender fingers.

At last his search was rewarded. He came upon a small opening in the floor, level with the cement. It was perfectly round and somewhat larger than a silver dollar. This was the way the rats had gone. He put his fingers deep into the opening; it seemed to be a disused drainage pipe and was dry and dusty.

Having satisfied himself on this point, he sat on the bed again for an hour, then made another inspection of his surroundings through the small cell window. One of the outside guards stood directly opposite, beside the wall, and happened to be looking at the window of Cell 13 when the head of The Thinking Machine appeared. But the scientist didn't notice the guard.

Noon came and the jailer appeared with the prison dinner of repulsively plain food. At home The Thinking Machine merely ate to live; here he took what was offered without comment. Occasionally he spoke to the jailer who stood outside the door watching him.

"Any improvements made here in the last few years?" he asked.

"Nothing particularly," replied the jailer.

"New wall was built four years ago."

"Anything done to the prison proper?"

"Painted the woodwork outside, and I believe about seven years ago a new system of plumbing was put in."

"Ah!" said the prisoner. "How far is the river over there?"

"About three hundred feet. The boys have a baseball ground between the wall and the river."

The Thinking Machine had nothing further to say just then, but when the jailer was ready to go he asked for some water.

"I get very thirsty here," he explained. "Would it be possible for you to leave a little water in a bowl for me?"

"I'll ask the warden," replied the jailer, and he went away.

Half an hour later he returned with water in a small earthen bowl.

"The warden says you may keep this bowl," he informed the prisoner. "But you must show it to me when I ask for it. If it is broken, it will be the last."

"Thank you," said The Thinking Machine. "I shan't break it."

The jailer went on about his duties. For just the fraction of a second it seemed that The Thinking Machine wanted to ask a question, but he didn't.

Two hours later this same jailer, in passing the door of Cell No. 13, heard a noise inside and stopped. The Thinking Machine was down on his hands and knees in a corner of the cell, and from that same corner came several frightened squeaks. The jailer looked on interestedly.

"Ah, I've got you," he heard the prisoner say.

"Got what?" he asked, sharply.

"One of these rats," was the reply. "See?" And between the scientist's long fingers the jailer saw a small gray rat struggling. The prisoner brought it over to the light and looked at it closely.

"It's a water rat," he said.

"Ain't you got anything better to do than to catch rats?" asked the jailer.

"It's disgraceful that they should be here at all," was the irritated reply. "Take this one away and kill it. There are dozens more where it came from."

The jailer took the wriggling, squirmy rodent and flung it down on the floor violently. It gave one squeak and lay still. Later he reported the incident to the warden, who only smiled.

Still later that afternoon the outside armed guard on the Cell 13 side of the prison looked up again at the window and saw the prisoner looking out. He saw a hand raised to the barred window and then something white fluttered to the ground, directly under the window of Cell 13. It was a little roll of linen, evidently of white shirting material, and tied around it was a five-dollar bill. The guard looked up at the window again, but the face had disappeared.

With a grim smile he took the little linen roll and the five-dollar bill to the warden's office. There together they deciphered something which was written on it with a queer sort of ink, frequently blurred. On the outside was this:

"Finder of this please deliver to Dr. Charles Ransome."

"Ah," said the warden, with a chuckle. "Plan of escape number one has gone wrong." Then, as an afterthought: "But why did he address it to Dr. Ransome?"

"And where did he get the pen and ink to write with?" asked the guard.

The warden looked at the guard and the

guard looked at the warden. There was no apparent solution of that mystery. The warden studied the writing carefully, then shook his head.

"Well, let's see what he was going to say to Dr. Ransome," he said at length, still puzzled, and he unrolled the inner piece of linen.

"Well, if that—what—what do you think of that?" he asked, dazed.

The guard took the bit of linen and read this:—

"Epa cseot d'net niiy awe
htto n'si sih. T."

The warden spent an hour wondering what sort of a cipher it was, and half an hour wondering why his prisoner should attempt to communicate with Dr. Ransome, who was the cause of his being there. After this the warden devoted some thought to the question of where the prisoner got writing materials, and what sort of writing materials he had. With the idea of illuminating this point, he examined the linen again. It was a torn part of a white shirt and had ragged edges.

Now it was possible to account for the linen, but what the prisoner had used to write with was another matter. The warden knew it would have been impossible for him to have either pen or pencil, and, besides, neither pen nor pencil had been used in this writing. What, then? The warden decided to investigate personally. The Thinking Machine was his prisoner; he had orders to hold his prisoners; if this one sought to escape by sending cipher messages to persons outside, he would stop it, as he would have stopped it in the case of any other prisoner.

The warden went back to Cell 13 and found The Thinking Machine on his hands and knees on the floor, engaged in nothing more alarming than catching rats. The prisoner heard the warden's step and turned to him quickly.

"It's disgraceful," he snapped, "these rats. There are scores of them."

"Other men have been able to stand them," said the warden. "Here is another shirt for you—let me have the one you have on."

"Why?" demanded The Thinking Machine, quickly. His tone was hardly natural, his manner suggested actual perturbation.

"You have attempted to communicate with Dr. Ransome," said the warden severely. "As my prisoner, it is my duty to put a stop to it."

The Thinking Machine was silent for a moment.

"All right," he said, finally. "Do your duty."

The warden smiled grimly. The prisoner arose from the floor and removed the white shirt, putting on instead a striped convict shirt the warden had brought. The warden took the white shirt eagerly, and then and there compared the pieces of linen on which was written the cipher with certain torn places in the shirt. The Thinking Machine looked on curiously.

"The guard brought *you* those, then?" he asked.

"He certainly did," replied the warden triumphantly. "And that ends your first attempt to escape."

The Thinking Machine watched the warden as he, by comparison, established to his own satisfaction that only two pieces of linen had been torn from the white shirt.

"What did you write this with?" demanded the warden.

"I should think it a part of your duty to find out," said The Thinking Machine, irritably.

The warden started to say some harsh things, then restrained himself and made a minute search of the cell and of the prisoner instead. He found absolutely nothing; not even a match or toothpick which might have been used for a pen. The same mystery surrounded the fluid with which the cipher had been written. Although the warden left Cell 13 visibly annoyed, he took the torn shirt in triumph.

"Well, writing notes on a shirt won't get him out, that's certain," he told himself with some complacency. He put the linen scraps into his desk to await developments. "If that man escapes from that cell I'll—hang it—I'll resign."

On the third day of his incarceration The Thinking Machine openly attempted to bribe his way out. The jailer had brought his dinner and was leaning against the barred door, waiting, when The Thinking Machine began the conversation.

"The drainage pipes of the prison lead to the river, don't they?" he asked.

"Yes," said the jailer.

"I suppose they are very small."

"Too small to crawl through, if that's what you're thinking about," was the grinning response.

There was silence and The Thinking Machine finished his meal. Then:

"You know I'm not a criminal, don't you?"

"Yes."

"And that I've a perfect right to be freed if I demand it?"

"Yes."

"Well, I came here believing that I could make my escape," said the prisoner, and his squint eyes studied the face of the jailer. "Would you consider a financial reward for aiding me to escape?"

The jailer, who happened to be an honest man, looked at the slender, weak figure of the prisoner, at the large head with its mass of yellow hair, and was almost sorry.

"I guess prisons like these were not built for the likes of you to get out of," he said, at last.

"But would you consider a proposition to help me get out?" the prisoner insisted, almost beseechingly.

"No," said the jailer, shortly.

"Five hundred dollars," urged The Thinking Machine. "I am not a criminal."

"No," said the jailer.

"A thousand?"

"No," again said the jailer, and he started away hurriedly to escape further temptation. Then he turned back. "If you should give me ten thousand dollars I couldn't get you out. You'd have to pass through seven doors, and I only have the keys to two."

Then he told the warden all about it.

"Plan number two fails," said the warden, smiling grimly. "First a cipher, then bribery."

When the jailer was on his way to Cell 13 at six o'clock, again bearing food to The Thinking Machine, he paused, startled by the unmistakable scrape, scrape of steel against steel. It stopped at the sound of his steps, then craftily the jailer, who was beyond the prisoner's range of vision, resumed his tramping, the sound being apparently that of a man going away from Cell 13. As a matter of fact, he was in the same spot.

After a moment there came again the steady scrape, scrape, and the jailer crept cautiously on tiptoes to the door and peered between the bars. The Thinking Machine was standing on the iron bed working at the bars of the little window. He was using a file, judging from the backward and forward swing of his arms.

Cautiously the jailer crept back to the office, summoned the warden in person, and they returned to Cell 13 on tiptoes. The steady scrape was still audible. The warden listened to satisfy himself and then suddenly appeared at the door.

"Well?" he demanded, and there was a smile on his face.

The Thinking Machine glanced back from his perch on the bed and leaped suddenly to the floor, making frantic efforts to hide something. The warden went in, with hand extended.

"Give it up," he said.

"No," said the prisoner, sharply.

"Come, give it up," urged the warden. "I don't want to have to search you again."

"No," repeated the prisoner.

"What was it—a file?" asked the warden.

The Thinking Machine was silent and stood squinting at the warden with something very nearly approaching disappointment on his face—nearly, but not quite. The warden was almost sympathetic.

"Plan number three fails, eh?" he asked, good-naturedly. "Too bad, isn't it?"

The prisoner didn't say.

"Search him," instructed the warden.

The jailer searched the prisoner carefully. At last, artfully concealed in the waistband of the trousers, he found a piece of steel about two inches long, with one side curved like a half moon.

"Ah," said the warden, as he received it from the jailer. "From your shoe heel," and he smiled pleasantly.

The jailer continued his search and on the other side of the trousers waistband found another piece of steel identical with the first. The edges showed where they had been worn against the bars of the window.

"You couldn't saw a way through those bars with these," said the warden.

"I could have," said The Thinking Machine firmly.

"In six months, perhaps," said the warden, good-naturedly.

The warden shook his head slowly as he gazed into the slightly flushed face of his prisoner.

"Ready to give it up?" he asked.

"I haven't started yet," was the prompt reply.

Then came another exhaustive search of the cell. Carefully the two men went over it, finally turning out the bed and searching that. Nothing. The warden in person climbed upon the bed and examined the bars of the window where the prisoner had been sawing. When he looked he was amused.

"Just made it a little bright by hard rubbing," he said to the prisoner, who stood looking on with a somewhat crestfallen air. The warden grasped the iron bars in his strong hands and tried to shake them. They were immovable, set firmly in the solid granite. He examined each in turn and found them all satisfactory. Finally he climbed down from the bed.

"Give it up, Professor," he advised.

The Thinking Machine shook his head and the warden and jailer passed on again. As they disappeared down the corridor The Thinking Machine sat on the edge of the bed with his head in his hands.

"He's crazy to try to get out of that cell," commented the jailer.

"Of course he can't get out," said the warden. "But he's clever. I would like to know what he wrote that cipher with."

It was four o'clock next morning when an awful, heart-racking shriek of terror resounded through the great prison. It came from a cell, somewhere about the center, and its tone told a tale of horror, agony, terrible fear. The warden heard and with three of his men rushed into the long corridor leading to Cell 13.

As they ran there came again that awful cry. It died away in a sort of wail. The white faces of prisoners appeared at cell doors upstairs and down, staring out wonderingly frightened.

"It's that fool in Cell 13," grumbled the warden.

He stopped and stared in as one of the jailers flashed a lantern. "That fool in Cell 13" lay comfortably on his cot, flat on his back with his mouth open, snoring. Even as they looked there came again the piercing cry, from somewhere above. The warden's face blanched a little as he started up the stairs. There on the top floor he found a man in Cell 43, directly above Cell 13, but two floors higher, cowering in a corner of his cell.

"What's the matter?" demanded the warden.

"Thank God you've come," exclaimed the prisoner, and he cast himself against the bars of his cell.

"What is it?" demanded the warden again.

He threw open the door and went in. The prisoner dropped on his knees and clasped the warden about the body. His face was white with terror, his eyes were widely distended, and he was shuddering. His hands, icy cold, clutched at the warden's.

"Take me out of this cell, please take me out," he pleaded.

"What's the matter with you, anyhow?" insisted the warden, impatiently.

"I heard something—something," said the prisoner, and his eyes roved nervously around the cell.

"What did you hear?"

"I—I can't tell you," stammered the prisoner. Then, in a sudden burst of terror: "Take me out of this cell—put me anywhere—but take me out of here."

The warden and the three jailers exchanged glances.

"Who is this fellow? What's he accused of?" asked the warden.

"Joseph Ballard," said one of the jailers. "He's accused of throwing acid in a woman's face. She died from it."

"But they can't prove it," gasped the prisoner. "They can't prove it. Please put me in some other cell."

He was still clinging to the warden, and that official threw his arms off roughly. Then for a time he stood looking at the cowering wretch, who seemed possessed of all the wild, unreasoning terror of a child.

"Look here, Ballard," said the warden, finally, "if you heard anything, I want to know what it was. Now tell me."

"I can't, I can't," was the reply. He was sobbing.

"Where did it come from?"

"I don't know. Everywhere—nowhere. I just heard it."

"What was it—a voice?"

"Please don't make me answer," pleaded the prisoner.

"You must answer," said the warden, sharply.

"It was a voice—but—but it wasn't human," was the sobbing reply.

"Voice, but not human?" repeated the warden, puzzled.

"It sounded muffled and—and far away—and ghostly," explained the man.

"Did it come from inside or outside the prison?"

"It didn't seem to come from anywhere—it was just here, here, everywhere. I heard it. I heard it."

For an hour the warden tried to get the story, but Ballard had become suddenly obstinate and would say nothing—only pleaded to be placed in another cell, or to have one of the jailers remain near him until daylight. These requests were gruffly refused.

"And see here," said the warden, in conclusion, "if there's any more of this screaming I'll put you in the padded cell."

Then the warden went his way, a sadly puzzled man. Ballard sat at his cell door until daylight, his face, drawn and white with terror, pressed against the bars, and looked out into the prison with wide, staring eyes.

That day, the fourth since the incarceration of The Thinking Machine, was enlivened considerably by the volunteer prisoner, who spent most of his time at the little window of his cell. He began proceedings by throwing another piece of linen down to the guard, who picked it up dutifully and took it to the warden. On it was written:

"Only three days more."

The warden was in no way surprised at what he read; he understood that The Thinking Machine meant only three days more of his imprisonment, and he regarded the note as a boast. But how was the thing written? Where had The Thinking Machine found this new piece of linen? Where? How? He carefully examined the linen. It was white, of fine texture, shirting material. He took the shirt which he had taken and carefully fitted the two original pieces of the linen to the torn places. This third piece was entirely superfluous; it didn't fit anywhere, and yet it was unmistakably the same goods.

"And where—where does he get anything to write with?" demanded the warden of the world at large.

Still later on the fourth day The Thinking Machine, through the window of his cell, spoke to the armed guard outside.

"What day of the month is it?" he asked.

"The fifteenth," was the answer.

The Thinking Machine made a mental astronomical calculation and satisfied himself that the moon would not rise until after nine o'clock that night. Then he asked another question:

"Who attends to those arc lights?"

"Man from the company."

"You have no electricians in the building?"

"No."

"I should think you could save money if you had your own man."

"None of my business," replied the guard.

The guard noticed The Thinking Machine at the cell window frequently during that day, but always the face seemed listless and there was a certain wistfulness in the squint eyes behind the glasses. After a while he accepted the presence of the leonine head as a matter of course. He had seen other prisoners do the same thing; it was the longing for the outside world.

That afternoon, just before the day guard was relieved, the head appeared at the window again, and The Thinking Machine's hand held something out between the bars. It fluttered to the ground and the guard picked it up. It was a five-dollar bill.

"That's for you," called the prisoner.

As usual, the guard took it to the warden. That gentleman looked at it suspiciously; he looked at everything that came from Cell 13 with suspicion.

"He said it was for me," explained the guard.

"It's a sort of a tip, I suppose," said the warden. "I see no particular reason why you shouldn't accept—"

Suddenly he stopped. He had remembered that The Thinking Machine had gone into Cell 13 with one five-dollar bill and two ten-dollar bills; twenty-five dollars in all. Now a five-dollar bill had been tied around the first pieces of linen that came from the cell. The warden still had it, and to convince himself he took it out and looked at it. It was five dollars; yet here was another five dollars, and The Thinking Machine had only had ten-dollar bills.

"Perhaps somebody changed one of the bills for him," he thought at last, with a sigh of relief.

But then and there he made up his mind. He would search Cell 13 as a cell was never before searched in this world. When a man could write at will, and change money, and do other wholly inexplicable things, there was something radically wrong with his prison. He planned to enter the cell at night—three o'clock would be an excellent time. The Thinking Machine must do all the weird things he did sometime. Night seemed the most reasonable.

Thus it happened that the warden stealthily descended upon Cell 13 that night at three o'clock. He paused at the door and listened. There was no sound save the steady, regular breathing of the prisoner. The keys unfastened the double locks with scarcely a clank, and the warden entered, locking the door behind him. Suddenly he flashed his dark lantern in the face of the recumbent figure.

If the warden had planned to startle The Thinking Machine he was mistaken, for that individual merely opened his eyes quietly, reached for his glasses and inquired, in a most matter-of-fact tone:

"Who is it?"

It would be useless to describe the search that the warden made. It was minute. Not one inch of the cell or the bed was overlooked. He found the round hole in the floor, and with a flash of inspiration thrust his thick fingers into it. After a moment of fumbling there he drew up something and looked at it in the light of his lantern.

"Ugh!" he exclaimed.

The thing he had taken out was a rat—a dead rat. His inspiration fled as a mist before the sun. But he continued the search. The Thinking Machine, without a word, arose and kicked the rat out of the cell into the corridor.

The warden climbed on the bed and tried the steel bars in the tiny window. They were perfectly rigid; every bar of the door was the same.

Then the warden searched the prisoner's clothing, beginning at the shoes. Nothing hidden in them! Then the trousers waist-band. Still nothing! Then the pockets of the trousers. From one side he drew out some paper money and examined it.

"Five one-dollar bills," he gasped.

"That's right," said the prisoner.

"But the—you had two tens and a five—what the—how do you do it?"

"That's my business," said The Thinking Machine.

"Did any of my men change the money for you—on your word of honor?"

The Thinking Machine paused just a fraction of a second.

"No," he said.

"Well, do you make it?" asked the warden. He was prepared to believe anything.

"That's my business," again said the prisoner.

The warden glared at the eminent scientist fiercely. He felt—he knew—that this man was making a fool of him, yet he didn't know how. If he were a real prisoner he would get the truth—but, then, perhaps, those inexplicable things which had happened would not have been brought before him so sharply. Neither of the men spoke for a long time, then suddenly the warden turned fiercely and left the cell, slamming the door behind him. He didn't dare to speak, then.

He glanced at the clock. It was ten minutes to four. He had hardly settled himself in bed when again came that heartbreaking shriek through the prison. With a few muttered words, which, while not elegant, were highly expressive, he relighted his lantern and rushed through the prison again to the cell on the upper floor.

Again Ballard was crushing himself against the steel door, shrieking, shrieking at the top of his voice. He stopped only when the warden flashed his lamp in the cell.

"Take me out, take me out," he screamed.

"I did it, I did it, I killed her. Take it away."

"Take what away?" asked the warden.

"I threw the acid in her face—I did it—I confess. Take me out of here."

Ballard's condition was pitiable; it was only an act of mercy to let him out into the corridor. There he crouched in a corner, like an animal at bay, and clasped his hands to his ears. It took half an hour to calm him sufficiently for him to speak. Then he told incoherently what had happened. On the night before at four o'clock he had heard a voice—a sepulchral voice, muffled and wailing in tone.

"What did it say?" asked the warden, curiously.

"Acid—acid—acid!" gasped the prisoner. "It accused me. Acid! I threw the acid, and the woman died. Oh!" It was a long, shuddering wail of terror.

"Acid?" echoed the warden, puzzled. The case was beyond him.

"Acid. That's all I heard—that one word, repeated several times. There were other things, too, but I didn't hear them."

"That was last night, eh?" asked the warden. "What happened tonight—what frightened you just now?"

"It was the same thing," gasped the prisoner. "Acid—acid—acid!" He covered his face with his hands and sat shivering. "It was acid I used on her, but I didn't mean to kill her. I just heard the words. It was something accusing me—accusing me." He mumbled, and was silent.

"Did you hear anything else?"

"Yes—but I couldn't understand—only a little bit—just a word or two."

"Well, what was it?"

"I heard 'acid' three times, then I heard a long, moaning sound, then—then—I heard 'No. 8 hat.' I heard that twice."

"No. 8 hat," repeated the warden. "What the devil—No. 8 hat? Accusing voices of conscience have never talked about No. 8 hats, so far as I ever heard."

"He's insane," said one of the jailers, with an air of finality.

"I believe you," said the warden. "He must be. He probably heard something and got frightened. He's trembling now. No. 8 hat! What the—"

When the fifth day of The Thinking Machine's imprisonment rolled around the warden was wearing a hunted look. He was anxious for the end of the thing. He could not help but feel that his distinguished prisoner had been amusing himself. And if this were so, The Thinking Machine had lost none of his sense of humor. For on this fifth day he flung down another linen note to the outside guard, bearing the words: "Only two days more." Also he flung down a half dollar.

Now the warden knew—he *knew*—that the man in Cell 13 didn't have any half dollars—he *couldn't* have any half dollars, no more than he could have pen and ink and linen, and yet he did have them. It was a condition, not a theory; that is one reason why the warden was wearing a hunted look.

That ghastly, uncanny thing, too, about "Acid" and "No. 8 hat" clung to him tenaciously. They didn't mean anything, of course, merely the ravings of an insane murderer who had been driven by fear to confess his crime, still there were so many things that "didn't mean anything" happening in the prison now since The Thinking Machine was there.

On the sixth day the warden received a postal stating that Dr. Ransome and Mr. Fielding would be at Chisholm Prison on the following evening, Thursday, and in the event Professor Van Dusen had not yet escaped—and they presumed he had not because they had not heard from him—they would meet him there.

"In the event he had not yet escaped!" The warden smiled grimly. Escaped!

The Thinking Machine enlivened this day for the warden with three notes. They were on the usual linen and bore generally on the appointment at half past eight o'clock Thursday night, which appointment the scientist had made at the time of his imprisonment.

On the afternoon of the seventh day the warden passed Cell 13 and glanced in. The Thinking Machine was lying on the iron bed, apparently sleeping lightly. The cell appeared precisely as it always did from a casual glance. The warden would swear that no man was going to leave it between that hour—it was then four o'clock—and half past eight o'clock that evening.

On his way back past the cell the warden heard the steady breathing again, and coming close to the door looked in. He wouldn't have done so if The Thinking Machine had been looking, but now—well, it was different.

A ray of light came through the high window and fell on the face of the sleeping man. It occurred to the warden for the first time that his prisoner appeared haggard and weary. Just then The Thinking Machine stirred slightly and the warden hurried on up the corridor guiltily. That evening after six o'clock he saw the jailer.

"Everything all right in Cell 13?" he asked.

"Yes, sir," replied the jailer. "He didn't eat much, though."

It was with a feeling of having done his duty that the warden received Dr. Ransome and Mr. Fielding shortly after seven o'clock. He intended to show them the full story of his woes, which was a long one. But before this came to pass the guard from the river side of the prison yard entered the office.

"The arc light in my side of the yard won't light," he informed the warden.

"Confound it, that man's a hoodoo," thundered the official. "Everything has happened since he's been here."

The guard went back to his post in the darkness, and the warden phoned to the electric light company.

"This is Chisholm Prison," he said through the phone. "Send three or four men down here quick, to fix an arc light."

The reply was evidently satisfactory, for the warden hung up the receiver and passed out into the yard. While Dr. Ransome and Mr. Fielding sat waiting the guard at the outer gate came in with a special delivery letter. Dr. Ransome happened to notice the address, and, when the guard went out, looked at the letter more closely.

"By George!" he exclaimed.

"What is it?" asked Mr. Fielding.

Silently the doctor offered the letter. Mr. Fielding examined it closely.

"Coincidence," he said. "It must be."

It was nearly eight o'clock when the warden returned to his office. The electricians had arrived in a wagon, and were now at work. The warden pressed the buzz-button communicating with the man at the outer gate in the wall.

"How many electricians came in?" he asked, over the short phone. "Four? Three workmen in jumpers and overalls and the manager? Frock coat and silk hat? All right. Be certain that only four go out. That's all."

He turned to Dr. Ransome and Mr. Fielding.

"We have to be careful here—particularly," and there was broad sarcasm in his

tone, "since we have scientists locked up."

The warden picked up the special delivery letter carelessly, and then began to open it.

"When I read this I want to tell you gentlemen something about how— Great Caesar!" he ended, suddenly, as he glanced at the letter. He sat with mouth open, motionless, from astonishment.

"What is it?" asked Mr. Fielding.

"A special delivery letter from Cell 13," gasped the warden. "An invitation to supper."

"What?" and the two others arose, unanimously.

The warden sat dazed, staring at the letter for a moment, then called sharply to a guard outside in the corridor.

"Run down to Cell 13 and see if that man's in there."

The guard went as directed, while Dr. Ransome and Mr. Fielding examined the letter.

"It's Van Dusen's handwriting; there's no question of that," said Dr. Ransome. "I've seen too much of it."

Just then the buzz on the telephone from the outer gate sounded, and the warden, in a semi-trance, picked up the receiver.

"Hello! Two reporters, eh? Let 'em come in." He turned suddenly to the doctor and Mr. Fielding. "Why, the man *can't* be out. He must be in his cell."

Just at that moment the guard returned.

"He's still in his cell, sir," he reported. "I saw him. He's lying down."

"There, I told you so," said the warden, and he breathed freely again. "But how did he mail that letter?"

There was a rap on the steel door which led from the jail yard into the warden's office.

"It's the reporters," said the warden. "Let them in," he instructed the guard; then to the two other gentlemen: "Don't say anything about this before them, because I'd never hear the last of it."

The door opened, and the two men from the front gate entered.

"Good evening, gentlemen," said one. That was Hutchinson Hatch; the warden knew him well.

"Well?" demanded the other, irritably. "I'm here."

That was The Thinking Machine. He squinted belligerently at the warden, who sat with mouth agape. For the moment that official had nothing to say. Dr. Ransome and Mr. Fielding were amazed, but they didn't know what the warden knew. They were only amazed; he was paralyzed. Hutchinson Hatch, the reporter, took in the scene with greedy eyes.

"How—how—how did you do it?" gasped the warden, finally.

"Come back to the cell," said The Thinking Machine, in the irritated voice which his scientific associates knew so well.

The warden, still in a condition bordering on trance, led the way.

"Flash your light in there," directed The Thinking Machine.

The warden did so. There was nothing unusual in the appearance of the cell, and there—there on the bed lay the figure of The Thinking Machine. Certainly! There was the yellow hair! Again the warden looked at the man beside him and wondered at the strangeness of his own dreams.

With trembling hands he unlocked the cell door and The Thinking Machine passed inside.

"See here," he said.

He kicked at the steel bars in the bottom of the cell door and three of them were pushed out of place. A fourth broke off and rolled away in the corridor.

"And here, too," directed the erstwhile prisoner as he stood on the bed to reach the small window. He swept his hand across the opening and every bar came out.

"What's this in bed?" demanded the warden, who was slowly recovering.

"A wig," was the reply. "Turn down the cover."

The warden did so. Beneath it lay a large coil of strong rope, thirty feet or more, a dagger, three files, ten feet of electric wire, a thin, powerful pair of steel pliers, a small tack hammer with its handle, and—and a derringer pistol.

"How did you do it?" demanded the warden.

"You gentlemen have an engagement to supper with me at half past nine o'clock," said The Thinking Machine. "Come on, or we shall be late."

"But how did you do it?" insisted the warden.

"Don't ever think you can hold any man who can use his brain," said The Thinking Machine. "Come on; we shall be late."

It was an impatient supper party in the rooms of Professor Van Dusen and a somewhat silent one. The guests were Dr. Ransome, Alfred Fielding, the warden, and

Hutchinson Hatch, reporter. The meal was served to the minute, in accordance with Professor Van Dusen's instructions of one week before; Dr. Ransome found the artichokes delicious. At last the supper was finished and The Thinking Machine turned full on Dr. Ransome and squinted at him fiercely.

"Do you believe it now?" he demanded.

"I do," replied Dr. Ransome.

"Do you admit that it was a fair test?"

"I do."

With the others, particularly the warden, he was waiting anxiously for the explanation.

"Suppose you tell us how—" began Mr. Fielding.

"Yes, tell us how," said the warden.

The Thinking Machine readjusted his glasses, took a couple of preparatory squints at his audience, and began the story. He told it from the beginning logically; and no man ever talked to more interested listeners.

"My agreement was," he began, "to go into a cell, carrying nothing except what was necessary to wear, and to leave that cell within a week. I had never seen Chisholm Prison. When I went into the cell I asked for tooth powder, two ten- and one five-dollar bills, and also to have my shoes blacked. Even if these requests had been refused it would not have mattered seriously. But you agreed to them.

"I knew there would be nothing in the cell which you thought I might use to advantage. So when the warden locked the door on me I was apparently helpless, unless I could turn three seemingly innocent things to use. They were things which would have been permitted any prisoner under sentence of death, were they not, warden?"

"Tooth powder and polished shoes, yes, but not money," replied the warden.

"Anything is dangerous in the hands of a man who knows how to use it," went on The Thinking Machine. "I did nothing that first night but sleep and chase rats." He glared at the warden. "When the matter was broached I knew I could do nothing that night, so suggested next day. You gentlemen thought I wanted time to arrange an escape with outside assistance, but this was not true. I knew I could communicate with whom I pleased, when I pleased."

The warden stared at him a moment, then went on smoking solemnly.

"I was aroused next morning at six o'clock by the jailer with my breakfast," continued the scientist. "He told me dinner was at twelve and supper at six. Between these times, I gathered, I would be pretty much to myself. So immediately after breakfast I examined my outside surroundings from my cell window. One look told me it would be useless to try to scale the wall, even should I decide to leave my cell by the window, for my purpose was to leave not only the cell, but the prison. Of course, I could have gone over the wall, but it would have taken me longer to lay my plans that way. Therefore, for the moment, I dismissed all idea of that.

"From this first observation I knew the river was on that side of the prison, and that there was also a playground there. Subsequently these surmises were verified by a keeper. I knew then one important thing—that anyone might approach the prison wall from that side if necessary without attracting any particular attention. That was well to remember. I remembered it.

"But the outside thing which most attracted my attention was the feed wire to the arc light which ran within a few feet—probably three or four—of my cell window. I knew that would be valuable in the event

I found it necessary to cut off that arc light."

"Oh, you shut it off tonight, then?" asked the warden.

"Having learned all I could from that window," resumed The Thinking Machine, without heeding the interruption, "I considered the idea of escaping through the prison proper. I recalled just how I had come into the cell, which I knew would be the only way. Seven doors lay between me and the outside. So, also for the time being, I gave up the idea of escaping that way. And I couldn't go through the solid granite walls of the cell."

The Thinking Machine paused for a moment and Dr. Ransome lighted a new cigar. For several minutes there was silence, then the scientific jailbreaker went on:

"While I was thinking about these things a rat ran across my foot. It suggested a new line of thought. There were at least half a dozen rats in the cell—I could see their beady eyes. Yet I had noticed none come under the cell door. I frightened them purposely and watched the cell door to see if they went out that way. They did not, but they were gone. Obviously they went another way. Another way meant another opening.

"I searched for this opening and found it. It was an old drainpipe, long unused and partly choked with dirt and dust. But this was the way the rats had come. They came from somewhere. Where? Drainpipes usually lead outside prison grounds. This one probably led to the river, or near it. The rats must therefore come from that direction. If they came a part of the way, I reasoned that they came all the way, because it was extremely unlikely that a solid iron or lead pipe would have any hole in it except at the exit.

"When the jailer came with my luncheon he told me two important things, although he didn't know it. One was that a new system

of plumbing had been put in the prison seven years before; another that the river was only three hundred feet away. Then I knew positively that the pipe was a part of an old system; I knew, too, that it slanted generally toward the river. But did the pipe end in the water or on land?

"This was the next question to be decided. I decided it by catching several of the rats in the cell. My jailer was surprised to see me engaged in this work. I examined at least a dozen of them. They were perfectly dry; they had come through the pipe, and, most important of all, they were *not house rats, but field rats*. The other end of the pipe was on land, then, outside the prison walls. So far, so good.

"Then, I knew that if I worked freely from this point I must attract the warden's attention in another direction. You see, by telling the warden that I had come there to escape you made the test more severe, because I had to trick him by false scents."

The warden looked up with a sad expression in his eyes.

"The first thing was to make him think I was trying to communicate with you, Dr. Ransome. So I wrote a note on a piece of linen I tore from my shirt, addressed it to Dr. Ransome, tied a five-dollar bill around it and threw it out the window. I knew the guard would take it to the warden, but I rather hoped the warden would send it as addressed. Have you that first linen note, warden?"

The warden produced the cipher.

"What the deuce does it mean, anyhow?" he asked.

"Read it backward, beginning with the 'T' signature and disregard the division into words," instructed The Thinking Machine.

The warden did so.

"*T-h-i-s*, this," he spelled, studied it a moment, then read it off, grinning:

"This is not the way I intend to escape."

"Well, now what do you think o' that?" he demanded, still grinning.

"I knew that would attract your attention, just as it did," said The Thinking Machine, "and if you really found out what it was it would be a sort of gentle rebuke."

"What did you write it with?" asked Dr. Ransome, after he had examined the linen and passed it to Mr. Fielding.

"This," said the erstwhile prisoner, and he extended his foot. On it was the shoe he had worn in prison, though the polish was gone—scraped off clean. "The shoe blacking, moistened with water, was my ink; the metal tip of the shoelace made a fairly good pen."

The warden looked up and suddenly burst into a laugh, half of relief, half of amusement.

"You're a wonder," he said, admiringly. "Go on."

"That precipitated a search of my cell by the warden, as I had intended," continued The Thinking Machine. "I was anxious to get the warden into the habit of searching my cell, so that finally, constantly finding nothing, he would get disgusted and quit. This at last happened, practically."

The warden blushed.

"He then took my white shirt away and gave me a prison shirt. He was satisfied that those two pieces of the shirt were all that was missing. But while he was searching my cell I had another piece of that same shirt, about nine inches square, rolled into a small ball in my mouth."

"Nine inches of that shirt?" demanded the warden. "Where did it come from?"

"The bosoms of all stiff white shirts are of triple thickness," was the explanation. "I tore out the inside thickness, leaving the bosom only two thicknesses. I knew you wouldn't see it. So much for that."

There was a little pause, and the warden looked from one to another of the men with a sheepish grin.

"Having disposed of the warden for the time being by giving him something else to think about, I took my first serious step toward freedom," said Professor Van Dusen. "I knew, within reason, that the pipe led somewhere to the playground outside; I knew a great many boys played there; I knew that rats came into my cell from out there. Could I communicate with someone outside with these things at hand?

"First was necessary, I saw, a long and fairly reliable thread, so—but here," he pulled up his trousers legs and showed that the tops of both stockings, of fine, strong lisle, were gone. I unraveled those—after I got them started it wasn't difficult—and I had easily a quarter of a mile of thread that I could depend on.

"Then on half of my remaining linen I wrote, laboriously enough I assure you, a letter explaining my situation to this gentleman here," and he indicated Hutchinson Hatch. "I knew he would assist me—for the value of the newspaper story. I tied firmly to this linen letter a ten-dollar bill—there is no surer way of attracting the eye of anyone—and wrote on the linen: 'Finder of this deliver to Hutchinson Hatch, *Daily American,* who will give another ten dollars for the information.'

"The next thing was to get this note outside on that playground where a boy might find it. There were two ways, but I chose the best. I took one of the rats—I became adept in catching them—tied the linen and money firmly to one leg, fastened my lisle thread to another, and turned him loose in the drainpipe. I reasoned that the natural fright of the rodent would make him run until he was outside the pipe and then out on earth he would probably stop to gnaw off the linen and money.

"From the moment the rat disappeared into that dusty pipe I became anxious. I was taking so many chances. The rat might gnaw the string, of which I held one end; other rats might gnaw it; the rat might run out of the pipe and leave the linen and money where they would never be found; a thousand other things might have happened. So began some nervous hours, but the fact that the rat ran on until only a few feet of the string remained in my cell made me think he was outside the pipe. I had carefully instructed Mr. Hatch what to do in case the note reached him. The question was: Would it reach him?

"This done, I could only wait and make other plans in case this one failed. I openly attempted to bribe my jailer, and learned from him that he held the keys to only two of seven doors between me and freedom. Then I did something else to make the warden nervous. I took the steel supports out of the heels of my shoes and made a pretense of sawing the bars of my cell window. The warden raised a pretty row about that. He developed, too, the habit of shaking the bars of my cell window to see if they were solid. They were—then."

Again the warden grinned. He had ceased being astonished.

"With this one plan I had done all I could and could only wait to see what happened," the scientist went on. "I couldn't know whether my note had been delivered or even found, or whether the mouse had gnawed it up. And I didn't dare to draw back through the pipe that one slender thread which connected me with the outside.

"When I went to bed that night I didn't sleep, for fear there would come the slight signal twitch at the thread which was to tell me that Mr. Hatch had received the note. At half past three o'clock, I judge, I felt this twitch, and no prisoner actually under sentence of death ever welcomed a thing more heartily."

The Thinking Machine stopped and turned to the reporter.

"You'd better explain just what you did," he said.

"The linen note was brought to me by a small boy who had been playing baseball," said Mr. Hatch. "I immediately saw a big story in it, so I gave the boy another ten dollars, and got several spools of silk, some twine, and a roll of light, pliable wire. The professor's note suggested that I have the finder of the note show me just where it was picked up, and told me to make my search from there, beginning at two o'clock in the morning. If I found the other end of the thread I was to twitch it gently three times, then a fourth.

"I began the search with a small-bulb electric light. It was an hour and twenty minutes before I found the end of the drainpipe, half hidden in weeds. The pipe was very large there, say twelve inches across. Then I found the end of the lisle thread, twitched it as directed and immediately I got an answering twitch.

"Then I fastened the silk to this and Professor Van Dusen began to pull it into his cell. I nearly had heart disease for fear the string would break. To the end of the silk I fastened the twine, and when that had been pulled in I tied on the wire. Then that was drawn into the pipe and we had a substantial line, which rats couldn't gnaw, from the mouth of the drain into the cell."

The Thinking Machine raised his hand and Hatch stopped.

"All this was done in absolute silence," said the scientist. "But when the wire reached my hand I could have shouted. Then we tried another experiment, which Mr. Hatch was prepared for. We tested the pipe as a speaking tube. Neither of us could hear very clearly, but I dared not speak loud for fear of attracting attention in the prison. At last I made him understand what I wanted immediately. He seemed to have great difficulty in understanding when I asked for nitric acid, and I repeated the word 'acid' several times.

"Then I heard a shriek from a cell above me. I knew instantly that someone had overheard, and when I heard you coming, Mr. Warden, I feigned sleep. If you had entered my cell at that moment that whole plan of escape would have ended there. But you passed on. That was the nearest I ever came to being caught.

"Having established this improvised trolley it is easy to see how I got things in the cell and made them disappear at will. I merely dropped them back into the pipe. You, Mr. Warden, could not have reached the connecting wire with your fingers; they are too large. My fingers, you see, are longer and more slender. In addition I guarded the top of that pipe with a rat—you remember how."

"I remember," said the warden, with a grimace.

"I thought that if anyone were tempted to investigate that hole the rat would dampen his ardor. Mr. Hatch could not send me anything useful through the pipe until next night, although he did send me change for ten dollars as a test, so I proceeded with other parts of my plan. Then I evolved the method of escape which I finally employed.

"In order to carry this out successfully it was necessary for the guard in the yard to get accustomed to seeing me at the cell window.

I arranged this by dropping linen notes to him, boastful in tone, to make the warden believe, if possible, one of his assistants was communicating with the outside for me. I would stand at my window for hours gazing out, so the guard could see, and occasionally I spoke to him. In that way I learned that the prison had no electricians of its own, but was dependent upon the lighting company if anything should go wrong.

"That cleared the way to freedom perfectly. Early in the evening of the last day of my imprisonment, when it was dark, I planned to cut the feed wire which was only a few feet from my window, reaching it with an acid-tipped wire I had. That would make that side of the prison perfectly dark while the electricians were searching for the break. That would also bring Mr. Hatch into the prison yard.

"There was only one more thing to do before I actually began the work of setting myself free. This was to arrange final details with Mr. Hatch through our speaking tube. I did this within half an hour after the warden left my cell on the fourth night of my imprisonment. Mr. Hatch again had serious difficulty in understanding me, and I repeated the word 'acid' to him several times, and later on the words: 'No. 8 hat'—that's my size—and these were the things which made a prisoner upstairs confess to murder, so one of the jailers told me next day. This prisoner heard our voices, confused of course, through the pipe, which also went to his cell. The cell directly over me was not occupied, hence no one else heard.

"Of course the actual work of cutting the steel bars out of the window and door was comparatively easy with nitric acid, which I got through the pipe in tin bottles, but it took time. Hour after hour on the fifth and sixth and seventh days the guard below was looking at me as I worked on the bars of the window with the acid on a piece of wire. I used the tooth powder to prevent the acid spreading. I looked away abstractedly as I worked and each minute the acid cut deeper into the metal. I noticed that the jailers always tried the door by shaking the upper part, never the lower bars, therefore I cut the lower bars, leaving them hanging in place by thin strips of metal. But that was a bit of daredeviltry. I could not have gone that way so easily."

The Thinking Machine sat silent for several minutes.

"I think that makes everything clear," he went on. "Whatever points I have not explained were merely to confuse the warden and jailers. These things in my bed I brought in to please Mr. Hatch, who wanted to improve the story. Of course, the wig was necessary in my plan. The special delivery letter I wrote and directed in my cell with Mr. Hatch's fountain pen, then sent it out to him and he mailed it. That's all, I think."

"But your actually leaving the prison grounds and then coming in through the outer gate to my office?" asked the warden.

"Perfectly simple," said the scientist. "I cut the electric light wire with acid, as I said, when the current was off. Therefore when the current was turned on the arc didn't light. I knew it would take some time to find out what was the matter and make repairs. When the guard went to report to you, the yard was dark. I crept out the window—it was a tight fit, too—replaced the bars by standing on a narrow ledge and remained in a shadow until the force of electricians arrived. Mr. Hatch was one of them.

"When I saw him I spoke and he handed me a cap, a jumper and overalls, which I put on within ten feet of you, Mr. Warden, while you were in the yard. Later Mr. Hatch called me, presumably as a workman, and together we went out the gate to get something out of the wagon. The gate guard let us pass out readily as two workmen who had just passed in. We changed our clothing and reappeared, asking to see you. We saw you. That's all."

There was silence for several minutes. Dr. Ransome was first to speak.

"Wonderful!" he exclaimed. "Perfectly amazing."

"How did Mr. Hatch happen to come with the electricians?" asked Mr. Fielding.

"His father is manager of the company," replied The Thinking Machine.

"But what if there had been no Mr. Hatch outside to help?"

"Every prisoner has one friend outside who would help him escape if he could."

"Suppose—just suppose—there had been no plumbing system there?" asked the warden, curiously.

"There were two other ways out," said The Thinking Machine, enigmatically.

Ten minutes later the telephone bell rang. It was a request for the warden.

"Light all right, eh?" the warden asked, through the phone. "Good. Wire cut beside Cell 13? Yes, I know. One electrician too many? What's that? Two came out?"

The warden turned to the others with a puzzled expression.

"He only let in four electricians, he has let out two and says there are three left."

"I was the odd one," said The Thinking Machine.

"Oh," said the warden. "I see." Then through the phone: "Let the fifth man go. He's all right."

1. Which aspects of Van Dusen's personality aid him in his escape? Why is it important for the reader to be aware of these traits and abilities at the beginning of the story?

2. Explain the conditions of Van Dusen's test. What three requests does he make before he enters the cell?

3. Why does Van Dusen drop the coded message, try to bribe a guard, and try to file his prison bars?

4. How does Van Dusen use the elements in his surroundings to make his escape?

5. Suspense is maintained in this story not only because the escape seems impossible, but also because there are many unexpected surprises. What are these surprises?

6. What type of conflict is in this story (person against person or person against nature)? Whom or what is the conflict between?

7. This story was written from the omniscient point of view in which the author told anything he wanted to about any of the characters. How would the story have been different if it had been written from the third person limited point of view—from only Van Dusen's point of view?

Vocabulary

Context clues are hints that are given by surrounding words about the general meaning of an unfamiliar word. There are many different kinds of context clues. One of them is the WORD-SERIES CONTEXT CLUE. This is a list of three or more words placed together, one after another. For example:

George enjoyed playing *tennis, baseball,* and *quoits.*

Like other context clues, word-series context clues do not give exact meanings, but they do tell you in what general category of meaning a word belongs. In the sentence above, the familiar words *tennis* and *baseball* show that the unfamiliar word *quoits* must also be a sport or a game.

Here is another example:

Hank was *arrested, taken to police headquarters,* and *incarcerated.*

The word series in this sentence does not tell you whether *incarcerated* means "registered," "questioned," or "jailed." It does tell you, however, that *incarcerated* fits into the category of things that happen to people who get into trouble with the law. (The actual meaning of *incarcerated* is "imprisoned.")

Use word-series context clues to figure out the category of meaning for each *italicized* word below. On a separate sheet of paper, list each word-series and give the general category to which the word belongs. Write your answers this way:

tennis, baseball, quoits—games or sports

1. The Thinking Machine always seemed to speak impatiently, irritably, and *petulantly.*

2. "I have done more ridiculous, unreasonable, outrageous, and even *asinine* things than this," said Professor Van Dusen.

3. On the night before, at four o'clock, Ballard had heard a muffled, hollow, *sepulchral* voice wailing.

4. The note was meant to serve as a correction or criticism, a mild *rebuke,* to anyone who figured out its meaning.

5. No one else could have imagined or suspected, much less *surmised,* how the escape had been carried out.

Jacques Futrelle 1875—1912

Jacques Futrelle was born in Pike County, Georgia. While still in his twenties, he was a theatrical manager and worked as an editor for the *Boston American.* Futrelle's Thinking Machine, an amusingly clever and eccentric character, made his first appearance in the closing chapters of *The Chase of the Golden Plate.* Short stories about Augustus S.F.X. Van Dusen kept appearing in popular magazines until collected and published under the title of *The Thinking Machine.* Later the book was reissued as *The Problem of Cell 13,* the title of the first and best-known story in the collection. Futrelle died a heroic and tragic death in the *Titanic* catastrophe in 1912.

3 PLOT

Discussion

1. Which short stories in this unit are based on a conflict between persons? State the main characters involved in each conflict. Then briefly describe the nature of the conflict.

2. Setting can be an important part of the plot. An example of this is the sunless landscape on Venus in "All Summer in a Day." Explain how setting is also an essential part of the plot in other stories in this unit.

3. Explain how one event in some of the stories in this unit is the cause of other events. For example, Aunt Gertrude's wishes caused changes in Matilda's life in "All You've Ever Wanted."

4. Which other story in this unit, besides "All You've Ever Wanted," has elements of fantasy in it? What are those elements? Which story from this unit is the closest to reality? Explain why.

5. The story, "Without Words," is written from the third person limited point of view—from Jan's point of view. Which stories in this unit use first person point of view? Which stories use omniscient point of view in which the readers are told the thoughts and feelings of more than one major character?

Composition

1. Choose the story in this unit which you enjoyed the most, and write a brief summary of the plot. Then analyze the plot by discussing its major parts. For example: What is the story's conflict and whom is the conflict between? What problems stand in the way of the main character's resolving the conflict? What is the climax or turning point? How does the story conclude? In a final paragraph, tell how the plot captured and held your interest.

2. Now it is your turn to be an author. You do not have to write a whole short story, though. All you have to do is come up with a plot for a short story. Begin by writing a brief description of the setting. Does your story take place in a real or imaginary world? Who is the main character? Write a description of your character's physical appearance and personality. Next decide on a conflict. Whom will the main character confront? List some problems the main character will have to solve. Then briefly describe the climax of the story.

4

CONVERSATIONS *Ben Shahn* 1958 Collection, the Whitney Museum of American Art

Characterization

CHARACTERIZATION

Characters in stories are as different as people in real life. They vary in size, shape, age, and personality. Some are even like superheroes who seem almost perfect. In this unit you will meet some of these different kinds of people. You will also get to know them quite well in just a few pages. That's because authors have three ways to reveal a character's appearance and personality:

—by what they say directly about the character.
—by what the character actually does, says, or thinks.
—by what other characters do, say, or think about
the character.

It is because of these methods that you can often get to know a character in a story much better and much quicker than you can someone in real life. As a result, you probably will be able to actually feel some of the emotions of the characters. For example, you will understand the frustration of the boy who is told by his boss to do something he knows is wrong. You might even feel the shame of the boy who is embarrassed by his mother. The characters in this unit will strike you as realistic or fanciful, but they will all be unique personalities who will live in your imagination as you read their stories.

He knew what the boss told him to do was wrong, but he needed the job. What should he do?

Say It with Flowers

TOSHIO MORI

HE WAS A STRANGE ONE to come to the shop and ask Mr. Sasaki for a job, but at the time I kept my mouth shut. There was something about this young man's appearance which I could not altogether harmonize with a job as a clerk in a flower shop. I was a delivery boy for Mr. Sasaki then. I had seen clerks come and go, and although they were of various sorts of temperaments and conducts, all of them had the technique of waiting on the customers or acquired one eventually. You could never tell about a new one, however, and to be on the safe side I said nothing and watched our boss readily take on this young man. Anyhow we were glad to have an extra hand because the busy season was coming around.

Mr. Sasaki undoubtedly remembered last year's rush when Tommy, Mr. Sasaki, and I had to do everything and had our hands tied behind our backs from having so many things to do at one time. He wanted to be ready this time. "Another clerk and we'll be all set for any kind of business," he used to tell us. When Teruo came around looking for a job, he got it, and Morning Glory Flower Shop was all set for the year as far as our boss was concerned.

When Teruo reported for work the following morning Mr. Sasaki left him in Tommy's hands. Tommy had been our number one clerk for a long time.

"Tommy, teach him all you can," Mr. Sasaki said. "Teruo's going to be with us from now on."

"Sure," Tommy said.

"Tommy's a good florist. You watch and listen to him," the boss told the young man.

"All right, Mr. Sasaki," the young man said. He turned to us and said, "My name is Teruo." We shook hands.

We got to know one another pretty well after that. He was a quiet fellow with very little words for anybody, but his smile disarmed a person. We soon learned that he knew nothing about the florist business. He could identify a rose when he saw one, and gardenias and carnations too; but other flowers and materials were new to him.

"You fellows teach me something about this business and I'll be grateful. I want to start from the bottom," Teruo said.

Tommy and I nodded. We were pretty sure by then he was all right. Tommy eagerly went about showing Teruo the florist game. Every morning for several days Tommy repeated the prices of the flowers for him. He told Teruo what to do on telephone orders; how to keep the greens fresh; how to make bouquets, corsages, and sprays. "You need a little more time to learn how to make big funeral pieces," Tommy said. "That'll come later."

In a couple of weeks Teruo was just as good a clerk as we had had in a long time. He was curious almost to a fault, and was a glutton for work. It was about this time our boss decided to move ahead his yearly business trip to Seattle. Undoubtedly he was satisfied with Teruo, and he knew we could get along without him for a while. He went off and left Tommy in full charge.

During Mr. Sasaki's absence I was often in the shop helping Tommy and Teruo with the customers and the orders. One day Teruo learned that I once worked in the nursery and had experience in flower-growing.

"How do you tell when a flower is fresh or old?" he asked me. "I can't tell one from the other. All I do is follow your instructions and sell the ones you tell me to sell first, but I can't tell one from the other."

I laughed. "You don't need to know that, Teruo," I told him. "When the customers ask you whether the flowers are fresh, say firmly, 'Our flowers are always fresh, madam.'"

Teruo picked up a vase of carnations. "These flowers came in four or five days ago, didn't they?" he asked me.

"You're right. Five days ago," I said.

"How long will they keep if a customer bought them today?" Teruo asked.

"I guess in this weather they'll hold a day or two," I said.

"Then they're old," Teruo almost gasped. "Why, we have fresh ones that last a week or so in the shop."

"Sure, Teruo. And why should you worry about that?" Tommy said. "You talk right to the customers and they'll believe you. 'Our flowers are always fresh? You bet they are! Just came in a little while ago from the market.'"

Teruo looked at us calmly. "That's a hard thing to say when you know it isn't true."

"You've got to get it over with sooner or later," I told him. "Everybody has to do it. You, too, unless you want to lose your job."

"I don't think I can say it convincingly again," Teruo said. "I must've said yes forty times already when I didn't know any better. It'll be harder next time."

"You've said it forty times already so why can't you say yes forty million times more? What's the difference? Remember, Teruo, it's your business to live," Tommy said.

"I don't like it," Teruo said.

"Do we like it? Do you think we're any different from you?" Tommy asked Teruo. "You're just a green kid. You don't know any better so I don't get sore, but you got to play the game when you're in it. You understand, don't you?"

Teruo nodded. For a moment he stood and looked curiously at us for the first time, and then went away to water the potted plants.

In the ensuing weeks we watched Teruo develop into a slick salesclerk but for one thing. If a customer forgot to ask about the condition of the flowers Teruo did splendidly. But if someone should mention about the freshness of the flowers he wilted right in front of the customers. Sometimes he would splutter. He would stand gaping speechless on other occasions without a comeback. Sometimes, looking embarrassedly at us, he would take the customers to the fresh flowers in the rear and complete the sales.

"Don't do that any more, Teruo,"

Tommy warned him one afternoon after watching him repeatedly sell the fresh ones. "You know we got plenty of the old stuff in the front. We can't throw all that stuff away. First thing you know the boss'll start losing money and we'll all be thrown out."

"I wish . . . I could sell like you," Teruo said. "Whenever they ask me, 'Is this fresh?' 'How long will it keep?' I lose all sense about selling the stuff, and begin to think of the difference between the fresh and the old stuff. Then the trouble begins."

"Remember, the boss has to run the shop so he can keep it going," Tommy told him. "When he returns next week you better not let him see you touch the fresh flowers in the rear."

On the day Mr. Sasaki came back to the shop we saw something unusual. For the first time I watched Teruo sell some old stuff to a customer. I heard the man plainly ask him if the flowers would keep good, and very clearly I heard Teruo reply, "Yes, sir. These flowers'll keep good." I looked at Tommy, and he winked back. When Teruo came back to make it into a bouquet he looked as if he had a snail in his mouth. Mr. Sasaki came back to the rear and watched him make the bouquet. When Teruo went up front to complete the sale Mr. Sasaki looked at Tommy and nodded approvingly.

When I went out to the truck to make my last delivery for the day Teruo followed me. "Gee, I feel rotten," he said to me. "Those flowers I sold to the people, they won't last longer than tomorrow. I feel lousy. I'm lousy. The people'll get to know my word pretty soon."

"Forget it," I said. "Quit worrying. What's the matter with you?"

"I'm lousy," he said, and went back to the store.

Then one early morning the inevitable happened. While Teruo was selling the fresh flowers in the back to a customer Mr. Sasaki came in quietly and watched the transaction. The boss didn't say anything at the time. All day Teruo looked sick. He didn't know whether to explain to the boss or shut up.

While Teruo was out to lunch Mr. Sasaki called us aside. "How long has this been going on?" he asked us. He was pretty sore.

"He's been doing it off and on. We told him to quit it," Tommy said. "He says he feels rotten selling old flowers."

"Old flowers!" snorted Mr. Sasaki. "I'll tell him plenty when he comes back. Old flowers! Maybe you can call them old at the wholesale market but they're not old in a flower shop."

"He feels guilty fooling the customers," Tommy explained.

The boss laughed impatiently. "That's no reason for a businessman."

When Teruo came back he knew what was up. He looked at us for a moment and then went about cleaning the stems of the old flowers.

"Teruo," Mr. Sasaki called.

Teruo approached us as if steeled for an attack.

"You've been selling fresh flowers and leaving the old ones go to waste. I can't afford that, Teruo," Mr. Sasaki said. "Why don't you do as you're told? We all sell the flowers in the front. I tell you they're not old in a flower shop. Why can't you sell them?"

"I don't like it, Mr. Sasaki," Teruo said. "When the people ask me if they're fresh I hate to answer. I feel rotten after selling the old ones."

"Look here, Teruo," Mr. Sasaki said. "I don't want to fire you. You're a good boy, and I know you need a job, but you've got to

be a good clerk here or you're going out. Do you get me?"

"I get you," Teruo said.

In the morning we were all at the shop early. I had an eight o'clock delivery, and the others had to rush with a big funeral order. Teruo was there early. "Hello," he greeted us cheerfully as we came in. He was unusually high-spirited, and I couldn't account for it. He was there before us and had already filled out the eight o'clock package for me. He was almost through with the funeral frame, padding it with wet moss and covering it all over with brake fern, when Tommy came in. When Mr. Sasaki arrrived, Teruo waved his hand and cheerfully went about gathering the flowers for the funeral piece. As he flitted here and there he seemed as if he had forgotten our presence, even the boss. He looked at each vase, sized up the flowers, and then cocked his head at the next one. He did this with great deliberation, as if he were the boss and the last word in the shop. That was all right, but when a customer soon came in, he swiftly attended him as if he owned all the flowers in the world. When the man asked Teruo if he was getting fresh flowers, Teruo without batting an eye escorted the customer into the rear and eventually showed and sold the fresh ones. He did it with so much grace, dignity and swiftness that we stood around like his stooges. However, Mr. Sasaki went on with his work as if nothing had happened.

Along toward noon Teruo attended his second customer. He fairly ran to greet an old lady who wanted a cheap bouquet around fifty cents for a dinner table. This time he not only went back to the rear for the fresh ones but added three or four extras. To make it more irritating for the boss, who was watching every move, Teruo used an extra lot of maidenhair[1] because the old lady was appreciative of his art of making bouquets. Tommy and I watched the boss fuming inside of his office.

When the old lady went out of the shop Mr. Sasaki came out furious. "You're a blockhead. You have no business sense. What are you doing here?" he said to Teruo. "Are you crazy?"

Teruo looked cheerful. "I'm not crazy, Mr. Sasaki," he said. "And I'm not dumb. I just like to do it that way, that's all."

The boss turned to Tommy and me. "That boy's a sap," he said. "He's got no head."

Teruo laughed and walked off to the front with a broom. Mr. Sasaki shook his head. "What's the matter with him? I can't understand him," he said.

While the boss was out to lunch Teruo went on a mad spree. He waited on three customers at one time, ignoring our presence. It was amazing how he did it. He hurriedly took one customer's order and had him write a birthday greeting for it; jumped to the second customer's side and persuaded her to buy Columbia roses because they were the freshest of the lot. She wanted them delivered so he jotted it down on the sales book, and leaped to the third customer.

"I want to buy that orchid in the window," she stated without deliberation.

"Do you have to have an orchid, madam?" Teruo asked the lady.

"No," she said. "But I want something nice for tonight's ball, and I think the orchid will match my dress. Why do you ask?"

"If I were you I wouldn't buy that orchid," he told her. "It won't keep. I could sell it to you and make a profit but I don't want to do that and spoil your evening. Come to the back, madam, and I'll show you some of the nicest gardenias in the market today. We call them Belmont and they're fresh today."

He came to the rear with the lady. We watched him pick out three of the biggest gardenias and make them into a corsage. When the lady went out with her package a little boy about eleven years old came in and wanted a twenty-five-cent bouquet for his mother's birthday. Teruo waited on the boy. He was out in the front, and we saw him pick

---

1 maidenhair: a fine, delicate type of fern.

out a dozen of the two-dollar-a-dozen roses and give them to the kid.

Tommy nudged me. "If he was the boss he couldn't do those things," he said.

"In the first place," I said, "I don't think he could be a boss."

"What do you think?" Tommy said. "Is he crazy? Is he trying to get himself fired?"

"I don't know," I said.

When Mr. Sasaki returned, Teruo was waiting on another customer, a young lady.

"Did Teruo eat yet?" Mr. Sasaki asked Tommy.

"No, he won't go. He says he's not hungry today," Tommy said.

We watched Teruo talking to the young lady. The boss shook his head. Then it came. Teruo came back to the rear and picked out a dozen of the very fresh white roses and took them out to the lady.

"Aren't they lovely?" we heard her exclaim.

We watched him come back, take down a box, place several maidenhairs and asparagus, place the roses neatly inside, sprinkle a few drops, and then give it to her. We watched him thank her, and we noticed her smile and thanks. The girl walked out.

Mr. Sasaki ran excitedly to the front. "Teruo! She forgot to pay!"

Teruo stopped the boss on the way out.

"Wait, Mr. Sasaki," he said "I gave it to her."

"What!" the boss cried indignantly.

"She came in just to look around and see the flowers. She likes pretty roses. Don't you think she's wonderful?"

"What's the matter with you?" the boss said. "Are you crazy? What did she buy?"

"Nothing, I tell you," Teruo said. "I gave it to her because she admired it, and she's pretty enough to deserve beautiful things, and I liked her."

"You're fired! Get out!" Mr. Sasaki spluttered. "Don't come back to the store again."

"And I gave her fresh ones too," Teruo said.

Mr. Sasaki rolled out several bills from his pocketbook. "Here's your wages for this week. Now, get out," he said.

"I don't want it," Teruo said. "You keep it and buy some more flowers."

"Here, take it. Get out," Mr. Sasaki said.

Teruo took the bills and rang up the cash register. "All right, I'll go now. I feel fine. I'm happy. Thanks to you." He waved his hand to Mr. Sasaki. "No hard feelings."

On the way out Teruo remembered our presence. He looked back. "Goodbye. Good luck," he said cheerfully to Tommy and me.

He walked out of the shop with his shoulders straight, head high, and whistling. He did not come back to see us again.

Discussion

1. Who is the narrator of this story? What is his first impression of Teruo?

2. What does Teruo do that suggests he will be successful at his new job?

3. What is Teruo's one problem with his new job? How does he handle this problem?

4. Why is Tommy, the other clerk, so worried about Teruo's selling the fresh flowers?

5. Tell what happens during Teruo's last day at work.

6. What arguments can you state in support of Teruo's decision to sell the fresh flowers first? What arguments can you offer in support of Mr. Sasaki's decision to fire him?

Writer's Craft

Characters in stories are like people in real life. That's why some characters in stories are braver or stronger than others. In stories sometimes one character will show unusual physical or moral courage or accomplish some act of bravery. This type of character is called a HERO if a man or a HEROINE if a woman. Often the hero or heroine is the central character in a story.

1. Who is the hero in this story? Why?

2. What are Teruo's heroic qualities?

Composition

1. What happens after Teruo is fired? Use your imagination and take the story one step further. Does Teruo go home? If he does, his mother would want to know why he is home early. Write his explanation to his mother. Begin by having Teruo tell her everything he did at the shop that day. Then have him explain why he did those things. Write your explanation in the first person so that it sounds as if Teruo is talking.

2. To show his disapproval of Mr. Sasaki's business practices, Teruo gives away flowers, forcing Mr. Sasaki to fire him. Think of another way Teruo could have handled this situation. Write another end to this story, including your solution. Begin on the morning of Teruo's last day. Be sure to make it clear whether your solution would save Teruo's job or whether he would still be fired. Your ending should include any necessary description, action, or conversation.

More than anything else, Plummer wanted to be in the top band. The only problem was . . . he was the worst musician in town! But that small matter was not going to stop him!

The No-Talent Kid

KURT VONNEGUT, JR.

IT WAS AUTUMN, and the leaves outside Lincoln High School were turning the same rusty color as the bare brick walls in the band-rehearsal room. George M. Helmholtz, head of the music department and director of the band, was ringed by folding chairs and instrument cases; and on each chair sat a very young man, nervously prepared to blow through something, or, in the case of the percussion section, to hit something, the instant Mr. Helmholtz lowered his white baton.

Mr. Helmholtz, a man of forty, who believed that his great belly was a sign of health, strength and dignity, smiled angelically, as though he were about to release the most exquisite sounds ever heard by men. Down came his baton.

"*Blrooooomp!*" went the big sousaphones.

"*Blat! Blat!*" echoed the French horns, and the plodding, shrieking, querulous waltz was begun.

Mr. Helmholtz's expression did not change as the brasses lost their places, as the woodwinds' nerve failed and they became inaudible rather than have their mistakes heard, as the percussion section shifted into a rhythm pattern belonging to a march they knew and liked better.

"A-a-a-a-ta-ta, a-a-a-a-a-a, ta-ta-ta-ta!" sang Mr. Helmholtz in a loud tenor, singing the first-cornet part when the first cornetist, florid and perspiring, gave up and slouched in his chair, his instrument in his lap.

"Saxophones, let me hear you," called Mr. Helmholtz. "Good!"

This was the C Band, and, for the C Band, the performance was good; it couldn't have been more polished for the fifth session of the school year. Most of the youngsters were just starting out as bandsmen, and in the years ahead of them they would acquire artistry enough to move into the B Band, which met in the next hour. And finally the best of them would gain positions in the pride of the city, the Lincoln High School Ten Square Band.

The football team lost half its games and the basketball team lost two thirds of its, but the band, in the ten years Mr. Helmholtz had been running it, had been second to none until last June. It had been first in the state to use flag twirlers, the first to use choral as well as instrumental numbers, the first to use triple-tonguing extensively, the first to march in breathtaking double time, the first to put a light in its bass drum. Lincoln High School awarded letter sweaters to the members of the A Band, and the sweaters were deeply respected—and properly so. The band had won every statewide high school band competition in the last ten years—everyone save the one in June.

As the members of the C Band dropped out of the waltz, one by one, as though mustard gas[1] were coming out of the ventilators, Mr. Helmholtz continued to smile and wave his baton for the survivors, and to brood inwardly over the defeat his band had sustained in June, when Johnstown High School had won with a secret weapon, a bass drum seven feet in diameter. The judges, who were not musicians but politicians, had had eyes and ears for nothing but this eighth wonder of the world, and since then Mr. Helmholtz had thought of little else. But the school budget was already lopsided with band expenses. When the school board had given him the last special appropriation he'd begged for so desperately—money to wire the plumes of the bandsmen's hats with flashlight bulbs and batteries for night games—the board had made him swear that this was the last time.

Only two members of the C Band were playing now, a clarinetist and a snare drummer, both playing loudly, proudly, confidently, and all wrong. Mr. Helmholtz, coming out of his wistful dream of a bass drum bigger than the one that had beaten him, administered the *coup de grâce*[2] to the waltz by clattering his stick against his music stand. "All righty, all righty," he said cheerily, and he nodded his congratulations to the two

who had persevered to the bitter end.

Walter Plummer, the clarinetist, nodded back soberly, like a concert soloist receiving an ovation led by the director of a symphony orchestra. He was small, but with a thick chest developed in summers spent at the bottom of swimming pools, and he could hold a note longer than anyone in the A Band, much longer, but that was all he could do. He drew back his tired, reddened lips, showing the two large front teeth that gave him the look of a squirrel, adjusted his reed, limbered his fingers, and awaited the next challenge to his virtuosity.

This would be Plummer's third year in the C Band, Mr. Helmholtz thought, with a mixture of pity and fear. Nothing, apparently, could shake Plummer's determination to earn the right to wear one of the sacred letters of the A Band, so far, terribly far away.

Mr. Helmholtz had tried to tell Plummer how misplaced his ambitions were, to recommend other fields for his great lungs and enthusiasm, where pitch would be unimportant. But Plummer was blindly in love, not with music, but with the letter sweaters, and, being as tone-deaf as boiled cabbage, he could detect nothing in his own playing to be discouraged about.

"Remember, now," said Mr. Helmholtz to the C Band, "Friday is challenge day, so be on your toes. The chairs you have now were assigned arbitrarily.[3] On challenge day it'll be up to you to prove which chair you deserve." He avoided the narrowed, confident eyes of Plummer, who had taken the first clarinetist's chair without consulting the seating plan posted on the bulletin board. Challenge day

---

1 **mustard gas**: a poisonous gas.
2 *coup de grâce* (kü′ də gräs′): last stroke.

3 **arbitrarily**: without any rules or reasons.

occurred every two weeks, and on that day any bandsman could challenge anyone ahead of him to a contest for his position, with Mr. Helmholtz as the utterly dispassionate judge.

Plummer's hand was raised, its fingers snapping urgently.

"Yes, Plummer?" said Mr. Helmholtz, smiling bleakly. He had come to dread challenge days because of Plummer, and had come to think of it as Plummer's day. Plummer never challenged anybody in the C Band or even in the B Band, but stormed the organization at the very top, challenging, as was unfortunately the privilege of all, only members of the A Band. The waste of the A Band's time was troubling enough, but infinitely more painful for Mr. Helmholtz were Plummer's looks of stunned disbelief when he heard Mr. Helmholtz's decision that he hadn't outplayed the men he'd challenged. And Mr. Helmholtz was thus rebuked not just on challenge days, but every day, just before supper, when Plummer delivered the evening paper. "Something about challenge day, Plummer?" said Mr. Helmholtz uneasily.

"Mr. Helmholtz," said Plummer coolly, "I'd like to come to A Band session that day."

"All right—if you feel up to it." Plummer always felt up to it, and it would have been more of a surprise if Plummer had announced that he wouldn't be at the A Band session.

"I'd like to challenge Flammer."

The rustling of sheet music and clicking of instrument-case latches stopped. Flammer was the first clarinetist in the A Band, a genius that not even members of the A Band would have had the gall to challenge.

Mr. Helmholtz cleared his throat: "I admire your spirit, Plummer, but isn't that rather ambitious for the first of the year?

Perhaps you should start out with, say, challenging Ed Delaney." Delaney held down the last chair in the B Band.

"You don't understand," said Plummer patiently. "You haven't noticed I have a new clarinet."

"H'm'm? Oh—well, so you do."

Plummer stroked the satin-black barrel of the instrument as though it were like King Arthur's sword, giving magical powers to whoever possessed it. "It's as good as Flammer's," said Plummer. "Better, even."

There was a warning in his voice, telling Mr. Helmholtz that the days of discrimination were over, that nobody in his right mind would dare to hold back a man with an instrument like this.

"Um," said Mr. Helmholtz. "Well, we'll see, we'll see."

After practice, he was forced into close quarters with Plummer again in the crowded hallway. Plummer was talking darkly to a wide-eyed freshman bandsman.

"Know why the band lost to Johnstown High last June?" asked Plummer, seemingly ignorant of the fact that he was back to back with Mr. Helmholtz. "Because," said Plummer triumphantly, "they stopped running the band on the merit system. Keep your eyes open on Friday."

Mr. George Helmholtz lived in a world of music, and even the throbbing of his headaches came to him musically, if painfully, as the deep-throated boom of a cart-borne bass drum seven feet in diameter. It was late afternoon on the first challenge day of the new school year. He was sitting in his living room, his eyes covered, awaiting another sort of thump—the impact of the evening paper, hurled against the clapboard of the front of the house by Walter Plummer.

As Mr. Helmholtz was telling himself that

"Sure—why not?" said Plummer, shrugging. "Let bygones be bygones, is what I say." He gave a bitter imitation of an amiable chuckle. "Water over the dam. It's been two hours now since the knife was stuck in me and twisted."

Mr. Helmholtz sighed. "Have you got a moment? It's time we had a talk, my boy."

Plummer kicked down the standard on his bicycle, hid his papers under shrubbery, and walked in sullenly. Mr. Helmholtz gestured at the most comfortable chair in the room, the one in which he'd been sitting, but Plummer chose instead to sit on the edge of a hard one with a straight back.

Mr. Helmholtz, forming careful sentences in his mind before speaking, opened his newspaper, and laid it open on the coffee table.

"My boy," he said at last, "God made all kinds of people: some who can run fast, some who can write wonderful stories, some who can paint pictures, some who can sell anything, some who can make beautiful music. But He didn't make anybody who could do everything well. Part of the growing-up process is finding out what we can do well and what we can't do well." He patted Plummer's shoulder gently. "The last part, finding out what we can't do, is what hurts most about growing up. But everybody has to face it, and then go in search of his true self."

Plummer's head was sinking lower and lower on his chest and Mr. Helmholtz hastily pointed out a silver lining. "For instance, Flammer could never run a business like a paper route, keeping records, getting new customers. He hasn't that kind of a mind, and couldn't do that sort of thing if his life depended on it."

"You've got a point," said Plummer,

he would rather not have his newspaper on challenge day, since Plummer came with it, the paper was delivered with a crash that would have done credit to a siege gun.

"Plummer!" he cried furiously, shaken.

"Yes, sir?" said Plummer solicitously from the sidewalk.

Mr. Helmholtz shuffled to the door in his carpet slippers. "Please, my boy," he said plaintively, "can't we be friends?"

looking up suddenly with unexpected brightness. "A guy's got to be awful one-sided to be as good at one thing as Flammer is. I think it's more worthwhile to try to be better-rounded. No, Flammer beat me fair and square today, and I don't want you to think I'm a bad sport about that. It isn't that that gets me."

"That's very mature of you," said Mr. Helmholtz. "But what I was trying to point out to you was that we've all got weak points, and—"

Plummer charitably waved him to silence. "You don't have to explain to me, Mr. Helmholtz. With a job as big as you've got, it'd be a miracle if you did the whole thing right."

"Now, hold on, Plummer!" said Mr. Helmholtz.

"All I'm asking is that you look at it from my point of view," said Plummer. "No sooner'd I come back from challenging A Band material, no sooner'd I come back from playing my heart out, than you turned those C Band kids loose on me. You and I know we were just giving 'em the feel of challenge days, and that I was all played out. But did you tell them that? Heck, no, you didn't, Mr. Helmholtz; and those kids all think they can play better than me. That's all I'm sore about, Mr. Helmholtz. They think it means something, me in the last chair of the C Band."

"Plummer," said Mr. Helmholtz evenly, "I have been trying to tell you something as kindly as possible, but apparently the only way to get it across to you is to tell it to you straight."

"Go ahead and quash[4] criticism," said Plummer, standing.

"Quash?"

---

4 **quash**: put a stop to.

"Quash," said Plummer with finality. He headed for the door. "I'm probably ruining my chances for getting into the A Band by speaking out like this, Mr. Helmholtz, but frankly, it's incidents like what happened to me today that lost you the band competition last June."

"It was a seven-foot bass drum!"

"Well, get one for Lincoln High and see how you make out then."

"I'd give my right arm for one!" said Mr. Helmholtz, forgetting the point at issue and remembering his all-consuming dream.

Plummer paused on the threshold. "One like the Knights of Kandahar use in their parades?"

"That's the ticket!" Mr. Helmholtz imagined the Knights of Kandahar's huge drum, the showpiece of every local parade. He tried to think of it with the Lincoln High School black panther painted on it. "Yes, sir!" When he returned to earth, Plummer was on his bicycle.

Mr. Helmholtz started to shout after Plummer, to bring him back and tell him bluntly that he didn't have the remotest chance of getting out of C Band ever; that he would never be able to understand that the mission of a band wasn't simply to make noises, but to make special kinds of noises. But Plummer was off and away.

Temporarily relieved until next challenge day, Mr. Helmholtz sat down to enjoy his paper, to read that the treasurer of the Knights of Kandahar, a respected citizen, had disappeared with the organization's funds, leaving behind and unpaid the Knights' bills for the past year and a half. "We'll pay a hundred cents on the dollar, if we have to sell everything but the Sacred Mace," the Sublime Chamberlain of the Inner Shrine was on record as saying.

Mr. Helmholtz didn't know any of the people involved, and he yawned and turned to the funnies. He gasped suddenly, turned to the front page again, looked up a number in the phone book, and dialed feverishly.

"Zum-zum-zum-zum," went the busy signal in his ear. He dropped the telephone clattering into its cradle. Hundreds of people, he thought, must be trying to get in touch with the Sublime Chamberlain of the Inner Shrine of the Knights of Kandahar at this moment. He looked up at his flaking ceiling in prayer. But none of them, he prayed, were after a bargain in a cart-borne bass drum.

He dialed again and again, always getting the busy signal, and walked out on his porch to relieve some of the tension building up in him. He would be the only one bidding on the drum, he told himself, and he could name his own price. If he offered fifty dollars for it, he could probably have it! He'd put up his own money, and get the school to pay him back in three years, when the plumes with the electric lights in them were paid for in full.

He lit a cigarette, and laughed like a department-store Santa Claus at this magnificent stroke of fortune. As he exhaled happily, his gaze dropped from heaven to his lawn, and he saw Plummer's undelivered newspapers lying beneath the shrubbery.

He went inside and called the Sublime Chamberlain again, with the same results. To make the time go, and to do a Christian good turn, he called Plummer's home to let him know where the papers were mislaid. But the Plummers' line was busy too.

He dialed alternately the Plummers' number and the Sublime Chamberlain's number for fifteen minutes before getting a ringing signal.

"Yes?" said Mrs. Plummer.

"This is Mr. Helmholtz, Mrs. Plummer. Is Walter there?"

"He was here a minute ago, telephoning, but he just went out of here like a shot."

"Looking for his papers? He left them under my spiraea."[5]

"He did? Heavens, I have no idea where he was going. He didn't say anything about his papers, but I thought I overheard something about selling his clarinet." She sighed and then laughed nervously. "Having money of their own makes them awfully independent. He never tells me anything."

"Well, you tell him I think maybe it's for the best, his selling his clarinet. And tell him where his papers are."

It was unexpected good news that Plummer had at last seen the light about his musical career, and Mr. Helmholtz now called the Sublime Chamberlain's home again for more good news. He got through this time, but was momentarily disappointed to learn that the man had just left on some sort of lodge business.

For years Mr. Helmholtz had managed to smile and keep his wits about him in C Band practice sessions. But on the day after his fruitless efforts to find out anything about the Knights of Kandahar's bass drum, his defenses were down, and the poisonous music penetrated to the roots of his soul.

"No, no, no!" he cried in pain, and he threw his white baton against the brick wall. The springy stick bounded off the bricks and fell into an empty folding chair at the rear of the clarinet section—Plummer's empty chair.

As Mr. Helmholtz, red-faced and apologetic, retrieved the baton, he found himself unexpectedly moved by the symbol of the empty chair. No one else, he realized, no

---

5 **spiraea** (spī rē′ ə): a shrub.

matter how untalented, could ever fill the last chair in the organization as well as Plummer had. He looked up to find many of the bandsmen contemplating the chair with him, as though they, too, sensed that something great, in a fantastic way, had disappeared, and that life would be a good bit duller on account of it.

During the ten minutes between the C Band and B Band sessions, Mr. Helmholtz hurried to his office and again tried to get in touch with the Sublime Chamberlain of the Knights of Kandahar, and was again told what he'd been told substantially several times during the night before and again in the morning.

"Lord knows where he's off to now. He was in for just a second, but went right out again. I gave him your name, so I expect he'll call you when he gets a minute. You're the drum gentleman, aren't you?"

"That's right—the drum gentleman."

The buzzers in the hall were sounding, marking the beginning of another class period. Mr. Helmholtz wanted to stay by the phone until he'd caught the Sublime Chamberlain and closed the deal, but the B Band was waiting—and after that it would be the A Band.

An inspiration came to him. He called Western Union, and sent a telegram to the man, offering fifty dollars for the drum, and requesting a reply collect.

But no reply came during B Band practice. Nor had one come by the halfway point of the A Band session. The bandsmen, a sensitive, high-strung lot, knew immediately that their director was on edge about something, and the rehearsal went badly. Mr. Helmholtz was growing so nervous about the drum that he stopped a march in the middle because of a small noise coming from the large double

doors at one end of the room, where someone out-of-doors was apparently working on the lock.

"All right, all right, let's wait until the racket dies down so we can hear ourselves," he said.

At that moment, a student messenger handed him a telegram. Mr. Helmholtz beamed, tore open the envelope and read:

DRUM SOLD STOP COULD YOU USE A STUFFED CAMEL ON WHEELS STOP

The wooden doors opened with a shriek of rusty hinges, and a snappy autumn gust showered the band with leaves. Plummer stood in the great opening, winded and perspiring, harnessed to a drum on wheels that could have contained a dozen youngsters his size.

"I know this isn't challenge day," said Plummer, "but I thought you might make an exception in my case."

He walked in with splendid dignity, the huge apparatus grumbling along beside him.

Mr. Helmholtz rushed to meet him, and crushed Plummer's right hand between both of his. "Plummer, boy! You got it for us! Good boy! I'll pay you whatever you paid for it," he cried, and in his joy he added rashly, "and a nice little profit besides. Good boy!"

Plummer laughed modestly. "Sell it?" he said. "Heck fire, I'll give it to you when I graduate," he said grandly. "All I want to do is play it in the A Band while I'm here."

"But, Plummer," said Mr. Helmholtz uneasily, "you don't know anything about drums."

"I'll practice hard," said Plummer reassuringly. He started to back his instrument into an aisle between the tubas and the trombones—like a man backing a trailer truck into

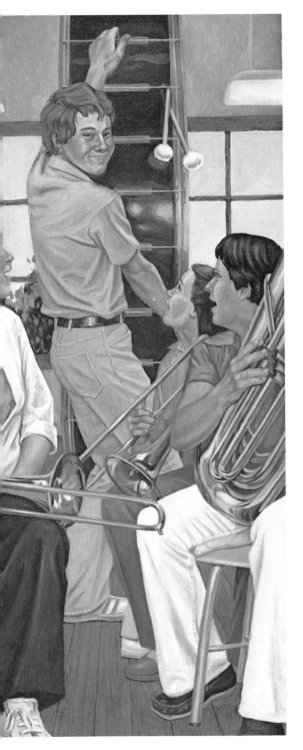

a narrow alley—backing it toward the percussion section, where the amazed musicians were hastily making room.

"Now, just a minute," said Mr. Helmholtz, chuckling as though Plummer were joking, and knowing full well he wasn't. "There's more to drum playing than just lambasting[6] the thing whenever you take a notion to, you know. It takes years to be a drummer."

"Well," said Plummer cheerfully, "the quicker I get at it, the quicker I'll get good."

"What I meant was that I'm afraid you won't be quite ready for the A Band for a little while."

Plummer stopped his backing. "How long?" he asked suspiciously.

"Oh, sometime in your senior year, perhaps. Meanwhile, you could let the band have your drum to use until you're ready."

Mr. Helmholtz's skin began to itch all over as Plummer stared at him coldly, appraisingly. "Until hell freezes over?" Plummer said at last.

Mr. Helmholtz sighed resignedly. "I'm afraid that's about right." He shook his head sadly. "It's what I tried to tell you yesterday afternoon: nobody can do everything well, and we've all got to face up to our limitations. You're a fine boy, Plummer, but you'll never be a musician—not in a million years. The only thing to do is what we all have to do now and then: smile, shrug, and say, 'Well, that's just one of those things that's not for me.'"

Tears formed on the rims of Plummer's eyes, but went no farther. He walked slowly toward the doorway, with the drum tagging after him. He paused on the doorsill for one more wistful look at the A Band that would

6 lambasting: beating.

The No-Talent Kid   293

never have a chair for him. He smiled feebly and shrugged. "Some people have eight-foot drums," he said kindly, "and other's don't, and that's just the way life is. You're a fine man, Mr. Helmholtz, but you'll never get this drum in a million years, because I'm going to give it to my mother for a coffee table."

"Plummer!" cried Mr. Helmholtz. His plaintive voice was drowned out by the rumble and rattle of the big drum as it followed its small master down the school's concrete driveway.

Mr. Helmholtz ran after him with a floundering, foot-slapping gait. Plummer and his drum had stopped at an intersection to wait for a light to change, and Mr. Helmholtz caught him there, and seized his arm. "We've got to have that drum," he panted. "How much do you want?"

"Smile," said Plummer. "Shrug! That's what I did." Plummer did it again. "See? So I can't get into the A Band, so you can't have the drum. Who cares? All part of the growing-up process."

"The situations aren't the same!" said Mr. Helmholtz furiously. "Not at all the same!"

"You're right," said Plummer, without a smile. "I'm growing up, and you're not."

The light changed, and Plummer left Mr. Helmholtz on the corner, stunned.

Mr. Helmholtz had to run after him again. "Plummer," he said sweetly, "you'll never be able to play it well."

"Rub it in," said Plummer, bitterly.

"But you're doing a beautiful job of pulling it, and if we got it, I don't think we'd ever be able to find anybody who could do it as well."

Plummer stopped, backed and turned the instrument on the narrow sidewalk with speed and hair-breadth precision, and headed back for Lincoln High School, skipping once to get in step with Mr. Helmholtz.

As they approached the school they both loved, they met and passed a group of youngsters from the C Band, who carried unscarred instrument cases and spoke self-consciously of music.

"Got a good bunch of kids coming up this year," said Plummer judiciously. "All they need's a little seasoning."

Discussion

1. What is Mr. Helmholtz's main problem? What does he think will solve it?

2. What is Plummer's main desire? Why is he unable to achieve it?

3. How does Plummer solve Mr. Helmholtz's problem? What are Plummer's terms for the deal? What is the final solution for both of them?

4. Why does Plummer accept Mr. Helmholtz's final solution so easily?

5. What kind of person is Plummer? What aspects of his personality help him achieve his goal?

Vocabulary

DENOTATIONS are the dictionary definitions of words. CONNOTATIONS are the implied meanings of words. Two words which have almost exactly the same denotation could have entirely different connotations. For example, the words *heavyset* and *fat* both have the same denotation: *overweight.* Yet their connotations are altogether different. Most overweight people probably would not mind being called *heavyset,* but they would resent being called *fat.* Of the two words, *heavyset* has a more pleasant, positive connotation, while *fat* has a more unpleasant, negative connotation.

A. On a separate sheet of paper, make two columns. Label the left-hand column *Positive* and the right-hand column *Negative.* Then write the more pleasant word from each pair in the *Positive* column and the more unpleasant word in the *Negative* column.

1. skinny—slender
2. idea—notion
3. noise—racket
4. modern—new-fangled
5. fake—imitation
6. ask—interrogate
7. plan—scheme
8. economical—cheap
9. obtain—grab
10. blunder—error

B. Each of the following passages, based on "The No-Talent Kid," includes one *italicized* word. Following each word is either the word *positive* or *negative* in parentheses ( ). These words show which kind of connotation the word is intended to have in the passage.

   On the same paper, copy each *italicized* word and give a synonym—a word that means the same—for each one. If the word has a positive connotation in the passage, choose a synonym that has a negative connotation. If the word is negative in the passage, choose a synonym with a positive connotation. If you need help, use a dictionary.

EXAMPLE: Mr. Helmholtz believed that his great *belly* (negative) was a sign of health, strength, and dignity.
ANSWER: belly—stomach

1. *Perspiring* (positive), the first cornetist gave up and slouched in his chair.
2. The school budget was already *lopsided* (negative) with band expenses.
3. He was small, but had a *thick* (positive) chest developed in summers spent at the bottom of swimming pools.

4. The chairs you have now were assigned *arbitrarily* (positive). On challenge day it'll be up to you to prove which chair you deserve.

5. There's more to drum playing than just *lambasting* (negative) the thing whenever you take a notion to.

6. Mr. Helmholtz was sitting in his living room, his eyes covered, awaiting another sort of thump—the impact of the evening paper, *hurled* (negative) against the front of the house by Walter Plummer.

7. Mr. Helmholtz *gestured* (positive) at the most comfortable chair in the room, the one in which he'd been sitting.

8. Mr. Helmholtz believed that Plummer would never be able to understand that the mission of a band wasn't simply to make *noises* (negative).

9. Plummer's mother told Mr. Helmholtz, "Having money of their own makes them awfully *independent*" (positive).

10. At the intersection, Mr. Helmholtz caught him and *seized* (negative) his arm.

Kurt Vonnegut, Jr. 1922—

In his novel, *Mother Night,* Kurt Vonnegut wrote, "We are what we pretend to be, so we must be careful what we pretend to be." During the 1960s, Vonnegut emerged as one of the most popular and influential writers of American fiction. His writing frequently concerns the control of machines and society over people. He often uses science-fiction and futuristic settings to develop unforgettable commentaries on modern life.

Vonnegut did not set out to be a writer. After studying chemistry for three years, he went into the army. His experience as a prisoner of war during the bombing of Dresden gave him the basis for the novel, *Slaughterhouse Five.* His other novels include: *Player Piano, The Sirens of Titan,* and *Breakfast of Champions.*

Harry met the postman on the corner. Searching through the mail, he found the invitation and tore it up into small pieces. Now his mother would never know. What was Harry hiding?

The Torn Invitation

NORMAN KATKOV

AT FIFTEEN, in the spring of his sophomore year at Hamilton High School, Harry Wojick was as big as a college senior, a long, thin, big-boned left-hander, who could anchor a leg in first base and stretch halfway to right field for a bad throw from his shortstop.

Now, in the waning daylight, he turned into Glover Street toward his home, his arms swinging as he moved onto the unpaved road. For a few feet he ran easily, bringing his knees up high, until, without warning, he stopped short and bent low to field the imaginary ball cleanly, beating the runner by a mile. He straightened up, grinning in the half darkness, blushing a little from the applause at the brilliant play he had made.

Harry Wojick came off the street onto the opposite sidewalk. He passed the four-family flat in the middle of the block. He passed the empty lot and beyond it the condemned building with all the windows long since broken, and then he turned into the cement walk which ran the length of his house.

The windows were raised in the kitchen and he smelled the roast. He smelled the asparagus for the roast and the fried potatoes with onions that nobody made like Ma, and he was suddenly terribly hungry after the three hours of baseball practice.

When he came into the kitchen, Theresa Wojick turned from the stove, smiling at her son, rubbing her hands on her apron as she walked to meet him. She held him at the elbows, examining him carefully, her face warm and her eyes gentle, welcoming him as though he had returned from a long and perilous journey. She was a tall woman with large, capable hands and black, unkempt hair shot through with gray. She held Harry and she said, "Hello, my little son. Will you eat supper?" joking with him as always.

He put his cheek to hers, noticing again the redness of her chapped hands. She could try to do something about it, he said to himself, as she released him, remembering the mothers of his teammates who lived above the flats on Livingston Drive and Harding Boulevard and scattered through Maple Heights. They were mothers with manicures and they were thin—and their hair was always set just right.

Harry went to the sink to wash and, turning, saw the table set for three. He thought for an instant that his father was home, that Peter Wojick had not gone to his night watchman's job in the office building downtown. But he saw the hooks on the wall near the door empty of cap and coat.

"For Frankie Thomas," his mother whispered, looking at her son. "His mother is gone again till half the night, and leaves cold cuts. Boy like Frankie to eat cold cuts," she whispered. "You call him, Harry."

"Why can't she learn to speak English?" he asked himself savagely, turning away. "She's been here long enough!"

Harry walked through the short hall and stood under the arch which led into the living room. He saw the frail, black-haired boy with whom he had grown up, sitting in the chair under the lamp. "Hey, Frankie," Harry said. "Come on and eat." Harry whistled shrilly and came back into the kitchen.

He pulled the chair out and held it suspended off the clean, bare floor, his fingers tightening on the wood. There, next to his plate, was the white, square envelope, and atop it, covered by a transparent sheet of thin paper, was the embossed invitation.

Harry looked at his mother, who had her back to him, busy at the stove. He heard Frankie coming through the house and knew it was Frankie's work, *knew* it. He moved the chair at last and sat down and, without touching it, his hands holding his knees, he read the invitation from the faculty of Hamilton High School to an open house in honor of all the students' mothers.

It was for tomorrow.

Harry knew *that,* all right. Had known it for ten days and had kept it secret. He looked up as Frankie sat down across the table.

Harry's mother was sitting between them,

and as she handed her son the roast she said, "I asked Frankie maybe he has this invitation, Harry. I heard by Celusik, the grocery man, about this open house. Must be open house for junior, senior mothers." Frankie had skipped a grade.

Harry was busy with the roast. "It's for everyone," he said, watching the roast. "Didn't you get one, Ma?" He turned to his mother. "They mailed them out," Harry said, remembering now that morning when he had waited for the postman on the corner, taken the envelopes from him, searched for the square, white one, and had torn it, scattering the pieces in the empty lot before running home and dropping the rest of the mail in the black metal box beside the door.

"Maybe they make a mistake," his mother said.

She reached for a thick slice of the rye bread she baked herself and held it flat in her left hand. She buttered it completely and thickly and brought it to her mouth, taking a large bite, and Harry wanted to leave the table and this house. He remembered the homes on Maple Heights to which he had been invited, where they called it dinner and ate in a dining room with tablecloths; where George Sidley's mother sat at one end of the table and broke her bread piece by piece, buttering it lightly and eating slowly.

"Frankie's ma got this invitation," Theresa Wojick said, nodding at their guest, who lived with his mother in one of the upstairs apartments of the four-family flat. "How long she got the open house, Frankie?"

"Mother had it," Frankie said. "She—we didn't talk about it."

She turned to Harry, smiling at her son. "You eat, Harry. Big ballplayer must eat good," she said.

Harry ate. The three sat in silence.

Later, while Theresa Wojick set out the dessert plates, Frankie said, "How's practice going, Harry?"

"All right, I guess." He wanted this supper finished.

Theresa Wojick filled the dessert plates with pudding. As she sat down she said to Frankie, "Your ma goes to this open house?"

"I don't know," he answered. "She—well, you know, she's pretty busy. One of my aunts is sick and I think she's going to be with her for a few days. She packed her suitcase when she left today."

"Ma," Harry said.

She set her coffee cup down.

"I wanted to tell you, Ma," he said. "I meant to tell you about it and then I forgot, I guess."

"Easy to forget," she said.

"It wouldn't make any difference anyway,

Ma," Harry lied. "We've got that game with Central next week and the coach is worried. He's been working us hard all week. He's got a game for tomorrow. You know, he picks two teams from the squad and we play each other."

"I've got to go," Frankie said. "Thanks very much for supper, Mrs. Wojick."

"You're welcome, Frankie. Here"—she reached across the table—"here is the invitation, Frankie," and she offered it to him.

He held it, shifting it from one hand to the other. "Thanks," he said, moving toward the kitchen door. "Thanks. Thanks." And he was gone.

"I won't be finished until about six o'clock, Ma," Harry said.

She nodded. Harry watched her walking to the sink. "Do you want me to miss practice, Ma?" he asked.

She had her back to him.

"We'll go next year, Ma. I'll be a regular on the team then. We can go next year," he said, but she didn't turn, nor move, nor did she answer him, and he left the kitchen quickly. He went into the living room and stood before the windows. He tried to blame Frankie and couldn't, and he tried to blame Theresa Wojick and couldn't. He was seldom a liar, but he just didn't want her there with George Sidley's mother and Eric Portland's mother.

Harry heard the water running in the sink and the clatter of dishes, and he went back into the kitchen. He opened the cabinet door, reaching for one of the dish towels his mother had cut from sugar sacks and washed white and soft. She took it from his hand.

"You rest, Harry," his mother said. "Big ball game tomorrow. You must rest up for the ball game." She turned from him to the sink.

"All right," he thought, and now he left the house, going out into the vestibule and then to the rear porch. "Let her wash her own dishes," he thought, and walked out to the sidewalk.

Frankie said, "Hi, Harry." He was leaning against the fence in front of Harry's house. He said, "I didn't want to jam you up, Harry."

"You didn't jam me up."

"That ought to be a pretty good game tomorrow, that intrasquad game," Frankie said. "Think I'll watch it."

"There isn't any intrasquad game," Harry muttered.

"You said—"

"I said. I say a lot of things." He felt the meanness in him. He started to walk away, but Frankie took his arm.

"I've got enough for a movie," Frankie said.

"I'm busy," Harry said, jerking his arm free. He left Frankie there, walking down Glover Street. He passed the corner and went on aimlessly.

When he came home he entered the house through the front door and moved through the living room in darkness, turning into his bedroom. He could see the cracks of light below the bathroom door and heard the water running; he wondered if there was ever a time in this house when the water *wasn't* running. He made it to his bedroom and undressed in the darkness, dropping his clothes on the floor and crawling into the turned-down bed.

"All right," he thought; "this time tomorrow it'll be over." He heard the bathroom door open and his mother moving around the house. He lay still, his eyes closed, his breath coming evenly as he simulated sleep, but the sound of her footsteps faded.

For a bad moment he thought of his ma, saw her again at the kitchen table, but he chased the scene from his mind and went, instead, to baseball, seeing himself leading infield practice, and thus, at last, fell asleep.

The first thing he noticed in the morning was his clothes, arranged neatly on the chair beside the bed, the shoes together on the floor and clean socks across them. He dressed quickly.

The kitchen was deserted. He saw his cornflakes and the orange juice and the milk before his chair, but he stood behind it, gulping the juice. As he set the empty glass on the table his mother came in from the rear porch.

"You didn't eat, Harry," she said.

"I'm late, Ma. I've got a test this morning. I've got to study for the test." He wanted to be out of here now as he turned from the table, saw that her hands were full.

She held the clean, freshly dried sweatshirt and the two pairs of wool socks, and he knew now why the water had been running in the bathroom last night. "For your game today, Harry," she said. "You bring me tonight your dirty stuff."

Harry watched her wrap the bundle and he wanted to kiss her, suddenly. He wanted to put his arms around her and hold her as she tied the bundle carefully with the string she always saved. But he only took the package from her and said thanks, and left.

All the way up to school he promised he'd make it up to her. He'd start tonight. He'd sit in the kitchen with Ma; she liked him there studying while she worked. He'd take her for a walk if she wanted. Saturday and Sunday he was staying home the whole time, that's all.

He came into school on the Livingston Drive side. His locker was on the first floor. He put the package inside, took his books,

and slammed the locker shut. The bell sounded for first hour and Harry went to English.

Pete Overholt, the team's catcher, sat behind Harry. As they waited for the tardy bell, he nudged Harry. "Look at the women, man," he whispered. "Look at 'em, Harry!"

Harry looked. Not a girl in the class wore saddle shoes, or blue jeans, or boys' shirts with the sleeves rolled above the elbows. They were in Sunday dresses and suits, and high heels.

"The open house," Pete whispered. "All of them showing off for their mothers."

The tardy bell sounded, and Harry saw Miss Liggett look up from the desk. He wasn't called on during the hour, and afterward, on his way to study hall, he waved to George Sidley, who played third base, and to Bernie Cremmens, the right-fielder. They were both wearing sports jackets and regular shirts, and they wore ties. Harry looked down at his sweater worn over the skivvy shirt. His corduroys were clean, but they were corduroys, and around him, in the study hall, was a sea of gray flannels.

There was only one lunch period today because they had to get the cafeteria ready for the open house. Harry bought a sandwich and a glass of milk. Then he saw that half the guys on the team, sitting at the table they shared every day, were dressed up, too. He sat down in a far corner with two guys he didn't know, ate quickly, and left by the side door so he wouldn't have to pass Sidley and Cremmens and the others.

He went to his locker for his afternoon books. He had only a French class left, because, for today, school was over after fifth hour. He sat half hearing Miss Formanek, gazing out the window until his name was called sharply.

Harry turned to the teacher, his face red, feeling the eyes of the whole class on him as Miss Formanek smiled. "Let's look alive there," said Miss Formanek. "Your mother will find her way, Harry," and she told him the place in the French book.

The bell sounded at last and Harry hurried to his locker. He saw the cafeteria cleared of tables, the floor bare and chairs lining the walls. He saw the huge coffeepots steaming, and then he got his package out and threw his books into the locker and slammed it shut.

He was half running for the door when George Sidley stopped him: "Hey, where you headed for?"

Harry stared at him. "Headed for?" he asked. "Where do you think I'm headed for? Aren't you going to practice?"

"Not me," George grinned. "Coach said anybody who wanted to could be excused. Isn't your mother coming?"

"She had to go downtown," Harry said. "She had to see a doctor. She hasn't been feeling well."

"Hey, that's not good," George said, frowning. Then his face brightened. "Well, hang around anyway. Lots of fun."

Harry shook his head. He swung his left arm. "It feels like it's stiffening up," he said. "Guess I'll work out. See you."

He walked down Livingston Drive toward the baseball field. He crossed the playing area, moving toward the Quonset hut that served as dressing room for the team. There was nobody inside but Art Hughes, the student manager.

"You alone, Harry?" Art asked.

"Yup."

Art turned and opened the doors of the uniform rack. "Anybody that's coming better come quick—that's all I got to say," he announced. "My mother is over at school waiting for me. I'm not keeping her waiting too long."

Harry sat down on the bench before the lockers and unwrapped the package. He pulled his sweater off and he was in his pants and skivvy shirt, standing in his socks on the cement floor when Oscar Anderson walked in. In a few minutes they were joined by Chuck Kellerman, the shortstop, and Mr. Quint, who taught chemistry and was assistant baseball coach.

Mr. Quint came over to the bench. "Look, you fellows, my wife's outside in the car. It seems there are only three of you here. You won't mind if I go back to school, will you?"

"Go ahead, Mr. Quint," Chuck said.

"I don't want to run out on you," Mr. Quint said. "It's just—well, with only three of you here, there doesn't seem to be much we could do."

"Can I get a ride back?" Art Hughes said. "You guys can check out your own uniforms today."

"Come ahead, Art," Mr. Quint said.

When they were gone, Chuck Kellerman slammed his baseball cap down on the cement floor. "All the way over here for nothing," he said.

He looked at Oscar Anderson. "How about you?" he asked. "Aren't you going to Mamma's Day and eat cookies?"

"Listen; I've got six brothers and sisters and I'm the baby," Oscar said. "My mother's tired of this stuff. I'm going home and get the grass cut, and then I got Saturday for myself."

"How about you, Harry?" Chuck asked.

"How about *you*, wise guy?" Harry said, beginning to tie his shoelaces.

Chuck got up from the bench and reached for a bat. "My mother is dead," he said, and he swung the bat desperately, as though he were hitting a line drive. Then he dropped the bat into the wicker basket. Harry watched him pick up his books and walk to the door and leave without turning to them.

"Will you lock up, Harry?" Oscar asked.

Harry saw his mother in the kitchen, and he reached for his sweater.

"Will you, Harry?"

He remembered the light under the bathroom door and the sound of water as she washed the sweatshirt and the socks.

"HARRY!"

"It isn't too late yet," Harry said. He had his sweater on.

"Are you nuts?" Oscar asked.

He'd call her. He'd use the phone in the principal's office. "See you tomorrow," he said, and he ran out of the Quonset hut. Far off, walking in left-center field, Harry saw Chuck Kellerman, and then he began to run.

He could call her, he thought as he ran, and she could even take a taxi. Just this once a taxi; Pa wouldn't care. Harry knew that. She could get dressed and be up there in half an hour, and he was suddenly breathless with anticipation. He'd wait out in front of the school, on Hamilton Avenue, and help her from the cab and hold her arm and lead her to the front door. He didn't care about the bread any more, or how she talked. She was his ma.

Harry was out of the alley now, running across Livingston Drive. There were cars all around the school, almost like it was graduation night. He cut across the grass, toward the long flight of steps that led up to the second floor. He was gasping for breath when he reached the door.

He stood there a moment, then pulled the heavy door open and stepped into the deserted corridor. There was nobody on the second floor, but from the cafeteria below he heard the murmur of a hundred voices.

The principal's door was open. There was a phone in the outer office, an ancient upright that Miss Tibbetts, the principal's secretary, used. Harry took the receiver off the hook, set it on the desk and, holding the upright with his left hand, dialed his home number.

He grinned with excitement thinking of her when she answered. Ma didn't like phones and couldn't hear good on them, but she'd hear this. He could see her listening and her face lighting up, and then, afterward, ordering Pa around to help her, getting the gray dress ready and her coat. She never wore a hat, but let the wind command her hair, and Harry didn't care.

But she didn't answer.

Aloud he said, "Wrong number," but felt the first, tiny stabs of alarm in his chest. He dialed again, slowly now, holding the receiver to his ear, hearing the first ring, the second, the third, the eighth, the ninth, and finally, the operator's voice telling him there was no answer.

He felt the ache in his chest now, and his hands were wet. "Maybe Ma is sick or something," he thought, and he knew who had to take the blame. He dialed the 0 and asked the operator to check the number; maybe the phone was out of order. But all the time he knew it wasn't.

At last he thanked the operator and replaced the receiver and stood listlessly at the desk, wondering what to do. Now he remembered his ma helping him with fractions when he was at Crowley School. He remembered her at graduation, Ma and Pa sitting alone in the back row, and after he had his diploma, when the other guys were bringing their parents up to the front of the auditorium, he had led them out to the hall and home immediately. He remembered her walking over to the skating rink on Inverness Street, standing in a corner beside the fence to watch him skate under the floodlights, careful not to be seen, but he had seen her, all right. Seen her and kept away from that corner.

It seemed to him now, alone in the principal's office, that he had been hiding his ma all his life, and he was sick inside then, with a physical distaste in his mouth. He grimaced with self-hatred, wanting, somehow, to feel a sharper pain, to hurt himself deliberately; and he left the office and almost ran into Mr. Quint and a woman.

"Hello, Harry," Mr. Quint said. "I thought you were practicing."

"I guess not, sir."

"This is my wife, Harry," Mr. Quint said. "Harry Wojick, Emma," he said. "Harry's our first baseman."

Mrs. Quint smiled and shook hands with him.

"Mrs. Quint wants to use the phone," the assistant coach said. "She's worried about our little girl . . . I'll see you in the cafeteria, dear," he said to his wife.

She nodded, and Mr. Quint took Harry's arm. "Let's get some of those cookies, Harry."

"I can't, sir. My mother isn't there," Harry said.

"Oh, yes. One of the boys told me. She's seeing a doctor. Hasn't been feeling well, eh?"

Harry pulled his arm away. "That's a lie," he said. "I didn't want her to come today."

Mr. Quint started laughing. He put his arm around Harry's shoulders and they walked toward the stairs. "You guys," he said, shaking his head. He looked at Harry. "Do I really look that old, Harry? An old fossil whose leg you all enjoy pulling?"

"What's the difference?" Harry thought. "What difference does it make now?" And his heart leaped as he thought of next year. There'd be an open house next year, but Ma wouldn't go. If she never went anywhere with him, he'd deserve it. If she never talked with him, he had that coming, too. "Just let me get away from Mr. Quint," he thought. Get out of here without trouble and without a fuss. But now they were in the cafeteria, in the midst of mothers and daughters and sons and teachers, and Mr. Quint was pulling him through the mob.

But they got separated and Harry was alone. He wanted to get out quickly now, away from all the laughter and gaiety. He saw Miss Formanek, the French teacher. He saw her wave at him, her finger curved beckoning him. He saw Frankie Thomas standing beside her and the woman between them. He was moving sideways, pushing through the people, and he looked up for Miss Formanek again, and then felt his heart stop. For a long time he remembered his heart stopping dead as he saw the woman in the gray dress.

He thought his legs would give away. His legs were shaking and he was shaking, and he couldn't move until someone pushed him clear and he was standing there before them. He couldn't get his hands free of sweat. He rubbed his hands up and down against the corduroys and looked at his ma.

"I was telling your mother how you were watching for her, Harry. You have a devoted son, Mrs. Wojick," the French teacher said.

Harry saw his ma smile and nod. She was beautiful.

Frankie was wearing a jacket and a tie. How come *he* was dressed up?

"And you're pinch-hitting for Frankie's mother, too," Miss Formanek said. "Frankie was my best student, Mrs. Wojick."

"Frankie's a good boy," Theresa Wojick said.

"They're all good boys," Miss Formanek said, and she excused herself and left them then.

"Ma," Harry said. He had to tell her.

She had her hand in Frankie's arm. She was smiling, and her hair was pulled back neat, and she was the loveliest women he had ever seen. "Ma, I tore up the invitation," he said, and he looked right at her.

"I know," she said. "But Frankie has an

invitation. We are two orphans: mother without a son, and son without a mother."

"I'm your son, Ma," Harry said, and saw Frankie slipping away, but his mother held the black-haired boy.

She was wearing white gloves and she looked right at him, and he was more afraid than he had ever been in his life.

"Ma." He held her elbows as she had held his and he didn't drop his eyes. He said, "Please, Ma, I'm your son. Please, Ma, let's get something to eat. There's my coach there. I want to introduce you to my coach."

"Yes," she said, and she smiled at him then, and for him. "Yes," she said, and put one hand through his arm and the other through Frankie's. "Introduce, please, to this coach, my little son."

Discussion

1. Why doesn't Harry want his mother to come to the open house at school?

2. How does Harry try to prevent his mother from going to the open house?

3. Harry later wants his mother to be at the open house. Why does he change his mind?

4. When Harry is trying to reach his mother on the phone, he thinks about how he has treated her during his school life. What things had he done to her? At the end of the story, how does he feel about his past treatment of his mother?

5. It is a tense moment when Harry sees his mother with Frankie at the open house. What does Harry confess to his mother? What is her first reaction to him? How does her attitude change by the end of the story? What causes this change? What is Frankie's reaction to Harry's conversation with his mother?

Vocabulary

Instead of learning just one new word at a time, you can learn several new words—if you learn them in groups or WORD FAMILIES. A word family is any set of words that has two common features:

1. All the words in the group contain a word part that is the same, or they have the same series of letters which are drawn from some other language.

2. All the words in the group have meanings that relate somehow to that same word part.

For example:

uniform   union   unit   universal   disunited

Each of the words at the bottom of the previous page contains the same word part, *uni,* which was brought into English from Latin. The meaning of this word part in English is the same as it is in Latin: "oneness," or "being joined together into one."

A. On a separate sheet of paper, copy the five *uni* family words listed on the previous page. After each word try to write its definition. Use a dictionary only if necessary. Then underline the part of your definition that relates to "oneness" or to "being joined together into one." Write your answers this way:

unison—"joined together in speech or song, as if with one voice"

B. Here are five other members of the *uni* word family:

unicolor   unicycle   unidirectional   unipersonal   unipolar

Even if you have never seen these words before, you should be able to figure out their meanings for two reasons. First, you know what *uni* means. Second, you probably know the meaning of the rest of each word.

Copy the five words above on the same sheet of paper. After each one, write what you think its definition is. Then check a dictionary. If any guess you made is wrong, correct it. Write your answers this way:

word—unisex   guessed definition—"one sex"
dictionary definition—"suitable for either sex" (like a cap for both men and women)

Norman Katkov 1918——

Norman Katkov was born in Russia, grew up in St. Paul, Minnesota, and graduated from the University of Minnesota. During his service in the United States Army, he worked on the *Yank* newspaper. Later he was a reporter for the St. Paul *Pioneer Press.* Katkov is also the author of the movie script, *It Happened to Jane,* as well as television scripts for *Ben Casey, The Virginian,* and other shows. His books include: *Eagle at My Eyes, A Little Sleep a Little Slumber, Eric Matteson,* and *With These Hands.*

If you think Superman can do spectacular things,
wait until you read about Pecos Bill. He could
gallop faster than a speeding locomotive
. . . without a horse!

Pecos Bill Invents Modern Cowpunching

JAMES CLOYD BOWMAN

ALL THE MEN of the I. X. L. were eating out of Pecos Bill's hand within less than a week after he arrived. He took to the life of a cowboy like a duck to water. He learned their best tricks, then went on to do better. Gun Smith and Chuck and the rest were very soon like children before him. Among themselves, they bragged about their noble deeds; but when Pecos was around, they couldn't help thinking that they were mere bridled cayuses.[1]

He could stand on the ground beside a broncho, turn an air flop, and land astride the pony before it had time to tighten a muscle. He could ride bareback without a bridle. He could urge his pony at top speed over ground so rough and uneven that Gun Smith and the others were afraid even to attempt it with bit and saddle. And he was so casual and modest about everything he did that they thought Pecos the eighth wonder of the world. Almost at once he was full of ideas. And what ideas!

Up to Pecos Bill's day, when a man wanted to capture a horse or a steer, he would lay a piece of rope down on the ground, make a loop in one end of it, sit down behind a tree or a blind, and by laying a bait, try to coax the wild critter to step within the loop. He would then jerk sharply on the rope, and perhaps one time in a dozen, if he was lucky, he would succeed in making a catch. It was no uncommon thing for a man to wait around and lose an entire month's time without laying hold of a single animal.

"Well, this sort of thing has got to be changed," said Pecos Bill to himself when no one was near to hear him. "A man can't be expected to waste his entire lifetime catching a single horse or cow."

Without further delay, Pecos got hold of the longest piece of rope he could find around the ranch, and began to throw it through the air. Next he rode off alone where the others could not see what he was doing. After three days of constant practice, he found that he could lasso almost anything. He was limited only by the reach of his line.

Pecos Bill would just make a large loop in one end of his rope, swing it wildly about his head three or four times, and then, with a quick flip of his forearm and wrist, send it

---

1 **cayuses** (kī yüs′ ez): horses.

flying like a bullet. And as he grew more and more skilled, he added rapidly to the length of his rope.

As soon as he was entirely sure of himself, Pecos asked the boys to come out and let him show them his new invention.

"See that roan steer across there? That's Old Crook-horn, our wildest critter, ain't it?" Pecos asked quietly.

Before anyone was aware of what he was doing, Pecos had whirled his loop about his head and had sent it so fast in the direction of the four-year-old, that the eye could scarcely follow it.

In an instant the old steer began to jump and bellow, and Pecos Bill to tow in the rope. Soon the astonished steer stood with lowered head before the even more surprised cowboys.

Not content with this great skill, Pecos began practicing from horseback.

In another week, he again called his cowboys out to see what he could do. They watched, with popping eyes, as he gave his rope a double turn around his saddle-bow. He then started his broncho at a hard gallop. They saw him quickly approach a rather tall, scraggly mesquite tree, whirl his loop wildly about his head and then fling it into the air. When he dragged a great hawk down from the topmost branch with the noose about its neck, the men were unable to believe their eyes.

"What sort o' wonder worker is this anyway?" they asked each other. "No human could ever throw the rope like that!"

Then Pecos Bill showed the men how it was done, and after two or three months of hard practice, each of them was able to make frequent catches at a distance of from ten to not more than twenty feet.

In the meantime, Pecos Bill had become

dissatisfied with the fact that he couldn't find a longer rope. So he began to braid himself a cowhide lariat. This is how he went to work. First he looked up some old horned steers that had lived so many years within the depths of the trees that there were green algae on their backs—moss-backs, sure enough. What's more, these steers were so old their faces were gray and wrinkled.

Whenever Pecos Bill got hold of one of these old fellows, he first loosened the hide behind the ears. He then grasped the steer by the tail and with a flip of his wrist and forearm and a wild yowl, he frightened the animal so that it jumped out of its skin. The tough hides of these old moss-backs were just what Pecos needed.

Three or four years later when he had it finished, his loyal ranchers declared on all sides that the lariat was as long as the equator, and that Pecos could lasso anything this side of China.

It was thus that Pecos Bill solved one of the problems that had worried cowhands and their bosses for years.

Another thing that Pecos very soon learned was that every ranch outfit was a bitter enemy of every other outfit. When two neighboring ranchers happened to meet anywhere near the supposed boundary of their pasture lands, they would begin to complain about missing cattle. Soon one would accuse the other of rustling—a polite word for stealing—his stock. Then there would be a sudden flashing of pistols, and one or the other, and often both men would bite the dust.

"Why do they all make such fools of themselves?" Pecos Bill asked. "Why don't they invent some way of marking their horses and cattle so that they will know them wherever they happen to meet them? All this fighting and killing is sheer nonsense. The spirit of the Coyote pack is entirely lacking."

While Pecos Bill was trying to invent a plan for marking the animals, a deer fly gave him just the right suggestion when it nipped him sharply on the arm. In chasing the fly away, he naturally happened to notice the tattooed star that was his own mark of identification. "Mother was wiser than all these cowmen put together," Pecos declared, laughing at himself for having been so slow in finding the right idea! "Why of course cattle and horses can be tattooed the same way. Then they'll be marked for life."

That very evening Pecos Bill explained his plans to Bean Hole. The cook listened, then shook his head. "But tattooin' is too infernal slow," declared Bean Hole, looking at the purple markings up and down the backs of his own arms. "It wasted more'n a whole week of my time to do these pictures. It'd be quicker to burn the mark on. I ain't been cookin' all these years for nothin'. I know that if you burn the skin deep enough, it'll leave an everlastin' scar. Look at this mark now—I've been carryin' it on my wrist for more'n twenty-seven years, and it's just as plain now as ever it was."

"You're right," shouted Pecos. "Together we've invented a new system of bookkeeping for every cowhand in the world."

That evening Pecos explained the new invention to the cowboys, who were open-mouthed at the cleverness of the plan. Rusty Peters, who was a blacksmith by trade, was set immediately to make the brands. He bent the iron so that it would read I X L when burnt upon the side of a horse or a cow.

The next morning all the men were as excited as boys. They herded and roped the cattle, dragging them near the heated irons and throwing them on their side to apply the stinging brand. All day long the smoke curled. All day long the cattle bellowed.

"Keep that iron a cherry red, I'm a-tellin' you," shouted Bean Hole, as he gave directions. "Hold it on long enough to do more'n singe the hair. Wait till it smells like the Devil's own stithy, and looks like the whole critter was burned to a cracklin'. That's not near long enough. She'll shed that mark before the snow flies. There, that's about right. Let her bawl her fill. The loss of a few mouthfuls of hot air ain't going to hurt her any."

"Keep quiet, you old bag o' wind," shouted Rusty Peters, hard at work. "I ain't a blacksmith for nothin'! I'll burn a brand across your mouth in a minute if you don't keep quiet."

By evening the entire job was complete. It was found that the I. X. L. outfit possessed fifty-seven steers of various ages, forty-one cows, some fat and sleek, some spindly and thin, and twenty-four calves.

"This small herd ain't really enough to bother with," Pecos Bill observed in disappointment. "I thought you cowmen said you had a real ranch. Why, the woods are full of wild cattle that belong to nobody in particular. I'll just go out and drive in a few thousand of them. We'll put our trademark on them, and then they'll be ours."

"But how in tarnation will we ever keep these longhorns from runnin' straight away again?" asked Gun Smith with a doubting stare. "What's the use of goin' through all this trouble disfigurin' the sides of all these cattle with our silly I. X. L. advertisement, if we're goin' to turn 'em back to the wild prairies again?"

Pecos Bill had not thought of this. The general custom among the cowmen had been to allow all the cattle to go and come whenever they liked. The ranch shack was nearly always built beside running water, and naturally, a few of the timid and lazy cows and steers would make this their home. The more ambitious stock would just as naturally wander off across the prairies and mesa and take refuge within the mesquite woods. Soon they would be as wild as deer and as difficult to catch.

This careless way of doing things meant that each ranch had a mere handful of shifting population, as far as the cattle were concerned. When the pasture and the water elsewhere were scarce, the cattle would flock to the ranch; but most of the time they would not even trouble themselves to take a French leave.

"It's dead wrong," said Pecos Bill to himself as he squatted on his haunches. "The problem to be solved is this: How are the cattle to be kept together in a herd after they are branded?"

While he was trying to work out the answer, he loped off alone to the top of a small mountain one morning before the others were awake. Far over the rolling prairies he could see many small wandering herds of cows and steers.

"Of course, if bad should come to worse, I could just round the herd up every night and throw my noose about them, and tie the cattle up till morning," he smiled. "But that ain't a good solution, for I can't bind myself that close to the ranch. I've got to reserve my energy for bigger work. All kinds of things are waiting to be invented."

At first as he sat and thought, his mind was just one grazing herd after another. He saw cattle scattered all over the prairies; he saw cattle stampeded, and he saw cattle leaving the herd to get lost in the wild mesa. But after a little things cleared up and he knew what he was going to do.

He got up, stretched the kinks out of his muscles and started at a brisk gallop for the ranch house. As soon as he arrived he called for everybody to come.

"Here's the plan," he said excitedly. "The way to keep the herd together is for you men to ride out with the cattle every day. By waking up the drags and by holding back the leaders, the herd can be kept together and can be made to go to the best feeding grounds every day."

"You mean," said Gun Smith, with an ironical smile, "that us cowpunchers has got to be ordinary bovine[2] critters the rest of our lives?"

"And stay with the herd all night and sleep with the hoot owl?" asked Moon Hennessey sourly.

"Oh, yes," and the musical Mushmouth sang with a pretense of tears in his voice:

"The centipede runs 'cross my head,
The vinegaroon crawls in my bed,
Tarantulas jump and scorpions play,
The bronchs are grazin' far away,
The rattlesnake sounds his noisy cry,
And the Coyotes sing their lullaby,
While I *sleep* soundly beneath the sky."

"It don't appeal to me," complained Moon Hennessey.

"Oh, well, you'll be just crazy about it when you've tried it—especially if the herd stampedes in your direction," suggested Gun Smith with irony. "It's goin' to be a regular picnic, Sundays and weekdays together, an' there's no doubt about it."

"And if the herd gets stampeded you'll be on hand to turn the leaders and start them millin' until they are bitterly disappointed in

---

2 **bovine:** cow or ox.

trying to run away," added Pecos Bill quietly. "Besides, sleeping out under the stars is wonderful, once you've acquired the knack. I know from long experience."

"It'll all be easier than handlin' a month-old heifer calf," laughed Gun Smith bitterly.

"Well, now that we have decided what to do, I'll go out and drive in the cattle to be branded. And while I'm away Gun Smith will be your foreman. He'll keep you out of mischief. We can't get started too soon. So, with your permission, I'll be going right away. I'll have a herd ready to be branded first thing in the morning."

As soon as Pecos Bill had darted out into the night, the men began to wonder whether his coming to them had been a blessing or a curse.

"Chuck, before this monstrosity of yours arrived," began Moon Hennessey, "we was leadin' a peaceful and easy life. All we expected to do was swap lies, and eat juicy tobacco. Now, it seems, we're goin' to be set at hard labor!"

"To my way of thinkin', the change will be all to the good," answered Chuck. "And who knows—it may bring us glory and honor—and gold!"

"Well, then, since I'm the appointed foreman of this outfit until Pecos returns," Gun Smith drawled as he put his hands on his guns, "I'm goin' to give you, Chuck, the place of highest honor. While the rest of us turn in for the night, you, Chuck, will take your Old Pepper and make contact with our branded herd. If they object to your presence and attempt to trample you and your noble steed to smithereens by startin' a wild stampede, you'll simply turn the leaders and set the herd millin'. If they show signs of thirst, you will lead them beside the still water!"

"Thank you very much for the honor,"

answered Chuck, as he rose promptly to carry out the assigned task.

"The rest of us motherless mavericks," Gun Smith continued, "will remain here, so's to be on hand with the ropes and the brandin' irons when Old Pecos returns any minute with his promised herd of wild cattle."

"Well," added Moon Hennessey with a bored yawn, "Old Pecos will be doin' splendid if he shows up by the end of next week. There'll be no herd here tomorrow mornin', I can promise you that."

"Don't fool yourself," replied Chuck spiritedly as he turned on his heel. "You evidently ain't yet acquainted with my brother."

"Brother!" fairly hissed Moon Hennessey in a rage. "Cut out your star identification talk and go on about your business!"

Next morning the men were awakened at early dawn by the dull thud, thud, thud of innumerable hoofs, and by the monotonous bawling of the weary cattle. As the men rubbed the sleep out of their eyes and looked about, they discovered, to their astonishment, that Pecos Bill had actually returned with a herd so large that they couldn't begin to see either its beginning or end.

"What, aren't you boys up yet?" Pecos called with a smile. "I've been having a wonderful night. And I've got enough cattle here to keep all of us busy for a while, anyway."

"Enough wild critters to keep the brandin' irons sizzlin' and the smoke risin' for a month of Sundays, I'd say," conceded Gun Smith, none too happily.

But Pecos Bill had no use for conversation just then. Breakfast was gulped down, cattle struggling and bellowing; the alkali dust flying mountain high; Bean Hole rushing about like a chicken with its head off, shouting his

directions amid the din and waving his kettles and pans, and Rusty Peters keeping the smoking brands busy. This was the way it went all day long. By the time the sun had set, the tired men had added three hundred and thirty-eight cattle to their herd. Three hundred and thirty-eight—hurrah for Pecos Bill!

Pecos Bill himself was so happy over the results that frequently during the following months he would go out for an evening adventure, returning promptly the following morning with hundreds more bawling wild cattle. By the end of the season the I. X. L. ranch was one living sea of four-footed beasts.

As soon as his men had finished branding the incoming herd with the I. X. L. trademark, Pecos Bill at once began looking around to find other worlds to conquer. He instructed the men how to live in the saddle, and how to take cat naps astride their grazing ponies. He showed them how to soothe the cattle by crooning songs to them, and how to keep the herd together without annoying even the leaders.

When the herd stampeded, as it was sure to do at times, Pecos taught the men how to turn the leaders, and thus start the entire herd milling in a circle until the cattle finally winded themselves, and stopped through sheer weariness in the very spot from which they had started in the first place.

During these days, Bean Hole was the busiest man this side of Mars. After trying for a week to feed the men by carrying food out to them from the ranch shack, he finally gave up. On four or five different occasions, as he was starting out with his kettles and pans, he actually met himself on the trail coming back with the empty dishes of the previous afternoon. If he hadn't stopped his foolishness of trying to work twenty-seven hours a day just when he did, most likely his ghost would still be wandering on the wind over the same trails.

In the despair of complete exhaustion, Bean Hole finally hitched two spans of mules to the chuck wagon, loaded it down with enough food to last a fortnight, and left the ranch shack to take care of itself. He hadn't been gone half an hour before the place looked as deserted as the ruins of Pompeii.

Very soon the entire life of the ranch was going along according to the new plan. Everything was clicking like clockwork and Pecos Bill was so pleased, for the present at least, that he couldn't think of anything left to invent. So he decided to go out and tell the world about what he had been doing, not for the sake of his own fame, but for the benefit of the cowmen of the entire range country.

One evening, after the cattle had settled down for the first sleep of the night, Pecos Bill announced to Gun Smith, his foreman, that it would be necessary for him to go away from the ranch for a few days. "If anybody asks where I am" he whispered, "just tell them that I'll be back for breakfast, like as not."

Pecos then took his boots under his arm, threw his coiled rope over his shoulder, and went bounding off across the rolling prairie. When he came to a strange ranch, he would quickly put on his boots and walk in great dignity, with jangling spurs, up to the boss of the outfit. Very soon he would be telling the wide-eyed cowman his story. In this way he easily covered forty or fifty miles in an hour and a half or two hours.

Pecos Bill thus visited all the ranches of the entire Southwest within two or three months. Not forgetting a single detail, he told the men everywhere what he had done. At first they thought him the biggest liar that had ever been invented in the whole world of cowmen. But when he had limbered up his lariat, and when they had witnessed his performance, they were quite willing to believe everything he told them.

What they saw was even more wonderful than what he had said. For with perfect ease, he would lasso any animal within reach of their vision. He could lasso a grazing or galloping steer, or lay his flying noose around the neck of a bald eagle in full flight.

The flying visits led later to many heated disputes among the puzzled ranchers: "You say this Pecos Bill left Hub's Ferry at nine o'clock? But he was at Slippery Mike's by eleven, and that's a good forty miles as the crow flies, ain't it? And he was alone and on foot, wasn't he? Who is this Pecos Bill, anyway?" Every rancher seemed to have a bigger yarn to tell than his neighbor.

But they were all true—certainly! And through the efforts of Pecos Bill, ranchmen began to have a spring roundup and fall roundup. Pecos persuaded the ranchers of a given range section or river valley to drive together all the cattle of their entire district. They then sorted them into individual herds according to the particular brand of each owner. After this work was completed, each owner branded all of his calves. The strays, with no brand, and the orphan mavericks were then distributed equally and branded so that they could never again go astray. And every bit of the plan was Pecos Bill's.

In the fall the roundup was repeated so that the stray cattle could be located and given back to their rightful owners. After all the exchanges were made, the cowmen, as they took their herds back to their individual feeding grounds, found it easy to count the number of steers that were in condition for the market and the number that they would have to pasture during the coming winter.

Thus it was that each owner was given what belonged to him, according to the laws of reason, and not in accordance with the earlier outlawry of the pistol.

And so it came about very naturally, through the organization of all the scattered cowmen, that the fame of Pecos Bill rapidly spread to the four corners of the range country. From the valley of the Rio Grande, through Texas and New Mexico, Arizona and Colorado, Kansas and Nebraska, and far into the wilderness of Montana and Wyoming, cowboys, when they met, would carelessly throw one foot free from its stirrup and in a resting position shout to their nearest companion: "Say, have you heard about the rope Uncle Bill is still braidin' down on the Pecos? Why, it's already twice as long as the equator! You know, if Old Pecos Bill could only get a toe hold on the moon, he'd turn in and lasso this wanderin' planet of ours and bring it back into the Milky Way, where it belongs! Yes, and Pecos could do it easier than you or I could lasso a year-old heifer calf!"

Discussion

1. When Pecos Bill first arrives at the I. X. L. ranch, why do the men think he is the "eighth wonder of the world"?

2. Describe the "old" way of capturing a horse or steer. What does Pecos Bill invent that changes this old system?

3. What does Pecos Bill use to make his own lasso? How does he get the necessary material to make the lasso? How long did men say the lasso was?

4. Pecos Bill invents branding cattle because neighboring ranchers were always accusing each other of stealing cattle. It bothers Pecos Bill that "the spirit of the Coyote pack is entirely lacking." What do you think that statement means?

5. After branding is invented, another problem arises. How can the men keep the cattle together? What is Pecos Bill's first solution to this problem? Why does he reject that idea? What is his second solution? Why don't some of the men like this second idea?

6. Where does Pecos Bill go when he leaves the I. X. L. for a few days? Why does he make this trip? How do people first react to him when he tells them about his inventions? By the time he leaves a particular place, how do people feel about him?

7. Within a short period of time, "each owner was given what belonged to him, according to the laws of reason." What had these "laws of reason" replaced?

Sometimes when you are about to tell something that happened to you, you are tempted to exaggerate the situation just enough to make it seem more important or funnier than it really was. You explain, for example, about the monster fish you recently caught. You tell how you struggled with it for hours. It was so strong, it dragged you halfway down the stream and broke your pole. However, before the fish swam away, it jumped out of the water. As it did a back flip, you were able to catch it in midair with your hands.

Such a fish tale is very similar to the kind of highly exaggerated story found in early American folktales. These stories are usually humorous and are called TALL TALES. The main characters in tall tales may be fictitious people such as Pecos Bill, Paul Bunyan, or Windwagon Smith. They also may be actual historical heroes such as Annie Oakley and Davy Crockett. These characters usually have impossible tasks to do or problems to solve, and they usually solve them in unusual ways. The personalities, the abilities, and the deeds of the main characters are also usually exaggerated to make them seem more powerful than ordinary people.

1. Within the first two paragraphs, what exaggerations do you see that suggest that "Pecos Bill . . ." is going to be a tall tale?

2. Great exaggeration is used throughout this story to describe Pecos Bill. Find at least three examples.

3. How does Pecos Bill become a legendary figure in the last part of the story?

1. Look back over the story, and choose the invention of Pecos Bill which you think is most ingenious or clever. Write a description of that invention. Begin by explaining why the invention was needed; then tell about the invention. Finally, summarize the results of the invention.

2. Create the basis for a tall tale. In the first paragraph, describe the main character's personality and physical appearance. Be sure to give your character a name, and tell if he or she has any unusual powers or abilities. In the next paragraph, explain the problem the main character must solve, and then briefly tell how he or she will solve it. Finally, think of a good title for your tall tale.

People in Sleepy Hollow talked about a headless horseman and ghosts. Were they just stories, or did Ichabod Crane really see them?

The Legend of Sleepy Hollow

WASHINGTON IRVING

IN THE BOSOM OF ONE of those spacious coves which indent the eastern shore of the Hudson, there lies a small market town, which by some is called Greensburgh, but which is more generally and properly known by the name of Tarrytown. This name was given by the good housewives of the adjacent country, from the tendency of their husbands to linger about the village tavern on market days. Not far from this village, perhaps about two miles, there is a little valley among high hills, which is one of the quietest places in the whole world. A small brook glides through it, with just murmur enough to lull one to repose, and the occasional whistle of a quail, or tapping of a woodpecker, is almost the only sound that ever breaks in upon the uniform tranquillity.

From the listless repose of the place, and the peculiar character of its inhabitants, who are descendants from the original Dutch settlers, this glen has long been known by the name of Sleepy Hollow, and its lads are called the Sleepy Hollow Boys throughout all the neighboring country. A drowsy, dreamy influence seems to hang over the land. The whole neighborhood abounds with local tales, haunted spots, and twilight superstitions; and the nightmare seems to make it the favorite scene of her gambols.[1]

The dominant spirit, however, that haunts this enchanted region, and seems to be commander in chief of all the powers of the air, is the apparition of a figure on horseback without a head. It is said by some to be the ghost of a Hessian trooper[2] whose head had been carried away by a cannonball, in some nameless battle during the Revolutionary War, and who is ever and anon seen by the country folk, hurrying along in the gloom of night, as if on the wings of the wind. His haunts are not confined to the valley, but extend at times to the adjacent roads, and especially to the vicinity of a church at no great distance. Certain historians of those parts claim that the body of the trooper having been buried in the churchyard, the ghost rides forth to the scene of battle in

---

1 **nightmare . . . gambols:** People used to believe that nightmares were caused by an evil spirit who often suffocated people while they slept. This spirit's *gambols* are "playful" activities.
2 **Hessian** (hesh' ən) **trooper:** A German soldier.

ICHABOD CRANE AND THE HEADLESS HORSEMAN attributed to *J. W. Wilgus*

nightly quest of his head; and that the rushing speed with which he sometimes passes along the Hollow, like a midnight blast, is owing to his being late, and in a hurry to get back to the churchyard before daybreak. The specter[3] is known, at all the country firesides, by the name of the Headless Horseman of Sleepy Hollow.

In this by-place of nature, there abode, some thirty years since, a worthy fellow of the name of Ichabod Crane, who sojourned, or, as he expressed it, "tarried," in Sleepy Hollow, for the purpose of instructing the children of the vicinity. The name of Crane was not inapplicable to his person. He was tall, but exceedingly lank, with narrow shoulders, long arms and legs, hands that dangled a mile out of his sleeves, feet that might have served for shovels, and his whole frame most loosely hung together. His head was small, and flat at top, with huge ears, large green glassy eyes, and a long snipe[4] nose, so that it looked like a weathercock, perched upon his spindle neck, to tell which way the wind blew. To see him striding along the profile of a hill on a windy day, with his clothes bagging and fluttering about him, one might have mistaken him for the spirit of famine descending upon the earth, or some scarecrow eloped from a cornfield.

3 **specter:** ghost.

4 **snipe:** a bird.

His schoolhouse was a low building of one large room, rudely constructed of logs; the windows partly glazed, and partly patched with leaves of old copybooks. It stood in a rather lonely but pleasant situation, just at the foot of a woody hill, with a brook running close by, and a formidable birch tree growing at one end of it. From here the low murmur of his pupils' voices, conning over[5] their lessons, might be heard in a drowsy summer's day, like the hum of a beehive; interrupted now and then by the authoritative voice of the master, in the tone of menace or command; or, perhaps, by the appalling sound of the birch,[6] as he urged some tardy loiterer along the flowery path of knowledge. Truth to say, he was a conscientious man, and ever bore in mind the golden maxim, "Spare the rod and spoil the child." Ichabod Crane's scholars certainly were not spoiled.

I would not have it imagined, however, that he was one of those cruel tyrants of the school who joy in the smart[7] of their subjects. On the contrary, he administered justice with discrimination rather than severity, taking the burden off the backs of the weak and laying it on those of the strong. Your mere puny stripling[8] that winced at the least flourish of the rod was passed by. The claims of justice were satisfied by inflicting a double portion on some little, tough, wrong-headed Dutch urchin, who sulked and swelled and grew dogged and sullen beneath the birch. All this he called "doing his duty by their parents," and he never inflicted a chastisement without following it by the assurance, so consoling to the smarting urchin, that "he

would remember it, and thank him for it, the longest day he had to live."

When school hours were over, he was even the companion and playmate of the larger boys; and on holiday afternoons would convoy some of the smaller ones home who happened to have pretty sisters, or good housewives for mothers, noted for the comforts of the cupboard. Indeed it behooved him to keep on good terms with his pupils. The revenue arising from his school was small, and would have been scarcely sufficient to furnish him with daily bread, for he was a huge feeder. To help out his maintenance, he was, according to country custom in those parts, boarded and lodged at the houses of the farmers whose children he instructed. With these he lived successively a week at a time, thus going the rounds of the neighborhood, with all his wordly effects tied up in a cotton handkerchief.

That all this might not be too hard on the purses of his patrons, who are apt to consider the costs of schooling a grievous burden, and schoolmasters as mere drones, he had varied ways of rendering himself both useful and agreeable. He assisted the farmers occasionally in the lighter labors of their farms; helped to make hay; mended the fences; took the horses to water; drove the cows from pasture; and cut wood for the winter fire. He found favor in the eyes of the mothers by petting the children, particularly the youngest. He would sit with a child on one knee, and rock a cradle with his foot for whole hours together.

In addition to his other vocations, he was the singing master of the neighborhood, and picked up many bright shillings by instructing the young folks in psalmody.[9] It was a

---

5 conning over: memorizing.
6 birch: stick or rod from a birch tree used to punish pupils.
7 smart: pain.
8 stripling: youth.

---

9 psalmody (sä′ mə dē): psalm singing.

matter of no little vanity to him, on Sundays, to take his station in front of the church gallery, with a band of chosen singers, where, in his own mind, he completely carried away the palm[10] from the parson. Certain it is, his voice resounded far above all the rest of the congregation; and there are peculiar quavers still to be heard in that church, and even half a mile off, quite to the opposite side of the millpond, on a still Sunday morning, which are said to be descended from the nose of Ichabod Crane. Thus, by various little makeshifts, the worthy pedagogue[11] got on tolerably enough, and was thought, by all who understood nothing of the labor of headwork, to have a wonderfully easy life of it.

The schoolmaster is generally a man of some importance in the female circle of a rural neighborhood, being considered of vastly superior taste and accomplishments to the rough country swains, and, indeed, inferior in learning only to the parson. Our man of letters, therefore, was peculiarly happy in the smiles of all the country damsels. How he would figure among them in the churchyard, between services on Sundays, gathering grapes for them from the wild vines that overran the surrounding trees; reciting for their amusement all the epitaphs on the tombstones; or sauntering, with a whole bevy of them, along the banks of the adjacent millpond; while the more bashful country bumpkins hung sheepishly back, envying his superior elegance and address.[12]

From his half-itinerant life, also, he was a kind of traveling gazette, carrying the whole store of local gossip from house to house, so that his appearance was always greeted with satisfaction. He was, moreover, esteemed by the women as a man of great learning, for he had read several books quite through, and was a perfect master of Cotton Mather's *History of New England Witchcraft,* in which, by the way, he most firmly believed.

He was, in fact, an odd mixture of small shrewdness and simple credulity. His appetite for the marvelous, and his powers of digesting it, were equally extraordinary; and both had been increased by his residence in this spellbound region. It was often his delight, after his school was dismissed in the afternoon, to stretch himself on the rich bed of clover bordering the little brook that whimpered by his schoolhouse, and there con over old Mather's direful tales, until the gathering dusk of the evening made the printed page a mere mist before his eyes. Then, as he took his way, by swamp and stream and awful woodland, to the farmhouse where he happened to be quartered, every sound of nature, at that witching hour, fluttered his excited imagination: the moan of the whippoorwill from the hillside; the boding cry of the tree toad; the dreary hooting of the screech owl; or the sudden rustling in the thicket of birds frightened from their roost. His only resource on such occasions, either to drown thought, or drive away evil spirits, was to sing psalm tunes; and the good people of Sleepy Hollow, as they sat by their doors of an evening, were often filled with awe, at hearing his nasal melody, floating from the distant hill, or along the dusky road.

Another of his sources of fearful pleasure was to pass long winter evenings with the old Dutch wives, as they sat spinning by the fire, with a row of apples roasting and spluttering along the hearth, and listen to their marvelous tales of ghosts and goblins, and haunted fields, and haunted brooks, and haunted

---

10 **palm**: glory; triumph.
11 **pedagogue** (ped'ə gog): school teacher.
12 **address**: here, manner of speaking.

bridges, and haunted houses, and particularly of the headless horseman, or Galloping Hessian of the Hollow, as they sometimes called him. He would delight them equally by his anecdotes of witchcraft, and would frighten them woefully with speculations upon comets and shooting stars, and with the alarming fact that the world did absolutely turn round, and that they were half the time topsy-turvy!

But if there was a pleasure in all this, while snugly cuddling in the chimney corner of a chamber that was all of a ruddy glow from the crackling wood fire, and where, of course, no specter dared to show his face, it was dearly purchased by the terrors of his walk homewards later. What fearful shapes and shadows beset his path amidst the dim and ghastly glare of a snowy night!—How often was he appalled by some shrub covered with snow, which, like a sheeted specter, beset his very path!—How often did he shrink with curdling awe at the sound of his own steps on the frosty crust beneath his feet, and dread to look over his shoulder, lest he should behold some uncouth being tramping close behind him!—And how often was he thrown into complete dismay by some rushing blast, howling among the trees, in the idea that it was the Galloping Hessian on one of his nightly scourings![13]

All these, however, were mere terrors of the night, phantoms of the mind that walk in darkness; and though he had seen many specters in his time, yet daylight put an end to all these evils. He would have passed a pleasant life of it, if his path had not been crossed by a being that causes more perplexity to mortal man than ghosts, goblins, and the whole race of witches put together, and that was—a woman.

Among the musical disciples who assembled, one evening in each week, to receive his instructions in psalmody was Katrina Van Tassel, the daughter and only child of a prosperous Dutch farmer. She was a blooming lass of fresh eighteen; plump as a partridge; ripe and melting and rosy-cheeked as one of her father's peaches; and universally famed, not merely as a beauty, but as an heiress. She was a little of a coquette,[14] as might be perceived even in her dress, which was a mixture of ancient and modern fashions, as most suited to set off her charms. She wore the ornaments of pure yellow gold which her great-great-grandmother had brought over from Holland; the tempting stomacher[15] of the olden time; and a provokingly short petticoat, to display the prettiest foot and ankle in the country round.

Ichabod Crane had a soft and foolish heart towards the sex; and it is not to be wondered at that so tempting a morsel soon found favor

---

14 **coquette** (kō ket′): a flirt.
15 **stomacher**: a decorated triangular cloth which fastens around the waist and hangs over the stomach.

---

13 **scourings** (skour′ ings): rides to search for something.

in his eyes, more especially after he had visited her in her paternal mansion. Old Baltus Van Tassel was a perfect picture of a thriving, contented, liberal-hearted farmer. He was satisfied with his wealth, but not proud of it, and prided himself upon the hearty abundance rather than the style in which he lived. His stronghold was situated on the banks of the Hudson, in one of those green, sheltered, fertile nooks, in which the Dutch farmers are so fond of nestling. A great elm tree spread its broad branches over it, at the foot of which bubbled up a spring of the softest and sweetest water, in a little well formed of a barrel. Close by the farmhouse was a vast barn that might have served for a church, every window and crevice of which seemed bursting forth with the treasures of the farm. Rows of pigeons were enjoying the sunshine on the roof. Sleek, unwieldy porkers were grunting in the repose and abundance of their pens. A stately squadron of snowy geese were riding in an adjoining pond, convoying whole fleets of ducks. Regiments of turkeys were gobbling through the farmyard and guinea fowls fretting about it with their peevish, discontented cry. Before the barn door strutted the gallant cock, clapping his burnished wings, and crowing in the pride and gladness of his heart—sometimes tearing up the earth with his feet, and then generously calling his ever-hungry family of wives and children to enjoy the rich morsel which he had discovered.

The pedagogue's mouth watered as he looked upon this sumptuous promise of luxurious winter fare. In his devouring mind's eye he pictured to himself every roasting-pig running about him with a pudding in his belly, and an apple in his mouth. The pigeons were snugly put to bed in a comfortable pie, and tucked in with a coverlet of crust; the geese were swimming in their own gravy; and the ducks pairing cozily in dishes, with a decent competency of onion sauce. In the porkers he saw carved out the future sleek side of bacon, and juicy, relishing ham; not a turkey but he beheld daintily trussed up, with its gizzard under its wing, and, perhaps, a necklace of savory sausages; and even bright chanticleer[16] himself lay sprawling on his back, in a side dish, with uplifted claws.

As the enraptured Ichabod fancied all this, and as he rolled his great green eyes over the fat meadowlands, the rich fields of wheat, of rye, of buckwheat, and Indian corn, and the orchard burdened with ruddy fruit, which surrounded the warm tenement of Van Tassel, his heart yearned after the damsel who was to inherit these domains.

When he entered the house, the conquest of his heart was complete. It was one of those spacious farmhouses, with high-ridged but lowly sloping roofs, built in the style handed down from the first Dutch settlers, the low, projecting eaves forming a piazza[17] along the front, capable of being closed up in bad weather. Under this were hung flails,[18] harnesses, various utensils of husbandry, and nets for fishing in the neighboring river. Benches were built along the sides for summer use; and a great spinning wheel at one end, and a churn at the other, showed the various uses to which this important porch might be devoted. From this piazza the wondering Ichabod entered the hall, which formed the center of the mansion and the place of usual residence. Here rows of resplendent pewter, ranged on a long dresser, dazzled his eyes. In one corner stood a huge bag of wool ready to

---

16 **chanticleer** (chan′ tə klir): a rooster.
17 **piazza** (pē az′ ə): a porch.
18 **flails** (flālz): tools for threshing grain.

be spun; in another a quantity of linsey-woolsey just from the loom; ears of Indian corn and strings of dried apples and peaches hung in gay festoons along the walls, mingled with red peppers; and a door left ajar gave him a peep into the best parlor, where the claw-footed chairs and dark mahogany tables shone like mirrors; and a corner cupboard, knowingly left open, displayed immense treasures of old silver and well-mended china.

From the moment that Ichabod laid his eyes upon these regions of delight, the peace of his mind was at an end, and his only study was how to gain the affections of the peerless daughter of Van Tassel. In this enterprise, however, he had more real difficulties than generally fell to the lot of a knight-errant of yore, who seldom had anything but giants, enchanters, fiery dragons, and such like easily conquered adversaries to contend with. Ichabod, on the contrary, had to win his way to the heart of a country coquette, beset with whims and caprices which were forever presenting new difficulties; and he had to encounter a host of fearful adversaries of real flesh and blood, the numerous admirers who beset every portal to her heart, keeping a watchful and angry eye upon each other, but ready to fly out in the common cause against any new competitor.

Among these the most formidable was a burly, roaring, roistering blade,[19] of the name of Abraham, or, according to the Dutch abbreviation, Brom Van Brunt, the hero of the country round, which rang with his feats of strength and hardihood. He was broad-shouldered and double-jointed, with curly black hair, and a bluff but not unpleasant countenance, having a mingled air of fun and arrogance. From his Herculean frame and great powers of limb, he had received the nickname of "Brom Bones," by which he was universally known. He was famed for great knowledge and skill in horsemanship. He was foremost at all races and cockfights. He was always ready for either a fight or a frolic, but had more mischief than ill will in his composition; and, with all his overbearing roughness, there was a strong dash of waggish good humor at bottom. He had three or four boon companions, who regarded him as their model, and at the head of whom he scoured the country, attending every scene of feud or merriment for miles round. In cold weather he was distinguished by a fur cap, surmounted with a flaunting fox's tail; and when the folks at a country gathering spied this well-known crest at a distance, whisking about among a squad of hard riders, they always stood by for a squall.[20] Sometimes his crew would be heard dashing along past the farmhouses at midnight, with whoop and halloo; and the old dames, startled out of their sleep, would listen for a moment till the hurry-scurry had clattered by, and then exclaim, "Aye, there goes Brom Bones and his gang!" The neighbors looked upon him with a mixture of awe, admiration, and good will; and when any madcap prank or brawl occurred in the vicinity, always shook their heads, and warranted Brom Bones was at the bottom of it.

This reckless hero had for some time singled out the blooming Katrina for the object of his gallantries, and it was whispered that she did not altogether discourage his hopes. Certain it is, his advances were signals for

---

19 **roistering blade** (roi′ stə ring blād): a young man given to wild, destructive fun.

20 **squall**: storm; here, a fight or disturbance.

rival candidates to retire. When his horse was seen tied to Van Tassel's paling,[21] on a Sunday night, a sure sign that his master was courting or, as it is termed, "sparking," within, all other suitors passed by in despair.

Such was the formidable rival with whom Ichabod Crane had to contend, and, considering all things, a stouter[22] man than he would have shrunk from the competition, and a wiser man would have despaired. He had, however, a happy mixture of pliability and perseverance in his nature.

To have taken the field openly against his rivals would have been madness. Ichabod, therefore, made his advances in a quiet and gently insinuating manner. Under cover of his character of singing master, he made frequent visits at the farmhouse; not that he had anything to fear from the meddlesome interference of parents, which is so often a stumbling block in the path of lovers. Balt Van Tassel was an easy, indulgent soul; he loved his daughter better even than his pipe, and, like a reasonable man and an excellent father, let her have her way in everything. His notable little wife, too, had enough to do to attend to her housekeeping and manage her poultry; for, as she sagely observed, ducks and geese are foolish things, and must be looked after, but girls can take care of themselves. Thus, while the busy dame bustled about the house, or plied her spinning wheel at one end of the piazza, honest Balt would sit smoking his evening pipe at the other. In the meantime, Ichabod would carry on his suit with the daughter by the side of the spring under the great elm, or sauntering along in the twilight—that hour so favorable to the lover's eloquence.

I profess not to know how women's hearts are wooed and won. To me they have always been matters of riddle and admiration. He who wins a thousand common hearts is entitled to some renown; but he who keeps undisputed sway over the heart of a coquette is indeed a hero. Certain it is, this was not the case with the redoubtable Brom Bones. From the moment Ichabod Crane made his advances, the interests of the former evidently declined. His horse was no longer seen tied at the palings on Sunday nights, and a deadly feud gradually arose between him and the schoolmaster of Sleepy Hollow.

Brom, who had a degree of rough chivalry in his nature, would have carried matters to open warfare, and have settled their pretensions to the lady according to the mode of the knights-errant of yore—by single combat; but Ichabod was too conscious of the superior might of his adversary to enter the lists[23] against him. He had overheard a boast of Bones, that he would "double the schoolmaster up, and lay him on a shelf of his own schoolhouse"; and he was too wary to give him an opportunity. There was something extremely provoking in this obstinately pacific system; it left Brom no alternative but to play boorish practical jokes upon his rival. Ichabod became the object of whimsical persecution to Bones and his gang of roughriders. They harried his hitherto peaceful domains; smoked out his singing school, by stopping up the chimney; broke into the schoolhouse at night and turned everything topsy-turvey; so that the poor schoolmaster began to think all the witches in the country held their meetings there. But what was still more annoying, Brom took opportunities of turning him into ridicule in the presence of his mistress, and

---

21 **paling:** fencing.
22 **stouter:** here, braver.

23 **the lists:** the areas of combat.

had a scoundrel dog whom he taught to whine in the most ludicrous manner and introduced as a rival of Ichabod's to instruct her in psalmody.

In this way matters went on for some time, without producing any material effect on the relative situation of the rivals. On a fine autumn afternoon, Ichabod, in pensive mood, sat enthroned on the lofty stool whence he usually watched all the concerns of his little literary realm. In his hand he swayed a ferule, that scepter of despotic power,[24] the birch of justice reposed on three nails, behind the throne, a constant terror to evildoers. Apparently there had been some appalling act of justice recently inflicted, for his scholars were all busily intent upon their books, or slyly whispering behind them with one eye kept upon the master; and a kind of buzzing stillness reigned throughout the schoolroom. It was suddenly interrupted by the appearance of a man who came clattering up to the school door with an invitation to Ichabod to attend a merrymaking, or "quilting frolic," to be held that evening at Mynheer[25] Van Tassel's.

All was now bustle and hubbub in the late quiet schoolroom. The scholars were hurried through their lessons, without stopping at trifles; those who were nimble skipped over half with impunity,[26] and those who were tardy had a smart application now and then in the rear, to quicken their speed, or help them over a tall word. Books were flung aside without being put away on the shelves, inkstands were overturned, benches thrown down, and the whole school was turned loose an hour before the usual time, bursting forth like a legion of young imps, yelping and racketing about the green, in joy of their early emancipation.

The gallant Ichabod now spent at least an extra half hour at his toilet, brushing up his best and indeed only suit of rusty black, and arranging his locks by a bit of broken looking glass that hung up in the schoolhouse. That he might make his appearance before his mistress in the true style of a cavalier, he borrowed a horse from the farmer with whom he was living, a choleric[27] old Dutchman, of the name of Hans Van Ripper, and, thus gallantly mounted, issued forth, like a knight-errant in quest of adventures. But it is proper that I should, in the true spirit of romantic story, give some account of the looks and equipment of my hero and his steed. The animal he bestrode was a broken-down plow horse that had outlived almost everything but his viciousness. He was gaunt and shaggy, with a thin neck and a head like a hammer; his rusty mane and tail were tangled and knotted with burrs; one eye had lost its pupil, and was glaring and spectral; but the other had the gleam of a genuine devil in it. Still, he must have had fire and mettle in his day, if we may judge from the name he bore of Gunpowder. Old and broken-down as he looked, there was more of the lurking devil in him than in any young filly in the country.

Ichabod was a suitable figure for such a steed. He rode with short stirrups, which brought his knees nearly up to the pommel of the saddle; his sharp elbows stuck out like grasshoppers'. He carried his whip perpendicularly in his hand, like a scepter, and, as his horse jogged on, the motion of his arms was not unlike the flapping of a pair of wings. A small wool hat rested on the top of his nose,

---

24 **ferule . . . power:** a ruler that represented absolute power.
25 **Mynheer** (mīn her'): Dutch for "mister."
26 **impunity** (im pyū' nə tē): without fear of punishment.

---

27 **choleric** (kol' ər ik): bad-tempered.

for so his scanty strip of forehead might be called; and the skirts of his black coat fluttered out almost to the horse's tail. Such was the appearance of Ichabod and his steed as they shambled out of the gate of Hans Van Ripper, and it was altogether such an apparition as is seldom to be met with in broad daylight.

As Ichabod jogged slowly on his way, his eye ranged with delight over the treasures of jolly autumn. On all sides he beheld vast stores of apples: some hanging on the trees; some gathered into baskets and barrels for the market; others heaped up in rich piles for the cider press. Farther on he beheld great fields of Indian corn, with its golden ears peeping from their leafy coverts, and holding out the promise of cakes and hasty pudding; and the yellow pumpkins lying beneath them, turning up their fair round bellies to the sun, and giving ample prospects of the most luxurious of pies. Next he passed the fragrant buckwheat fields, breathing the odor of the beehive, and as he beheld them, soft anticipations stole over his mind of dainty slapjacks, well buttered and garnished with honey by the delicate little dimpled hands of Katrina Van Tassel.

It was toward evening that Ichabod arrived at the castle of the Heer Van Tassel, which he found thronged with the pride and flower of the adjacent country. Old farmers, a spare, leathern-faced race, in homespun coats and breeches, blue stockings, huge shoes, and magnificent pewter buckles. Their brisk, withered little dames, in close-crimped caps, long-waisted gowns, homespun petticoats, with scissors and pincushions and gay calico pockets hanging on the outside. Buxom lasses, almost as old-fashioned as their mothers, except for a straw hat, a fine ribbon, or perhaps a white frock. The sons, in short

square-skirted coats with rows of stupendous brass buttons, and their hair generally queued[28] in the fashion of the times.

Brom Bones, however, was a hero of the scene, having come to the gathering on his favorite steed, Daredevil, a creature, like himself, full of mettle and mischief, which no one but himself could manage. He held a tractable, well-broken horse as unworthy of a lad of spirit.

I pause to dwell upon the world of charms that burst upon the enraptured gaze of my hero as he entered the state parlor of Van Tassel's mansion. Not those of the bevy of buxom lasses, with their luxurious display of red and white; but the ample charms of a genuine Dutch country tea table, in the sumptuous time of autumn. Such heaped-up

28 **queued** (kyūd): gathered in a ponytail or pigtail style.

platters of cakes of various and almost inde- scribable kinds, known only to experienced Dutch housewives! There was the doughty doughnut, the tenderer olykoek,[29] and the crisp and crumbling cruller; sweet cakes and shortcakes, ginger cakes and honey cakes, and the whole family of cakes. And then there were apple pies and peach pies and pumpkin pies; besides slices of ham and smoked beef; and moreover delectable dishes of preserved plums, and peaches, and pears, and quinces, not to mention broiled shad and roasted chickens; together with bowls of milk and cream; all mingled higgledy-piggledy, pretty much as I have enumerated them, with the motherly teapot sending up its clouds of vapor from the midst.

I want breath and time to discuss this banquet as it deserves, and am too eager to get on with my story. Happily, Ichabod Crane was not in so great a hurry as his historian, but did ample justice to every dainty.

He was a kind and thankful creature, whose heart dilated in proportion as his skin was filled with good cheer, and whose spirits rose with eating as some men's do with drink. He could not help, too, rolling his large eyes round him as he ate, and chuckling with the possibility that he might one day be lord of all this scene of almost unimaginable luxury and splendor. Then, he thought, how soon he'd turn his back upon the old schoolhouse, snap his fingers in the face of Hans Van Ripper and every other niggardly[30] patron, and kick any itinerant pedagogue out-of-doors that should dare to call him comrade!

Old Baltus Van Tassel moved about among his guests with a face dilated with content and good humor, round and jolly as the harvest moon. His hospitable attentions were brief, but expressive, being confined to a shake of the hand, a slap on the shoulder, a loud laugh, and a pressing invitation to fall to and help themselves.

And now the sound of the music from the common room, or hall, summoned to the dance. Ichabod prided himself upon his dancing as much as upon his vocal powers. Not a limb, not a fiber about him was idle; and to have seen his loosely hung frame in full motion, and clattering about the room, you would have thought Saint Vitus himself, that blessed patron of the dance, was figuring before you in person. How could the flogger of urchins be otherwise than animated and joyous? The lady of his heart was his partner in the dance, and smiling graciously in reply to all his amorous looks, while Brom Bones, sorely smitten with love and jealousy, sat brooding by himself in one corner.

When the dance was at an end, Ichabod was attracted to a knot of the sager folks, who, with old Van Tassel, sat smoking at one end of the piazza, gossiping over former times, and drawing out long stories about the war. But all these were nothing to the tales of ghosts and apparitions that succeeded. The neighborhood is rich in legendary treasures of the kind. The immediate cause of the preva- lence of supernatural stories in these parts was doubtless owing to the vicinity of Sleepy Hollow. There was a contagion in the very air that blew from that haunted region; it breathed forth an atmosphere of dreams and fancies infecting all the land. Several of the Sleepy Hollow people were present at Van Tassel's, and, as usual, were doling out their wild and wonderful legends. Many dismal tales were told about funeral trains and mourning cries and wailings heard and seen

---

29 **olykoek**: another type of donut.
30 **niggardly**: stingy.

about the great tree where the unfortunate Major André was taken, and which stood in the neighborhood. Some mention was made also of the woman in white that haunted the dark glen at Raven Rock, and was often heard to shriek on winter nights before a storm, having perished there in the snow. The chief part of the stories, however, turned upon the favorite specter of Sleepy Hollow, the headless horseman, who had been heard several times of late, patrolling the country, and, it was said, tethered his horse nightly among the graves in the churchyard.

The lonely situation of this church seems always to have made it a favorite haunt of troubled spirits. It stands on a knoll, surrounded by locust trees and lofty elms, from among which its decent whitewashed walls shine modestly forth. A gentle slope descends from it to a silver sheet of water, bordered by high trees. To look upon its grass-grown yard, where the sunbeams seem to sleep so quietly, one would think that there at least the dead might rest in peace. On one side of the church extends a wide woody dell, along which pours a large brook among broken rocks and trunks of fallen trees. Over a deep black part of the stream, not far from the church, was formerly thrown a wooden bridge. The road that led to it, and the bridge itself, were thickly shaded by overhanging trees, which cast a gloom about it, even in the daytime, but caused a fearful darkness at night. This was one of the favorite haunts of the headless horseman, and the place where he was most frequently encountered. The tale was told of old Brouwer, a most heretical disbeliever in ghosts, how he met the horseman returning from his foray into Sleepy Hollow, and was obliged to get up behind him; how they galloped over bush and brake, over hill and swamp, until they reached the

bridge, when the horseman suddenly turned into a skeleton, threw old Brouwer into a brook, and sprang away over the treetops with a clap of thunder.

This story was immediately matched by a thrice-marvelous adventure of Brom Bones, who made light of the Galloping Hessian as an arrant[31] jockey. He affirmed that, on returning one night from the neighboring village of Sing Sing, he had been overtaken by this midnight trooper; that he had offered to race with him for a bowl of punch, and should have won it, too, for Daredevil beat

31 **arrant:** notorious.

the goblin horse all hollow, but, just as they came to the church bridge, the Hessian bolted, and vanished in a flash of fire.

All these tales, told in that drowsy undertone with which men talk in the dark, the countenance of the listeners only now and then receiving a casual gleam from the glare of a pipe, sank deep in the mind of Ichabod. He repaid them in kind with large extracts from his invaluable author, Cotton Mather, and added many fearful sights which he had seen in his nightly walks about Sleepy Hollow.

The revel now gradually broke up. The old farmers gathered together their families in their wagons, and were heard for some time rattling along the hollow roads, and over the distant hills. The late scene of noise and frolic was all silent and deserted. Ichabod only lingered behind, according to the custom of country lovers, to have a tête-à-tête[32] with the heiress, fully convinced that he was now on the high road to success. What passed at this interview I will not pretend to say, for in fact I do not know. Something, however, must have gone wrong, for he certainly sallied forth, after no very great interval, with an air quite desolate and chopfallen.— Oh, these women! these women! Could that girl have been playing any of her coquettish tricks? Was her encouragement to the poor pedagogue all a mere sham to secure her conquest of his rival?—Heaven only knows, not I!—Let it suffice to say, Ichabod stole forth with the air of one who had been sacking a hen roost rather than a fair lady's heart. Without looking to the right or left to notice the scene of rural wealth on which he had so often gloated, he went straight to the stable, and with several hearty cuffs and

kicks, roused his steed most uncourteously from the comfortable quarters in which he was soundly sleeping, dreaming of mountains of corn and oats, and whole valleys of timothy and clover.

It was the very witching time of night that Ichabod, heavy-hearted and crestfallen, pursued his travel homewards, along the sides of the lofty hills which rise above Tarrytown, and which he had traversed so cheerily in the afternoon. The hour was as dismal as himself. In the dead hush of midnight, he could even hear the barking of the watchdog from the opposite shore of the Hudson; but it was so vague and faint as only to give an idea of his distance from this faithful companion of man. Now and then, too, the long-drawn crowing of a cock would sound far, far off, from some farmhouse away among the hills—but it was like a dreaming sound in his ear. No signs of life occurred near him but occasionally the melancholy chirp of a cricket, or perhaps the gutteral twang of a bullfrog, from a neighboring marsh, as if sleeping uncomfortably and turning suddenly in his bed.

All the stories of ghosts and goblins that he had heard in the afternoon now came crowding upon his recollection. The night grew darker and darker; the stars seemed to sink deeper in the sky, and driving clouds occasionally hid them from his sight. He had never felt so lonely and dismal. He was, moreover, approaching the very place where many of the scenes of the ghost stories had been laid. In the center of the road stood an enormous tulip tree, which towered like a giant above all the other trees of the neighborhood, and formed a kind of landmark. Its limbs were gnarled and fantastic, large enough to form trunks for ordinary trees, twisting down almost to the earth, and rising

---

32 **tête-à-tête:** (tāt′ə tāt′): a private talk.

again into the air. It was connected with the tragical story of the unfortunate André, who had been taken prisoner close by, and was universally known by the name of Major André's Tree. The common people regarded it with a mixture of respect and superstition, partly out of sympathy for the fate of its ill-starred namesake, and partly from the tales of strange sights and doleful lamentations told concerning it.

As Ichabod approached this fearful tree, he began to whistle; he thought his whistle was answered—it was but a blast sweeping sharply through the dry branches. As he approached a little nearer, he thought he saw something white, hanging in the midst of the tree—he paused and ceased whistling, but on looking more closely perceived that it was a place where the tree had been struck by lightning, and the white wood laid bare. Suddenly he heard a groan—his teeth chattered and his knees smote against his saddle; it was but the rubbing of one huge bough upon another as they were swayed about by the breeze. He passed the tree in safety; but new perils lay before him.

About two hundred yards from the tree a small brook crossed the road, and ran into a marshy and thickly wooded glen, known by the name of Wiley's Swamp. A few rough logs, laid side by side, served for a bridge over this stream. On that side of the road where the brook entered the wood, a group of oaks and chestnuts, matted thick with wild grapevines, threw a cavernous gloom over it. To pass this bridge was the severest trial. It was at this identical spot that the unfortunate André was captured, and under cover of those chestnuts and vines were the sturdy yeomen[33] concealed who surprised him. This

has ever since been considered a haunted stream, and fearful are the feelings of the schoolboy who has to pass it alone after dark.

As he approached the stream his heart began to thump. He summoned up, however, all his resolution, gave his horse half a score of kicks in the ribs, and attempted to dash briskly across the bridge. But instead of starting forward, the perverse old animal made a lateral movement, and ran broadside against the fence. Ichabod, whose fears increased with the delay, jerked the reins on the other side and kicked lustily with the opposite foot. It was all in vain. His steed started, it is true, but it was only to plunge to the opposite side of the road into a thicket of brambles and alder bushes. The schoolmaster now bestowed both whip and heel upon the starveling ribs of old Gunpowder, who dashed forward, snuffing and snorting, but came to a stand just by the bridge, with a suddenness that had nearly sent his rider sprawling over his head. Just at this moment a splashing step by the side of the bridge caught the sensitive ear of Ichabod. In the dark shadow of the grove, on the margin of the brook, he beheld something huge, misshapen, black, and towering. It stirred not, but seemed gathered up in the gloom, like some gigantic monster ready to spring upon the traveler.

The hair of the affrighted pedagogue rose upon his head with terror. What was to be done? To turn and fly was now too late; and besides, what chance was there of escaping ghost or goblin, if such it was, which could ride upon the wings of the wind? Summoning up, therefore, a show of courage, he demanded in stammering accents, "Who are you?" He received no reply. He repeated his demand in a still more agitated voice. Still there was no answer. Once more he cudgeled the sides of the inflexible Gunpowder, and,

---

33 **yeomen** (yō′ mən): here, farmers.

shutting his eyes, broke forth with involuntary fervor into a psalm tune. Just then the shadowy object of alarm put itself in motion, and, with a scramble and a bound, stood at once in the middle of the road. Though the night was dark and dismal, yet the form of the unknown might now in some degree be made out. He appeared to be a horseman of large dimensions, and mounted on a black horse of powerful frame. He made no offer of harm or sociability, but kept aloof on one side of the road, jogging along on the blind side of old Gunpowder, who had now got over his fright and waywardness.

Ichabod, who had no relish for this strange midnight companion, and bethought himself of the adventure of Brom Bones with the Galloping Hessian, now quickened his steed, in hopes of leaving him behind. The stranger, however, quickened his horse to an equal pace. Ichabod pulled up and fell into a walk, thinking to lag behind—the other did the same. His heart began to sink within him. He endeavored to resume his psalm tune, but his parched tongue clove to the roof of his mouth, and he could not utter a stave.[34] There was something in the moody and dogged silence of this persistent companion that was mysterious and appalling. It was soon fearfully accounted for. On mounting a rising ground, which brought the figure of his fellow traveler in relief against the sky, gigantic in height, and muffled in a cloak, Ichabod was horror-struck on perceiving that he was headless—but his horror was still more increased on observing that the head, which should have rested on his shoulders, was carried before him on the pommel of the saddle. His terror rose to desperation. He rained a shower of kicks and blows upon Gunpowder, hoping, by sudden movement, to give his companion the slip—but the specter started full jump with him. Away then they dashed through thick and thin, stones flying and sparks flashing at every bound. Ichabod's flimsy garments fluttered in the air as he stretched his long lank body away over his horse's head in the eagerness of his flight.

They had now reached the road which turns off to Sleepy Hollow; but Gunpowder, who seemed possessed with a demon, instead of keeping on it, made an opposite turn, and plunged headlong downhill to the left. This road leads through a sandy hollow, shaded by trees for about a quarter of a mile, where it crosses the bridge famous in goblin story, and just beyond swells the green knoll on which stands the whitewashed church.

As yet the panic of the steed had given his unskillful rider an apparent advantage in the chase; but just as he had got halfway through the hollow the girths of the saddle gave way, and he felt it slipping from under him. He seized it by the pommel, and endeavored to hold it firm, but in vain; and he had just time to save himself by clasping old Gunpowder round the neck, when the saddle fell to the earth, and he heard it trampled underfoot by his pursuer. For a moment the terror of Hans Van Ripper's wrath passed across his mind— for it was his Sunday saddle; but this was no time for petty fears. The goblin was hard on his haunches; and (unskillful rider that he was!) he had much ado to maintain his seat, sometimes slipping on one side, sometimes on another, and sometimes jolted on the high ridge of his horse's backbone, with a violence that he feared would cleave him asunder.[35]

An opening in the trees now cheered him

---

34 **stave** (stāv): stanza of music.

35 **cleave him asunder**: split him in two.

with the hopes that the church bridge was at hand. He saw the walls of the church dimly glaring under the trees beyond. He recollected the place where Brom Bones's ghostly competitor had disappeared. "If I can but reach that bridge," thought Ichabod, "I am safe." Just then he heard the black steed panting and blowing close behind him; he even fancied that he felt his hot breath. Another convulsive kick in the ribs, and old Gunpowder sprang upon the bridge; he thundered over the resounding planks; he gained the opposite side; and now Ichabod cast a look behind to see if his pursuer would vanish, according to the rule, in a flash of fire and brimstone. Just then he saw the goblin rising in his stirrups, and in the very act of hurling his head at him. Ichabod endeavored to dodge the horrible missile, but too late. It encountered his cranium with a tremendous crash—he was tumbled headlong into the dust, and Gunpowder, the black steed, and the goblin rider passed by like a whirlwind.

The next morning the old horse was found

without his saddle, and with the bridle under his feet, soberly cropping the grass at his master's gate. Ichabod did not make his appearance at breakfast—dinner hour came, but no Ichabod. The boys assembled at the schoolhouse, and strolled idly about the banks of the brook, but no schoolmaster. Hans Van Ripper now began to feel some uneasiness about the fate of poor Ichabod and his saddle. An inquiry was set on foot, and after diligent investigation they came upon his traces. In one part of the road leading to the church was found the saddle trampled in the dirt. The tracks of horses' hoofs deeply dented in the road, and evidently at furious speed, were traced to the bridge, beyond which, on the bank of a broad part of the brook, where the water ran deep and black, was found the hat of the unfortunate Ichabod, and close beside it a shattered pumpkin.

The brook was searched, but the body of the schoolmaster was not to be discovered. The mysterious event caused much speculation at the church on the following Sunday. Knots of gazers and gossips were collected in the churchyard, at the bridge, and at the spot where the hat and pumpkin had been found. The stories of Brouwer, of Bones, and a whole store of others, were called to mind; and when they had diligently considered them all, and compared them with the symptoms of the present case, they shook their heads, and came to the conclusion that Ichabod had been carried off by the Galloping Hessian. As he was a bachelor, and in nobody's debt, nobody troubled his head any more about him. The school was removed to a different quarter of the Hollow, and another pedagogue reigned in his stead.

It is true, an old farmer, who had been down to New York on a visit several years after, and from whom this account of the ghostly adventure was received, brought home word that Ichabod Crane was still alive; that he had left the neighborhood, partly through fear of the goblin and Hans Van Ripper and partly in mortification at having been suddenly dismissed by the heiress; that he had changed his quarters to a distant part of the country; had kept school and studied law at the same time, had been admitted to the bar, turned politician, electioneered, written for the newspapers, and finally had been made a justice of the Ten Pound Court.[36] Brom Bones, too, who shortly after his rival's disappearance conducted the blooming Katrina in triumph to the altar, was observed to look exceedingly knowing whenever the story of Ichabod was related, and always burst into a hearty laugh at the mention of the pumpkin, which led some to suspect that he knew more about the matter than he chose to tell.

The old country wives, however, who are the best judges of these matters, maintain to this day that Ichabod was spirited away by supernatural means; and it is a favorite story often told about the neighborhood round the winter-evening fire. The bridge became more than ever an object of superstitious awe, and that may be the reason why the road has been altered of late years, so as to approach the church by the border of the millpond. The schoolhouse, being deserted, soon fell to decay, and was reported to be haunted by the ghost of the unfortunate pedagogue; and the plowboy, loitering homeward of a still summer evening, has often fancied his voice at a distance, chanting a melancholy psalm tune among the tranquil solitudes of Sleepy Hollow.

---

36 **Ten Pound Court:** a small claims court.

1. Why is Ichabod Crane so interested in Katrina Van Tassel?

2. What advantage does Ichabod have over the other young men in courting the girls?

3. What does Brom Bones have against Ichabod Crane? Why doesn't Brom ever fight with Ichabod? What does Brom do instead?

4. What evidence is there that Brom Bones dressed as the Headless Horseman and ran Ichabod out of town?

5. In this story, do you learn about Ichabod's appearance and personality by what other characters say about him or by what the author says about him?

6. What aspect of Ichabod's personality turns out to be his downfall? Explain.

Vocabulary

You can learn new words faster and with less effort if you learn them in groups, or WORD FAMILIES. All the words in a word family contain a word part that is the same, or they have the same series of letters which are drawn from another language. The words in a word family also have definitions which relate in some way to the identical word part.

Here are nine members of one word family:

superman	supernatural	superannuated
supersonic	superstructure	superfluous
superfine	supersensitive	superscribe

As you can see, all of these words are related because they contain the same word part, *super. Super* also has several closely related meanings, such as "beyond," "over," "above," and "more than." Definitions of four other words from the *super* family are used below to show how these meanings apply:

superstition: a belief that goes beyond anything that can be proven true
superintendent: a person who oversees the work of other people
superb: far above the ordinary
superlative: more than any other; most

A. Draw two lines across a sheet of paper, roughly dividing it into three equal parts. On the top third of the paper, list any of the nine words above which you can define without help. Then in the middle third of your paper, list all the words whose meanings you can guess. Finally in the bottom third, list any remaining words.

Now go back to the top third of the paper. After each word, write a definition that includes one or more of the words: *beyond, over, above,* and *more than.*

B. In the middle third of the paper, write the definitions you would guess to be correct. Once again, in each definition use one or more of the words such as *beyond* or *over.* When you finish these two sections, check a dictionary to make sure that your definitions are correct. If they are not, change them. (NOTE: Definitions differ from dictionary to dictionary. Perhaps your dictionary will not use such words as *beyond* or *over.* By thinking carefully, however, you should be able to see the "sense" of these words in each definition.)

C. After each word in the bottom third of your paper, write the dictionary definition.

Washington Irving 1783–1859

Washington Irving, the youngest of eleven children in a wealthy merchant family, was born in New York City. Although he went into a law practice, he quickly lost interest and began writing for newspapers. His earliest major work, *History of New York,* was one of the first books of comic literature written by an American. In 1816, he moved to England where he went bankrupt in an unsuccessful business venture. As a result, he once again turned to writing for a living, and in 1820, he published his most successful work, *The Sketch Book.* It contains the unforgettable tales, "Rip Van Winkle" and "The Legend of Sleepy Hollow." Irving has been called the "Father of American Literature."

Before he had run to get awards and to hear the cheers of the crowds. Now he was running to save lives. This was the one race in his life he had to win . . . but could he?

Going to Run All Night

HARRY SYLVESTER

THEY BROUGHT HIM IN before the commanding officer, a lieutenant colonel, and stood him there, almost as though he were a prisoner, a slight man, whose face, they now remembered, had been curiously harassed and marked by strain before this campaign had begun. He noticed that they walked on either side as if guarding him, as if, indeed, he were a prisoner or someone valued. And since he could think of nothing he had done or left undone for which they should make him a prisoner, he was driven to the incredible conclusion that at last he had come to be of value.

He looked at the lieutenant colonel, seeing that the officer's face was hardly less harassed than his own. All day, in the midst of the danger which constantly encircled them and intermittently killed some of them, the new legend of the lieutenant colonel's irascibility[1] had grown, so that now, standing before the man, the corporal could wonder he was not ripped up and down with words as scores of men had been that day.

The lieutenant colonel looked at him,

blinking and staring, as though making some kind of adjustment from rage to calm. Which it was, perhaps, for to Nilson's amazement he said rather mildly, "They tell me that you used to be a runner, Corporal?"

"Why, yes," Nilson said. "Yes, sir, I mean."

"You used to run distances? I mean road races and such?"

"Yes, sir."

"Ever run in marathon races or anything like that?"

"Yes, sir," the corporal said. He was thinking: There is nothing "like" the marathon. Just the figures alone mean something: 26 miles, 385 yards. "I ran seventh one year in the Boston Marathon." Right after he said it, he could see that the lieutenant colonel was not impressed, that he did not know running seventh in the Boston Marathon was not the same as running seventh in another foot race.

"Well," the officer said, as though making the best of a bad bargain, rubbing his eyes tiredly and slowly with the heels of his hands. "Well, as you know, they've sort of got us over a barrel here. The one radio we still have that is working has been damaged so

---

1 irascibility (i ras′ə bil′ə tē): bad humor; grumpiness.

that we cannot vary the frequency enough to keep the enemy from picking it up rather often."

He went on like that, rubbing his eyes, explaining to the corporal as if the corporal were a general—someone who ought to be told of what the situation was. "We think we can break out at dawn, if we can synchronize our attack with some sort of aid coming from our main forces opposite the point of our own attack. Break through the ring," he said vaguely. Then: "Look! You think you could run across the hills by dark and carry them a message?"

Nilson began to think, for some reason, about how his grandmother used to talk about lightning and how you never knew where or when it was going to strike. Fear was not in him, although for a little while he would think it was fear. His gasp was silent, so that his mouth was open before he began to speak. He said, "Why, I guess so. I mean, I'm not in very good shape. I—"

"But in no worse shape than anyone else here," the lieutenant colonel said. "And you used to be a runner. How long since you stopped active competition?"

"Oh, I was running all the time. Right up until my induction, and even then, when I was still in the States and could get leave, I was competing some."

The officer nodded. "Well, that's about all. There'll be no written message . . . in case you might be taken. You'll be picked up by one of our own patrols probably. Just tell them we can't last another day here and that we're going to try to come through at dawn. It's possible they won't believe you. But that's a chance we'll have to take. If they have time, they can send a plane over with a message, to let us know that they understand, although it hasn't been very healthy here for planes.

There won't be much trouble getting you through their lines at night. I'll send a guard with you until you're beyond their lines and then you'll be on your own. Just follow the road. The main idea is to get there before dawn. I figure it's thirty-five or forty miles before they'll pick you up. We won't attack for six hours. You think you could make it in, say, five hours?"

"Why, if I was in shape," Nilson said, "I could, maybe, easy."

"Still," the officer said, "you're the best we have. Good luck."

"Yes, sir," Nilson said, and saluted and turned.

Outside, the two sergeants stood on either side of him, and the tall one said, "Well, what are you gonna need?"

"I dunno," Nilson said. "I guess I won't need anything. Maybe I'll take a canteen, maybe not." He knew that thirst for water and the actual need for water were not necessarily the same thing; he was already weighing in his mind the weight of the canteen against the necessity for water.

"Well, let's get going, then," the other sergeant said.

The tall sergeant got Nilson a canteen filled with water, and they moved out into the darkness beyond where the tanks and cars stood in a shallow arc like great animals huddled in the dark.

They were more than halfway across the three-mile plain that separated them from the hills holding the enemy, when Nilson said, "Look, this isn't any good for you two, is it? I mean, if they see us, three isn't going to be much better than one?"

"Stop being noble," the tall sergeant said. "Someone's got to show you through the hills."

"I see what you mean," Nilson said.

It was simpler than he had thought it would be. You could neither hear nor see the enemy, who needed no pickets to hear tanks approaching, or a plane.

The three moved upward over the dry hills, the soil crumbling under foot as they climbed, so that at the crest the sergeants were bushed, panting in the heat and the altitude like animals, and even Nilson was sweating. In the moonlight, below them and to the west and right, they could see the road.

"I guess this is where we get off," the tall sergeant said. "You better get going."

"All right," Nilson said. "I gotta get ready, though."

He undressed in the cloud-broken dark, until he sat there in his underwear, his socks and shoes and his dog tag. The other sergeant handed him the canteen.

"I'll take a drink now," Nilson said, "and that'll have to hold me. The canteen's too heavy—"

"You take that canteen," the tall sergeant said. "You're gonna need it."

"Look," Nilson said, then stopped. He saw that they did not know about water and running or any violent exercise. You could be thirsty for an awfully long time without actually needing water, but this was no time to start explaining that to them. "Well," he said, "I'll go along then."

"Good luck," they said. They watched him move, still walking down the slope toward the road a half mile away. They thought it was because he couldn't run down a slope that steep, but Nilson was walking until the water was out of his stomach and he could be sure he wouldn't get a stitch when he started to run.

Watching him, the tall sergeant said, "You think he's gonna do any good?"

"No, I don't," the other sergeant said.

"Even if he gets through their patrols, he'll drop before he gets to our people—or quit and go hide."

"What do you say that for?" the tall sergeant said.

"Because you're probably thinking the same thing I am!"

In the darkness, the tall sergeant nodded. "We both know we could go along, too, now and hide until this is over, because they're not going to get through tomorrow morning."

"But we go back, instead," the other sergeant said. "And I don't know why."

"I don't know why, either," the tall sergeant said.

Then they turned and began to go back the way they had come.

Nearing the road, the feeling of great adventure began to leave Nilson. Not fear but a sense of futility took him—of his own littleness in the night and the desert that was also the enemy's country. At the edge of the road he paused, although he could not tell why and attributed it to fear. It was not fear so much as an unwillingness to undergo one more futility.

He had not been a very good runner, and he was now thirty-one. Like many of the young men of the Scandinavian colonies in Brooklyn, he had run more because it was a tradition among their people. He had liked it, although after almost fifteen years of little or no glory, he had begun to feel that he was too old to keep losing that often, had begun to realize that, after a while, it did something to a man. Not that it was any fault of his; after all, you'd have to be pretty special to run well Saturdays or Sundays after being on your feet all day as a post-office clerk.

He still hesitated on the edge of the road; there was in his hesitation a quality of sullenness, a shadowy resentment against some large amorphous[2] body or group that somehow had become identified with the long years of defeat.

Without quite knowing what the resentment was, he knew it to be, if not wrong, at least inappropriate now and here. He sighed and at the edge of the road did a curious little exercise that relatives of his also had done three hundred years before in Norway. He bent over, touching his toes five or six times and each time straightening up and flinging his arms wide. The idea was to open his lungs quickly and limber the muscles of his chest and arms. Although he was not a very good runner, he knew all about running; he knew that a man ran as much with his arms as with his legs.

He stepped onto the road and in a reflexive gesture pawed at the crude paving as though it were hard-packed cinders, and the heavy G.I. shoes were the short-spiked ones of the distance runner. He felt sheepish, and in the darkness his mouth twisted into a grin. He began to run.

Almost immediately he felt easier; felt confidence flow through him as though it were his blood; felt that now, at last, he was in his own country, or, more accurately, in his own medium. There are mediums of action that vary with the individual; some feel best moving in an automobile, others on a horse, some walking, a few running or flying.

As he ran, he felt with his feet for the part of the tar-and-gravel road that was best suited to him. The road was slightly crowned in the center and in places pocked lightly by machine-gun bullets from the planes that had gone over it. As on most roads, he found that the shoulder was best for running. It was softer, the spikeless shoes slipped less, and its resilience would save him from shin splints tomorrow. He thought with irony that it was of no importance whether he got the little pains along the shin from bruising or pulling the tendons that held the muscle to the bone. Certainly he would run no more tomorrow, come what might; indeed, there might not be a tomorrow.

This started him thinking of what he called fear—but what was really an ennui,[3] a saturation in himself of having for so many years done things to no purpose. He wondered if this, too, would be to no purpose; if some burial detail, an indefinite number of days from now, would find his twisted body some place along this road.

Then he began to think that it would be worse to get to where he was going and not be believed. There was nothing he could think of to do about that, so he stopped thinking of it. Like many Scandinavians, he was a fatalist,[4] and the war had not helped overcome that.

The night—soft, warm and windless—was all around him. In its blackness, there was a quality of brown; or perhaps he imagined this, for all day the hills were brown, so that afterward you associated the color with thirst, with violence and with the imminence[5] of death. He had discovered, only recently and to his relief, that he was not afraid of death; after all, he had no responsibilities in life, no dependents; disablement, though, was something else.

Then suddenly he began to think of the time he had run seventh in the Boston

---

2 **amorphous** (ə môr′ fəs): shapeless.

3 **ennui** (än′ wē): weary boredom.
4 **fatalist**: one who believes that events are fixed in advance.
5 **imminence** (im′ə nəns): nearness, proximity.

Marathon; the cold day and the girls unexpectedly lining the road at Wellesley, and the tremendous lift they had given his spirit, just standing there, calling to the runners, the wind moving their hair and their bright skirts.

He was running faster, too fast, he thought. He was beginning to breathe hard. It was too early to be breathing so hard; but he knew that would pass soon, and the thing called second wind would come to him. He slackened his pace a little, feeling the weight of the shoes and trying to reject the thought before it took too much form; trying not to think of it.

He began to think of the enemy and where the enemy might be; all around him, surely, but probably not too near the road, because, by night, planes could see a road. Still, there might be patrols knowing a man running steadily by night was a strange and unaccountable thing. But they might never see him; only hear him and the pounding of his feet on the road. So, deviously, his mind came back to the thought which he could no longer avoid: there was only one thing to do, take the G.I. shoes off and run without them.

He slowed gradually until he was walking, and walked perhaps thirty yards before he stopped. Then he sat on the ground and took off his shoes.

When he stood up, he hesitated again. Once, he had lost a shoe and had finished the race, but the cinders had taken their toll of that foot.

The road here was bad, but principally what he feared was stepping on one of the scorpions. He wondered if they were out by night—and then he began to run again.

Now the element of strangeness about this man running in the night, this Brooklyn Norwegian in a strange land, was intensified by the silence, in which only his regular, heavy breathing made a sound.

Without knowing it, he ran at times in a kind of stupor. The nights of little or fitful sleep, the days of too little food and water, were beginning to affect him, and he began to take refuge from exhaustion and pain in something at times close to unconsciousness.

Twice he passed tanks not far from the road, their crews sleeping, he himself not knowing he passed them. Like a dun ghost, he drifted with the short, effortless stride he had developed over the long years of competition and training. These little spells of semi-consciousness no longer occurred; effort was too much to permit them, too sustained and by now terrible, so that his senses became acute again, his thoughts long-ranging, sharp and filled with color. It was perhaps this return to acute consciousness, induced by pain, that saved him.

He had begun to think of the long dreams of his youth, of passing through lines of people at the end of the Boston Marathon, as he strode in, tired but easily first; of the Olympic Marathon and the laurel wreath he had read of.

Some place there was sound and a hoarse shouting. He could not tell for a moment whether they were in his thoughts or in the reality of the night all around him. Then the sound, now long familiar to him, but still terrible, of an automatic rifle coughing in the night.

He glanced about him, flinching, his eyes, already strained open by the night, trying to open wider, so that the muscles near them hurt. The shouting, the firing were above him—here the road was sunken—behind and to the right.

The firing sounded again, farther away. He neither heard nor felt bullets. In one of those sudden lifts of speed—instinctive and desperate now—with which a distance runner sometimes in the middle of a race tries to break the heart of his opponents, Nilson started to sprint.

The road ran downhill here, and now through the warm, dark night, the little man let his feet shoot out ahead of him, carrying his legs out with the controlled abandon of the cross-country runner going downhill.

He ran with almost no sound, although he was not aware of this. The shouting and the sound of guns continued behind him. With a faint pleasure, he realized that it was his passing that had alarmed the enemy.

There was an eeriness about him as he moved in the night. Perhaps it was this, perhaps only the adrenalin further secreted in his body by his fear when the shots sounded—but he found a new strength. The legs, the rhythmically moving arms recovered the thing of which, in his boyhood, he and the other runners had made a fetish[6]—the thing called form.

So, going downhill now, the enemy all around him, he experienced a sense of power, as though he were invisible, as though he were fleeter and stronger than anything that could seek to kill or hinder him.

Sweat bathed him, he glistened as though oiled, and there was a slight froth at his lips. He moved with a machinelike rhythm and his eyes—if they could have been seen—might have seemed mad.

The road leveled, ran flat for perhaps a quarter-mile, then began to mount again. He became aware of this only gradually. The first change he noted was in himself, first the mind, then the body. The sense of power, of superhuman ability was gone, almost

---

6 fetish (fet' ish): object of devotion.

abruptly, his lungs began to hurt badly, and the cords in his neck. He was, he suddenly realized, nothing special; he was Pete Nilson from Brooklyn, and he was bushed; he was just about done.

He shook his head, like a trapped, bewildered animal. The desire, the need to stop was extraordinarily strong in him. He tried an old trick: he tried to analyze his pain, knowing this sometimes made it disappear. There was the pain in his lungs, in his throat, in the muscles of his eyes, but not yet where his arms went into the shoulders, not yet just above the knees where the thigh muscles overlapped.

His stride had shortened with the hill and his body leaned forward. He had not been above quitting in a few races, when he was hopelessly outdistanced, when he had not been trained right, when he had not enough rest the previous week to make him strong.

It seemed that he had never been so exhausted as now, and his mind sought excuses to stop. First, came the thought that if only he knew how long he had to run, he might endure it. Twenty-six miles, 385 yards—that was the distance of the Marathon, and in Boston, in Toronto, you always knew within a few hundred yards how far you had come, how far you had to go. But now, no one knew or had known, not within four or five miles. The enemy was in the hills, and the hills were all around the lieutenant colonel and his men, and beyond the hills that held the enemy were more of your own men, some place. So late in his life he learned that it is important to all men in their various endeavors to see an end, to know how far off that end is.

Fatigue blurred his vision and he started to deviate from a straight line, veering slightly from side to side. Although he did not know

it, he was beyond the enemy, and had only to combat himself. But he had forgotten about the enemy, and his mind sought reasons to stop, old resentments that could possess the weight of argument. What had they ever done for him? He should have been a sergeant by now.

Anger formed in him: he could not tell its nature or its object. He realized it might be at himself; then, that it was at himself. He must have been crazy, he thought; he supposed that, all his life, his efforts had been directed obscurely toward achieving a sense of usefulness, corrupted sometimes into what was called a sense of glory. And now, close to it, he had almost rejected it.

When the change occurred, the sudden insight, he was on top of a hill and looking down into a plain full of great shadows; there was a paleness in the sky over the shadows. He was on top of this hill, but whether he was running or standing still, he could not tell, for it was as great an effort to stand as to run.

He began to move downhill again, still veering. He sensed, if he did not see, that there were no more hills beyond and that his own people must be somewhere near, perhaps at the bottom of the hill he now descended.

As he staggered, half-blind in the dim light, to the foot of the hill, he thought of the Athenian runner finishing the first Marathon and, as he collapsed, crying, "Rejoice, we conquer!" Nilson realized how much that image, those words had been with him, influencing him all his life. They heartened him now, sealed the sense of meaning in him.

A sentry challenged as the road leveled out into the plain, and Nilson, not knowing the password, reasoned that this was the place for him to collapse. Pheidippides, finishing the first Marathon, had cried, "Rejoice, we conquer!" but Pete Nilson, thinking this, and finishing his own run, said in a kind of prayer, "Buddy, don't shoot," knelt and quietly fell forward in the dust.

He didn't remember exactly what he said to them, but they took him to another lieutenant colonel. And the miracle was not over. He could not believe it then; all the rest of his life, he could hardly believe it. They believed him. They believed him, and some place near him as he sat stupefied on a canvas stool in a tent, he heard all around him, in the first light, the sound of armor beginning to move, the clatter and roar of the tanks.

A staff sergeant tried to explain. "Look," he said, "nobody comes down here in the shape you're in to lie to somebody else. You see?" Especially the feet, the sergeant thought.

But all Nilson did was sit on the canvas stool and stare.

"Look," the sergeant said again, "you'll get something big for this. Don't you catch?"

Nilson stared at him. He was beginning to catch, but it would be a long time, if ever, before he could make anyone understand. The big thing, the most important thing in his life, was that he had come down here, without credentials of any sort, and they had believed him. The citation, the medal, nothing was ever going to mean that much.

"Look," the sergeant said. "They're getting you a doctor. You want anything now, though? Coffee or something?" Don't the guy know about his feet, he thought.

The little froth still at his lips, Nilson shook his head. He looked like a madman, and the sergeant thought that maybe he was mad. But all Nilson was doing was sitting there listening to the roar and thinking that he, Pete Nilson, had set it in motion. He didn't want anything right then, only to sit there and listen.

Discussion   1. When Corporal Nilson is brought before the commanding officer, what are his thoughts?

2. What is Nilson's mission? Why is he selected? Why is this mission so important to his unit?

3. Why do the escorts say of Corporal Nilson, "Even if he gets through their patrols, he'll drop before he gets to our people—or quit and go hide."?

4. What physical and mental strategies does Nilson use to run the forty miles through enemy lines?

5. What new insights does Nilson gain about himself during and after his run?

6. Although Nilson's run is successful, he feels the real miracle is that the lieutenant colonel of the main forces believes him. Why is Nilson's story believed? Why is it difficult for Nilson to accept their belief in him?

7. At the end of the story, the sergeant tells Nilson that he will be honored for his bravery. What means more than the citation and medal to Nilson?

Composition

1. Imagine you are a successful runner, and a friend of yours is going to run in his or her first marathon race. He or she wants some advice on running the race. Write a letter to your friend, passing along any useful running techniques mentioned in this selection. Discuss both the physical and mental strategies necessary to be competitive in the race. End by commenting on the feeling of success when a race is won.

2. Winning or achieving a goal is a wonderful feeling—whether it is winning a race or earning an *A* on a vocabulary test. Think of some goal you or a friend of yours has achieved. Begin by stating the goal. In the next paragraph, tell about the things that might have prevented you from achieving that goal. In the next paragraph, tell what you did—what strategies you used—to assure your success. Finally, relate the feeling you had when you won or achieved your goal.

Vocabulary

Context clues are hints about the meaning of an unknown word that are given by familiar words surrounding it. There are many different kinds of context clues. One of them is the EXAMPLE CONTEXT CLUE. As its name implies, an example context clue suggests the general meaning of an unfamiliar word by using an illustration. For example:

Pete Nilson deserves a *citation*. He should be honored with a handsome gold medal.

The *gold medal* in the second sentence suggests the general meaning of *citation:* "an award for outstanding service."

A. Use example context clues to figure out the meaning of each *italicized* word on this page. On a separate sheet of paper, copy the *italicized* words and write possible meanings for them. Then write the example context clues that you used to figure out the meanings. Write your answers this way:

citation: "some kind of honor"—handsome gold medal

1. Fatigue blurred his vision, and he started to *deviate* from a straight line. First toward the left his body moved; then toward the right.

2. The legend of the lieutenant colonel's *irascibility* had grown. Standing before the officer now, the corporal expected to be ripped up and down with words.

3. He thought of his *ennui.* For so many years he had done things to no purpose. He wondered if this, too, would be to no purpose.

4. He ran at times in a kind of *stupor.* He took refuge from exhaustion and pain in a state close to unconsciousness.

5. His senses became *acute* again. His thoughts grew sharp and filled with color.

B. Use a dictionary to check the accuracy of the guesses you made in Exercise A. Write the correct definition if an answer is wrong.

Harry Sylvester 1908—

Harry Sylvester was born in Brooklyn, New York, and graduated from Notre Dame. Upon graduation he wrote for three New York City newspapers, but he gave up journalism to write on his own. His novels include: *Big Football Man, Dearly Beloved, Dayspring,* and *Moon Gafney.* Sylvester once commented that he would have liked to write more novels, but he had to sell over 150 short stories to support his family. Eventually Sylvester returned to journalism for his living.

Life was very different for women in 1891 when this story was written. Equal rights was an unheard-of issue. Women not only could not vote, but they were expected to obey their husbands in all matters. The strangest thing was . . . most people in this New England town accepted this practice without question. That is, until Mother revolted.

The Revolt of "Mother"

MARY E. WILKINS FREEMAN

"Father!"

"What is it?"

"What are them men diggin' over there in the field for?"

There was a sudden dropping and enlarging of the lower part of the old man's face, as if some heavy weight had settled therein; he shut his mouth tight and went on harnessing the great bay mare. He hustled the collar on to her neck with a jerk.

"Father!"

The old man slapped the saddle upon the mare's back.

"Look here, Father, I want to know what them men are diggin' over in the field for, an' I'm goin' to know."

"I wish you'd go into the house, Mother, an' 'tend to your own affairs," the old man said then. He ran his words together, and his speech was almost as inarticulate as a growl.

But the woman understood; it was her native tongue. "I ain't goin' into the house till you tell me what them men are doin' over there in the field," said she.

Then she stood waiting. She was a small woman, short and straight-waisted like a child in her brown cotton gown. Her forehead was mild and benevolent between the smooth curves of gray hair; there were meek downward lines about her nose and mouth; but her eyes, fixed upon the old man, looked as if the meekness had been the result of her own will, never of the will of another.

They were in the barn, standing before the wide open doors. The spring air, full of the smell of growing grass and unseen blossoms, came in their faces. The deep yard in front was littered with farm wagons and piles of wood; on the edges, close to the fence and the house, the grass was a vivid green, and there were some dandelions.

The old man glanced doggedly at his wife as he tightened the last buckles on the harness. She looked as immovable to him as one of the rocks in his pasture land, bound to the earth with generations of blackberry vines.

He slapped the reins over the horse, and started forth from the barn.

"*Father*!" said she.

The old man pulled up. "What is it?"

"I want to know what them men are diggin' over there in that field for."

"They're diggin' a cellar, I s'pose, if you've got to know."

"A cellar for what?"

"A barn."

"A barn? You ain't goin' to build a barn over there where we was goin' to have a house, Father?"

The old man said not another word. He hurried the horse into the farm wagon and clattered out of the yard, jouncing as sturdily on his seat as a boy.

The woman stood a moment looking after him, then she went out of the barn across a corner of the yard to the house. The house, standing at right angles with the great barn and a long reach of sheds and outbuildings, was infinitesimal¹ compared with them. It was scarcely as commodious² for people as the little boxes under the barn eaves were for doves.

A pretty girl's face, pink and delicate as a flower, was looking out of one of the house windows. She was watching three men who were digging over in the field which bounded the yard near the road line. She turned quietly when the woman entered.

"What are they digging for, Mother?" said she. "Did he tell you?"

"They're diggin' for—a cellar for a new barn."

"Oh, Mother, he ain't going to build another barn?"

"That's what he says."

A boy stood before the kitchen glass combing his hair. He combed slowly and painstakingly, arranging his brown hair in a smooth hillock³ over his forehead. He did not seem to pay any attention to the conversation.

"Sammy, did you know Father was going to build a new barn?" asked the girl.

The boy combed assiduously.

"Sammy!"

He turned and showed a face like his father's under his smooth crest of hair.

"Yes, I s'pose I did," he said reluctantly.

"How long have you known it?" asked his mother.

"'Bout three months, I guess."

"Why didn't you tell of it?"

"Didn't think 'twould do no good."

"I don't see what Father wants another

barn for," said the girl, in her sweet, slow voice. She turned again to the window and stared out at the digging men in the field. Her tender, sweet face was full of gentle distress. Her forehead was as bald and innocent as a baby's, with the light hair strained back from it in a row of curl papers. She was quite large, but her soft curves did not look as if they covered muscles.

Her mother looked sternly at the boy. "Is he goin' to buy more cows?" said she.

The boy did not reply; he was tying his shoes.

"Sammy, I want you to tell me if he's goin' to buy more cows."

"I s'pose he is."

"How many?"

"Four, I guess."

His mother said nothing more. She went into the pantry, and there was a clatter of dishes. The boy got his cap from a nail behind the door, took an old arithmetic from the shelf, and started for school. He was lightly built, but clumsy. He went out of the yard with a curious spring in the hips, that made his loose homemade jacket tilt up in the rear.

The girl went to the sink and began to wash the dishes that were piled up there. Her mother came promptly out of the pantry and shoved her aside. "You wipe 'em," said she; "I'll wash. There's a good many this mornin'."

The mother plunged her hands vigorously into the water; the girl wiped the plates slowly and dreamily. "Mother," said she, "don't you think it's too bad Father's going to build that new barn, much as we need a decent house to live in?"

Her mother scrubbed a dish fiercely. "You ain't found out yet we're womenfolks, Nanny Penn," said she. "You ain't seen enough of menfolks yet to. One of these days

---

1 infinitesimal (in′ fi nə tes′ə məl) very small.
2 commodious (kə mō′ dē əs): comfortable; spacious.
3 hillock: a small mound.

you'll find it out, an' then you'll know that we know only what menfolks think we do, so far as any use of it goes, an' how we'd ought to reckon menfolks in with Providence[4] an' not complain of what they do any more than we do of the weather."

"I don't care; I don't believe George is anything like that, anyhow," said Nanny. Her delicate face flushed pink, her lips pouted softly, as if she were going to cry.

"You wait an' see. I guess George Eastman ain't no better than other men. You hadn't ought to judge Father, though. He can't help it, 'cause he don't look at things jest the way we do. An' we've been pretty comfortable here, after all. The roof don't leak—ain't never but once—that's one thing. Father's kept it shingled right up."

"I do wish we had a parlor."

"I guess it won't hurt George Eastman any to come to see you in a nice clean kitchen. I guess a good many girls don't have as good a place as this. Nobody's ever heard me complain."

"I ain't complained either, Mother."

"Well, I don't think you'd better, a good father an' a good home as you've got. S'pose your father made you go out an' work for your livin'? Lots of girls have to that ain't no stronger an' better able to than you be."

Sarah Penn washed the frying pan with a conclusive air. She scrubbed the outside of it as faithfully as the inside. She was a masterly keeper of her box of a house. Her one living room never seemed to have in it any of the dust which the friction of life with inanimate matter produces. She swept, and there seemed to be no dirt to go before the broom; she cleaned, and one could see no difference. She was like an artist so perfect that he has

apparently no art. Today she got out a mixing bowl and a board and rolled some pies, and there was no more flour upon her than upon her daughter who was doing finer work. Nanny was to be married in the fall, and she was sewing on some white cambric[5] and embroidery. She sewed industriously while her mother cooked; her soft milk-white hands and wrists showed whiter than her delicate work.

"We must have the stove moved out in the shed before long," said Mrs. Penn. "Talk about not havin' things, it's been a real blessin' to be able to put a stove up in that shed in hot weather. Father did one good thing when he fixed that stovepipe out there."

Sarah Penn's face as she rolled her pies had that expression of meek vigor which might have characterized one of the New Testament saints. She was making mince pies. Her husband, Adoniram Penn, liked them better than any other kind. She baked twice a week. Adoniram often liked a piece of pie between meals. She hurried this morning. It had been later than usual when she began, and she wanted to have a pie baked for dinner. However deep a resentment she might be forced to hold against her husband, she would never fail in sedulous attention to his wants.

Nobility of character manifests itself at loopholes when it is not provided with large doors. Sarah Penn's showed itself today in flaky dishes of pastry. So she made the pies faithfully, while across the table she could see, when she glanced up from her work, the sight that rankled in her patient and steadfast soul—the digging of the cellar of the new barn in the place where Adoniram forty years

---

4 **Providence:** Divine power; God.

5 **cambric:** a fine, thin white linen.

ago had promised her their new house should stand.

The pies were done for dinner. Adoniram and Sammy were home a few minutes after twelve o'clock. The dinner was eaten with serious haste. There was never much conversation at the table in the Penn family. Adoniram asked a blessing, and they ate promptly, then rose up and went about their work.

Sammy went back to school, taking soft sly lopes out of the yard like a rabbit. He wanted a game of marbles before school and feared his father would give him some chores to do. Adoniram hastened to the door and called after him, but he was out of sight.

"I don't see what you let him go for, Mother," said he. "I wanted him to help me unload that wood."

Adoniram went to work out in the yard unloading wood from the wagon. Sarah put away the dinner dishes, while Nanny took down her curl papers and changed her dress. She was going down to the store to buy some more embroidery and thread.

When Nanny was gone, Mrs. Penn went to the door. "Father!" she called.

"Well, what is it!"

"I want to see you jest a minute, Father."

"I can't leave this wood nohow. I've got to git it unloaded an' go for a load of gravel afore two o'clock. Sammy had ought to have helped me. You hadn't ought to let him go to school so early."

"I want to see you jest a minute."

"I tell ye I can't, nohow, Mother."

"Father, you come here." Sarah Penn stood in the door like a queen; she held her head as if it bore a crown; there was that patience which makes authority royal in her voice. Adoniram went.

Mrs. Penn led the way into the kitchen and pointed to a chair. "Sit down, Father," said she; "I've got somethin' I want to say to you."

He sat down heavily; his face was quite stolid, but he looked at her with restive[6] eyes. "Well, what is it, Mother?"

"I want to know what you're buildin' that new barn for, Father?"

"I ain't got nothin' to say about it."

"It can't be you think you need another barn?"

"I tell ye I ain't got nothin' to say about it, Mother; an' I ain't goin' to say nothin'."

"Be you goin' to buy more cows?"

Adoniram did not reply; he shut his mouth tight.

"I know you be, as well as I want to. Now, Father, look here"—Sarah Penn had not sat down; she stood before her husband in the humble fashion of a Scripture woman—"I'm goin' to talk real plain to you; I never have sence I married you, but I'm goin' to now. I ain't never complained, an' I ain't goin' to complain now, but I'm goin' to talk plain. You see this room here, Father; you look at it well. You see there ain't no carpet on the floor, an' you see the paper is all dirty an' droppin' off the walls. We ain't had no new paper on it for ten year, an' then I put it on myself, an' it didn't cost but ninepence a roll. You see this room, Father; it's all the one I've had to work in an' eat in an' sit in sence we was married. There ain't another woman in the whole town whose husband ain't got half the means you have but what's got better. It's all the room Nanny's got to have her company in; an' there ain't one of her mates but what's got better, an' their fathers not so able as hers is. It's all the room she'll have to be married in. What would you have thought, Father, if we had had our weddin' in a room

---

6 restive: stubborn.

no better than this? I was married in my mother's parlor, with a carpet on the floor, an' stuffed furniture, an' a mahogany card table. An' this is all the room my daughter will have to be married in. Look here, Father!"

Sarah Penn went across the room as though it were a tragic stage. She flung open a door and disclosed a tiny bedroom, only large enough for a bed and bureau, with a path between. "There, Father," said she—"there's all the room I've had to sleep in forty year. All my children were born there—the two that died, an' the two that's livin'. I was sick with a fever there."

She stepped to another door and opened it. It led into the small, ill-lighted pantry. "Here," said she, "is all the buttery I've got—every place I've got for my dishes, to set away my victuals[7] in, an' to keep my milk pans in. Father, I've been takin' care of the milk of six cows in this place, an' now you're going to build a new barn, an' keep more cows, an' give me more to do in it."

She threw open another door. A narrow crooked flight of stairs wound upward from it. "There, Father," said she, "I want you to look at the stairs that go up to them two unfinished chambers that are all the places our son an' daughter have had to sleep in all their lives. There ain't a prettier girl in town nor a more ladylike one than Nanny, an' that's the place she has to sleep in. It ain't so good as your horse's stall; it ain't so warm an' tight."

Sarah Penn went back and stood before her husband. "Now, Father," said she, "I want to know if you think you're doin' right an' accordin' to what you profess. Here,

when we was married, forty year ago, you promised me faithful that we should have a new house built in that lot over in the field before the year was out. You said you had money enough, an' you wouldn't ask me to live in no such place as this. It is forty year now, an' you've been makin' more money, an' I've been savin' of it for you ever sence, an' you ain't built no house yet. You've built sheds an' cow houses an' one new barn an' now you're goin' to build another. Father, I want to know if you think it's right. You're lodgin' your dumb beasts better than you are your own flesh an' blood. I want to know if you think it's right."

"I ain't got nothin' to say."

"You can't say nothin' without ownin' it ain't right, Father. An' there's another thing—I ain't complained; I've got along forty year, an' I s'pose I should forty more, if it wa'n't for that—if we don't have another house, Nanny she can't live with us after she's married. She'll have to go somewheres else to live away from us, an' it don't seem as if I could have it so, noways, Father. She wa'n't ever strong. She's got considerable color, but there wa'n't never any backbone to her. I've always took the heft of everything off her, an' she ain't fit to keep house an' do everything herself. She'll be all worn out inside of a year. Think of her doin' all the washin' an' ironin' an' bakin' with them soft white hands an' arms, an' sweepin'! I can't have it so, noways, Father."

Mrs. Penn's face was burning; her mild eyes gleamed. She had pleaded her little cause like a Webster;[8] she had ranged from severity to pathos; but her opponent employed that obstinate silence which makes eloquence

---

7 **victuals**: food.

8 **Webster**: Daniel Webster, a famous public speaker of the 19th century.

futile with mocking echoes. Adoniram arose clumsily.

"Father, ain't you got nothin' to say?" said Mrs. Penn.

"I've got to go off after that load of gravel. I can't stan' here talkin' all day."

"Father, won't you think it over an' have a house built there instead of a barn?"

"I ain't got nothin' to say."

Adoniram shuffled out. Mrs. Penn went into her bedroom. When she came out, her eyes were red. She had a roll of unbleached cotton cloth. She spread it out on the kitchen table and began cutting out some shirts for her husband. The men over in the field had a team to help them this afternoon; she could hear their halloos. She had a scanty pattern for the shirts; she had to plan and piece the sleeves.

Nanny came home with her embroidery and sat down with her needlework. She had taken down her curl papers and there was a soft roll of fair hair like an aureole⁹ over her forehead; her face was as delicately fine and clear as porcelain. Suddenly she looked up, and the tender red flamed all over her face and neck. "Mother," said she.

"What say?"

"I've been thinking—I don't see how we're goin' to have any—wedding in this room. I'd be ashamed to have his folks come if we didn't have anybody else."

"Mebbe we can have some new paper before then; I can put it on. I guess you won't have no call to be ashamed of your belongin's."

"We might have the wedding in the new barn," said Nanny, with gentle pettishness. "Why, Mother, what makes you look so?"

Mrs. Penn had started, and was staring at her with a curious expression. She turned again to her work and spread out a pattern carefully on the cloth. "Nothin'," said she.

Presently Adoniram clattered out of the yard in his two-wheeled dump cart, standing as proudly upright as a Roman charioteer. Mrs. Penn opened the door and stood there a minute looking out; the halloos of the men sounded louder.

It seemed to her all through the spring months that she heard nothing but the halloos and the noises of saws and hammers. The new barn grew fast. It was a fine edifice for this little village. Men came on pleasant Sundays, in their meeting suits and clean shirt bosoms, and stood around it admiringly. Mrs. Penn did not speak of it, and Adoniram did not mention it to her, although sometimes, upon a return from inspecting it, he bore himself with injured dignity.

"It's a strange thing how your mother feels about the new barn," he said, confidentially, to Sammy one day.

Sammy only grunted after an odd fashion for a boy; he had learned it from his father.

The barn was all completed ready for use by the third week in July. Adoniram had planned to move his stock in on Wednesday; on Tuesday he received a letter which changed his plans. He came in with it early in the morning. "Sammy's been to the post office," said he, "an' I've got a letter from Hiram." Hiram was Mrs. Penn's brother, who lived in Vermont.

"Well," said Mrs. Penn, "what does he say about the folks?"

"I guess they're all right. He says he thinks if I come up country right off there's a chance to buy jest the kind of a horse I want." He stared reflectively out of the window at the new barn.

---

9 aureole (ôr' ē ōl): halo.

Mrs. Penn was making pies. She went on clapping the rolling pin into the crust, although she was very pale, and her heart beat loudly.

"I dun' know but what I'd better go," said Adoniram. "I hate to go off jest now, right in the midst of hayin', but the ten-acre lot's cut, an' I guess Rufus an' the others can git along without me three or four days. I can't get a horse round here to suit me, nohow, an' I've got to have another for all that wood haulin' in the fall. I told Hiram to watch out, an' if he got wind of a good horse to let me know. I guess I'd better go."

"I'll get out your clean shirt an' collar," said Mrs. Penn calmly.

She laid out Adoniram's Sunday suit and his clean clothes on the bed in the little bedroom. She got his shaving water and razor ready. At last she buttoned on his collar and fastened his black cravat.[10]

Adoniram never wore his collar and cravat except on extra occasions. He held his head high, with a rasped dignity. When he was all ready, with his coat and hat brushed, and a lunch of pie and cheese in a paper bag, he hesitated on the threshold of the door. He looked at his wife, and his manner was defiantly apologetic. "If them cows come today, Sammy can drive 'em into the new barn," said he; "an' when they bring the hay up, they can pitch it in there."

"Well," replied Mrs. Penn.

Adoniram set his shaven face ahead and started. When he had cleared the doorstep, he turned and looked back with a kind of nervous solemnity. "I shall be back by Saturday if nothin' happens," said he.

"Do be careful, Father," replied his wife. She stood in the door with Nanny at her elbow and watched him out of sight. Her eyes had a strange, doubtful expression in them; her peaceful forehead was contracted. She went in and about her baking again. Nanny sat sewing. Her wedding day was drawing nearer, and she was getting pale and thin with her steady sewing. Her mother kept glancing at her.

"Have you got that pain in your side this mornin'?" she asked.

"A little."

Mrs. Penn's face, as she worked, changed, her perplexed forehead smoothed, her eyes were steady, her lips firmly set. She formed a maxim for herself, although incoherently with her unlettered thoughts. "Unsolicited opportunities are the guideposts of the Lord to the new roads of life," she repeated in effect, and she made up her mind to her course of action.

"S'posin' I *had* wrote to Hiram," she muttered once, when she was in the pantry—"s'posin' I had wrote an' asked him if he knew of any horse? But I didn't an' Father's goin' wa'n't none of my doin'. It looks like a providence." Her voice rang out quite loud at the last.

"What you talkin' about, Mother?" called Nanny.

"Nothin'."

Mrs. Penn hurried her baking; at eleven o'clock it was all done. The load of hay from the west field came slowly down the cart track and drew up at the new barn. Mrs. Penn ran out.

"Stop!" she screamed—"stop!"

The men stopped and looked; Sammy upreared from the top of the load and stared at his mother.

"Stop!" she cried out again. "Don't you put the hay in that barn; put it in the old one."

"Why, he said to put it in here," returned

---

10 **cravat** (krə vat′): tie.

one of the haymakers, wonderingly. He was a young man, a neighbor's son, whom Adoniram hired by the year to help on the farm.

"Don't you put the hay in the new barn; there's room enough in the old one, ain't there?" said Mrs. Penn.

"Room enough," returned the hired man, in his thick, rustic tones. "Didn't need the new barn, nohow, far as room's concerned. Well, I s'pose he changed his mind." He took hold of the horses' bridles.

Mrs. Penn went back to the house. Soon the kitchen windows were darkened, and a fragrance like warm honey came into the room.

Nanny laid down her work. "I thought Father wanted them to put the hay into the new barn?" she said wonderingly.

"It's all right," replied her mother.

Sammy slid down from the load of hay and came in to see if dinner was ready.

"I ain't goin' to get a regular dinner today, as long as Father's gone," said his mother. "I've let the fire go out. You can have some bread an' milk an' pie. I thought we could get along." She set out some bowls of milk, some bread, and a pie on the kitchen table. "You better eat your dinner now," said she. "You might jest as well get through with it. I want you to help me afterward."

Nanny and Sammy stared at each other. There was something strange in their mother's manner. Mrs. Penn did not eat anything herself. She went into the pantry, and they heard her moving dishes while they ate. Presently she came out with a pile of plates. She got the clothes basket out of the shed and packed them in it. Nanny and Sammy watched. She brought out cups and saucers and put them in with the plates.

"What you goin' to do, Mother?" inquired Nanny, in a timid voice. A sense of some-thing unusual made her tremble, as if it were a ghost. Sammy rolled his eyes over his pie.

"You'll see what I'm goin' to do," replied Mrs. Penn. "If you're through, Nanny, I want you to go upstairs an' pack up your things; an' I want you, Sammy, to help me take down the bed in the bedroom."

"Oh, Mother, what for?" gasped Nanny.

"You'll see."

During the next few hours a feat was performed by the simple, pious New England mother which was equal in its way to Wolfe's storming of the Heights of Abraham.[11] It took no more genius and audacity of bravery for Wolfe to cheer his wondering soldiers up those steep precipices, under the sleeping eyes of the enemy, than for Sarah Penn, at the head of her children, to move all their little household goods into the new barn while her husband was away.

Nanny and Sammy followed their mother's instructions without a murmur; indeed, they were over-awed. There is a certain uncanny and superhuman quality about all such purely original undertakings as their mother's was to them. Nanny went back and forth with her light loads, and Sammy tugged with sober energy.

At five o'clock in the afternoon the little house in which the Penns had lived for forty years had emptied itself into the new barn.

Every builder builds somewhat for unknown purposes and is in a measure a prophet. The architect of Adoniram Penn's barn, while he designed it for the comfort of four-footed animals, had planned better than he knew for the comfort of humans. Sarah Penn saw at a glance its possibilities. Those great box stalls, with quilts hung before them,

---

11 **Wolfe's . . . Abraham:** refers to a flat area on top of steep cliffs outside of Quebec where, in 1759, the British General Wolfe defeated the French.

would make better bedrooms than the one she had occupied for forty years, and there was a tight carriage room. The harness room, with its chimney and shelves, would make a kitchen of her dreams. The great middle space would make a parlor, by and by, fit for a palace. Upstairs there was as much room as down. With partitions and windows, what a house would there be! Sarah looked at the row of stanchions[12] before the allotted space for the cows and reflected that she would have her front entry there.

At six o'clock the stove was up in the harness room, the kettle was boiling, and the table was set for tea. It looked almost as homelike as the abandoned house across the yard had ever done. The young hired man milked, and Sarah directed him calmly to bring the milk to the new barn. He came gaping, dropping little blots of foam from the brimming pails on the grass. Before the next morning he had spread the story of Adoniram Penn's wife moving into the new barn all over the little village. Men assembled in the store and talked it over, women with shawls over their heads scuttled into each other's houses before their work was done. Any deviation from the ordinary course of life in this quiet town was enough to stop all progress in it. Everybody paused to look at the staid, independent figure on the side track. There was a difference of opinion with regard to her. Some held her to be insane; some, of a lawless and rebellious spirit.

Friday the minister went to see her. It was in the forenoon, and she was at the barn door shelling peas for dinner. She looked up and returned his salutation with dignity, then she went on with her work. She did not invite him in. The saintly expression of her face remained fixed, but there was an angry flush over it.

The minister stood awkwardly before her and talked. She handled the peas as if they were bullets. At last she looked up, and her eyes showed the spirit that her meek front had covered for a lifetime.

"There ain't no use talkin', Mr. Hersey," said she. "I've thought it all over, an' I believe I'm doin' what's right. I've made it the subject of prayer, an' it's betwixt me an' the Lord an' Adoniram. There ain't no call for nobody else to worry about it."

"Well, of course, if you have brought it to the Lord in prayer and feel satisfied that you are doing right, Mrs. Penn," said the minister, helplessly. His thin gray-bearded face was pathetic. He was a sickly man; his youthful confidence had cooled; he had to scourge himself up to some of his pastoral duties as relentlessly as a Catholic ascetic, and then he was prostrated by the smart.

"I think it's right jest as much as I think it was right for our forefathers to come over from the old country 'cause they didn't have what belonged to 'em," said Mrs. Penn. She arose. The barn threshold might have been Plymouth Rock from her bearing. "I don't doubt you mean well, Mr. Hersey," said she, "but there are things people hadn't ought to interfere with. I've been a member of the church for over forty years. I've got my own mind an' my own feet, an' I'm goin' to think my own thoughts an' go my own ways, an' nobody but the Lord is goin' to dictate to me unless I've a mind to have him. Won't you come in an' set down? How is Mis' Hersey?"

"She is well, I thank you," replied the minister. He added some more perplexed apologetic remarks; then he retreated.

---

12 **stanchions** (stan' shənz): devices that fit loosely around cows' necks to limit their movement.

He could expound the intricacies of every character study in the Scriptures, he was competent to grasp the Pilgrim Fathers and all historical innovators, but Sarah Penn was beyond him. He could deal with primal cases, but parallel ones worsted him. But, after all, although it was aside from his province, he wondered more how Adoniram Penn would deal with his wife than how the Lord would. Everybody shared the wonder. When Adoniram's four new cows arrived, Sarah ordered three to be put in the old barn, the other in the house shed where the cooking stove had stood. That added to the excitement. It was whispered that all four cows were domiciled in the house.

Toward sunset on Saturday, when Adoniram was expected home, there was a knot of men in the road near the new barn. The hired man had milked, but he still hung around the premises. Sarah Penn had supper all ready. There were brown bread and baked beans and a custard pie; it was the supper that Adoniram loved on a Saturday night. She had on a clean calico, and she bore herself imperturbably. Nanny and Sammy kept close at her heels. Their eyes were large, and Nanny was full of nervous tremors. Still there was to them more pleasant excitement than anything else. An inborn confidence in their mother over their father asserted itself.

Sammy looked out of the harness room window. "There he is," he announced, in an awed whisper. He and Nanny peeped around the casing. Mrs. Penn kept on about her work. The children watched Adoniram leave the new horse standing in the drive while he went to the house door. It was fastened. Then he went around to the shed. That door was seldom locked, even when the family was away. The thought how her father would be confronted by the cow flashed upon Nanny.

There was a hysterical sob in her throat. Adoniram emerged from the shed and stood looking about in a dazed fashion. His lips moved. He was saying something, but they could not hear what it was. The hired man was peeping around a corner of the old barn, but nobody saw him.

Adoniram took the new horse by the bridle and led him across the yard to the new barn. Nanny and Sammy slunk close to their mother. The barn doors rolled back, and there stood Adoniram, with the long mild face of the great Canadian farm horse looking over his shoulder.

Nanny kept behind her mother, but Sammy stepped suddenly forward and stood in front of her.

Adoniram stared at the group. "What on airth you all down here for?" said he. "What's the matter over to the house?"

"We've come here to live, Father," said Sammy. His shrill voice quavered out bravely.

"What"—Adoniram sniffed—"what is it smells like cookin'?" said he. He stepped forward and looked in the open door of the harness room. Then he turned to his wife. His old bristling face was pale and frightened. "What on airth does this mean, Mother?" he gasped.

"You come in here, Father," said Sarah. She led the way into the harness room and shut the door. "Now, Father," said she, "you needn't be scared. I ain't crazy. There ain't nothin' to be upset over. But we've come here to live, an' we're goin' to live here. We've got jest as good a right here as new horses an' cows. The house wa'n't fit for us to live in any longer, an' I made up my mind I wa'n't goin' to stay there. I've done my duty by you forty year, an' I'm goin' to do it now; but I'm goin' to live here. You've got to put in some windows and partitions; an' you'll have to buy some furniture."

"Why, Mother!" the old man gasped.

"You'd better take your coat off an' get washed—there's the washbasin—and then we'll have supper."

"Why, Mother!"

Sammy went past the window, leading the new horse to the old barn. The old man saw him and shook his head speechlessly. He tried to take off his coat, but his arms seemed to lack the power. His wife helped him. She poured some water into the tin basin and put in a piece of soap. She got the comb and brush and smoothed his thin gray hair after he had washed. Then she put the beans, hot bread, and tea on the table. Sammy came in, and the family drew up. Adoniram sat looking dazedly at his plate, and they waited.

"Ain't you goin' to ask a blessin', Father?" said Sarah. And the old man bent his head and mumbled.

All through the meal he stopped eating at intervals and stared furtively at his wife, but he ate well. The home food tasted good to him, and his old frame was too sturdily healthy to be affected by his mind. But after supper he went out and sat down on the step of the smaller door at the right of the barn,

through which he had meant his Jerseys to pass in stately file, but which Sarah designed for her front house door, and he leaned his head on his hands.

After the supper dishes were cleared away and the milk pans washed, Sarah went out to him. The twilight was deepening. There was a clear green glow in the sky. Before them stretched the smooth level of field; in the distance was a cluster of haystacks like the huts of a village; the air was very cool and calm and sweet. The landscape might have been an ideal one of peace.

Sarah bent over and touched her husband on one of his thin, sinewy shoulders. "Father!"

The old man's shoulder heaved; he was weeping.

"Why, don't do so, Father," said Sarah.

"I'll—put up the—partitions, an'—everything you—want, Mother."

Sarah put her apron up to her face; she was overcome by her own triumph.

Adoniram was like a fortress whose walls had no active resistance and went down the instant the right besieging tools were used. "Why, Mother," he said, hoarsely, "I hadn't no idee you was so set on't as all this comes to."

Discussion

1. What kind of person is Sarah Penn? In what ways is she like her husband? Select examples from the story that show each quality.

2. What reasons does Sarah give her husband for wanting a new house?

3. How do the townspeople react to Sarah's move into the barn?

4. When her husband returns home, what further demands does Sarah make?

5. What is her husband's reaction to the move when he first returns home? What is his reaction after dinner?

6. How is it possible that in forty years Sarah's husband never understood how much she wanted a new house?

Writer's Craft

Fables, as you know, usually end with a moral—a short statement that summarizes the main idea of the fable. Other kinds of literature have summaries of their main ideas as well. However, unlike the moral of a fable which is usually stated at the end, the main idea of a story, poem, or play is not actually written by the author. It is implied in the story. The reader must decide the main idea. This type of summary is called the THEME of the story. For example, a theme for "The No-Talent Kid" might be: *Often the most important talent is knowing how to get what you want.* Or, for "The Torn Invitation" the theme might be: *A boy becomes a man when he accepts his own heritage proudly and lovingly.* It is important to remember, though, that several variations of a theme are possible. Different readers see different things in stories, based on their own personal experiences and backgrounds.

1. One possible theme for "The Revolt of 'Mother'" could be: *It is important for people to be true to their own feelings and to assert their rights.* Using examples from the story, explain why this statement might summarize the main idea of this story.

2. What could be another possible theme for this story?

Mary E. Wilkins Freeman 1852—1930

Mary Freeman was born in Randolph, Massachusetts. Because of her frail health, her formal education was limited. Her haphazard self-education was primarily based on her reading. Nevertheless, she is credited with writing 238 short stories, 12 novels, a play, and a couple volumes of poetry. Two collections of short stories, *A Humble Romance and Other Stories* and *A New England Nun and Other Stories,* are usually thought to be her best works. Although she wrote very little during the decade before her death, she was awarded the Howells Medal for fiction and was made a member of the National Institute of Arts and Letters.

4 CHARACTERIZATION

Discussion

1. Who is the central character in the following stories: "The No-Talent Kid," "Pecos Bill . . . ," "Going to Run All Night," and "The Revolt of 'Mother'"? Which of these central characters can be considered a hero or heroine? Explain why.

2. What is the main motivation or reason behind the actions of both Plummer in "The No-Talent Kid" and Pecos Bill? Explain how their motivations relate to their personalities.

3. Compare the stories, "Pecos Bill . . ." and "The Legend of Sleepy Hollow." Why is the first story a tall tale and the second one not a tall tale?

4. In "Going to Run All Night," Corporal Nilson undergoes a change from an undistinguished nonachiever to a winner and a man of accomplishment. Select another central character from this unit who also had a change of character or personality. Explain what the change was.

5. What do you think would be a good theme for "Say It with Flowers"?

Composition

1. Select the main character from this unit who you think is the most realistic. In one or two paragraphs, give examples from the story that support your choice. Your examples could include the character's physical appearance, actions, feelings, or motivations. Be sure to put your examples in your own words. End with your own opinion of the character.

2. Create a humorous character such as Ichabod Crane in "The Legend of Sleepy Hollow." First describe his or her physical appearance. Include some humorous aspects. Be careful, however, not to make your character so ridiculous that he or she would not seem real or believable. Give your character a name and an occupation. Finally write a single incident which is humorous because of the character's actions and words.

PLAYS

Plays, costumes, acting—none of these are new to you. You may have even had first-hand experience putting on school plays. This familiarity is one of the reasons why plays are so much fun to see or even to read.

There is, of course, a great difference between seeing a play in a theater and reading a play from a book. In the theater you can see the characters, their costumes, and the scenery. But when you read a play, all you have is the original version of the play, the SCRIPT, which contains very little description of the setting or the characters. What a script mostly contains is the dialogue—the conversations between the characters.

What little description or explanation the playwright does give is limited to STAGE DIRECTIONS. These brief notes usually indicate how an actor or actress should say a certain line, such as "cheerfully" or "gloomily." Stage directions can also indicate a character's actions. He or she could be told to "read the newspaper," "sit down," or "move to the left." Since stage directions are often the playwright's only help to the visual understanding of a play, they should not be ignored.

When you read a play, your imagination is also very important. First you should try to picture in your mind what each character looks like. Then, when you read aloud, you should try to imitate the voice and the expression that person would use. This combination will make reading a play seem a lot more like seeing it on the stage. It will make the play come alive for you.

The Princess was disguised as Dulcibella, and the King thought Carlo was the Prince. There was so much confusion in the court that no one could really be sure who was who.

The Ugly Duckling

A. A. MILNE

Characters

King   **Dulcibella**
Queen   **Prince Simon**
Princess Camilla   **Carlo**
Chancellor

Scene: *The Throne Room of the Palace; a room of many doors, or, if preferred, curtain-openings: simply furnished with three thrones for Their Majesties and Her Royal Highness the* Princess Camilla—*in other words, with three handsome chairs. At each side is a long seat: reserved, as it might be, for His Majesty's Council (if any), but useful as today, for other purposes. The* King *is asleep on his throne with a handkerchief over his face. He is a king of any country from any storybook in whatever costume you please. But he should be wearing his crown.*

A Voice (*announcing*). His Excellency the Chancellor!

[*The* Chancellor, *an elderly man in horn-rimmed spectacles, enters, bowing. The* King *wakes up with a start and removes the handkerchief from his face.*]

King (*with simple dignity*). I was thinking.

Chancellor (*bowing*). Never, Your Majesty, was greater need for thought than now.

King. That's what I was thinking. (*He struggles into a more dignified position.*) Well, what is it? More trouble?

Chancellor. What we might call the old trouble, Your Majesty.

King. It's what I was saying last night to the Queen. "Uneasy lies the head that wears a crown," was how I put it.

Chancellor. A profound and original thought, which may well go down to posterity.

King. You mean it may go down well with posterity. I hope so. Remind me to tell you sometime of another little thing I said to Her Majesty: something about a fierce light beating on a throne. Posterity would like that, too. Well, what is it?

Chancellor. It is in the matter of Her Royal Highness's wedding.

King. Oh . . . yes.

Chancellor. As Your Majesty is aware, the young Prince Simon arrives today to seek Her Royal Highness's hand in marriage. He has been traveling in distant lands and, as I understand, has not—er—has not—

King. You mean he hasn't heard anything.

Chancellor. It is a little difficult to put this tactfully, Your Majesty.

King. Do your best, and I will tell you afterwards how you got on.

Chancellor. Let me put it this way. The Prince Simon will naturally assume that Her Royal Highness has the customary—so customary as to be in my own poor opinion, slightly monotonous—has what one might call the inevitable—so inevitable as to be, in my opinion again, almost mechanical—will assume, that she has the, as *I* think of it, faultily faultless, icily regular, splendidly—

King. What you are trying to say in the fewest words possible is that my daughter is not beautiful.

Chancellor. Her beauty is certainly elusive, Your Majesty.

King. It is. It has eluded you, it has eluded me, it has eluded everybody who has seen her. It even eluded the Court Painter. His last words were, "Well, I did my best." His successor is now painting the view across the water-meadows from the West Turret. He says that his doctor has advised him to keep to landscape.[1]

Chancellor. It is unfortunate, Your Majesty, but there it is. One just cannot understand how it could have occurred.

King. You don't think she takes after *me*, at all? You don't detect a likeness?

Chancellor. Most certainly not, Your Majesty.

King. Good. . . . Your predecessor did.

Chancellor. I have often wondered what happened to my predecessor.

King. Well, now you know.

[*There is a short silence.*]

Chancellor. Looking at the bright side, although Her Royal Highness is not, strictly speaking, beautiful—

King. Not, truthfully speaking, beautiful—

Chancellor. Yet she has great beauty of character.

King. My dear Chancellor, we are not considering Her Royal Highness's character, but her chances of getting married. You observe that there is a distinction.

Chancellor. Yes, Your Majesty.

King. Look at it from the suitor's point of view. If a girl is beautiful, it is easy to assume

---

1 **keep to landscape:** Paint no more portraits for fear of suffering revenge.

that she has, tucked away inside her, an equally beautiful character. But it is impossible to assume that an unattractive girl, however elevated in character, has, tucked away inside her, an equally beautiful face. That is, so to speak, not where you want it—tucked away.

Chancellor. Quite so, Your Majesty.

King. This doesn't, of course, alter the fact that the Princess Camilla is quite the nicest person in the Kingdom.

Chancellor (*enthusiastically*). She is, indeed, Your Majesty. (*Hurriedly*) With the exception, I need hardly say, of Your Majesty—and Her Majesty.

King. Your exceptions are tolerated for their loyalty and condemned for their extreme fatuity.[2]

Chancellor. Thank you, Your Majesty.

King. As an adjective for your King, the word "nice" is ill-chosen. As an adjective for Her Majesty, it is—ill-chosen.

[*At which moment Her Majesty comes in. The* King *rises. The* Chancellor *puts himself at right angles.*]

Queen (*briskly*). Ah. Talking about Camilla?

[*She sits down.*]

King (*returning to his throne*). As always, my dear, you are right.

Queen (*to* Chancellor). This fellow, Simon—What's he like?

Chancellor. Nobody has seen him, Your Majesty.

Queen. How old is he?

Chancellor. Five-and-twenty, I understand.

Queen. In twenty-five years he must have been seen by somebody.

King (*to the* Chancellor). Just a fleeting glimpse.

Chancellor. I meant, Your Majesty, that no detailed report of him has reached this country, save that he has the usual personal advantages and qualities expected of a Prince, and has been traveling in distant and dangerous lands.

Queen. Ah! Nothing gone wrong with his eyes? Sunstroke or anything?

Chancellor. Not that I am aware of, Your Majesty. At the same time, as I was venturing to say to His Majesty, Her Royal Highness's character and disposition are so outstandingly—

Queen. Stuff and nonsense. You remember what happened when we had the Tournament of Love last year.

Chancellor. I was not myself present, Your Majesty. I had not then the honor of—I was abroad, and never heard the full story.

Queen. No, it was the other fool. They all rode up to Camilla to pay their homage—it was the first time they had seen her. The heralds blew their trumpets and announced that she would marry whichever Prince was left master of the field when all but one had been unhorsed. The trumpets were blown again; they charged enthusiastically into the fight, and—(*The* King *looks nonchalantly at the ceiling and whistles a few bars.*)—don't do that.

King. I'm sorry, my dear.

2 fatuity (fə tü′ ə tē): foolishness.

The Ugly Duckling **365**

Queen (*to* Chancellor). And what happened? They all simultaneously fell off their horses and assumed a posture of defeat.

King. One of them was not quite so quick as the others. I was very quick. I proclaimed him the victor.

Queen. At the Feast of Betrothal[3] held that night—

King. We were all very quick.

Queen. The Chancellor announced that by the laws of the country the successful suitor had to pass a further test. He had to give the correct answer to a riddle.

Chancellor. Such undoubtedly is the fact, Your Majesty.

King. There are times for announcing facts, and times for looking at things in a broad-minded way. Please remember that, Chancellor.

Chancellor. Yes, Your Majesty.

Queen. I invented the riddle myself. Quite an easy one. What is it which has four legs and barks like a dog? The answer is, "A dog."

King (*to* Chancellor). You see that?

Chancellor. Yes, Your Majesty.

King. It isn't difficult.

Queen. He, however, seemed to find it so. He said an eagle. Then he said a serpent; a very high mountain with slippery sides; two peacocks; a moonlight night; the day after tomorrow—

King. Nobody could accuse him of not trying.

Queen. *I* did.

King. I *should* have said that nobody could fail to recognize in his attitude an appearance of doggedness.[4]

Queen. Finally he said "Death." I nudged the King—

King. Accepting the word "nudge" for the moment, I rubbed my ankle with one hand, clapped him on the shoulder with the other, and congratulated him on the correct answer. He disappeared under the table, and, personally, I never saw him again.

Queen. His body was found in the moat next morning.

Chancellor. But what was he doing in the moat, Your Majesty?

King. Bobbing about. Try not to ask needless questions.

Chancellor. It all seems so strange.

Queen. What does?

Chancellor. That Her Royal Highness, alone of all the princesses one has ever heard of, should lack that invariable attribute of royalty, supreme beauty.

Queen (*to the* King). That was your Great-Aunt Malkin. She came to the christening. You know what she said.

King. It was cryptic. Great-Aunt Malkin's besetting weakness. She came to *my* christening—she was one hundred and one then, and that was fifty-one years ago. (*To the* Chancellor) How old would that make her?

Chancellor. One hundred and fifty-two, Your Majesty.

King (*after thought*). About that, yes. She

---

3 **Betrothal:** engagement to marry.

4 **doggedness:** determination.

promised me that when I grew up, I should have all the happiness which my wife deserved. It struck me at the time—well, when I say "at the time," I was only a week old—but it did strike me as soon as anything could strike me—I mean of that nature—well, work it out for yourself, Chancellor. It opens up a most interesting field of speculation. Though naturally I have not liked to go into it at all deeply with Her Majesty.

Queen. I never heard anything less cryptic. She was wishing you extreme happiness.

King. I don't think she was *wishing* me anything. However . . .

Chancellor (*to the* Queen). But what, Your Majesty, did she wish Her Royal Highness?

Queen. Her other godmother—on my side—had promised her the dazzling beauty for which all the women in my family are famous—

[*She pauses, and the* King *snaps his fingers surreptitiously in the direction of the* Chancellor.]

Chancellor (*hurriedly*). Indeed, yes, Your Majesty.

[*The* King *relaxes.*]

Queen. And Great-Aunt Malkin said—(*to the* King)—what were the words?

King. I give you with this kiss
A wedding-day surprise.
Where ignorance is bliss
'Tis folly to be wise.
I thought the last two lines rather neat. But what it *meant*—

Queen. We can all see what it meant. She was given beauty—and where is it? Great-Aunt Malkin took it away from her. The

wedding-day surprise is that there will never be a wedding day.

King. Young men being what they are, my dear, it would be much more surprising if there *were* a wedding day. So how—

[*The* Princess *comes in. She is young, happy, healthy, but not beautiful. Or let us say that by some trick of makeup or arrangement of hair she seems plain to us: unlike the* Princess *of the storybooks.*]

Princess (*to the* King). Hello, darling! (*Seeing the others*) Oh, I say! Affairs of state? Sorry.

King (*holding out his hands*). Don't go, Camilla.

[*She takes his hands.*]

Chancellor. Shall I withdraw, Your Majesty?

Queen. You are aware, Camilla, that Prince Simon arrives today?

Princess. He has arrived. They're just letting down the drawbridge.

King (*jumping up*). Arrived! I must—

Princess. Darling, you know what the drawbridge is like. It takes at *least* half an hour to let it down.

King (*sitting down*). It wants oil. (*To the* Chancellor) Have *you* been grudging it oil?

Princess. It wants a new drawbridge, darling.

Chancellor. Have I Your Majesty's permission—

King. Yes, yes.

[*The* Chancellor *bows and goes out.*]

Queen. You've told him, of course? It's the only chance.

King. Er—no. I was just going to, when—

Queen. Then I'd better. *(She goes to the door.)* You can explain to the girl; I'll have her sent to you. You've told Camilla?

King. Er—no. I was just going to, when—

Queen. Then you'd better tell her now.

King. My dear, are you sure—

Queen. It's the only chance left. *(Dramatically to heaven)* My daughter!

[*She goes out. There is a little silence when she is gone.*]

King. Camilla, I want to talk seriously to you about marriage.

Princess. Yes, Father.

King. It is time that you learnt some of the facts of life.

Princess: Yes, Father.

King. Now the great fact about marriage is that once you're married, you live happy ever after. All our history books affirm this.

Princess. And your own experience too, darling.

King *(with dignity)*. Let us confine ourselves to history for the moment.

Princess. Yes, Father.

King. Of course, there *may* be an exception here and there, which, as it were, proves the rule; just as—oh, well, never mind.

Princess *(smiling)*. Go on, darling. You were going to say that an exception here and there proves the rule that all princesses are beautiful.

King. Well—leave that for the moment. The point is that it doesn't matter *how* you marry, or *who* you marry, as long as you *get* married. Because you'll be happy ever after in any case. Do you follow me so far?

Princess. Yes, Father.

King. Well, your mother and I have a little plan—

Princess. Was that it, going out of the door just now?

King. Er—yes. It concerns your waiting maid.

Princess. Darling, I have several.

King. Only one that leaps to the eye, so to speak. The one with the—well, with everything.

Princess. Dulcibella?

King. That's the one. It is our little plan that at the first meeting she should pass herself off as the Princess—a harmless ruse,[5] of which you will find frequent record in the history books—and allure Prince Simon to his—that is to say, bring him up to the— In other words, the wedding will take place immediately afterwards, and as quietly as possible— well, naturally in view of the fact that your Aunt Malkin is one hundred and fifty-two; and since you will be wearing the family bridal veil—which is no doubt how the custom arose—the surprise after the ceremony will be his. Are you following me at all? Your attention seems to be wandering.

Princess. I was wondering why you needed to tell me.

King. Just a precautionary measure, in case

---

5 **ruse:** trick.

you happened to meet the Prince or his attendant before the ceremony; in which case, of course, you would pass yourself off as the maid—

Princess. A harmless ruse, of which, also, you will find frequent record in the history books.

King. Exactly. But the occasion need not arise.

A Voice *(announcing)*. The woman Dulcibella!

King. Ah! *(To the Princess)* Now, Camilla, if you will just retire to your own apartments, I will come to you there when we are ready for the actual ceremony. *(He leads her out as he is talking, and as he returns, calls out:)* Come in, my dear! *(Dulcibella comes in. She is beautiful, but dumb.)* Now don't be frightened, there is nothing to be frightened about. Has Her Majesty told you what you have to do?

Dulcibella. Y-yes, Your Majesty.

King. Well now, let's see how well you can do it. You are sitting here, we will say. *(He leads her to a seat.)* Now imagine that I am Prince Simon. *(He curls his moustache and pulls in his stomach. She giggles.)* You are the beautiful Princess Camilla whom he has never seen. *(She giggles again.)* This is a serious moment in your life, and you will find that a giggle will not be helpful. *(He goes to the door.)* I am announced: "His Royal Highness Prince Simon!" That's me being announced. Remember what I said about giggling. You should have a faraway look upon the face. *(She does her best.)* Farther away than that. *(She tries again.)* No, that's too far. You are sitting there, thinking beautiful thoughts—in maiden meditation, fancy-free, as I remember saying to Her Majesty once . . . speaking of somebody else . . . fancy-free, but with the mouth definitely shut—that's better. I advance and fall upon one knee. *(He does so.)* You extend your hand graciously—*graciously*; you're not trying to push him in the face—that's better, and I raise it to my lips—so—and I kiss it—*(He kisses it warmly.)*—no, perhaps not so ardently as that, more like this *(He kisses it again.)* and I say, "Your Royal Highness, this is the most—er—Your Royal Highness, I shall ever be—no—Your Royal Highness, it is the proudest—" Well, the point is that *he* will say it, and it will be something complimentary, and then he will take your hand in both of his, and press it to his heart. *(He does so.)* And then—what do *you* say?

Dulcibella. Coo!

King. No, *not* Coo!

Dulcibella. Never had anyone do *that* to me before.

King. That also strikes the wrong note. What you want to say is, "Oh, Prince Simon!" . . . Say it.

Dulcibella *(loudly)*. Oh, Prince Simon!

King. No, no. You don't need to shout until he has said "What?" two or three times. Always consider the possibility that he *isn't* deaf. Softly, and giving the words a dying fall, letting them play around his head like a flight of doves.

Dulcibella *(still a little overloud)*. O-o-o-h, Prinsimon!

King. Keep the idea in your mind of a flight of *doves* rather than a flight of panic-stricken elephants, and you will be all right. Now I'm going to get up, and you must, as it were, *waft* me into a seat by your side. *(She starts*

wafting.) Not rescuing a drowning man, that's another idea altogether, useful at times, but at the moment inappropriate. Wafting. Prince Simon will put the necessary muscles into play—all you're required to do is to indicate by gracious movement of the hand the seat you require him to take. Now! *(He gets up, a little stiffly, and sits next to her.)* That was better. Well, here we are. Now, I think you give me a look: something, let us say, halfway between the breathless adoration of a nun and the voluptuous abandonment of a woman of the world; with an undertone of regal dignity, touched, as it were, with good comradeship. Now try that. *(She gives him a vacant look of bewilderment.)* Frankly, that didn't quite get it. There was just a little something missing. An absence, as it were, of all the qualities I asked for, and in their place an odd resemblance to an unsatisfied fish. Let us try to get it another way. Dulcibella, have you a young man of your own?

Dulcibella (*eagerly, seizing his hand*). Oo, yes, he's ever so smart; he's an archer, well not as you might say a real archer, he works in the armory, but old Bottlenose, *you* know who I mean, the Captain of the Guard, says the very next man they ever has to shoot, my Eg shall take his place, knowing Father and how it is with Eg and me, and me being maid to Her Royal Highness and can't marry me till he's a real soldier, but ever so loving, and funny like, the things he says. I said to him once, "Eg," I said—

King (*getting up*). I rather fancy, Dulcibella, that if you think of Eg all the time, *say* as little as possible, and, when thinking of Eg, see that the mouth is not more than partially open, you will do very well. I will show you where you are to sit and wait for His Royal Highness. (*He leads her out. On the way he is saying:*) Now remember—*waft*—*waft*—not hoick.

[Prince Simon *wanders in from the back unannounced. He is a very ordinary-looking young man in rather dusty clothes. He gives a deep sigh of relief as he sinks into the* King's *throne. . . .* Camilla, *a new and strangely beautiful* Camilla, *comes in.*]

Princess (*surprised*). Well!

Prince. Oh, hello!

Princess. Ought you?

Prince (*getting up*). Do sit down, won't you?

Princess. Who are you, and how did you get here?

Prince. Well, that's rather a long story. Couldn't we sit down? You could sit here if you liked, but it isn't very comfortable.

Princess. That is the King's throne.

Prince. Oh, is that what it is?

Princess. Thrones are not meant to be comfortable.

Prince. Well, I don't know if they're meant to be, but they certainly aren't.

Princess. Why were you sitting on the King's throne, and who are you?

Prince. My name is Carlo.

Princess. Mine is Dulcibella.

Prince. Good. And now couldn't we sit down?

Princess (*sitting down on the long seat to the left of the throne, and, as it were, wafting him to a place next to her*). You may sit here, if you like. Why are you so tired?

[*He sits down.*]

Prince. I've been taking very strenuous exercise.

Princess. Is that part of the long story?

Prince. It is.

Princess (*settling herself*). I love stories.

Prince. This isn't a story really. You see, I'm attendant on Prince Simon, who is visiting here.

Princess. Oh? I'm attendant on Her Royal Highness.

Prince. Then you know what he's here for.

Princess. Yes.

Prince. She's very beautiful, I hear.

Princess. Did you hear that? Where have you been lately?

Prince. Traveling in distant lands—with Prince Simon.

Princess. Ah! All the same, I don't understand. Is Prince Simon in the palace now? The drawbridge *can't* be down yet!

Prince. I don't suppose it is. *And* what a noise it makes coming down!

Princess. Isn't it terrible?

Prince. I couldn't stand it any more. I just had to get away. That's why I'm here.

Princess. But how?

Prince. Well, there's only one way, isn't there? That beech tree, and then a swing and a grab for the battlements, and don't ask me to remember it all—

[*He shudders.*]

Princess. You mean you came across the moat by that beech tree?

Prince. Yes. I got so tired of hanging about.

Princess. But it's terribly dangerous!

Prince. That's why I'm so exhausted. Nervous shock.

[*He lies back and breathes loudly.*]

Princess. Of course, it's different for *me*.

Prince (*sitting up*). Say that again. I must have got it wrong.

Princess. It's different for me because I'm used to it. Besides, I'm so much lighter.

Prince. You don't mean that *you*—

Princess. Oh, yes, often.

Prince. And I thought I was a brave man! At least, I did until five minutes ago, and now I don't again.

Princess. Oh, but you are! And I think it's wonderful to do it straight off the first time.

Prince. Well, *you* did.

Princess. Oh, no, not the first time. When I was a child—

Prince. You mean that you crashed?

Princess. Well, you only fall into the moat.

Prince. Only! Can you *swim*?

Princess. Of course.

Prince. So you swam to the castle walls, and yelled for help, and they fished you out and walloped you. And next day you tried again. Well, if *that* isn't pluck[6]—

Princess. Of course, I didn't. I swam back, and did it at once; I mean I tried again at once. It wasn't until the third time that I actually did it. You see, I was afraid I might lose my nerve.

Prince. Afraid she might lose her nerve!

Princess. There's a way of getting over from this side, too; a tree grows out from the wall and you jump into another tree—I don't think it's quite so easy.

Prince. Not quite so easy. Good. You must show me.

Princess. Oh, I will.

Prince. Perhaps it might be as well if you taught me how to swim first. I've often heard about swimming, but never—

Princess. You can't swim?

Prince. No. Don't look so surprised. There are a lot of other things which I can't do. I'll tell you about them as soon as you have a couple of years to spare.

Princess. You can't swim and yet you

---

6 **pluck:** courage.

crossed by the beech tree! And you're *ever* so much heavier than I am! Now who's brave?

Prince *(getting up)*. You keep talking about how light you are. I must see if there's anything in it. Stand up! *(She stands obediently and he picks her up.)* You're right, Dulcibella. I could hold you here forever. *(Looking at her)* You're very lovely. Do you know how lovely you are?

Princess. Yes.

[*She laughs suddenly and happily.*]

Prince. Why do you laugh?

Princess. Aren't you tired of holding me?

Prince. Frankly, yes. I exaggerated when I said I could hold you forever. When you've been hanging by the arms for ten minutes over a very deep moat, wondering if it's too late to learn how to swim—*(He puts her down.)*—what I meant was that I should *like* to hold you forever. Why did you laugh?

Princess. Oh, well, it was a little private joke of mine.

The Ugly Duckling   **373**

Prince. If it comes to that, I've got a private joke too. Let's exchange them.

Princess. Mine's very private. One other woman in the whole world knows, and that's all.

Prince. Mine's just as private. One other man knows, and that's all.

Princess. What fun. I love secrets. . . . Well, here's mine. When I was born, one of my godmothers promised that I should be very beautiful.

Prince. How right she was.

Princess. But the other one said this:

> I give you with this kiss
> A wedding-day surprise.
> Where ignorance is bliss
> 'Tis folly to be wise.

And nobody knew what it meant. And I grew up very plain. And then, when I was about ten, I met my godmother in the forest one day. It was my tenth birthday. Nobody knows this—except you.

Prince. Except us.

Princess. Except us. And she told me what her gift meant. It meant that I *was* beautiful—but everybody else was to go on being ignorant, and thinking me plain, until my wedding day. Because, she said, she didn't want me to grow up spoiled and willful and vain, as I should have done if everybody had always been saying how beautiful I was; and the best thing in the world, she said, was to be quite sure of yourself, but not to expect admiration from other people. So ever since then my mirror has told me I'm beautiful, and everybody else thinks me ugly, and I get a lot of fun out of it.

Prince. Well, seeing that Dulcibella is the result, I can only say that your godmother was very, very wise.

Princess. And now tell me *your* secret.

Prince. It isn't such a pretty one. You see, Prince Simon was going to woo Princess Camilla, and he'd heard that she was beautiful and haughty and imperious—all *you* would have been if your godmother hadn't been so wise. And being a very ordinary-looking fellow himself, he was afraid she wouldn't think much of him, so he suggested to one of his attendants, a man called Carlo, of extremely attractive appearance, that *he* should pretend to be the Prince and win the Princess' hand; and then at the last moment they would change places—

Princess. How would they do that?

Prince. The Prince was going to have been married in full armor—with his visor down.

Princess (*laughing happily*). Oh, what fun!

Prince. Neat, isn't it?

Princess (*laughing*). Oh, very . . . very . . . very.

Prince. Neat, but not so terribly *funny*. Why do you keep laughing?

Princess. Well, that's another secret.

Prince. If it comes to that, *I've* got another one up my sleeve. Shall we exchange again?

Princess. All right. You go first this time.

Prince. Very well . . . I am not Carlo. (*Standing up and speaking dramatically*) I am Simon! —*ow!*

[*He sits down and rubs his leg violently.*]

Princess (*alarmed*). What is it?

Prince. Cramp. *(In a mild voice, still rubbing)* I was saying that I was Prince Simon.

Princess. Shall I rub it for you?

[*She rubs.*]

Prince *(still hopefully)*. I am Simon.

Princess. Is that better?

Prince *(despairingly)*. I am Simon.

Princess. I know.

Prince. How did you know?

Princess. Well, you told me.

Prince. But oughtn't you to swoon or something?

Princess. Why? History records many similar ruses.

Prince *(amazed)*. Is that so? I've never read history. I thought I was being profoundly original.

Princess. Oh, no! Now I'll tell you *my* secret. For reasons very much like your own the Princess Camilla, who is held to be extremely plain, feared to meet Prince Simon. Is the drawbridge down yet?

Prince. Do your people give a faint, surprised cheer every time it gets down?

Princess. Naturally.

Prince. Then it came down about three minutes ago.

Princess. Ah! Then at this very moment your man Carlo is declaring his passionate love for my maid, Dulcibella. That, I think, is funny. *(So does the* Prince. *He laughs heartily.)* Dulcibella, by the way, is in love with a man she calls Eg, so I hope Carlo isn't getting carried away.

Prince. Carlo is married to a girl he calls "the little woman," so Eg has nothing to fear.

Princess. By the way, I don't know if you've heard, but I said, or as good as said, that I am the Princess Camilla.

Prince. I wasn't surprised. History, of which I read a good deal, records many similar ruses.

Princess *(laughing)*. Simon!

Prince *(laughing)*. Camilla! *(He stands up.)* May I try holding you again? *(She nods. He takes her in his arms and kisses her.)* Sweetheart!

Princess. You see when you lifted me up before, you said, "You're very lovely," and my godmother said that the first person to whom I would seem lovely was the man I should marry; so I knew then that you were Simon and I should marry you.

Prince. I knew directly when I saw you that I should marry you, even if you were Dulcibella. By the way, which of you *am* I marrying?

Princess. When she lifts her veil, it will be Camilla. *(Voices are heard outside.)* Until then it will be Dulcibella.

Prince *(in a whisper)*. Then good-bye, Camilla, until you lift your veil.

Princess. Good-bye, Simon, until you raise your visor.

[*The* King *and* Queen *come in arm-in-arm, followed by* Carlo *and* Dulcibella, *also arm-in-arm. The* Chancellor *precedes them, walking backwards, at a loyal angle.*]

Prince *(supporting the* Chancellor *as an accident seems inevitable)*. Careful!

[*The* Chancellor *turns indignantly round.*]

King. Who and what is this? More accurately who and what are all these?

Carlo. My attendant, Carlo, Your Majesty. He will, with Your Majesty's permission, prepare me for the ceremony.

[*The* Prince *bows.*]

King. Of course, of course!

Queen. (*to* Dulcibella). Your maid, Dulcibella, is it not, my love? (Dulcibella *nods violently.*) I thought so. (*To* Carlo) *She* will prepare Her Royal Highness.

[*The* Princess *curtsies.*]

King. Ah, yes. Yes. *Most* important.

Princess (*curtsying*). I beg pardon, Your Majesty, if I've done wrong, but I found the gentleman wandering—

King (*crossing to her*). Quite right, my dear, quite right. (*He pinches her cheek and takes advantage of this kingly gesture to say in a loud whisper:*) We've pulled it off!

[*They sit down; the* King *and* Queen *on their thrones,* Dulcibella *on the* Princess' *throne.* Carlo *stands behind* Dulcibella, *the* Chancellor *on the right of the* Queen, *and the* Prince *and* Princess *behind the long seat on the left.*]

Chancellor (*consulting documents*). H'r'm! Have I Your Majesty's authority to put the final test to His Royal Highness?

Queen (*whispering to* King). Is this safe?

King (*whispering*). Perfectly, my dear. I told him the answer a minute ago. (*Over his shoulder to* Carlo) Don't forget. *Dog.* (*Aloud*) Proceed, Your Excellency. It is my desire that the affairs of my country should ever be conducted in a strictly constitutional manner.

Chancellor (*oratorically*). By the constitution of the country, a suitor to Her Royal Highness' hand cannot be deemed successful until he has given the correct answer to a riddle. (*Conversationally*) The last suitor answered incorrectly, and thus failed to win his bride.

King. By a coincidence he fell into the moat.

Chancellor (*to* Carlo). I have now to ask Your Royal Highness if you are prepared for the ordeal?

Carlo (*cheerfully*). Absolutely.

Chancellor. I may mention, as a matter, possibly, of some slight historical interest to our visitor, that by the constitution of the country the same riddle is not allowed to be asked on two successive occasions.

King (*startled*). What's that?

Chancellor. This one, it is interesting to recall, was propounded[7] exactly a century ago, and we must take it as a fortunate omen that it was well and truly solved.

King (*to* Queen). I may want my sword directly.

Chancellor. The riddle is this. What is it which has four legs and mews like a cat?

Carlo (*promptly*). A dog.

King (*still more promptly*). Bravo, bravo!

[*He claps loudly and nudges the* Queen, *who claps too.*]

Chancellor (*peering at his documents*). According to the records of the occasion to which I referred, the correct answer would seem to be—

---

7 **propounded:** proposed.

Princess (*to the* Prince). Say something, quick!

Chancellor. —not dog, but—

Prince. Your Majesty, have I permission to speak? Naturally His Royal Highness could not think of justifying himself on such an occasion, but I think that with Your Majesty's gracious permission, I could—

King. Certainly, certainly.

Prince. In our country, we have an animal to which we have given the name "dog," or, in the local dialect of the more mountainous districts, "doggie." It sits by the fireside and purrs.

Carlo. That's right. It purrs like anything.

Prince. When it needs milk, which is its staple food, it mews.

Carlo (*enthusiastically*). Mews like nobody's business.

Prince. It also has four legs.

Carlo. One at each corner.

Prince. In some countries, I understand, this animal is called a "cat." In one distant country to which His Royal Highness and I penetrated, it was called by the very curious name of "hippopotamus."

Carlo. That's right. (*To the* Prince) Do you remember that ginger-colored hippopotamus which used to climb onto my shoulder and lick my ear?

Prince. I shall never forget it, sir. (*To the* King) So you see, Your Majesty—

King. Thank you. I think that makes it perfectly clear. (*Firmly to the* Chancellor) You are about to agree?

Chancellor. Undoubtedly, Your Majesty.

May I be the first to congratulate His Royal Highness on solving the riddle so accurately?

King. You may be the first to see that all is in order for an immediate wedding.

Chancellor. Thank you, Your Majesty.

[*He bows and withdraws. The* King *rises, as do the* Queen *and* Dulcibella.]

King (*to* Carlo). Doubtless, Prince Simon, you will wish to retire and prepare yourself for the ceremony.

Carlo. Thank you, sir.

Prince. Have I Your Majesty's permission to attend His Royal Highness? It is the custom of his country for princes of the royal blood to be married in full armor, a matter which requires a certain adjustment—

King. Of course, of course. (Carlo *bows to the* King *and* Queen *and goes out. As the* Prince *is about to follow, the* King *stops him.*) Young man, you have a quality of quickness which I admire. It is my pleasure to reward it in any way which commends itself to you.

Prince. Your Majesty is ever gracious. May I ask for my reward after the ceremony?

[*He catches the eye of the* Princess, *and they give each other a secret smile.*]

King. Certainly. (*The* Prince *bows and goes out. To* Dulcibella) Now, young woman, make yourself scarce. You've done your work excellently, and we shall see that you and your—what was his name?

Dulcibella. Eg, Your Majesty.

King. —that you and your Eg are not forgotten.

Dulcibella. Coo!

The Ugly Duckling 377

[*She curtsies and goes out.*]

Princess *(calling)*. Wait for me, Dulcibella!

King *(to* Queen*)*. Well, my dear, we may congratulate ourselves. As I remember saying to somebody once, "You have not lost a daughter, you have gained a son." How does he strike you?

Queen. Stupid.

King. They made a very handsome pair, I thought, he and Dulcibella.

Queen. Both stupid.

King. I said nothing about stupidity. What I *said* was that they were both extremely handsome. That is the important thing. *(Struck by a sudden idea)* Or isn't it?

Queen. What do *you* think of Prince Simon, Camilla?

Princess. I adore him. We shall be so happy together.

King. Well, of course, you will. I told you so. Happy ever after.

Queen. Run along now and get ready.

Princess. Yes, Mother.

[*She throws a kiss to them and goes out.*]

King *(anxiously)*. My dear, have we been wrong about Camilla all this time? It seemed to me that she wasn't looking *quite* so plain as usual just now. Did *you* notice anything?

Queen *(carelessly)*. Just the excitement of the marriage.

King *(relieved)*. Ah, yes, that would account for it.

Curtain

Discussion

1. What do Princess Camilla's two godmothers promise her at her christening?

2. What does her Godmother Malkin's wish mean? Why does she give Camilla that wish?

3. In the preceding year's Tournament of Love, how do Camilla's suitors show that none of them want to marry her? Why do they behave that way?

4. What almost prevents the Prince and Princess from marrying? How is this problem solved?

5. Why do the Prince and the Princess seem well suited for each other?

Writer's Craft

The movie or play is over. You are walking out of the theater still chuckling to yourself. "That really was funny," you say to your friend. "It sure was, and didn't you like how everything worked out all right at the end?" That little bit of conversation indicates that you have just seen a COMEDY. It was humorous and it had a happy ending.

The two most common sources of humor in a comedy are situation and character. An audience seeing a situation comedy laughs either at errors which its players make or at the ridiculous predicaments they get themselves into. An audience seeing a comedy of character, on the other hand, laughs at the characters' unusual behavior or the exaggeration of their minor faults or weaknesses. Most playwrights, however, usually mix these two kinds of comedy in one play.

1. Tell which of the following events in the *The Ugly Duckling* may be called an example of situation comedy and which is an example of comedy of character:

   a. Dulcibella reveals her stupidity as the King shows her how to behave when Prince Simon arrives.

   b. Carlo is all ready to answer the question: "What has four legs and barks like a dog?" But instead of asking that, the Chancellor poses a different question: "What has four legs and mews like a cat?"

2. One type of error that often provides humor in situation comedies is mistaken identity. An example of mistaken identity would be: Character A dresses up as Character B and fools one or more members of the cast with the disguise. Point out the mistaken identity in *The Ugly Duckling*.

3. Another source of situation comedy is the ridiculous predicaments that players get themselves into. Tell what ridiculous predicaments the King and Queen get themselves into when they hold the Tournament of Love.

4. What oddities, faults, or weaknesses make the Chancellor and the Queen suitable as players in a comedy of characters?

5. In addition to humor, comedy requires a happy ending. Tell why the Prince and Princess will be even happier than the King and Queen realize at the end of the play.

Composition

1. The King says, "It doesn't matter *how* you marry, or *who* you marry, as long as you *get* married. Because you'll be happy ever after in any case." Do the characters and events in *The Ugly Duckling* support or contradict the King's viewpoint? Write your opinion. Include specific examples of what people say and do in the play to support your position.

2. The play ends before the actual wedding takes place. Write a final scene for this play. You may write it either in play form or in story form. Pick up the action as the Prince and Princess are entering the room in which they will be married. Emphasize the moment in which their true identities are revealed. How do the King and Queen react when they learn that Carlo is not the real Prince? What happens when they also find out that the Prince and Princess already know each other? The end of your scene should indicate that everyone finally sees the Princess's beauty.

Vocabulary

The Ugly Duckling contains many examples of a special kind of language called EUPHEMISMS. A euphemism is a mild or indirect word or phrase used in place of a direct or unpleasant one. For example:

EUPHEMISM: Maria's uncle is a *sanitation engineer.*
ORDINARY LANGUAGE: Maria's uncle is a *garbage collector.*

Euphemisms are used to avoid hurting people's feelings, to avoid making people angry, and to avoid embarrassment. They most often deal with subjects such as personal lives, physical functions, financial matters, or death. We say, for example, that a person wears *dentures* rather than *false teeth.* We talk about the *underprivileged* rather than the *poor. Old people* have become *senior citizens,* and an *undertaker* is called a *funeral director.*

A. Below are sentences in ordinary language. On a separate sheet of paper, change the *italicized* words to euphemisms.

1. The boy *stole* the ball from the gym.
2. The person next door is *crippled*.
3. Some students are *rude*.
4. The child was *clumsy*.
5. *Rich* people always live in expensive houses.

B. In the lines below from *The Ugly Duckling*, the euphemisms are *italicized*. Rewrite them using ordinary language. Use a dictionary if you need help.

1. **King** (*to* Chancellor). Your exceptions are *tolerated* for their *loyalty* and *condemned* for their *extreme fatuity*.
2. **Queen** (*to* Chancellor). I *nudged* the King . . .
3. **King** (*to* Camilla). It is our little plan that at the first meeting she should *pass herself off* as the Princess—*a harmless ruse,* of which you will find frequent *record* in the history books.
4. **King** (*to* Dulcibella). Frankly, *that didn't quite get it. There was just a little something missing. An absence,* as it were, *of all the qualities I asked for,* and in their place an *odd resemblance to an unsatisfied fish.*
5. **King** (*to* Carlo). *By a coincidence* he (the last young man who gave the wrong answer) *fell into the moat.*

Alan Alexander Milne 1882—1936

A. A. Milne was a successful novelist, playwright, poet, journalist, short story writer, and screenplay writer. He is most famous for his Christopher books, including *Winnie the Pooh* and *The House at Pooh Corner*. His plays, stories, and poetry have been illustrated, made into both live and animated films, and shown on stage, in theaters, and on television throughout the world. Although Milne was highly successful in all types of writing, he once commented, "The most exciting writing is the writing of plays."

Today both men and women serve on juries in criminal and civil trials. This, however, was not always the case. In fact, in 1950, when Twelve Angry Men *was written, juries in New York were made up completely of men. This jury, though, could be any jury of men and women today. Human beings would still have to decide whether the young defendant was guilty or innocent. They would still have to face the fear of locking up an innocent man or setting a guilty man free.*

Twelve Angry Men

REGINALD ROSE
Stage Version by SHERMAN L. SERGEL

Characters

Foreman of the Jury	**Juror No. Nine**
Juror No. Two	**Juror No. Ten**
Juror No. Three	**Juror No. Eleven**
Juror No. Four	**Juror No. Twelve**
Juror No. Five	**Guard**
Juror No. Six	**Judge** ⎫
Juror No. Seven	**Clerk** ⎬ *offstage voices*
Juror No. Eight	

Place: *A jury room.*
Time: *The present. Summer.*

Synopsis
Act I: *Late afternoon.*
Act II: *A second or two later.*
Act III: *Immediately following Act II.*

© Copyright MCMLV by Reginald Rose, Based upon the Television Show TWELVE ANGRY MEN, All Rights Reserved

CAUTION: It is against the law to make copies of this play. Playbooks may be ordered from the play publisher with whom royalty arrangements must be made prior to any performance. For the right to produce this play contact THE DRAMATIC PUBLISHING COMPANY, 4150 N. Milwaukee Avenue, Chicago, IL 60641

Foreman: He is a small, petty man who is impressed with the authority he has and handles himself quite formally. He is not overly bright, but dogged.[1]

Juror No. Two: He is a meek, hesitant man who finds it difficult to maintain any opinions of his own. He is easily swayed and usually adopts the opinion of the last person to whom he has spoken.

Juror No. Three: He is a very strong, very forceful, extremely opinionated man within whom can be detected a streak of sadism. Also, he is a humorless man who is intolerant of opinions other than his own, and he is accustomed to forcing his wishes and views upon others.

Juror No. Four: He seems to be a man of wealth and position and a practiced speaker who presents himself well at all times. He seems to feel a little bit above the rest of the jurors. His only concern is with the facts in this case, and he is appalled[2] with the behavior of the others.

Juror No. Five: He is a naïve, very frightened young man who takes his obligations in this case very seriously but who finds it difficult to speak up when his elders have the floor.

Juror No. Six: He is an honest but dull-witted man who comes upon his decisions slowly and carefully. He is a man who finds it difficult to create positive opinions, but who must listen to and digest and accept those opinions offered by others which appeal to him most.

Juror No. Seven: He is a loud, flashy, glad-handed salesman type who has more important things to do than to sit on a jury. He is quick to show temper and equally quick to form opinions on things about which he knows nothing. He is a bully and, of course, a coward.

Juror No. Eight: He is a quiet, thoughtful, gentle man—a man who sees all sides of every question and constantly seeks the truth. He is a man of strength tempered with compassion. Above all, he is a man who wants justice to be done, and he will fight to see that it is.

Juror No. Nine: He is a mild, gentle old man, long since defeated by life, and now merely waiting to die. He recognizes himself for what he is, and mourns the days when it would have been possible to be courageous without shielding himself behind his many years.

Juror No. Ten: He is an angry, bitter man—a man who antagonizes[3] almost at sight. He is also a bigot[4] who places no values on any human life save his own. Here is a man who has been nowhere and is going nowhere and knows it deep within him.

Juror No. Eleven: He is a refugee from Europe. He speaks with an accent and is ashamed, humble, almost subservient[5] to the people around him. He will honestly seek justice because he has suffered through so much injustice.

Juror No. Twelve: He is a slick, bright advertising man who thinks of human beings in terms of percentages, graphs and polls, and has no real understanding of people. He is a superficial snob, but he is trying to be a good fellow.

---

1 **dogged:** determined.
2 **appalled** (ə pôld'): shocked.

3 **antagonizes:** arouses other people's dislike.
4 **bigot:** a prejudiced person.
5 **subservient** (səb sėr' vē ənt): acting like a servant.

ACT I

[AT RISE OF CURTAIN: *The curtain comes up on a dark stage; then as the lights start to come up on the scene, we hear the voice of the* Judge, *off stage.*]

Judge (*off stage*). Murder in the first degree . . . premeditated[6] homicide . . . is the most serious charge tried in our criminal courts. You have heard a long and complex case, gentlemen, and it is now your duty to sit down to try and separate the facts from the fancy. One man is dead. The life of another is at stake. If there is a reasonable doubt in your minds as to the guilt of the accused—then you must declare him not guilty. If—however—there is no reasonable doubt, then he must be found guilty. Whichever way you decide, the verdict must be unanimous. I urge you to deliberate honestly and thoughtfully. You are faced with a grave responsibility. Thank you, gentlemen.

[*There is a long pause. The lights are now up full in the jury room. There is a door L and a window in the R wall of the room. Over the door L is an electric clock. A water cooler is DR, with a wastebasket beside it. A container with paper cups is attached to the wall nearby. A long conference table is slightly upstage of C stage. About it are twelve uncomfortable-looking straight chairs. There is a chair at either end of the table, seven at the upstage side and three at the downstage side of the table. (*Note: *This arrangement of the chairs about the table will enable most of the action to be directed toward the audience, with a minority of the characters placed with their backs toward the audience.) There are two more straight chairs*

---

6 **premeditated**: deliberate; planned ahead.

against the wall DL and one in the UR corner of the room. It is a bare, unpleasant room. After a pause, the door L opens and the Guard walks in. As he opens the door, the lettering "Jury Room" can be seen on the outside of the door. The Guard walks across the room and opens the window R as the Clerk drones out, off-stage L.]

Clerk (*offstage* L). The jury will retire.

Guard (*surveying room, shaking his head*). He doesn't stand a chance. (*Moves L again*)

[*The* Jurors *file in L. The Guard stands upstage of the door and counts them. Four or five of the Jurors light cigarettes as they enter the room. Juror Five lights a pipe which he smokes constantly. Jurors Two, Nine, and Twelve go to the water cooler for a drink. Juror Seven goes to the window and opens it wider. The rest of the Jurors begin to take seats around the table, though some of them stand and lean forward, with both hands on the backs of the chairs. Juror Seven produces a pack of gum and offers a piece to the men by the water cooler.*]

Seven. Chewing gum? Gum? Gum?

Nine. Thank you, but no. (*Jurors Two and Twelve shake their heads.*)

Seven. Y'know something?

Twelve. I know lots of things. I'm in advertising.

Seven (*tugging at collar*). Y'know, it's hot.

Twelve (*to Two, mildly sarcastic*). I never would have known that if he hadn't told me. Would you?

Two (*missing sarcasm*). I suppose not. I'd kind of forgotten.

Twelve. All I've done all day is sweat.

Three (calling out). I bet you aren't sweating like that kid who was tried.

Seven. You'd think they'd at least air-condition the place. I almost dropped dead in court.

Twelve. My taxes are high enough.

Seven. This should go fast, anyway. (Moves to table, as Eight goes to window)

Nine (nodding to himself, then, as he throws his paper water cup into wastebasket). Yes, it's hot.

Guard. Okay, gentlemen. Everybody's here. If there's anything you want, I'm right outside. Just knock. (He goes out L, closing door. They all look at door, silently. The lock is turned.)

Three. Did he lock that door?

Four. Yes, he did.

Three. What do they think we are, crooks?

Foreman (seated at left end of table). They lock us up for a little while. . . .

Three (breaking in). And then they lock that kid up forever and that's okay by me.

Five (motioning toward door). I never knew they did that.

Ten (blowing his nose). Sure, they lock the door. What did you think?

Five (a bit irritated). I just didn't know. It never occurred to me.

Four. Shall we all admit right now that it is hot and humid and our tempers are short?

Eight (turning from window). It's been a pretty hard week. (Turns back and continues looking out)

Three. I feel just fine.

Twelve. I wonder what's been going on down at the office. You know how it is in advertising. In six days my job could be gone, and the whole company, too. They aren't going to like this.

[Jurors start to take off their suit coats and hang them over backs of chairs.]

Foreman. Well, figure this is our duty.

Twelve. I didn't object to doing my duty. I just mentioned that I might not have a job by the time I get back. (He and Nine move to table and take their places. Nine sits near right end of table.)

Three (motioning to Four). Ask him to hire you. He's rich. Look at the suit.

Foreman (to Four, as he tears off slips of paper for a ballot). Is it custom-tailored?

Four. Yes, it is.

Foreman. I have an uncle who's a tailor. (Four takes his jacket off, places it carefully over back of chair and sits.)

Four. How does he do?

Foreman (shaking his head). Not too well. Y'know, a friend of his, that's a friend of my uncle, the tailor—well—this friend wanted to be on this jury in my place.

Seven. Why didn't you let him? I would have done anything to miss this.

Foreman. And get caught, or something? Y'know what kind of a fine you could pay for anything like that? Anyway, this friend of my uncle's was on a jury once, about ten years ago—a case just about like this one.

Twelve. So what happened?

Foreman. They let him off. Reasonable doubt. And do y'know, about eight years later they found out that he'd actually done it, anyway. A guilty man—a murderer—was turned loose in the streets.

Three. Did they get him?

Four. They couldn't.

Three. Why not?

Four. A man can't be held in double jeopardy.[7] Unless it's a hung jury, they can't try a man twice for the same crime.

Seven. That isn't going to happen here.

Three. Six days. They should have finished it in two. *(Slapping back of one hand into palm of other)* Talk! Talk! Talk! *(Gets up and starts for water cooler)* Did you ever hear so much talk about nothing?

Two *(laughing nervously).* Well—I guess—they're entitled. . . .

Three. Everybody gets a fair trial. . . . *(Shakes his head)* That's the system. *(Downs his drink)* Well, I suppose you can't say anything against it. *(He tosses his water cup toward wastebasket and misses.* Two *picks cup up and puts it in wastebasket as* Three *returns to his seat.)*

Seven *(to* Ten*).* How did you like that business about the knife? Did you ever hear a phonier story?

Ten *(wisely).* Well, look, you've gotta expect that. You know what you're dealing with. . . .

Seven. He bought a switch knife that night. . . .

Ten *(with a sneer).* And then he lost it.

Seven. A hole in his pocket.

Ten. A hole in his father.

Two. An awful way to kill your father—a knife in his chest. *(Crosses to table)*

Ten. Look at the kind of people they are—you know them. *(Gets handkerchief out again)*

Seven. What's the matter? You got a cold?

Ten *(blowing).* A lulu! These hot weather colds can kill you.

Seven. I had one last year, while I was on vacation, too.

Foreman *(briskly).* All right, gentlemen, let's take seats.

Seven. Right. This better be fast. I've got tickets to—*(insert name of any current Broadway hit)*—for tonight. I must be the only guy in the world who hasn't seen it yet. *(Laughs and sits down, as do others still not seated)* Okay, your honor, start the show.

Foreman *(to* Eight, *who is still looking out window).* How about sitting down? *(Eight doesn't hear him.)* The gentleman at the window. *(Eight turns, startled.)* How about sitting down?

Eight. Oh, I'm sorry. *(Sits at right end of table, opposite* Foreman*)*

Ten. It's tough to figure, isn't it? A kid kills his father. Bing! Just like that. Well, it's the element. They let the kids run wild. Maybe it serves 'em right.

Four. There are better proofs than some emotion you may have—perhaps a dislike for some group.

Seven. We all agreed that it was hot.

Nine. And that our tempers will get short.

Three. That's if we disagree—but this is open

---

7 **hung jury:** a jury which cannot agree on a verdict.

and shut.[8] Let's get it done.

Foreman. All right. Now—you gentlemen can handle this any way you want to. I mean, I'm not going to make any rules. If we want to discuss it first and then vote, that's one way. Or we can vote right now and see how we stand.

Seven. Let's vote now. Who knows, maybe we can all go home.

Ten. Yeah. Let's see who's where.

Three. Right. Let's vote now.

Eight. All right. Let us vote.

Foreman. Anybody doesn't want to vote? (*He looks around table. There is a pause as All look at each other.*)

---

8 **open and shut:** a simple, clear-cut matter.

Seven. That was easy.

Foreman. Okay. All those voting guilty raise your hands. (*Jurors Three, Seven, Ten and Twelve put their hands up instantly. The Foreman and Two, Four, Five and Six follow a second later. Then Eleven raises his hand and a moment later Nine puts his hand up.*) Eight—nine—ten—eleven—that's eleven for guilty. Okay. Not guilty? (*Eight's hand goes up. All turn to look at him.*)

Three. Hey, you're in left field!

Foreman. Okay. Eleven to one. Eleven guilty, one not guilty. Now we know where we stand.

Three (*rising, to* Eight). Do you really believe he's not guilty?

Eight (*quietly*). I don't know.

Seven (*to* Foreman). After six days, he doesn't know.

Twelve. In six days I could learn calculus. This is A, B, C.

Eight. I don't believe that it is as simple as A, B, C.

Three. I never saw a guiltier man in my life. (*Sits again*)

Eight. What does a guilty man look like? He is not guilty until we say he is guilty. Are we to vote on his face?

Three. You sat right in court and heard the same things I did. The man's a dangerous killer. You could see it.

Eight. Where do you look to see if a man is a killer?

Three (*irritated by him*). Oh, well! . . .

Eight (*with quiet insistence*). I would like to know. Tell me what the facial characteristics of a killer are. Maybe you know something I don't know.

Four. Look! What is there about the case that makes you think the boy is innocent?

Eight. He's nineteen years old.

Three. That's old enough. He knifed his own father. Four inches into the chest. An innocent little nineteen-year-old kid.

Four (*to* Three). I agree with you that the boy is guilty, but I think we should try to avoid emotionally colored arguments.

Three. All right. They proved it a dozen different ways. Do you want me to list them?

Eight. No.

Ten (*rising, putting his feet on seat of chair and sitting on back of it, then, to* Eight). Well, do you believe that stupid story he told?

Four (*to* Ten). Now, now.

Ten. Do you believe the kid's story?

Eight. I don't know whether I believe it or not. Maybe I don't.

Seven. So what'd you vote not guilty for?

Eight. There were eleven votes for guilty—it's not so easy for me to raise my hand and send a boy off to die without talking about it first.

Seven. Who says it's easy for me?

Four. Or me?

Eight. No one.

Foreman. He's still just as guilty, whether it's an easy vote or a hard vote.

Seven (*belligerently*). Is there something wrong because I voted fast?

Eight. Not necessarily.

Seven. I think the guy's guilty. You couldn't change my mind if you talked for a hundred years.

Eight. I don't want to change your mind.

Three. Just what are you thinking of?

Eight. I want to talk for a while. Look—this boy's been kicked around all his life. You know—living in a slum—his mother dead since he was nine. That's not a very good head start. He's a tough, angry kid. You know why slum kids get that way? Because we knock 'em over the head once a day, every day. I think maybe we owe him a few words. That's all. *(He looks around table and is met by cold looks.* Nine *nods slowly while* Four *begins to comb his hair.)*

Four. All right, it's hard, sure—it was hard for me. Everything I've got I fought for. I worked my way through college. That was a long time ago, and perhaps you do forget. I fought, yes, but I never killed.

Three. I know what it's like. I never killed nobody.

Twelve. I've been kicked around, too. Wait until you've worked in an ad agency and the big boy that buys the advertising walks in. We all know.

Eleven *(who speaks with an accent)*. In my country, in Europe, kicking was a science, but let's try to find something better than that.

Ten *(to* Eight*)*. I don't mind telling you this, mister. We don't owe the kid a thing. He got a fair trial, didn't he? You know what that trial cost? He's lucky he got it. Look, we're all grown-ups here. You're not going to tell us that we're supposed to believe him, knowing what he is. I've lived among 'em all my life—

You can't believe a word they say. You know that.

Nine *(to* Ten, *very slowly)*. I don't know that. What a terrible thing for a man to believe! Since when is dishonesty a group characteristic? You have no monopoly on the truth!

Three *(interrupting)*. All right. It's not Sunday. We don't need a sermon.

Nine *(not heeding)*. What this man says is very dangerous.

[Eight *puts his hand on* Nine's *arm and stops him.* Nine *draws a deep breath and relaxes.*]

Four. I don't see any need for arguing like this. I think we ought to be able to behave like gentlemen.

Seven. Right!

Twelve *(smiling up at* Four*)*. Oh, all right, if you insist.

Four *(to* Twelve*)*. Thank you.

Twelve. Sure.

Four. If we're going to discuss this case, why, let's discuss the facts.

Foreman. I think that's a good point. We have a job to do. Let's do it.

Eleven. If you gentlemen don't mind, I'm going to close the window. *(Gets up and does so, then, apologetically as he moves back to table)* It was blowing on my neck. *(*Ten *blows his nose fiercely as he gets down from back of chair and sits again.)*

Seven. If you don't mind, I'd like to have the window open.

Eleven. But it was blowing on me.

Seven. Don't you want a little air? It's summer—it's hot.

Eleven. I was very uncomfortable.

Seven. There are twelve of us in this room; it's the only window. If you don't mind!

Eleven. I have some rights, too.

Seven. So do the rest of us.

Four (*to* Eleven). Couldn't you trade chairs with someone at the other end of the table?

Eleven. All right, I will open the window, if someone would trade. (*He goes to window and opens it.* Two *gets up and goes to* Eleven's *chair, near right end of table.*)

Two (*motioning*). Take my chair.

Eleven. Thank you. (*Goes to* Two's *chair, near left end of table*)

Foreman. Shall we get back to the case?

Three. Yeah, let's.

Twelve. I may have an idea here. I'm just thinking out loud now, but it seems to me that it's up to us to convince this gentleman—(*motioning toward* Eight)—that we're right and he's wrong. Maybe if we each talk for a minute or two. You know—try it on for size.

Foreman. That sounds fair enough.

Four. Very fair.

Foreman. Supposing we go once around the table.

Seven. Okay—let's start it off.

Foreman. Right. (*To* Two) We'll start with you.

Two (*timidly*). Oh. Well . . . (*There is a long pause.*) I just think he's guilty. I thought it was obvious.

Eight. In what way was it obvious?

Two. I mean that nobody proved otherwise.

Eight (*quietly*). Nobody has to prove otherwise; innocent until proven guilty. The burden of proof is on the prosecution. The defendant doesn't have to open his mouth. That's in the Constitution. The Fifth Amendment. You've heard of it.

Four. Everyone has.

Two (*flustered*). Well, sure—I've heard of it. I know what it is . . . I . . . what I meant . . . well, anyway . . . I think he's guilty!

Eight (*looking at* Two, *shaking his head slowly*). No reasons—just guilty. There is a life at stake here.

Three. Okay, let's get to the facts. Number one: let's take the old man who lived on the second floor right underneath the room where the murder took place. At ten minutes after twelve on the night of the killing, he heard loud noises in the upstairs apartment. He said it sounded like a fight. Then he heard the kid say to his father, "I'm gonna kill you." A second later he heard a body falling, and he ran to the door of his apartment, looked out and saw the kid running downstairs and out of the house. Then he called the police. They found the father with a knife in his chest.

Foreman. And the coroner fixed the time of death at around midnight.

Three. Right. Now what else do you want?

Eight. It doesn't seem to fit.

Four. The boy's entire story is flimsy. He claimed he was at the movies. That's a little ridiculous, isn't it? He couldn't even remember what picture he saw.

Three. That's right. Did you hear that? (*To*

Four. You're absolutely right.

Five. He didn't have any ticket stub.

Eight. Who keeps a ticket stub at the movies?

Four (*to* Five). That's true enough.

Five. I suppose, but the cashier didn't remember him.

Three. And the ticket taker didn't, either.

Ten. Look—what about the woman across the street? If her testimony don't prove it, then nothing does.

Twelve. That's right. She saw the killing, didn't she?

Foreman (*rapping on table*). Let's go in order.

Ten (*loudly*). Just a minute. Here's a woman who's lying in bed and can't sleep. It's hot, you know. (*Gets up and begins to walk around at L stage, blowing his nose and talking*) Anyway, she wakes up and she looks out the window, and right across the street she sees the kid stick the knife into his father.

Eight. How can she really be sure it was the kid when she saw it through the windows of a passing elevated train?[9]

Ten (*pausing DL*). She's known the kid all his life. His window is right opposite hers—across the el tracks—and she swore she saw him do it.

Eight. I heard her swear to it.

Ten. Okay. And they proved in court that you can look through the windows of a passing el train at night, and see what's

---
9 **elevated train:** a city streetcar which has tracks built high above the street, allowing traffic to pass underneath.

happening on the other side. They proved it.

Eight. Weren't you telling us just a minute or two ago that you can't trust *them*? That you can't believe *them*?

Ten (*coldly*). So?

Eight. Then I'd like to ask you something. How come you believed her? She's one of *them*, too, isn't she? (Ten *crosses up to* Eight.)

Ten. You're a pretty smart fellow, aren't you?

Foreman (*rising*). Now take it easy. (Three *gets up and goes to* Ten.)

Three. Come on. Sit down. (*Leads* Ten *back to his seat*) What're you letting him get you all upset for? Relax. (Ten *and* Three *sit down.*)

Four. Gentlemen, they did take us out to the woman's room and we looked through the windows of a passing el train—(*to* Eight)—didn't we?

Eight. Yes. (*Nods*) We did.

Four. And weren't you able to see what happened on the other side?

Eight. I didn't see as well as they told me I would see, but I did see what happened on the other side.

Ten (*snapping at* Eight). You see—do you see?

Foreman (*sitting again*). Let's calm down now. (*To* Five) It's your turn.

Five. I'll pass it.

Foreman. That's your privilege. (*To* Six) How about you?

Six (*slowly*). I don't know. I started to be convinced, you know, with the testimony from those people across the hall. Didn't they say something about an argument between the father and the boy around seven o'clock that night? I mean, I can be wrong.

Eleven. I think it was eight o'clock. Not seven.

Eight. That's right. Eight o'clock.

Four. They heard the father hit the boy twice and then saw the boy walk angrily out of the house.

Six. Right.

Eight. What does that prove?

Six. Well, it doesn't exactly prove anything. It's just part of the picture. I didn't say it proved anything.

Foreman. Anything else?

Six. No. *(Rises, goes to water cooler for a drink and then sits again)*

Seven. I don't know—most of it's been said already. We can talk all day about this thing, but I think we're wasting our time.

Eight. I don't.

Four. Neither do I. Go on.

Seven. Look at the kid's record. He stole a car. He's been arrested for mugging. I think they said he stabbed somebody in the arm.

Four. They did.

Seven. He was picked up for knife fighting. At fifteen he was in reform school.

Three. And they sent him to reform school for stabbing someone!

Seven *(with sarcasm)*. This is a very fine boy.

Eight. Ever since he was five years old, his father beat him up regularly. He used his fists.

Seven. So would I! On a kid like that.

Three. You're right. It's the kids. The way they are—you know? They don't listen. *(Bitterly)* I've got a kid. When he was eight years old, he ran away from a fight. I saw him. I was so ashamed. I told him right out, "I'm gonna make a man out of you or I'm gonna bust you up into little pieces trying." When he was fifteen, he hit me in the face. He's big, you know? I haven't seen him in three years. Rotten kid! I hate tough kids! You work your heart out. . . . *(Pauses)* All right. Let's get on with it. . . . *(Gets up and goes to window, very embarrassed)*

Four. We're missing the point here. This boy—let's say he's a product of a filthy neighborhood and a broken home. We can't help that. We're not here to go into the reasons why slums are breeding grounds for criminals; they are. I know it. So do you. The children who come out of slum backgrounds are potential menaces to society.

Ten. You said it there. I don't want any part of them, believe me. *(There is dead silence for a moment, and then* Five *speaks haltingly.)*

Five. I've lived in a slum all my life. . . .

Ten. Now wait a second!

Five. I used to play in a backyard that was filled with garbage. Maybe it still smells on me.

Foreman. Now, let's be reasonable. There's nothing personal—

Five *(rising, slamming his hand down on table)*. There is something personal! *(Then he catches himself, and, seeing* Everyone *looking at him, sits down, fists clenched.)*

Three *(turning from window)*. Come on,

now. He didn't mean you, feller. Let's not be so sensitive. (*There is a long pause.*)

Eight (*breaking silence*). Who did he mean?

Eleven. I can understand this sensitivity.

Foreman. Now let's stop the bickering.

Twelve. We're wasting time.

Foreman (*to* Eight). It's your turn.

Eight. All right. I had a peculiar feeling about this trial. Somehow I felt that the defense counsel never really conducted a thorough cross-examination. Too many questions were left unasked.

Four. While it doesn't change my opinion about the guilt of the kid, still, I agree with you that the defense counsel was bad.

Three. So-o-o-o? (*Crosses back to table and sits*)

Eight. This is a point.

Three. What about facts?

Eight. So many questions were never answered.

Three (*annoyed*). What about the questions that were answered? For instance, let's talk about that cute little switch knife. You know, the one that fine, upright kid admitted buying.

Eight. All right, let's talk about it. Let's get it in here and look at it. I'd like to see it again, Mr. Foreman. (Foreman *looks at him questioningly and then gets up and goes to door* L.)

[*During the following dialogue the* Foreman *knocks. The* Guard *unlocks the door and comes in* L *and the* Foreman *whispers to him. The* Guard *nods and leaves, locking the door. The* Foreman *returns to his seat.*]

Three. We all know what it looks like. I don't see why we have to look at it again. (*To* Four) What do you think?

Four. The gentleman has a right to see exhibits in evidence.

Three (*shrugging*). Okay with me.

Four (*to* Eight). This knife is a pretty strong piece of evidence, don't you agree?

Eight. I do.

Four. Now let's get the sequence of events right as they relate to the switch knife.

Twelve. The boy admits going out of his house at eight o'clock, after being slapped by his father.

Eight. Or punched.

Four. Or punched. (*Gets up and begins to pace at* R *stage, moving* DR *to* UR *and back again*) He went to a neighborhood store and bought a switch knife. The storekeeper was arrested the following day when he admitted selling it to the boy.

Three. I think everyone agrees that it's an unusual knife. Pretty hard to forget something like that.

Four. The storekeeper identified the knife and said it was the only one of its kind he had in stock. Why did the boy get it?

Seven (*sarcastically*). As a present for a friend of his, he says.

Four (*pausing in his pacing*). Am I right so far?

Eight. Right.

Three. You bet he's right. (*To* All) Now listen to this man. He knows what he's talking about.

Four (*standing at R stage*). Next, the boy claims that on the way home the knife must have fallen through a hole in his coat pocket, that he never saw it again. Now there's a story, gentlemen. You know what actually happened. The boy took the knife home, and a few hours later stabbed his father with it and even remembered to wipe off the fingerprints.

[*The door L opens and the Guard walks in with an oddly designed knife with a tag on it. Four crosses L and takes the knife from him. The Guard goes out L, closing and locking the door.*]

Four (*at LC, holding up knife*). Everyone connected with the case identified this knife. Now are you trying to tell me that someone picked it up off the street and went up to the boy's house and stabbed his father with it just to be amusing?

Eight. No. I'm saying that it's possible that the boy lost the knife, and that someone else stabbed his father with a similar knife. It's possible. (*Four flips knife open and jams it into wall just downstage of door L.*)

Four. (*standing back to allow others to see*). Take a look at that knife. It's a very strange knife. I've never seen one like it before in my life. Neither had the storekeeper who sold it to him. (*Eight reaches casually into his pocket and withdraws an object. No one notices him. He stands up.*) Aren't you trying to make us accept a pretty incredible coincidence?

Eight (*moving toward Four*). I'm not trying to make anyone accept it. I'm just saying it's possible.

Three (*rising, shouting*). And I'm saying it's *not* possible! (*Eight swiftly flicks open blade of a switch knife, jams it into wall next to first knife and steps back. They are exactly alike. There are*

several gasps and Everyone *stares at knife. There is a long silence.* Three *continues, slowly, amazed.*) What are you trying to do?

Ten (*loudly*). Yeah, what is this? Who do you think you are? (*A flow of ad lib conversation bursts forth.*)

Five. Look at it! It's the same knife!

Foreman. Quiet! Let's be quiet. (*Jurors quiet down.* Three *sits again.*)

Four. Where did you get it?

Eight. I got it in a little junk shop around the corner from the boy's house. It cost two dollars.

Three. Now listen to me!

Eight (*turning to him*). I'm listening.

Three. You pulled a real smart trick here, but you proved absolutely zero. Maybe there are ten knives like that, so what?

Eight. Maybe there are.

Three. The boy lied and you know it.

Eight (*crossing back to his seat, sitting*). And maybe he didn't lie. Maybe he did lose the knife and maybe he did go to the movies. Maybe the reason the cashier didn't see him was because he sneaked into the movies, and maybe he was ashamed to say so. (*Looks around*) Is there anybody here who didn't sneak into the movies once or twice when they were young? (*There is a long silence.*)

Eleven. I didn't.

Four. Really, not even once?

Eleven. We didn't have movies.

Four. Oh. (*Crosses back to his place and sits*

Eight. Maybe he did go to the movies—maybe he didn't. And—he may have lied.

(*To* Ten) Do you think he lied?

Ten (*violently*). Now that's a stupid question. Sure, he lied!

Eight (*to* Four). Do you?

Four. You don't have to ask me that. You know my answer. He lied.

Eight (*to* Five). Do you think he lied? (Five *can't answer immediately. He looks around nervously.*)

Five. I—I don't know.

Seven. Now wait a second. What are you—the guy's lawyer? Listen—there are still eleven of us who think he's guilty. You're alone. What do you think you're going to accomplish? If you want to be stubborn and hang this jury, he'll be tried again and found guilty sure as he's born.

Eight. You're probably right.

Seven. So what are you going to do about it? We can be here all night.

Nine. It's only one night. A man may die.

Seven. Oh, now. Come on.

Eight (*to* Nine). Well, yes, that's true.

Foreman. I think we ought to get on with it now.

Three. Right. Let's get going here.

Ten (*to* Three). How do you like this guy? (Three *shrugs and turns to* Eight.)

Three. Well, what do you say? You're the one holding up the show.

Four (*to* Eight). Obviously you don't think the boy is guilty.

Eight. I have a doubt in my mind.

Four. But you haven't really presented anything to us that makes it possible for us to understand your doubt. There's the old man downstairs. He heard it. He heard the kid shriek it out.

Three. The woman across the el tracks—she saw it!

Seven. We know he bought a switch knife that night and we don't know where he really was. At the movies?

Foreman. Earlier that night the kid and his father did have a fight.

Four. He's been a violent kid all the way, and while that doesn't prove anything . . .

Ten. Still, you know . . .

Eight (*standing*). I've got a proposition to make. (Five *stands and puts his hands on back of his chair. Several* Jurors *glare at him. He sinks his head down a bit, then sits down.*) I want to call for a vote. I want you eleven men to vote by secret ballot. I'll abstain.[10] If there are still eleven votes for guilty, I won't stand alone. We'll take in a guilty verdict right now.

Seven. Okay. Let's do it.

Foreman. That sounds fair. Is everyone agreed?

Four. I certainly am.

Twelve. Let's roll it.

Eleven (*slowly*). Perhaps this is best.

[Eight *walks over to window and stands there for a moment looking out, then turns as* Foreman *passes ballot slips down table to all of them.* Eight *tenses as* Jurors *begin to write. Then folded ballots are passed back to* Foreman. *He flips through*

---

10 **abstain**: refrain; not take part in.

folded ballots, counts them to be sure he has eleven and then he begins to open them, reading verdict each time.]

Foreman. Guilty. Guilty. Guilty. Guilty. Guilty. Guilty.

Three. That's six.

Foreman. Please. *(Fumbles with one ballot)* Six guilty. Guilty. Guilty. Guilty. *(Pauses for a moment at tenth ballot and then reads)* Not guilty. *(Three slams his hand down hard on table. Eight starts for table, as Foreman reads final ballot.)* Guilty.

Ten *(angrily)*. How do you like that!

Seven *(standing, snarling)*. Who was it? I think we have a right to know. *(He looks about. No one moves.)*

Curtain

Discussion

1. What details of action and dialogue tell the audience that this play takes place during the summer? Why do you think the season of the year is emphasized?

2. Which two jurors show prejudice against the defendant? What are their prejudices?

3. Who were the two most important witnesses at the trial? What testimony did each of them give?

4. What was the murder weapon? What information about the weapon was presented by (a) the shopkeeper, (b) the defendant, and (c) Juror Eight?

5. The defendant's past behavior and police record are discussed in the jury room. How does this discussion make many of the jurors believe that the defendant is guilty? What information does Juror Eight bring up that helps explain the defendant's behavior and record?

6. Which of the eleven jurors presents the most sensible, unemotional reasons for wanting the defendant punished? Explain by giving some specific examples.

7. What are some of the problems—apart from the trial—that the jurors must overcome before they can agree on a verdict?

ACT II

[AT RISE OF CURTAIN: *It is only a second or two later. The* Jurors *are in the same positions as they were at the end of Act I.*]

Three *(after brief pause).* All right! Who did it? What idiot changed his vote?

Eight. Is that the way to talk about a man's life? *(Sits at his place again)*

Three. Whose life are you talking about? The life of the dead man or the life of a murderer?

Seven. I want to know. Who?

Three. So do I.

Eleven. Excuse me. This was a secret ballot.

Three. No one looked while we did it, but now I want to know.

Eleven. A secret ballot—we agreed on that point, no? If the gentleman wants it to remain a secret—

Three *(standing up angrily).* What do you mean? There are no secrets in here! I know who it was. *(Turns to Five)* What's the matter with you? You come in here and you vote guilty and then this—*(nods toward Eight)*—slick preacher starts to tear your heart out with stories about a poor little kid who just couldn't help becoming a murderer. So you change your vote. If that isn't the most sickening—*(Five edges away in his chair.)*

Foreman. Now hold it. *(Seven sits again slowly.)*

Four *(to Three).* I agree with you that the man is guilty, but let's be fair.

Three. Hold it? Be fair? That's just what I'm saying. We're trying to put a guilty man into the chair where he belongs—and all of a sudden we're paying attention to fairy tales.

Five. Now, just a minute—

Three *(bending toward Five, wagging finger at him).* Now, you listen to me—

Foreman *(rapping on table).* Let's try to keep this organized, gentlemen.

Four. It isn't organized, but let's try to be civilized.

Eleven. Please. I would like to say something here. I have always thought that a man was entitled to have unpopular opinions in this country. This is the reason I came here. I wanted to have the right to disagree.

Three. Do you disagree with us?

Eleven. Usually, I would. In this one case I agree with you, but the point I wish to make is that in my own country, I am ashamed to say—

Ten. Oh, now-w-w, what do we have to listen to—the whole history of your country? *(Three sits again in disgust.)*

Four. It's always wise to bear in mind what has happened in other countries, when people aren't allowed to disagree; but we are, so let's stick to the subject.

Seven. Yeah, let's stick to the subject. *(To Five)* I want to ask you, what made you change your vote?

Three. I want to know, too. You haven't told us yet.

Five. Why do you think I changed my vote?

Seven. Because I do. Now get on with it.

Nine *(quietly)*. There's nothing for him to tell you. He didn't change his vote. I did. *(All look at* Nine.*)*

Five *(to* Three*)*. I was going to tell you, but you were so sure of yourself.

Three. Sorry. *(To* Nine*)* Okay, now . . .

Nine. Maybe you'd like to know why.

Three *(not giving him a chance)*. Let me tell you why that kid's a—

Foreman. The man wants to talk. *(Three subsides.)*

Nine *(to* Foreman*)*. Thank you. *(Points at* Eight*)* This gentleman chose not to stand alone against us. That's his right. It takes a great deal of courage to stand alone even if you believe in something very strongly. He left the verdict up to us. He gambled for support and I gave it to him. I want to hear more. The vote is ten to two. *(Jurors* Two *and* Four *get up at about same instant and walk to water cooler as* Ten *speaks.)*

Ten. That's fine. If the speech is over, let's go on. *(Foreman* gets up, goes to door L, pulls tagged knife from wall and then knocks on door.*)*

[*The door is opened by the* Guard. *The* Foreman *hands the* Guard *the tagged switch knife. The* Guard *goes out and the* Foreman *takes the other switch knife, closes it and puts it in the middle of the table. He sits again. The other* Jurors *talk on, in pantomime, as* Two *and* Four *stand by the water cooler.*]

Four *(filling cup)*. If there was anything in the kid's favor, I'd vote not guilty.

Two. I don't see what it is.

Four *(handing cup to* Two, *then drawing drink for himself)*. Neither do I. They're clutching at straws.

Two. As guilty as they get—that's the kid, I suppose.

Four. It's that one juror that's holding out, but he'll come around. He's got to and, fundamentally, he's a very reasonable man.

Two. I guess so.

Four. They haven't come up with one real fact yet to back up a not guilty verdict.

Two. It's hard, you know.

Four. Yes, it is. And what does "guilty beyond a reasonable doubt" really mean?

Two. What's a reasonable doubt?

Four. Exactly. When a life is at stake, what is a reasonable doubt? You've got to have law and order; you've got to draw the line somewhere; if you don't, everyone would start knifing people.

Two. Not much doubt here.

Four. Two men think so. I wonder why. I really wonder why.

Two. You do hear stories about innocent men who have gone to jail—or death, sometimes—then years later things turn up.

Four. And then on the other hand, some killers get turned loose and they go and do it again. They squeeze out on some technicality and kill again. *(He throws his cup into wastebasket, walks back and sits. We then hear* Three *say to* Five:*)*

Three. Look, buddy, now that we've kind of cooled off, why—ah—I was a little excited a minute ago. Well, you know how it is—I didn't mean to get nasty. Nothing personal.

[Two *trails back to his place and sits again.*]

Five (*after staring at* Three *for a moment*). Okay.

Seven (*to* Eight). Look. Supposing you answer me this. If the kid didn't kill him, who did?

Eight. As far as I know, we're supposed to decide whether or not the boy on trial is guilty. We're not concerned with anyone else's motives here.

Seven. I suppose, but who else had a motive?

Eight. The kid's father was along in years; maybe an old grudge.

Nine. Remember, it is "guilty beyond a reasonable doubt." This is an important thing to remember.

Three (*to* Ten). Everyone's a lawyer. (*To* Nine) Supposing you explain to us what your reasonable doubts are.

Nine. This is not easy. So far, it's only a feeling I have. A feeling. Perhaps you don't understand.

Three (*abruptly*). No. I don't.

Ten. A feeling! What are we gonna do, spend the night talking about your feelings? What about the facts?

Three. You said a mouthful. (*To* Nine) Look, the old man heard the kid yell, "I'm gonna kill you." A second later he heard the father's body falling, and he saw the boy running out of the house fifteen seconds after that.

Seven. Where's the reasonable doubt in that?

Twelve. That's right. And let's not forget the woman across the street. She looked into the open window and saw the boy stab his father. She saw it!

Three. Now, if that's not enough for you—

Eight (*quietly firm*). It's not enough for me.

Four. What is enough for you? I'd like to know.

Seven. How do you like him? It's like talking into a dead phone.

Four. The woman saw the killing through the windows of a moving elevated train. The train had five cars and she saw it through the windows of the last two cars. She remembers the most insignificant details.

Three. Well, what have you got to say about that?

Eight. I don't know. It doesn't sound right to me.

Three. Well, supposing you think about it. (*To* Twelve) Lend me your pencil. (*Twelve hands him a pencil.*) Let's play some tic-tac-toe. (*Draws an* X *on a piece of paper, then hands pencil and paper to* Twelve.) We might as well pass the time.

Eight. This isn't a game. (*He rises and snatches paper away.* Three *jumps up.*)

Three. Now, wait a minute!

Eight. This is a man's life.

Three (*angrily*). Who do you think you are?

Seven (*rising*). All right, let's take it easy. (Eight *sits again.*)

Three. I've got a good mind to walk around this table and belt him one!

Foreman. Now, please. I don't want any fights in here.

Three. Did you see him? The nerve! The absolute nerve!

Ten. All right. Forget it. It don't mean anything.

Six. How about sitting down?

Three. "This isn't a game." Who does he think he is? (Six *and* Ten *urge* Three *back into his seat.* Seven *sits again, and* All *are seated once more.*)

Four (*when quiet is restored*). Weren't we talking about elevated trains?

Eight. Yes, we were.

Four. So?

Eight. All right. How long does it take an elevated train going at top speed to pass a given point?

Four. What has that got to do with anything?

Eight. How long would it take? Guess.

Four. I wouldn't have the slightest idea.

Seven. Neither would I.

Nine. I don't think they mentioned it.

Eight (*to* Five). What do you think?

Five. About ten or twelve seconds—maybe.

Eight. I'd say that was a fair guess. (*Looks about*) Anyone else?

Eleven. I would think about ten seconds, perhaps . . .

Two (*reflectively*). About ten seconds, yes.

Four. All right, we're agreed. Ten seconds. (*To* Eight) What are you getting at?

Eight. This. An el train passes a given point in ten seconds. That given point is the window of the room in which the killing took place. You can almost reach out of the window of that room and touch the el. Right?

Foreman. That's right. I tried it.

Four. So?

Eight. All right. Now let me ask you this. Did anyone here ever live right next to the el tracks?

Five. I've lived close to them.

Eight. They make a lot of noise, don't they? (Five *nods.*) I've lived right by the el tracks. When your window is open, and the train goes by, the noise is almost unbearable. You can't hear yourself think.

Ten (*impatiently*). Okay. You can't hear yourself think. Get to the point.

Eight. The old man who lived downstairs heard the boy say—

Three (*interrupting*). He didn't *say* it, he screamed it.

Eight. The old man heard the boy scream, "I'm going to kill you," and one second later he heard a body fall. (*Slight pause*) One second. That's the testimony. Right?

Two. Right.

Eight. The woman across the street looked through the windows of the last two cars of the el and saw the body fall. Right?

Four. Right.

Twelve. So?

Eight (*slowly*). The last two cars. (*Slight pause, then repeats*) The last two cars.

Ten. What are you giving us here?

Eight. An el train takes ten seconds to pass a

given point, or two seconds per car. That el had been going by the old man's window for at least six seconds and maybe more *before the body fell*, according to the woman. The old man would have had to hear the boy say, "I'm going to kill you," while the front of the el was roaring past his nose. It's not possible that he could have heard it.

Three. What do you mean! Sure, he could have heard it.

Eight. With an el train going by?

Three. He said the boy yelled it out.

Eight. An el train makes a lot of noise.

Three. It's enough for me.

Four. It's enough for me, too.

Nine. I don't think he could have heard it.

Two. Maybe the old man didn't hear it. I mean with the el noise . . .

Three. What are you people talking about? Are you calling the old man a liar?

Eight (*shaking his head*). Something doesn't fit.

Five. Well, it stands to reason—

Three. You're crazy! Why would he lie? What's he got to gain?

Nine. Attention . . . maybe.

Three. You keep coming up with these bright sayings. Why don't you send one into the newspaper? They pay two dollars.

Eight (*hard, to* Three). What does that have to do with a man's life? (*Then, to* Nine) Why might the old man have lied? You have a right to be heard.

Nine (*after a moment's hesitation*). It's just that I looked at him for a very long time. The seam of his jacket was split under his arm. Did you notice that? He was a very old man with a torn jacket, and he carried two canes. (*Gets up, moves R and leans against wall*) I think I know him better than anyone here. This is a quiet, frightened, insignificant man who has been nothing all his life—who has never had recognition—his name in the newspapers. Nobody knows him after seventy-five years. This is a very sad thing. A man like this needs to be recognized—to be questioned, and listened to, and quoted just once. This is very important. . . .

Twelve. And you're trying to tell us he lied about a thing like this just so he could be important?

Nine. No, he wouldn't really lie. But perhaps he'd make himself believe that he heard those words and recognized the boy's face.

Three. Well— (*loud and brassy*)—that's the most fantastic story I've ever heard. How can you make up a thing like that?

Nine (*doggedly*). I'm not making it up.

Three. You must be making it up. People don't lie about a thing like that.

Nine. He made himself believe he told the truth.

Three. What do you know about it?

Nine (*low but firm*). I speak from experience.

Seven. What!

Nine. I am the same man.

Four. I think we all understand now. Thank you. (Nine *moves slowly back to table and sits.*)

Three (*as* Nine *sits*). If you want to admit you're a liar, it's all right by me.

Eight. Now, that is too much!

Three. He's a liar. He just told us so.

Eight. He did not say he was a liar; he was explaining.

Three (to Nine). Didn't you admit that you're a liar?

Eight (to Three). Please—he was explaining the circumstances so that we could understand why the old man might have lied. There is a difference.

Three. A liar is a liar, that's all there is to it.

Eight. Please—have some compassion.

Foreman. Gentlemen, please, we have our job and our duty here.

Four. I think they've covered it.

Eight. I hope we have.

Foreman (to Eight). All right. Is there anything else? (Two *holds up a box of cough drops and speaks to* Foreman.)

Two. Cough drop?

Foreman (waving it aside). No, thank you.

Two (hesitantly). Anybody—want a cough—drop? (Offers box around)

Foreman (sharply). Come on. Let's get on with it.

Eight. I'll take one. (Two *hands him box.*) Thank you. (Takes one and returns box) Now—there's something else I'd like to point out here. I think we proved that the old man couldn't have heard the boy say, "I'm going to kill you."

Three. Well, I disagree.

Four (to Three). Let's hear him through, anyway.

Eight. But supposing the old man really did hear the boy say, "I'm going to kill you." This phrase—how many times has each of you used it? Probably hundreds. "If you do that once more, Junior, I'm going to murder you." "Come on, Rocky, kill him!" We say it every day. This doesn't mean that we're really going to kill someone.

Four. Don't the circumstances alter that somewhat?

Twelve. The old man was murdered.

Three. One thing more. The phrase was, "I'm going to kill you." And the kid screamed it out at the top of his lungs.

Four. That's the way I understand it.

Three. Now don't try and tell me he didn't mean it. Anybody says a thing like that the way he said it—they mean it.

Ten. And how they mean it!

Eight. Well, let me ask you this. Do you really think the boy would shout out a thing like that so the whole neighborhood would hear it? I don't think so. He's much too bright for that.

Ten (exploding). Bright! He's a common, ignorant slob. He don't even speak good English!

Eleven (slowly). He *doesn't* even speak good English.

Four. The boy is clever enough. (Four's *line is spoken as* Ten *rises and glowers at* Eleven. *There is a momentary pause.* Ten *sits again as* Five *gets up and looks around. He is nervous.*)

Five. I'd like to change my vote to not guilty. (Three *slams his fist into his hand, then walks to window and does it again.*)

Foreman. Are you sure?

Five. Yes. I'm sure.

Foreman. The vote is nine to three in favor of guilty.

Four (*to* Five). I'd like to know why you've changed your vote.

Five. I think there's a doubt.

Three (*turning abruptly from window, snarling*). Where? What is the doubt?

Five. There's the knife . . .

Seven (*slamming his hand down on table*). Oh, fine!

Ten. He—(*motioning at* Eight)—he talked you into believing a fairy tale.

Four (*to* Five). Go on. Give us the reasons.

Five. The old man, too. Maybe he didn't lie, but then just *maybe* he did. Maybe the old man doesn't like the kid.

Seven. Well, if that isn't the end.

Five. I believe that there is reasonable doubt. (*Sits again*)

Seven. What are you basing it on? Stories that this guy—(*indicates* Eight)—made up! He ought to write for *Amazing Detective Monthly*. He'd make a fortune. Listen, the kid had a lawyer, didn't he? Why didn't his lawyer bring up all these points?

Five. Lawyers can't think of everything.

Seven. Oh, brother! (*To* Eight) You sit in here and pull stories out of thin air. Now we're supposed to believe that the old man didn't get out of bed, run to the door and see the kid beat it downstairs fifteen seconds after the killing.

Four. That's the testimony, I believe.

Seven. And the old man swore to this— yes—he swore to this only so he could be important. (*Looks over at* Nine)

Five. Did the old man say he *ran* to the door?

Seven. Ran. Walked. What's the difference? He got there.

Five. I don't remember what he said. But I don't see how he could run.

Four. He said he *went*. I remember it now. He *went* from his bedroom to the front door. That's enough, isn't it?

Eight. Where was his bedroom, again?

Ten (*disinterested*). Down the hall somewhere.

Eight (*mad*). Down the hall! Are we to send a man off to die because it's down the hall *somewhere*?

Ten. I thought you remembered everything. Don't you remember that?

Eight. No, I don't.

Nine. I don't remember, either.

Eight. Mr. Foreman, I'd like to take a look at the diagram of the apartment.

Seven. Why don't we have them run the trial over just so you can get everything straight?

Eight. The bedroom is down the hall somewhere. Do you *know*—do you know exactly where it is? Please. A man's life is at stake. Do you *know*?

Seven. Well, ah . . .

Eight. Mr. Foreman.

Foreman (*rising*). I heard you. (*Goes to door L and knocks on door*)

[*During the ensuing dialogue the* Guard *opens*

the door L. The Foreman *whispers to him. The* Guard *nods and then closes the door.*]

Three *(stepping away from window, moving a few steps toward* Eight*).* All right. What's this one for? How come you're the only one in the room who wants to see exhibits all the time?

Five. I want to see this one, too.

Nine. So do I.

Three. And I want to stop wasting time.

Four. Are we going to start wading through all that nonsense about where the body was found?

Eight. We're not. We're going to find out how a man who's had two strokes in the past three years and who walks with a pair of canes could get to his front door in fifteen seconds.

Three. He said twenty seconds.

Two. He said fifteen.

Three. How does he know how long fifteen seconds is? You can't judge that kind of thing.

Nine. He said fifteen. He was very positive about it.

Three *(angrily).* He's an old man. You saw that. Half the time he was confused. How could he be positive about—anything? *(Looks around sheepishly, unable to cover his blunder)* Well, ah—you know.

Eight. No, I don't know. Maybe you know.

[*The door* L *opens and the* Guard *walks in carrying a large pen-and-ink diagram of the apartment done on heavy drawing board stock. It is a railroad flat. A bedroom faces the el tracks. Behind it is a series of rooms off a long hall. In the front bedroom there is a mark where the body was*

found. *At the back of the apartment we see the entrance into the apartment hall from the building hall. We see a flight of stairs in the building hall. The diagram is clearly labeled, and included in the information on it are the various dimensions of the various rooms. The* Guard *gives the diagram to the* Foreman, *who has remained by the door* L.]

Guard. Is this what you wanted?

Foreman. That's right. Thank you.

Guard. Sure, that's my job. *(He nods and goes out* L, *closing and locking door as he goes.* Eight *rises and starts toward* Foreman.*)*

Foreman. You want this?

Eight. Yes, please.

[Foreman *nods.* Eight *takes diagram and crosses* UR. *He takes chair from* UR *corner and brings it* RC, *half facing table. He sets diagram up on chair so that* All *can see it.* Eight *looks it over. Several* Jurors *get up to see it better.* Foreman *comes over to look.* Three, Ten, *and* Seven, *however, barely bother to look at it.* Three *sits abruptly again at table.*]

Seven *(to* Ten*).* Do me a favor. *(Slumps in chair)* Wake me up when this is over.

Ten. I looked at that diagram for two hours; enough is enough.

Four. Some of us are interested. Go ahead.

Eight. All right. This is the apartment in which the killing took place. The old man's apartment is directly beneath it, and exactly the same. *(Pointing)* Here are the el tracks. The bedroom. Another bedroom. Living room. Bathroom. Kitchen. And this is the hall. Here's the front door to the apartment, and here are the steps. *(Points to front bedroom and then to front door)* Now, the old man was in bed in this room. He says he got up, went out into the hall, down the hall to the front door and opened it and looked out just in time to see the boy racing down the stairs. Am I right?

Four. That's the story.

Seven. That's what happened!

Eight. Fifteen seconds after he heard the body fall.

Eleven. Correct. (Foreman *and other* Jurors *who have come over to look at diagram now drift back to table and sit again.*)

Eight (*still by diagram at* RC). His bed was at the window. (*Looking closer*) It's twelve feet from his bed to the bedroom door. The length of the hall is forty-three feet, six inches. He had to get up out of bed, get his canes, walk twelve feet, open the bedroom door, walk forty-three feet and open the front door—all in fifteen seconds. Do you think this possible?

Ten. You know it's possible.

Four. I don't see why not.

Three. He would have been in a hurry. He did hear the scream.

Eleven. He can only walk very slowly. They had to help him into the witness chair.

Three. You make it sound like a long walk. It's not. (Eight *goes* DL *and takes two chairs. He crosses* DR, *near water cooler, and puts them together to indicate a bed.*)

Nine. For an old man who uses canes, it's a long walk.

Three (*to* Eight). What are you doing?

Eight. I want to try this thing. Let's see how long it took him. I'm going to pace off twelve feet—the length of the bedroom. (*Begins to do*

so, *pacing from* DR, *across stage, toward* DC)

Three. You're crazy! You can't recreate a thing like that.

Eleven. Perhaps if we could see it—this is an important point.

Three (*angrily*). It's a ridiculous waste of time!

Six. Let him do it.

Four. I can't see any harm in it. Foolish, but go ahead.

Eight. Hand me a chair, please. (Nine *pushes chair from right end of table to* Eight *and then sits again.*) All right. (*Places chair at point he has paced off*) This is the bedroom door. How far would you say it is from here to the door of this room?

Six (*as* All *look*). I'd say it was twenty feet. (*Several* Jurors, *excluding* Three, Seven, *and* Ten, *rise and stand near their places, watching.*)

Two. Just about.

Eight. Twenty feet is close enough. All right, from here to the door and back is about forty feet. It's shorter than the length of the hall the old man had to move through. Wouldn't you say that?

Nine. A few feet, maybe.

Ten. Look, this is absolutely insane. What makes you think you can do this?

Foreman. We can't stop him.

Eight. Do you mind if I try it? According to you, it'll only take fifteen seconds. We can spare that. (*Walks over to two chairs and lies down on them*) Who's got a watch with a second hand?

Two. I have. (*Indicates wrist watch*)

Eight. When you want me to start, stamp your foot. That'll be the body falling.

Two. We'll time you from there.

Eight (*lying down on two chairs*). Let's say he keeps his canes right at his bedside. Right?

Four. Right!

Eight. Okay. I'm ready.

Two (*explaining*). I'm waiting for the hand to get to sixty.

[All *watch carefully; then* Two *stamps his foot, loudly.* Eight *begins to get up. Slowly, he swings his legs over edges of chairs, reaches for imaginary canes and struggles to his feet.* Two *stares at his watch.* Eight *walks as a crippled old man would walk now. He goes toward chair which is serving as bedroom door. He gets to it and pretends to open it.*]

Ten (*shouting*). Speed it up. He walked twice as fast as that.

[Eight, *not having stopped for this outburst, begins to walk simulated forty-foot hallway, to door L and back to chair.*]

Eleven. This is, I think, even more quickly than the old man walked in the courtroom.

Three. No, it isn't.

Eight. If you think I should go faster, I will.

Four. Speed it up a little.

[Eight *speeds up his pace slightly. He reaches door L and turns now, heading back, hobbling as an old man would hobble, bent over his imaginary canes. All* watch him tensely. *He hobbles back to chair, which also serves as front door. He stops there and pretends to unlock door. Then he pretends to push it open.*]

Eight (*loudly*). Stop.

Two (*his eyes glued to watch*). Right.

Eight. What's the time?

Two. Fifteen—twenty—thirty—thirty-five—thirty-nine seconds, exactly. (*He moves toward* Eight. *Other* Jurors *now move in toward* Eight, *also.*)

Three. That can't be!

Eleven. Thirty-nine seconds!

Four. Now, that's interesting.

Seven (*looking at* Jurors). Hey, now—you know . . .

Nine. What do you think of that!

Eleven (*nodding*). Thirty-nine seconds. Thirty-nine.

Four. And the old cripple swore, on his oath, that it was fifteen.

Eleven (*pointing to* Eight). He may have been a little bit off on the speed that the old cripple moved at—but twenty-four seconds off . . . well, now, you know . . .

Foreman. Far be it from me to call anyone a liar, and even allowing for quite a difference in speed between the old man and you. . . . (*Motions at* Eight) Why, still, there's quite a—

Four. Quite a discrepancy.

Eight. It's my guess that the old man was trying to get to the door, heard someone racing down the stairs and *assumed* that it was the boy.

Six. I think that's possible.

Three (*infuriated*). Assumed? Now, listen to me, you people. I've seen all kinds of dishonesty in my day—but this little display takes the cake.

Eight. What dishonesty?

Three *(to* Four*).* Tell him! *(Four turns away DR and sits silently in one of the two chairs there. Three looks at him and then he strides to Eight.)* You come in here with your heart bleeding all over the floor about slum kids and injustice and you make up these wild stories, and you've got some soft-hearted old ladies listening to you. Well, I'm not. I'm getting real sick of you. *(To All)* What's the matter with you people? This kid is guilty! He's got to burn! We're letting him slip through our fingers.

Eight *(calmly).* Our fingers. Are you his executioner?

Three *(raging).* I'm one of 'em!

Eight. Perhaps you'd like to pull the switch.

Three *(shouting).* For this kid? You bet I'd like to pull the switch!

Eight *(shaking his head sadly).* I'm sorry for you.

Three *(shouting).* Don't start with me!

Eight. What it must feel like to want to pull the switch!

Three. Shut up!

Eight. You're a sadist.[11] . . .

Three *(louder).* Shut up!

Eight *(his voice strong).* You want to see this boy die because you personally want it—not because of the facts. *(Spits out words)* You are a beast. You disgust me.

Three *(shouting).* Shut up! *(He lunges at Eight, but is caught by two of the Jurors and is held. He struggles as Eight watches calmly. Then he screams.)* Let me go! I'll kill him! I'll kill him!

Eight *(softly).* You don't really mean you'll kill me, do you?

[Three *stops struggling now and stares at* Eight, *and all the* Jurors *watch in silence, as:*]

Curtain

---

11 **sadist** (sā′ dist): a person who takes pleasure in making others suffer pain.

Discussion

1. At the beginning of Act II, which jurors assume that Juror Five has changed his vote? Who really had changed his vote? Why?

2. At the water cooler, Jurors Two and Four discuss problems that *all* jurors must face if they are to do their job properly. What are these problems?

3. According to the testimony of the old man downstairs, one second before he heard the body fall, the defendant shouted, "I'm going to kill you." Why does Juror Eight question the truth of this testimony?

4. Why does Juror Nine think the old man might have lied in his testimony?

5. Several times during Act II, Juror Three makes childish and irresponsible remarks. What are some of those remarks?

6. At the end of Act II, Jurors Three and Eight are both angry for different reasons. What are those reasons?

7. At the end of Act II, Juror Three shouts at Eight, "I'll kill him! I'll kill him!" Why is this statement so important at this point in the play?

ACT III

[AT RISE OF CURTAIN: *We see the same scene as at the end of Act II. There has been no time lapse. Three glares angrily at Eight. He is still held by two* Jurors. *After a long pause* Three *shakes himself loose and turns away. He walks to the window. The other* Jurors *move away and stand around the room now; they are shocked by this display of anger. There is silence. Then the door L opens and the* Guard *enters. He looks around the room.*]

Guard. Is there anything wrong, gentlemen? I heard some noise.

Foreman. No. There's nothing wrong. *(Points to large diagram of apartment)* You can take that back. We're finished with it.

[Guard *nods and takes diagram. He looks curiously at some of* Jurors *and then goes out.* Jurors *still are silent; some of them begin to sit down slowly at table.* Four *is still seated* DR. Three *still stands at window. He turns around now.* Jurors *look at him.*]

Three *(loudly).* Well, what are you looking at?

[*They turn away. He goes back to his seat now.* Eight *puts his chair back at right end of table. Silently, rest of* Jurors, *including* Four *but excluding* Eleven, *take their seats.* Twelve *begins to doodle on a piece of paper.* Eleven *moves* DL *and leans reflectively against wall.* Ten *blows his nose but no one speaks. Then, finally:*]

Four. I don't see why we have to behave like children here.

Eleven. Nor do I. We have a responsibility. This is a remarkable thing about democracy. That we are—what is the word? . . . ah, notified! That we are notified by mail to come down to this place—and decide on the guilt or innocence of a man; of a man we have not known before. We have nothing to gain or lose by our verdict. This is one of the reasons why we are strong. We should not make it a personal thing. . . .

Nine (slowly). Thank you, very much.

Eleven (slight surprise). Why do you thank me?

Nine. We forget. It's good to be reminded. (Eleven nods and leans against wall again.)

Four. I'm glad that we're going to be civilized about this.

Twelve. Well, we're still nowhere.

Eight. No, we're somewhere, or getting there—maybe.

Four. Maybe.

Twelve. Who's got an idea?

Six. I think maybe we should try another vote. (Turns to Foreman) Mr. Foreman?

Foreman. It's all right with me. Anybody doesn't want to vote? (He looks around table. Most of them shake their heads. Eleven has moved to table and takes his seat.)

Four. Let's vote.

Twelve. Yes, vote.

Seven. So all right, let's do it.

Three. I want an open ballot. Let's call out our votes. I want to know who stands where.

Foreman. That sounds fair. Anyone object? (He looks around. There is a general shaking of heads.) All right. I'll call off your jury numbers. (Takes a pencil and paper and makes marks in one of two columns after each vote) I vote guilty. Number two?

Two. Not guilty.

Foreman. Three?

Three. Guilty.

Foreman. Four?

Four. Guilty.

Foreman. Five?

Five. Not guilty.

Foreman. Six?

Six. Not guilty.

Foreman. Seven?

Seven. Guilty.

Foreman. Eight?

Eight. Not guilty.

Foreman. Nine?

Nine. Not guilty.

Foreman. Ten?

Ten. Guilty.

Foreman. Eleven?

Eleven. Not guilty.

Foreman. Twelve?

Twelve. Guilty.

Four. That's six to six.

Ten (mad). I'll tell you something. The crime is being committed right in this room.

Foreman. The vote is six to six.

Three. I'm ready to walk into court right now and declare a hung jury. There's no point in this going on any more.

Four (to Eleven). I'd like to know why you changed your mind. (To Two) And why you changed your mind. (To Six) And why you did. There are six men here who think that we may be turning a murderer loose in the streets. Emotion won't do. Why? (Two, Eleven and Six look at each other.)

Six. It would seem that the old man did not see the boy run downstairs. I do not think it likely that the old man heard someone scream, "I'm going to kill you." Old men dream. And if the boy did scream that he was going to kill, then we have the authority of this man— *(motions at* Three*)* —to prove that it might not really mean he's going to kill.

Seven. Why don't we take it in to the judge and let the kid take his chances with twelve other guys?

Foreman. Six to six. I don't think we'll ever agree—on anything.

Three. It's got to be unanimous— *(motioning at* Eight*)* —and we're never going to convince him.

Eight. At first I was alone. Now five others agree; there is a doubt.

Three. You can't ever convince me that there's a doubt, because I know there isn't no doubt.

Twelve. I tell you what, maybe we are a hung jury. It happens sometimes.

Eight. We are not going to be a hung jury.

Seven. But we are, right now, a perfect balance. Let's take it in to the judge.

Four *(to* Eight*)*. If there is a reasonable doubt, I don't see it.

Nine. The doubt is there, in my mind.

Foreman. Maybe we should vote.

Twelve. What do you mean—vote?

Three. Not again!

Ten. I still want to know. Vote on what?

Foreman. Are we or aren't we a hung jury?

Eight. You mean that we vote yes, we are a hung jury, or no, we are not a hung jury?

Foreman. That's just what I was thinking of.

Eleven *(bitterly)*. We can't even agree about whether or not the window should be open.

Foreman. Let's make it a majority vote. The majority wins.

Four. If seven or more of us vote yes, that we are a hung jury, then we take it in to the judge and tell him that we are a hung jury.

Foreman. Right. And if seven or more vote no, that means that we aren't a hung jury, and we go on discussing it.

Four. It doesn't seem quite right to me.

Three. It's the only solution.

Seven. I agree, it's the only way.

Twelve. Anything to end this.

Foreman *(looking around table)*. Are we agreed then? Seven or more vote yes and we take it in to the judge. (All *nod.*)

Three. Let's call our votes out.

Foreman. I vote yes, we're a hung jury. *(Makes a mark on a sheet of paper)* Two?

Two. No.

Foreman. Three?

Three. Yes.

Foreman. Four?

Four. Yes.

Foreman. Five?

Five. No.

Foreman. Six?

Six. No.

Foreman. Seven?

Seven. Yes.

Foreman. Eight?

Eight. No.

Foreman. Nine?

Nine. No.

Foreman. Ten?

Ten. Yes.

Foreman. Eleven?

Eleven. No.

Foreman. Twelve?

Twelve. Yes.

Three (*with a groan*). Oh, no!

Foreman. It's six to six.

Nine. We can't even get a majority to decide whether or not we're a hung jury.

Four (*rising*). I went along with the majority vote on this question. And I didn't agree with voting that way, not really, and I still don't. So I'm changing my vote. I say no, we are not a hung jury. I believe that the boy is guilty beyond a reasonable doubt. There are some things I want to find out from those gentlemen that changed their minds. (*Sits again*)

Foreman. Then we aren't a hung jury—so we go on.

Eight. Good! We go on.

Four (*to* Two). Why did you change your mind?

Two (*hesitating a moment*). He—(*points to* Eight)—he seems so sure. And he has made a number of good points. While he—(*points to* Three)—only gets mad and insults everybody.

Four. Does the anger and the insult change the guilt of the boy? He did do it. Are you going to turn a murderer loose because one of the jurors gets angry when he thinks a murderer is being turned loose?

Two. That's true.

Five. There is a doubt.

Four. I don't think so. The track is straight in front of the window. Let's take that point. So the el train would have made a low rumbling noise. El trains screech when they go around curves. So the old man could have heard a scream, which is high-pitched. And it is a tenement and they have thin walls.

Three. Good. Good. That's it. That's it.

Four. And what if the old man was wrong about the time it took him to get to the door, but right about whom he saw? Please remember that there weren't any fingerprints on the knife, and it is summer, so gloves seem unlikely.

Three (*to* Eight). Now I want you to listen to this man. (*Motions at* Four) He's got the goods.

Four. And it might have taken a few seconds to get a handkerchief out and wipe the fingerprints away.

Eight. This is a point.

Three. Why don't we just time this one, to see?

Five. Just what are we timing?

Eight. Yes, let's be exact, please.

Four. I am saying that the old man downstairs might have been wrong about how long it took him to get to the door, but that he was right about whom he saw running down the stairs. Now it may have taken the murderer about thirty-nine seconds to wipe away all the fingerprints and get down the stairs to the place where the old man saw him—the boy, that is.

Three. This is right.

Foreman. We reconstructed the old man getting out of bed and going to the door, and we timed that; now let's reconstruct the actual crime.

Nine. As well as we can reconstruct it.

Seven. I think a murderer could use up thirty or forty seconds pretty easily at that point.

Four. Let's reconstruct the killing.

Seven. Yes, let's.

Three (*taking knife from table, giving it to* Eight). Here, you do the stabbing.

Four (*taking knife*). No. I'll do it.

Three (*to* Seven). Why don't you be the one that gets stabbed? You're younger than I am. And don't forget, you take one second to fall.

Four (*rising, moving toward* R, *turning*). And he was found on his side—his right side—so fall and roll onto your right side. (*To* Eight) If someone hates another person enough to kill them, don't you think that it's reasonable to suppose that the murderer would look at his victim for a second or two?

Twelve (*to* Eight). Divorce yourself from this particular case—just human nature.

Eight. Yes, it seems reasonable.

Three. Hey, wait a minute! (*All* look at Three.) He falls and he ends up on his right side, the father did, but stabbing someone isn't like shooting them, even when it's right in the heart. The father would have worked around for a few seconds—lying there on the floor—writhing, maybe.

Four. That's quite possible. There would have been enough oxygen in his system to carry him for two or three seconds, I should think.

Eleven. Wouldn't the father have cried out?

Three. Maybe the kid held his mouth.

Eight. That also seems possible.

Four. Also, there's another point we might bring out. Anyone who is clear enough mentally to wipe the fingerprints away after murdering someone, well, that person is also clear enough mentally to look around the apartment, or the room in this case, to see if there are any other clues. It would just be for a second or two I should think, but still he would look around.

Three. This gets better and better.

Four. We're trying to make it clear. One doesn't talk about quality when murder is involved. Well, let's do it.

Foreman. About this on the fingerprints—the kid wiped the fingerprints off the knife. Well, what about the doorknob? If I saw a man coming into my home, a man that hated me, and if he was wiping the doorknob with a handkerchief as he came in, it would give me an uneasy feeling. (*All* smile.) So the doorknobs must have been wiped after the killing, and this, too, would take some time.

Four (*to* Two). You timed the last one. Why don't you time this one, too?

Two. All right.

Four (*as Seven takes his position in front of Four at R stage; Four has knife in his hand*). Stamp your foot when you want me to start.

Two (*waiting a few seconds*). I want the hand to be at sixty. (*Waits another second, then stamps foot*)

Four (*not screaming, but still loud*). I'm going to kill you. (*Brings knife down overhand. Blade is collapsed. Seven catches knife in his hands and falls to floor a second after shout. He writhes a bit, then rolls onto his right side. Four stares at him for a few moments, then digs into his pocket and produces a handkerchief. It takes him a moment or two to unfold handkerchief; then he bends down and wipes handle of knife. He looks about, as though checking to be sure that he has done everything. Then he rushes to door L that leads out of jury room and wipes doorknob. Then he turns around a full circle and wipes knob again.*) He would have wiped both knobs. (*Then he rushes R and goes back to door of jury room and repeats double process on doorknob. Then he stamps his foot and cries out.*) Stop!

Two (*checking watch*). Twenty—yeah, twenty, twenty-five— twenty-nine— about twenty-nine and a half seconds, I'd say.

Four (*moving to behind Foreman's chair at left end of table*). And whoever did murder the old man, and I think it was the kid, he still had to run down the hall and down the stairs—at least one flight of stairs.

Three. You see! You see! (*Seven rises from floor and dusts himself off.*)

Four. The old man downstairs may have been wrong on the time, but in view of this I think it's quite reasonable to assume that he did see the kid run downstairs.

Twelve (*to Eight*). So now both time sequences check—the one you did and the one we did; what with running downstairs and everything, it does pretty much check out on times.

Seven. Sure—he's an old man who wants attention. . . . (*Motions at Nine*) He's probably right, but the old man feels the way everyone does—a life is at stake. (*Sits again at table, placing knife back on table*)

Four. So the story of the old man may well be true.

Eight. Except for the fact that he absolutely swore, under oath, that it was only fifteen seconds.

Nine. We seem to all agree that it was twenty-five to forty seconds later.

Eight. You are now admitting that the old man lied in one case and told the truth in the other. I admit that this does tend to confirm the story of the old man, but in part he is now a proven liar—and this is by your own admission.

Two (*to Eight*). That may be true, that the old man lies in part, but I think it will change my vote once more. (*To Foreman*) Guilty.

Three (*to Six*). What about you? What do you think now?

Six (*getting up, crossing to water cooler*). I'm not just sure what I think. I want to talk some more. At first I thought guilty, then I changed. Now—I'm sort of swinging back to guilty. (*Takes a drink*)

Three (*to Eleven*). And what about you?

Eleven. No. (*Shakes his head*) I am now in real doubt—real doubt. . . .

Five. I say guilty. I was right the first time.

Three. Now we're beginning to make sense in here.

Foreman. It seems to be about nine guilty to three not guilty. (Four *sits again.*)

Eight. One more question about the old man downstairs. How many of you live in apartment buildings? (Eight *hands go up, including his own.*)

Eleven (*to* Eight). I don't know what you're thinking, but I know what I'm thinking.

Four (*to* Eleven). What's that?

Eleven. I do not live in a tenement, but it is close and there is just enough light in the hall so you can see the steps, no more—the light bulbs are so small—and this murder took place in a tenement. Remember how we stumbled on the steps?

Eight. The police officers were using big bulbs and one even had a flashlight. Remember?

Eleven. An old man who misjudged the time by twenty seconds, on this we all agree, this old man looked down the dark hallway of a tenement and recognized a running figure?

Eight. He was one hundred per cent wrong about the time; it took twice as long as he thought.

Eleven. Then could not the old man be one hundred per cent wrong about who he saw?

Three. That's the most iodiotic thing I've ever heard of. You're making that up out of thin air.

Twelve. We're a hung jury. Let's be honest about it.

Eleven (*to* Seven). Do you truly feel that there is no room for reasonable doubt?

Seven. Yes, I do.

Eleven. I beg your pardon, but maybe you don't understand the term, "reasonable doubt."

Seven (*angrily*). What do you mean, I don't understand it? Who do you think you are to talk to me like that? (*To* All) How do you like this guy? He comes over here running for his life, and before he can even take a big breath, he's telling us how to run the show. The arrogance of him!

Four. No one here is asking where anyone came from.

Seven. I was born right here.

Four. Or where your father came from. (*Looks at* Seven, *who looks away*)

Eight. Maybe it wouldn't hurt us to take a few tips from people who come running here! Maybe they learned something we don't know. We're not so perfect.

Eleven. Please . . . I am used to this. . . . It's all right. Thank you.

Eight. It's not all right.

Seven. Okay—okay—I apologize. Is that what you want?

Eight (*grimly*). That's what I want.

Foreman. All right. Let's stop the arguing. Who's got something constructive to say?

Two (*hesitantly*). Well, something's been bothering me a little. This whole business about the stab wound, and how it was made—the downward angle of it, you know?

Three. Don't tell me we're going to start that. They went over it and over it in court.

Two. I know they did—but I don't go along with it. The boy is five feet, eight inches tall. His father was six feet, two inches tall. That's a difference of six inches. It's a very awkward thing to stab *down* into the chest of someone who's half a foot taller than you are. (Three *grabs knife from table and jumps up.*)

Three (*moving* LC). Look, you're not going to be satisfied till you see it again. I'm going to give you a demonstration. Somebody get up. (*He looks toward table.* Eight *stands up and walks toward him.* Three *closes knife and puts it in his pocket. They stand face to face and look at each other for a moment.*) Okay. (*To* Two) Now watch this. I don't want to have to do it again. (*Crouches down until he is quite a bit shorter than* Eight) Is that six inches?

Twelve. That's more than six inches.

Three. Okay, let it be more. (*He reaches into his pocket and takes out knife. He flicks it open, changes its position in his hand and holds knife aloft, ready to stab. He and* Eight *look steadily into each other's eyes. Then he stabs downward, hard.*)

Two (*shouting*). Look out! (*He reaches short just as the blade reaches* Eight's *chest.* Three *laughs.*)

Six. That's not funny. (*Crosses back to table and sits*)

Five. What's the matter with you?

Three. Now just calm down. Nobody's hurt, are they?

Eight (*low*). No. Nobody's hurt. (*Turns, crosses back to his place but does not sit*)

Three. All right. There's your angle. Take a look at it. (*Illustrates*) Down and in. That's how I'd stab a taller man in the chest, and that's how it was done. (*Crosses back to his*

place at table) Take a look at it, and tell me I'm wrong. (Two *doesn't answer.* Three *looks at him for a moment, then jams knife into table and sits down. All look at knife.*)

Six. Down and in. I guess there's no argument. (Eight *picks knife out of table and closes it. He flicks it open and, changing its position in his hand, stabs downward with it.*)

Eight (*to* Six). Did you ever stab a man?

Six. Of course not.

Eight (*to* Three). Did you?

Three. All right, let's not be silly.

Eight (*insistently*). Did you?

Three (*loudly*). No. I didn't!

Eight. Where do you get all your information about how it's done?

Three. What do you mean? It's just common sense.

Eight. Have you ever seen a man stabbed?

Three (*pausing, looking around rather nervously, finally*). No.

Eight. All right. I want to ask you something. The boy was an experienced knife-fighter. He was even sent to reform school for knifing someone. Isn't that so?

Twelve. That's right.

Eight. Look at this. (*Closes knife, flicks it open and changes position of knife so that he can stab overhand*) Doesn't it seem like an awkward way to handle a knife?

Three. What are you asking me for? (Eight *closes blade and flicks it open, holding knife ready to slash underhanded.*)

Five. Wait a minute! What's the matter

with me? Give me that knife. *(Reaches out for knife)*

Eight. Have you ever seen a knife fight?

Five. Yes, I have.

Eight. In the movies? *(Passes knife to Five)*

Five. In my backyard. On my stoop. In the vacant lot across the street. Too many of them. Switch knives came with the neighborhood where I lived. Funny that I didn't think of it before. I guess you try to forget those things. *(Flicks knife open)* Anyone who's ever used a switch knife would never have stabbed downward. You don't handle a switch knife that way. You use it underhanded. *(Illustrates)*

Eight. Then he couldn't have made the kind of wound that killed his father.

Five. I suppose it's conceivable that he could have made the wound, but it's not likely, not if he'd ever had any experience with switch knives, and we know that the kid had a lot of experience with switch knives.

Three. I don't believe it.

Ten. Neither do I. You're giving us a lot of mumbo-jumbo.

Eight *(to Twelve)*. What do you think?

Twelve *(hesitantly)*. Well—I don't know.

Eight *(to Seven)*. What about you?

Seven. Listen, I'll tell you all something. I'm a little sick of this whole thing already. We're getting nowhere fast. Let's break it up and go home.

Eight. Before we decide anything more, I would like to try to pull this together.

Three. This should be good.

Four. He has a right. Let him go ahead.

Two. Do you want me to time this, too? *(Eight looks at Two.)*

Foreman. Let's hear him.

Twelve *(getting comfortable)*. I'm in advertising. I'm used to the big shots pulling things together. Let's chip up a few shots to see if any of them land on the green.

Eight. I want you all to look at this logically and consistently.

Three. We have. Guilty.

Eight. I want to know—is the kid smart or is the kid dumb?

Four. What do you mean?

Eight *(moving UC, so that he is standing back of men at upstage side of table)*. This is a kid who has gone to the reform school for knife fighting. The night of the murder he bought a knife, a switch knife. It would then take a very stupid kid to go and murder a man, his father, with an instrument that everyone would associate with the kid.

Three. I quite agree, he's dumb.

Eight. However, if he were dumb, then why did he make the kind of wound that an inexperienced man would make with a knife?

Foreman. I'm not sure I understand.

Eight. To murder someone must take a great emotion, great hatred. *(Moves over to left of Foreman)* And at that moment he would handle the knife as best he could and a trained knife-fighter would handle it as he had been trained, underhand. . . . *(Makes underhanded motion)* A man who had not been trained would go overhand. . . .

(Makes overhanded motion) But the kid is being very smart. Everyone knows that he is an experienced knife-fighter—so he is smart enough at that moment to make the wound that an amateur would make. That man is a smart man. Smart enough to wipe the fingerprints away, perhaps even smart enough to wait until an el train was going by in order to cover the noise. Now, is the kid smart, or is he dumb? *(Looks around)*

Three. Hey, now, wait a minute!

Nine. Well, the woman across the el tracks saw the murder through the el train, so someone in that el train could have seen the murder, too.

Eight. A possibility, but no one did that we know of.

Nine. It would take an awfully dumb man to take that chance, doing the murder as the train went by.

Eight. Exactly. A dumb man, a very stupid man, a man swept by emotion. Probably he heard nothing; he probably didn't even hear the train coming. And whoever did murder the father did it as well as he could.

Four. So?

Eight *(moving back to his place, at right end of table, not sitting)*. The kid is dumb enough to do everything to associate himself with the switch knife—a switch knife murder—and then a moment after the murder he becomes smart. The kid is smart enough to make a kind of wound that would lead us to suspect someone else, and yet at the same instant he is dumb enough to do the killing as an el train is going by, and then a moment later he is smart enough to wipe fingerprints away. To make this boy guilty, you have to say he is dumb from eight o'clock until about midnight and then about midnight he is smart one second, then dumb for a few seconds and then smart again and then once again he becomes stupid, so stupid that he does not think of a good alibi. Now is this kid smart or is he dumb? To say that he is guilty, you have to toss his intelligence like a pancake. There is doubt, doubt, doubt. *(Beats table with fist as he emphasizes word "doubt")*

Four. I hadn't thought of that.

Eight. And the old man downstairs. On the stand he swore that it was fifteen seconds; he insisted on fifteen seconds, but we all agree that it must have been almost forty seconds.

Nine. Does the old man lie half the time and then does he tell the truth the other half of the time?

Eight. For the kid to be guilty he must be stupid, then smart, then stupid and then smart and so on, and, also, for the kid to be guilty the old man downstairs must be a liar half of the time and the other half of the time he must tell the truth. You can reasonably doubt. *(He sits again. There is a moment of silence.)*

Seven *(breaking silence)*. I'm sold on "reasonable doubt."

Two. I think I am, too.

Six. I wanted more talk, and now I've had it.

Eight *(fast)*. I want another vote.

Foreman. Okay, there's another vote called for. I guess the quickest way is a show of hands. Anybody object? *(No one does.)* All right. All those voting not guilty raise your hands. (Jurors Two, Five, Six, Seven, Eight, Nine, Eleven *and* Twelve *raise their hands* *immediately.* Foreman *looks around table carefully and then he, too, raises his hand. He looks around table, counting silently.)* Nine. *(Hands go down.)* All those voting guilty. *(Jurors Three, Four and Ten raise their hands.)* Three. *(They lower their hands.)* The vote is nine to three in favor of acquittal.[12]

Ten. I don't understand you people. How can you believe this kid is innocent? Look, you know how those people lie. I don't have to tell you. They don't know what the truth is. And let me tell you, they— *(Five gets up from table, turns his back to it and goes to window.)* — don't need any real big reason to kill someone, either. You know, they get drunk, and bang, someone's lying in the gutter. Nobody's blaming them. That's how they are. You know what I mean? Violent! *(Nine gets up and goes to window and looks out. He is followed by Eleven.)* Human life don't mean as much to them as it does to us. Hey, where are you all going? Look, these people're drinking and fighting all the time, and if somebody gets killed, so somebody gets killed. They don't care. Oh, sure, there are some good things about them, too. Look, I'm the first to say that. *(Eight gets up and then Two and Six follow him to window.)* I've known a few who were pretty decent, but that's the exception. Most of them, it's like they have no feelings. They can do anything. What's going on here? *(Foreman gets up and goes to window, followed by Seven and Twelve.)* I'm speaking my piece, and you— listen to me! They're no good. There's not a one of 'em who's any good. We better watch out. Take it from me. This kid on trial . . . *(Three sits at table toying with knife as Four gets up and starts toward Ten. All the other*

Jurors *have their backs turned on* Ten.) Well, don't you know about them? Listen to me! What are you doing? I'm trying to tell you something. . . . *(Four stands over him as he trails off. There is a dead silence. Then* Four *speaks softly.)*

Four. I've had enough. If you open your mouth again, I'm going to split your skull. *(He stands there and looks at him. No one moves or speaks.* Ten *looks at* Four *and then looks down at table.)*

Ten *(softly).* I'm only trying to tell you . . . *(There is a long pause as* Four *stares down at* Ten.)

Four *(to* Jurors *at window).* All right. Sit down, everybody. *(All move back to their seats. When they are all seated,* Four *takes a stand behind men on upstage side of table. He speaks quietly.)* I still believe the boy is guilty of murder. I'll tell you why. To me, the most damning evidence was given by the woman across the street who claimed she actually saw the murder committed.

Three. That's right. As far as I'm concerned, that's the most important testimony.

Eight. All right. Let's go over her testimony. What exactly did she say?

Four *(moving toward window).* I believe I can recount it accurately. She said that she went to bed at about eleven o'clock that night. Her bed was next to the open window, and she could look out of the window while lying down and see directly into the window across the street. She tossed and turned for over an hour, unable to fall asleep. Finally she turned toward the window at about twelve-ten and, as she looked out, she saw the boy stab his father. As far as I can see, this is unshakable testimony.

---

12 **acquittal:** judgment of innocence.

Three. That's what I mean. That's the whole case. (Four *takes off his eyeglasses and begins to polish them as they* All *sit silently watching him.*)

Four (*to* All *of them*). Frankly, in view of this, I don't see how you can vote for acquittal. (*To* Twelve *as he sits again*) What do you think about it?

Twelve. Well—maybe . . . There's so much evidence to sift. . . .

Three. What do you mean, maybe? He's absolutely right. You can throw out all the other evidence.

Four. That was my feeling. I don't deny the validity of the points that he has made. (*Motions at* Eight) Shall we say that on one side of the tracks there is doubt? But what can you say about the story of the woman? She saw it. (Two, *while he is polishing his glasses, too, squints at clock.*)

Two. What time is it?

Eleven. Ten minutes of six.

Six. You don't suppose they'd let us go home and finish it in the morning. I've got a kid with mumps. . . .

Five. Not a chance.

Eight (*to* Two). Can't you see the clock without your glasses?

Two. Not clearly.

Eight. Oh.

Four. Glasses are a nuisance, aren't they?

Eight (*an edge of excitement in his tone*). Well, what do you all do when you wake up at night and want to know what time it is?

Two. I put my glasses on and look at the clock.

Four. I just lie in bed and wait for the clock to chime. My father gave it to me when we married, my wife and I. It was ten years before we had a place to put it.

Eight (*to* Two). Do you wear your glasses to bed?

Two. Of course not. No one wears eyeglasses to bed.

Eight. The woman who testified that she saw the killing wears glasses. What about her?

Four. Did she wear glasses?

Eleven (*excitedly*). Of course! The woman wore bifocals. I remember this very clearly. They looked quite strong.

Nine. That's right. Bifocals. She never took them off.

Four. Funny. I never thought of that.

Eight. I think it's logical to say that she was not wearing her glasses in bed, and I don't think she'd put them on to glance casually out the window. . . . She testified that the murder took place the instant she looked out, and that the lights went out a split second later. She couldn't have had time to put on her glasses then. Now perhaps this woman honestly thought she saw the boy kill his father. (*Rises*) I say that she only saw a blur.

Three. How do you know what she saw? Maybe she's farsighted. . . . (*He looks around. No one answers. Loudly*) How does he know all these things? (*There is silence.*)

Eight. Does anyone think there still is not a reasonable doubt? (*He looks around room, then squarely at* Ten. Ten *looks down at table for a moment; then he looks up at* Eight.)

Ten. I will always wonder. But there is a reasonable doubt.

Three (*loudly*). I think he's guilty!

Eight (*calmly*). Does anyone else?

Four (*quietly*). No. I'm convinced now. There is a reasonable doubt.

Eight (*to* Three). You're alone.

Foreman. Eleven votes, not guilty; one, guilty.

Three. I don't care whether I'm alone or not! I have a right. . . .

Eight. Yes, you have a right. (*All* stare at Three.)

Three. Well, I told you. I think the kid's guilty. What else do you want?

Eight. Your arguments. (*All* look at Three *after glancing at* Eight.)

Three. I gave you my arguments.

Eight. We're not convinced. We're waiting to hear them again. We have time. (*He sits down again.* Three *runs to* Four *and grabs his arm.*)

Three (*pleading*). Listen. What's the matter with you? You're the guy. You made all the arguments. You can't turn now. A guilty man's going to be walking the streets. A murderer! He's got to die! Stay with me! . . .

Four (rising). I'm sorry. I'm convinced. I don't think I'm wrong often, but I guess I was this once. (Crosses R) There is a reasonable doubt in my mind.

Eight. We're waiting. . . . (Three turns violently on him.)

Three (shouting). You're not going to intimidate me! (They are All staring at Three.) I'm entitled to my opinion! (No one answers him.) It's gonna be a hung jury! (Turns abruptly and sits in his chair again) That's it!

Eight. There's nothing we can do about that except hope that some night, maybe in a few months, why, you might get some sleep.

Five. You're all alone.

Nine. It takes a great deal of courage to stand alone.

Four (moving back to table, sitting). If it is a hung jury, there will be another trial and some of us will point these things out to the various lawyers.

[Three looks around table at All of them. As Three's glance goes from Juror to Juror, each one of them shakes his head in his direction. Then, suddenly, Three's face contorts and he begins to pound on table with his fist. He seems about to cry.]

Three (thundering). All right! (He jumps up quickly and moves DR, his back to all of them as Foreman goes to door L and knocks. The other Jurors now rise.)

[The Guard opens the door L and looks in and sees them All standing. The Guard holds the door open for them as they All file past and out L; that is, All except Three and Eight. The Guard waits for them. Eight moves toward the door L, pausing at LC.]

Eight (to Three). They're waiting. (Three sees that he is alone. He moves to table and pulls switch knife out of table and walks over to Eight with it. Three is holding knife in approved knife-fighter fashion. Three looks long and hard at juror Eight and weaves a bit from side to side as he holds knife with point of it in direction of Eight's belly. Eight speaks quietly, firmly.) Not guilty. (Three turns knife around and Eight takes it by handle. Eight closes knife and puts it away.)

Three. Not guilty!

[Three walks out of room. Eight glances around quickly, sighs, then turns and moves out through door. Guard goes out, closing door.]

Curtain

Discussion

1. Why are two votes taken at the beginning of Act III? What are the results of each vote?
2. Juror Eight tells the other jurors, "To say that he (the defendant) is guilty, you have to toss his intelligence like a pancake." What does he mean?
3. During Juror Ten's long speech in Act III, why do the other jurors turn their backs on him?

4. How do the jurors test parts of the evidence? What is the result of each testing?

5. What finally convinces Jurors Four and Ten to change their votes to "Not Guilty"?

6. At the beginning of the play, Juror Eight is alone in voting "Not Guilty." At the end, Juror Three is alone in voting "Guilty." What character traits or attitudes enable Eight to stand alone? On the other hand, why does Three give in?

Writer's Craft

A play often opens with a slow-paced scene which introduces the characters and establishes the setting and mood. This scene also gives the audience all the background information it needs to know to understand what is going to happen in the rest of the play. This introductory material as a whole is called the EXPOSITION.

1. The exposition of *Twelve Angry Men* begins in darkness. The audience hears a voice that would have been heard in the courtroom rather than in the jury room. Whose voice is heard? Why are this person's words important?

2. Much of the exposition of this play deals with such things as the temperature, the length of the trial, outside time pressures, and details of the jurors' lives. In what sense are these elements important to the play as a whole?

3. The exposition of *Twelve Angry Men* ends with the first vote on the defendant's guilt or innocence. Explain why.

Composition

1. *Twelve Angry Men* may be said to be two stories in one. First, there is the story of the jurors themselves. In addition, there is also the story of the defendant, his murdered father, and the neighbors who testify during the trial. Details of this second story are scattered throughout the play. They are never gathered together and fully summed up in one place. Write a summary which brings all these details together. Arrange the facts in order of their occurrence. Begin, for example, with the defendant's being mistreated at the age of five by his father, and end with the defendant's arrest on the murder charge. Limit your summary to facts presented in the play.

2. Notice that you—along with the jurors—never know for certain whether the accused man is guilty or innocent. Assume, for the sake of discussion, that the man on trial *is* guilty. Now decide whether or not Eight acted correctly in persuading the other jurors to change their votes. Write the reasons for your opinion.

Twelve Angry Men **423**

Vocabulary

Various occupations and professions have SPECIALIZED VOCABULARIES of their own. A specialized vocabulary, in this case, means a set of words that are known to and used by everyone who earns a living in a certain field. The same words, however, may be unknown to most people outside that field.

The specialized vocabulary of the legal profession is more widely known than most because nearly everybody has a great interest in justice. Legal terms such as *trial, juror, witness,* and *prosecution* are understood by almost all people who speak English. Nevertheless, there are many words in the specialized vocabulary of law that may not commonly be used or known by most people. For example:

abstain	acquittal	foreman	open-and-shut
counsel	double jeopardy	premeditated	technicality

On a separate sheet of paper, list all the terms above. Using a dictionary, write a definition for each word. As you look for definitions, be sure to read every entry completely. Write only the definitions that would apply to the law or the courts. Then write a sentence using each word. Try to make the meaning of each word clear in the sentence.

Reginald Rose 1921 —

Reginald Rose, a native New Yorker, is best known as a television writer. He gained fame during the early 1950s, television's "Golden Age" of drama, when all programing was live. He wrote plays for *Studio One, Playhouse 90, CBS Playhouse,* and the *Elgin Hour.* In 1961, he created and wrote several scripts for the Emmy-winning television series, *The Defenders.* Rose has also written several hour-long original scripts including *Twelve Angry Men,* which received three Emmy Awards.

Discussion

1. In *The Ugly Duckling*, the exposition ends with the Queen's exit, just after Princess Camilla's first entrance. By this time, how much does the audience know about the problem of finding a marriage partner for the Princess?

2. What is a possible theme for *The Ugly Ducking?* for *Twelve Angry Men?*

3. Following are stage directions from Act I of *Twelve Angry Men*. Tell why you think they are important to a reader's understanding of the play.

   a. (AT RISE OF CURTAIN: *The curtain comes up on a dark stage; then as the lights start to come up on the scene, we hear the voice of the* Judge, *off stage.*)

   b. **Seven** *(tugging at collar).* Y'know, it's hot.

   c. **Three** *(motioning to* Four*).* Ask him to hire you. He's rich, look at the suit!

   d. **Foreman.** Anybody doesn't want to vote? *(He looks around the table. There is a pause as* All *look at each other.)*

   e. **Five** *(rising, slamming his hand down on table).* There is something personal! *(Then he catches himself, and, seeing* Everyone *looking at him, sits down, fists clenched.)*

Composition

1. Contrast Juror Three and Juror Eight. By using examples from *Twelve Angry Men,* show differences in their personalities, their attitudes toward the defendant, and their individual arguments. Conclude by explaining why you think the personalities of these men might have affected their influence on the other jurors.

2. It will not be too long before you could be on a jury. In most states eligibility corresponds with the voting age. Write your views of jury duty. First state any advantages and then explain any disadvantages. (If you can, you first might want to talk with someone who has been on a jury.) Then end by stating whether you think our present jury system is either good or bad. Give reasons for your opinion.

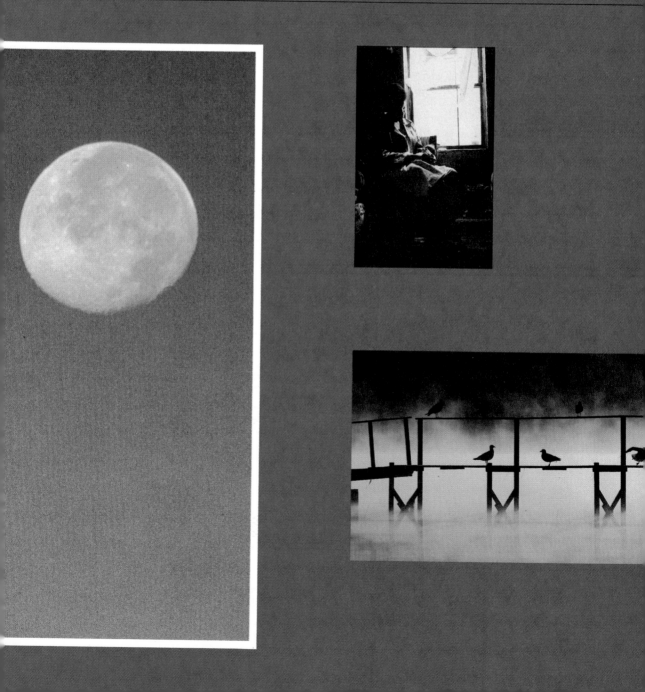

POETRY

Poetry is a special way of using language. Poems do all the things a short story can do—tell a story, create suspense, cause you to laugh—but poetry can do even more. Poems can help you see people and things more clearly than a photograph. They can also help you feel the softness of a cat's fur or smell and taste a Thanksgiving dinner.

But if this seeing and feeling is going to happen, you must be able to see and feel with a poet's eyes. In the following poem, the writer shows you one way to use a poet's eyes.

To Look at Any Thing

To look at any thing,
If you would know that thing,
You must look at it long:
To look at this green and say,
"I have seen spring in these
Woods," will not do—you must
Be the thing you see:
You must be the dark snakes of
Stems and ferny plumes of leaves,
You must enter in
To the small silences between
The leaves,
You must take your time
And touch the very peace
They issue from.

John Moffitt

The poet first suggests that you look at things "long." If you really want to know about them, "You must take your time . . ."

Then the poet gives the example of a fern leaf. At first glance, it is nothing more than a "thing." Looking a little harder, the poet sees that it is "green." Then the green thing is seen as "spring." Finally, the poet looks even closer and actually becomes a part of the snakelike stems and the plumelike leaves. It is then that you and the poet together can share the "silences" and "peace" of the fern leaf.

This unit invites you to a new way of seeing—with the mind and eyes of a poet. Take your time . . . take a long look . . . and become a part of the poets' experiences and feelings.

One of the earliest kinds of poetry was NARRATIVE POETRY—*poems which tell a story. Narrative poems have all the interest and suspense of a short story. They tell exciting stories about people—their weaknesses, their heroism, their adventures, their loves, and their deaths. For example, the first poem in this section is a love story that ends tragically.*

The Highwayman

ALFRED NOYES

PART 1

The wind was a torrent of darkness among the gusty trees.
The moon was a ghostly galleon[1] tossed upon cloudy seas.
The road was a ribbon of moonlight over the purple moor,[2]
And the highwayman came riding—
      Riding—riding—   5
The highwayman came riding, up to the old inn-door.

He'd a French cocked-hat on his forehead, a bunch of lace at his chin,
A coat of the claret[3] velvet, and breeches of brown doe-skin.
They fitted with never a wrinkle; his boots were up to the thigh.
And he rode with a jewelled twinkle,   10
      His pistol butts a-twinkle,
His rapier hilt a-twinkle, under the jewelled sky.

---

1 **galleon** (gal' ē ən): ship.
2 **moor**: a broad area of open land.
3 **claret** (klar' ət): red color.

Over the cobbles he clattered and clashed in the dark inn-yard.
He tapped with his whip on the shutters, but all was locked and barred.
He whistled a tune to the window, and who should be waiting there   15
But the landlord's black-eyed daughter,
        Bess, the landlord's daughter,
Plaiting a dark red love-knot into her long black hair.

And dark in the dark old inn-yard a stable-wicket creaked
Where Tim, the ostler,[4] listened; his face was white and peaked.   20
His eyes were hollows of madness, his hair like moldy hay,
But he loved the landlord's daughter,
        The landlord's red-lipped daughter.
Dumb as a dog he listened, and he heard the robber say—

"One kiss, my bonny sweetheart, I'm after a prize to-night,   25
But I shall be back with the yellow gold before the morning light.
Yet, if they press me sharply, and harry me through the day,
Then look for me by moonlight,
        Watch for me by moonlight,
I'll come to thee by moonlight, though hell should bar the way."   30

He rose upright in the stirrups. He scarce could reach her hand,
But she loosened her hair in the casement.[5] His face burnt like a brand
As the black cascade of perfume came tumbling over his breast,
And he kissed its waves in the moonlight,
        (O, sweet black waves in the moonlight!)   35
Then he tugged at his reins in the moonlight, and galloped away to the west.

PART 2

He did not come in the dawning; he did not come at noon,
And out of the tawny sunset, before the rise of the moon,
When the road was a gypsy's ribbon, looping the purple moor,
A red-coat troop came marching—   40
        Marching—marching—
King George's men came marching, up to the old inn-door.

---

4 **ostler** (os′ lər): a groom for horses.
5 **casement**: a window that opens outward.

THE SCOTTISH HORSEMAN *Gustave Moreau*

They said no word to the landlord; they drank his ale instead,
But they gagged his daughter, and bound her, to the foot of her narrow bed.
Two of them knelt at her casement, with muskets at the side.   45
There was death at every window;
        And hell at one dark window;
For Bess could see, through her casement, the road that *he* would ride.

They had tied her up to attention, with many a sniggering jest.
They had bound a musket beside her, with the barrel beneath her breast!   50
"Now, keep good watch!" and they kissed her. She heard the dead man say—
Look for me by moonlight,
        Watch for me by moonlight;
I'll come to thee by moonlight, though hell should bar the way!

She twisted her hands behind her, but all the knots held good!   55
She writhed her hands till her fingers were wet with sweat or blood!
They stretched and strained in the darkness, and the hours crawled by like years,
Till, now, on the stroke of midnight,
        Cold, on the stroke of midnight,
The tip of one finger touched it! The trigger at least was hers!   60

The tip of one finger touched it; she strove no more for the rest.
Up, she stood up to attention, with the barrel beneath her breast.
She would not risk their hearing; she would not strive again;
For the road lay bare in the moonlight,
        Blank and bare in the moonlight,   65
And the blood of her veins, in the moonlight, throbbed to her love's refrain.

Tlot-tlot, tlot-tlot! Had they heard it? The horse-hoofs ringing clear;
Tlot-tlot, tlot-tlot, in the distance? Were they deaf that they did not hear?
Down the ribbon of moonlight, over the brow of the hill,
The highwayman came riding—   70
        Riding—riding—
The red-coats looked to their priming! She stood up, straight and still.

Tlot-tlot, in the frosty silence! *Tlot-tlot*, in the echoing night!
Nearer he came and nearer. Her face was like a light.
Her eyes grew wide for a moment; she drew one last deep breath,   75
Then her finger moved in the moonlight,
     Her musket shattered the moonlight,
Shattered her breast in the moonlight, and warned him—with her death.

He turned. He spurred to the west; he did not know who stood
Bowed with her head o'er the musket, drenched with her own red blood!   80
Not till the dawn he heard it, and his face grew gray to hear
How Bess, the landlord's daughter,
     The landlord's black-eyed daughter,
Had watched for her love in the moonlight, and died in the darkness there.

Back, he spurred like a madman, shouting a curse to the sky,   85
With the white road smoking behind him, and his rapier[6] brandished high.
Blood-red were his spurs in the golden noon; wine-red was his velvet coat,
When they shot him down on the highway,
     Down like a dog on the highway,
And he lay in his blood on the highway, with a bunch of lace at his throat.   90

And still of a winter's night, they say, when the wind is in the trees,
When the moon is a ghostly galleon tossed upon cloudy seas,
When the road is a ribbon of moonlight over the purple moor,
A highwayman comes riding—
     Riding—riding—   95
A highwayman comes riding, up to the old inn-door.

Over the cobbles he clatters and clangs in the dark inn-yard.
He taps with his whip on the shutters, but all is locked and barred.
He whistles a tune to the window, and who should be waiting there
But the landlord's black-eyed daughter,   100
     Bess, the landlord's daughter,
Plaiting a dark red love-knot into her long black hair.

---

6 rapier: sword.

Discussion

1. In lines 19–30, Tim overhears the conversation between the highwayman and Bess. What does he find out? What does he do with this information? Why?
2. How does Bess warn the highwayman of the trap?
3. What happens when the highwayman learns that Bess has killed herself to warn him?
4. What words does the poet use to imitate a sound in this poem?
5. What sound is he imitating?

Writer's Craft

Sometimes poets use a special kind of sound effect in their poems. They repeat the same consonant sound at the beginnings of two or more words in a row. For example, you probably remember twisting your tongue over "Peter Piper picked a peck of pickled peppers." This repetition of consonant sounds is called ALLITERATION. Poets use alliteration to create a special sound, to create rhythm, and to make a passage easier to remember.

1. What consonant is repeated in line 13?
2. How is alliteration used in line 15?
3. Find another example of alliteration in this poem.

Vocabulary

Poetry can create pictures in your mind because the poet uses descriptive words. Those descriptive words which mainly describe nouns are called ADJECTIVES. Adjectives generally come right before the nouns they describe. Another way to find adjectives is to ask the questions: which one? what kind? how many? For example, in the following lines from "The Highwayman," the *italicized* words are adjectives.

> The wind was a torrent of darkness among the *gusty* trees.
> The moon was a *ghostly* galleon tossed upon *cloudy* seas.
> The road was a ribbon of moonlight over the *purple* moor,
> And the highwayman came riding—
>   Riding—riding—
> The highwayman came riding, up to the *old* inn-door.

A. Each *italicized* word in the stanza on the next page from "The Highwayman" is a noun. Each one has one or more adjectives which describe it. On a separate sheet of paper, list all the adjectives.

He'd a French *cocked-hat* on his forehead, a bunch of lace at his chin,
A coat of the claret *velvet,* and breeches of brown *doe-skin.*
They fitted with never a wrinkle; his boots were up to the thigh.
And he rode with a jewelled *twinkle,*
        His pistol butts a-twinkle,
His rapier hilt a-twinkle, under the jewelled *sky.*

B. On the same paper copy all the adjectives in the stanza following of
   "The Highwayman." Beside each adjective, write the noun the
   adjective describes.

Back, he spurred like a madman, shouting a curse to the sky.
With the white road smoking behind him, and his rapier brandished
    high.
Blood-red were his spurs in the golden noon; wine-red was his velvet
    coat,
When they shot him down on the highway,
        Down like a dog on the highway,
And he lay in his blood on the highway, with a bunch of lace at his
    throat.

Alfred Noyes 1880—1958

Alfred Noyes was born at Staffordshire, England, and was educated at
Exeter College in Oxford. At school he excelled in athletics although
he took part in literary activities. After college he went to London and
soon became a writer. His epic poem, *Drake,* soon became his best
known work. In addition to his shorter poems and *Drake,* he also
wrote *Tales of the Mermaid Tavern* and *The Torch Bearers.* His
autobiography, *Two Worlds for Memory,* was published in 1953.

The Charge of the Light Brigade [1]

ALFRED, LORD TENNYSON

Half a league, half a league,
Half a league onward,
All in the valley of Death
    Rode the six hundred.
"Forward the Light Brigade!   5
Charge for the guns!" he said.
Into the valley of Death
    Rode the six hundred.

"Forward, the Light Brigade!"
Was there a man dismayed?   10
Not tho' the soldier knew
    Someone had blundered.
Theirs not to make reply,
Theirs not to reason why,
Theirs but to do and die.   15
Into the valley of Death
    Rode the six hundred.

Cannon to right of them,
Cannon to left of them,
Cannon in front of them   20
    Volleyed and thundered;
Stormed at with shot and shell,
Boldly they rode and well,
Into the jaws of Death,
Into the mouth of hell   25
    Rode the six hundred.

Flashed all their sabers bare,
Flashed as they turned in air
Sabring the gunners there,
Charging an army, while   30
    All the world wondered.
Plunged in the battery smoke
Right thro' the line they broke;
Cossack and Russian
Reeled from the saber-stroke   35
    Shattered and sundered. [2]
Then they rode back, but not,
    Not the six hundred.

Cannon to right of them,
Cannon to left of them,   40
Cannon behind them
    Volleyed and thundered;
Stormed at with shot and shell,
While horse and hero fell,
They that had fought so well   45
Came thro' the jaws of Death,
Back from the mouth of hell,
All that was left of them,
    Left of six hundred.

When can their glory fade?   50
O the wild charge they made!
    All the world wondered.
Honor the charge they made!
Honor the Light Brigade,
    Noble six hundred!   55

1 **Brigade:** a large unit of soldiers. In this poem the British brigade of soldiers fought against the Russians in the Crimean War in 1854. Because the officer in charge made an error, most of the soldiers were killed.

2 **sundered:** separated.

1. Who were the "six hundred"?
2. Who said, "Forward the Light Brigade!/Charge for the guns!" in lines 5 and 6?
3. Who "blundered" in line 12?
4. Who are "they" in line 37?
5. Why did most of the soldiers ride to their deaths? What lines in the poem indicate this?
6. Do you think the purpose of this poem is to criticize the British officers or to praise the common soldiers? How do you know?
7. In the middle of each stanza, what rhyme sound is repeated? What sound effect do you think is being imitated with the repetition of these hard rhyming sounds?

Alfred, Lord Tennyson 1809—1892

Alfred Tennyson was the fourth of twelve children. He did much reading in his father's parsonage at Lincolnshire, England, and began composing poems while a youth and later as a student at Cambridge University. After the death of his father, Tennyson assumed the responsibility of caring for his mother and sisters. He published a volume of poety in 1832, but it was not until a second volume appeared in 1842 that he was recognized as the leading poet of his day. He became poet laureate of England in 1850, and in 1884 received the title Lord (Baron) Tennyson.

The Glove and the Lions

LEIGH HUNT

King Francis was a hearty king, and loved a royal sport,
And one day as his lions fought, sat looking on the court;
The nobles filled the benches, and the ladies in their pride,
And 'mongst them sat the Count de Lorge, with one for
    whom he sighed:
And truly 'twas a gallant thing to see that crowning show,   5
Valor and love, and a king above, and the royal beasts below.

Detail of a French tapestry from the mid–1400s.

Ramped and roared the lions, with horrid laughing jaws;
They bit, they glared, gave blows like beams, a wind went
   with their paws;
With wallowing might and stifled roar they rolled on one
   another,
Till all the pit with sand and mane was in a thunderous
   smother;   10
The bloody foam above the bars came whisking through
   the air;
Said Francis then, "Faith, gentlemen, we're better here
   than there."

De Lorge's love o'erheard the King, a beauteous lively dame
With smiling lips and sharp bright eyes, which always
   seemed the same;
She thought, "The Count my lover is brave as brave can be;   15
He surely would do wondrous things to show his love of me;
King, ladies, lovers, all look on; the occasion is divine;
I'll drop my glove, to prove his love; great glory will be
   mine."

She dropped her glove, to prove his love, then looked at
   him and smiled;
He bowed, and in a moment leaped among the lions wild: 20
The leap was quick, return was quick, he has regained his
   place,
Then threw the glove, but not with love, right in the lady's
   face.
"By God!" said Francis, "rightly done!" and he rose from
   where he sat:
"No love," quoth he, "but vanity, sets love a task like that."

Discussion

1. What sporting event is going on at the beginning of the poem?

2. Who are the two men named in this poem? Who is the unnamed woman?

3. What does the woman overhear the King say? What does she then decide to do? Why?

4. How does the Count respond to her action? What is the King's opinion of what the Count does?

Writer's Craft

Rhyme, the repetition of similar sounds, is familiar to almost everyone. From your earliest childhood, you can remember hearing nursery rhymes such as:

Twinkle, twinkle, little *star,*
How I wonder what you *are.*

Rhyme is not used in all poems, but when it is, it usually appears in a pattern that repeats itself with each stanza. This pattern is called a RHYME SCHEME. A poem's rhyme scheme is shown by using a small letter *a* for the first rhyming sound, a *b* for the second rhyming sound, and consecutive letters for any other rhyming sounds. Within a stanza, the letters are repeated each time the same rhyming sound is repeated. For example, look at the first two stanzas of "Casey at the Bat" below:

The outlook wasn't brilliant for the Mudville nine that day;	*a*
The score stood four to two, with but one inning more to play;	*a*
And so, when Cooney died at first, and Barrows did the same,	*b*
A sickly silence fell upon the patrons of the game.	*b*
A straggling few got up to go in deep despair. The rest	*a*
Clung to the hope which springs eternal in the human breast;	*a*
They thought, if only Casey could but get a whack; at that,	*b*
They'd put up even money now, with Casey at the bat.	*b*

The rhyme scheme for this poem is *aabb* because in the first stanza "day" and "play" rhyme together, and "same" and "game" rhyme together. In the second stanza, "rest" and "breast" rhyme together, and "that" and "bat" rhyme together. Notice that the lettering starts over again with each new stanza.

1. In the first stanza of "The Glove and the Lions," what words at the end of each line rhyme together?
2. What is the rhyme scheme of the first stanza? of the other stanzas?

Leigh Hunt 1784–1859

Born in London, Leigh Hunt was unable to continue his education beyond a few years because of his frail health and nervousness. At thirteen, he began writing poems, and four years later he had enough for a volume. He did not receive any real success, however, until the performance of his play, *A Legend of Florence,* in 1840.

aesop revised by archy [1]

DON MARQUIS

a wolf met a spring
lamb drinking
at a stream
and said to her
you are the lamb   5
that muddied this stream
all last year
so that i could not get
a clean fresh drink
i am resolved that   10
this outrage
shall not be enacted again
this season
i am going to kill you
just a moment   15
said the lamb
i was not born last
year so it could not
have been i
the wolf then pulled   20
a number of other
arguments as to why the lamb
should die
but in each case the lamb
pretty innocent that she was   25
easily proved
herself guiltless

well well said the wolf
enough of argument
you are right and i am wrong   30
but i am going to eat
you anyhow
because i am hungry
stop exclamation point
cried a human voice   35
and a man came over
the slope of the ravine
vile lupine marauder [2]
you shall not kill that
beautiful and innocent   40
lamb for i shall save her
exit the wolf
left upper entrance
snarling
poor little lamb   45
continued our human hero
sweet tender little thing
it is well that i appeared
just when i did
it makes my blood boil   50
to think of the fright
to which you have been
subjected in another
moment i would have been
too late come home with me   55
and the lamb frolicked

---

1 **aesop . . . archy:** Aesop was a famous storyteller who
lived around 6 B.C. Archy is a cockroach who is a main
character in a series of poems written by Don Marquis.
Archy does the typing, but due to his size and condition, he
can never reach the capital letter key on the typewriter. That
is why all the poems are written with small letters and no
punctuation.

---

2 **lupine marauder** (lü′ pən mər ôd′ ər): wolf thief.

about her new found friend
gamboling³ as to the sound
of a wordsworthian tabor⁴
and leaping for joy   60
as if propelled by a stanza
from william blake⁵
these vile and bloody wolves
went on our hero
in honest indignation   65
they must be cleared out
of the country
the meads⁶ must be made safe
for sheepocracy
and so jollying her along   70
with the usual human hokum⁷
he led to his home
and the son of a gun
did not even blush when
they passed the mint bed   75

gently he cut her throat
all the while inveighing⁸
against the inhuman wolf
and tenderly he cooked her
and lovingly he sauced her   80
and meltingly he ate her
and piously he said a grace
thanking his gods
for their bountiful gifts to him
and after dinner   85
he sat with his pipe
before the fire meditating
on the brutality of wolves
and the injustice of
the universe   90
which allows them to harry⁹
poor innocent lambs
and wondering if he
had not better
write to the papers   95
for as he said
for god s sake can t
something be done about it
                          archy

---

3 **gamboling**: skipping and leaping.
4 **tabor**: a small drum.
5 **william blake**: William Blake, an English poet
(1757–1827) who often wrote about lambs.
6 **meads**: meadows.
7 **hokum**: insincere flattery.

8 **inveighing** (in vā′ ing): complaining.
9 **harry**: to bother in a destructive way.

Discussion

1. What reason does the wolf first give for wanting to kill the lamb?
How does the lamb know he is lying? What is the wolf's real
reason?

2. Why doesn't the wolf kill the lamb?

3. What happens when the man takes the lamb home with him?

4. Why does the end of this poem come as a surprise?

5. Aesop's fables usually end with morals. What moral could you
apply to this modern fable?

Don Marquis 1878—1937

As a young man, Don Marquis tried his hand at many occupations before becoming an editorial writer on the *Atlanta Constitution.* Joel Chandler Harris, the editor and author of the *Uncle Remus* stories, took an interest in Marquis and directed him to creative writing. In 1912, Marquis went to work for the *New York Sun* and later he wrote for the *Herald Tribune.* From his columns on these two newspapers, many of his best-known characters developed. His most popular work is the sequence of books beginning with *archy and mehitabel,* consisting of the poetry and prose of a cockroach and a cat. In addition, he wrote several novels, including *The Cruise of Jasper B* and the semi-autobiographical *Sons of the Puritans.*

Casey at the Bat

ERNEST LAWRENCE THAYER

The outlook wasn't brilliant for the Mudville nine that day;
The score stood four to two, with but one inning more to play;
And so, when Cooney died[1] at first, and Barrows did the same,
A sickly silence fell upon the patrons of the game.

A straggling few got up to go in deep despair. The rest   5
Clung to the hope which springs eternal in the human breast;
They thought, if only Casey could but get a whack; at that,
They'd put up even money now, with Casey at the bat.

---

1 **died:** was called out.

But Flynn preceded Casey, as did also Jimmy Blake;
And the former was a pudding,[2] and the latter was a fake;
So upon that stricken multitude grim melancholy sat,
For there seemed but little chance of Casey's getting to the bat.   10

But Flynn let drive a single, to the wonderment of all,
And Blake, the much despisèd, tore the cover off the ball;
And when the dust had lifted, and they saw what had occurred,   15
There was Jimmy safe on second, and Flynn a-hugging third.

Then from the gladdened multitude went up a joyous yell;
It bounded from the mountaintop and rattled in the dell;
It struck upon the hillside and recoiled upon the flat,
For Casey, mighty Casey, was advancing to the bat.   20

There was ease in Casey's manner as he stepped into his place;
There was pride in Casey's bearing and a smile on Casey's face;
And when, responding to the cheers, he lightly doffed his hat,
No stranger in the crowd could doubt 'twas Casey at the bat.

Ten thousand eyes were on him as he rubbed his hands with dirt;   25
Five thousand tongues applauded when he wiped them on his shirt;
Then, while the writhing pitcher ground the ball into his hip,
Defiance gleamed in Casey's eye, a sneer curled Casey's lip.

And now the leather-covered sphere came hurtling through the air,
And Casey stood a-watching it in haughty grandeur there;   30
Close by the sturdy batsman the ball unheeded sped.
"That ain't my style," said Casey. "Strike one," the umpire said.

From the benches, black with people, there went up a muffled roar,
Like the beating of the storm waves on a stern and distant shore;
"Kill him! Kill the umpire!" shouted someone in the stand.   35
And it's likely they'd have killed him had not Casey raised his hand.

With a smile of Christian charity great Casey's visage[3] shone;
He stilled the rising tumult; he bade the game go on;
He signaled to the pitcher, and once more the spheroid flew;
But Casey still ignored it, and the umpire said, "Strike two."   40

---

2 **pudding:** a weakling.
3 **visage** (viz' ij): face; appearance.

"Fraud!" cried the maddened thousands, and the echo answered, "Fraud!"
But one scornful look from Casey, and the audience was awed;
They saw his face grow stern and cold; they saw his muscles strain;
And they knew that Casey wouldn't let that ball go by again.

The sneer is gone from Casey's lips; his teeth are clenched in hate;   45
He pounds with cruel violence his bat upon the plate;
And now the pitcher holds the ball, and now he lets it go,
And now the air is shattered by the force of Casey's blow.

Oh, somewhere in this favored land the sun is shining bright;
The band is playing somewhere, and somewhere hearts are light,   50
And somewhere men are laughing, and somewhere children shout;
But there is no joy in Mudville—mighty Casey has struck out!

Discussion

1. Why is the crowd so gloomy in the first three stanzas? What is the crowd's mood in stanzas 4 and 5? Why has the mood changed?

2. How does Casey make his first two strikes? his last strike?

3. What is the reaction of the crowd to Casey's striking out?

4. The poet takes great care in building up Casey's image. What words or phrases reveal Casey's personality? Do you think this is a serious or a light-hearted poem? Explain your answer.

Composition

1. Select one of the narrative poems in this section and rewrite it in a regular story fashion. Do not use any rhyme or repetition. You may invent conversation between characters and add additional details. However, use the order of events found in the poem, and keep the same point of view and speaker.

2. Write two poems that have four lines each. The rhyme scheme for the first poem should be *aabb*, and the rhyme scheme for the second one should be *abab*. These poems can be about any subject.

Vocabulary

Expressions whose meanings are not clear by merely understanding the meanings of the words within them are called IDIOMS. For example:

IDIOM: We have *put up with* this nonsense long enough.
MEANING: We have *tolerated* or *accepted* this nonsense long enough.
IDIOM: There is *no use crying over spilled milk.*
MEANING: There is *nothing to be gained by feeling regret.*

A. On a separate sheet of paper, write the meanings of the *italicized* idioms below.

1. My great uncle *kicked the bucket.*
2. Don't worry. *It's in the bag!*
3. He *threw in the sponge.*
4. She *blew her top.*
5. Don't *spill the beans!*

B. Some idioms are regional or geographical. Others belong to a specialized area such as music or sports. Below are some of the sports idioms found in "Casey at the Bat." On the same paper, explain the meaning of each *italicized* idiom below.

1. Cooney *died at first.*
2. Blake, the much despisèd, *tore the cover off the ball.*
3. The former was a *pudding,* and the latter was a fake.
4. They'd *put up even money* now, with Casey at the bat.

Ernest Lawrence Thayer 1863—1940

Ernest Thayer was born in Worcester, Massachusetts. While he attended Harvard, he worked on the student humor magazine *Lampoon* as editor-in-chief. When he left Harvard to take up journalism, he went to work with his former classmate, William Randolph Hearst, on the *San Francisco Examiner.* Although he contributed a number of poems to various newspapers, he is remembered mainly for his poem, "Casey at the Bat." Many players claimed to be the real "Casey," but Thayer contended he had no special player in mind when he wrote the poem.

Besides telling stories, poems also describe people, things, events, and emotions. When poets write descriptive poetry, they almost paint. They create colorful pictures so that readers can see what they are describing in a closer, more detailed way than ever before. In the first poem in this section, for instance, you will see how a poet describes a crow so clearly that you almost shiver with it in the cold.

Absolutes

(From an ink painting by Seiho)

GUSTAVE KEYSER

black on white
crow in snow
        hunched
          wet lump
on brittle branch
remembering warmth
remembering corn
miserable
as life
is
black on white

Desert Noon

ELIZABETH COATSWORTH

When the desert lies
Pulsating with heat
And even the rattlesnakes
Coil among the roots of the mesquite[1]
And the coyotes pant at the waterholes—   5

Far above,
Against the sky,
Shines the summit of San Jacinto,[2]
Blue-white and cool as a hyacinth
With snow.   10

1 **mesquite** (me skēt′): a scrubby tree.
2 **San Jacinto:** the highest peak in southwestern California.

1. What is the setting of "Absolutes"?
2. Where is the crow? What is it doing?
3. What is the setting of the first stanza of "Desert Noon"? of the second stanza?
4. How does the author emphasize the heat in the first stanza? What words add to the cool feeling of the second stanza?

Writer's Craft

Sometimes authors and poets want to emphasize an idea or a feeling. Maybe they want their readers, for example, to feel and understand the smallness of a fly. To do this, they first might describe the fly. Then they might place this insect next to a large object such as a chair or a door to emphasize its minuteness. Placing opposites side by side is called CONTRAST.

1. What colors are contrasted in "Absolutes"? What seasons are contrasted?
2. What is contrasted with "warmth" and "food"?
3. The word *absolutes* means "pure" and "free from mixture." Why is this word a good title for this poem?
4. What scenes are contrasted in the two stanzas of "Desert Noon"?
5. Why do you think the poet contrasted the two scenes?

Elizabeth Coatsworth 1893 ——

During her early years, Elizabeth Coatsworth traveled frequently to the Alps, the Egyptian deserts, and the Aztec ruins of Mexico. She was known as an authority on the Orient while still in her twenties. Much of her work such as "Desert Noon," came from the images she saw in her travels. Her poetry collections include: *Fox Footsprings, Atlas and Beyond,* and *Compass Rose.* She also wrote a novel, *Here I Stay.* Coatsworth's poems are said to have appeared more frequently in magazines than any other American poet's.

Song of the Truck

DORIS FRANKEL

This is the song that the truck drivers hear
In the grinding of brake and the shifting of gear,
From the noise of the wheel and the clarion[1] horn,
From the freight and the weight—

                         a song has been born:
Mohair and cotton and textiles and silk,   5
Chickens and onions and apples and milk,
Rubber and clothing and coffee and tires,
Harness and hay and molasses and wires,
Petroleum, vinegar, furniture, eggs,
Race horses, stoves, and containers and kegs,   10
Chemicals, cantaloupes, canned goods and seeds—
Song of the cargo America needs!
Song of the wheels in the well-traveled grooves—
Coastline to coastline—

                  America moves!

---

1 **clarion** (klar′ ē ən): loud and clear.

Crossing

PHILIP BOOTH

STOP LOOK LISTEN
as gate stripes swing down,
  count the cars hauling distance
   upgrade through town:
    warning whistle, bellclang,   5
     engine eating steam,
      engineer waving,
       a fast–freight dream:
        B&M boxcar,
         boxcar again,   10
          Frisco gondola,
eight-nine-ten,
 Erie and Wabash,
  Seaboard, U.P.,
   Pennsy tankcar,   15
twenty-two, three,
 Phoebe Snow, B&O,
thirty-four, five,
 Santa Fe cattle
  shipped alive,   20
   red cars, yellow cars,
   orange cars, black,
    Youngstown steel
     down to Mobile
      on Rock Island track,   25
fifty-nine, sixty,
 hoppers of coke,
  Anaconda copper,
  hotbox smoke,

eighty-eight,   30
 red-ball freight,
  Rio Grande,
   Nickel Plate,
   Hiwatha,
    Lackawanna,   35
    rolling fast
    and loose,
ninety-seven,
 coal car,
  boxcar,   40
   CABOOSE!

1. In "Song of the Truck," what words create the sounds of a truck beginning to move?
2. How does the poet create the feeling of the hugeness and heaviness of the trucks?
3. What do you think the last line means?
4. What is the rhyme scheme of "Song of the Truck"?
5. Where is the speaker in "Crossing"?
6. What happens in this poem? How many cars are in the train?
7. How does the author make you feel that the train is gaining speed?

Composition

1. There are several similarities between "Song of the Truck" and "Crossing." Analyze the poems—their subject matter, the techniques the authors use, and the impressions that readers get after reading them. End by stating which poem you liked the most and explain why.

2. The authors of "Song of the Truck" and "Crossing" use many sense impressions in their poems. Readers of their poems can *see* and *hear* boxcar after boxcar going by. They can *smell* the coffee and vinegar and practically *taste* the apples and cantaloupes. They can almost even *touch* the textures of the textiles and silk. Now it is your turn to use this sense technique in a small, five-line poem of your own. First, pick an emotion and give it a color. Then tell how it smells, tastes, sounds, and feels. Use the examples below as your guide.

Happiness is a rainbow of color.
It smells like the first rose of summer
And tastes like a hot fudge sundae.
Happiness sounds gentle like a bluebird
And feels like a strong handshake.

Fear is black like midnight on Halloween.
It smells of sauerkraut cooking on the stove
And tastes like oily sardines.
Fear sounds like the silence of an empty room
And feels slimy like anchovies.

Sea Lullaby

ELINOR WYLIE

The old moon is tarnished
With smoke of the flood,
The dead leaves are varnished
With color like blood,

A treacherous smiler   5
With teeth white as milk,
A savage beguiler[1]
In sheathings of silk,

1 **beguiler** (bi gil′ ər): deceiver, cheat.

MOONLIGHT, WOOD'S ISLAND LIGHT *Winslow Homer*

The sea creeps to pillage,
She leaps on her prey;   10
A child of the village
Was murdered today.

She came up to meet him
In a smooth golden cloak,
She choked him and beat him   15
To death, for a joke.

Her bright locks were tangled,
She shouted for joy,
With one hand she strangled
A strong little boy.   20

Now in silence she lingers
Beside him all night
To wash her long fingers
In silvery light.

Silver

WALTER DE LA MARE

Slowly, silently, now the moon
Walks the night in her silver shoon;[1]
This way, and that, she peers, and sees
Silver fruit upon silver trees;
One by one the casements[2] catch
Her beams beneath the silvery thatch;[3]
Couched in his kennel, like a log,
With paws of silver sleeps the dog;
From their shadowy cote[4] the white breasts peep
Of doves in a silver-feathered sleep;
A harvest mouse goes scampering by,
With silver claws and a silver eye;
And moveless fish in the water gleam,
By silver reeds in a silver stream.

1 **shoon** (shün): shoes.
2 **casements**: windows.
3 **thatch**: a straw roof.
4 **cote** (kōt): a small shelter for birds.

1. What happens in "Sea Lullaby"?

2. What words or phrases in the first two stanzas create a feeling of fright or terror?

3. In "Sea Lullaby," the sea is described as a person. Who is that person? What does she do? Why does she do it?

4. Why do you think "Sea Lullaby" is a good title for this poem even though such a violent occurrence takes place in it?

5. In the first four lines of "Silver," the moon is compared to a person. Who is that person? What is that person doing?

6. In what lines does the poet of "Silver" use alliteration—the repetition of consonant sounds at the beginning of words? What one word is repeated most often?

7. The *s* sound is repeated within many words in "Silver." What effect is created by using this *s* sound so much throughout the poem?

Writer's Craft

Poets and authors can describe things in several different ways. They can picture a tree, for example, by describing it exactly as it is—similar to a photograph. They can also describe a tree by giving it human characteristics. An author could say, for instance, "The tree waved its long arms in the wind." Instead of branches, the tree has *arms,* and the tree is *waving* them—a human action. Giving human characteristics to things is called PERSONIFICATION. Comparisons such as personification, metaphors, and similes are called FIGURES OF SPEECH. The reader understands that the poet or author is saying that two things have some similar characteristics, but they are not identical.

1. In "Sea Lullaby," the sea is personified as a woman who has just murdered a child. What do the following personifications actually represent?
   a. "treacherous smiler/With teeth white as milk"
   b. "sea creeps to pillage/She leaps on her prey"
   c. "She came up to meet him/In a smooth golden cloak"
   d. "Her bright locks were tangled"
   e. "To wash her long fingers"

2. The figure of speech, personification, is also used in "Silver." Find examples of the moon personified as a woman.

3. Another figure of speech used in both poems is the simile. This comparison uses the word *like* or *as.* Find some examples.

1. Without using personification, write what happens in "Sea Lullaby" and "Silver." How do you think the use of personification makes the incident in "Sea Lullaby" more tragic? How do you think the use of personification in "Silver" makes this poem more interesting?

2. Select some common, everyday object such as a comb, a book, or a chair. In several paragraphs write a short incident in which you personify that object. For example, give the object human feelings and a voice. A chair, for instance, could complain terribly when little children bounce up and down because it hurts the chair's stomach (springs). Give as many human characteristics as you can to your object.

Elinor Wylie 1885—1928

Elinor Wylie was born in Somerville, New Jersey, but she grew up in Pennsylvania and Washington, D.C. While at school, Wylie secretly composed poetry and painted. She did not begin to publish in journals until shortly before the appearance of her book, *Nets to Catch the Wind,* in 1921. The next seven years of her life were devoted entirely to writing. During this period her poetry collections included: *Black Armour, Trivial Breath,* and *Angels and Other Creatures.*

Walter de la Mare 1873—1956

Walter de la Mare was born in Charlton, England. At sixteen, he founded and edited the *Chorister's Journal.* Then in 1890, his formal education ended, and he went to work for Standard Oil as a book-keeper. Even while working in business, he considered himself a writer, and in his spare time he wrote short stories and a novel. Finally in 1908, his literary accomplishments were recognized, and he received a government pension to write. His most important novel, *Memoirs of a Midget,* won the James Tait Black Memorial Prize in 1922.

Tree

LENORE MARSHALL

They were felling[1] the dead tree. It was necessary.
On the hard ground
Men stamped and clapped for warmth.
Wind, otherwise, hurling against old rot
The winter wind at unresisting rot   5
Would knock the neighbor beeches[2] headlong with it.
The man in a red plaid coat secured a cable
The man, blue-hooded, hacked a deeper notch
Men stamped and clapped for warmth and tied the noose.
It was all familiar. Cold air, frozen earth,   10
The patch of woods, familiar, and the crack
Of axe, the buzz of saw; it was necessary.
Hacked branches lay there first. It was a cold day.
Men shouted. A woman came and stood.
It was all familiar. There was a splintering.   15
There was a crack and crash. Men leapt and laughed,
    the woman shuddered.
There was an empty hole
Roots stiff as corpses
Sprang out, like arms and legs stiffened in the air,   20
And unfamiliar.

---

1 **felling**: cutting down.
2 **beeches**: hardwood trees.

Discussion

1. What is the setting of "Tree"?
2. What are the men doing? Why is it necessary?
3. What are the roots of the tree compared to at the end of the poem? What effect does this comparison create?

The Double Play

ROBERT WALLACE

In his sea-lit
distance, the pitcher winding
like a clock about to chime comes down with

the ball, hit
sharply, under the artificial   5
banks of arc lights, bounds like a vanishing string

over the green
to the shortstop magically
scoops to his right whirling above his invisible

shadows   10
in the dust redirects
its flight to the running poised second baseman

pirouettes[1]
leaping, above the slide, to throw   15
from mid-air, across the colored tightened interval,

to the leaning-
out first baseman ends the dance
drawing it disappearing into his long brown glove

stretches. What   20
is too swift for deception
is final, lost, among the loosened figures

jogging off the field
(the pitcher walks), casual
in the space where the poem has happened.

---

1 **pirouettes** (pir′ ü ets′): full turns on the toe or ball of the
foot in ballet.

1. What similes describe the pitcher? the hit ball? What do the similes mean?
2. How does the poet compare the movements of the second and first basemen with those of a ballet dancer?
3. Why do you think this poem is not punctuated between stanzas?

Lenore Marshall 1899—1971

As a young woman, Lenore Marshall wrote poetry and did book reviews, but she compromised her writing for her marriage and a family. However, in the late 1920s, she took a job in a publishing house. The high point in her job came when she discovered a new book by a then unknown author. The book was *The Sound and the Fury* by William Faulkner. During this time, Marshall also wrote poems which began to appear in periodicals. In 1935, her first book of poems, *Only the Fear,* was published. This was followed by another collection, *No Boundary,* and a novel, *Hall of Mirrors.* In later life Marshall turned to the Quaker religion and worked for peace and minority rights.

Robert Wallace 1932—

Born in Springfield, Missouri, Robert Wallace graduated from Harvard College and Cambridge University with honors. He has taught English at four colleges and is a reader for the Book-of-the-Month Club and the Educational Testing Service. He was awarded the William Rose Benét Memorial Award in 1957 and *Approach* magazine's Bragdon Prize in 1965. His poetry collections include: *This Various World and Other Poems, Ungainly Things,* and *Views from a Ferris Wheel.*

Fog

CARL SANDBURG

The fog comes
on little cat feet.

It sits looking
over harbor and city
on silent haunches
and then moves on.

Song of the Sky Loom

TEWA INDIAN

Oh our Mother the Earth, oh our Father the Sky,
Your children are we, and with tired backs
We bring you the gifts that you love.

Then weave for us a garment of brightness;

May the warp[1] be the white light of morning,   5
May the weft[2] be the red light of evening,
May the fringes be the falling rain,
May the border be the standing rainbow.

Thus weave for us a garment of brightness
That we may walk fittingly where birds sing,   10
That we may walk fittingly where grass is green,

Oh our Mother the Earth, oh our Father the Sky!

---

1 **warp**: the yarn that extends lengthwise on the loom.
2 **weft**: the yarns that are woven through the warp.

Discussion

1. What does Carl Sandburg compare with the fog?
2. In what ways is the fog like a cat?
3. What do you think is Sandburg's attitude toward the fog?
4. "Song of the Sky Loom" is a Tewa prayer. To whom is the prayer addressed?
5. In your own words, what do the Tewas request? What do they offer in return?
6. Describe the four items that make up the "garment of brightness."

Writer's Craft

"The sun is a big, orange balloon in the sky." That, as you know, is a metaphor. It is a comparison of two dissimilar things without using the word *like* or *as*. Poets use metaphors frequently to better describe something. However, sometimes instead of using just a one-line metaphor, poets may use one comparison throughout an entire poem. Or, they may base an entire poem on a single comparison. This is called an EXTENDED METAPHOR.

1. What is the extended metaphor in "Fog"?
2. What is the extended metaphor in "Song of the Sky Loom"?

Carl Sandburg 1878–1967

In many ways Carl Sandburg represented the frontier spirit. Like his predecessor, Samuel Clemens (Mark Twain), he was largely a self-taught writer. Experience seemed to be his teacher. He was a milk delivery boy, barber shop porter, fireman, truck operator, film salesman, house painter, motion picture editor, political organizer, reporter, lecturer, and folk singer. Sandburg remained virtually unknown until 1914 when his book *Poetry* was published. It contained a number of his short pieces including "Chicago." In 1916, *Chicago Poems,* a collection of poems about ordinary people and commonplace things, was published. This book was followed by *Cornhuskers,* which won a special Pulitzer Prize in 1919. In 1950, he was again honored with the Pulitzer Prize for his poetry in *Complete Poems.* Besides his poetry and journalism, Sandburg devoted much time and careful research to his biography of Abraham Lincoln. His four-volume work, *Abraham Lincoln: The War Years,* won another Pulitzer Prize in 1939.

American Gothic

SAMUEL ALLEN

TO SATCH[1]

Sometimes I feel like I will *never* stop
Just go on forever
'Til one fine mornin'
I'm gonna reach up and grab me a handfulla stars
Swing out my long lean leg
And whip three hot strikes burnin' down the heavens
And look over at God and say
How about that!

---

1 **Satch**: the nickname for Satchel Paige, a famous Black baseball player during the 1930s and 1940s.

Discussion

1. Who is talking in this poem?
2. What does he plan to do when he dies? What is his attitude toward death?
3. How do you think the use of everyday language, such as "grab me a handfulla stars," makes this poem more realistic?

Samuel Allen (Paul Vesey) 1917 —

Samuel Allen practiced and taught law before becoming a professor of English in 1971. He now teaches at Boston University and writes under the name of Paul Vesey. His first collection of poetry was *Ivory Tusks.* He is also well known for his translation of Jean Paul Sartre's *Black Orpheus.* Essays and poems, such as "American Gothic," have been included in more than sixty anthologies. Allen also recorded his poetry for the Library of Congress in 1972.

Catalogue

ROSALIE MOORE

Cats sleep fat and walk thin.
Cats, when they sleep, slump;
When they wake, stretch and begin
Over, pulling their ribs in.
Cats walk thin.   5

Cats wait in a lump,
Jump in a streak.
Cats, when they jump, are sleek
As a grape slipping its skin—
They have technique.   10
Oh, cats don't creak.
They sneak.

Cats sleep fat.
They spread out comfort underneath them
Like a good mat,   15
As if they picked the place
And then sat;
You walk around one
As if he were the City Hall
After that.   20

If male,
A cat is apt to sing on a major scale;
This concert is for everybody, this
Is wholesale.
For a baton, he wields a tail.   25

(He is also found,
When happy, to resound
With an enclosed and private sound.)

A cat condenses.
He pulls in his tail to go under bridges,   30
And himself to go under fences.
Cats fit
In any size box or kit,
And if a large pumpkin grew under one,
He could arch over it.   35

When everyone else is just ready to go out,
The cat is just ready to come in.
He's not where he's been.
Cats sleep fat and walk thin.

Reprinted by permission, © 1940, 1978 The New Yorker Magazine, Inc.

Discussion

1. Why is "Catalogue" a good title for this poem?
2. What do you think the author means by "Cats sleep fat and walk thin."?
3. How is the cat musical?
4. What do you think is the author's attitude toward cats? Explain your answer.

Rosalie Moore (Rosalie Brown) 1910—

Rosalie Moore is a poet and writer. Using the name, Rosalie Brown, she collaborated with her husband to write children's books, including: *Forest Fireman, Big Rig,* and *The Hippopotamus That Wanted To Be a Baby.* Her own poetry has been frequently anthologized and published in several well-known magazines. Since her husband's death, Moore has been teaching and writing. Although her love for cats still remains, she commented, "I no longer keep any cats, but my daughter Camas has five."

Sea Fever

JOHN MASEFIELD

I must go down to the seas again, to the lonely sea and the sky,
And all I ask is a tall ship and a star to steer her by,
And the wheel's kick and the wind's song and the white sail's shaking,
And a gray mist on the sea's face and a gray dawn breaking.

I must go down to the seas again, for the call of the running tide   5
Is a wild call and a clear call that may not be denied;
And all I ask is a windy day with the white clouds flying,
And the flung spray and the blown spume[1] and the sea gulls crying.

I must go down to the seas again to the vagrant gypsy life,
To the gull's way and the whale's way where the wind's like a whetted[2] knife;   10
And all I ask is a merry yarn from a laughing fellow rover,
And quiet sleep and a sweet dream when the long trick's[3] over.

---

1 **spume** (spyūm): foam, froth.
2 **whetted** (hwet' əd): sharpened.
3 **trick**: turn of duty; for example, steering or standing watch.

Discussion

1. What is meant by the lines: "I must go down to the seas again, for the call of the running tide/. . . may not be denied;"?

2. In the last line, the speaker says he will have "quiet sleep" and a "sweet dream" when he returns from his duties at sea. What does he mean?

3. What is this sailor's attitude toward sea life? Do you think this is a true picture of all sailors' lives? Explain.

ON A LEE SHORE   *Winslow Homer*

Words in English that have more than one meaning are called MULTIPLE-MEANING WORDS. For example, in "Sea Fever," the poet uses the word *yarn* to refer to "a story" or "tale," but the same word can also mean "a thread woven from wool, cotton, or silk."

A. Find the word *sweet* in a dictionary. Then on a separate sheet of paper, copy the meaning that applies to the last line of the poem: "And quiet sleep and a sweet dream." Then copy at least three other definitions for *sweet* from the dictionary. Write a sentence for each definition.

B. Look through "Sea Fever," and find at least three other multiple-meaning words. On the same paper copy these words, and give at least two different definitions for each.

John Masefield 1878—1967

John Masefield was born in Ledbury, England, and at thirteen he ran away to the sea. He remained a sailor for three years until he left his ship when it docked in New York City. While in New York, he worked in a bakery, a saloon, a livery stable, a carpet factory, and on the waterfront. Finally in 1897, he returned to England and became an editor and writer. In 1902, he published his first book of poetry, *Salt Water Ballads,* which contains the poem, "Sea Fever." His list of poems, novels, short stories, plays, and essays is remarkably long. In 1930, King George appointed Masefield poet laureate of England, and in 1935, he received the Order of Merit.

In order for life to continue to exist on this earth, prophets for centuries have said that people must show concern for others. This idea has appeared as a theme in poetry throughout all ages, in all languages, and in all cultures. In this section, different areas of concern are examined. For example, in the first poem a boy tries to help his awkward friend feel a part of the neighborhood football games.

The Sleeper

EDWARD FIELD

When I was the sissy of the block who nobody wanted on their team
Sonny Hugg persisted in believing that my small size was an asset
Not the liability and curse I felt it was
And he saw a use for my swift feet with which I ran away from fights.

He kept putting me into complicated football plays   5
Which would have been spectacular if they worked:
For instance, me getting clear in front and him shooting the ball over—
Or the sensation of the block, the Sleeper Play
In which I would lie down on the sidelines near the goal
As though resting and out of action, until the scrimmage began   10
And I would step onto the field, receive the long throw
And to the astonishment of all the tough guys in the world
Step over the goal line for a touchdown.

That was the theory anyway. In practice
I had the fatal flaw of not being able to catch   15
And usually had my fingers bent back and the breath knocked out of me
So the plays always failed, but Sonny kept on trying
Until he grew up out of my world into the glamorous
Varsity crowd, the popular kids at Lynbrook High.

But I will always have this to thank him for: 20
That when I look back on childhood
(That four psychiatrists haven't been able to help me bear the thought of)
There is not much to be glad for
Besides his foolish and delicious faith
That, with all my oddities, there was a place in the world for me 25
If only he could find the special role.

Discussion

1. Describe the speaker. Describe Sonny Hugg.

2. How does Sonny try to include the speaker in the neighborhood football games? Why don't his plans work?

3. In later years, how does the speaker feel about Sonny's attempts to help him?

Edward Field 1924——

Edward Field's two books, *Stand Up, Friend, with Me* and *Variety Photoplays*, contain some of the best poems published during the 1960s. He is a master storyteller who relates childhood experiences with realistic thought and feeling. Field held many part-time jobs while writing and acted in various theater groups. He wrote the narrative for *To Be Alive*, the award-winning documentary shown at the New York World's Fair. In 1962, he received the Lamont Poetry Selection Award for *Stand Up, Friend, with Me*.

A Time to Talk

ROBERT FROST

When a friend calls to me from the road
And slows his horse to a meaning walk,
I don't stand still and look around
On all the hills I haven't hoed,
And shout from where I am, "What is it?" 5

No, not as there is a time to talk.
I thrust my hoe in the mellow ground,
Blade-end up and five feet tall,
And plod: I go up to the stone wall
For a friendly visit. 10

Discussion

1. What does the speaker do when a friend calls to him from the road?
2. What does this tell you about him?
3. Instead of walking over to his friend, what could the speaker have done?

Robert Frost 1874—1963

Although Robert Frost is considered by many as the chief interpreter of New England life, he lived in San Francisco until he was eleven years old. When his father died, he and his mother returned to Lawrence, Massachusetts. In 1912, he moved to England. There he published two works, *A Boy's Will* and *North of Boston*. When both books were published in the United States, Frost reportedly said to his wife, "My books have gone home; we must go, too." Frost won three Pulitzer Prizes: in 1923 for *New Hampshire*, in 1930 for *Collected Poems*, and in 1936 for *A Further Range*.

if you have had your midnights

MARI EVANS

if you have had
    your midnights
and they have drenched
    your barren guts
        with tears

I sing you sunrise
    and love
and someone to touch

Discussion

1. Who is the speaker talking to in this poem?
2. What does "midnights" mean? What is the result of the midnights?
3. What alternative to midnight tears does the speaker offer?
4. What things are contrasted in the first five lines and the last three lines?

Mari Evans

Recently for several years Mari Evans was the producer-director for "The Black Experience," a weekly television program in Indianapolis, Indiana. Like her television work, Evans's poetry reflects the Black experience. Some of her poems have even been choreographed and used on record albums, filmstrips, television specials, and off-Broadway shows. In 1970, while teaching at Indiana-Purdue University, she received the Black Academy of Arts and Letters first annual poetry award for *I Am a Black Woman*. Her other works include the poetry collection, *Where Is All the Music*, and the children's books, *I Look at Me* and *Rap Stories*.

An Easy Decision

KENNETH PATCHEN

I had finished my dinner
Gone for a walk
It was fine
Out and I started whistling

It wasn't long before   5

I met a

Man and his wife riding on
A pony with seven
Kids running along beside them

I said hello and   10

Went on
Pretty soon I met another
Couple
This time with nineteen
Kids and all of them   15
Riding on
A big smiling hippopotamus

I invited them home

1. Where is the speaker going? How does the speaker feel?
2. What is the first family the speaker meets doing? How does the speaker react?
3. What is the second family doing? How does the speaker react?
4. Why do you think the speaker treats the two families differently?
5. Why do you think this poem is called "An Easy Decision"?

Kenneth Patchen 1911—1972

Kenneth Patchen held many jobs during his youth, including working in the fields and in a steel mill. His artistic talents were as varied as his work experiences. He was skilled in prose, poetry, and art. For his poems in *The Dark Kingdom,* he painted corresponding watercolors, and his poems often created forms which were designed by the words themselves. For many years Patchen suffered from a spinal injury incurred in his youth. Despite his illness, he managed to publish more than one book a year, including *Cloth of the Tempest* and *Collected Poems.*

Those Winter Sundays

ROBERT HAYDEN

Sundays too my father got up early
and put his clothes on in the blueblack cold,
then with cracked hands that ached
from labor in the weekday weather made
banked fires blaze. No one ever thanked him.   5

I'd wake and hear the cold splintering, breaking.
When the rooms were warm, he'd call,
and slowly I would rise and dress,
fearing the chronic angers of that house,

Speaking indifferently to him,   10
who had driven out the cold
and polished my good shoes as well.
What did I know, what did I know
of love's austere and lonely offices?

Discussion

1. What things does the speaker's father do each Sunday morning?
2. How does the speaker treat his or her father?
3. What do you think the last two lines mean? How can love be "lonely"?

Robert Hayden 1913—1980

Robert Hayden's poetry was his life. In a conversation from *How I Write*, he said, "If one could answer the question 'Why do you go on living?' then perhaps one could come up with a convincing answer to 'Why do you write poetry?'" Although some of Hayden's poems contain many of the characteristics of Black folk poetry, he wrote about a variety of topics and in a number of forms. His poetry is universal. At the core of his work is the theme of oppression, but the oppression is not limited to any one kind. His poetry includes: *The Lion and the Archer, Selected Poems,* and *A Ballad of Remembrance,* which won the grand prize for poetry in English at the first World Festival of Negro Arts in 1966.

The Twenty-third Psalm

The Lord *is* my shepherd; I shall not want.
He maketh me to lie down in green pastures:
He leadeth me beside the still waters.
He restoreth my soul:
He leadeth me in the paths of righteousness for his name's sake.   5
Yea, though I walk through the valley of the shadow of death,
I will fear no evil: for thou *art* with me;
Thy rod and thy staff they comfort me.
Thou preparest a table before me in the presence of mine enemies:
Thou anointest my head with oil;   10
My cup runneth over.
Surely goodness and mercy shall follow me all the days of my life:
And I will dwell in the house of the Lord forever.

Discussion

1. What is the extended metaphor in "The Twenty-third Psalm"? Explain how these two things are compared throughout the psalm.

2. What feelings are associated with words such as *green pastures* and *still waters*?

3. What is meant by "the valley of the shadow of death"?

4. According to "The Twenty-third Psalm," what part of a person's life is guided by the Lord?

Given the same situation—a problem, a success, a decision—different people will react and respond in various ways. The first poem in this section, for example, shows how a woman remains hopeful in spite of her poverty and hard life. Other people, of course, might become bitter or resentful in the same situation. This section will explore some of these differing viewpoints of life.

Taught Me Purple

EVELYN TOOLEY HUNT

My mother taught me purple
    Although she never wore it.
Wash-gray was her circle,
    The tenement her orbit.

My mother taught me golden   5
    And held me up to see it,
Above the broken molding,
    Beyond the filthy street.

My mother reached for beauty
    And for its lack she died,   10
Who knew so much of duty
    She could not teach me pride.

Dream Variation

LANGSTON HUGHES

To fling my arms wide
In some place of the sun,
To whirl and to dance
Till the white day is done.
Then rest at cool evening   5
Beneath a tall tree
While night comes on gently,
   Dark like me—
That is my dream!

To fling my arms wide   10
In the face of the sun,
Dance! Whirl! Whirl!
Till the quick day is done.
Rest at pale evening . . .
A tall, slim tree . . .   15
Night coming tenderly
   Black like me.

Discussion

1. What is the mother's life like in "Taught Me Purple"?
2. What does she try to teach her child? What is the *one* thing she cannot teach her child? Why?
3. In both stanzas of "Dream Variation," the speaker flings his arms wide, whirls, and dances. What feelings do these movements express? Why do you think the speaker feels this way?
4. The title, "Dream Variation," suggests that the speaker had the same dream twice, but the second dream was slightly different. What word differences do you see in the two dreams?
5. Which of the two dreams is more active? What do you think this increased action means?
6. In this poem "night" could mean death. How does the author feel about death? Why?
7. What are the contrasting viewpoints toward life in these two poems?

Langston Hughes 1902—1967

Langston Hughes wrote novels, short stories, plays, musical lyrics, children's books, history books, news columns, and poetry. Born in Joplin, Missouri, Hughes lived in numerous Midwest cities and Mexico. He attended Columbia University for a year but left to take a seafaring journey to Africa and Europe. He wrote when possible but spent much of his time working. While later working in Washington, D.C., his poetry was recognized. After his first books of poetry, *The Weary Blues* and *Fine Clothes to the Jew*, were published in 1926 and 1927, he devoted all of his time to writing. His other works include a novel, *Not without Laughter;* his autobiography, *The Big Sea;* and a poetry collection, *Selected Poems.* His last book, *The Panther and the Lash*, a collection of poetry, was published after his death.

A Psalm of Life

HENRY WADSWORTH LONGFELLOW

Tell me not, in mournful numbers,
  Life is but an empty dream!—
For the soul is dead that slumbers,
  And things are not what they seem.

Life is real! Life is earnest!   5
  And the grave is not its goal;
Dust thou art, to dust returnest,
  Was not spoken of the soul.

Not enjoyment, and not sorrow,
  Is our destined end or way;   10
But to act, that each to-morrow
  Find us farther than to-day.

Art is long, and Time is fleeting,
  And our hearts, though stout and brave,
Still, like muffled drums, are beating   15
  Funeral marches to the grave.

In the world's broad field of battle,
  In the bivouac[1] of Life,
Be not like dumb, driven cattle!
  Be a hero in the strife!   20

---

1 **bivouac** (biv′ wak): temporary military shelter.

Trust no Future, howe'er pleasant!
   Let the dead Past bury its dead!
Act,—act in the living Present!
   Heart within, and God o'erhead!

Lives of great men all remind us   25
   We can make our lives sublime,
And, departing, leave behind us
   Footprints on the sands of time;

Footprints, that perhaps another,
   Sailing o'er life's solemn main,   30
A forlorn and shipwrecked brother,
   Seeing, shall take heart again.

Let us, then, be up and doing,
   With a heart for any fate;
Still achieving, still pursuing,   35
   Learn to labor and to wait.

Discussion

1. What attitudes toward life does the speaker in this poem reject? Give examples from the poem. What attitudes does the speaker encourage? Give examples.
2. What advice for living is given? Explain why you think this advice might be difficult to follow.
3. What do lines 25–28 mean to you? Explain why you think this statement is true or false.

Vocabulary

An ANTONYM is a word that means the opposite, or nearly the opposite, of another word. For example:

life—death   empty—full   happy—sad

Below are five lines from "A Psalm of Life." Each line contains one *italicized* word. Below each sentence are four other words, one of which is an antonym for the *italicized* word. On a separate sheet of paper, copy both the *italicized* word and its antonym.

1. And our hearts, though *stout* and brave . . .
   thin   weak   green   cool
2. Be a hero in the *strife!*
   sport   city   past   peace
3. We can make our lives *sublime.*
   shameful   bitter   forgettable   unholy
4. Sailing o'er life's *solemn* main . . .
   dry   amusing   sweet   unimportant
5. A *forlorn* and shipwrecked brother . . .
   courageous   cheerful   strong   safe

Death at Suppertime

PHYLLIS McGINLEY

Between the dark and the daylight,
  When the night is beginning to lower,
Comes a pause in the day's occupation,
  That is known as the Children's Hour.

Then endeth the skipping and skating,   5
  The giggles, the tantrums, and tears,
When, the innocent voices abating,
  Alert grow the innocent ears.

The little boys leap from the stairways,
  Girls lay down their dolls on the dot,   10
For promptly at five o'er the airways
  Comes violence geared to the tot.

Comes murder, comes arson, come G-men
  Pursuing unspeakable spies;
Come gangsters and tough-talking he-men   15
  With six-shooters strapped to their thighs.

Comes the corpse in the dust, comes the dictum
  "Ya' better start singin', ya' rat!"
While the torturer leers at his victim,
  The killer unleashes his gat.[1]   20

With mayhem the twilight is reeling.
  Blood spatters; the tommy guns bark.
Hands reach for the sky or the ceiling
  As the dagger strikes home in the dark.

---

1 **gat**: slang for gun or pistol.

And lo! with what rapturous wonder   25
   The little ones hark to each tale
Of gambler shot down with his plunder
   Or outlaw abducting the mail.

Between the news and the tireless
   Commercials, while tempers turn sour,   30
Comes a season of horror by wireless
   That is known as the Children's Hour.

Discussion

1. What is the author criticizing?
2. What is the children's reaction to the programs?
3. The word "wireless" is used in line 31. It refers to the radio in its early days. How is the problem presented in this poem still true today? Do you think the problem was worse then or now?

Phyllis McGinley 1905 —

Phyllis McGinley first started writing poems when she was six. "I always wanted to be a poet," she once said. "I cut my teeth on a pencil." After teaching school for a little over four years in New Rochelle, New York, McGinley began writing poetry. When the *New Yorker* magazine started to accept her poems, she moved to New York City. There she made her living by writing before she got married. Then she became a housewife-writer. Her witty poems have not only appeared in the *New Yorker* and *Saturday Review*, but they have also been collected into numerous volumes including the winner of the 1960 Pulitzer Prize, *Times Three: Selected Verse from Three Decades*, which contains the poem, "Death at Suppertime."

The Immigrant Experience

RICHARD OLIVAS

I'm sitting in my history class,
The instructor commences rapping,
I'm in my U.S. History class,
And I'm on the verge of napping.

The *Mayflower* landed on Plymouth Rock.   5
Tell me more! Tell me more!
Thirteen colonies were settled.
I've heard it all before.

What did he say?
Dare I ask him to reiterate?   10
Oh, why bother,
It sounded like he said,
George Washington's my father.

I'm reluctant to believe it,
I suddenly raise my *mano*.   15
If George Washington's my father,
Why wasn't he Chicano?

Discussion

1. Where is the speaker in this poem? Why is the speaker bored?
2. What particular statement by the teacher catches the speaker's interest? What is the speaker's reaction to the statement?
3. If you were the teacher, how would you answer the speaker's question?

To Kate, Skating Better Than Her Date

DAVID DAICHES

Wait, Kate! You skate at such a rate
You leave behind your skating mate.
Your splendid speed won't you abate?[1]
He's lagging far behind you, Kate.
He brought you on this skating date   5
His shy affection thus to state,
But you on skating concentrate
And leave him with a woeful weight
Pressed on his heart. Oh, what a state
A man gets into, how irate   10
He's bound to be with life and fate
If, when he tries to promulgate[2]
His love, the loved one turns to skate
Far, far ahead to demonstrate
Superior speed and skill. Oh, hate   15
Is sure to come of love, dear Kate,
If you so treat your skating mate.
Turn again, Kate, or simply wait
Until he comes, then him berate
(Coyly) for catching up so late.   20
For, Kate, he *knows* your skating's great,
He's *seen* your splendid figure eight,
He is not here to contemplate
Your supersonic skating rate—
That is not why he made the date.   25
He's anxious to expatiate[3]
On how he wants you for his mate.
And don't you want to hear him, Kate?

---

1 **abate:** to reduce.
2 **promulgate** (prom′ əl gāt): to announce.
3 **expatiate** (ek spā′ shē āt): to speak more.

Reprinted by permission; © 1957 The New Yorker Magazine, Inc.

1. Why was Kate asked to go skating?
2. What problems does Kate's boyfriend have?
3. What do you think is Kate's answer to the question in the last line? Support your answer by explaining what kind of person Kate is.

David Daiches 1912——

David Daiches is both a successful writer and teacher. He began writing poetry, plays, and stories at nine, and at eighteen he wrote and helped produce a musical comedy. His studies at the University of Edinburgh turned his literary interests to education, and he has since taught and lectured at several well-known universities in the United States and England. Besides his critical studies, including *The Place of Meaning in Poetry* and *The Idea of a New University,* Daiches has contributed several poems, sketches, and short stories to the *New Yorker* and other magazines.

The Choice

DOROTHY PARKER

He'd have given me rolling lands,
    Houses of marble, and billowing farms,
Pearls, to trickle between my hands,
    Smoldering rubies, to circle my arms.
You—you'd only a lilting song.   5
    Only a melody, happy and high,
You were sudden and swift and strong—
    Never a thought for another had I.

He'd have given me laces rare,
    Dresses that glimmered with frosty sheen,   10
Shining ribbons to wrap my hair,
    Horses to draw me, as fine as a queen.
You—you'd only to whistle low,
    Gayly I followed wherever you led.
I took you, and I let him go—   15
    Somebody ought to examine my head!

Discussion

1. What does each suitor have to offer the speaker in this poem?
2. Which of the two suitors does she eventually choose? Why?
3. What do you think the last line means?
4. Do you think she made the right choice? Explain your answer.

Dorothy Parker 1893–1967

Dorothy Parker began her literary career in 1917 as a drama critic for *Vanity Fair* magazine. Ten years later she was book critic for the *New Yorker,* but she resigned when her first book of poetry became a best-seller. After that, she spent all her time writing stories, poems, plays, and screenplays. Parker's works include: the poetry collection, *Death and Taxes;* the short story collection, *Laments for the Living;* and the Broadway play, *Ladies of the Corridor.* She won the O. Henry Memorial Award in 1929 for the story, "Big Blond."

Poets write about all subjects, but the basic experiences of growing up and growing old are two favorite themes. In the first four poems in this section, you will see how some poets from different ethnic groups in America treat the theme of sharing between generations. Then in the last four poems, you will read about young people—their individual problems and their problems with the older generation.

Carriers of the Dream Wheel

N. SCOTT MOMADAY

This is the Wheel of Dreams
Which is carried on their voices,
By means of which their voices turn
And center upon being.
It encircles the First World,   5
This powerful wheel.
They shape their songs upon the wheel
And spin the names of the earth and sky,
The aboriginal[1] names.
They are old men, or men   10
Who are old in their voices,
And they carry the wheel among the camps,
Saying: Come, come,
Let us tell the old stories,
Let us sing the sacred songs.   15

---

1 **aboriginal** (ab'ə rij'ə nəl): the original people who settled
in an area; the natives.

Aunt Sue's Stories

LANGSTON HUGHES

Aunt Sue has a head full of stories.
Aunt Sue has a whole heart full of stories.
Summer nights on the front porch
Aunt Sue cuddles a brown-faced child to her bosom
And tells him stories.   5

Black slaves
Working in the hot sun,
And black slaves
Walking in the dewy night,
And black slaves   10
Singing sorrow songs on the banks of a mighty river
Mingle themselves softly
In the flow of old Aunt Sue's voice,
Mingle themselves softly

In the dark shadows that cross and recross   15
Aunt Sue's stories.

And the dark-faced child, listening,
Knows that Aunt Sue's stories are real stories.
He knows that Aunt Sue never got her stories
Out of any book at all,   20
But that they came
Right out of her own life.

The dark-faced child is quiet
Of a summer night
Listening to Aunt Sue's stories.   25

1. In "Carriers of the Dream Wheel," what is the "Wheel of Dreams"? Who are the "carriers"? What do they do?
2. What are Aunt Sue's stories about? Why do these stories mean so much to the young boy who hears them?
3. How could Aunt Sue be considered a "carrier of the dream wheel"?

N. Scott Momaday 1934—

N. Scott Momaday has emerged as a strong literary voice of the Native American. His interest in the arts came from his father, a painter and art teacher, and his mother, a painter and a writer. Momaday once said, "I am an American Indian and am vitally interested in American Indian art, history, and culture." He left his Lawton, Oklahoma, home to pursue his interests at the University of New Mexico and Stanford. In 1963, he became a professor at the University of California. In addition to his teaching and editing, Momaday has published a novel, *House Made of Dawn,* which won the Pulitzer Prize for fiction in 1969.

My Grandmother Would Rock Quietly and Hum

LEONARD ADAMÉ

in her house
she would rock quietly and hum
until her swelled hands
calmed

in summer   5
she wore thick stockings
sweaters
and grey braids

mornings
sunlight barely lit   10
the kitchen.
flour tortillas
were rolled quietly;
the papas
cracking in hot lard   15
wakened me,
and where
there were shadows
it was not cold

with bread soaked   20
in cafe,
she sat and talked
of girlhood—
of things strange to me:
    Mexico   25
    epidemics
    relatives shot
    her father's hopes
      of this country,

and how they sank   30
with cement dust
to his insides

now,
at the old house,
there are   35
worn spots by the stove
where she shuffled:
and Mexico
hangs in her
fading calendar pictures . . .   40

piñones

LEROY V. QUINTANA

when i was young
we would sit by
an old firewood stove
watching my grandmother make candy,
listening to the stories   5
my grandparents would tell
about "the old days"
        and eat piñones

now we belong
to a supersonic age
and have college degrees.   10
we sit around color t.v. sets
watching the super bowl
listening to howard cosell,
new stories of rioting, war, inflation
        and eat piñones

Discussion

1. Describe the setting of "My Grandmother Would Rock Quietly and Hum." Describe the grandmother.

2. What had life been like in Mexico for the grandmother's family? What is life like in America? Find the lines in the poem that answer these questions.

3. Do you think the grandmother was sorry her family had moved to America?

4. In "piñones," the poet makes his point by contrasting different times. Which time seems more attractive—the past or the present? Explain your answer.

5. Why is "piñones" a good title for this poem? Using the meaning of the title as the basis of your answer, what do you think this poem means?

6. Both of these poems contrast the past with the present. How do the poets' opinions differ about which time period is better? Do you think life is better now or when your parents were young? Explain your answer.

A Spring Night

ROBERT BELOOF

His son meant something that he couldn't name.
He had his picture in his wallet,
but never remembered taking out the wallet
for anything but cash, or an address, or a name.

He could have hated him, but didn't,   5
even though the boy reminded him
how stuck he was because of him.
He could have loved him, too, but didn't.

When Mr. Cuff came home at night
there was reading, or sitting on the stoop till dark,   10
watching the dead-end street he lived on fade to dark,
so they didn't talk together much at night.

Sitting as usual this April evening
watching an impassively dying sun,
he became aware that hesitantly his son   15
was coming to him out of the evening.

They sat awhile together, then quietly
the boy asked him, "Do you really like boys?
I'd just like to know that, if you really like boys."
Mr. Cuff was stunned. The sun set quietly.   20

Communication was a rusted hinge to Cuff.
He sought someway convincingly to say
"There's just the word I've wanted long to say
but couldn't say." "'Like' is the word," thought Cuff.

"I'm damned," said Mr. Cuff under his breath.   25
Finally, the boy shuffled off. Cuff went to bed.
"What's that you're mumbling over there in bed?"
asked Mrs. Cuff in the dark. Cuff lay still as death.

1. How does Mr. Cuff feel toward his son?

2. Mr. Cuff feels he could have hated his son. What reason does he give?

3. What does Mr. Cuff do in the evenings? What does this tell you about his attitude toward his family?

4. What question does Mr. Cuff's son ask him? Although he does not answer his son, what does Mr. Cuff think he should have said?

5. What is the meaning of the metaphor, "Communication was a rusted hinge to Cuff."?

Writer's Craft

Writing poetry sometimes can be more difficult than writing a whole short story. Often poets can use only three or four words to create a feeling or describe a scene, while short-story writers can use several paragraphs to do the same thing. Because a poem is so much shorter, every word counts.

That is why it is so important that poets—and their readers—understand the *exact* meaning of each word as well as its *implied* meaning. For example, a thin girl might not mind being described as "slender" because that word implies a model-like appearance. But, if you were to call the same girl "skinny," she would probably be hurt and offended because this word implies uncomplimentary and negative images. The exact meaning of a word is called its DENOTATION, and its implied meaning is called its CONNOTATION. Poets must carefully consider both of these if they are to convey a particular meaning to a reader.

1. The words in "A Spring Night" were carefully chosen by the poet. The most simple change could make a difference in the overall meaning of the poem. For example, in line 24, Mr. Cuff answers his son's question by thinking to himself, "There's just the word I've wanted long to say/but couldn't say." "'Like' is the word." How would this poem be different if the word *love* had been used instead of *like*?

2. When Cuff's son received no answer from his father in the last stanza, he "shuffled off." What different connotations do *shuffled* and *walked* have? What would readers not learn if *walked* had been used instead of *shuffled*?

3. Explain the importance of the wording in the last sentence of the poem: "Cuff lay still as death." What do these words imply that a sentence such as "Cuff didn't answer," does not?

Fifteen

WILLIAM STAFFORD

South of the Bridge on Seventeenth
I found back of the willows one summer
day a motorcycle with engine running
as it lay on its side, ticking over
slowly in the high grass. I was fifteen.   5

I admired all that pulsing gleam, the
shiny flanks, the demure headlights
fringed where it lay; I led it gently
to the road and stood with that
companion, ready and friendly. I was fifteen.   10

We could find the end of a road, meet
the sky out on Seventeenth. I thought about
hills, and patting the handle got back a
confident opinion. On the bridge we indulged
a forward feeling, a tremble. I was fifteen.   15

Thinking, back farther in the grass I found
the owner, just coming to, where he had flipped
over the rail. He had blood on his hand, was pale—
I helped him walk to his machine. He ran his hand
over it, called me good man, roared away.   20

I stood there, fifteen.

1. What happens in this poem?
2. What animal does the speaker compare with the motorcycle? Find specific examples which support your answer.
3. What sentence is repeated throughout the poem? Why do you think the poet repeats this sentence?
4. How do you know that the speaker wants to take a ride on the motorcycle? What prevents him?

Robert Beloof 1923——

Since 1948, Robert Beloof has taught and lectured at the University of California in Berkeley, and from 1959–1960, he was the Fulbright professor of American literature at Oriental Institute in Naples. His volume of poetry, *One-eyed Gunner,* was published in 1956. In 1966, he also published *The Performing Voice in Literature.* Beloof has contributed articles and poems to numerous literary magazines both in this country and abroad.

William Stafford 1914——

William Stafford was born in Kansas. During World War II, he was a conscientious objector. Since then he has been active in many pacifist organizations. Stafford published his first book of poetry, *West of Your City: Poems,* in 1960. Since then he has published over a dozen or more collections, including *Traveling through the Dark,* which won the National Book Award for poetry in 1963. As the subject of his poems, Stafford often contrasts modern mechanical civilization with more natural cultures, as in the poem, "Fifteen." He once commented, "My poetry seems to me direct and communicative, with some oddity and variety. It is usually not formal. It is much like talk, with some enhancement."

Advice to a Girl

SARA TEASDALE

No one worth possessing
Can be quite possessed;
Lay that on your heart,
My young angry dear;
This truth, this hard and precious stone,   5
Lay it on your hot cheek,
Let it hide your tear.

Hold it like a crystal
When you are alone
And gaze in the depths of the icy stone.   10
Long, look long and you will be blessed:
No one worth possessing
Can be quite possessed.

Discussion

1. What do you think the girl in this poem did that is now causing her to be angry and to cry?

2. What advice does the author give the girl?

3. The author compares her advice to "a hard and precious stone" which can appear as a "crystal" (a fortuneteller's crystal ball). How is her advice like these two things?

Discussion

1. Find examples of alliteration in the poems "Casey at the Bat" and "Silver."

2. Many poems in this unit contain figures of speech. Find an example of a simile in "The Double Play" and "Catalogue." Find an example of a metaphor in "A Psalm of Life" and "Advice to a Girl." Find an example of personification in "Crossing" and "Sea Fever."

3. How does the use of contrast contribute to the meaning of "Taught Me Purple" and "piñones"?

4. What are the different rhyme schemes of "Song of the Truck," "Sea Lullaby," and "To Kate, Skating Better Than Her Date"?

5. What is the rhyme scheme of "A Spring Night"? What is unusual about this particular rhyme scheme?

Composition

1. You learned in this unit that personification is the giving of human characteristics to objects. Write a description of the two women personified in "Sea Lullaby" and "Silver." Then contrast these two women. Use as many specific examples from the poems as you can.

2. Select an idea or a scene. Then try to see it and its opposite. For example, you might choose *cocoon* and its opposite *butterfly*, or *joy* and *sadness*. Once you have done this, fit your ideas into a diamond poem. Use the examples below as your guide.

Car	Stranger
shiny, new	new, different
cruising, stopping, revving	seeing, meeting, talking
driver, friends—admirers, darers	acquaintance, associate—member, pal
racing, cornering, skidding	liking, enjoying, seeking
crumpled, smashed	familiar, trusted
Wreck	Friend

Nonfiction Narrative

NONFICTION NARRATIVE

You have probably heard the familiar expression, "Truth is stranger than fiction." In this unit you will see how that statement is true. You will read accounts of real people doing things that seem impossible. For example, you will read about a teenage girl and the problems she has on her first job as a newspaper reporter and about a poor boy from Puerto Rico who becomes a superstar. Literature which is based on true events and people is called NONFICTION NARRATIVE. It is nonfiction because it is true, and it is a narrative because it is a story. The excitement of reading nonfiction narrative comes from sharing the unusual adventures of outstanding people.

I saw him play so often. I watched the grace of his movements and the artistry of his reflexes from who knows how many press boxes. None of us really appreciated how pure an athlete he was until he was gone. What follows is a personal retracing of the steps that took Roberto Clemente from the narrow, crowded streets of his native Carolina to the local ball parks in San Juan and on to the major leagues. But it is more. It is a remembrance formed as I stood at the water's edge in Puerto Rico and stared at daybreak into the waves that killed him. It is all the people I met in Puerto Rico who knew and loved him.

Roberto Clemente— A Bittersweet Memoir

JERRY IZENBERG

THE RECORD BOOK will tell you that Roberto Clemente collected 3,000 hits during his major-league career. It will say that he came to bat 9,454 times, that he drove in 1,305 runs, and played 2,433 games over an eighteen-year span.

But it won't tell you about Carolina, Puerto Rico, and the old square, and the narrow, twisting streets, and the roots that produced him. It won't tell you about the Julio Coronado School and a remarkable woman named María Isabella Casares, whom he called "Teacher" until the day he died and who helped to shape his life in times of despair and depression. It won't tell you

about a man named Pedro Zarrilla, who found him on a country softball team and put him in the uniform of the Santurce club and who nursed him from a promising young athlete to a major-league superstar.

And most of all, those cold numbers won't begin to delineate[1] the man Roberto Clemente was. To even begin to understand what this magnificent athlete was all about, you have to work backward. The search begins at the site of its ending.

The car moves easily through the predawn streets of San Juan. It turns down a bumpy

---

1 **delineate:** describe; represent.

secondary road and moves past small shanty-towns. Then there is another turn, onto hard-packed dirt and sand, and although the light has not yet quite begun to break, you can sense the nearness of the ocean. You can hear its waves, pounding harshly against the jagged rocks. You can smell its saltiness. The car noses to a stop, and the driver says, "From here you must walk." The place is called Punta Maldonado.

"This is the nearest place," the driver tells me. "This is where they came by the thousands on that New Year's Eve and New Year's Day. Out there," he says, gesturing with his right hand, "out there, perhaps a mile and a half from where we stand. That's where we think the plane went down."

The final hours of Roberto Clemente

were like this. Just a month or so before, he had agreed to take a junior-league baseball team to Nicaragua and manage it in an all-star game in Managua. He had met people and made friends there. He was not a man who made friends casually. He had always said that the people you wanted to give your friendship to were the people to whom you had to be willing to give something—no matter what the price.

Just two weeks after he returned from that trip, Managua, Nicaragua, exploded into flames. The earth trembled, and people died. It was the worst earthquake anywhere in the hemisphere in a long time.

Back in Puerto Rico, a television personality named Luis Vigereaux heard the news and was moved to try to help the victims. He needed someone to whom the people would listen, someone who could say what had to be said and get the work done that had to be done and help the people who had to be helped.

"I knew," Luis Vigereaux said, "that Roberto was such a person, perhaps the only such person who would be willing to help."

And so the mercy project, which would eventually claim Roberto's life, began. He appeared on television. But he needed a staging area. The city agreed to give him Sixto Escobar Stadium.

"Bring what you can," he told the people. "Bring medicine . . . bring clothes . . . bring food . . . bring shoes . . . bring yourself to help us load. We need so much. Whatever you bring, we will use."

And the people of San Juan came. They walked through the heat, and they drove old cars and battered little trucks, and the mound of supplies grew and grew. Within two days, the first mercy planes left for Nicaragua.

Meanwhile, a ship had been chartered and

loaded. And as it prepared to steam away, unhappy stories began to drift back from Nicaragua. Not all the supplies that had been flown in, it was rumored, were getting through. Puerto Ricans, who had flown the planes, had no passports, and Nicaragua was in a state of panic.

"We have people there who must be protected. Black-market types must not be allowed to get their hands on these supplies," Clemente told Luis Vigereaux. "Someone must make sure—particularly before the ship gets there. I'm going on the next plane."

The plane they had rented was an old DC-7. It was scheduled to take off at 4 P.M. on December 31, 1972. Long before takeoff time, it was apparent that the plane needed more work. It had even taxied onto the runway and then turned back. The trouble, a mechanic who was at the airstrip that day conjectured, "had to do with both port[2] engines. We worked on them most of the afternoon."

The departure time was delayed an hour, and then two, and then three. At 9 P.M., even as the first stirrings of the annual New Year's Eve celebration were beginning in downtown San Juan, the DC-7 taxied onto the runway, received clearance, rumbled down the narrow concrete strip, and pulled away from the earth. It headed out over the Atlantic and banked toward Nicaragua, and its tiny lights disappeared on the horizon.

Just ninety seconds later, the tower at San Juan International Airport received this message from the DC-7 pilot, "We are coming back around."

Just that.

Nothing more.

And then there was a great silence.

---

2 **port:** left side.

"It was almost midnight," recalls Rudy Hernández, a former teammate of Roberto's. "We were having this party in my restaurant. Somebody turned on the radio, and the announcer was saying that Roberto's plane was feared missing. And then, because my place is on the beach, we saw these giant floodlights crisscrossing the waves, and we heard the sound of the helicopters and the little search planes."

Drawn by a common sadness, the people of San Juan began to make their way toward the beach, toward Punta Maldonado. A cold rain had begun to fall. It washed their faces and blended with the tears.

They came by the thousands, and they watched for three days. Towering waves boiled up and made the search virtually impossible. The U.S. Navy sent a team of expert divers into the area, but the battering of the waves defeated them too. Midway through the week, the pilot's body was found in the swift-moving currents to the north. On Saturday, bits of the cockpit were sighted.

And then—nothing else.

Rudy Hernández said, "I have never seen a time or a sadness like that. The streets were empty, the radios silent, except for the constant bulletins about Roberto. Traffic? Forget it. All of us cried. All of us who knew him, and even those who didn't, wept that week. There will never be another like Roberto."

Who was he . . . I mean really?

He was born in Carolina, Puerto Rico. Today the town has about 125,000 people, but when Roberto was born there in 1934, it was roughly one-sixth its current size.

María Isabella Casares is a school teacher. She has taught the children of Carolina for thirty years. Most of her teaching has been done in tenth-grade history classes. Carolina is her home, and its children are her children. And among all of those whom she calls her own (who are all the children she taught), Roberto Clemente was something even more special to her.

"His father was an overseer on a sugar plantation. He did not make much money," she explained in an empty classroom at Julio Coronado School. "But then, there are no rich children here. There never have been. Roberto was typical of them. I had known him when he was a small boy because my father had run a grocery store in Carolina and Roberto's parents used to shop there."

There is this thing that you have to know about María Isabella Casares before we hear more from her. What you have to know is that she is the model of what a teacher should be. Between her and her students even now, as back when Roberto attended her school, there is this common bond of mutual respect. Earlier in the day, I had watched her teach a class in the history of the Abolition Movement[3] in Puerto Rico. I don't speak much Spanish, but even to me it was clear that this is how a class should be, this is the kind of person who should teach, and these are the kinds of students such a teacher will produce.

With this as a background, what she has to say about Roberto Clemente carries much more impact.

"Each year," she said, "I let my students choose the seats they want to sit in. I remember the first time I saw Roberto. He was a very shy boy, and he went straight to the back of the room and chose the very last seat. Most of the time he would sit with his eyes down. He was an average student. But there was something very special about him. We would talk after class for hours. He wanted to

be an engineer, you know, and perhaps he could have been. But then he began to play softball, and one day he came to me and said, 'Teacher, I have a problem.'

"He told me that Pedro Zarrilla, who was one of our most prominent baseball people, had seen him play and that Pedro wanted him to sign a professional contract with the Santurce Crabbers. He asked me what he should do.

"I have thought about that conversation many times. I believe Roberto could have been almost anything, but God gave him a gift that few have, and he chose to use that gift. I remember that on that day I told him, 'This is your chance, Roberto. We are poor people in this town. This is your chance to do something. But if in your heart you prefer not to try, then, Roberto, that will be your problem—and your decision.'"

There was and there always remained a closeness between this boy-soon-to-be-a-man and his favorite teacher.

"Once, a few years ago, I was sick with a very bad back. Roberto, not knowing this, had driven over from Río Piedras, where his house was, to see me," Mrs. Casares recalled.

"Where is the teacher?" Roberto asked Mrs. Casares's stepdaughter that afternoon.

"Teacher is sick, Roberto. She is in bed."

"Teacher," Roberto said, pounding on the bedroom door, "get up and put on your clothes. We are going to the doctor whether you want to or not."

"I got dressed," Mrs. Casares told me, "and he picked me up like a baby and carried me in his arms to the car. He came every day for fifteen days, and most days he had to carry me. But I went to the doctor, and he treated me. Afterward, I said to the doctor that I wanted to pay the bill.

"'Mrs. Casares,' he told me, 'please don't

---

3 **Abolition Movement:** the movement to abolish slavery.

start with that Clemente or he will kill me. He has paid all your bills, and don't you dare tell him I have told you.'

"Well, Roberto was like that. We had been so close. You know, I think I was there the day he met Vera, the girl he later married. She was one of my students too. I was working part-time in the pharmacy, and he was already a baseball player by then, and one day Vera came into the store.

"'Teacher,' Roberto asked me, 'who is that girl?'

"'That's one of my students,' I told him. 'Now, don't you dare bother her. Go out and get someone to introduce you. Behave yourself.'

"He was so proper, you know. That's just what he did, and that's how he met her, and they were married here in Carolina in the big church on the square."

On the night Roberto Clemente's plane disappeared, Mrs. Casares was at home, and a delivery boy from the pharmacy stopped by and told her to turn on the radio and sit down. "I think something has happened to someone who is very close to you, Teacher, and I want to be here in case you need help."

María Isabella Casares heard the news. She is a brave woman, and months later, standing in front of the empty crypt in the cemetery at Carolina where Roberto Clemente was to have been buried, she said, "He was like a son to me. This is why I want to tell you about him. This is why you must make people—particularly our people, our Puerto Rican children—understand what he was. He was like my son, and he is all our sons in a way. We must make sure that the children never forget how beautiful a man he was."

The next person to touch Roberto Clemente was Pedro Zarrilla, who owned the Santurce club. He was the man who discovered Clemente on the country softball team, and he was the man who signed him for a four-hundred-dollar bonus.

"He was a skinny kid," Pedro Zarrilla recalls, "but even then he had those large, powerful hands, which we all noticed right away. He joined us, and he was nervous. But I watched him, and I said to myself, 'This kid can throw, and this kid can run, and this kid can hit. We will be patient with him.' The season had been through several games before I finally sent him in to play."

Luis Olmo remembers that game. Luis Olmo had been a major-league outfielder with the Brooklyn Dodgers. He had been a splendid ballplayer. Today he is in the insurance business in San Juan. He sat in his office and recalled very well that first moment when Roberto Clemente stepped up to bat.

"I was managing the other team. They had a man on base, and this skinny kid comes out. Well, we had never seen him, so we didn't really know how to pitch to him. I decided to throw him a few bad balls and see if he'd bite.

"He hit the first pitch. It was an outside fast ball and he never should have been able to reach it. But he hit it down the line for a double. He was the best bad-ball hitter I have ever seen, and if you ask major-league pitchers who are pitching today, they will tell you the same thing. After a while, it got so that I just told my pitchers to throw the ball down the middle because he was going to hit it no matter where they put it, and at least if he decided not to swing, we'd have a strike on him.

"I played in the big leagues. I know what I am saying. He was the greatest we ever had . . . maybe one of the greatest anyone ever had. Why did he have to die?"

Once Pedro Zarrilla turned him loose,

there was no stopping Roberto Clemente. As Clemente's confidence grew, he began to get better and better. He was the one the crowds came to see out at Sixto Escobar Stadium.

"You know, when Clemente was in the line-up," Pedro Zarrilla says, "there was always this undercurrent of excitement in the ball park. You knew that if he was coming to bat, he would do something spectacular. You knew that if he was on first base, he was going to try to get to second base. You knew that if he was playing right field and there was a man on third base, then that man on third base already knew what a lot of men on third base in the majors were going to find out— you don't try to get home against Roberto Clemente's arm."

Soon the major-league scouts began to make their moves, and in 1955 Roberto Clemente came to the Pittsburgh Pirates. He was the finest prospect the club had had in a long, long time. But the Pirates of those days were spectacular losers, and even Roberto Clemente couldn't turn them around overnight.

"I will never forget how fast he became a superstar in this town," says Bob Friend, who became a great Pirate pitcher. "Later he would have troubles because he was either hurt or thought he was hurt, and some people would say that he was loafing. But I know he gave it his best shot, and he helped make us winners."

The first winning year was 1960, when the Pirates won the pennant and went on to beat the Yankees in the seventh game of the World Series. Whitey Ford, who pitched against him twice in that Series, recalls that Roberto actually made himself look bad on an outside pitch to encourage Whitey to come back with it. "I did," Ford recalls, "and he unloaded. Another thing I remember is the way he ran out a routine ground ball in the last game, and when we were a little slow covering, he beat it out. It was something most people forget, but it made the Pirates' victory possible."

The season was over. Roberto Clemente had hit safely in every World Series game. He had batted over .300. He had been a superstar. But when they announced the Most Valuable Player Award voting, Roberto had finished a distant third.

"I really don't think he resented the fact that he didn't win it," Bob Friend says. "What hurt—and in this he was right—was how few votes he got. He felt that he simply wasn't being accepted. He brooded about that a lot. I think his attitude became one of 'well, I'm going to show them from now on so that they will never forget.'

"And you know, he sure did."

Roberto Clemente went home and married Vera. He felt less alone. Now he could go on and prove what it was he had to prove. And he was determined to prove it.

His moment finally came. It took eleven years for the Pirates to win a World Series berth again, and when they did in 1971, it was Roberto Clemente who led the way. I will never forget him as he was during that 1971 Series with the Orioles, a Series that the Pirates figured to lose and in which they, in fact, dropped the first two games down in Baltimore.

When they got back to Pittsburgh for the middle slice of the tournament, Roberto Clemente went to work and led his team. He was a superstar during the five games that followed. He was the big man in the Series. He was the MVP. He was everything he had ever dreamed of being on a ball field.

Most important of all, the entire country saw him do it on network television, and never again—even though nobody knew it would end so tragically soon—was anyone ever to doubt his ability.

The following year, Clemente ended the season by collecting his three thousandth hit. Only ten other men had ever done that in the entire history of baseball.

"When I think of Roberto now," says Willie Stargell, his closest friend on the Pirates, "I think of the kind of man he was. There was nothing phony about him. He had his own ideas about how life should be lived, and if you didn't see it that way, then he let you know in so many ways, without words, that it was best you each go your separate ways.

"He was a man who chose his friends carefully. His was a friendship worth having. I don't think many people took the time and the trouble to try to understand him, and I'll admit it wasn't easy. But he was worth it.

"The way he died, you know, I mean on that plane carrying supplies to Nicaraguans who'd been dying in that earthquake, well, I wasn't surprised he'd go out and do something like that. I wasn't surprised he'd go. I just never thought what happened could happen to him.

"But I know this. He lived a full life. And if he knew at that moment what the Lord had decided, well, I really believe he would have said, 'I'm ready.'"

He was thirty-eight years old when he died. He touched the heart of Puerto Rico in a way that few people ever could. He touched a lot of other hearts too. He touched hearts that beat inside people of all colors of skin.

Discussion

1. What events led up to Clemente's death on December 31, 1972?

2. How did the people of Puerto Rico react to the news of Clemente's missing plane? Why do you think they reacted this way?

3. What two people contributed most to Clemente's success? Explain how.

4. Give one example of Clemente's kindness and thoughtfulness for others.

5. During Clemente's early career in Puerto Rico, why did one team manager tell his players to throw the ball down the middle when they pitched to him?

6. In 1960, even though Clemente hit safely in every World Series game, he was not voted the Most Valuable Player Award. Why did this hurt him so much? When did he finally win the MVP Award?

7. Almost from the beginning, you knew that Clemente died tragically. Did this knowledge spoil the rest of the narrative for you? Explain why or why not.

Composition

1. Pretend you are a baseball coach. Write the advice you would give to your team members. In one paragraph tell what personality traits they will need to become successful players. Use specific examples from Clemente's life to support your points.

2. "Those who really want to be winners . . . can be!" Write several paragraphs in which you either agree or disagree with this statement. Begin by briefly describing how Roberto Clemente's experiences support this statement. Then state whether you think he is an example for all people, or just an exception to the rule. Then in one or more paragraphs give reasons why you think the statement is true or false by using examples from the story or other true-life incidents—perhaps even a personal experience. In a final paragraph, summarize what you have written.

Vocabulary

A SYNONYM is a word which means the same, or nearly the same, as another word. One synonym, though, is sometimes better than another in certain instances. For example, some synonyms for *small* are: "minute," "petite," "tiny," and "miniature." If you were describing a baby's hand, the word *tiny* obviously would be better than *minute* or *miniature*.

A. On a separate sheet of paper, write the words below from "Roberto Clemente—A Bittersweet Memoir." Then copy two synonyms of each word from a dictionary.

carelessly	location	supervisor
present	curved	touched
surmised	leading	tragically

B. In each sentence below, based on the Roberto Clemente story, one word is *italicized*. On the same paper, replace the *italicized* word with a synonym from the list in Exercise A.

1. The author began his story at the *site* of Clemente's death.
2. Clemente was not a man to make friends *casually*.
3. The mechanic *conjectured* that the problem with Clemente's plane had to do with both port engines.
4. The plane headed out over the Atlantic and *banked* toward Nicaragua.
5. At the time of Clemente's birth, his hometown was only one-sixth of its *current* size.
6. Clemente's father was an *overseer* on a sugar plantation.
7. Pedro Zarrilla, a *prominent* sportsman, first approached Clemente about a baseball career.

The desert diamondback snake is feared for its deadly poison by both animals and people. But what about the snake itself . . . what does it fear? Who are its enemies?

The Life and Death of a Western Gladiator

CHARLES G. FINNEY

HE WAS BORN on a summer morning in the shady mouth of a cave. Three others were born with him, another male and two females. Each was about five inches long and slimmer than a lead pencil.

Their mother left them a few hours after they were born. A day after that his brother and sisters left him also. He was all alone. Nobody cared whether he lived or died. His tiny brain was very dull. He had no arms or legs. His skin was delicate. Nearly everything that walked on the ground or burrowed in it, that flew in the air or swam in the water or climbed trees was his enemy. But he didn't know that. He knew nothing at all. He was aware of his own existence, and that was the sum of his knowledge.

The direct rays of the sun could, in a short time, kill him. If the temperature dropped too low, he would freeze. Without food he would starve. Without moisture he would die of dehydration. If a man or a horse stepped on him, he would be crushed. If anything chased him, he could run neither very far nor very fast.

Thus it was at the hour of his birth. Thus it would be, with modifications, all his life.

But against these drawbacks he had certain qualifications that fitted him to be a competitive creature of this world and equipped him for its warfare. He could exist a long time without food or water. His very smallness at birth protected him when he most needed protection. Instinct provided him with what he lacked in experience. In order to eat he first had to kill, and he was eminently adapted for killing. In sacs in his jaws he secreted a virulent[1] poison. To inject that poison he had two fangs, hollow and pointed. Without that poison and those fangs he would have been among the most helpless creatures on earth. With them he was among the deadliest.

He was, of course, a baby rattlesnake, a desert diamondback, named Crotalus atrox by the herpetologists Baird and Girard and so listed in the *Catalogue of North American Reptiles* in its issue of 1853. He was grayish brown in color with a series of large dark

---

1 **virulent** (vir′ yə lənt): deadly.

diamond-shaped blotches on his back. His tail was white with five black crossbands. It had a button on the end of it.

Little Crotalus lay in the dust in the mouth of his cave. Some of his kinfolk lay there too. It was their home. That particular tribe of rattlers had lived there for scores of years.

The cave had never been seen by a white man.

Sometimes as many as two hundred rattlers occupied the den. Sometimes the numbers shrunk to as few as forty or fifty.

The tribe members did nothing at all for each other except breed. They hunted singly; they never shared their food. They derived some automatic degree of safety from their numbers, but their actions were never concerted toward using their numbers to any end. If an enemy attacked one of them, the others did nothing about it.

Young Crotalus's brother was the first of the litter to go out into the world and the first to die. He achieved a distance of fifty feet from the den when a Sonoran racer, four feet long and hungry, came upon him. The little rattler, despite his poison fangs, was a tidbit. The racer, long skilled in such arts, snatched him up by the head and swallowed him down. Powerful digestive juices in the racer's stomach did the rest. Then the racer, appetite whetted, prowled around until it found one of Crotalus's little sisters. She went the way of the brother.

Nemesis[2] of the second sister was a chaparral cock. This cuckoo, or road runner as it is called, found the baby amid some rocks, uttered a cry of delight, scissored it by the neck, shook it until it was almost lifeless, banged and pounded it upon a rock until life

had indeed left it, and then gulped it down.

Crotalus, somnolent[3] in a cranny of the cave's mouth, neither knew nor cared. Even if he had, there was nothing he could have done about it.

On the fourth day of his life he decided to go out into the world himself. He rippled forth uncertainly, the transverse plates on his belly serving as legs.

He could see things well enough within his limited range, but a five-inch-long snake can command no great field of vision. He had an excellent sense of smell. But, having no ears, he was stone deaf. On the other hand, he had a pit, a deep pock mark between eye and nostril. Unique, this organ was sensitive to animal heat. In pitch blackness, Crotalus, by means of the heat messages recorded in his pit, could tell whether another animal was near and could also judge its size. That was better than an ear.

The single button on his tail could not, of course, yet rattle. Crotalus wouldn't be able to rattle until that button had grown into three segments. Then he would be able to buzz.

He had a wonderful tongue. It looked like

---

2 **Nemesis** (nem′ə sis): one who brings disaster.

3 **somnolent** (som′ nə lənt): drowsy.

an exposed nerve and was probably exactly that. It was forked, and Crotalus thrust it in and out as he traveled. It told him things that neither his eyes nor his nose nor his pit told him.

Snake fashion, Crotalus went forth, not knowing where he was going, for he had never been anywhere before. Hunger was probably his prime mover. In order to satisfy that hunger he had to find something smaller than himself and kill it.

He came upon a baby lizard sitting in the sand. Eyes, nose, pit, and tongue told Crotalus it was there. Instinct told him what it was and what to do. Crotalus gave a tiny one-inch strike and bit the lizard. His poison killed it. He took it by the head and swallowed it. Thus was his first meal.

During his first two years Crotalus grew rapidly. He attained a length of two feet; his tail had five rattles on it and its button. He rarely bothered with lizards any more, preferring baby rabbits, chipmunks, and round-tailed ground squirrels. Because of his slow locomotion he could not run down these agile little things. He had to contrive, instead, to be where they were when they would pass. Then he struck swiftly, injected his poison, and ate them after they died.

At two he was formidable. He had grown past the stage where a racer or a road runner could safely tackle him. He had grown to the size where other desert dwellers—coyotes, foxes, coatis, wildcats—knew it was better to leave him alone.

And, at two, Crotalus became a father, his life being regulated by cycles. His cycles were plantlike. The peach tree does not "know" when it is time to flower, but flower it does because its cycle orders it to do so.

In the same way, Crotalus did not "know" when it was time for young desert diamond-back rattlers to pair off and breed. But his cycle knew.

He found "her" on a rainy morning. Crotalus's courtship at first was sinuous and subtle, slow and stealthy. Then suddenly it became dynamic. A period of exhaustion followed. Two metabolic machines had united to produce new metabolic machines.

Of that physical union six new rattlesnakes were born. Thus Crotalus, at two, had carried out his major primary function: he had reproduced his kind. In two years he had experienced everything that was reasonably possible for desert diamondback rattlesnakes to experience except death.

He had not experienced death for the simple reason that there had never been an opportunity for anything bigger and stronger than himself to kill him. Now, at two, because he was so formidable, that opportunity became more and more unlikely.

He grew more slowly in the years following his initial spurt. At the age of twelve he was five feet long. Few of the other rattlers in his den were older or larger than he.

He had a castanet of fourteen segments. It had been broken off occasionally in the past, but with each new molting a new segment appeared.

His first skin-shedding back in his babyhood had been a bewildering experience. He did not know what was happening. His eyes clouded over until he could not see. His skin thickened and dried until it cracked in places. His pit and his nostrils ceased to function. There was only one thing to do and that was to get out of that skin.

Crotalus managed it by nosing against the bark of a shrub until he forced the old skin down over his head, bunching it like the rolled top of a stocking around his neck. Then he pushed around among rocks and

The Life and Death of a Western Gladiator **511**

sticks and branches, literally crawling out of his skin by slow degrees. Wriggling free at last, he looked like a brand-new snake. His skin was bright and satiny, his eyes and nostrils were clear, his pit sang with sensation.

For the rest of his life he was to molt three or four times a year. Each time he did it he felt as if he had been born again.

At twelve he was a magnificent reptile. Not a single scar defaced his rippling symmetry. He was diabolically beautiful and deadly poison.

His venom was his only weapon, for he had no power of constriction. Yellowish in color, his poison was odorless and tasteless. It was a highly complex mixture of proteids,[4] each in itself direly toxic. His venom worked on the blood. The more poison he injected with a bite, the more dangerous the wound. The pain rendered by his bite was instantaneous, and the shock accompanying it was profound. Swelling began immediately, to be followed by a ghastly oozing. Injected directly into a large vein, his poison brought death quickly, for the victim died when it reached his heart.

At the age of twenty Crotalus was the oldest and largest rattler in his den. He was six feet long and weighed thirteen pounds. His whole world was only about a mile in radius. He had fixed places where he avoided the sun when it was hot and he was away from his cave. He knew his hunting grounds thoroughly, every game trail, every animal burrow.

He was a fine old machine, perfectly adapted to his surroundings, accustomed to a life of leisure and comfort. He dominated his little world.

---

4 **proteids**: substances in plants and animals necessary for life.

The mighty seasonal rhythms of the desert were as vast pulsations, and the lives of the rattlesnakes were attuned to them. Spring sun beat down, spring rains fell, and, as the plants of the desert ended their winter hibernations, so did the vipers in their lair. The plants opened forth and budded; the den "opened" too, and the snakes crawled forth. The plants fertilized each other, and new plants were born. The snakes bred, and new snakes were produced. The desert was repopulated.

In the autumn the plants began to close; in the same fashion the snake den began to close, the reptiles returned to it, lay like lingering blossoms about its entrance for a while, then disappeared within it when winter came. There they slept until summoned forth by a new spring.

Crotalus was twenty years old. He was in the golden age of his viperhood.

But men were approaching. Spilling out of their cities, men were settling in that part of the desert where Crotalus lived. They built roads and houses, set up fences, dug for water, planted crops.

They homesteaded the land. They brought new animals with them—cows, horses, dogs, cats, barnyard fowl.

The roads they built were death traps for the desert dwellers. Every morning new dead bodies lay on the roads, the bodies of the things the men had run over and crushed in their vehicles.

That summer Crotalus met his first dog. It was a German shepherd which had been reared on a farm in the Midwest and there had gained the reputation of being a snake-killer. Black snakes, garter snakes, pilots, water snakes; it delighted in killing them all. It would seize them by the middle, heedless of their tiny teeth, and shake them violently until they died.

This dog met Crotalus face to face in the desert at dusk. Crotalus had seen coyotes aplenty and feared them not. Neither did the dog fear Crotalus, although Crotalus then was six feet long, as thick in the middle as a motorcycle tire, and had a head the size of a man's clenched fist. Also this snake buzzed and buzzed and buzzed.

The dog was brave, and a snake was a snake. The German shepherd snarled and attacked. Crotalus struck him in the under-jaw; his fangs sank in almost half an inch and squirted big blobs of hematoxic[5] poison into the tissues of the dog's flesh.

The shepherd bellowed with pain, backed off, groveled with his jaws in the desert sand, and attacked again. He seized Crotalus somewhere by the middle of his body and tried to flip him in the air and shake him as, in the past, he had shaken slender black snakes to their death. In return, he received another poison-blurting stab in his flank and a third in the belly and a fourth in the eye as the terrible, writhing snake bit wherever it could sink its fangs.

The German shepherd had enough. He dropped the big snake and in sick, agonizing bewilderment crawled somehow back to his master's homestead and died.

The homesteader looked at his dead dog and became alarmed. If there was a snake around big enough to kill a dog that size, it could also kill a child and probably a man. It was something that had to be eliminated.

The homesteader told his fellow farmers, and they agreed to initiate a war of extermination against the snakes.

The campaign during the summer was sporadic. The snakes were scattered over the desert, and it was only by chance that the men came upon them. Even so, at summer's end, twenty-six of the vipers had been killed.

When autumn came, the men decided to look for the rattlers' den and execute mass slaughter. The homesteaders had become desert-wise and knew what to look for.

They found Crotalus's lair without too much trouble—a rock outcropping on a slope that faced the south. Castoff skins were in evidence in the bushes. Bees flew idly in and out of the den's mouth. Convenient benches and shelves of rock were at hand where the snakes might lie for a final sunning in the autumn air.

5 **hematoxic**: poisoning the blood.

The Life and Death of a Western Gladiator **513**

They killed the three rattlers they found at the den when they first discovered it. They made plans to return in a few more days when more of the snakes had congregated. They decided to bring along dynamite with them and blow up the mouth of the den so that the snakes within would be sealed there forever and the snakes without would have no place to find refuge.

On the day the men chose to return nearly fifty desert diamondbacks were gathered at the portals of the cave. The men shot them, clubbed them, smashed them with rocks. Some of the rattlers escaped the attack and crawled into the den.

Crotalus had not yet arrived for the autumn rendezvous. He came that night. The den's mouth was a shattered mass of rock, for the men had done their dynamiting well. Dead members of his tribe lay everywhere. Crotalus nosed among them, tongue flicking as he slid slowly along.

There was no access to the cave anymore. He spent the night outside among the dead. The morning sun warmed him and awakened him. He lay there at full length. He had no place to go.

The sun grew hotter upon him and instinctively he began to slide toward some dark shade. Then his senses warned him of some animal presence near by; he stopped, half coiled, raised his head and began to rattle. He saw two upright figures. He did not know what they were because he had never seen men before.

"That's the granddaddy of them all," said one of the homesteaders. "It's a good thing we came back." He raised his shotgun.

Discussion

1. What factors threaten the survival of a baby rattlesnake? What things provide the rattlesnake with some chance of survival?

2. The author wants the reader to understand why a snake behaves the way it does. He makes it clear that the snake does not do something because it *decides* to do it. Rather, the snake's natural instincts direct its life. Find examples in the narrative which prove this fact.

3. Why do you think Crotalus and the dog have no fear of each other?

4. How is Crotalus like a gladiator?

5. How do you know the men kill Crotalus? Why did they have to kill him?

6. What do you think is the author's attitude toward snakes?

7. How does this narrative account of rattlesnakes differ from a discussion of rattlesnakes that you might find in an encyclopedia or textbook? What would be the same in both accounts?

Vocabulary   Words have jobs to do in sentences. In these jobs, called WORD FUNCTIONS, words work as nouns, which are naming words; verbs, which are action or linking words; or adjectives which are describing words.

A. On a separate sheet of paper, make three columns. Label the column at the left *Nouns,* the column in the middle *Adjectives,* and the column at the right *Verbs.* Put each word from the list below into the proper column. (Note: A word might fit into more than one column. If you need help, use a dictionary.)

black	forked	rattle	strike
buzz	formidable	ripple	subtle
crawl	grayish	sac	swallow
Crotalus	hibernate	satiny	toxic
deadly	hunt	sinuous	venom
deaf	inject	slim	viper
diamondback	instinct	snake	virulent
dull	pit (pock mark)	somnolent	water
fangs	racer	stealthy	writhe

B. Choose four words from each list of your answers for Exercise A. Write a sentence for each word, using it correctly.

Charles G. Finney 1905 —

Charles Finney was born in Sedalia, Missouri, and attended the University of Missouri for a year and a half before enlisting in the army. He spent his time in the service stationed with the 15th Infantry in China. His best-known book, *The Circus of Dr. Lao,* which was awarded the first American Booksellers' Association prize for most original novel, resulted mostly from his experiences in China. His short story, "The Life and Death of a Western Gladiator," first appeared in *Harper's* magazine in 1958. Not surprisingly, one of Finney's hobbies is catching snakes.

from A Peculiar Treasure

EDNA FERBER

THERE NEVER had been a woman reporter in Appleton. The town, broad-minded though it was, put me down as definitely cuckoo. Not crazy, but strange. Big-town newspapers, such as the *Chicago Tribune* and the *Milwaukee Sentinel,* employed women on their editorial and re-portorial staffs, but usually these were what is known as special or feature writers, or they conducted question-and-answer columns, advice to the lovelorn, society columns or woman's pages. But at seventeen on the *Appleton Crescent,* I found myself covering a regular news beat like any man reporter.

I often was embarrassed, sometimes frightened, frequently offended and offensive, but I enjoyed it, and knowing what I know today, I wouldn't swap that year and a half of small-town newspaper reporting for any four years of college education. I'm a blank when it comes to Latin, I can't bound[1] New York State, and I count on my fingers, but in those eighteen months I learned to

read what lay behind the look that veiled people's faces, I learned how to sketch in human beings with a few rapid words, I learned to see, to observe, to remember; learned, in short, the first rules of writing. And I was the town scourge.[2] . . .

Those three dollars per week were earned. Eight in the morning found me at my desk. Lest that should have a rich and commanding sound I hasten to add that my desk was a shaky pine table in the darkest, smallest and dustiest corner of that dark, small and dusty room which constituted the *Crescent* editorial department. We worked underground, like moles. Why, in this sunny little Wisconsin town, Sam Ryan and his father James Ryan before him had chosen to install their newspaper plant in a basement, I can't imagine. Thrift, probably. There it was below the street level at the corner of College Avenue and Morrison Street.

There were five little stone steps leading down to the front office. By the very way in

---

1 **bound:** here, name the states that have common boundary lines with New York.

2 **scourge:** one who inflicts pain.

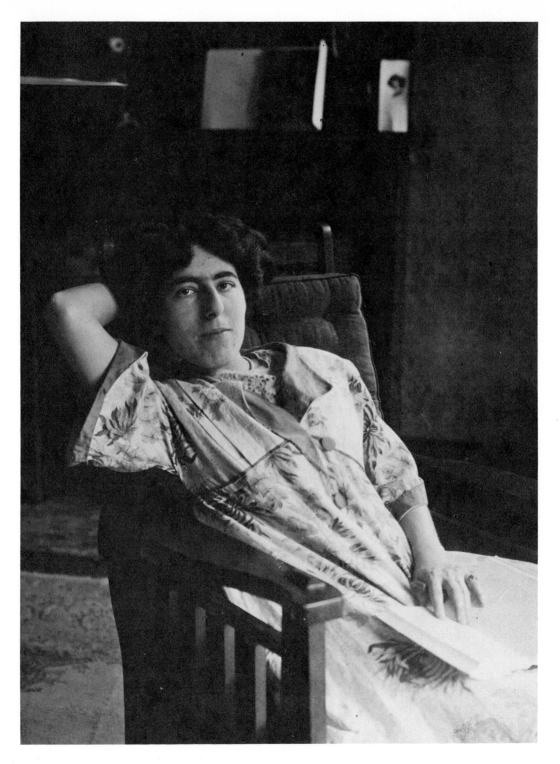

from *A Peculiar Treasure* 517

which a reporter hurled himself down those steps, you could sense whether he had a good story or not. . . .

Eight o'clock found me pounding down Morrison Street on my way to the office. Before eight-thirty the city editor had handed me my assignment sheet for the day. Dull-enough stuff, usually, for I was the least important cog in the *Crescent* office machine. When it came to news stories, the city editor came first. He had his regular run—the juiciest one, of course. Next came Byron Beveridge. All the really succulent bits fell to them—the Elks Club up above Wharton's China Store on College Avenue, where the gay blades of the town assembled; Moriarty's pool shack, the Sherman House, the city jail, the fire-engine house, the Hub Clothing Store, the coroner's office, the mayor's office, Peter Thom's stationery and tobacco store, Little's Drug Store, the Sherman Barber Shop—these were the rich cupboards from which the real food of the day's news was dispensed. There you found the facts and gossip of business, politics, scandal, petty crime.

To me fell the crumbs. They gave me the daily courthouse run, and I wondered why until I discovered that it was up in the Chute at the far end of town, a good mile and a half distant. You could take the bumpy little local street car, but that cost five cents one way, and the office furnished no carfare for daily scheduled runs. Sixty cents a week was too serious a bite out of a three-dollar weekly wage. I walked it. I walked miles and miles and miles, daily. At the end of that first year my plumpness had melted almost to streamline proportions. . . .

The courthouse, the county jail up in Chute at the other end of town, these weren't nourishing news sources, but I had to cover them. Such criminals as were housed in the tree-shaded county jail were there for crimes which already had been disposed of as news. Courthouse records were made up of dry bits such as real-estate transfers in the town and the near-by farm districts. There was nothing very exhilarating about jotting down items such as "State of Wisconsin, Winnebago County, Such-and-Such Township, sixty acres northeast section, etc." But having plodded the mile and a half up there, I gleaned what I could. Bailiffs, clerks, courthouse hangers-on were a roughish tobacco-chewing crew with little enough to do. I was fair game for them. As I clattered up and down the long corridors paved with tiles, in and out of the land record office, the county clerk's office, here and there, making a lot of noise with my hurried determined step, one of the men in a group called out to me in greeting one morning, "Hi, Boots!" And Boots I remained as long as I worked on the *Appleton Crescent*.

I ranged the town, ferreting out corners too obscure or too obvious for the loftier glance of Meyer or Beveridge. Sometimes rich morsels repaid me for my pains. If space permitted, I was allowed such feature or special stories as struck my fancy. This sort of half-imaginative writing turned out to be excellent practice for later fiction-writing use. I raked up tear-jerkers about the Poor Farm at the edge of town; when Barnum & Bailey's circus came to town, I spent the day in the back tents with the performers. I ate dinner with the Living Skeleton, the Fat Lady, the clowns and the trapeze artists, and very good it was, too. The tents were miracles of cleanliness, the circus people friendly and warmhearted. My story was the trite and shopworn stuff about the bareback rider in the pink tights and spangles sitting in her tent just before the show sewing a fine seam on her baby's dress or mending her lion-tamer husband's socks, or some such matter. But it was all new to me, and true, so perhaps it had something of freshness, as well. . . .

Celebrities didn't come our way often. When Houdini, the Handcuff King, arrived with his show, he got shorter shrift than he deserved, being a home-town boy. Before my day he had been a local product, Harry Weiss, the son of a Russian Jewish rabbi. Failing to find him at his hotel or at the theater, I encountered him by chance on College Avenue at the drugstore corner just across from the *Crescent* office. Outside the store was the usual slot machine containing chocolate and chewing gum. As he chatted affably with me, Houdini leaned carelessly against this. At the end of the interview he dropped a cold metal object into my hand.

"There's the padlock to this slot machine," he said. "Better give it to the drugstore man. Somebody'll steal all his chewing gum."

I hadn't seen so much as a movement of his fingers. Tottering with admiration, I went back to the office to write my story. . . .

Big news rarely broke in our well conducted little town. I used to pray for a murder, but I never got an answer to prayer. In all the years of our life there, not a single murder or even a robbery of anything more than a turnip field, an apple orchard or perhaps a trinket filched from a store counter ever marred the peace of the thriving Wisconsin town. The Appletonians worked, lived, were content, behaved as civilization does when it is not frightened and resentful.

I must have been quite obnoxious but I did bring in the news. As an amateur detective in a farce gets down on his knees to examine footprints in a cracker-barrel robbery, so I made much of small events and motivations.

Housewives fled at my approach, clerks dodged behind counters, policemen turned their coats inside out and hid their badges, my best friends grew wary of confidences. Life for me narrowed down to this. It was news or it was nothing. I talked to everyone; the railroad-crossing gatekeeper, the farmers in town, the interurban-car motorman. . . .

By two-thirty or three the paper was put to bed, the press was rolling. The chatter of the linotype, the locking of the forms, the thump-thump of the press were plain in our ears as we sat at our typewriters in the front office, for the open door between us and the back shop made one big room of the whole.

Townspeople slammed and scuffed up and down the stone steps, in and out of the office, all day long. I early learned that the big story isn't the one that is brought to you. The things people want you to print in your paper usually are the things of interest to few besides themselves. One of the angles that makes newspaper reporting so chancy, exhilarating and absorbing is the chase. The person you want most to talk to frequently doesn't want to talk to you, though it is an amazing fact that almost everyone, properly approached, will tell you almost anything.

Half the people I encountered preferred not to have me discover the very thing I wanted most to know. It wasn't long before I learned, from that quick appraising look at my victim's face, to gauge his character and to shape my approach in accordance. If he didn't want to talk, he must be made to talk by wheedling, bribing, cajoling, threatening, playing for sympathy. Roughly, the approach was one of these:

1. I understand your reluctance to talk about this. But I have to turn in some kind of story. I can't go back to the office without

from *A Peculiar Treasure* **519**

it. Don't you think we'd better get it straight from you?

2. It's going to be in the newspaper anyway. Take my advice. Talk.

3. I wish you'd help me out on this. If I come back without a story, I'll lose my job.

4. I think—if you don't mind my saying so—that you've taken a wonderful stand in this matter. I'd like to be able to write it from your viewpoint because it seems to me to be the only one worth while.

5. Perhaps if you'll tell me all about this, frankly, we can help you.

If all this sounds revolting, it is as nothing compared to coming into the office without your story. . . .

I learned to see and remember details without taking notes. If I had to take them, it was done as surreptitiously[3] as possible in the presence of the person being interviewed, or after I had left and was on my way back to the office. A trained reporter, in an interview, takes notes only if he must. It is only on the stage that a reporter whips out a notebook and begins to scribble feverishly. Most newspaper people do their note-taking on a little folded sheaf of yellow copy paper grabbed up on their way out of the office. If he must use this homemade pad, he usually lets his pencil scrawl unguided, his gaze meeting the eye of the person speaking, and responding to it. To one being interviewed there is something disconcerting about the sight of that busy pencil traveling over the blank paper. His speech hesitates, falters, the flow of revelation ceases. People tell you more when you are looking at them with understanding or sympathy. It is a kind of hypnotism. . . .

Now Meyer, the little blond city editor, left for his old job in Milwaukee, fed up with his small-town experience. He turned over to me his job as Appleton correspondent for the *Milwaukee Journal.* It became my duty to telegraph or telephone the briefest possible line on any local happening of consequence. This was called *querying* the paper. If they found the story of sufficient importance, they would telephone or telegraph an order for the number of words they thought the story rated. Less immediate stuff I mailed in on the afternoon southbound train. Semi-feature stuff I pasted up and mailed in from time to time.

I felt enormously important and professional. Among other things the Lawrence University football games had to be covered, as well as the Ryan High School games. This was a tough assignment for a girl. It had to be caught play by play. At first I was guilty of using such feminine adjectives as *splendid* and *lovely,* but after a bit I caught on to the sport writer's lingo, and I don't think that the *Milwaukee Journal* readers found the Appleton football correspondence too sissy.

Paul Hunter was the new city editor, imported from out of town. A moist, loose-hung man, eyeglassed, loquacious.[4] He didn't like me. He didn't want a self-dramatizing Girl Reporter around the place. He began a systematic campaign. My run was cut down. My stories were slashed. My suggestions were ignored or pooh-poohed. I was in the doghouse. Midway through my summer vacation of two weeks I got word that I needn't return. I was fired. I can see why Hunter didn't want a girl around the place when a second man reporter could cover more varied ground. My rather embellished style of writing had no appeal for Hunter. He wanted the news and no nonsense.

---

3 **surreptitiously:** secretly.

4 **loquacious** (lō kwā′ shəs): very talkative.

The bottom had dropped right out of my world and I was left dangling in space. . . .

I had been fired just in time, but I didn't know it then. My heart was broken.

That summer I tried to interest myself in Appleton life (as a layman. I! I who had once walked so proud as a newspaper reporter!). But the world was flat and flavorless. Eighteen years old. In another six months I would be nineteen. Withered old age stared me in the face.

At the very nadir[5] of this despair there appeared a message timed like a last-minute reprieve in a bad melodrama. It was from Henry Campbell, the managing editor of the *Milwaukee Journal*. He asked me to come to work on the *Journal* immediately at fifteen dollars a week, and to call him on the telephone in Milwaukee at once.

In order to telephone long-distance one had to go to the main office of the telephone company. I held the telegram in my hand. The family sat there, looking at me—my father, my mother, my sister. There is a curiously strong bond in Jewish families. They cling together. Jewish parents are

possessive, Jewish sons and daughters are filial[6] to the point of sentimentality. I wonder how I ever had the courage to leave. . . . Until now we had clung together, we four Ferbers. I am certain I never should have written if I had not gone. I was wrung by an agony of pity as I looked at my father's face.

"You go on, Pete," he said. "You go if you want to."

It is lucky that youth is ruthless, or the work of the world never would be done.

I walked down to the telephone company's office and put in my call for the *Journal*'s managing editor. It took some minutes to get him. As I waited in the booth, my heart beating fast, a townsman who had come into the office stood chatting with the chief operator.

"That's Feber's girl, isn't it?"

"Yeh."

"She the one is a reporter?"

"Yeh, she's calling up Milwaukee, the *Journal* there, she says they want her to go to work for them in Milwaukee."

The other man ruminated. "Wonder a girl like that wouldn't try to do something decent, like teaching school."

---

5 **nadir** (nā′ dər): the lowest point.

6 **filial** (fil′ ē əl): loyalty and respect for parents.

Discussion

1. In her first job as a reporter on the *Appleton Crescent,* Edna Ferber refers to herself as the "town scourge." Explain how this phrase was an accurate description of her.

2. Why was the "courthouse run" a difficult assignment?

3. What were some ways Edna Ferber got people to talk when they didn't want to?

4. Why was she fired from the *Appleton Crescent?*

5. How did the local townspeople feel about a woman being a reporter? Find specific examples from the story. Why do you think they felt that way?

Writer's Craft

You are a great fan of a particular movie star. You want to know as much about that person as you can. Then you hit the jackpot! In the library you see a book which was written by the star, telling about his or her background and early experiences. You have just found the star's AUTOBIOGRAPHY.

Most autobiographers deal with their public lives. In other words, the facts a person includes in his or her autobiography are mainly about how he or she became, for example, a movie star, a writer, a doctor, or a scientist. Autobiographies also tell the highlights of a person's career.

1. This selection is only one chapter in Edna Ferber's autobiography. What is her age in this chapter?
2. What are the three major events that happened in this section of her autobiography that helped her develop as a famous writer?
3. Which aspects of Ferber's personality contributed to her being a good reporter? Why do you think there are no negative traits presented?

Composition

1. Pretend you are the editor of your local newspaper. Members of a high school journalism class visit you because they are interested in becoming reporters. Based on this selection, write the advice you would give them. First tell them some of the personal qualities necessary in becoming successful reporters. Then end by giving them some practical advice about writing for their own high school newspaper. You might, for instance, tell them how to take notes and how to get people to talk.
2. Imagine yourself as a famous person forty years from now. Select two or three incidents from your junior high school years which you would want to emphasize in *your* autobiography. Write about these incidents in the order in which they occurred in your life. Explain why each incident helped make you the person you are.

Vocabulary

CONTEXT CLUES are hints about the general meaning of an unfamiliar word that are given by the words surrounding it. There are many different types of context clues. Several of these types have been covered in earlier pages of this book. If you need more practice, review the information on the following pages before starting the exercise.

Each sentence below, based on this selection from *A Peculiar Treasure,* contains one *italicized* word. On a separate sheet of paper, copy all the *italicized* words and write their general meanings. If you do not know a word, look for context clues.

1. The man *ruminated,* or wondered, why a girl wouldn't try something decent, like teaching school.

2. I walked miles and miles, daily. At the end of that first year my *obesity* had melted away and my figure had taken on a streamlined appearance.

3. Housewives fled at my approach, clerks dodged behind counters, policemen hid their badges, and my best friends grew *wary* about telling me their secrets.

4. I ranged the town *ferreting* out corners too obscure for the other reporters.

5. The person I interviewed often had to be threatened, bribed, or *cajoled* to give me a story.

6. Since I couldn't let them see me take notes, I did it as *surreptitiously* as possible.

7. My rather *embellished* style of writing bothered Hunter, who wanted straight news and nothing more.

Edna Ferber 1887—1968

Edna Ferber was a novelist, short story writer, journalist, and playwright. Rather than attend college she worked on newspapers in Milwaukee and Chicago. Her first novel, *Dawn O'Hara,* was based on her journalistic experiences. Then in 1924, she received the Pulitzer Prize for the novel, *So Big.* Many of her books such as *Giant* and *Showboat* were made into movies. She also wrote numerous short stories, a number of Broadway plays, and two autobiographies including *A Peculiar Treasure.*

A scientist is not always a white-coated man in a fancy laboratory full of bottles, machines, and computers. In fact, one of the greatest scientific discoveries ever made—one which opened the door to the Atomic Age—was made by a woman and her husband working in a freezing, broken-down shed.

Four Years in a Shed

EVE CURIE

A MAN CHOSEN at random from a crowd to read an account of the discovery of radium would not have doubted for one moment that radium existed. . . .

The physicist colleagues of the Curies received the news in slightly different fashion. The special properties of polonium and radium upset fundamental theories in which scientists had believed for centuries. How was one to explain the spontaneous radiation of the radioactive bodies? The discovery upset a world of acquired knowledge and contradicted the most firmly established ideas on the composition of matter. Thus the physicist kept on the reserve. He was violently interested in Pierre and Marie's work; he could perceive its infinite developments, but before being convinced he awaited the acquisition of decisive results.

The attitude of the chemist was even more downright. By definition, a chemist only believes in the existence of a new substance when he has seen the substance, touched it, weighed and examined it, confronted it with acids, bottled it, and when he has determined its "atomic weight."[1]

Now, up to the present, nobody had "seen" radium. Nobody knew the atomic weight of radium. And the chemists, faithful to their principles, concluded: "No atomic weight, no radium. Show us some radium and we will believe you."

To show polonium and radium to the incredulous,[2] to prove to the world the existence of their "children," and to complete their own conviction, M. and Mme.[3] Curie were now to labor for four years.

The aim was to obtain pure radium and polonium. In the most strongly radioactive products the scientists had prepared, these substances figured only in imperceptible traces. Pierre and Marie already knew the

---

1 **atomic weight:** the average weight of an atom of an element.
2 **incredulous** (in krej′ ə ləs): disbelieving.
3 **M. and Mme.:** Mister and Mrs. (*Monsieur* and *Madame* in French).

method by which they could hope to isolate the new metals, but the separation could not be made except by treating very large quantities of crude material.

Here arose three agonizing questions:

How were they to get a sufficient quantity of ore? What premises could they use to effect their treatment? What money was there to pay the inevitable cost of the work?

Pitchblende, in which polonium and radium were hidden, was a costly ore, treated at the St. Joachimsthal mines in Bohemia for the extraction of uranium salts used in the manufacture of glass. Tons of pitchblende would cost a great deal: a great deal too much for the Curie household.

Ingenuity was to make up for wealth. According to the expectation of the two scientists, the extraction of uranium should leave, intact in the ore, such traces of polonium and radium as the ore contains. There was no reason why these traces should not be found in the residue.[4] And, whereas crude pitchblende was costly, its residue after treatment had very slight value. By asking an Austrian colleague for a recommendation to the directors of the mine of St. Joachimsthal, would it not be possible to obtain a considerable quantity of such residue for a reasonable price?

It was simple enough, but somebody had to think about it.

It was necessary, of course, to buy this crude material and pay for its transportation to Paris. Pierre and Marie appropriated the required sum from their very slight savings. They were not so foolish as to ask for official credits. . . .

But at least could there not be found, in the numerous buildings attached to the Sorbonne, some kind of suitable workroom to lend to the Curie couple? Apparently not. After vain attempts, Pierre and Marie staggered back to their point of departure, which is to say to the School of Physics where Pierre taught, to the little room where Marie had done her first experiments. The room opened onto a courtyard, and on the other side of the yard there was a wooden shack, an abandoned shed, with a skylight roof in such bad condition that it admitted the rain. The Faculty of Medicine had formerly used the place as a dissecting room, but for a long time now it had not even been considered fit to house the cadavers. No floor: an uncertain layer of bitumen[5] covered the earth. It was furnished with some worn kitchen tables, a blackboard which had landed there for no known reason, and an old cast-iron stove with a rusty pipe.

A workman would not willingly have worked in such a place; Marie and Pierre, nevertheless, resigned themselves to it. The shed had one advantage: it was so untempting, so miserable, that nobody thought of refusing them the use of it. Schutzenberger, the director of the school, had always been very kind to Pierre Curie and no doubt regretted that he had nothing better to offer. However that may be, he offered nothing else; and the couple, very pleased at not being put out into the street with their material, thanked him, saying that "this would do" and that they would "make the best of it."

As they were taking possession of the shed, a reply arrived from Austria. Good news! By extraordinary luck, the residue of recent extractions of uranium had not been scattered. The useless material had been piled up

---

4 **residue:** what remains after separation.

5 **bitumen** (bə tü' mən): here, an asphalt-type flooring.

in a no-man's-land planted with pine trees, near the mine of St. Joachimsthal. Thanks to the intercession of Professor Suess and the Academy of Science of Vienna, the Austrian government, which was the proprietor of the State factory there, decided to present a ton of residue to the two French lunatics who thought they needed it. If, later on, they wished to be sent a greater quantity of the material, they could obtain it at the mine on the best terms. For the moment the Curies had to pay only the transportation charges on a ton of ore.

One morning a heavy wagon, like those which deliver coal, drew up in the Rue Lhomond before the School of Physics. Pierre and Marie were notified. They hurried bare-headed into the street in their laboratory gowns. . . .

There was where radium was hidden. It was from there that Marie must extract it, even if she had to treat a mountain of this inert stuff like dust on the road.

Marya Sklodovska[6] had lived through the most intoxicating moments of her student life in a garret; Marie Curie was to know wonderful joys again in a dilapidated shed. It was a strange sort of beginning over again, in which a sharp subtle happiness (which probably no woman before Marie had ever experienced) twice elected the most miserable setting.

The shed in the Rue Lhomond surpassed the most pessimistic expectations of discomfort. In summer, because of its skylights, it was as stifling as a hothouse. In winter one did not know whether to wish for rain or frost; if it rained, the water fell drop by drop with a soft, nerve-racking noise, on the ground or on the worktables, in places which the physicists had to mark in order to avoid putting apparatus there. If it froze, one froze. There was no recourse. The stove, even when it was stoked white, was a complete disappointment. If one went near enough to touch it, one received a little heat, but two steps away and one was back in the zone of ice.

It was almost better for Marie and Pierre to get used to the cruelty of the outside temperature, since their technical installation—hardly existent—possessed no chimneys to carry off noxious gases, and the greater part of their treatment had to be made in the open air—in the courtyard. When a shower came, the physicists hastily moved their apparatus inside. To keep on working without being suffocated, they set up draughts[7] between the opened door and windows. . . .

We had no money, no laboratory and no help in the conduct of this important and difficult task [she was to write later]. It was like creating something out of nothing, and if Casimir Dluski once called my student years "the heroic years of my sister-in-law's life," I may say without exaggeration that this period was, for my husband and myself, the heroic period of our common existence.

. . . And yet it was in this miserable old shed that the best and happiest years of our life were spent, entirely consecrated to work. I sometimes passed the whole day stirring a mass in ebullition,[8] with an iron rod nearly as big as myself. In the evening I was broken with fatigue.

In such conditions M. and Mme. Curie worked for four years—from 1898 to 1902.

During the first year they busied themselves with the chemical separation of radium

---

6 **Marya Sklodovska**: Marie Curie's maiden name.

7 **draughts** (drafts): drafts.
8 **ebullition** (eb'ə lish' ən): a boiling mass.

and polonium, and they studied the radiation of the products (more and more active) thus obtained. Before long they considered it more practical to separate their efforts. Pierre Curie tried to determine the properties of radium and to know the new metal better. Marie continued those chemical treatments which would permit her to obtain salts of pure radium.

In this division of labor Marie had chosen the "man's job." She accomplished the toil of a day laborer. Inside the shed her husband was absorbed by delicate experiments. In the courtyard, dressed in her old dust-covered and acid-stained smock, her hair blown by the wind, surrounded by smoke which stung her eyes and throat, Marie was a sort of factory all by herself.

I came to treat as many as twenty kilograms of matter at a time [she writes], which had the effect of filling the shed with great jars full of precipitates[9] and liquids. It was killing work to carry the receivers, to pour off the liquids and to stir, for hours at a stretch, the boiling matter in a smelting basin.

Radium showed no intention of allowing itself to be known by human creatures. Where were the days when Marie naïvely expected the radium content of pitchblende to be *one per cent?* The radiation of the new substance was so powerful that a tiny quantity of radium, disseminated through the ore, was the source of striking phenomena which could be easily observed and measured. The difficult, the impossible thing, was to isolate this minute quantity, to separate it from the gangue[10] in which it was so intimately mixed.

The days became months and years; Pierre and Marie were not discouraged. This material which resisted them, which defended its secrets, fascinated them. United by their tenderness, united by intellectual passions, they had, in a wooden shack, the "anti-natural" existence for which they had both been made, she as well as he. . . .

Whenever Pierre and Marie, alone in this poor place, left their apparatus for a moment and quietly let their tongues run on, their talk about their beloved radium passed from the transcendent to the childish.

"I wonder what *It* will be like, what *It* will look like," Marie said one day with the feverish curiosity of a child who has been promised a toy. "Pierre, what form do you imagine *It* will take?"

"I don't know," the physicist answered gently. "I should like it to have a very beautiful color. . . ."

Marie to Bronya,[11] 1899:
Our life is always the same. We work a lot but we sleep well, so our health does not suffer. The evenings are taken up by caring for the child. In the morning I dress her and give her her food, then I can generally go out at about nine. During the whole of this year we have not been either to the theater or a concert, and we have not paid one visit. . . . I miss my family enormously, above all you, my dears, and Father. I often think of my isolation with grief. I cannot complain of anything else, for our health is not bad, the child is growing well, and I have the best husband one could dream of; I could never have imagined finding one like him. He is a true gift of heaven, and the more we live together the more we love each other.

Our work is progressing. I shall soon have a lecture to deliver on the subject. It should have been last Saturday, but I was prevented from

---

9 **precipitates** (pri sip′ə tāts): here, the results of their separation of elements.
10 **gangue** (gang): worthless rock material.

11 **Bronya:** Marie's sister who lived in Warsaw.

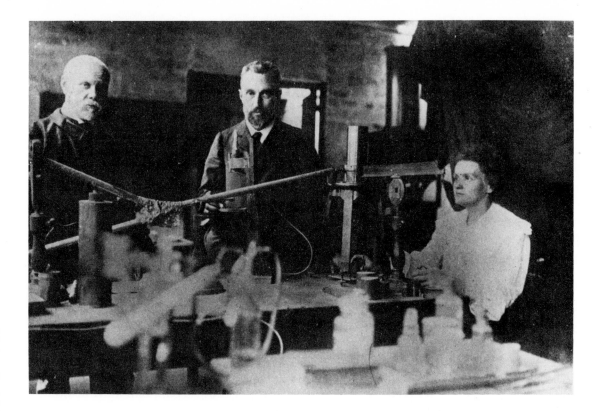

giving it, so it will no doubt be this Saturday, or else in a fortnight.

This work, which is so dryly mentioned in passing, was in fact progressing magnificently. In the course of the years 1899 and 1900, Pierre and Marie Curie published a report on the discovery of "induced radioactivity" due to radium, another on the effects of radioactivity, and another on the electric charge carried by the rays. And at last they drew up, for the Congress of Physics of 1900, a general report on the radioactive substances, which aroused immense interest among the scientists of Europe.

The development of the new science of radioactivity was rapid, overwhelming—the Curies needed fellow workers. Up to now they had had only the intermittent help of a laboratory assistant named Petit, an honest man who came to work for them outside his hours of service—working out of personal enthusiasm, almost in secret. But they now required technicians of the first order. Their discovery had important extensions in the domain of chemistry, which demanded attentive study. They wished to associate competent research workers with them.

Our work on radioactivity began in solitude [Marie was to write]. But before the breadth of the task it became more and more evident that collaboration would be useful. Already in 1898, one of the laboratory chiefs of the school, G. Bémont, had given us some passing help. Toward 1900, Pierre Curie entered into relations with a young chemist, André Debierne, assistant in the laboratory of Professor Friedel, who esteemed him highly.

André Debierne willingly accepted work on radioactivity. He undertook especially the research of a new radio element, the existence of which was suspected in the group of iron and rare clays. He discovered this element, named "actinium." Even though he worked in the physicochemical laboratory at the Sorbonne directed by Jean Perrin, he frequently came to see us in our shed and soon became a very close friend to us, to Dr. Curie, and later on to our children.

Thus, even before radium and polonium were isolated, a French scientist, André Debierne, had discovered a "brother," *actinium*.

At about the same period [Marie tells us], a young physicist, Georges Sagnac, engaged in studying X rays, came frequently to talk to Pierre Curie about the analogies that might exist between these rays, their secondary rays, and the radiation of radioactive bodies. Together they performed a work on the electric charge carried by these secondary rays.

Marie continued to treat, kilogram by kilogram, the tons of pitchblende residue which were sent her on several occasions from St. Joachimsthal. With her terrible patience, she was able to be, every day for four years, a physicist, a chemist, a specialized worker, an engineer and a laboring man all at once. Thanks to her brain and muscle, the old tables in the shed held more and more concentrated products—products more and more rich in radium. . . . She was now at the stage of purification and of the "fractional crystallization" of strongly radioactive solutions. But the poverty of her haphazard equipment hindered her work more than ever. It was now that she needed a spotlessly clean workroom and apparatus perfectly protected against cold, heat, and dirt. In this shed, open to every wind, iron and coal dust was afloat which, to Marie's despair, mixed itself into the products purified with so much care. . . .

Pierre was so tired of the interminable struggle that he would have been quite ready to abandon it. Of course, he did not dream of dropping the study of radium and of radioactivity. But he would willingly have renounced, for the time being, the special operation of preparing pure radium. The obstacles seemed insurmountable. Could they not resume this work later on, under better conditions? . . .

In 1902, forty-five months after the day on which the Curies announced the probable existence of radium, Marie finally carried off the victory in this war of attrition:[12] she succeeded in preparing a decigram of pure radium, and made a first determination of the atomic weight of the new substance, which was 225.

The incredulous chemists—of whom there were still a few—could only bow before the facts, before the superhuman obstinacy of a woman.

Radium officially existed.

It was nine o'clock at night. Pierre and Marie Curie were in their little house at 108 Boulevard Kellermann, where they had been living since 1900. . . .

Old Dr. Curie, who lived with the couple, had retired to his room. Marie had bathed her child and put her to bed, and had stayed for a long time beside the cot. This was a rite. When Irène did not feel her mother near her at night, she would call out for her incessantly, with "Mé!" which was to be our substitute for "Mamma" always. And Marie, yielding to the implacability[13] of the four-year-old baby, climbed the stairs, seated

---

12 **attrition** (ə trish′ ən): a gradual wearing down.
13 **implacability**: unreasonable insistence.

herself beside the child and stayed in the darkness until the young voice gave way to light, regular breathing. Only then would she go down again to Pierre, who was growing impatient. In spite of his kindness, he was the most possessive and jealous of husbands. He was so used to the constant presence of his wife that her least eclipse kept him from thinking freely. If Marie delayed too long near her daughter, he received her on her return with a reproach so unjust as to be comic:

"You never think of anything but that child!"

Pierre walked slowly about the room. Marie sat down and made some stitches on the hem of Irène's new apron. One of her principles was never to buy ready-made clothes for the child; she thought them too fancy and impractical. In the days when Bronya was in Paris, the two sisters cut out their children's dresses together, according to patterns of their own invention. These patterns still served for Marie.

But this evening she could not fix her attention. Nervous, she got up; then, suddenly:

"Suppose we go down there for a moment?" . . .

The day's work had been hard, and it would have been more reasonable for the couple to rest. But Pierre and Marie were not always reasonable. As soon as they had put on their coats and told Dr. Curie of their flight, they were in the street. They went on foot, arm in arm, exchanging few words. After the crowded streets of this queer district, with its factory buildings, wastelands, and poor tenements, they arrived in the Rue Lhomond and crossed the little courtyard. Pierre put the key in the lock. The door squeaked, as it had squeaked thousands of times, and admitted them to their realm, to their dream.

"Don't light the lamps!" Marie said in the darkness. Then she added with a little laugh:

"Do you remember the day when you said to me 'I should like radium to have a beautiful color'?"

The reality was more entrancing than the simple wish of long ago. Radium had something better than "a beautiful color": it was spontaneously luminous.[14] And in the somber shed where, in the absence of cupboards, the precious particles in their tiny glass receivers were placed on tables or on shelves nailed to the walls, their phosphorescent bluish outlines gleamed, suspended in the night.

"Look . . . Look!" the young woman murmured.

She went forward cautiously, looked for and found a straw-bottomed chair. She sat down in the darkness and silence. Their two faces turned toward the pale glimmering, the mysterious sources of radiation, toward radium—their radium. Her body leaning forward, her head eager, Marie took up again the attitude which had been hers an hour earlier at the bedside of her sleeping child.

---

14 **luminous:** glowing light.

Discussion

1. What were the "three agonizing questions" that faced the Curies at the beginning of their work?

2. Why didn't other scientists and chemists support the Curies' work?

3. Describe the conditions under which the Curies worked for four years. What was the only advantage to the shed?

4. Why was the hiring of assistants a significant moment in the Curies' research?

5. Describe the moment when the Curies realized they had actually discovered radium.

6. Marie Curie once wrote that she wanted "to prove to the world the existence of their 'children'." What did she mean?

Writer's Craft

When a person's life story is written by another person, the book is called a BIOGRAPHY. Writing about the life of another person is very difficult. In order to do an honest job, the biographer must find all the facts about the person's life, personality, and accomplishments. Then the author must select which facts to include. What would you select, for example, if you were to write a biography of your mother or father? How would you go about finding the important events of their lives? How would you choose which facts would go into the book and which would be omitted? Biographers must deal with these and other difficult questions.

1. The biographer of the Curies was their daughter, Eve Curie. Explain why being the child of the subjects of a biography is both an advantage and a disadvantage.

2. What feature of autobiography is included in this biography? Why do you think Eve Curie included this?

3. Although the Curies were partners on this project, this selection stresses the activities of Marie. How does the biographer do this?

Vocabulary

When Marie and Pierre Curie began their work, many other physicists refused to believe that radium existed. Eve Curie, the author of "Four Years in a Shed," used the word *incredulous* to describe their attitude. *Incredulous* means "unwilling to believe." *Incredulous* is a member of a WORD FAMILY that came from the Latin root *cred*, which means "believe."

A. On a separate sheet of paper, copy the following words from the *cred* word family. Then explain how "belief" relates to the meaning of each one. Use a dictionary only if you need help.

incredible   credit   credential

B. Here is a second list of *cred* family words. These are probably less familiar to you.

credence   credible   credo   credulous   discredit

On the same paper write each of the above words. Then copy the dictionary definition of each word. Underline the part of each definition which relates to "believing" or "belief."

C. Each word you defined in Exercise B fits correctly into a blank in one of the sentences below. On the same paper, write the word that best fits each blank.

1. The first paragraph of "Four Years in a Shed" says that ordinary people who lived during the Curies' time would have found it perfectly _____ that radium existed.

2. The author then goes on to say that physicists besides the Curies placed less _____ in radium's existence than ordinary people would have.

3. Chemists felt that only a very _____ person could believe in the existence of anything that could not be measured: "No atomic weight, no radium."

4. Nevertheless, Marie Curie lived and worked according to this _____ : that her husband's theory was right, that radium did exist, and that sooner or later she could prove it.

5. "Four Years in a Shed" does not say that the Curies' fellow physicists made enormous efforts to _____ the Curies' work.

Eve Curie 1904—

Unlike her parents, Marie and Pierre, Eve Curie found her career in the arts rather than in science. In her early years she was a concert pianist in France and Belgium, but then she eventually became a music critic for *Candide* weekly. From 1940–1945, she fought for the French Underground and after World War II, she co-published a daily newspaper, *Paris-Presse.* Her major work, *Madame Curie,* which received the National Book Award for nonfiction in 1937, was later made into a movie. In 1954, Eve Curie married Henry R. Labouisse; two years later she became a United States citizen.

The young boy had to remain alone in a pit in the ground—without food or water. He had to wait for a vision. He had to do these things to become a man.

from Lame Deer: Seeker of Visions

JOHN FIRE/LAME DEER

I WAS ALL ALONE on the hilltop. I sat there in the vision pit, a hole dug into the hill, my arms hugging my knees as I watched old man Chest, the medicine man who had brought me there, disappear far down in the valley. He was just a moving black dot among the pines, and soon he was gone altogether.

Now I was all by myself, left on the hilltop for four days and nights without food or water until he came back for me. You know, we Indians are not like some white folks—a man and a wife, two children, and one baby sitter who watches the TV set while the parents are out visiting somewhere.

Indian children are never alone. They are always surrounded by grandparents, uncles, cousins, relatives of all kinds, who fondle the kids, sing to them, tell them stories. If the parents go some place, the kids go along.

But here I was, crouched in my vision pit, left alone by myself for the first time in my life. I was sixteen then, still had my boy's name and, let me tell you, I was scared. I was shivering and not only from the cold. The nearest human being was many miles away, and four days and nights is a long, long time.

Of course, when it was all over, I would no longer be a boy, but a man. I would have had my vision. I would be given a man's name.

Sioux men are not afraid to endure hunger, thirst and loneliness, and I was only ninety-six hours away from being a man. The thought was comforting. Comforting, too, was the warmth of the star blanket which old man Chest had wrapped around me to cover my nakedness. My grandmother had made it especially for this, my first *hanblechia,* my first vision-seeking. It was a beautifully designed quilt, white with a large morning star made of many pieces of brightly colored cloth. That star was so big it covered most of the blanket. If *Wakan Tanka,* the Great Spirit, would give me the vision and the power, I would become a medicine man and perform many ceremonies wrapped in that quilt. I am an old man now and many times a grandfather, but I still have that star blanket my grandmother made for me. I treasure it; some day I shall be buried in it.

The medicine man had also left a peace pipe with me, together with a bag of *kinnickkinnick*—our kind of tobacco made of red willow bark. This pipe was even more of a friend to me than my star blanket. To us the pipe is like an open Bible. White people need a church house, a preacher and a pipe organ to get into a praying mood. There are so many things to distract you: who else is in the church, whether the other people notice that you have come, the pictures on the wall, the sermon, how much money you should give and did you bring it with you. We think you can't have a vision that way.

For us Indians there is just the pipe, the earth we sit on and the open sky. The spirit is everywhere. Sometimes it shows itself through an animal, a bird or some trees and hills. Sometimes it speaks from the Badlands, a stone, or even from the water. That smoke from the peace pipe, it goes straight up to the spirit world. But this is a two-way thing. Power flows down to us through that smoke, through the pipe stem. You feel that power as you hold your pipe; it moves from the pipe right into your body. It makes your hair stand up. That pipe is not just a thing; it is alive. Smoking this pipe would make me feel good and help me to get rid of my fears.

As I ran my fingers along its bowl of smooth red pipestone, red like the blood of my people, I no longer felt scared. That pipe had belonged to my father and to his father before him. It would someday pass to my son and, through him, to my grandchildren. As long as we had the pipe, there would be a Sioux nation. As I fingered the pipe, touched it, felt its smoothness that came from long use, I sensed that my forefathers who had once smoked this pipe were with me on the hill, right in the vision pit. I was no longer alone.

Besides the pipe, the medicine man had also given me a gourd. In it were forty small squares of flesh which my grandmother had cut from her arm with a razor blade. I had seen her do it. Blood had been streaming down from her shoulder to her elbow as she carefully put down each piece of skin on a handkerchief, anxious not to lose a single one. It would have made those anthropologists[1] mad. Imagine, performing such an ancient ceremony with a razor blade instead of a flint knife! To me it did not matter. Someone dear to me had undergone pain, given me something of herself, part of her body, to help me pray and make me strong-hearted. How could I be afraid with so many people—living and dead—helping me?

One thing still worried me. I wanted to become a medicine man, a *yuwipi*, a healer carrying on the ancient ways of the Sioux nation. But you cannot learn to be a medicine man like a white man going to medical school. An old holy man can teach you about herbs and the right ways to perform a ceremony where everything must be in its proper place, where every move, every word has its own, special meaning. These things you can learn—like spelling, like training a horse. But by themselves these things mean nothing. Without the vision and the power this learning will do no good. It would not make me a medicine man.

What if I failed, if I had no vision? Or if I dreamed of the Thunder Beings, or lightning struck the hill? That would make me at once into a *heyoka,* a contrarywise, an upside-down man, a clown. "You'll know it, if you get the power," my Uncle Chest had told me. "If you are not given it, you won't lie about it, you won't pretend. That would kill you, or kill somebody close to you, somebody you love."

---

1 **anthropologists** (an′ thrə pol′ə jists): scientists who study human beings—their customs, language, origins, and physical characteristics.

from *Lame Deer: Seeker of Visions*

Night was coming on. I was still light-headed and dizzy from my first sweat bath in which I had purified myself before going up the hill. I had never been in a sweat lodge before. I had sat in the little beehive-shaped hut made of bent willow branches and covered with blankets to keep the heat in. Old Chest and three other medicine men had been in the lodge with me. I had my back against the wall, edging as far away as I could from the red-hot stones glowing in the center. As Chest poured water over the rocks, hissing white steam enveloped me and filled my lungs. I thought the heat would kill me, burn the eyelids off my face! But right in the middle of all this swirling steam I heard Chest singing. So it couldn't be all that bad. I did not cry out, "All my relatives!"—which would have made him open the flap of the sweat lodge to let in some cool air—and I was proud of this. I heard him praying for me: "Oh, holy rocks, we receive your white breath, the steam. It is the breath of life. Let this young boy inhale it. Make him strong."

The sweat bath had prepared me for my vision-seeking. Even now, an hour later, my skin still tingled. But it seemed to have made my brains empty. Maybe that was good, plenty of room for new insights.

Darkness had fallen upon the hill. I knew that hanhepiwi had risen, the night sun, which is what we call the moon. Huddled in my narrow cave, I did not see it. Blackness was wrapped around me like a velvet cloth. It seemed to cut me off from the outside world, even from my own body. It made me listen to the voices within me. I thought of my forefathers who had crouched on this hill before me, because the medicine men in my family had chosen this spot for a place of meditation and vision-seeking ever since the day they had crossed the Missouri to hunt for buffalo in the White River country some two hundred years ago. I thought that I could sense their presence right through the earth I was leaning against. I could feel them entering my body, feel them stirring in my mind and heart.

Sounds came to me through the darkness: the cries of the wind, the whisper of the trees, the voices of nature, animal sounds, the hooting of an owl. Suddenly I felt an overwhelming presence. Down there with me in my cramped hole was a big bird. The pit was only as wide as myself, and I was a skinny boy, but that huge bird was flying around me as if he had the whole sky to himself. I could hear his cries, sometimes near and sometimes far, far away. I felt feathers or a wing touching my back and head. This feeling was so overwhelming that it was just too much for me. I trembled and my bones turned to ice. I grasped the rattle with the forty pieces of my grandmother's flesh. It also had many little stones in it, tiny fossils picked up from an ant heap. Ants collect them. Nobody knows why. These little stones are supposed to have a power in them. I shook the rattle and it made a soothing sound, like rain falling on rock. It was talking to me, but it did not calm my fears. I took the sacred pipe in my other hand and began to sing and pray: "Tunka-shila, grandfather spirit, help me." But this did not help. I don't know what got into me, but I was no longer myself. I started to cry. Crying, even my voice was different. I sounded like an older man; I couldn't even recognize this strange voice. I used long-ago words in my prayer, words no longer used nowadays. I tried to wipe away my tears, but they wouldn't stop. In the end I just pulled that quilt over me, rolled myself up in it. Still I felt the bird wings touching me.

Slowly I perceived that a voice was trying

from *Lame Deer: Seeker of Visions* **537**

to tell me something. It was a bird cry, but I tell you, I began to understand some of it. That happens sometimes. I know a lady who had a butterfly sitting on her shoulder. That butterfly told her things. This made her become a great medicine woman.

I heard a human voice, too, strange and high-pitched, a voice which could not come from an ordinary, living being. All at once I was way up there with the birds. The hill with the vision pit was way above everything. I could look down even on the stars, and the moon was close to my left side. It seemed as though the earth and the stars were moving below me. A voice said, "You are sacrificing yourself here to be a medicine man. In time you will be one. You will teach other medicine men. We are the fowl people, the winged ones, the eagles and the owls. We are a nation and you shall be our brother. You will never kill or harm anyone of us. You are going to understand us whenever you come to seek a vision here on this hill. You will learn about herbs and roots, and you will heal people. You will ask them for nothing in return. A man's life is short. Make yours a worthy one."

I felt that these voices were good, and slowly my fear left me. I had lost all sense of time. I did not know whether it was day or night. I was asleep, yet wide awake. Then I saw a shape before me. It rose from the darkness and the swirling fog which penetrated my earth hole. I saw that this was my great-grandfather, Tahca Ushte, Lame Deer, old man chief of the Minneconjou. I could see the blood dripping from my great-grandfather's chest where a white soldier had shot him. I understood that my great-grandfather wished me to take his name. This made me glad beyond words.

We Sioux believe that there is something within us that controls us, something like a second person almost. We call it *nagi,* what other people might call soul, spirit or essence. One can't see it, feel it or taste it, but that time on the hill—and only that once—I knew it was there inside of me. Then I felt the power surge through me like a flood. I cannot describe it, but it filled all of me. Now I knew for sure that I would become a *wicasa wakan,* a medicine man. Again I wept, this time with happiness.

I didn't know how long I had been up there on that hill—one minute or a lifetime. I felt a hand on my shoulder gently shaking me. It was old man Chest, who had come for me. He told me that I had been in the vision pit four days and four nights and that it was time to come down. He would give me something to eat and water to drink and then I was to tell him everything that had happened to me during my *hanblechia.* He would interpret my visions for me. He told me that the vision pit had changed me in a way that I would not be able to understand at that time. He told me also that I was no longer a boy, that I was a man now. I was Lame Deer.

Discussion   1. Why was Lame Deer taken out into the woods and left alone? How long did he have to remain there? Why is it more difficult for a Sioux child to be alone than for a white child?

2. How old is Lame Deer when he recalls this experience of seeking a vision? How old was he when he went to seek his vision?

3. Do you think Lame Deer wrote this autobiographical account for other Sioux or for non-Indian people? How do you know?

4. What is the purpose of the peace pipe to a Sioux? How important is the pipe to the future of the Sioux nation?

5. What major difference exists between the training of a Sioux medicine man and the training of a doctor in a medical school?

6. What was Lame Deer's vision like? What were the two forms that he saw? What did each one mean to him?

Vocabulary

CONTEXT CLUES are hints about the general meaning of an unfamiliar word that are given by the words surrounding it. When a written work contains words from a foreign language, context clues may be the only way of figuring out what these words mean. For example, in the selection from *Lame Deer,* the author includes several words from the Sioux language. These words are not found in English dictionaries. Therefore, to understand them you must rely entirely on context clues.

Each sentence below from the selection from *Lame Deer* contains one *italicized* word. Study the context clues for the meaning of that word. On a separate sheet of paper, write the best definition you can for each *italicized* word.

EXAMPLE: My grandmother had made it especially for this, my first *hanblechia,* my first vision-seeking.
ANSWER: a search for a vision.

1. The medicine man had also left a peace pipe with me, together with a bag of *kinnickinnick*—our kind of tobacco made of red willow bark.

2. One thing still worried me. I wanted to become a medicine man, a *yuwipi,* a healer carrying on the ancient ways of the Sioux nation.

3. That would make me at once into a *heyoka,* a contrarywise, an upside-down man, a clown.

4. I knew that *hanhepiwi* had risen, the night sun, which is what we call the moon.

5. We Sioux believe that there is something within us that controls us, something like a second person almost. We call it *nagi,* what other people might call soul, spirit or essence.

6. Now I knew for sure that I would become a *wicasa wakan,* a medicine man.

from *Lame Deer: Seeker of Visions* **539**

The leopard was going to kill the baby baboon. Its mother defended it. At first, it was an even fight. . . .

Battle by the Breadfruit Tree

THEODORE J. WALDECK

SMITH AND I were anxious to procure motion pictures of a herd of baboons. We had tried and tried, with no success whatever, though we saw many of these creatures. Our camp was some miles from a little ravine through which a stream ran. Beyond the ravine was a plateau leading back to thick woods. The baboons, scores of them, came out of these woods with their young to play on the plateau, to drink from the stream, and to fight for the favors of the females. Often Smith and I watched them, tried to photograph them, but could never get close enough. The baboons enjoyed what we were doing. They thought it was a game of some sort.

Once we set up the camera at the edge of the plateau, in order to take them when they came through the woods at dawn to greet the sun. We didn't even come close, for when the baboons saw us they charged like a shrieking army of savages. They threw sticks and stones at us, and we fled as though the devil and all his imps were at our heels. A grown bull baboon could have torn either of us to shreds. We didn't even stop to take our camera. We felt sure that our camera would be a wreck when we returned, which could not be until the baboons had retired from the plateau. We went back then, to find it exactly as we had left it. They had not so much as touched it.

"We *must* get those pictures," said Smith, "and I think I know the answer. Those breadfruit trees this side of the ravine. That big one, with the leafy top . . ."

"Yes?"

"We go there now and build a platform, up among the leaves, set up our camera, take blankets, a thermos bottle filled with hot tea, and spend the night. Then, when they come out in the morning, we'll be looking right down on them."

I saw that he was right, and we set about it. The trekkers[1] got boards from the camp and carried them to the tree. Big limbs were cut off and lashed high among the leaves at the top of the breadfruit tree. Then the boards were laid across the limbs, the camera set up. We had supper, took our blankets, and went to the tree to spend an uncomfortable night; but however uncomfortable it might be, it

---

1 **trekkers:** hired men.

would not matter if we got our pictures.

Night. We sat hunched up with our blankets over us listening to the sounds of the night. Now and again we dozed off. Then we'd waken. I'd have a cigarette; Smith would smoke his pipe. The wind blew steadily toward us from the plateau, which we could see dimly in the moonlight. The hours wore on.

Finally, animals began to greet the growing morning, though it would be some time, if they stuck to schedule, before the baboons appeared. I sat back on my blanket now—it was already warm enough to do without it—and watched the day break. I never tired of doing that. The sun comes up in a different way in Africa. First the leaves would be

black. Then a grayish haze would outline their shapes. Then the gray would lighten into the green of the leaves. Then the sun itself would strike through and morning would be with us, covering that part of Africa with a mixture of colors that ran through all the spectrum. Sunlight played upon colors like a mighty organist upon the keys, and the keys were everything the sunlight touched; when the dawn was come, it was music made visible. Not just the music that men played, but the music of Nature herself, with all the sounds that Nature used. A great sword of crimson was like a bloodcurdling scream you could not hear, because you came before it sounded, or after the sound had passed—and the sword struck deeply into the ravine, and raised itself to slash across the plateau on which the baboons usually played. The green of the trees was light, and like a touch of agony somehow—not the agony of pain, but the agony of an unexplainable kind of ecstasy. Far away and all around were the mounded hills, with the veldt[2] between them, and some of the hills wore caps of crimson, or orange, or gold, and some were still touched with the mystery of distance, or the night that had not yet left them. Whatever color or combination of colors you cared to mention, you could find there. And they came out of the east in a magical rush, like paint of all colors flung across the world by a painter bigger than all the earth itself.

I sighed and drank it in. Smith was looking out through the leaves, watching for the baboons to appear. Then he nudged me, and I made an end, for the moment, of dreaming. I parted the leaves in utter silence, making sure that my lens was uncovered and aimed at the plateau, and looked through. The baboon herd had not come, but a single baboon and her baby. Smith had not actually seen her coming. One moment he had been watching, seeing nothing. Then he had blinked his eyes and she was there. He signaled me to start the camera. I noted that the wind was toward us. I felt sure that the rest of the baboons would come, following this one. The mother baboon, while her baby played across the plateau behind her, came down to its edge to peer into the ravine, perhaps to dash down for a drink. I started the camera. It was almost silent, but not quite. And with the first whirring sound, which we ourselves could scarcely hear, though we were right beside it, the mother jumped up and looked around. Her ears had caught the little sound. She looked in all directions, twisting her head swiftly, and even in this her eyes kept darting to her young one. I stilled the whirring. We did not move or make a sound, even a whisper. She was so close we could see her nose wrinkling as she tried to get our scent. But the wind was toward us, and she got nothing. She even looked several times at the breadfruit tree that hid us.

I was about to start grinding again when a terrific squall came from the baby. It caught at my heart, that sound. I know it caught at the heart of Smith, too, for I could see it in his face. The mother baboon whirled around, so fast one could scarcely see the movement. The baby was jumping swiftly to the top of a rock, which was all too low to be of any use to him, as protection against the creature that was close behind him.

That creature was a hunting leopard, and it, like the baboon, had come so softly and silently that we had not seen it. It was simply there, a murderous streak behind the baby baboon. Did the female hesitate for a single moment? Not at all. If the leopard were a streak, so was the mother baboon. She shot toward that leopard and was in the air above him, reaching for his neck, while he was in mid-leap behind the baby, which now sat upon the rock and uttered doleful screams of terror.

The great cat instantly had his work cut out for him. For the baboon, by gripping his neck from behind, beyond reach of those talons,[3] could break it. And that was what she tried, with hands and feet and killing incisors.[4] But while I knew nothing of this fighting combination, the leopard must have,

---

2 **veldt** (velt): African grasslands.

3 **talons** (tal′ ənz): claws.
4 **incisors** (in sī′ zərz): sharp front teeth.

for he did what any cat would instinctively do in such a case. He spun to his back and reached for the baboon with all four of his brutally armed paws. One stroke across the abdomen of the baboon and she would be killed outright. But she knew something of leopards.

Smith did not make a sound, nor did I. I don't think we even breathed. The great cat recovered himself as the baboon jumped free of the leopard and ran toward her baby. The leopard charged the baboon. The baboon waited until the last minute, shot into the air, allowed the cat to go under her, turned in the air, and dropped back for the killing hold on the back of the neck again.

She got some hair in her mouth, which she spat out disgustedly. The baby kept on squalling. As nearly as I could tell—though I probably would not have heard even the trumpeting of elephants or the roaring of lions—there was no sound other than the screaming of the female baboon, the squalling of her baby, and the spitting and snarling of the leopard.

This time, when the leopard whirled to his back to dislodge the baboon, he managed to sink his claws into the baboon. I saw the blood spurt from the baboon's body, dyeing her fur. I knew that the smell of blood would drive the leopard mad, and it did. He would just as soon eat the meat of a grown baboon, if he could not have the baby.

Both stood off for a second, regarding each other, to spit out fur and hair. Then the leopard charged once more. Again the baboon leaped high, started down, reaching for that neck. And this time, when she came down, the leopard had already turned, and she could not entirely avoid landing among those fearful talons. Even a baboon could not jump from a spot in midair. For a brief moment there was a terrific flurry of in-fighting, from which came the snarling of the leopard, the screaming of the she-baboon. Now we could see the leopard, now the baboon, the latter trying with all her strength and agility to escape a disemboweling stroke from one of the four feet of the killer. Then both were so mixed up, and fighting so much all over the plateau, that we could not distinguish them. We could tell they were together, because they formed a ball of fighting fury, and the sounds of the two animals came out of the pinwheel of murderous action.

How long it lasted I do not know. To the she-baboon and her baby it must have seemed ages. It may have been seconds, even a minute. And then they were standing off, catching their breath, spitting out fur, regarding each other again. Both were tired. To my utter amazement the baboon was holding her own with the leopard. At that moment I would not have known which one had the edge, if either. For both were panting, weary, and stained with blood.

Neither gave ground. By common consent they stood for a few seconds, the baboon on her hindlegs, the leopard crouching on all fours. Then the leopard charged. Again the baboon went into the air to let the leopard go under her. She knew better, at this stage of the game, than to run away or jump to either side. The leopard could overtake her if she ran, could turn instantly and follow her if she jumped to either side. So up and over was her only chance. Again she came down. But this time she was expecting the cat to whip upon his back and present his talons, and was ready. She twisted aside a little, and to the front, perhaps with some idea of reaching for the neck from the underside, now upper-most. The forepaws of the leopard lashed at

her. The sun gleamed on the exposed talons, and showed that they were red with baboon blood. I could see long weals across the abdomen of the baboon. She had evaded those slashes at the last moment, each time. Feeling the talons' touch she had got away, just enough to escape disemboweling, not enough to escape deep, parallel gashes that reached inward for her life.

Now I began to see how the fight was going to go, though neither Smith nor I could have done anything about it, because we were spellbound, rooted to our place in the breadfruit tree, watching something that few explorers had ever seen: a battle between a leopard and a baboon! And for the best reason in the world—the baboon to protect her baby.

But now the she-baboon was tiring. It was obvious in all her movements, though I knew and the leopard knew that as long as she stood upright and could see him, she was dynamite—fury incarnate, capable of slaying if she got in the blows she wanted. So far she had not made it.

Now she panted more than the leopard did. She did not entirely evade his rushes, though she jumped over him as before. But she did not go as high or twist as quickly in the air. She couldn't. Her body was beginning to weigh too much for her tiring muscles. She was like an arm-weary prizefighter who has almost fought himself out. But her little eyes still glared defiance, her screaming still informed him that she was ready for more. Now there were other slashes upon her face, her head, her chest, and her abdomen—clear down even to her hands and feet. She was a bloody mess. But she never even thought of quitting. They drew apart once more, spitting fur. They glared at each other. Several times I saw the orange eyes of the leopard, and there was hell in them—the hell of hate and fury, and thwarted hunger.

Now he charged before the baboon had rested enough. He was getting stronger, the baboon weaker. His second wind came sooner perhaps, and he sorely needed it. Even yet the baboon could break his neck, given the one chance.

Again the baboon went into the air, came down, and was caught in the midst of those four paws. Again the battle raged, the two animals all mixed up together, all over the plateau. The little one squalled from his boulder, and there was despair in his voice. He cried hopeless encouragement to his mother. She heard, I knew she did, and tried to find some reserve with which to meet the attacks of the killer.

That last piece of in-fighting lasted almost too long. There was no relief from it, and the nerves of the two men who watched were strained to the breaking point, though neither was aware of it. How long they had held their breath they did not know.

The two beasts broke apart, and I saw instantly that the leopard had at last succeeded, managing the stroke he had been trying for since the battle began. He had raked deeply into the abdomen of the baboon. The result may be well imagined. The baboon drew off slowly, and looked down at herself. What she saw told her the truth—that even if the leopard turned and ran away this minute, she was done.

But did she expect mercy? Death did not grant mercy in Africa—certainly not on this particular morning.

The baboon noted the direction of the leopard's glance. The great cat was crouched well back, but facing the rock on which the baby squalled. He licked his chops, looked at the dying she-baboon, and growled, and it was as though he said, "Not much time now. And when you are gone, nothing will keep me from getting him!"

As if the leopard had actually screamed those words, I got the thought which raced through his evil head. And the baboon got it too. For she turned slowly, like a dead thing walking, and moved to turn her back toward the rock, so that now the baby was almost over her head.

Then she looked at the leopard once more, and screamed, as though she answered: "Perhaps, but over my dead body!"

The leopard charged again, for the last time. It would be easy now. And as the she-baboon set herself against that last charge, the strangest, most nearly human cry I ever heard went keening out across the veldt. It bounced against the breadfruit trees, dipped into the ravine; it went back through the forest whence the other baboons usually came to play and drink. It went out in all directions, that cry, across the plain. It rolled across the mounded hills. It was a cry that could never be forgotten by those that heard it.

And then, in the midst of the cry—like

none she had uttered while the fight had been so fierce—the leopard struck her down. She sprawled, beaten to a pulp, at the base of the boulder, while that last cry of hers still moved across the veldt.

And now, sure that the she-baboon was dead, the leopard backed away, crouched, lifted his eyes to the baby on the rock.

I came to life then, realizing for the first time what I was seeing. I couldn't have moved before. But now, somehow, my rifle was in my hands, at my shoulder, and I was getting the leopard in my sights. Why had I not done it before, saved the life of the mother? I'll never know. Certainly, and sincerely, I had not allowed the fight to continue simply in order to see which would win out. I had simply become a statue, possessing only eyes and ears.

I got the leopard in my sights as he crouched to spring. I had his head for a target. I'd get him before he moved, before he sprang. The baby—looking down, sorrow in his cries, with a knowledge of doom too—had nowhere to go. I tightened the trigger. And then . . .

On the instant the leopard was blotted out, and for several seconds I could not understand what had happened, what the mother's last cry had meant. But now I did. For living baboons, leaping, screaming, had appeared out of nowhere. They came, the whole herd of them, and the leopard was invisible in their midst. I did not even hear the leopard snarl and spit. I heard nothing save the baboons, saw nothing save the big blur of their bodies, over and around the spot where I had last seen the leopard.

How long that lasted I do not know. But when it was over, another she-baboon jumped to the rock, gathered up the baby, and was gone. After her trailed all the other baboons. Smith and I looked at each other, and if my face was as white and shocked as his, it was white and shocked indeed. Without a word, because we both understood, we slipped down from the tree, crossed the ravine, climbed its far side, crossed the plateau, looked down at the dead she-baboon, then looked away again. One mother had fought to the death for the life of her baby and had saved that life. We looked around for the leopard who had slain her. We couldn't find a piece of it as big as an average man's hand! So the baboons had rallied to the dying cry of the mother baboon.

We went slowly back to the tree, got our camera down, returned with it to our camp. Not until we were back did we realize that neither of us, from the beginning of that fight to its grim and savage end, had thought of the camera, much less touched it.

One of the greatest fights any explorer ever saw was unrecorded.

Discussion
1. How does the author contrast the African setting with the battle that followed? What effect is created by this contrast? What figures of speech—similes and metaphors—does the author use to describe the sunrise?

2. How is the reader able to accept the fact that the baboon has a chance against the leopard?

3. When were you reasonably sure that the baboon had lost the battle? Find the exact moment in the story.

4. What stopped the narrator from killing the leopard with his rifle? Why hadn't he killed the leopard sooner?

5. Whose side was the narrator on during the battle? How do you know? Find examples to support your view.

Writer's Craft

One of the most important decisions authors have to make is how they will tell their stories—in what order they will arrange the events. Many writers simply relate the events in the order they actually happened. When a story is told with the events in their natural order, it is described as having CHRONOLOGICAL ORDER. Stating the events exactly as they occur helps the reader to follow and understand the narrative more easily.

1. Following are the major events from "Battle by the Breadfruit Tree." Arrange them in chronological order.
   a. the fight
   b. the construction of the platform in the breadfruit tree
   c. the destruction of the leopard by the baboons
   d. the attack of the baboons on the explorers and their cameras
   e. the sunrise

2. Consider what the story might have been like if the narrative had started with the paragraph on p. 546, beginning, "I got the leopard in my sights as he crouched to spring." If the ending were told first, how would you bring in the other information? Which time order do you think would be more effective? Why?

Theodore J. Waldeck 1894——

Rather than become a doctor, Theodore Waldeck went to Africa on an expedition when he was eighteen. After recovering from an illness, he set out on his own safari. Because his venture was successful, he continued his explorer's life. He recorded his experiences in a series of books, among them are *Lions on the Hunt* and *On Safari*.

The wave was almost as big as a tidal wave. But he had to ride it to shore on his surfboard . . . even if it cost him his life.

That Legendary Ride

DUKE KAHANAMOKU

MUCH SEEMS to have been made of that once-in-a-lifetime ride of mine from the outer steamer lane off Waikiki, and now is as good a time as any to put the record straight. The incident has been written up before but might bear repeating. I can remember the details as though it all happened yesterday, for, in retrospect, I have relived the ride many a time. I think my memory plays me no tricks on this one.

Pride was in it with me those days, and I was still striving to build bigger and better boards, ride taller and faster waves, and develop more dexterity from day to day. Also, vanity probably had much to do with my trying to delight the crowds at Waikiki with spectacular rides on the long, glassy, sloping waves.

But the day I caught the Big One was a day when I was not thinking in terms of awing any tourists or *kamaainas*[1] on Waikiki Beach. It was simply an early morning when mammoth ground swells were rolling in sporadically from the horizon, and I saw that no one was paddling out to try them.

Frankly, they were the largest I'd ever seen. The yell of "The surf is up!" was the understatement of the century.

In fact, it was that rare morning when the word was out that the big "bluebirds" were rolling in; this is the name for gigantic waves that sweep in from the horizon on extraordinary occasions. Sometimes years elapse with no evidence of them. They are spawned far out at sea and are the result of certain cataclysms of nature—either great atmospheric disturbances or subterranean agitation like underwater earthquakes and volcanic eruptions.

True, as waves go, the experts will agree that bigness alone is not what supplies outstandingly good surfing. Sometimes giant waves make for bad surfing in spite of their size, and the reason often is that there is an onshore wind that pushes the top of the waves down and makes them break too fast with lots of white water. It takes an offshore wind to make the waves stand up to their full height. This day we had stiff trade winds blowing from the high Koolau Range, and they were making those bluebirds tower up like the Himalayas. Man, I was pulling my breath from way down at the sight of them.

---

1 *kamaainas* (kä mä′ ä ē′ näz): native-born or old residents of Hawaii.

It put me in mind of the winter storm waves that roar in at Kaena Point on the North Shore. Big-wave surfers, even then, were doing much speculating on whether those Kaena waves could be ridden with any degree of safety. The bluebirds facing me were easily thirty-plus waves, and they looked as though, with the right equipment—plus a lot of luck—they just might be makable.

The danger lay in the prone-out or wipe-out. Studying the waves made me wonder if any person's body could withstand the unbelievable force of a thirty-to-fifty-foot wall of water when it crashes. And, too, could even a top swimmer like myself manage to battle the currents and explosive water that would necessarily accompany the aftermath of such a wave?

Well, the answer seemed to be simply— *don't get wiped out!*

From the shore you could see those high glassy ridges building up in the outer Diamond Head region. The bluebirds were swarming across the bay in a solid line as far northwest as Honolulu Harbor. They were tall, steep, and fast. The closer-in ones crumbled and showed their teeth with a fury that I had never seen before. I wondered if I could even push through the acres of white water to get to the outer area where the build-ups were taking place.

But, like the mountain climbers with Mount Everest, you try it "just because it's there." Some days you do not take time to analyze what motivates you. All I knew was that I was suddenly trying to shove through that incoming sea—and having the fight of my life. I was using my *Papa-nui,* the sixteen-foot, 114-pound semihollow board, and it was like trying to jam a log through the flood of a dam break.

Again and again it was necessary to turn turtle with the big board and hang on tightly underneath—arms and legs wrapped around a thing that bucked like a bronco gone berserk. The shoreward-bound torrents of water ground overhead, making all the racket of a string of freight cars roaring over a trestle. The prone paddling between combers was a demanding thing because the water was wild. It was a case of wrestling the board through block-busting breakers, and it was a miracle that I ever gained the outlying waters.

Bushed from the long fight to get seaward, I sat on my board and watched the long humps of water peaking into ridges that marched like animated foothills. I let a slew of them lift and drop me with their silent, threatening glide. I could hardly believe that such perpendicular walls of water could be built up like that. The troughs between the swells had the depth of elevator shafts, and I wondered again what it would be like to be buried under tons of water when it curled and detonated. There was something eerie about watching the shimmering backs of the ridges as they passed me and rolled on toward Waikiki.

I let a lot of them careen by, wondering in my own heart whether I was passing them up because of their unholy height or whether I was really waiting for the big right one. One begins to doubt oneself at a time like that. Then I was suddenly wheeling and turning to catch the towering blue ridge bearing toward me. I was prone and stroking hard at the water with my hands.

Strangely, it was more as though the wave had selected me, rather than I had chosen it. It seemed like a very personal and special wave—the kind I had seen in my mind's eye during a night of tangled dreaming. There

was no backing out on this one; the two of us had something to settle between us. The rioting breakers between me and shore no longer bugged me. There was just this one ridge and myself—no more. Could I master it? I doubted it, but I was willing to die in the attempt to harness it.

Instinctively I got to my feet when the pitch, slant, and speed seemed right. Left foot forward, knees slightly bent, I rode the board down that precipitous slope like a person tobogganing down a glacier. Sliding left along the watery monster's face, I didn't know I was at the beginning of a ride that would become a celebrated and memoried thing. All I knew was that I had come to grips with the tallest, bulkiest, fastest wave I had ever seen. I realized, too, more than ever, that to be trapped under its curling bulk would be the same as letting a factory cave in upon you.

This lethal avalanche of water swept shoreward swiftly and spookily. The board began hissing from the traction as the wave leaned forward with greater and more incredible speed and power. I shifted my weight, cut left at more of an angle, and shot into the big Castle Surf which was building and adding to the wave I was on. Spray was spuming up wildly from my rails, and I had never before seen it spout up like that. I rode it for city-long blocks, the wind almost sucking the breath out of me. Diamond Head itself seemed to have come alive and was leaping in at me from the right.

Then I was slamming into Elk's Club Surf, still sliding left and still fighting for balance, for position, for everything and anything that would keep me upright. The drumming of the water under the board had become a mad tattoo. Elk's Surf rioted me along, high and steep, until I skidded and slanted through into Public Baths Surf. By then it amounted to three surfs combined into one; big, rumbling, and exploding. I was not sure I could make it on this ever-steepening ridge. A curl broke to my right and almost engulfed me, so I swung even farther left, shuffled back a little on the board to keep from purling.

Left it was; left and more left, with the board veeing a jet of water on both sides and making a snarl that told of speed and stress and thrust. The wind was tugging my hair with frantic hands. Then suddenly it looked as if I might, with more luck, make it into the back of Queen's Surf! The build-up had developed into something approximating what I had heard of tidal waves, and I wondered if it would ever flatten out at all. White water was pounding to my right, so I angled farther from it to avoid its wiping me out and burying me in the sudsy depths.

Borrowing on the Cunha Surf for all it was worth—and it was worth several hundred yards—I managed to manipulate the board into the now towering Queen's Surf. One mistake—just one small one—could well spill me into the maelstrom[2] to my right. I teetered for some panic-ridden seconds, caught control again, and made it down on that last forward rush, sliding and bouncing through lunatic water. The breaker gave me all the tossing of a bucking bronco. Still luckily erect, I could see the people standing there on the beach, their hands shading their eyes against the sun, and watching me complete this crazy, unbelievable one-and-three-quarter-mile ride.

I made it into the shallows in one last surging flood. A little dazedly I wound up in hip-deep water, where I stepped off and pushed my board shoreward through the bubbly surf. That improbable ride gave me the sense of being an unlickable guy for the moment. I heisted my board to my hip, locked both arms around it, and lugged it up the beach.

Without looking at the people clustered around, I walked on, hearing them murmur fine, exciting things which I wanted to remember in days to come. I told myself this was the ride to end all rides. I grinned my thanks to those who stepped close and slapped me on the shoulders, and I smiled to those who told me this was the greatest. I trudged on and on, knowing this would be a shining memory for me that I could take out in years to come and relive in all its full glory. This had been *it*.

I never caught another wave anything like that one. And now with the birthdays piled up on my back, I know I never shall. But they cannot take that memory away from me. It is a golden one that I treasure, and I'm grateful that God gave it to me.

---

2 **maelstrom** (māl′ strəm): a powerful whirlpool.

Discussion

1. What motivated Duke to take on big waves?

2. What two things does Duke say are necessary for experienced surfers to ride the big waves successfully? What are the two biggest dangers of surfing?

3. Duke compares surfing to mountain climbing. He says, ". . . like the mountain climbers with Mount Everest, you try it 'just because it's there.'" What does he mean by this statement?

4. What thoughts went through Duke's mind as he waited for the big wave?

5. Throughout this selection, Duke personifies the water and the wind—he gives them human characteristics. Find examples of personification.

6. How did the people on the beach react to Duke's ride? Do you think Duke would have ridden the big wave if no one had been on the beach that day?

7. Do you think Duke's accomplishment was worth the risk he took? Explain your answer.

Duke Kahanamoku 1890–1968

Duke Kahanamoku is known to surfers everywhere. As a former Olympic swimming champion, Kahanamoku was the first to introduce surfing to the mainland of the United States and Australia. A pure-blooded Hawaiian, his ancestry goes back to King Kamehameha.

Throughout his later life, Kahanamoku was elected to thirteen consecutive terms as Sheriff of Honolulu. He was also Ambassador-at-large for Hawaii and Official Greeter of the City and County of Honolulu until his death. In his book, *World of Surfing,* Kahanamoku writes a complete guide to surfing, including a chapter on ancient surfing and body surfing which the Polynesian Islanders call *kala nahu.* "That Legendary Ride" is also a chapter from his book.

7 NONFICTION NARRATIVE

Discussion

1. An anecdote is a very short narrative about a single incident. It can be amusing, curious, or revealing, but it is always short and interesting. Long, nonfiction biographies and autobiographies may be collections of anecdotes about a person. Find some anecdotes included in the selections in this unit.

2. What selections in this unit are clearly autobiographical? What selectons are biographical? Explain the reasons for your answers.

3. Which one of these narratives used chronological order: "Roberto Clemente—A Bittersweet Memoir," "The Life and Death of a Western Gladiator," or the selection from *Lame Deer: Seeker of Visions*? Explain why these other two selections are not written in chronological order?

Composition

1. In the introduction to this unit, the expression, "Truth is stranger than fiction" was used to describe the unusual nature of some nonfiction narratives. How does this statement particularly apply to "Roberto Clemente—A Bittersweet Memoir"? Write examples from this selection that, in your opinion, would not be believable if presented as fiction. Explain why readers would not easily believe the events in the story. End by explaining why you think readers *do* believe them when they are labeled "nonfiction."

2. Earlier in this unit you saw some of the problems you would have to resolve if you wrote a biography of one of your parents. Do some investigating about the background of one of your parents or relatives. After you have collected enough information, choose one experience that would make an interesting or humorous anecdote in your biography. Write the anecdote, including both description and conversation.

The Novel

THE NOVEL

"Deep in the forest a call was sounding, and as often as he heard this call, mysteriously thrilling and luring, he felt compelled to turn his back upon the fire and the beaten earth around it, and to plunge into the forest, and on and on, he knew not where or why. . . ." And so the dog Buck, the hero of Jack London's famous tale of the Klondike, hears the "call of the wild."

As you read this classic tale of Buck and the gold rush in Alaska, you will learn what it takes to survive in the wild. That's because Jack London pulls no punches in providing you with a vivid picture of what life was really like when the law of "the club and fang" ruled and when "survival of the fittest" most often meant life or death.

The Call of the Wild is a short novel. Since even a short novel is usually longer than most other forms of literature, the author has a greater opportunity to give you more details about the characters in the story. Also, you can often see these characters from different sides or points of view. This enables you to more accurately understand and evaluate the motives and actions of the characters. This is certainly true of *The Call of the Wild*. Although you may have read other animal stories, you probably have not had the chance to learn about the mind, character, and heart of an animal character as thoroughly as you will in this story. Jack London seems to put you right into the mind of Buck—you know his actions, thoughts, feelings, almost as if you were Buck yourself.

With these increased insights, you will not only learn about life during the Klondike gold rush, but you will also probably learn something about yourself. You certainly will learn that a book of fiction contains realistic situations and characters.

The Call of the Wild

JACK LONDON

Chapter 1

INTO THE PRIMITIVE

> "Old longings nomadic leap,
>   Chafing at custom's chain;
> Again from its brumal sleep
>   Wakens the ferine strain."

BUCK DID NOT READ the newspapers or he would have known that trouble was brewing, not alone for himself, but for every tidewater dog, strong of muscle and with warm, long hair, from Puget Sound to San Diego. Because men, groping in the Arctic darkness, had found a yellow metal, and because steamship and transportation companies were booming the find, thousands of men were rushing into the Northland. These men wanted dogs, and the dogs they wanted were heavy dogs with strong muscles by which to toil and furry coats to protect them from the frost.

Buck lived at a big house in the sun-kissed Santa Clara Valley. Judge Miller's place, it was called. It stood back from the road, half hidden among the trees through which glimpses could be caught of the wide, cool veranda that ran around its four sides. The house was approached by graveled driveways which wound about through wide-spreading lawns and under the interlacing boughs of tall poplars. At the rear, things were on even a more spacious scale than at the front. There were great stables where a dozen grooms and boys held forth, rows of vine-clad servants' cottages, and an endless and orderly array of outhouses, long grape arbors, green pastures, orchards, and berry patches. Then there was the pumping plant for the artesian well and the big cement tank where Judge Miller's boys took their morning plunge and kept cool in the hot afternoon.

And over this great demesne, Buck ruled. Here he was born, and here he had lived the four years of his life. It was true, there were other dogs. There could not but be other dogs on so vast a place, but they did not count. They came and went, resided in the populous kennels, or lived obscurely in the recesses of the house after the fashion of Toots, the Japanese pug, or Ysabel, the Mexican hairless—strange creatures that rarely put nose out of doors or set foot to ground. On the other hand, there were the fox terriers, a score of them at least, who yelped fearful promises at Toots and Ysabel looking out of the windows at them and protected by a legion of housemaids armed with brooms and mops.

But Buck was neither house dog nor kennel dog. The whole realm was his. He plunged into the swimming tank or went hunting with the Judge's sons; he escorted Mollie and Alice, the Judge's daughters, on long twilight or early morning rambles; on wintry nights he lay at the Judge's feet before the roaring library fire; he carried the Judge's grandsons on his back, or rolled them in the grass, and guarded their footsteps through wild adventures down to the fountain in the stable yard, and even beyond where the paddocks were and the berry patches. Among the terriers he stalked imperiously, and Toots and Ysabel he utterly ignored, for he was king—king over all creeping, crawling, flying things of Judge Miller's place, humans included.

His father Elmo, a huge St. Bernard, had been the Judge's inseparable companion, and Buck bid fair to follow in the way of his father. He was not so large—he weighed only one hundred and forty pounds—for his mother Shep had been a Scotch shepherd dog. Nevertheless, one hundred and forty pounds, to which was added the dignity that comes of good living and universal respect, enabled him to carry himself in right royal fashion. During the four years since his puppyhood, he had lived the life of a sated[1] aristocrat; he had a fine pride in himself, was even a trifle egotistical, as country gentlemen sometimes become because of their insular[2] situation. But he had saved himself by not becoming a

mere pampered house dog. Hunting and kindred outdoor delights had kept down the fat and hardened his muscles; and to him, as to the cold-tubbing races, the love of water had been a tonic and a health preserver.

And this was the manner of dog Buck was in the fall of 1897, when the Klondike strike dragged men from all the world into the frozen North. But Buck did not read the

---

1 **sated:** fully satisfied.
2 **insular:** protected; isolated.

The Call of the Wild **559**

newspapers, and he did not know that Manuel, one of the gardener's helpers, was an undesirable acquaintance. Manuel had one besetting sin. He loved to play Chinese lottery. Also, in his gambling he had one besetting weakness—faith in a system, and this made his damnation certain. For to play a system requires money, while the wages of a gardener's helper do not lap over the needs of a wife and numerous progeny.[3]

The Judge was at a meeting of the Raisin Growers' Association, and the boys were busy organizing an athletic club on the memorable night of Manuel's treachery. No one saw him and Buck go off through the orchard on what Buck imagined was merely a stroll. And with the exception of a solitary man, no one saw them arrive at the little flag station known as College Park. This man talked with Manuel, and money chinked between them.

"You might wrap up the goods before you deliver 'm," the stranger said gruffly, and Manuel doubled a piece of stout rope around Buck's neck under the collar.

"Twist it, an' you'll choke 'm plentee," said Manuel, and the stranger grunted a ready affirmative.

Buck had accepted the rope with quiet dignity. To be sure, it was an unwonted performance, but he had learned to trust in men he knew and to give them credit for a wisdom that outreached his own. But when the ends of the rope were placed in the stranger's hands, he growled menacingly. He had merely intimated his displeasure, in his pride believing that to intimate was to command. But to his surprise the rope tightened around his neck, shutting off his breath. In quick rage he sprang at the man, who met him halfway, grappled him close by the throat, and with a deft twist threw him over on his back. Then the rope tightened mercilessly while Buck struggled in a fury, his tongue lolling out of his mouth and his great chest panting futilely.[4] Never in all his life had he been so vilely treated, and never in all his life had he been so angry. But his strength ebbed, his eyes glazed, and he knew nothing when the train was flagged and the two men threw him into the baggage car.

The next he knew, he was dimly aware that his tongue was hurting and that he was being jolted along in some kind of a conveyance. The hoarse shriek of a locomotive whistling a crossing told him where he was. He had traveled too often with the Judge not to know the sensation of riding in a baggage car. He opened his eyes, and into them came the unbridled anger of a kidnapped king. The man sprang for his throat, but Buck was too quick for him. His jaws closed on the hand, nor did they relax till his senses were choked out of him once more.

"Yep, has fits," the man said, hiding his mangled hand from the baggageman, who had been attracted by the sounds of struggle. "I'm takin' 'm up for the boss to 'Frisco. A crack dog doctor there thinks that he can cure 'm."

Concerning that night's ride, the man spoke most eloquently for himself in a little shed back of a saloon on the San Francisco waterfront.

"All I get is fifty for it," he grumbled, "an' I wouldn't do it over for a thousand, cash."

His hand was wrapped in a bloody handkerchief, and the right trouser leg was ripped from knee to ankle.

"How much did the other mug get?" the saloonkeeper demanded.

---

3 **progeny** (proj' ə nē): children.

4 **futilely**: uselessly.

"A hundred," was the reply. "Wouldn't take a sou less, so help me."

"That makes a hundred and fifty," the saloonkeeper calculated, "and he's worth it, or I'm a squarehead."

The kidnapper undid the bloody wrappings and looked at his lacerated hand. "If I don't get the hydrophoby[5] —"

"It'll be because you was born to hang," laughed the saloonkeeper. "Here, lend me a hand before you pull your freight," he added.

Dazed, suffering intolerable pain from throat and tongue, with the life half throttled out of him, Buck attempted to face his tormentors. But he was thrown down and choked repeatedly till they succeeded in filing the heavy brass collar from off his neck. Then the rope was removed, and he was flung into a cagelike crate.

There he lay for the remainder of the weary night, nursing his wrath and wounded pride. He could not understand what it all meant. What did they want with him, these strange men? Why were they keeping him pent up in this narrow crate? He did not know why, but he felt oppressed by the vague sense of impending calamity. Several times during the night he sprang to his feet when the shed door rattled open, expecting to see the Judge or the boys at least. But each time it was the bulging face of the saloonkeeper that peered in at him by the sickly light of a tallow candle. And each time the joyful bark that trembled in Buck's throat was twisted into a savage growl.

But the saloonkeeper let him alone, and in the morning four men entered and picked up the crate. More tormentors, Buck decided, for they were evil-looking creatures, ragged and unkempt; and he stormed and raged at

them through the bars. They only laughed and poked sticks at him, which he promptly assailed with his teeth till he realized that that was what they wanted. Whereupon he lay down sullenly and allowed the crate to be lifted into a wagon. Then he and the crate in which he was imprisoned began a passage through many hands. Clerks in the express office took charge of him; he was carted about in another wagon; a truck carried him with an assortment of boxes and parcels upon a ferry steamer; he was trucked off the steamer into a great railway depot; and finally he was deposited in an express car.

For two days and nights this express car was dragged along at the tail of shrieking locomotives, and for two days and nights Buck neither ate nor drank. In his anger he had met the first advances of the express messengers with growls, and they had retaliated by teasing him. When he flung himself against the bars, quivering and frothing, they laughed at him and taunted him. They growled and barked like detestable dogs, mewed, and flapped their arms and crowed. It was all very silly, he knew, but therefore the more outrage to his dignity, and his anger waxed[6] and waxed. He did not mind the hunger so much, but the lack of water caused him severe suffering and fanned his wrath to fever pitch. For that matter, high-strung and finely sensitive, the ill treatment had flung him into a fever, which was fed by the inflammation of his parched and swollen throat and tongue.

He was glad for one thing: the rope was off his neck. That had given them an unfair advantage, but now that it was off, he would show them. They would never get another

---

5 **hydrophoby:** Here he means *hydrophobia* or rabies.

6 **waxed:** grew.

rope around his neck. Upon that he was resolved. For two days and nights he neither ate nor drank, and during those two days and nights of torment, he accumulated a fund of wrath that boded ill for whoever first fell foul of him. His eyes turned bloodshot, and he was metamorphosed[7] into a raging fiend. So changed was he that the Judge himself would not have recognized him, and the express messengers breathed with relief when they bundled him off the train at Seattle.

Four men gingerly carried the crate from the wagon into a small, high-walled back-yard. A stout man, with a red sweater that sagged generously at the neck, came out and signed the book for the driver. That was the man, Buck divined, the next tormentor, and he hurled himself savagely against the bars. The man smiled grimly and brought a hatchet and a club.

"You ain't going to take him out now?" the driver asked.

"Sure," the man replied, driving the hatchet into the crate for a pry.

There was an instantaneous scattering of the four men who had carried it in, and from safe perches on top of the wall they prepared to watch the performance.

Buck rushed at the splintering wood, sinking his teeth into it, surging and wrestling with it. Wherever the hatchet fell on the outside, he was there on the inside, snarling and growling, as furiously anxious to get out as the man in the red sweater was calmly intent on getting him out.

"Now, you red-eyed devil," he said, when he had made an opening sufficient for the passage of Buck's body. At the same time he dropped the hatchet and shifted the club to his right hand.

And Buck was truly a red-eyed devil as he drew himself together for the spring, hair bristling, mouth foaming, a mad glitter in his bloodshot eyes. Straight at the man he launched his one hundred and forty pounds of fury, surcharged with the pent passion of two days and nights. In midair, just as his jaws were about to close on the man, he received a shock that checked his body and brought his teeth together with an agonizing clip. He whirled over, fetching the ground on his back and side. He had never been struck by a club in his life and did not understand. With a snarl that was part bark and more scream, he was again on his feet and launched into the air. And again the shock came and he was brought crushingly to the ground. This time he was aware that it was the club, but his madness knew no caution. A dozen times he charged, and as often the club broke the charge and smashed him down.

After a particularly fierce blow, he crawled to his feet, too dazed to rush. He staggered limply about, the blood flowing from nose and mouth and ears, his beautiful coat sprayed and flecked with bloody slaver. Then the man advanced and deliberately dealt him a frightful blow on the nose. All the pain he had endured was as nothing compared with the exquisite agony of this. With a roar that was almost lionlike in its ferocity, he again hurled himself at the man. But the man, shifting the club from right to left, coolly caught him by the underjaw, at the same time wrenching downward and backward. Buck described a complete circle in the air, and half of another, then crashed to the ground on his head and chest.

For the last time he rushed. The man struck the shrewd blow he had purposely withheld for so long, and Buck crumpled up and went down, knocked utterly senseless.

7 **metamorphosed**: changed.

"He's no slouch at dog-breakin', that's wot I say," one of the men on the wall cried enthusiastically.

"Druther break cayuses[8] any day, and twice on Sundays," was the reply of the driver, as he climbed on the wagon and started the horses.

Buck's senses came back to him, but not his strength. He lay where he had fallen, and from there he watched the man in the red sweater.

"'Answers to the name of Buck,'" the man soliloquized,[9] quoting from the saloon-keeper's letter which had announced the consignment of the crate and contents. "Well, Buck, my boy," he went on in a genial voice, "we've had our little ruction, and the best thing we can do is to let it go at that. You've learned your place, and I know mine. Be a good dog, and all 'll go well and the goose hang high.[10] Be a bad dog, and I'll whale the stuffin' outa you. Understand?"

As he spoke, he fearlessly patted the head he had so mercilessly pounded, and though Buck's hair involuntarily bristled at the touch of the hand, he endured it without protest. When the man brought him water, he drank eagerly, and later bolted a generous meal of raw meat, chunk by chunk, from the man's hand.

He was beaten (he knew that), but he was not broken. He saw, once for all, that he stood no chance against a man with a club. He had learned a lesson, and in all his after-life he never forgot it. That club was a revelation. It was his introduction to the reign of primitive law, and he met the introduction halfway. The facts of life took on a fiercer aspect, and while he faced that aspect uncowed,[11] he faced it with all the latent cunning of his nature aroused. As the days went by, other dogs came in crates and at the ends of ropes, some docilely, and some raging and roaring as he had come; and, one and all, he watched them pass under the dominion of the man in the red sweater. Again and again, as he looked at each brutal performance, the lesson was driven home to Buck: a man with a club was a lawgiver, a master to be obeyed, though not necessarily conciliated.[12] Of this last Buck was never guilty, though he did see beaten dogs that fawned upon the man, and wagged their tails, and licked his hand. Also he saw one dog, that would neither conciliate nor obey, finally killed in the struggle for mastery.

Now and again men came, strangers, who talked excitedly, wheedlingly, and in all kinds of fashions to the man in the red sweater. And at such times that money passed between them, the strangers took one or more of the dogs away with them. Buck wondered where they went, for they never came back, but the fear of the future was strong upon him, and he was glad each time when he was not selected.

Yet his time came in the end, in the form of a little weazened man who spat broken English and many strange and uncouth exclamations which Buck could not understand.

"Look at dat!" he cried, when his eyes lit upon Buck. "Dat one darn bully dog! Eh? How moch?"

"Three hundred, and a present at that," was the prompt reply of the man in the red sweater. "And seein' it's government money, you ain't got no kick coming, eh, Perrault?"

---

8 **cayuses** (kī yüs′ ez): horses.
9 **soliloquized** (sə lil′ə kwīzd): talked to himself.
10 **goose hang high**: an expression meaning "All is well."

11 **uncowed**: unafraid.
12 **conciliated**: made friends with.

Perrault grinned. Considering that the price of dogs had been boomed skyward by the unwonted demand, it was not an unfair sum for so fine an animal. The Canadian government would be no loser, nor would its despatches travel the slower. Perrault knew dogs, and when he looked at Buck, he knew that he was one in a thousand— "One in ten t'ousand," he commented mentally.

Buck saw money pass between them and was not surprised when Curly, a good-natured Newfoundland, and he were led away by the little weazened man. That was the last he saw of the man in the red sweater, and as Curly and he looked at receding Seattle from the deck of the *Narwhal,* it was the last he saw of the warm Southland. Curly and he were taken below by Perrault and turned over to a black-faced giant called François. Perrault was a French-Canadian, and swarthy; but François was a French-Canadian half-breed, and twice as swarthy. They were a new kind of men to Buck (of which he was destined to see many more), and while he developed no affection for them, he nonetheless grew honestly to respect them. He speedily learned that Perrault and François were fair men, calm and impartial in administering justice, and too wise in the way of dogs to be fooled by dogs.

In the 'tween-decks of the *Narwhal,* Buck and Curly joined two other dogs. One of them was a big, snow-white fellow from Spitzbergen who had been brought away by a whaling captain and who had later accompanied a geological survey into the Barrens.

He was friendly, in a treacherous sort of way, smiling into one's face while he meditated some underhand trick, for instance, when he stole from Buck's food at the first meal. As Buck sprang to punish him, the lash of François's whip sang through the air, reaching the culprit first, and nothing remained to Buck but to recover the bone. That was fair of François, he decided, and the half-breed began his rise in Buck's estimation.

The other dog made no advances nor received any; also, he did not attempt to steal from the newcomers. He was a gloomy, morose fellow, and he showed Curly plainly that all he desired was to be left alone, and further, that there would be trouble if he were not left alone. "Dave" he was called, and he ate and slept or yawned between times and took interest in nothing, not even when the *Narwhal* crossed Queen Charlotte Sound and rolled and pitched and bucked like a thing possessed. When Buck and Curly grew excited, half wild with fear, he raised his head as though annoyed, favored them with an incurious glance, yawned, and went to sleep again.

Day and night the ship throbbed to the tireless pulse of the propeller, and though one day was very like another, it was apparent to Buck that the weather was steadily growing colder. At last, one morning the propeller was quiet, and the *Narwhal* was pervaded with an atmosphere of excitement. He felt it, as did the other dogs, and knew that a change was at hand. François leashed them and brought them on deck. At the first step upon the cold surface, Buck's feet sank into a white mushy something very like mud. He sprang back with a snort. More of this white stuff was falling through the air. He shook himself, but more of it fell upon him. He sniffed it curiously, then licked some up on his tongue. It bit like fire, and the next instant was gone. This puzzled him. He tried it again with the same result. The onlookers laughed uproariously, and he felt ashamed, he knew not why, for it was his first snow.

Chapter 2

THE LAW OF CLUB AND FANG

Buck's first day on the Dyea beach was like a nightmare. Every hour was filled with shock and surprise. He had been suddenly jerked from the heart of civilization and flung into the heart of things primordial.[1] No lazy, sun-kissed life was this, with nothing to do but loaf and be bored. Here was neither peace, nor rest, nor a moment's safety. All was confusion and action, and every moment life and limb were in peril. There was imperative need to be constantly alert, for these dogs and men were not town dogs and men. They were savages, all of them, who knew no law but the law of club and fang.

He had never seen dogs fight as these wolfish creatures fought, and his first experience taught him an unforgettable lesson. It is true, it was a vicarious experience,[2] else he would not have lived to profit by it. Curly was the victim. They were camped near the log store, where she, in her friendly way, made advances to a husky dog the size of a full-grown wolf, though not half so large as she. There was no warning, only a leap in like a flash, a metallic clip of teeth, a leap out equally swift, and Curly's face was ripped open from eye to jaw.

It was the wolf manner of fighting, to strike and leap away, but there was more to it than this. Thirty or forty huskies ran to the spot and surrounded the combatants in an intent and silent circle. Buck did not com-

prehend that silent intentness, nor the eager way with which they were licking their chops. Curly rushed her antagonist, who struck again and leaped aside. He met her next rush with his chest, in a peculiar fashion that tumbled her off her feet. She never regained them. This was what the onlooking huskies had waited for. They closed in upon her, snarling and yelping, and she was buried, screaming with agony, beneath the bristling mass of bodies.

So sudden was it, and so unexpected, that Buck was taken aback. He saw Spitz run out his scarlet tongue in a way he had of laughing; and he saw François, swinging an axe, spring into the mess of dogs. Three men with clubs were helping him to scatter them. It did not take long. Two minutes from the time Curly went down, the last of her assailants was clubbed off. But she lay there limp and lifeless in the bloody, trampled snow, almost literally torn to pieces, the swart half-breed standing over her and cursing horribly. The scene often came back to Buck to trouble him in his sleep. So that was the way. No fair play. Once down, that was the end of you. Well, he would see to it that he never went down. Spitz ran out his tongue and laughed again, and from that moment Buck hated him with a bitter and deathless hatred.

Before he had recovered from the shock caused by the tragic passing of Curly, he received another shock. François fastened upon him an arrangement of straps and buckles. It was a harness, such as he had seen

---

1 **primordial** (prī môr′ dē əl): existing at the very beginning; primitive; original.
2 **vicarious experience**: experience gained by observing someone else go through the actual experience.

the grooms put on the horses at home. And as he had seen horses work, so he was set to work, hauling François on a sled to the forest that fringed the valley and returning with a load of firewood. Though his dignity was sorely hurt by thus being made a draught animal, he was too wise to rebel. He buckled down with a will and did his best, though it was all new and strange. François was stern, demanding instant obedience, and by virtue of his whip receiving instant obedience; while Dave, who was an experienced wheeler, nipped Buck's hindquarters whenever he was in error. Spitz was the leader, likewise experienced, and while he could not always get at Buck, he growled sharp reproof now and again, or cunningly threw his weight in the traces[3] to jerk Buck into the way he should go. Buck learned easily, and under the combined tuition of his two mates and François made remarkable progress. Ere they returned to camp, he knew enough to stop at "ho," to go ahead at "mush," to swing wide on the bends and to keep clear of the wheeler when the loaded sled shot downhill at their heels.

"T'ree vair' good dogs," François told Perrault. "Dat Buck, heem pool lak ever't'ing. I tich heem queek as anyt'ing."

By afternoon Perrault, who was in a hurry to be on the trail with his despatches, returned with two more dogs. "Billee" and "Joe" he called them, two brothers, and true huskies both. Sons of the one mother though they were, they were as different as day and night. Billee's one fault was his excessive good nature, while Joe was the very opposite, sour and introspective, with a perpetual snarl and a malignant[4] eye. Buck received them in comradely fashion, Dave ignored them,

while Spitz proceeded to thrash first one and then the other. Billee wagged his tail appeasingly, turned to run when he saw that appeasement was of no avail, and cried (still appeasingly) when Spitz's sharp teeth scored his flank. But no matter how Spitz circled, Joe whirled around on his heels to face him, mane bristling, ears laid back, lips writhing and snarling, jaws clipping together as fast as he could snap, and eyes diabolically gleaming—the incarnation of belligerent fear. So terrible was his appearance that Spitz was forced to forego disciplining him; but to cover his own discomfiture he turned upon the inoffensive and wailing Billee and drove him to the confines of the camp.

By evening Perrault secured another dog, an old husky, long and lean and gaunt, with a battle-scarred face and a single eye which flashed a warning of prowess that commanded respect. He was called Sol-leks, which means the Angry One. Like Dave, he asked nothing, gave nothing, expected nothing; and when he marched slowly and deliberately into their midst, even Spitz left him alone. He had one peculiarity which Buck was unlucky enough to discover. He did not like to be approached on his blind side. Of this offence Buck was unwittingly guilty, and the first knowledge he had of his indiscretion was when Sol-leks whirled upon him and slashed his shoulder to the bone for three inches up and down. Forever after Buck avoided his blind side, and to the last of their comradeship had no more trouble. His only apparent ambition, like Dave's, was to be left alone; though, as Buck was afterward to learn, each of them possessed one other and even more vital ambition.

That night Buck faced the great problem of sleeping. The tent, illuminated by a candle, glowed warmly in the midst of the white

---

3 **traces:** straps which harness an animal to a sled.
4 **malignant** (mə lig' nənt): very evil.

plain; and when he, as a matter of course, entered it, both Perrault and François bombarded him with curses and cooking utensils, till he recovered from his consternation and fled ignominiously into the outer cold. A chill wind was blowing that nipped him sharply and bit with especial venom into his wounded shoulder. He lay down on the snow and attempted to sleep, but the frost soon drove him shivering to his feet. Miserable and disconsolate, he wandered about among the many tents, only to find that one place was as cold as another. Here and there savage dogs rushed upon him, but he bristled his neck hair and snarled (for he was learning fast), and they let him go his way unmolested.

Finally an idea came to him. He would return and see how his own teammates were making out. To his astonishment, they had disappeared. Again he wandered about through the great camp, looking for them, and again he returned. Were they in the tent? No, that could not be, else he would not have been driven out. Then where could they possibly be? With drooping tail and shivering body, very forlorn indeed, he aimlessly circled the tent. Suddenly the snow gave way beneath his forelegs and he sank down. Something wriggled under his feet. He sprang back, bristling and snarling, fearful of the unseen and unknown. But a friendly little yelp reassured him, and he went back to investigate. A whiff of warm air ascended to his nostrils, and there, curled up under the snow in a snug ball, lay Billee. He whined placatingly,[5] squirmed and wriggled to show his good will and intentions, and even ventured, as a bribe for peace, to lick Buck's face with his warm, wet tongue.

Another lesson. So that was the way they did it eh? Buck confidently selected a spot, and with much fuss and wasted effort, proceeded to dig a hole for himself. In a trice[6] the heat from his body filled the confined space and he was asleep. The day had been long and arduous, and he slept soundly and comfortably, though he growled and barked and wrestled with bad dreams.

Nor did he open his eyes till roused by the noises of the waking camp. At first he did not know where he was. It had snowed during the night and he was completely buried. The snow walls pressed him on every side, and a great surge of fear swept through him—the fear of the wild thing for the trap. It was a token that he was harking back through his own life to the lives of his forebearers; for he was a civilized dog, an unduly civilized dog, and of his own experience knew no trap and so could not of himself fear it. The muscles of his whole body contracted spasmodically and instinctively, the hair on his neck and shoulders stood on end, and with a ferocious snarl he bounded straight up into the blinding day, the snow flying about him in a flashing cloud. Ere he landed on his feet, he saw the white camp spread out before him and knew where he was and remembered all that had passed from the time he went for a stroll with Manuel to the hole he had dug for himself the night before.

A shout from François hailed his appearance. "Wot I say?" the dog driver cried to Perrault. "Dat Buck for sure learn queek as anyt'ing."

Perrault nodded gravely. As courier for the Canadian government, bearing important despatches, he was anxious to secure the best dogs, and he was particularly gladdened by the possession of Buck.

---

5 **placatingly:** soothingly; offering peace.

6 **trice:** a short period of time.

Three more huskies were added to the team inside an hour, making a total of nine, and before another quarter of an hour had passed, they were in harness and swinging up the trail toward the Dyea Cañon. Buck was glad to be gone, and though the work was hard, he found he did not particularly despise it. He was surprised at the eagerness which animated the whole team and which was communicated to him, but still more surprising was the change wrought in Dave and Sol-leks. They were new dogs, utterly transformed by the harness. All passiveness and unconcern had dropped from them. They were alert and active, anxious that the work should go well, and fiercely irritable with whatever, by delay or confusion, retarded that work. The toil of the traces seemed the supreme expression of their being, and all that they lived for and the only thing in which they took delight.

Dave was wheeler or sled dog, pulling in front of him was Buck, then came Sol-leks; the rest of the team was strung out ahead, single file to the leader, which position was filled by Spitz.

Buck had been purposely placed between Dave and Sol-leks so that he might receive instruction. Apt scholar that he was, they were equally apt teachers, never allowing him to linger long in error and enforcing their teaching with their sharp teeth. Dave was fair and very wise. He never nipped Buck without cause, and he never failed to nip him when he stood in need of it. As François's whip backed him up, Buck found it to be cheaper to mend his ways than to retaliate. Once, during a brief halt, when he got tangled in the traces and delayed the start, both Dave and Sol-leks flew at him and administered a sound trouncing. The resulting tangle was even worse, but Buck took

good care to keep the traces clear thereafter; and ere the day was done, so well had he mastered his work, his mates about ceased nagging him. François's whip snapped less frequently, and Perrault even honored Buck by lifting up his feet and carefully examining them.

It was a hard day's run, up the Cañon, through Sheep Camp, past the Scales and the timberline, across glaciers and snowdrifts hundreds of feet deep, and over the great Chilcoot Divide, which stands between the salt water and the fresh and guards forbiddingly the sad and lonely North. They made good time down the chain of lakes which fills the craters of extinct volcanoes, and late that night pulled into the huge camp at the head of Lake Bennett, where thousands of gold seekers were building boats against the breakup of the ice in the spring. Buck made his hole in the snow and slept the sleep of the exhausted just, but all too early was routed out in the cold darkness and harnessed with his mates to the sled.

That day they made forty miles, the trail being packed; but the next day and for many days to follow, they broke their own trail, worked harder, and made poorer time. As a rule, Perrault traveled ahead of the team, packing the snow with webbed shoes to make it easier for them. François, guiding the sled at the gee-pole, sometimes exchanged places with him, but not often. Perrault was in a hurry, and he prided himself on his knowledge of ice, which knowledge was indispensable, for the fall ice was very thin, and where there was swift water, there was no ice at all.

Day after day for days unending, Buck toiled in the traces. Always they broke camp in the dark, and the first gray of dawn found them hitting the trail with fresh miles reeled

off behind them. And always they pitched camp after dark, eating their bit of fish, and crawling to sleep into the snow. Buck was ravenous. The pound and a half of sun-dried salmon, which was his ration for each day, seemed to go nowhere. He never had enough and suffered from perpetual hunger pangs. Yet the other dogs, because they weighed less and were born to the life, received a pound only of the fish and managed to keep in good condition.

He swiftly lost the fastidiousness[7] which had characterized his old life. A dainty eater, he found that his mates, finishing first, robbed him of his unfinished ration. There was no defending it. While he was fighting off two or three, it was disappearing down the throats of the others. To remedy this, he ate as fast as they; and, so greatly did hunger compel him, he was not above taking what did not belong to him. He watched and

learned. When he saw Pike, one of the new dogs, a clever malingerer[8] and thief, slyly steal a slice of bacon when Perrault's back was turned, he duplicated the performance the following day, getting away with the whole chunk. A great uproar was raised, but he was unsuspected, while Dub, an awkward blunderer who was always getting caught, was punished for Buck's misdeed.

This first theft marked Buck as fit to survive in the hostile Northland environment. It marked his adaptability, his capacity to adjust himself to changing conditions, the lack of which would have meant swift and terrible death. It marked, further, the decay or going to pieces of his moral nature, a vain thing and a handicap in the ruthless struggle for existence. It was all well enough in the Southland, under the law of love and fellowship, to respect private property and personal feelings; but in the Northland, under the law

---

7 **fastidiousness:** hard-to-please attitude.

8 **malingerer:** one who pretends to be sick or injured to escape work.

of club and fang, whosoever took such things into account was a fool, and in so far as he observed them he would fail to prosper.

Not that Buck reasoned it out. He was fit, that was all, and unconsciously he accommodated himself to the new mode of life. All his days, no matter what the odds, he had never run from a fight. But the club of the man in the red sweater had beaten into him a more fundamental and primitive code. Civilized, he could have died for a moral consideration, say the defense of Judge Miller's riding whip; but the completeness of his decivilization was now evidenced by his ability to flee from the defense of a moral consideration and so save his hide. He did not steal for the joy of it, but because of the clamor of his stomach. He did not rob openly, but stole secretly and cunningly, out of respect for club and fang. In short, the things he did were done because it was easier to do them than not to do them.

His development (or retrogression)[9] was rapid. His muscles became hard as iron and he grew callous[10] to all ordinary pain. He achieved an internal as well as external economy. He could eat anything, no matter how loathsome or indigestible; and, once eaten, the juices of his stomach extracted the last least particle of nutriment; and his blood carried it to the farthest reaches of his body, building it into the toughest and stoutest of tissues. Sight and scent became remarkably keen, while his hearing developed such acuteness that in his sleep he heard the faintest sound and knew whether it heralded peace or peril. He learned to bite the ice out with his teeth when it collected between his toes; and when he was thirsty and there was a thick scum of ice over the water hole, he would break it by rearing and striking it with stiff forelegs. His most conspicuous trait was an ability to scent the wind and forecast it a night in advance. No matter how breathless the air when he dug his nest by tree or bank, the wind that later blew inevitably found him to leeward, sheltered and snug.

And not only did he learn by experience, but instincts long dead became alive again. The domesticated generations fell from him. In vague ways he remembered back to the youth of the breed, to the time the wild dogs ranged in packs through the primeval forest and killed their meat as they ran it down. It was no task for him to learn to fight with cut and slash and the quick wolf snap. In this manner had fought forgotten ancestors. They quickened the old life within him, and the old tricks which they had stamped into the heredity of the breed were his tricks. They came to him without effort or discovery, as though they had been his always. And when, on the still cold nights, he pointed his nose at a star and howled long and wolflike, it was his ancestors, dead and dust, pointing nose at star and howling down through the centuries and through him. And his cadences[11] were their cadences, the cadences which voiced their woe and what to them was the meaning of the stillness and the cold and dark.

Thus, as token of what a puppet thing life is, the ancient song surged through him and he came into his own again; and he came because men had found a yellow metal in the North, and because Manuel was a gardener's helper whose wages did not lap over the needs of his wife and divers small copies of himself.

---

9 **retrogression**: movement backward especially to an earlier or less advanced condition.
10 **callous**: toughened.

---

11 **cadences**: rhythms.

1. Why were dogs like Buck so important in the Klondike during the gold rush?
2. What was Buck like when he lived on the Santa Clara estate of Judge Miller?
3. Within a short period of time in the Klondike, Buck learns two important lessons—the "law of club and fang." What incidents teach him each lesson? What does he learn from each incident?
4. Why does François think Buck is worth every penny that was spent on him?
5. In chapter 2, Buck steals food from François and Perrault. What personality traits does this act reveal? Why are these traits so important to Buck?
6. As early as chapter 2, the change of Buck into a primitive or primordial beast begins. What aspects of Buck's character, actions, and habits indicate this change?

1. François and Perrault turn out to be far better owners than others Buck will have later on. Write a brief character sketch of one of these men. Begin with a physical description, and then tell about the man's personality traits. Give proof of these traits by giving examples found in the first two chapters. End by explaining why you think François or Perrault was a good dog owner.
2. Changes in one's outward situation or circumstance often bring inward changes. This was certainly true of Buck. Think of an incident or a time when an outward change in your life or someone else's life created inward changes as well. The outward change might have been a move to a different town, a promotion to a new school, or the loss or gain of a family member. How did one of these or some other situation change you or someone you know? Begin by writing a description of the situation. Then tell about the inward changes that resulted and the causes of those changes. End by explaining why you think these inward changes were good, bad, or both.

Chaper 3

THE DOMINANT PRIMORDIAL BEAST

The dominant primordial beast was strong in Buck, and under the fierce conditions of trail life, it grew and grew. Yet it was a secret growth. His newborn cunning gave him poise and control. He was too busy adjusting himself to the new life to feel at ease, and not only did he not pick fights, but he avoided them whenever possible. A certain deliberateness characterized his attitude. He was not prone to rashness and precipitate action; and in the bitter hatred between him and Spitz, he betrayed no impatience, shunned all offensive acts.

On the other hand, possibly because he divined in Buck a dangerous rival, Spitz never lost an opportunity of showing his teeth. He even went out of his way to bully Buck, striving constantly to start the fight which could end only in the death of one or the other.

Early in the trip this might have taken place had it not been for an unwonted accident. At the end of this day, they made a bleak and miserable camp on the shore of Lake Le Barge. Driving snow, a wind that cut like a white-hot knife, and darkness had forced them to grope for a camping place. They could hardly have fared worse. At their backs rose a perpendicular wall of rock, and Perrault and François were compelled to make their fire and spread their sleeping robes on the ice of the lake itself. The tent had been discarded at Dyea in order to travel light. A few sticks of driftwood furnished them with a fire that thawed down through the ice and left them to eat supper in the dark.

Close in under the sheltering rock Buck made his nest. So snug and warm was it, that he was loath to leave it when François distributed the fish which he had first thawed over the fire. But when Buck finished his ration and returned, he found his nest occupied. A warning snarl told him that the trespasser was Spitz. Till now Buck had avoided trouble with his enemy, but this was too much. The beast in him roared. He sprang upon Spitz with a fury which surprised them both, and Spitz particularly, for his whole experience with Buck had gone to teach him that his rival was an unusually timid dog, who managed to hold his own only because of his great weight and size.

François was surprised, too, when they shot out in a tangle from the disrupted nest and he divined the cause of the trouble. "A-a-ah!" he cried to Buck. "Gif it to heem, by Gar! Gif it to heem, the dirty t'eef!"

Spitz was equally willing. He was crying with sheer rage and eagerness as he circled back and forth for a chance to spring in. Buck was no less eager, and no less cautious, as he likewise circled back and forth for the advantage. But it was then that the unexpected happened, the thing which projected their struggle for supremacy far into the future, past many a weary mile of trail and toil.

An oath from Perrault, the resounding impact of a club upon a bony frame, and a shrill yelp of pain, heralded the breaking

The Call of the Wild **573**

forth of pandemonium. The camp was suddenly discovered to be alive with skulking furry forms—starving huskies, four or five score of them, who had scented the camp from some Indian village. They had crept in while Buck and Spitz were fighting, and when the two men sprang among them with stout clubs, they showed their teeth and fought back. They were crazed by the smell of food. Perrault found one with head buried in the grub box. His club landed heavily on the gaunt ribs, and the grub box was capsized on the ground. On the instant a score of the famished brutes were scrambling for the bread and bacon. The clubs fell upon them unheeded. They yelped and howled under the rain of blows, but struggled nonetheless madly till the last crumb had been devoured.

In the meantime the astonished team dogs had burst out of their nests only to be set upon by the fierce invaders. Never had Buck seen such dogs. It seemed as though their bones would burst through their skins. They were mere skeletons, draped loosely in draggled hides, with blazing eyes and slavered fangs. But the hunger-madness made them terrifying, irresistible. There was no opposing them. The team dogs were swept back against the cliff at the first onset. Buck was beset by three huskies, and in a trice his head and shoulders were ripped and slashed. The din[1] was frightful. Billee was crying as usual. Dave and Sol-leks, dripping blood from a score of wounds, were fighting bravely side by side. Joe was snapping like a demon. Once his teeth closed on the foreleg of a husky, and he crunched down through the bone. Pike, the malingerer, leaped upon the crippled animal, breaking its neck with a quick flash of teeth and a jerk. Buck got a frothing adversary by the throat and was sprayed with blood when his teeth sank through the jugular. The warm taste of it in his mouth goaded him to greater fierceness. He flung himself upon another, and at the same time felt teeth sink into his own throat. It was Spitz, treacherously attacking from the side.

Perrault and François, having cleaned out their part of the camp, hurried to save their sled dogs. The wild wave of famished beasts rolled back before them, and Buck shook himself free. But it was only for a moment. The two men were compelled to run back to save the grub, upon which the huskies returned to the attack on the team. Billee, terrified into bravery, sprang through the savage circle and fled away over the ice. Pike and Dub followed on his heels, with the rest of the team behind. As Buck drew himself together to spring after them, out of the tail of his eye, he saw Spitz rush upon him with the evident intention of overthrowing him. Once off his feet and under that mass of huskies, there was no hope for him. But he braced himself to the shock of Spitz's charge, then joined the flight out on the lake.

Later, the nine team dogs gathered together and sought shelter in the forest. Though unpursued, they were in a sorry plight. There was not one who was not wounded in four or five places, while some were wounded grievously. Dub was badly injured in a hind leg; Dolly, the last husky added to the team at Dyea, had a badly torn throat; Joe had lost an eye; while Billee, the good-natured, with an ear chewed and rent to ribbons, cried and whimpered throughout the night. At daybreak they limped warily back to camp, to find the marauders gone and the two men in bad tempers. Fully half their grub supply was gone. The huskies had chewed through the sled lashings and canvas

---

1 din: loud, continuous noise.

coverings. In fact, nothing, no matter how remotely eatable, had escaped them. They had eaten a pair of Perrault's moose-hide moccasins, chunks out of the leather traces, and even two feet of lash from the end of François's whip. He broke from a mournful contemplation of it to look over his wounded dogs.

"Ah, my frien's," he said softly, "mebbe it mek you mad dog, dose many bites. Mebbe all mad dog, . . . ! Wot you t'ink, eh, Perrault?"

The courier shook his head dubiously. With four hundred miles of trail still between him and Dawson, he could ill afford to have madness break out among his dogs. Two hours of cursing and exertion got the harnesses into shape, and the wound stiffened team was under way, struggling painfully over the hardest part of the trail they had yet encountered, and for that matter, the hardest between them and Dawson.

The Thirty Mile River was wide open. Its wild water defied the frost, and it was in the eddies only and in the quiet places that the ice held at all. Six days of exhausting toil were required to cover those thirty terrible miles. And terrible they were, for every foot of them was accomplished at the risk of life to dog and man. A dozen times Perrault, nosing the way, broke through the ice bridges, being saved by the long pole he carried, which he so held that it fell each time across the hole made by his body. But a cold snap was on, the thermometer registering fifty below zero, and each time he broke through, he was compelled for very life to build a fire and dry his garments.

Nothing daunted[2] him. It was because nothing daunted him that he had been chosen for government courier. He took all manner of risks, resolutely thrusting his little weazened face into the frost and struggling on from dim dawn to dark. He skirted the frowning shores on rim ice that bent and crackled under foot and upon which they dared not halt. Once the sled broke through with Dave and Buck, and they were half-frozen and all but drowned by the time they were dragged out. The usual fire was necessary to save them. They were coated solidly with ice, and the two men kept them on the run around the fire, sweating and thawing so close that they were singed by the flames.

At another time Spitz went through, dragging the whole team after him up to Buck, who strained backward with all his strength, his forepaws on the slippery edge and the ice quivering and snapping all around. But behind him was Dave, likewise straining backward, and behind the sled was François, pulling till his tendons cracked.

Again, the rim ice broke away before and behind, and there was no escape except up the cliff. Perrault scaled it by a miracle, while François prayed for just that miracle; and with every thong and sled lashing and the last bit of harness rove into a long rope, the dogs were hoisted, one by one, to the cliff crest. François came up last, after the sled and load.

Then came the search for a place to descend, which descent was ultimately made by the aid of the rope, and night found them back on the river with a quarter of a mile to the day's credit.

By the time they made the Hootalinqua and good ice, Buck was played out. The rest of the dogs were in like condition, but Perrault, to make up lost time, pushed them late and early. The first day they covered thirty-five miles to the Big Salmon; the next day thirty-five more to the Little Salmon; the third day forty miles, which brought them well up toward the Five Fingers.

Buck's feet were not so compact and hard as the feet of the huskies. His had softened during the many generations since the day his last wild ancestor was tamed by a cave dweller or river man. All day long he limped in agony, and camp once made, lay down like a dead dog. Hungry as he was, he would not move to receive his ration of fish, which François had to bring to him. Also, the dog driver rubbed Buck's feet for half an hour each night after supper and sacrificed the tops of his own moccasins to make four moccasins for Buck. This was a great relief, and Buck caused even the weazened face of Perrault to twist itself into a grin one morning, when François forgot the moccasins and Buck lay on his back, his four feet waving appealingly in the air, and refused to budge without them. Later his feet grew hard to the trail, and the worn-out footgear was thrown away.

At the Pelly one morning, as they were harnessing up, Dolly, who had never been conspicuous for anything, went suddenly mad. She announced her condition by a long, heartbreaking wolf howl that sent every dog bristling with fear, then sprang straight for Buck. He had never seen a dog go mad, nor

---

2 **daunted**: discouraged.

did he have any reason to fear madness; yet he knew that here was horror, and he fled away from it in a panic. Straight away he raced, with Dolly, panting and frothing, one leap behind; nor could she gain on him, so great was his terror, nor could he leave her, so great was her madness. He plunged through the wooded breast of the island, fled down to the lower end, crossed a back channel filled with rough ice to another island, gained a third island, curved back to the main river, and in desperation started to cross it. And all the time, though he did not look, he could hear her snarling just one leap behind. François called to him a quarter of a mile away, and he doubled back, still one leap ahead, gasping painfully for air and putting all his faith in that François would save him. The dog driver held the axe poised in his hand, and as Buck shot past him the axe crashed down upon mad Dolly's head.

Buck staggered over against the sled, exhausted, sobbing for breath, helpless. This was Spitz's opportunity. He sprang upon Buck, and twice his teeth sank into his unresisting foe and ripped and tore the flesh to the bone. Then François's lash descended, and Buck had the satisfaction of watching Spitz receive the worst whipping as yet administered to any of the team.

"One devil, dat Spitz," remarked Perrault. "Some darn day heem keel dat Buck."

"Dat Buck two devils," was François's rejoinder. "All de tam I watch dat Buck I know for sure. Lissen: some darn fine day heem get mad . . . an' den heem chew dat Spitz all up an' spit heem out on de snow. Sure. I know."

From then on it was war between them. Spitz, as lead dog and acknowledged master of the team, felt his supremacy threatened by this strange Southland dog. And strange Buck was to him, for of the many Southland dogs he had known, not one had shown up worthily in camp and on the trail. They were all too soft, dying under the toil, the frost, and starvation. Buck was the exception. He alone endured and prospered, matching the husky in strength, savagery, and cunning. Then he was a masterful dog, and what made him dangerous was the fact that the club of the man in the red sweater had knocked all blind pluck and rashness out of his desire for mastery. He was preeminently cunning and could bide his time with a patience that was nothing less than primitive.

It was inevitable that the clash for leadership should come. Buck wanted it. He wanted it because it was his nature, because he had been gripped tight by that nameless, incomprehensible pride of the trail and trace—that pride which holds dogs in the toil to the last gasp, which lures them to die joyfully in the harness and breaks their hearts if they are cut out of the harness. This was the pride of Dave as wheel dog, of Sol-leks as he pulled with all his strength; the pride that laid hold of them at break of camp, transforming them from sour and sullen brutes into straining, eager, ambitious creatures; the pride that spurred them on all day and dropped them at pitch of camp at night, letting them fall back into gloomy unrest and uncontent. This was the pride that bore up Spitz and made him thrash the sled dogs who blundered and shirked in the traces or hid away at harness-up time in the morning. Likewise it was this pride that made him fear Buck as a possible lead dog. And this was Buck's pride, too.

He openly threatened the other's leadership. He came between him and the shirks he should have punished. And he did it deliberately. One night there was a heavy snowfall, and in the morning Pike, the malingerer, did not appear. He was securely hidden in his nest under a foot of snow. François called him and sought him in vain. Spitz was wild with wrath. He raged through the camp, smelling and digging in every likely place, snarling so frightfully that Pike heard and shivered in his hiding place.

But when he was at last unearthed and Spitz flew at him to punish him, Buck flew, with equal rage, in between. So unexpected was it, and so shrewdly managed, that Spitz was hurled backward and off his feet. Pike, who had been trembling abjectly, took heart at this open mutiny and sprang upon his overthrown leader. Buck, to whom fair play was a forgotten code, likewise sprang upon Spitz. But François, chuckling at the incident while unswerving in the administration of justice, brought his lash down upon Buck with all his might. This failed to drive Buck from his prostrate[3] rival, and the butt of the whip was brought into play. Half-stunned by the blow, Buck was knocked backward and the lash laid upon him again and again, while Spitz soundly punished the many times offending Pike.

In the days that followed, as Dawson grew closer and closer, Buck still continued to interfere between Spitz and the culprits; but he did it craftily, when François was not around. With the covert mutiny of Buck, a general insubordination sprang up and increased. Dave and Sol-leks were unaffected, but the rest of the team went from bad to worse. Things no longer went right. There was continual bickering and jangling. Trouble was always afoot, and at the bottom of it was Buck. He kept François busy, for the dog driver was in constant apprehension of the life-and-death struggle between the two which he knew must take place sooner or later; and on more than one night, the sounds of quarreling and strife among the other dogs turned him out of his sleeping robe, fearful that Buck and Spitz were at it.

But the opportunity did not present itself, and they pulled into Dawson one dreary afternoon with the great fight still to come. Here were many men and countless dogs, and Buck found them all at work. It seemed the ordained order of things that dogs should work. All day they swung up and down the main street in long teams, and in the night their jingling bells still went by. They hauled cabin logs and firewood, freighted up to the mines, and did all manner of work that horses did in the Santa Clara Valley. Here and there Buck met Southland dogs, but in the main they were the wild wolf husky breed. Every night regularly at nine, at twelve, at three, they lifted a nocturnal song, a weird and eerie chant, in which it was Buck's delight to join.

With the aurora borealis[4] flaming coldly overhead, or the stars leaping in the frost dance, and the land numb and frozen under its pall of snow, this song of the huskies might have been the defiance of life, only it was pitched in minor key, with long-drawn wailings and half sobs, and was more the pleading of life, the articulate travail[5] of existence. It was an old song, old as the breed itself—one of the first songs of the younger world in a day when songs were sad. It was invested with the woe of unnumbered generations, this plaint by which Buck was so strangely stirred. When he moaned and

---

3 **prostrate**: lying down.

4 **aurora borealis**: northern lights.
5 **articulate travail**: the clearly spoken sufferings.

sobbed, it was with the pain of living that was of old the pain of his wild fathers, and the fear and mystery of the cold and dark that was to them fear and mystery. And that he should be stirred by it marked the completeness with which he harked back through the ages of fire and roof to the raw beginnings of life in the howling ages.

Seven days from the time they pulled into Dawson, they dropped down the steep bank by the Barracks to the Yukon Trail, and pulled for Dyea and Salt Water. Perrault was carrying despatches if anything more urgent than those he had brought in; also, the travel pride had gripped him, and he purposed to make the record trip of the year. Several things favored him in this. The week's rest had recuperated the dogs and put them in thorough trim. The trail they had broken into the country was packed hard by later journeyers. And further, the police had arranged in two or three places deposits of grub for dog and man, and he was traveling light.

They made Sixty Mile, which is a fifty-mile run, on the first day; and the second day saw them booming up the Yukon well on their way to Pelly. But such splendid running was achieved not without great trouble and vexation on the part of François. The insidious revolt led by Buck had destroyed the solidarity of the team. It no longer was as one dog leaping in the traces. The encouragement Buck gave the rebels led them into all kinds of petty misdemeanors. No more was Spitz a leader greatly to be feared. The old awe departed, and they grew equal to challenging his authority. Pike robbed him of half a fish one night and gulped it down under the protection of Buck. Another night Dub and Joe fought Spitz and made him forego the punishment they deserved. And even Billee, the good-natured, was less good-natured,

and whined not half so placatingly as in former days. Buck never came near Spitz without snarling and bristling menacingly. In fact, his conduct approached that of a bully, and he was given to swaggering up and down before Spitz's very nose.

The breaking down of discipline likewise affected the dogs in their relations with one another. They quarreled and bickered more than ever among themselves, till at times the camp was a howling bedlam. Dave and Sol-leks alone were unaltered, though they were made irritable by the unending squabbling. François swore strange barbarous oaths and stamped the snow in futile rage, and tore his hair. His lash was always singing among the dogs, but it was of small avail. Directly when his back was turned, they were at it again. He backed up Spitz with his whip, while Buck backed up the remainder of the team. François knew he was behind all the trouble, and Buck knew he knew; but Buck was too clever ever again to be caught red-handed. He worked faithfully in the harness, for the toil had become a delight to him; yet it was a greater delight slyly to precipitate a fight amongst his mates and tangle the traces.

At the mouth of the Tahkeena one night after supper, Dub turned up a snowshoe rabbit, blundered it, and missed. In a second the whole team was in full cry. A hundred yards away was a camp of the Northwest Police, with fifty dogs, huskies all, who joined the chase. The rabbit sped down the river, turned off into a small creek, up the frozen bed of which it held steadily. It ran lightly on the surface of the snow, while the dogs ploughed through by main strength. Buck led the pack, sixty strong, around bend after bend, but he could not gain. He lay down low to the race, whining eagerly, his splendid body flashing forward, leap by leap, in the wan white moonlight. And leap by leap, like some pale frost wraith,[6] the snowshoe rabbit flashed on ahead.

All that stirring of old instincts which at stated periods drives men out from the sounding cities to forest and plain to kill things by chemically propelled leaden pellets, the blood lust, the joy to kill—all this was Buck's, only it was infinitely more intimate. He was ranging at the head of the pack, running the wild thing down, the living meat, to kill with his own teeth and wash his muzzle to the eyes in warm blood.

There is an ecstasy that marks the summit of life, and beyond which life cannot rise. And such is the paradox of living, this ecstasy comes when one is most alive, and it comes as a complete forgetfulness that one is alive. This ecstasy, this forgetfulness of living, comes to the artist, caught up and out of himself in a sheet of flame; it comes to the soldier, war-mad on a stricken field and refusing quarter; and it came to Buck, leading the pack, sounding the old wolf cry, straining after the food that was alive and that fled swiftly before him through the moonlight. He was sounding the deeps of his nature, and of the parts of his nature that were deeper than he, going back into the womb of Time. He was mastered by the sheer surging of life, the tidal wave of being, the perfect joy of each separate muscle, joint, and sinew,[7] in that it was everything that was not death, that it was aglow and rampant, expressing itself in movement, flying exultantly under the stars and over the face of dead matter that did not move.

But Spitz, cold and calculating even in his supreme moods, left the pack and cut across a narrow neck of land where the creek made a long bend around. Buck did not know of this, and as he rounded the bend, the frost wraith of a rabbit still flitting before him, he saw another and larger frost wraith leap from the overhanging bank into the immediate path of the rabbit. It was Spitz. The rabbit could not turn, and as the white teeth broke its back in midair, it shrieked as loudly as a stricken man may shriek. At sound of this, the cry of Life plunging down from Life's apex in the grip of Death, the full pack at Buck's heels raised a hell's chorus of delight.

Buck did not cry out. He did not check himself but drove in upon Spitz, shoulder to shoulder, so hard that he missed the throat. They rolled over and over in the powdery snow. Spitz gained his feet almost as though he had not been overthrown, slashing Buck down the shoulder and leaping clear. Twice his teeth clipped together, like the steel jaws of a trap, as he backed away for better footing, with lean and lifting lips that writhed and snarled.

In a flash Buck knew it. The time had come. It was to the death. As they circled about, snarling, ears laid back, keenly watchful for the advantage, the scene came to Buck with a sense of familiarity. He seemed to remember it all—the white woods, and earth, and moonlight, and the thrill of battle. Over the whiteness and silence brooded a ghostly calm. There was not the faintest whisper of air—nothing moved, not a leaf quivered, the visible breaths of the dogs rising slowly and lingering in the frosty air. They had made short work of the snowshoe rabbit, these dogs that were ill-tamed wolves, and they were now drawn up in an expectant circle. They, too, were silent, their eyes only gleaming and their breaths drifting slowly upward. To

6 **wraith** (rāth): ghost.
7 **sinew** (sin′ yü): nerve.

Buck it was nothing new or strange, this scene of old time. It was as though it had always been, the wonted way of things.

Spitz was a practiced fighter. From Spitzbergen through the Arctic and across Canada and the Barrens, he had held his own with all manner of dogs and achieved to mastery over them. Bitter rage was his, but never blind rage. In passion to rend and destroy, he never forgot that his enemy was in like passion to rend and destroy. He never rushed till he was prepared to receive a rush; never attacked till he had first defended that attack.

In vain Buck strove to sink his teeth in the neck of the big white dog. Wherever his fangs struck for the softer flesh, they were countered by the fangs of Spitz. Fang clashed fang, and lips were cut and bleeding, but Buck could not penetrate his enemy's guard. Then he warmed up and enveloped Spitz in a whirlwind of rushes. Time and time again he tried for the snow-white throat, where life bubbled near to the surface, and each time and every time Spitz slashed him and got away. Then Buck took to rushing, as though for the throat, when, suddenly drawing back his head and curving in from the side, he would drive his shoulder at the shoulder of Spitz, as a ram by which to overthrow him. But instead, Buck's shoulder was slashed down each time as Spitz leaped lightly away.

Spitz was untouched, while Buck was streaming with blood and panting hard. The fight was growing desperate. And all the while the silent and wolfish circle waited to finish off whichever dog went down. As Buck grew winded, Spitz took to rushing, and he kept him staggering for footing. Once Buck went over, and the whole circle of sixty dogs started up; but he recovered himself, almost in midair, and the circle sank down again and waited.

But Buck possessed a quality that made for greatness—imagination. He fought by instinct, but he could fight by head as well. He rushed, as though attempting the old shoulder trick, but at the last instant swept low to the snow and in. His teeth closed on Spitz's left foreleg. There was a crunch of breaking bone, and the white dog faced him on three legs. Thrice he tried to knock him over, then repeated the trick and broke the right foreleg. Despite the pain and helplessness, Spitz struggled madly to keep up. He saw the silent circle, with gleaming eyes, lolling tongues, and silvery breaths drifting upward, closing in upon him as he had seen similar circles close in upon beaten antagonists in the past. Only this time he was the one who was beaten.

There was no hope for him. Buck was inexorable.[8] Mercy was a thing reserved for gentler climes.[9] He maneuvered for the final rush. The circle had tightened till he could feel the breaths of the huskies on his flanks. He could see them, beyond Spitz and to either side, half crouching for the spring, their eyes fixed upon him. A pause seemed to fall. Every animal was motionless as though turned to stone. Only Spitz quivered and bristled as he staggered back and forth, snarling with horrible menace, as though to frighten off impending death. Then Buck sprang in and out, but while he was in, shoulder had at last squarely met shoulder. The dark circle became a dot on the moon-flooded snow as Spitz disappeared from view. Buck stood and looked on, the successful champion, the dominant primordial beast who had made his kill and found it good.

---

8 **inexorable**: relentless; showing no mercy.
9 **climes**: climates.

Chapter 4

WHO HAS WON TO MASTERSHIP

"Eh? Wot I say? I spik true w'en I say dat Buck two devils."

This was François's speech next morning when he discovered Spitz missing and Buck covered with wounds. He drew him to the fire and by its light pointed them out.

"Dat Spitz fight lak the devil," said Perrault, as he surveyed the gaping rips and cuts.

"An' dat Buck fight lak two devils," was François's answer. "An' now we make good time. No more Spitz, no more trouble, sure."

While Perrault packed the camp outfit and loaded the sled, the dog driver proceeded to harness the dogs. Buck trotted up to the place Spitz would have occupied as leader, but François, not noticing him, brought Sol-leks to the coveted position. In his judgment, Sol-leks was the best lead dog left. Buck sprang upon Sol-leks in a fury, driving him back and standing in his place.

"Eh? eh?" François cried, slapping his thighs gleefully. "Look at dat Buck. Heem keel dat Spitz, heem t'ink to take de job."

"Go 'way, Chook!" he cried, but Buck refused to budge.

He took Buck by the scruff of the neck, and though the dog growled threateningly, dragged him to one side and replaced Sol-leks. The old dog did not like it and showed plainly that he was afraid of Buck. François was obdurate,[1] but when he turned his back, Buck again displaced Sol-leks, who was not at all unwilling to go.

François was angry. "Now, by Gar, I feex

---

1 **obdurate** (ob' dər it): stubborn.

you!" he cried, coming back with a heavy club in his hand.

Buck remembered the man in the red sweater and retreated slowly, nor did he attempt to charge in when Sol-leks was once more brought forward. But he circled just beyond the range of the club, snarling with bitterness and rage; and while he circled, he watched the club so as to dodge it if thrown by François, for he had become wise in the way of clubs.

The driver went about his work, and he called to Buck when he was ready to put him in his old place in front of Dave. Buck retreated two or three steps. François followed him up, whereupon he again retreated. After some time of this, François threw down the club, thinking that Buck feared a thrashing. But Buck was in open revolt. He wanted, not to escape a clubbing, but to have the leadership. It was his by right. He had earned it, and he would not be content with less.

Perrault took a hand. Between them they ran him about for the better part of an hour. They threw clubs at him. He dodged. They cursed him, and his fathers and mothers before him, and all his seed to come after him down to the remotest generation, and every hair on his body and drop of blood in his veins; and he answered curse with snarl and kept out of their reach. He did not try to run away but retreated around and around the camp, advertising plainly that when his desire was met, he would come in and be good.

François sat down and scratched his head.

Perrault looked at his watch and swore. Time was flying, and they should have been on the trail an hour gone. François scratched his head again. He shook it and grinned sheepishly at the courier, who shrugged his shoulders in sign that they were beaten. Then François went up to where Sol-leks stood and called to Buck. Buck laughed, as dogs laugh, yet kept his distance. François unfastened Sol-leks's traces and put him back in his old place. The team stood harnessed to the sled in an unbroken line, ready for the trail. There was no place for Buck save at the front. Once more François called, and once more Buck laughed and kept away.

"T'row down de club," Perrault commanded.

François complied, whereupon Buck trotted in, laughing triumphantly, and swung around into position at the head of the team. His traces were fastened, the sled broken out, and with both men running, they dashed out onto the river trail.

Highly as the dog driver had forevalued Buck, with his two devils, he found, while the day was yet young, that he had undervalued. At a bound Buck took up the duties of leadership; and where judgment was required and quick thinking and quick acting, he showed himself the superior even of Spitz, of whom François had never seen an equal.

But it was in giving the law and making his mates live up to it, that Buck excelled. Dave and Sol-leks did not mind the change in leadership. It was none of their business. Their business was to toil, and toil mightily, in the traces. So long as that was not interfered with, they did not care what happened. Billee, the good-natured, could lead for all they cared so long as he kept order. The rest of the team, however, had grown unruly during the last days of Spitz, and their surprise was great now that Buck proceeded to lick them into shape.

Pike, who pulled at Buck's heels, and who never put an ounce more of his weight against the breast band than he was compelled to do, was swiftly and repeatedly shaken for loafing; and ere the first day was done, he was pulling more than ever before in his life. The first night in camp, Joe, the sour one, was punished roundly—a thing that Spitz had never succeeded in doing. Buck simply smothered him by virtue of superior weight and cut him up till he ceased snapping and began to whine for mercy.

The general tone of the team picked up immediately. It recovered its old-time solidarity, and once more the dogs leaped as one dog in the traces. At the Rink Rapids two native huskies, Teek and Koona, were added; and the celerity[2] with which Buck broke them in took away François's breath.

"Nevaire such a dog as dat Buck!" he cried. "No, nevaire! Heem worth one t'ousan' dollair, by Gar! Eh? Wot you say, Perrault?"

And Perrault nodded. He was ahead of the record then and gaining day by day. The trail was in excellent condition, well packed and hard, and there was no new-fallen snow with which to contend. It was not too cold. The temperature dropped to fifty below zero and remained there the whole trip. The men rode and ran by turn, and the dogs were kept on the jump, with but infrequent stoppages.

The Thirty Mile River was comparatively coated with ice, and they covered in one day going out what had taken them ten days coming in. In one run they made a sixty-mile dash from the foot of Lake Le Barge to the White Horse Rapids. Across Marsh, Tagish, and Bennett (seventy miles of lakes), they

---

2 **celerity:** speed.

flew so fast that the man whose turn it was to run towed behind the sled at the end of a rope. And on the last night of the second week, they topped White Pass and dropped down the sea slope with the lights of Skagway and the shipping at their feet.

It was a record run. Each day for fourteen days they had averaged forty miles. For three days Perrault and François threw chests up and down the main street of Skagway and were deluged with invitations to drink, while the team was the constant center of a worshipful crowd of dog-busters and mushers. Then three or four western bad men aspired to clean out the town, were riddled like pepper boxes for their pains, and public interest turned to other idols. Next came official orders. François called Buck to him, threw his arms around him, wept over him. And that was the last of François and Perrault. Like other men, they passed out of Buck's life for good.

A Scotch half-breed took charge of him and his mates, and in company with a dozen other dog teams he started back over the weary trail to Dawson. It was not light running now, nor record time, but heavy toil each day, with a heavy load behind; for this was the mail train, carrying word from the world to the men who sought gold under the shadow of the Pole.

Buck did not like it, but he bore up well to the work, taking pride in it after the manner of Dave and Sol-leks, and seeing that his mates, whether they prided in it or not, did their fair share. It was a monotonous life, operating with machinelike regularity. One day was very much like another. At a certain time each morning the cooks turned out, fires were built, and breakfast was eaten. Then, while some broke camp, others harnessed the dogs, and they were under way an hour or so before the darkness which gave warning of dawn. At night, camp was made. Some pitched the flies, others cut firewood and pine boughs for the beds, and still others carried water or ice for the cooks. Also, the dogs were fed. To them, this was the one feature of the day, though it was good to loaf around, after the fish was eaten, for an hour or so with the other dogs, of which there were fivescore and odd. There were fierce fighters among them, but three battles with the fiercest brought Buck to mastery, so that when he bristled and showed his teeth, they got out of his way.

Best of all, perhaps, he loved to lie near the fire, hind legs crouched under him, forelegs stretched out in front, head raised, and eyes blinking dreamily at the flames. Sometimes he thought of Judge Miller's big house in the sun-kissed Santa Clara Valley and of the cement swimming tank and Ysabel, the Mexican hairless, and Toots, the Japanese pug; but more often he remembered the man in the red sweater, the death of Curly, the great fight with Spitz, and the good things he had eaten or would like to eat. He was not homesick. The Sunland was very dim and distant, and such memories had no power over him. Far more potent were the memories of his heredity that gave things he had never seen before a seeming familiarity; the instincts (which were but the memories of his ancestors become habits) which had lapsed in later days, and still later in him, quickened and became alive again.

Sometimes as he crouched there, blinking dreamily at the flames, it seemed that the flames were of another fire, and that as he crouched by this other fire, he saw another and different man from the half-breed cook before him. This other man was shorter of leg and longer of arm, with muscles that were stringy and knotty rather than rounded and swelling. The hair of this man was long and matted, and his head slanted back under it from the eyes. He uttered strange sounds and seemed very much afraid of the darkness into which he peered continually, clutching in his hand, which hung midway between knee and foot, a stick with a heavy stone made fast to the end. He was all but naked, a ragged and fire-scorched skin hanging part way down his back, but on his body there was much hair. In some places, across the chest and shoulders and down the outside of the arms and thighs, it was matted into almost a thick fur. He did not stand erect, but with trunk inclined forward from the hips, on legs that bent at the knees. About his body there was a peculiar springiness or resiliency, almost catlike, and a quick alertness as of one who lived in perpetual fear of things seen and unseen.

At other times this hairy man squatted by the fire with head between his legs and slept. On such occasions his elbows were on his knees, his hands clasped above his head as though to shed rain by the hairy arms. And beyond that fire, in the circling darkness, Buck could see many gleaming coals, two by two, always two by two, which he knew to be the eyes of great beasts of prey. And he could hear the crashing of their bodies through the undergrowth and the noises they made in the night. And dreaming there by the Yukon bank, with lazy eyes blinking at the fire, these sounds and sights of another world would make the hair rise along his back and stand on end across his shoulders and up his neck, till he whimpered low and suppressedly or growled softly, and the half-breed cook shouted at him, "Hey, you Buck, wake up!" Whereupon the other world would vanish and the real world would come into his eyes, and he would get up and yawn and stretch as though he had been asleep.

It was a hard trip with the mail behind them, and the heavy work wore them down. They were short of weight and in poor condition when they made Dawson, and they should have had a ten days' or a week's rest at least. But in two days' time, they dropped down the Yukon bank from the Barracks, loaded with letters for the outside. The dogs were tired, the drivers grumbling, and to make matters worse, it snowed every day. This meant a soft trail, greater friction on the runners, and heavier pulling for the dogs; yet the drivers were fair through it all and did their best for the animals.

Each night the dogs were attended to first.

They ate before the drivers ate, and no man sought his sleeping robe till he had seen to the feet of the dogs he drove. Still, their strength went down. Since the beginning of the winter, they had traveled eighteen hundred miles, dragging sleds the whole weary distance, and eighteen hundred miles will tell upon life of the toughest. Buck stood it, keeping his mates up to their work and maintaining discipline, though he, too, was very tired. Billee cried and whimpered regularly in his sleep each night. Joe was more sour than ever, and Sol-leks was unapproachable, blind side or other side.

But it was Dave who suffered most of all. Something had gone wrong with him. He became more morose and irritable, and when camp was pitched, he at once made his nest where his driver fed him. Once out of the harness and down, he did not get on his feet again till harness-up time in the morning. Sometimes in the traces, when jerked by a sudden stoppage of the sled, or by straining to start it, he would cry out with pain. The driver examined him but could find nothing. All the drivers became interested in his case. They talked it over at mealtime and over their last pipes before going to bed, and one night they held a consultation. He was brought from his nest to the fire and was pressed and prodded till he cried out many times. Something was wrong inside, but they could locate no broken bones, could not make it out.

By the time Cassiar Bar was reached, he was so weak that he was falling repeatedly in the traces. The Scotch half-breed called a halt and took him out of the team, making the next dog, Sol-leks, fast to the sled. His intention was to rest Dave, letting him run free behind the sled. Sick as he was, Dave resented being taken out, grunting and growling while the traces were unfastened, and whimpering brokenheartedly when he saw Sol-leks in the position he had held and served so long. For the pride of trace and trail was his, and sick unto death, he could not bear that another dog should do his work.

When the sled started, he floundered in the soft snow alongside the beaten trail, attacking Sol-leks with his teeth, rushing against him and trying to thrust him off into the soft snow on the other side, striving to leap inside his traces and get between him and the sled, and all the while whining and yelping and crying with grief and pain. The half-breed tried to drive him away with the whip, but he paid no heed to the stinging lash, and the man had not the heart to strike harder. Dave refused to run quietly on the trail behind the sled, where the going was easy, but continued to flounder alongside in the soft snow, where the going was most difficult, till exhausted. Then he fell and lay where he fell, howling lugubriously[3] as the long train of sleds churned by.

With the last remnant of his strength, he managed to stagger along behind till the train made another stop, when he floundered past the sleds to his own, where he stood alongside Sol-leks. His driver lingered a moment to get a light for his pipe from the man behind. Then he returned and started his dogs. They swung out on the trail with remarkable lack of exertion, turned their heads uneasily, and stopped in surprise. The driver was surprised, too; the sled had not moved. He called his comrades to witness the sight. Dave had bitten through both of Sol-leks's traces and was standing directly in front of the sled in his proper place.

He pleaded with his eyes to remain there.

The driver was perplexed. His comrades talked of how a dog could break its heart through being denied the work that killed it, and recalled instances they had known, where dogs, too old for the toil or injured, had died because they were cut out of the traces. Also they held it a mercy, since Dave was to die anyway, that he should die in the traces, heart-easy and content. So he was harnessed in again, and proudly he pulled as of old, though more than once he cried out involuntarily from the bite of his inward hurt. Several times he fell down and was dragged in the traces, and once the sled ran upon him so that he limped thereafter in one of his hind legs.

But he held out till camp was reached, when his driver made a place for him by the fire. Morning found him too weak to travel. At harness-up time he tried to crawl to his driver. By convulsive efforts he got on his feet, staggered, and fell. Then he wormed his way forward slowly toward where the harnesses were being put on his mates. He would advance his forelegs and drag up his body with a sort of hitching movement, when he would advance his forelegs and hitch ahead again for a few more inches. His strength left him, and the last his mates saw of him, he lay gasping in the snow and yearning toward them. But they could hear him mournfully howling till they passed out of sight behind a belt of river timber.

Here the train was halted. The Scotch half-breed slowly retraced his steps to the camp they had left. The men ceased talking. A revolver shot rang out. The man came back hurriedly. The whips were snapped, the bells tinkled merrily, the sleds churned along the trail; but Buck knew, and every dog knew, what had taken place behind the belt of river trees.

---

3 **lugubriously** (lü gü′ brē əs lē): mournfully.

The Call of the Wild **589**

Chapter 5

THE TOIL OF TRACE AND TRAIL

Thirty days from the time it left Dawson, the Salt Water mail, with Buck and his mates at the fore, arrived at Skagway. They were in a wretched state, worn out and worn down. Buck's one hundred and forty pounds had dwindled to one hundred and fifteen. The rest of his mates, though lighter dogs, had lost relatively more weight than he. Pike, the malingerer, who, in his lifetime of deceit, had often successfully feigned a hurt leg, was now limping in earnest. Sol-leks was limping, and Dub was suffering from a wrenched shoulder blade.

They were all terribly footsore. No spring or rebound was left in them. Their feet fell heavily on the trail, jarring their bodies and doubling the fatigue of a day's travel. There was nothing the matter with them except that they were dead tired. It was not the dead tiredness that comes through brief and excessive effort, from which recovery is a matter of hours; but it was the dead tiredness that comes through the slow and prolonged strength drainage of months of toil. There was no power of recuperation left, no reserve strength to call upon. It had been all used, the last least bit of it. Every muscle, every fiber, every cell, was tired, dead tired. And there was reason for it. In less than five months they had traveled twenty-five hundred miles, during the last eighteen hundred of which they had had but five days' rest. When they arrived at Skagway, they were apparently on their last legs. They could barely keep the traces taut, and on the down grades just managed to keep out of the way of the sled.

"Mush on, poor sore feets," the driver encouraged them as they tottered down the main street of Skagway. "Dis is de las'. Den we get one long res'. Eh? For sure. One bully long res'."

The drivers confidently expected a long stopover. Themselves, they had covered twelve hundred miles with two days' rest, and in the nature of reason and common justice they deserved an interval of loafing. But so many were the men who had rushed into the Klondike, and so many were the sweethearts, wives, and kin that had not rushed in, that the congested mail was taking on Alpine proportions; also, there were official orders. Fresh batches of Hudson Bay dogs were to take the places of those worthless for the trail. The worthless ones were to be got rid of, and since dogs count for little against dollars, they were to be sold.

Three days passed, by which time Buck and his mates found how really tired and weak they were. Then on the morning of the fourth day, two men from the States came along and bought them, harness and all, for a song. The men addressed each other as "Hal" and "Charles." Charles was a middle-aged, lightish-colored man, with weak and watery eyes and a mustache that twisted fiercely and vigorously up, giving the lie to the limply drooping lip it concealed. Hal was a youngster of nineteen or twenty, with a big Colt revolver and a hunting knife strapped about

him on a belt that fairly bristled with cartridges. This belt was the most salient[1] thing about him. It advertised his callowness[2]—a callowness sheer and unutterable. Both men were manifestly out of place, and why they should adventure the North is part of the mystery of things that passes understanding.

Buck heard the chaffering,[3] saw the money pass between the man and the government agent, and knew that the Scotch half-breed and the mail train drivers were passing out of his life on the heels of Perrault and François and the others who had gone before. When driven with his mates to the new owners' camp, Buck saw a slipshod and slovenly affair, tent half stretched, dishes unwashed, everything in disorder; also, he saw a woman. "Mercedes" the men called her. She was Charles's wife and Hal's sister—a nice family party.

Buck watched them apprehensively as they proceeded to take down the tent and load the sled. There was a great deal of effort about their manner, but no businesslike method. The tent was rolled into an awkward bundle, three times as large as it should have been. The tin dishes were packed away unwashed. Mercedes continually fluttered in the way of her men and kept up an unbroken chattering of remonstrance[4] and advice. When they put a clothes sack on the front of the sled, she suggested it should go on the back; and when they had it put on the back and covered it over with a couple of other bundles, she discovered overlooked articles which could abide nowhere else but in that very sack, and they unloaded again.

1 **salient**: striking; most noticeable.
2 **callowness**: inexperience.
3 **chaffering**: bargaining.
4 **remonstrance**: protesting; complaining.

Three men from a neighboring tent came out and looked on, grinning and winking at one another.

"You've got a right smart load as it is," said one of them; "and it's not me should tell you your business, but I wouldn't tote that tent along if I was you."

"Undreamed of!" cried Mercedes, throwing up her hands in dainty dismay. "However in the world could I manage without a tent?"

"It's springtime, and you won't get any more cold weather," the man replied.

She shook her head decidedly, and Charles and Hal put the last odds and ends on top the mountainous load.

"Think it'll ride?" one of the men asked.

"Why shouldn't it?" Charles demanded rather shortly.

"Oh, that's all right, that's all right," the man hastened meekly to say. "I was just a-wonderin', that is all. It seemed a mite top-heavy."

Charles turned his back and drew the lashings down as well as he could, which was not in the least well.

"An' of course the dogs can hike along all day with that contraption behind them," affirmed a second of the men.

"Certainly," said Hal, with freezing politeness, taking hold of the gee-pole with one hand and swinging his whip from the other. "Mush!" he shouted. "Mush on there!"

The dogs sprang against the breast bands, strained hard for a few moments, then relaxed. They were unable to move the sled.

"The lazy brutes, I'll show them," he cried, preparing to lash out at them with the whip.

But Mercedes interfered, crying, "Oh, Hal, you mustn't," as she caught hold of the whip and wrenched it from him. "The poor dears! Now you must promise you won't be harsh with them for the rest of the trip, or I won't go a step."

"Precious lot you know about dogs," her brother sneered, "and I wish you'd leave me alone. They're lazy, I tell you, and you've got to whip them to get anything out of them. That's their way. You ask anyone. Ask one of those men."

Mercedes looked at them imploringly, untold repugnance at sight of pain written on her pretty face.

"They're weak as water, if you want to know," came the reply from one of the men. "Plum tuckered out, that's what's the matter. They need a rest."

"Rest be blanked," said Hal, with his beardless lips; and Mercedes said, "Oh!" in pain and sorrow at the oath.

But she was a clannish creature and rushed at once to the defense of her brother. "Never mind that man," she said pointedly. "You're driving our dogs, and you do what you think best with them."

Again Hal's whip fell upon the dogs. They threw themselves against the breast bands, dug their feet into the packed snow, got down low to it, and put forth all their strength. The sled held as though it were an anchor. After two efforts, they stood still, panting. The whip was whistling savagely when once more Mercedes interfered. She dropped on her knees before Buck, with tears in her eyes, and put her arms around his neck.

"You poor, poor dears," she cried sympathetically, "why don't you pull hard? Then you wouldn't be whipped." Buck did not like her, but he was feeling too miserable to resist her, taking it as part of the day's miserable work.

One of the onlookers, who had been clenching his teeth to suppress hot speech, now spoke up:—

"It's not that I care a whoop what becomes of you, but for the dogs' sakes I just want to tell you, you can help them a mighty lot by breaking out that sled. The runners are froze fast. Throw your weight against the gee-pole, right and left, and break it out."

A third time the attempt was made, but this time, following the advice, Hal broke out the runners which had been frozen in the snow. The overloaded and unwieldy sled forged ahead, Buck and his mates struggling frantically under the rain of blows. A hundred yards ahead the path turned and sloped steeply into the main street. It would have required an experienced man to keep the top-heavy sled upright, and Hal was not such a man. As they swung on the turn, the sled went over, spilling half its load through the loose lashings. The dogs never stopped. The lightened sled bounded on its side behind them. They were angry because of the ill treatment they had received and the unjust load. Buck was raging. He broke into a run, the team following his lead. Hal cried, "Whoa! whoa!" but they gave no heed. He tripped and was pulled off his feet. The capsized sled ground over him, and the dogs dashed on up the street, adding to the gaiety of Skagway as they scattered the remainder of the outfit along its chief thoroughfare.

Kindhearted citizens caught the dogs and gathered up the scattered belongings. Also, they gave advice. Half the load and twice the dogs, if they ever expected to reach Dawson, was what was said. Hal and his sister and brother-in-law listened unwillingly, pitched tent, and overhauled the outfit. Canned goods were turned out that made men laugh, for canned goods on the Long Trail is a thing to dream about. "Blankets for a hotel," quoth one of the men who laughed and helped. "Half as many is too much; get rid of them.

Throw away that tent and all those dishes—who's going to wash them anyway? Good Lord, do you think you're traveling on a Pullman?"[5]

And so it went, the inexorable elimination of the superfluous.[6] Mercedes cried when her clothes bags were dumped on the ground and article after article was thrown out. She cried in general, and she cried in particular over each discarded thing. She clasped hands about knees, rocking back and forth brokenheartedly. She averred she would not go an inch, not for a dozen Charleses. She appealed to everybody and to everything, finally wiping her eyes and proceeding to cast out even articles of apparel that were imperative necessities. And in her zeal, when she had finished with her own, she attacked the belongings of her men and went through them like a tornado.

This accomplished, the outfit, though cut in half, was still a formidable bulk. Charles and Hal went out in the evening and bought six outside dogs. These, added to the six of the original team, and Teek and Koona, the huskies obtained at the Rink Rapids on the record trip, brought the team up to fourteen. But the outside dogs, though practically broken in since their landing, did not amount to much. Three were short-haired pointers, one was a Newfoundland, and the other two were mongrels of indeterminate breed. They did not seem to know anything, these newcomers. Buck and his comrades looked upon them with disgust, and though he speedily taught them their places and what *not* to do, he could not teach them what to do. They did not take kindly to trace and trail. With the exception of the two mongrels, they were bewildered and spirit-broken by the strange savage environment in which they found themselves and by the ill treatment they had received. The two mongrels were without spirit at all; bones were the only things breakable about them.

With the newcomers hopeless and forlorn, and the old team worn out by twenty-five hundred miles of continuous trail, the outlook was anything but bright. The two men, however, were quite cheerful. And they were proud, too. They were doing the thing in style, with fourteen dogs. They had seen other sleds depart over the Pass for Dawson, or come in from Dawson, but never had they seen a sled with so many as fourteen dogs. In the nature of Arctic travel there was a reason why fourteen dogs should not drag one sled, and that was that one sled could not carry the food for fourteen dogs. But Charles and Hal did not know this. They had worked the trip out with a pencil, so much to a dog, so many dogs, and so many days, Q.E.D. Mercedes looked over their shoulders and nodded comprehensively; it was all so very simple.

Late next morning Buck led the long team up the street. There was nothing lively about it, no snap or go in him and his fellows. They were starting dead weary. Four times he had covered the distance between Salt Water and Dawson, and the knowledge that, jaded and tired, he was facing the same trail once more, made him bitter. His heart was not in the work, nor was the heart of any dog. The outsides were timid and frightened, the insides without confidence in their masters.

Buck felt vaguely that there was no depending upon these two men and the woman. They did not know how to do anything, and as the days went by, it became apparent that they could not learn. They were slack in all things, without order or

---

5 **Pullman**: a special passenger train car with sleeping accommodations.
6 **superfluous** (sù pėr' flü əs): needless; unnecessary.

discipline. It took them half the night to pitch a slovenly camp, and half the morning to break that camp and get the sled loaded in fashion so slovenly that for the rest of the day they were occupied in stopping and rearranging the load. Some days they did not make ten miles. On other days they were unable to get started at all. And on no day did they succeed in making more than half the distance used by the men as a basis in their dog food computation.

It was inevitable that they should go short on dog food. But they hastened it by over-feeding, bringing the day nearer when under-feeding would commence. The outside dogs, whose digestions had not been trained by chronic famine to make the most of little, had voracious appetites. And when, in addition to this, the worn-out huskies pulled weakly, Hal decided that the orthodox ration was too small. He doubled it. And to cap it all, when Mercedes, with tears in her pretty eyes and a quaver in her throat, could not cajole him into giving the dogs still more, she stole from the fish sacks and fed them slyly. But it was not food that Buck and the huskies needed, but rest. And though they were making poor time, the heavy load they dragged sapped their strength severely.

Then came the under-feeding. Hal awoke one day to the fact that his dog food was half gone and the distance only quarter covered; further, that for love or money no additional dog food was to be obtained. So he cut down even the orthodox ration and tried to increase the day's travel. His sister and brother-in-law seconded him, but they were frustrated by their heavy outfit and their own incompetence. It was a simple matter to give the dogs less food, but it was impossible to make the dogs travel faster, while their own inability to get under way earlier in the morning prevented them from traveling longer hours. Not only did they not know how to work dogs, but they did not know how to work themselves.

The first to go was Dub. Poor blundering thief that he was, always getting caught and punished, he had nonetheless been a faithful worker. His wrenched shoulder blade, untreated and unrested, went from bad to worse, till finally Hal shot him with the big Colt revolver. It is a saying of the country that an outside dog starves to death on the ration of the husky, so the six outside dogs under Buck could do no less than die on half the ration of the husky. The Newfoundland went first, followed by the three short-haired pointers, the two mongrels hanging more grittily on to life, but going in the end.

By this time all the amenities and gentlenesses of the Southland had fallen away from the three people. Shorn of its glamor and romance, Arctic travel became to them a reality too harsh for their manhood and womanhood. Mercedes ceased weeping over the dogs, being too occupied with weeping over herself and with quarreling with her husband and brother. To quarrel was the one thing they were never too weary to do. Their irritability arose out of their misery, increased with it, doubled upon it, outdistanced it. The wonderful patience of the trail which comes to men who toil hard and suffer sore, and remain sweet of speech and kindly, did not come to these two men and the woman. They had no inkling of such a patience. They were stiff and in pain; their muscles ached, their bones ached, their very hearts ached; and because of this they became sharp of speech, and hard words were first on their lips in the morning and last at night.

Charles and Hal wrangled whenever Mercedes gave them a chance. It was the cherished belief of each that he did more than his share of the work, and neither forbore to speak this belief at every opportunity. Sometimes Mercedes sided with her husband, sometimes with her brother. The result was a beautiful and unending family quarrel. Starting from a dispute as to which should chop a few sticks for the fire (a dispute which concerned only Charles and Hal), presently would be lugged in the rest of the family, fathers, mothers, uncles, cousins, people thousands of miles away, and some of them dead. That Hal's views on art, or the sort of society plays his mother's brother wrote, should have anything to do with the chopping of a few sticks of firewood, passes comprehension; nevertheless the quarrel was as likely to end in that direction as in the direction of Charles's political prejudices. And that Charles's sister's tale-bearing tongue should be relevant to the building of a Yukon fire, was apparent only to Mercedes, who disburdened herself of copious[7] opinions upon that topic, and incidentally upon a few other traits unpleasantly peculiar to her husband's family. In the meantime the fire remained unbuilt, the camp half pitched, and the dogs unfed.

Mercedes nursed a special grievance—the grievance of sex. She was pretty and soft and had been chivalrously treated all her days. But the present treatment by her husband and brother was everything save chivalrous. It was her custom to be helpless. They complained. Upon which impeachment of what to her was her most essential sex prerogative, she made their lives unendurable. She no longer considered the dogs, and because she was sore and tired, she persisted in riding on the sled. She was pretty and soft, but she

weighed one hundred and twenty pounds—a lusty last straw to the load dragged by the weak and starving animals. She rode for days, till they fell in the traces and the sled stood still. Charles and Hal begged her to get off and walk, pleaded with her, entreated; the while she wept and importuned Heaven with a recital of their brutality.

On one occasion they took her off the sled by main strength. They never did it again. She let her legs go limp like a spoiled child and sat down on the trail. They went on their way, but she did not move. After they had traveled three miles, they unloaded the sled, came back for her, and by main strength put her on the sled again.

In the excess of their own misery, they were callous to the suffering of their animals. Hal's theory, which he practiced on others, was that one must get hardened. He had started out preaching it to his sister and brother-in-law. Failing there, he hammered it into the dogs with a club. At the Five Fingers the dog food gave out, and a toothless old squaw offered to trade them a few pounds of frozen horsehide for the Colt revolver that kept the big hunting knife company at Hal's hip. A poor substitute for food was this hide, just as it had been stripped from the starved horses of the cattlemen six months back. In its frozen state it was more like strips of galvanized iron, and when a dog wrestled it into his stomach, it thawed into thin and innutritious leathery strings and into a mass of short hair, irritating and indigestible.

And through it all Buck staggered along at the head of the team as in a nightmare. He pulled when he could; when he could no longer pull, he fell down and remained down till blows from whip or club drove him to his feet again. All the stiffness and gloss had gone

---

7 **copious:** abundant; plentiful.

out of his beautiful furry coat. The hair hung down, limp and draggled, or matted with dried blood where Hal's club had bruised him. His muscles had wasted away to knotty strings, and the flesh pads had disappeared, so that each rib and every bone in his frame were outlined clearly through the loose hide that was wrinkled in folds of emptiness. It was heartbreaking, only Buck's heart was unbreakable. The man in the red sweater had proved that.

As it was with Buck, so was it with his mates. They were perambulating[8] skeletons. There were seven all together, including him. In their very great misery they had become insensible to the bite of the lash or the bruise of the club. The pain of the beating was dull and distant, just as the things their eyes saw and their ears heard seemed dull and distant. They were not half living, or quarter living. They were simply so many bags of bones in which sparks of life fluttered faintly. When a halt was made, they dropped down in the traces like dead dogs, and the spark dimmed and paled and seemed to go out. And when the club or whip fell upon them, the spark fluttered feebly up, and they tottered to their feet and staggered on.

There came a day when Billee, the good-natured, fell and could not rise. Hal had traded off his revolver, so he took the axe and knocked Billee on the head as he lay in the traces, then cut the carcass out of the harness and dragged it to one side. Buck saw, and his mates saw, and they knew that this thing was very close to them. On the next day Koona went, and but five of them remained: Joe, too far gone to be malignant; Pike, crippled and limping, only half conscious and not conscious enough longer to malinger; Sol-leks,

the one-eyed, still faithful to the toil of trace and trail, and mournful in that he had so little strength with which to pull; Teek, who had not traveled so far that winter and who was now beaten more than the others because he was fresher; and Buck, still at the head of the team, but no longer enforcing discipline or striving to enforce it, blind with weakness half the time and keeping the trail by the loom of it and by the dim feel of his feet.

It was beautiful spring weather, but neither dogs nor humans were aware of it. Each day the sun rose earlier and set later. It was dawn by three in the morning, and twilight lingered till nine at night. The whole long day was a blaze of sunshine. The ghostly winter silence had given way to the great spring murmur of awakening life. This murmur arose from all the land, fraught with the joy of living. It came from the things that lived and moved again, things which had been as dead and which had not moved during the long months of frost. The sap was rising in the pines. The willows and aspens were bursting out in young buds. Shrubs and vines were putting on fresh garbs of green. Crickets sang in the nights, and in the days all manner of creeping, crawling things rustled forth into the sun. Partridges and wood-peckers were booming and knocking in the forest. Squirrels were chattering, birds singing, and overhead honked the wild fowl, driving up from the south in cunning wedges that split the air.

From every hill slope came the trickle of running water, the music of unseen fountains. All things were thawing, bending, snapping. The Yukon was straining to break loose the ice that bound it down. It ate away from beneath; the sun ate from above. Air holes formed, fissures sprang and spread apart, while thin sections of ice fell through

---

8 **perambulating**: walking.

bodily into the river. And amid all this bursting, rending, throbbing of awakening life, under the blazing sun and through the soft sighing breezes, like wayfarers to death, staggered the two men, the woman, and the huskies.

With the dogs falling, Mercedes weeping and riding, Hal swearing innocuously, and Charles's eyes wistfully watering, they staggered into John Thornton's camp at the mouth of White River. When they halted, the dogs dropped down as though they had all been struck dead. Mercedes dried her eyes and looked at John Thornton. Charles sat down on a log to rest. He sat down very slowly and painstakingly what of his great stiffness. Hal did the talking. John Thornton was whittling the last touches on an axe handle he had made from a stick of birch. He whittled and listened, gave monosyllabic[9] replies, and, when it was asked, terse advice. He knew the breed, and he gave his advice in the certainty that it would not be followed.

"They told us up above that the bottom was dropping out of the trail and that the best thing for us to do was to lay over," Hal said, in response to Thornton's warning to take no more chances on the rotten ice. "They told us we couldn't make White River, and here we are." This last with a sneering ring of triumph in it.

"And they told you true," John Thornton answered. "The bottom's likely to drop out at any moment. Only fools, with the blind luck of fools, could have made it. I tell you straight, I wouldn't risk my carcass on that ice for all the gold in Alaska."

"That's because you're not a fool, I suppose," said Hal. "All the same, we'll go on to

Dawson." He uncoiled his whip. "Get up there, Buck! Hi! Get up there! Mush on!"

Thornton went on whittling. It was idle, he knew, to get between a fool and his folly; while two or three fools more or less would not alter the scheme of things.

But the team did not get up at the command. It had long since passed into the stage where blows were required to rouse it. The whip flashed out, here and there, on its merciless errands. John Thornton compressed his lips. Sol-leks was the first to crawl to his feet. Teek followed. Joe came next, yelping with pain. Pike made painful efforts. Twice he fell over when half up, and on the third attempt managed to rise. Buck made no effort. He lay quietly where he had fallen. The lash bit into him again and again, but he neither whined nor struggled. Several times Thornton started, as though to speak, but changed his mind. A moisture came into his eyes, and as the whipping continued, he arose and walked irresolutely up and down.

This was the first time Buck had failed, in itself a sufficient reason to drive Hal into a rage. He exchanged the whip for the customary club. Buck refused to move under the rain of heavier blows which now fell upon him. Like his mates, he was barely able to get up, but, unlike them, he had made up his mind not to get up. He had a vague feeling of impending doom. This had been strong upon him when he pulled into the bank, and it had not departed from him. What of the thin and rotten ice he had felt under his feet all day; it seemed that he sensed disaster close at hand, out there ahead on the ice where his master was trying to drive him. He refused to stir. So greatly had he suffered, and so far gone was he, that the blows did not hurt much. And as they continued to fall upon him, the spark of life within flickered and went down. It was

---

9 **monosyllabic** (mon′ ə sə lab′ ik): consisting of a word or words of one syllable, such as "yes" or "no."

nearly out. He felt strangely numb. As though from a great distance, he was aware that he was being beaten. The last sensations of pain left him. He no longer felt anything, though very faintly he could hear the impact of the club upon his body. But it was no longer his body, it seemed so far away.

And then suddenly, without warning, uttering a cry that was inarticulate and more like the cry of an animal, John Thornton sprang upon the man who wielded the club. Hal was hurled backward, as though struck by a falling tree. Mercedes screamed. Charles looked on wistfully, wiped his watery eyes, but did not get up because of his stiffness.

John Thornton stood over Buck, struggling to control himself, too convulsed with rage to speak.

"If you strike that dog again, I'll kill you," he at last managed to say in a choking voice.

"It's my dog," Hal replied, wiping the blood from his mouth as he came back. "Get out of my way, or I'll fix you. I'm going to Dawson."

Thornton stood between him and Buck and evinced no intention of getting out of the way. Hal drew his long hunting knife. Mercedes screamed, cried, laughed, and manifested the chaotic abandonment of hysteria. Thornton rapped Hal's knuckles with the axe handle, knocking the knife to the ground. He rapped his knuckles again as he tried to pick it up. Then he stooped, picked it up himself, and with two strokes cut Buck's traces.

Hal had no fight left in him. Besides, his hands were full with his sister, or his arms, rather; while Buck was too near dead to be of further use in hauling the sled. A few minutes later they pulled out from the bank and down the river. Buck heard them go and raised his head to see. Pike was leading, Sol-leks was at the wheel, and between were Joe and Teek. They were limping and staggering. Mercedes was riding the loaded sled. Hal guided at the gee-pole, and Charles stumbled along in the rear.

As Buck watched them, Thornton knelt beside him and with rough, kindly hands searched for broken bones. By the time his search had disclosed nothing more than many bruises and a state of terrible starvation, the sled was a quarter of a mile away. Dog and man watched it crawling along over the ice. Suddenly, they saw its back end drop down, as into a rut, and the gee-pole with Hal clinging to it, jerk into the air. Mercedes's scream came to their ears. They saw Charles turn and make one step to run back, and then a whole section of ice give way and dogs and humans disappear. A yawning hole was all that was to be seen. The bottom had dropped out of the trail.

John Thornton and Buck looked at each other.

"You poor devil," said John Thornton, and Buck licked his hand.

Discussion

1. Find two examples from chapter 4 which illustrate Buck's careful and cunning strategy to take the team's leadership away from Spitz.

2. What is Buck's first tactic during this battle with Spitz? When this method does not work, what does he do then? What personality trait does this ability to change tactics reveal in Buck?

3. Who do you think is the man that Buck dreams about who is "shorter of leg and longer in arm"? Why do you think this dream is important in the development of the book's plot?

4. Why do François and Perrault and the Scotch half-breed have to sell Buck?

5. Explain how and why Charles, Hal, and Mercedes mistreat Buck.

6. Why does Buck refuse to pull the sled at John Thornton's camp at the mouth of the White River?

Composition

1. John Thornton knew that "it was idle to get between a fool and his folly." Write a letter to a friend and tell about the unbelievably foolish things that Hal, Charles, and Mercedes did which finally led to their destruction in the White River. End your letter with some advice about survival in the Yukon.

2. John Thornton acted to save a dog, but he did not prevent the destruction of Hal, Charles, and Mercedes. In your opinion, was he justified or should he be criticized? In a short paragraph, give at least three reasons for your opinion.

Chapter 6

FOR THE LOVE OF A MAN

When John Thornton froze his feet the previous December, his partners had made him comfortable and left him to get well, going on themselves up the river to get out a raft of saw logs for Dawson. He was still limping slightly at the time he rescued Buck, but with the continued warm weather even the slight limp left him. And here, lying by the river bank through the long spring days, watching the running water, listening lazily to the songs of birds and the hum of nature, Buck slowly won back his strength.

A rest comes very good after one has traveled three thousand miles, and it must be confessed that Buck waxed lazy as his wounds healed; his muscles swelled out, and the flesh came back to cover his bones. For that matter, they were all loafing—Buck, John Thornton, and Skeet and Nig—waiting for the raft to come that was to carry them down to Dawson. Skeet was a little Irish setter who early made friends with Buck, who in a dying condition was unable to resent her first advances. She had the doctor trait which some dogs possess, and as a mother cat washes her kittens, so she washed and cleansed Buck's wounds. Regularly, each morning after he had finished his breakfast,

she performed her self-appointed task, till he came to look for her ministrations as much as he did for Thornton's. Nig, equally friendly, though less demonstrative, was a huge black dog, half bloodhound and half deerhound, with eyes that laughed and a boundless good nature.

To Buck's surprise these dogs manifested no jealousy toward him. They seemed to share the kindliness and largeness of John Thornton. As Buck grew stronger, they enticed him into all sorts of ridiculous games in which Thornton himself could not forbear to join, and in this fashion Buck romped through his convalescence[1] and into a new existence. Love, genuine passionate love, was his for the first time. This he had never experienced at Judge Miller's down in the sun-kissed Santa Clara Valley. With the Judge's sons, hunting and tramping, it had been a working partnership; with the Judge's grandsons, a sort of pompous guardianship; and with the Judge himself, a stately and dignified friendship. But love that was feverish and burning, that was adoration, that was madness, it had taken John Thornton to arouse.

This man had saved his life, which was something; but further, he was the ideal master. Other men saw to the welfare of their dogs from a sense of duty and business expediency; he saw to the welfare of his as if they were his own children because he could not help it. And he saw further. He never forgot a kindly greeting or a cheering word, and to sit down for a long talk with them ("gas" he called it) was as much his delight as theirs. He had a way of taking Buck's head roughly between his hands and resting his own head upon Buck's, of shaking him back and forth, the while calling him ill names that to Buck were love names. Buck knew no greater joy than that rough embrace and the sound of murmured oaths, and at each jerk back and forth, it seemed that his heart would be shaken out of his body so great was its ecstasy. And when released, he sprang to his feet, his mouth laughing, his eyes eloquent, his throat vibrant with unuttered sound, and in that fashion remained without movement, John Thornton would reverently exclaim, "My gosh! you can all but speak!"

Buck had a trick of love expression that was akin to hurt. He would often seize Thornton's hand in his mouth and close so fiercely that the flesh bore the impress of his teeth for some time afterward. And as Buck understood the oaths to be love words, so the man understood this feigned bite for a caress.

For the most part, however, Buck's love was expressed in adoration. While he went wild with happiness when Thornton touched him or spoke to him, he did not seek these tokens. Unlike Skeet, who was wont to shove her nose under Thornton's hand and nudge and nudge till petted, or Nig, who would stalk up and rest his great head on Thornton's knee, Buck was content to adore at a distance. He would lie by the hour, eager, alert, at Thornton's feet, looking up into his face, dwelling upon it, studying it, following with keenest interest each fleeting expression, every movement or change of feature. Or, as chance might have it, he would lie farther away, to the side or rear, watching the outlines of the man and the occasional movements of his body. And often, such was the communion in which they lived, the strength of Buck's gaze would draw John Thornton's head around, and he would return the gaze, without speech, his heart

---

1 **convalescence** (kon′ və les′ ns): time during which one recovers health and strength after an illness.

shining out of his eyes as Buck's heart shone out.

For a long time after his rescue, Buck did not like Thornton to get out of his sight. From the moment he left the tent to when he entered it again, Buck would follow at his heels. His transient masters since he had come into the Northland had bred in him a fear that no master could be permanent. He was afraid that Thornton would pass out of his life as Perrault and François and the Scotch half-breed had passed out. Even in the night, in his dreams, he was haunted by this fear. At such times he would shake off sleep and creep through the chill to the flap of the tent where he would stand and listen to the sound of his master's breathing.

But in spite of this great love he bore John Thornton, which seemed to bespeak the soft civilizing influence, the strain of the primitive, which the Northland had aroused in him, remained alive and active. Faithfulness and devotion, things born of fire and roof, were his; yet he retained his wildness and wiliness. He was a thing of the wild, come in from the world to sit by John Thornton's fire, rather than a dog of the soft Southland stamped with the marks of generations of civilization. Because of his very great love, he could not steal from this man, but from any other man, in any other camp, he did not hesitate an instant; while the cunning with which he stole enabled him to escape detection.

His face and body were scored by the teeth of many dogs, and he fought as fiercely as ever and more shrewdly. Skeet and Nig were too good-natured for quarreling—besides, they belonged to John Thornton—but the strange dog, no matter what the breed or valor, swiftly acknowledged Buck's supremacy or found himself struggling for life with a terrible antagonist. And Buck was merciless. He had learned well the law of club and fang, and he never forewent an advantage or drew back from a foe he had started on the way to Death. He had lessoned from Spitz and from the chief fighting dogs of the police and mail, and he knew there was no middle course. He must master or be mastered; while to show mercy was a weakness. Mercy did not exist in the primordial life. It was misunderstood for fear, and such misunderstandings made for death. Kill or be killed, eat or be eaten, was the law; and this mandate, down out of the depths of Time, he obeyed.

He was older than the days he had seen and breaths he had drawn. He linked the past with the present, and the eternity behind him throbbed through him in a mighty rhythm to which he swayed as the tides and seasons swayed. He sat by John Thornton's fire, a broad-breasted dog, white-fanged and long-furred; but behind him were the shades of all manner of dogs, half-wolves and wild wolves, urgent and prompting, tasting the savor of the meat he ate, thirsting for the water he drank, scenting the wind with him, listening with him and telling him the sounds made by the wild life in the forest, dictating his moods, directing his actions, lying down to sleep with him when he lay down, and dreaming with him and beyond him and becoming themselves the stuff of his dreams.

So peremptorily[2] did these shades beckon him, that each day mankind and the claims of mankind slipped farther from him. Deep in the forest a call was sounding, and as often as he heard this call, mysteriously thrilling and luring, he felt compelled to turn his back upon the fire and the beaten earth around it, and to plunge into the forest, and on and on,

---

2 **peremptorily** (pə remp′ tər ə lē): without choice.

he knew not where or why; nor did he wonder where or why, the call sounding imperiously,[3] deep in the forest. But as often as he gained the soft unbroken earth and the green shade, the love for John Thornton drew him back to the fire again.

Thornton alone held him. The rest of mankind was as nothing. Chance travelers might praise or pet him, but he was cold under it all, and from a too demonstrative man he would get up and walk away. When Thornton's partners, Hans and Pete, arrived on the long-expected raft, Buck refused to notice them till he learned they were close to Thornton; after that he tolerated them in a passive sort of way, accepting favors from them as though he favored them by accepting. They were of the same large type as Thornton, living close to the earth, thinking simply and seeing clearly; and ere they swung the raft into the big eddy by the sawmill at Dawson, they understood Buck and his ways and did not insist upon an intimacy such as obtained with Skeet and Nig.

For Thornton, however, his love seemed to grow and grow. He, alone among men, could put a pack upon Buck's back in the summer traveling. Nothing was too great for Buck to do when Thornton commanded. One day (they had grub-staked themselves from the proceeds of the raft and left Dawson for the headwaters of Tanana) the men and dogs were sitting on the crest of a cliff which fell away, straight down, to naked bedrock three hundred feet below. John Thornton was sitting near the edge, Buck at his shoulder. A thoughtless whim seized Thornton, and he drew the attention of Hans and Pete to the experiment he had in mind. "Jump, Buck!" he commanded, sweeping his arm out and over the chasm. The next instant he was grappling with Buck on the extreme edge, while Hans and Pete were dragging them back into safety.

"It's uncanny," Pete said, after it was over and they had caught their speech.

Thornton shook his head. "No, it is splendid, and it is terrible, too. Do you know, it sometimes makes me afraid."

"I'm not hankering to be the man that lays hands on you while he's around," Pete announced conclusively, nodding his head toward Buck.

"By Jingo!" was Hans's contribution. "Not mineself either."

It was at Circle City, ere the year was out, that Pete's apprehensions were realized. "Black" Burton, a man evil-tempered and malicious, had been picking a quarrel with a tenderfoot at the bar when Thornton stepped good-naturedly between. Buck, as was his custom, was lying in a corner, head on paws, watching his master's every action. Burton struck out without warning, straight from the shoulder. Thornton was sent spinning and saved himself from falling only by clutching the rail of the bar.

Those who were looking on heard what was neither bark nor yelp, but a something which is best described as a roar, and they saw Buck's body rise up in the air as he left the floor for Burton's throat. The man saved his life by instinctively throwing out his arm, but he was hurled backward to the floor with Buck on top of him. Buck loosed his teeth from the flesh of the arm and drove in again for the throat. This time the man succeeded only in partly blocking, and his throat was torn open. Then the crowd was upon Buck, and he was driven off; but while a surgeon checked the bleeding, he prowled up and down, growling furiously, attempting to rush

---

3 **imperiously:** urgently.

in, and being forced back by an array of hostile clubs. A "miners' meeting," called on the spot, decided that the dog had sufficient provocation,[4] and Buck was discharged. But his reputation was made, and from that day his name spread through every camp in Alaska.

Later on in the fall of the year, he saved John Thornton's life is quite another fashion. The three partners were lining a long and narrow poling boat down a bad stretch of rapids on the Forty-Mile Creek. Hans and Pete moved along the bank, snubbing with a thin Manila rope from tree to tree, while Thornton remained in the boat, helping its descent by means of a pole and shouting directions to the shore. Buck, on the bank, worried and anxious, kept abreast of the boat, his eyes never off his master.

At a particularly bad spot where a ledge of barely submerged rocks jutted out into the river, Hans cast off the rope, and, while Thornton poled the boat out into the stream, ran down the bank with the end in his hand to snub the boat when it had cleared the ledge. This it did and was flying downstream in a current as swift as a millrace when Hans checked it with the rope and checked too suddenly. The boat flirted over and snubbed into the bank bottom up, while Thornton, flung sheer out of it, was carried downstream toward the worst part of the rapids, a stretch of wild water in which no swimmer could live.

Buck had sprung in on the instant, and at the end of three hundred yards, amid a mad swirl of water, he overhauled Thornton. When he felt him grasp his tail, Buck headed for the bank, swimming with all his splendid strength. But the progress shoreward was slow; the progress downstream amazingly rapid. From below came the fatal roaring where the wild current went wilder and was rent in shreds and spray by the rocks which thrust through like the teeth of an enormous comb. The suck of the water as it took the beginning of the last steep pitch was frightful, and Thornton knew that the shore was impossible. He scraped furiously over a rock, bruised across a second, and struck a third with crushing force. He clutched its slippery top with both hands, releasing Buck, and above the roar of the churning water shouted, "Go, Buck! Go!"

Buck could not hold his own and swept on downstream, struggling desperately, but unable to win back. When he heard Thornton's command repeated, he partly reared out of the water, throwing his head high, as though for a last look, then turned obediently toward the bank. He swam powerfully and was dragged ashore by Pete and Hans at the very point where swimming ceased to be possible and destruction began.

They knew that the time a man could cling to a slippery rock in the face of that driving current was a matter of minutes, and they ran as fast as they could up the bank to a point far above where Thornton was hanging on. They attached the line with which they had been snubbing the boat to Buck's neck and shoulders, being careful that it should neither strangle him nor impede his swimming, and launched him into the stream. He struck out boldly, but not straight enough into the stream. He discovered the mistake too late when Thornton was abreast of him and a bare half dozen strokes away while he was being carried helplessly past.

Hans promptly snubbed with the rope, as though Buck were a boat. The rope tightening on him in the sweep of the current,

---

4 **provocation:** reason; cause.

he was jerked under the surface, and under the surface he remained till his body struck against the bank and he was hauled out. He was half drowned, and Hans and Pete threw themselves upon him, pounding the breath into him and the water out of him. He staggered to his feet and fell down. The faint sound of Thornton's voice came to them, and though they could not make out the words of it, they knew that he was in his extremity. His master's voice acted on Buck like an electric shock. He sprang to his feet and ran up the bank ahead of the men to the point of his previous departure.

Again the rope was attached and he was launched, and again he struck out, but this time straight into the stream. He had miscalculated once, but he would not be guilty of it a second time. Hans paid out the rope, permitting no slack, while Pete kept it clear of coils. Buck held on till he was on a line straight above Thornton; then he turned, and with the speed of an express train headed down upon him. Thornton saw him coming, and as Buck struck him like a battering ram with the whole force of the current behind him, he reached up and closed with both arms around the shaggy neck. Hans snubbed the rope around the tree, and Buck and Thornton were jerked under the water. Strangling, suffocating, sometimes one uppermost and sometimes the other, dragging over the jagged bottom, smashing against rocks and snags, they veered into the bank.

Thornton came to, belly downward and being violently propelled back and forth across a drift log by Hans and Pete. His first glance was for Buck, over whose limp and apparently lifeless body Nig was setting up a howl, while Skeet was licking the wet face and closed eyes. Thornton was himself bruised and battered, and he went carefully over Buck's body when he had been brought around, finding three broken ribs.

"That settles it," he announced. "We camp right here." And camp they did, till Buck's ribs knitted and he was able to travel.

That winter at Dawson, Buck performed another exploit, not so heroic, perhaps, but one that put his name many notches higher on the totem pole of Alaskan fame. This exploit was particularly gratifying to the three men; for they stood in need of the outfit which it furnished and were enabled to make a long-desired trip into the virgin East where miners had not yet appeared. It was brought about by a conversation in the Eldorado Saloon, in which men waxed boastful of their favorite dogs. Buck, because of his record, was the target for these men, and Thornton was driven stoutly to defend him. At the end of half an hour, one man stated that his dog could start a sled with five hundred pounds and walk off with it; a second bragged six hundred for his dog; and a third seven hundred.

"Pooh! pooh!" said John Thornton. "Buck can start a thousand pounds."

"And break it out? and walk off with it for a hundred yards?" demanded Matthewson, a Bonanza king, he of the seven hundred vaunt.

"And break it out, and walk off with it for a hundred yards," John Thornton said coolly.

"Well," Matthewson said, slowly and deliberately, so that all could hear, "I've got a thousand dollars that says he can't. And there it is." So saying, he slammed a sack of gold dust of the size of a bologna sausage down upon the bar.

Nobody spoke. Thornton's bluff, if bluff it was, had been called. He could feel a flush of warm blood creeping up his face. His tongue

had tricked him. He did not know whether Buck could start a thousand pounds. Half a ton! The enormousness of it appalled him. He had great faith in Buck's strength and had often thought him capable of starting such a load; but never, as now, had he faced the possibility of it; the eyes of a dozen men fixed upon him, silent and waiting. Further, he had no thousand dollars, nor had Hans or Pete.

"I've got a sled standing outside now, with twenty fifty-pound sacks of flour on it," Matthewson went on with brutal directness, "so don't let that hinder you."

Thornton did not reply. He did not know what to say. He glanced from face to face in the absent way of a man who has lost the power of thought and is seeking somewhere to find the thing that will start it going again. The face of Jim O'Brien, a Mastodon king and old-time comrade, caught his eyes. It was a cue to him, seeming to rouse him to do what he would never have dreamed of doing.

"Can you lend me a thousand?" he asked, almost in a whisper.

"Sure," answered O'Brien, thumping down a plethoric[5] sack by the side of Matthewson's. "Though it's little faith I'm having, John, that the beast can do the trick."

The Eldorado emptied its occupants into the street to see the test. The tables were deserted, and the dealers and gamekeepers came forth to see the outcome of the wager and to lay odds. Several hundred men, furred and mittened, banked around the sled within easy distance. Matthewson's sled, loaded with a thousand pounds of flour, had been standing for a couple of hours, and in the intense cold (it was sixty below zero) the runners had frozen fast to the hard-packed snow. Men offered odds of two to one that Buck

---

5 **plethoric** (ple thôr′ ik): very full; inflated.

could not budge the sled. A quibble arose concerning the phrase "break out." O'Brien contended it was Thornton's privilege to knock the runners loose, leaving Buck to "break it out" from a dead standstill. Matthewson insisted that the phrase included breaking the runners from the frozen grip of the snow. A majority of the men who had witnessed the making of the bet decided in his favor, whereat the odds went up to three to one against Buck.

There were no takers. Not a man believed him capable of the feat. Thornton had been hurried into the wager, heavy with doubt; and now that he looked at the sled itself, the concrete fact, with the regular team of ten dogs curled up in the snow before it, the more impossible the task appeared. Matthewson waxed jubilant.

"Three to one!" he proclaimed. "I'll lay you another thousand at that figure, Thornton. What d'ye say?"

Thornton's doubt was strong in his face, but his fighting spirit was aroused—the fighting spirit that soars above odds, fails to recognize the impossible, and is deaf to all save the clamor for battle. He called Hans and Pete to him. Their sacks were slim, and with his own the three partners could rake together only two hundred dollars. In the ebb of their fortunes, this sum was their total capital; yet they laid it unhesitatingly against Matthewson's six hundred.

The team of ten dogs was unhitched, and Buck, with his own harness, was put into the sled. He had caught the contagion of the excitement, and he felt that in some way he must do a great thing for John Thornton. Murmurs of admiration at his splendid appearance went up. He was in perfect condition, without an ounce of superfluous flesh, and the one hundred and fifty pounds that he weighed were so many pounds of grit and virility. His furry coat shone with the sheen of silk. Down the neck and across the shoulders, his mane, in repose as it was, half bristled and seemed to lift with every movement, as though excess of vigor made each particular hair alive and active. The great breast and heavy forelegs were no more than in proportion with the rest of the body, where the muscles showed in tight rolls underneath the skin. Men felt these muscles and proclaimed them hard as iron, and the odds went down to two to one.

"Gad, sir! Gad, sir!" stuttered a member of the latest dynasty, a king of the Skookum Benches. "I offer you eight hundred for him, sir, before the test, sir; eight hundred just as he stands."

Thornton shook his head and stepped to Buck's side.

"You must stand off from him," Matthewson protested. "Free play and plenty of room."

The crowd fell silent; only could be heard the voice of the gamblers vainly offering two to one. Everybody acknowledged Buck a magnificent animal, but twenty fifty-pound sacks of flour bulked too large in their eyes for them to loosen their pouch strings.

Thornton knelt down by Buck's side. He took his head in his hands and rested cheek on cheek. He did not playfully shake him, as was his wont, or murmur soft love curses; but he whispered in his ear. "As you love me, Buck. As you love me," was what he whispered. Buck whined with suppressed eagerness.

The crowd was watching curiously. The affair was growing mysterious. It seemed like a conjuration.[6] As Thornton got to his feet,

---

6 conjuration: magical chant.

Buck seized his mittened hand between his jaws, pressing in with his teeth and releasing slowly, half reluctantly. It was the answer, in terms, not of speech, but of love. Thornton stepped well back.

"Now, Buck," he said.

Buck tightened the traces, then slacked them for a matter of several inches. It was the way he had learned.

"Gee!" Thornton's voice rang out, sharp in the tense silence.

Buck swung to the right, ending the movement in a plunge that took up the slack and with a sudden jerk arrested his one hundred and fifty pounds. The load quivered, and from under the runners arose a crisp crackling.

"Haw!" Thornton commanded.

Buck duplicated the maneuver, this time to the left. The crackling turned into a snapping, the sled pivoting and the runners slipping and grating several inches to the side. The sled was broken out. Men were holding their breaths, intensely unconscious of the fact.

"Now, MUSH!"

Thornton's command cracked out like a pistol shot. Buck threw himself forward, tightening the traces with a jarring lunge. His whole body was gathered compactly together in the tremendous effort, the muscles writhing and knotting like live things under the silky fur. His great chest was low to the ground, his head forward and down, while his feet were flying like mad, the claws scarring the hard-packed snow in parallel grooves. The sled swayed and trembled, half-started forward. One of his feet slipped, and one man groaned aloud. Then the sled lurched ahead in what appeared a rapid succession of jerks, though it never really came to a dead stop again . . . half an inch . . . an inch . . . two inches. . . . The jerks perceptibly diminished; as the sled gained momentum, he caught them up, till it was moving steadily along.

Men gasped and began to breathe again, unaware that for a moment they had ceased to breathe. Thornton was running behind, encouraging Buck with short, cheery words. The distance had been measured off, and as he neared the pile of firewood which marked the end of the hundred yards, a cheer began to grow and grow, which burst into a roar as he passed the firewood and halted at command. Every man was tearing himself loose, even Matthewson. Hats and mittens were flying in the air. Men were shaking hands, it did not matter with whom, and bubbling over in a general incoherent babel.[7]

But Thornton fell on his knees beside Buck. Head was against head, and he was shaking him back and forth. Those who hurried up heard him cursing Buck, and he cursed him long and fervently, and softly and lovingly.

"Gad, sir! Gad, sir!" spluttered the Skookum Bench king. "I'll give you a thousand for him, sir, a thousand, sir—twelve hundred, sir."

Thornton rose to his feet. His eyes were wet. The tears were streaming frankly down his cheeks. "Sir," he said to the Skookum Bench king, "no, sir. You can forget it, sir. It's the best I can do for you, sir."

Buck seized Thornton's hand in his teeth. Thornton shook him back and forth. As though animated by a common impulse, the onlookers drew back to a respectful distance; nor were they again indiscreet enough to interrupt.

---

7 **babel:** jumbled noise; confusion.

Chapter 7

THE SOUNDING OF THE CALL

When Buck earned sixteen hundred dollars in five minutes for John Thornton, he made it possible for his master to pay off certain debts and to journey with his partners into the East after a fabled lost mine, the history of which was as old as the history of the country. Many men had sought it; few had found it; and more than a few there were who had never returned from the quest. This lost mine was steeped in tragedy and shrouded in mystery. No one knew of the first man. The oldest tradition stopped before it got back to him. From the beginning there had been an ancient and ramshackle cabin. Dying men had sworn to it, and to the mine the site of which it marked, clinching their testimony with nuggets that were unlike any known grade of gold in the Northland.

But no living man had looted this treasure house, and the dead were dead; wherefore John Thornton and Pete and Hans with Buck and half a dozen other dogs, faced into the East on an unknown trail to achieve where men and dogs as good as themselves had failed. They sledded seventy miles up the Yukon, swung to the left into the Stewart River, passed the Mayo and the McQuestion, and held on until the Stewart itself became a streamlet, threading the upstanding peaks which marked the backbone of the continent.

John Thornton asked little of man or nature. He was unafraid of the wild. With a handful of salt and a rifle he could plunge into the wilderness and fare wherever he pleased and as long as he pleased. Being in no haste, Indian fashion, he hunted his dinner in the course of the day's travel; and if he failed to find it, like the Indian, he kept on traveling, secure in the knowledge that sooner or later he would come to it. So, on this great journey into the East, straight meat was the bill of fare, ammunition and tools principally made up the load on the sled, and the time card was drawn upon the limitless future.

To Buck it was boundless delight, this hunting, fishing, and indefinite wandering through strange places. For weeks at a time they would hold on steadily, day after day, and for weeks upon end they would camp, here and there, the dogs loafing and the men burning holes through frozen muck and gravel and washing countless pans of dirt by the heat of the fire. Sometimes they went hungry, sometimes they feasted riotously, all according to the abundance of game and the fortune of hunting. Summer arrived, and dogs and men packed on their backs, rafted across blue mountain lakes and descended or ascended unknown rivers in slender boats whipsawed from the standing forest.

The months came and went, and back and forth they twisted through the uncharted vastness where no men were and yet where men had been if the Lost Cabin were true. They went across divides in summer blizzards, shivered under the midnight sun on naked mountains between the timber line and the eternal snows, dropped into summer valleys amid swarming gnats and flies, and in

the shadows of glaciers picked strawberries and flowers as ripe and fair as any the Southland could boast. In the fall of the year they penetrated a weird lake country, sad and silent, where wild fowl had been, but where then there was no life nor sign of life—only the blowing of chill winds, the forming of ice in sheltered places, and the melancholy rippling of waves on lonely beaches.

And through another winter they wandered on the obliterated trails of men who had gone before. Once they came upon a path blazed through the forest, an ancient path, and the Lost Cabin seemed very near. But the path began nowhere and ended nowhere, and it remained a mystery, as the man who made it, and the reason he made it remained a mystery. Another time they chanced upon the time-graven wreckage of a hunting lodge, and amid the shreds of rotted blankets John Thornton found a long-barreled flintlock. He knew it for a Hudson Bay Company gun of the young days in the Northwest when such a gun was worth its height in beaver skins packed flat. And that was all—no hint as to the man who in an early day had reared the lodge and left the gun among the blankets.

Spring came on once more, and at the end of all their wandering they found, not the Lost Cabin, but a shallow placer in a broad valley where the gold showed like yellow butter across the bottom of the washing pan. They sought no farther. Each day they worked earned them thousands of dollars in clean dust and nuggets, and they worked every day. The gold was packed in moosehide bags, fifty pounds to the bag, and piled like so much firewood outside the spruce bough lodge. Like giants they toiled, days flashing on the heels of days like dreams as they heaped the treasure up.

There was nothing for the dogs to do, save the hauling in of meat now and again that Thornton killed, and Buck spent long hours musing by the fire. The vision of the short-legged hairy man came to him more frequently, now that there was little work to be done; and often, blinking by the fire, Buck wandered with him in that other world which he remembered.

The salient thing of this other world seemed fear. When he watched the hairy man sleeping by the fire, head between his knees and hands clasped above, Buck saw that he slept restlessly, with many starts and awakenings, at which times he would peer fearfully into the darkness and fling more wood upon the fire. Did they walk by the beach of a sea, where the hairy man gathered shellfish and ate them as he gathered; it was with eyes that roved everywhere for hidden danger and with legs prepared to run like the wind at its first appearance. Through the forest they crept noiselessly, Buck at the hairy man's heels; and they were alert and vigilant, the pair of them, ears twitching and moving and nostrils quivering, for the man heard and smelled as keenly as Buck. The hairy man could spring up into the trees and travel ahead as fast as on the ground, swinging by the arms from limb to limb, sometimes a dozen feet apart, letting go and catching, never falling, never missing his grip. In fact, he seemed as much at home among the trees as on the ground, and Buck had memories of nights of vigil spent beneath trees wherein the hairy man roosted, holding on tightly as he slept.

And closely akin to the visions of the hairy man was the call, still sounding in the depths of the forest. It filled him with a great unrest and strange desires. It caused him to feel a vague, sweet gladness, and he was aware of wild yearnings and stirrings for he knew not what. Sometimes he pursued the call into the forest, looking for it as though it were a tangible[1] thing, barking softly or defiantly, as the mood might dictate. He would thrust his nose into the cool wood moss or into the black soil where long grasses grew, and snort with joy at the fat earth smells; or he would crouch for hours, as if in concealment, behind fungus-covered trunks of fallen trees, wide-eyed to all that moved and sounded about him. It might be, lying thus, that he hoped to surprise this call he could not understand. But he did not know why he did these various things. He was impelled to do them and did not reason about them at all.

Irresistible impulses seized him. He would be lying in camp, dozing lazily in the heat of the day, when suddenly his head would lift and his ears pick up, intent and listening, and he would spring to his feet and dash away, and on and on, for hours through the forest aisles and across the open spaces. He loved to run down dry watercourses and creep and spy upon the bird life in the woods. For a day at a time he would lie in the underbrush where he could watch the partridges drumming and strutting up and down. But especially he loved to run in the dim twilight of the summer midnights, listening to the subdued and sleepy murmurs of the forest, reading signs and sounds as man may read a book, and seeking for the mysterious something that called—called, waking or sleeping, at all times, for him to come.

One night he sprang from sleep with a start, eager-eyed, nostrils quivering and scenting, his mane bristling in recurrent waves. From the forest came the call (or one note of it, for the call was many-noted), distinct and definite as never before—a long-drawn howl, like, yet unlike, any noise made by a husky dog. And he knew it, in the old familiar way, as a sound heard before. He sprang through the sleeping camp and in swift silence dashed through the woods. As he drew closer to the cry, he went more slowly, with caution in every movement, till he came to an open place among the trees, and looking out saw, erect on haunches with nose pointed to the sky, a long, lean timber wolf.

He had made no noise, yet it ceased from its howling and tried to sense his presence. Buck stalked into the open, half crouching, body gathered compactly together, tail straight and stiff, feet falling with unwonted care. Every movement advertised commingled threatening and overture of friendliness. It was the menacing truce that marks the meeting of wild beasts that prey. But the wolf fled at sight of him. He followed with wild leapings in a frenzy to overtake. He ran him into a blind channel in the bed of the creek, where a timber jam barred the way. The wolf whirled about, pivoting on his hind legs after the fashion of Joe and of all cornered husky dogs, snarling and bristling, clipping his teeth together in a continuous and rapid succession of snaps.

Buck did not attack but circled him about and hedged him in with friendly advances. The wolf was suspicious and afraid, for Buck made three of him in weight, while his head barely reached Buck's shoulder. Watching his chance, he darted away, and the chase was resumed. Time and again he was cornered and the thing repeated, though he was in poor condition or Buck could not so easily have overtaken him. He would run till Buck's head was even with his flank, when he would whirl around at bay, only to dash away again at the first opportunity.

---

1 **tangible:** that which can be touched or felt; real.

But in the end, Buck's pertinacity[2] was rewarded; for the wolf, finding that no harm was intended, finally sniffed noses with him. Then they became friendly and played about in the nervous, half-coy way with which fierce beasts belie their fierceness. After some time of this, the wolf started off at an easy lope in a manner that plainly showed he was going somewhere. He made it clear to Buck that he was to come, and they ran side by side through the somber twilight, straight up the creek bed, into the gorge from which it issued, and across the bleak divide where it took its rise.

On the opposite slope of the watershed, they came down into a level country where there were great stretches of forest and many streams, and through these great stretches they ran steadily, hour after hour, the sun rising higher and the day growing warmer. Buck was wildly glad. He knew he was at last answering the call, running by the side of his wood brother toward the place from where the call surely came. Old memories were coming upon him fast, and he was stirring to them as of old he stirred to the realities of which they were the shadows. He had done this thing before, somewhere in that other and dimly remembered world, and he was doing it again, now, running free in the open, the unpacked earth underfoot, the wide sky overhead.

They stopped by a running stream to drink, and stopping, Buck remembered John Thornton. He sat down. The wolf started on toward the place from where the call surely came, then returned to him, sniffing noses and making actions as though to encourage him. But Buck turned about and started slowly on the back track. For the better part

2 **pertinacity** (pėrt′ n as′ ə tē): great persistence.

of an hour the wood brother ran by his side, whining softly. Then he sat down, pointed his nose upward, and howled. It was a mournful howl, and as Buck held steadily on his way, he heard it grow faint and fainter until it was lost in the distance.

John Thornton was eating dinner when Buck dashed into camp and sprang upon him in a frenzy of affection, overturning him, scrambling upon him, licking his face, biting his hand—"playing the general tom-fool," as John Thornton characterized it, the while he shook Buck back and forth and cursed him lovingly.

For two days and nights Buck never left camp, never let Thornton out of his sight. He followed him about at his work, watched him while he ate, saw him into his blankets at night and out of them in the morning. But after two days the call in the forest began to sound more imperiously than ever. Buck's restlessness came back on him, and he was haunted by recollections of the wood brother, and of the smiling land beyond the divide, and of the run side by side through the wide forest stretches. Once again he took to wandering in the woods, but the wild brother came no more; and though he listened through long vigils, the mournful howl was never raised.

He began to sleep out at night, staying away from camp for days at a time, and once he crossed the divide at the head of the creek and went down into the land of timber and streams. There he wandered for a week, seeking vainly for a fresh sign of the wild brother, killing his meat as he traveled and traveling with the long, easy lope that seemed never to tire. He fished for salmon in a broad stream that emptied somewhere into the sea, and by this stream he killed a large black bear, blinded by the mosquitoes while

likewise fishing, and raging through the forest helpless and terrible. Even so, it was a hard fight, and it aroused the last latent remnants of Buck's ferocity. And two days later, when he returned to his kill and found a dozen wolverines quarreling over the spoil, he scattered them like chaff;[3] and those that fled left two behind who would quarrel no more.

The blood-longing became stronger than ever before. He was a killer, a thing that preyed, living on the things that lived, unaided, alone, by virtue of his own strength and prowess, surviving triumphantly in a hostile environment where only the strong survive. Because of all this, he became possessed of a great pride in himself, which communicated itself like a contagion to his physical being. It advertised itself in all his movements, was apparent in the play of every muscle, spoke plainly in speech in the way he carried himself, and made his glorious furry coat if anything more glorious. But for the stray brown on his muzzle and above his eyes and for the splash of white hair that ran midmost down his chest, he might well have been mistaken for a gigantic wolf, larger than the largest of the breed. From his St. Bernard father, he had inherited size and weight, but it was his shepherd mother who had given shape to that size and weight. His muzzle was the long wolf muzzle, save that it was larger than the muzzle of any wolf; and his head, somewhat broader, was the wolf head on a massive scale.

His cunning was wolf cunning and wild cunning; his intelligence, shepherd intelligence and St. Bernard intelligence, and all this, plus an experience gained in the fiercest

---

3 **chaff:** husks of wheat, oats, etc., especially when separated from the grain by threshing.

of schools, made him as formidable a creature as any that roamed the wild. A carnivorous animal, living on a straight meat diet, he was in full flower, at the high tide of his life, overspilling with vigor and virility. When Thornton passed a caressing hand along his back, a snapping and crackling followed the hand, each hair discharging its pent magnetism at the contact. Every part, brain and body, nerve tissue and fiber, was keyed to the most exquisite pitch; and between all the parts there was a perfect equilibrium or adjustment. To sights and sounds and events which required action, he responded with lightninglike rapidity. Quickly as a husky dog could leap to defend from attack or to attack, he could leap twice as quickly. He saw the movement, or heard sound, and responded in less time than another dog required to compass the mere seeing or hearing. He perceived and determined and responded in the same instant. In point of fact, the three actions of perceiving, determining, and responding were sequential; but so infinitesimal[4] were the intervals of time between them, that they appeared simultaneous. His muscles were surcharged with vitality and snapped into play sharply, like steel springs. Life streamed through him in splendid flood, glad and rampant, until it seemed that it would burst him asunder in sheer ecstasy and pour forth generously over the world.

"Never was there such a dog," said John Thornton one day, as the partners watched Buck marching out of camp.

"When he was made, the mold was broke," said Pete.

"By jingo! I t'ink so mineself," Hans affirmed.

They saw him marching out of camp, but they did not see the instant and terrible transformation which took place as soon as he was within the secrecy of the forest. He no longer marched. At once he became a thing of the wild, stealing along softly, cat-footed, a passing shadow that appeared and disappeared among the shadows. He knew how to take advantage of every cover, to crawl on his belly like a snake, and like a snake to leap and strike. He could take a ptarmigan[5] from its nest, kill a rabbit as it slept, and snap in midair the little chipmunks fleeing a second too late for the trees. Fish in open pools were not too quick for him, nor were the beaver, mending their dams, too wary. He killed to eat, not from wantonness, but he preferred to eat what he killed himself. So a lurking humor ran through his deeds, and it was his delight to steal upon the squirrels, and when he all but had them, to let them go, chattering in mortal fear to the tree tops.

As the fall of the year came on, the moose appeared in greater abundance, moving slowly down to meet the winter in the lower and less rigorous valleys. Buck had already dragged down a stray part-grown calf, but he wished strongly for larger and more formidable quarry, and he came upon it one day on the divide at the head of the creek. A band of twenty moose had crossed over from the land of streams and timber, and chief among them was a great bull. He was in a savage temper and, standing over six feet from the ground, was as formidable an antagonist as ever Buck could desire. Back and forth the bull tossed his great palmated antlers, branching to fourteen points and embracing seven feet within the tips. His small eyes burned with a vicious and bitter light while he roared with fury at sight of Buck.

---

4 **infinitesimal** (in' fi nə tes' ə məl): extremely small.

5 **ptarmigan** (tär' mə gən): any of several kinds of grouse.

From the bull's side, just forward of the flank, protruded a feathered arrow-end, which accounted for his savageness. Guided by that instinct which came from the old hunting days of the primordial world, Buck proceeded to cut the bull out from the herd. It was no slight task. He would bark and dance about in front of the bull, just out of reach of the great antlers and of the terrible splay of hoofs which could have stamped his life out with a single blow. Unable to turn his back on the fanged danger and go on, the bull would be driven into paroxysms of rage. At such moments he charged Buck, who retreated craftily, luring him on by a simulated inability to escape. But when he was thus separated from his fellows, two or three of the younger bulls would charge back upon Buck and enable the wounded bull to rejoin the herd.

There is a patience of the wild—dogged, tireless, persistent as life itself—that holds motionless for endless hours the spider in its web, the snake in its coils, the panther in its ambuscade; this patience belongs peculiarly to life when it hunts its living food; and it belonged to Buck as he clung to the flank of the herd, retarding its march, irritating the young bulls, worrying the cows with their half-grown calves, and driving the wounded bull mad with helpless rage. For half a day this continued. Buck multiplied himself, attacking from all sides, enveloping the herd in a whirlwind of menace, cutting out his victim as fast as it could rejoin its mates, wearing out the patience of creatures preyed upon, which is a lesser patience than that of the creatures preying.

As the day wore along and the sun dropped to its bed in the northwest (the darkness had come back and the fall nights were six hours long), the young bulls retraced their steps more and more reluctantly to the aid of their beset leader. The downcoming winter was harrying them on to the lower levels, and it seemed they could never shake off this tireless creature that held them back. Besides, it was not the life of the herd or of the young bulls, that was threatened. The life of only one member was demanded, which was a remoter interest than their lives, and in the end they were content to pay the toll.

As twilight fell, the old bull stood with lowered head, watching his mates—the cows he had known, the calves he had fathered, the bulls he had mastered—as they shambled on at a rapid pace through the fading light. He could not follow, for before his nose leaped the merciless fanged terror that would not let him go. Three hundredweight, more than half a ton, he weighed; he had lived a long, strong life, full of fight and struggle, and at the end he faced death at the teeth of a creature whose head did not reach beyond his great knuckled knees.

From then on, night and day, Buck never left his prey, never gave it a moment's rest, never permitted it to browse the leaves of trees or the shoots of young birch and willow. Nor did he give the wounded bull opportunity to slake his burning thirst in the slender trickling streams they crossed. Often in desperation, he burst into long stretches of flight. At such times Buck did not attempt to stay him but loped easily at his heels, satisfied with the way the game was played, lying down when the moose stood still, attacking him fiercely when he strove to eat or drink.

The great head drooped more and more under its tree of horns, and the shambling trot grew weaker and weaker. He took to standing for long periods with nose to the ground and dejected ears dropped limply, and Buck found more time in which to get water for himself and in which to rest. At such moments, panting with red lolling tongue and with eyes fixed upon the big bull, it appeared to Buck that a change was coming over the face of things. He could feel a new stir in the land. As the moose were coming into the land, other kinds of life were coming in. Forest and stream and air seemed palpitant[6] with their presence. The news of it was borne in upon him, not by sight or sound or smell, but by some other and subtler sense. He heard nothing, saw nothing, yet knew that the land was somehow different, that through it strange things were afoot and ranging; and he resolved to investigate after he had finished the business in hand.

At last, at the end of the fourth day, he pulled the great moose down. For a day and a night he remained by the kill, eating and sleeping, turn and turn about. Then, rested, refreshed, and strong, he turned his face toward camp and John Thornton. He broke into the long easy lope and went on, hour after hour, never at loss for the tangled way, heading straight home through strange country with a certitude of direction that put man and his magnetic needle to shame.

As he held on, he became more and more conscious of the new stir in the land. There was life abroad in it, different from the life which had been there throughout the summer. No longer was this fact borne in upon him in some subtle, mysterious way. The birds talked of it, the squirrels chattered about it, the very breeze whispered of it. Several times he stopped and drew in the fresh morning air in great sniffs, reading a message which made him leap on with greater speed. He was oppressed with a sense of calamity happening, if it were not calamity already happened; and as he crossed the last watershed and dropped down into the valley toward camp, he proceeded with greater caution.

Three miles away he came upon a fresh trail that sent his neck hair rippling and bristling. It led straight toward camp and John Thornton. Buck hurried on, swiftly and stealthily, every nerve straining and tense, alert to the multitudinous details which told a story—all but the end. His nose gave him a varying description of the passage of the life on the heels of which he was traveling. He remarked the pregnant silence of the forest. The bird life had flitted. The squirrels were in hiding. One only he saw—a sleek gray fellow, flattened against a gray dead limb so that he seemed a part of it, a woody excrescence[7] upon the wood itself.

As Buck slid along with the obscureness of a gliding shadow, his nose was jerked suddenly to the side as though a positive force had gripped and pulled it. He followed the new scent into a thicket and found Nig. He was lying on his side, dead where he had dragged himself, an arrow protruding, head and feathers, from either side of his body.

A hundred yards farther on, Buck came upon one of the sled dogs Thornton had bought in Dawson. This dog was thrashing about in a death struggle directly on the trail, and Buck passed around him without stopping. From the camp came the faint sound of many voices, rising and falling in a singsong chant. Bellying forward to the edge of the clearing, he found Hans, lying on his face, feathered with arrows like a porcupine. At the same instant Buck peered out where the

---

6 **palpitant:** beating very rapidly; trembling.

7 **excrescence** (ek skres′ ns): unnatural growth.

spruce bough lodge had been and saw what made his hair leap straight up on his neck and shoulders. A gust of overpowering rage swept over him. He did not know that he growled, but he growled aloud with a terrible ferocity. For the last time in his life he allowed passion to usurp[8] cunning and reason, and it was because of his great love for John Thornton that he lost his head.

The Yeehats were dancing about the wreckage of the spruce bough lodge when they heard a fearful roaring and saw rushing upon them an animal the like of which they had never seen before. It was Buck, a live hurricane of fury, hurling himself upon them in a frenzy to destroy. He sprang at the foremost man (it was the chief of the Yeehats), ripping the throat wide open till the rent jugular spouted a fountain of blood. He did not pause to worry the victim, but ripped in passing with the next bound, tearing wide the throat of a second man. There was no withstanding him. He plunged about in their very midst, tearing, rending, destroying, in constant and terrific motion which defied the arrows they discharged at him. In fact, so inconceivably rapid were his movements and so closely were the Indians tangled together, that they shot one another with the arrows; and one young hunter, hurling a spear at Buck in midair, drove it through the chest of another hunter with such force that the point broke through the skin of the back and stood out beyond. Then a panic seized the Yeehats, and they fled in terror to the woods, proclaiming as they fled the advent[9] of the Evil Spirit.

And truly Buck was the Fiend incarnate,[10]

---

8 **to usurp** (yü zėrp'): to seize and hold by power or without right.
9 **advent**: arrival.
10 **incarnate**: in human form.

raging at their heels and dragging them down like deer as they raced through the trees. It was a fateful day for the Yeehats. They scattered far and wide over the country, and it was not till a week later that the last of the survivors gathered together in a lower valley and counted their losses. As for Buck, wearying of the pursuit, he returned to the desolated camp. He found Pete where he had been killed in his blankets in the first moment of surprise. Thornton's desperate struggle was freshly written on the earth, and Buck scented every detail of it down to the edge of a deep pool. By the edge, head and forefeet in the water, lay Skeet, faithful to the last. The pool itself, muddy and discolored from the sluice boxes, effectually hid what it contained, and it contained John Thornton; for Buck followed his trace into the water, from which no trace led away.

All day Buck brooded by the pool or roamed restlessly about the camp. Death, as a cessation of movement, as a passing out and away from the lives of the living, he knew, and he knew John Thornton was dead. It left a great void in him, somewhat akin to hunger, but a void which ached and ached and which food could not fill. At times when he paused to contemplate the carcasses of the Yeehats, he forgot the pain of it; and at such times he was aware of a great pride in himself—a pride greater than any he had yet experienced. He had killed man, the noblest game of all, and he had killed in the face of the law of club and fang. He sniffed the bodies curiously. They had died so easily. It was harder to kill a husky dog than them. They were no match at all, were it not for their arrows and spears and clubs. Thenceforward he would be unafraid of them except when they bore in their hands their arrows, spears, and clubs.

Night came on, and a full moon rose high over the trees into the sky, lighting the land till it lay bathed in ghostly day. And with the coming of the night, brooding and mourning by the pool, Buck became alive to a stirring of the new life in the forest other than that which the Yeehats had made. He stood up, listening and scenting. From far away drifted a faint, sharp yelp, followed by a chorus of similar yelps. As the moments passed, the yelps grew closer and louder. Again Buck knew them as things heard in that other world which persisted in his memory. He walked to the center of the open space and listened. It was the call, the many-noted call, sounding more luringly and compelling than ever before. And as never before, he was ready to obey. John Thornton was dead. The last tie was broken. Man and the claims of man no longer bound him.

Hunting their living meat, as the Yeehats were hunting it, on the flanks of the migrating moose, the wolf pack had at last crossed over from the land of streams and timber and invaded Buck's valley. Into the clearing where the moonlight streamed, they poured in a silvery flood; and in the center of the clearing stood Buck, motionless as a statue, waiting their coming. They were awed, so still and large he stood, and a moment's pause fell, till the boldest one leaped straight for him. Like a flash Buck struck, breaking the neck. Then he stood, without movement as before, the stricken wolf rolling in agony behind him. Three others tried it in sharp succession, and one after the other they drew back, streaming blood from slashed throats or shoulders.

This was sufficient to fling the whole pack forward, pell-mell, crowded together, blocked and confused by its eagerness to pull down the prey. Buck's marvelous quickness and agility stood him in good stead. Pivoting on his hind legs and snapping and gashing, he was everywhere at once, presenting a front which was apparently unbroken, so swiftly did he whirl and guard from side to side. But to prevent them from getting behind him, he was forced back, down past the pool and into the creek bed, till he was brought up against a high gravel bank. He worked along to a right angle in the bank which the men had made in the course of mining, and in this angle he came to bay, protected on three sides and with nothing to do but face the front.

And so well did he face it, that at the end of half an hour the wolves drew back discomfited. The tongues of all were out and lolling, the white fangs showing cruelly white in the moonlight. Some were lying down with heads raised and ears pricked forward; others stood on their feet, watching him; and still others were lapping water from the pool. One wolf, long and lean and gray, advanced cautiously in a friendly manner, and Buck recognized the wild brother with whom he had run for a night and a day. He was whining softly, and as Buck whined, they touched noses.

Then an old wolf, gaunt and battle-scarred, came foward. Buck writhed his lips into the preliminary of a snarl, but sniffed noses with him. Whereupon the old wolf sat down, pointed nose at the moon, and broke out the long wolf howl. The others sat down and howled. And now the call came to Buck in unmistakable accents. He, too, sat down and howled. This over, he came out of his angle and the pack crowded around him, sniffing in half-friendly, half-savage manner. The leaders lifted the yelp of the pack and sprang away into the woods. The wolves swung in behind, yelping in chorus. And Buck ran with them, side by side with the wild brother, yelping as he ran.

And here may well end the story of Buck. The years were not many when the Yeehats noted a change in the breed of timber wolves, for some were seen with splashes of brown on head and muzzle and with a rift of white centering down the chest. But more remarkable than this, the Yeehats tell of a Ghost Dog that runs at the head of the pack. They are afraid of this Ghost Dog, for it has cunning greater than they, stealing from their camps in fierce winters, robbing their traps, slaying their dogs, and defying their bravest hunters.

Nay, the tale grows worse. Hunters there are who fail to return to the camp, and hunters there have been whom their tribesmen found with throats slashed cruelly open and with wolf prints about them in the snow greater than the prints of any wolf. Each fall, when the Yeehats follow the movement of the moose, there is a certain valley which they never enter. And women there are who become sad when the word goes over the fire of how the Evil Spirit came to select that valley for an abiding place.

In the summers there is one visitor, however, to that great valley, of which the Yeehats do not know. It is a great, gloriously coated wolf, like, and yet unlike, all other wolves. He crosses alone from the smiling timber land and comes down into an open space among the trees. Here a yellow stream flows from rotted moose-hide sacks and sinks into the ground, with long grasses growing through it and vegetable mold overrunning it and hiding its yellow from the sun; and here he muses for a time, howling once, long and mournfully, ere he departs.

But he is not always alone. When the long winter nights come on and the wolves follow their meat into the lower valleys, he may be seen running at the head of the pack through the pale moonlight or glimmering borealis, leaping gigantic above his fellows, his great throat a-bellow as he sings a song of the younger world, which is a song of the pack.

Discussion

1. Explain the difference between Buck's relationship with Judge Miller and his relationship with John Thornton.
2. Pete says to Thornton, "I'm not hankering to be the man that lays hands on you when he's (Buck's) around." What two future events does this statement predict?
3. Thornton saves Buck's life by rescuing him from the three foolish travelers. Name two times when Buck saves John Thornton's life.
4. Thornton could have made an easy $1000 by selling Buck to "a king of the Skookum Benches." Why doesn't he sell Buck?
5. What does Buck discover about men in his final battle with the Yeehats?

6. What is Buck's life like after Thornton's death? How do you know?

7. What do the Yeehats think Buck is? Why?

1. In chapter 6, Thornton uses Buck to win a bet by giving Buck the task of pulling a 1000-pound sled by himself from a frozen start. How does this differ from Buck's pulling the overloaded sled for Charles, Hal, and Mercedes? Do you think they are both examples of mistreatment? Explain your answer by pointing out differences between Thornton's treatment of Buck in accomplishing the task and the trio's treatment.

2. Buck performs several acts of courage to protect Thornton. Write an account of a true incident where an animal performed a heroic act. Begin by briefly describing the animal, then tell about the incident, and end by stating the outcome.

Jack London 1876—1916

Three years before his death, California-born Jack London was the highest-paid author in the world. Much of his writing is based on personal experiences that included working as a common sailor, prospecting for gold in the Klondike, and serving as a war correspondent during the Russo-Japanese War. His novels, *The Call of the Wild* and *The Sea Wolf,* and his short stories, "All Gold Canyon" and "To Build a Fire," will always ensure him a place as one of America's best adventure writers.

8 THE NOVEL

Discussion

1. Explain why Buck is a clear example of a traditional hero. Give incidents from the story to support your answer.

2. The characters in *The Call of the Wild*—dogs as well as people—are presented with very clearly defined personality traits. Match the following characters with the most suitable descriptive phrase. After you have matched them, find an example from the book which supports each answer.

   1. Spitz
   2. Perrault
   3. Sol-leks
   4. Pike
   5. John Thornton
   6. Mercedes

   a. lazy, a malingerer
   b. jealous, bossy
   c. selfish, ignorant
   d. experienced, fair, affectionate
   e. fearless, hardworking
   f. devoted entirely to work

3. What special contributions does each of the following men make to Buck's change into a "dominant primordial beast": Judge Miller, the man in the red sweater, Perrault, Hal, John Thornton?

4. The events of this novel are presented in chronological order. However, many times throughout the story you are made aware of events in the distant past, and you are forewarned of events to come in the future. Find at least one example of a past event and one example of a predicted future event.

Composition

1. From the beginning to the end of this book, Buck changes from a protected family pet to a wild, primitive beast. Write a brief account of the major steps—including the people, incidents, or experiences—that contributed to this great change. End by writing a short paragraph which describes Buck's life at the end of the book.

2. Many authors such as Jack London give human qualities of thought, motive, emotion, and feelings to their animal characters. Write an incident involving an animal—possibly your own pet—from the animal's point of view. Describe the animal's thoughts and feelings, as well as its actions.

623

*alliteration: (page 434) the repetition of consonant sounds at the beginnings of two or more words that are close together. Alliteration can give a poem a musical quality, and it can also emphasize the words having the same sound. The alliteration of the *s* sound in these lines from "Aunt Sue's Stories" (page 488) does both of these things:

> *And black slaves*
> *Singing sorrow songs on the banks of a mighty river.*

attitude: the feelings an author expresses about the subject or characters he or she writes about; also, the feelings of a character about a subject or another character. Some attitudes an author may reveal, for example, are admiration, dislike, amusement, affection, pity and anger. Writers convey attitude by the descriptive terms they use. In "The Charge of the Light Brigade" (page 436), Tennyson describes the action of the British soldiers:

> *Boldly they rode and well*
> *Into the jaws of Death.*

The words *boldly and well* convey Tennyson's attitude of admiration.

*autobiography: (page 522) a person's written account of his or her own life. Autobiographers usually write about the most important things that have happened to them—the highlights of their careers, for example, and the influences of childhood experiences. In the section from her autobiography, *A Peculiar Treasure* (page 516), Edna Ferber concentrates on the early experiences that contributed to her successful writing career.

ballad: a narrative poem written in highly rhythmic stanzas and concerned with adventure and deep emotion. The ballad is a very old form of poetry. Ballads were originally sung, and only later were they written down. Common ballad

subjects are physical courage or tragic love. Although ballads may be concerned with nobles, they are usually about common people. There is little characterization or description, and the action generally moves forward through dialogue. The plot is seldom given in detail; readers must use their imaginations to fill in the gaps.

Ballads are usually written in **ballad stanzas.** Each stanza has four lines; the fourth line rhymes with the second. In typical **ballad rhythm,** the second and fourth lines of each stanza have three accented syllables each. In the first and third lines of the stanza, there are four accented syllables.

ballad rhythm: See **ballad.**

ballad stanza: See **ballad.**

*biography: (page 532) a person's life story written by another person. Biographers must find as much information as possible about the life of the person they are writing about. Then they must decide which facts to include and which to leave out. Since Harriet Tubman is famous for helping runaway slaves escape, her biographer in *Pioneers in Protest* (page 110) emphasizes those parts of her life relating to this achievement.

central character: See **character.**

character: a person in a work of literature. Occasionally, an animal may be a character, as in *The Call of the Wild* (page 558). While all the characters are important, the reader is most interested in the thoughts and deeds of the **central character.** Matilda is the central character in "All You've Ever Wanted" (page 241). Although her aunts are interesting, especially Aunt Gertrude, the story focuses on Matilda's experiences.

characterization: (page 278) the method by which a writer shows a character's personality. Writers characterize people by the way they describe them. Also, a character's actions, thoughts, and words all reveal something about his or her personality. Professor Van Dusen, in "The Problem of Cell 13" (248), is described as "The Thinking Machine." Furthermore, he says that

---

An asterisk (*) indicates a literary term that is discussed in this book.

"Nothing is impossible. . . . The mind is the master of all things." The description and his own statement both show that Professor Van Dusen is totally confident in the power of his own intelligence. In addition, a writer may characterize a person by showing how others feel about him or her. Dr. Watson, for example, in "The Red-headed League" (page 179), describes Jabez Wilson by saying, ". . . there was nothing remarkable about the man save his blazing red head and the expression of extreme chagrin and discontent upon his features."

*chronological order: (page 547) the arrangement of the events in a story in the order in which they actually happened. In "How I Learned to Speak," (page 167), for example, Helen Keller describes in chronological order the steps by which she learned to communicate with others. First she tells how her teacher, Anne Sullivan, taught her to associate words with the things they represent. Then Helen Keller tells how she acquired the ability to speak out loud.

Not all works of literature are arranged in chronological order. Sometimes an author may choose to introduce a character as an adult, and later describe the character's childhood. "Roberto Clemente—A Bittersweet Memoir" (page 501) is a good example of this. This story begins with his death and then goes back to tell about his childhood and successes as a baseball player.

climax: the turning point in a story or play; the point at which the reader learns how things will turn out. The reader's interest and suspense are highest at this point. The climax of *The Call of the Wild* (page 619) occurs when Buck discovers that John Thornton has been killed by Indians, and Buck then joins the wolf pack.

*comedy: (page 379) a play that is humorous and usually has a happy ending. A comedy may be funny because of the humorous situations it presents. Also, the characters themselves may be funny because of their personality traits. Most comedies use both humorous situations and funny characters.

comparison: an examination of two things to discover how they are alike. Similes and metaphors are two kinds of comparison writers often use.

conflict: (page 197) the struggle between opposing forces around which the action of a work of literature revolves. The central charater may struggle against another character, as in "Without Words" (page 230). In "Leiningen versus the Ants" (page 5), the struggle, however, takes place between people and some aspect of nature. The opposing forces may even be within a character's mind. In "The Long Way Around" (page 199), Patty runs away from home because of a mental conflict; she has difficulty accepting her new stepmother and new school.

*connotation: (page 493) the suggested or implied meaning of a word; the feelings that a word may produce that go beyond the word's dictionary meaning, or **denotation.** *Odor* and *scent* have basically the same meaning: "smell." But *scent* has a more pleasant connotation. Consider this passage from "A Wild Strain" (page 97): "Cool winds . . . carried the scent of wild flowers down the open slopes." If the writer had used *odor* instead of *scent* the effect would have been quite different.

Poets must often create an effect with only a very few words. Therefore, connotations are especially important in poetry because they enrich the dictionary meanings of words. (See also **denotation.**)

*contrast: (page 449) the technique of showing the differences between two things. A work of literature is often based on contrast of character, setting, or ideas. A good example of contrast appears in "All Summer in a Day" (page 208). The climate of Venus is constantly contrasted to the climate of Earth. It is this very contrast that makes the children lock Margot in the closet.

*denotation: (page 493) the exact meaning of a word, as given in the dictionary. (See also **connotation.**)

descriptive poetry: (page 447) a poem about a person, scene, situation, or occasion which reveals the poet's feelings about the thing described. In "Fog" (page 460), Carl Sandburg conveys his impression of fog through an extended metaphor that compares fog to a cat.

dialogue: the words spoken by the characters in a play or a story.

exaggeration: stretching the facts beyond the actual truth. Exaggeration usually has a humorous effect. In "The Ransom of Red Chief" (page 229), for example, Bill describes how fast he will run to get away from Red Chief: "In ten minutes I shall cross the Central, Southern, and Middle Western States, and be legging it trippingly for the Canadian border."

*exposition: (page 423) the introductory section in a play or story that presents the characters, setting, and mood and gives the reader or audience any information necessary for understanding what is happening. At the beginning of *The Ugly Duckling* (page 363), for example, the audience learns that Princess Camilla is to marry Prince Simon and that her parents are worried that he will reject her because she is not pretty. A humorous mood is created by the dialogue and actions of the characters.

*extended metaphor: See **metaphor.**

fable: a short story that teaches a useful lesson about life and how to live it. The characters in a fable are usually animals that talk. In one of Aesop's fables, a slow but steady tortoise beats a hare in a race. The fable's moral is that it is better to be slow and persistent than swift and careless.

fantasy: (page 247) a work of literature that deals with an unreal world. Though events in the plot—and perhaps some of the characters—may not be true to life as we know it, the author usually supplies enough recognizable details to make the story or the play believable. Science fiction, for example, is based on fantasy. A story, such as "All Summer in a Day," (page 208) that

deals in fantasy is, in effect, saying something like this: Events like these cannot and do not happen in the real world, but if they could happen, they might well happen this way.

*fiction: (page 178) a work of literature that has imaginary characters, events, or setting. A fictional story may sometimes contain real people or events, and it may have a setting that actually exists or existed. But fiction is not an account of things as they actually happened. The writer changes things in some way. *The Call of the Wild* (page 558), for example, takes place during the Klondike Gold Rush, an event that actually happened. But the story is fiction because most of the characters and events are products of the author's imagination.

*figure of speech: (page 455) the imaginative comparison between two things that are basically unlike, but that have some similar characteristics. Similes, metaphors, and personfication are figures of speech that writers often use.

first-person point of view: See **point of view.**

folktale: a story that reflects the life of the people of a particular region. Before they were ever written down, folktales were passed on orally from person to person for many generations. Folktales include fairy tales, such as "Snow White" and "Cinderella," and they are usually concerned with typical human situations. "Pinocchio," for example, is about a person who could not stop lying.

Haiku: a three-line poem that describes a single image in no more than seventeen syllables. The first line has five syllables, the second line has seven, and the third line has five. Haiku originated in Japan.

*hero/heroine: (page 285) a character in a work of literature who shows exceptional physical or moral courage. *Hero* refers to a male character, *heroine* to a female character. In "Going to Run All Night" (page 336), Nilson is a hero because he keeps runing until he reaches his destination, in spite of exhaustion and the threat of enemy soldiers. The major character of a story is not necessarily a hero or heroine. There is nothing heroic about Ichabod Crane in "The Legend of Sleepy Hollow" (page 317), for instance.

limerick: a humorous five-line poem. The first, second, and fifth lines rhyme with each other, and they each have three beats. The third and fourth lines rhyme, and they each have two beats.

metaphor: a suggested or implied comparison between two things. This kind of comparison, unlike a simile, does not use the word *like* or *as*. Rather, a metaphor suggests that something *is* something else. A metaphor in "The Highwayman" (page 429) compares the moon to a ship and the clouds to the ocean: "The moon was a ghostly galleon tossed upon cloudy seas."

An **extended metaphor** (page 462) is a metaphor that extends throughout an entire poem. "O Captain! My Captain!" (page 122) has an extended metaphor in which the assassinated President Lincoln is compared to a captain who has just brought his ship safely to port.

mood: the atmosphere or feeling of a work of literature. One way in which a writer creates mood is by the choice of setting. The isolated, snowbound dugout in "Prairie Winter" (page 77) helps establish a mood of loneliness and apprehension. Details about how things look, sound, feel, taste, and smell also contribute to the mood of a work of literature. In "The Twenty-third Psalm" (page 476), a mood of peace and security is created by such descriptive details as "green pastures" and "still waters."

motivation: the reasons why a character acts as he or she does. In "Without Words" (page 230), Jan's motivation for pursuing Mathieu is the wish for revenge because Mathieu stole Jan's food.

myth: a story about superhuman beings—gods, goddesses, or heroes. Often myths are imaginative explanations of natural occurrences.

narrative poetry: (page 429) a poem that tells

a story. "The Glove and the Lions" (page 438), for example, tells the story of a lady who, out of vanity, throws her glove among fighting lions to see whether her lover is brave enough to recover it.

narrator: the person who tells a story or poem. The narrator may be the author or a character in the story. (See also **point of view.**)

*nonfiction narrative: (page 500) a true story; a narrative about real events and people. "Battle by the Breadfruit Tree" (page 540), the story of a mother baboon's fight with a leopard, is a nonfiction narrative. As with all nonfiction, the events in the story happen just as the writer describes them. Unlike fiction, a nonfiction narrative is not the creation of the author's imagination.

novel: (page 556) a long narrative, written in prose, about fictional characters and events. A **novella** is a short novel—shorter than a full-length novel, but longer than a short story. A novel, like a short story, has a plot, characters, conflict, and setting, but all of these elements are generally much more complex than in a short story. A novel may have many characters and several of them may be presented in detail. While novels, like short stories, generally focus on one major conflict, there may be several other minor conflicts. The action of a novel often takes place in several different settings.

novella: See **novel.**

omniscient point of view: See **point of view.**

*pace: (page 219) the rate at which a story moves; its beat or rhythm. When there is much action, a story has a fast pace. A lot of description and dialogue usually produce a slow pace. Different parts of the same story may have different paces. At the beginning of "The Black Stallion and the Red Mare" (page 46), when the writer describes the wild horses and Donald's conflicting feelings about them, the pace is relatively slow. Later, when the men chasing the horse begin to close in on the stallion and the mare, the pace becomes much faster.

*personification: (page 455) giving human characteristics to something that is not human. In "Midwest Town" (page 142), stores are personified as people having a conversation, or tête-á-tête: "The stores hold tête-á-tête across Main Street." This personification conveys the dignified, leisurely, close-knit atmosphere characteristic of a small town.

play: (page 362) the acting out of a narrative or story by a person or persons who move or speak in front of an audience or camera. A **playwright** is a person who writes a play.

plot: (page 178) the arrangement of actions in a story, play, or narrative poem. Most writers follow one basic plot pattern to relate the events of their stories. First they let readers know something about the main conflict of the story. The conflict places the main character against an opposing force. Next authors reveal some of the problems that prevent the main character from resolving the conflict. Suspense continues to build until the climax or turning point of the story. That is the moment when readers finally learn if the main character will win or lose the struggle. Writers usually end their stories soon after the climax. The conclusion of the story just ties up the loose ends.

point of view: (page 238) the position or standpoint from which a narrative is presented; in other words, the voice through which a writer tells the story. The author, of course, is really the person telling the story, but sometimes an author will make one of the characters in the story narrate the events that happen. Such a story has **first-person point of view.** The term "first person" refers to the pronouns "I" and "we"; the narrator is the "I" of a story with a first-person point of view. A. Conan Doyle is the author of "The Redheaded League" (page 179), but the character, Watson, narrates the story of how Sherlock Holmes solves the mystery of the league. The narrator does not have to be the central character, or even a major character; Sherlock Holmes, not Watson, is the central character in "The Redheaded League."

Often, rather than having a character tell the story, the author will act as narrator. When the narrator knows everything that goes on and sees into the minds of all the characters, the story has an **omniscient point of view.** *Omniscient* means "knowing everything." "The Revolt of 'Mother'" (page 346) is written in the omniscient point of view. While the author focuses on Sarah Penn's thoughts and feelings, she also lets the reader know directly how other characters—Nanny and the minister, for instance—feel when Sarah moves into the barn.

When the reader sees into the mind of only one character, even though no character in the story acts as narrator, the point of view is ***third-person limited.** As in the first-person point of view, the writer reveals the thoughts of only one character, and the reader knows only what this character knows. But unlike first-person point of view, no "I" character narrates the story. For example, the reader of "The Torn Invitation" (page 297) knows only what is in Harry's mind. The author never directly shows what is going on in the minds of Harry's mother or Frankie.

refrain: a line or phrase repeated at regular points in a poem, usually at the end of each stanza. A refrain can also be an entire stanza repeated at certain points in a poem.

rhyme: the repetition of words or syllables with similar sounds. This repetition occurs at specific places in a poem, usually at the ends of lines. A poem's ***rhyme scheme** (page 440), or pattern of rhyme, is indicated by letters. The small letter *a* is used for the first rhyming sound, *b* for the second rhyming sound, and so forth. Each stanza of "Sea Lullaby" (page 453) has the rhyme scheme *abab.*

rhythm: the pattern in which accented and unaccented syllables are repeated in each line of a poem; the beat of a poem. Each line of "Taught Me Purple" (page 477) has three accented syllables alternating with four unaccented ones. Each line begins and ends with an unaccented syllable.

*script: (page 362) the written version of a play, movie, or television program. It usually includes a list of the characters, as well as the dialogue and the stage directions. The script of *Twelve Angry Men* begins on page 382.

setting: the time and place in which a work of literature takes place. The setting of "Paul Revere's Ride" (page 71) is Boston and nearby towns on the night before the battles of Lexington and Concord.

*short story: (page 178) a short work of fiction that usually can be read in one sitting. Short stories generally have only a few characters and events, with the conflict centering on one main character. "Prairie Winter" (page 77), for example, has one major character—Caroline. Her struggle to ensure that she and her baby survive the bitter prairie winter constitutes the story's conflict.

simile: a comparison using the word *like* or *as*. In this simile from "Catalogue" (page 464), jumping cats are compared to grapes:

Cats, when they jump, are sleek
As a grape slipping its skin.

stage directions: (page 362) the playwright's instructions within a play to the director and actors, indicating how something should be done. Stage directions may indicate what the stage or set should look like, how an actor or actress should say a certain line, or what actions characters should perform. In Act I of *Twelve Angry Men* (page 385), for instance, a stage direction says: Jurors *start to take off their suitcoats and hang them over backs of chairs.*

stanza: a division in a poem consisting of a group of related lines. Every stanza in a poem usually has the same number of lines, as well as the same pattern of rhyme and rhythm. For example,

"Casey at the Bat" (page 443) has stanzas of four lines each. The rhyme scheme in each stanza is *aabb*.

surprise ending: an unexpeted conclusion to a work of literature. "The Choice" (page 485) has such an unexpected ending. For most of the poem, the poet implies that it is best to choose romance in preference to riches, as she did. Then, in the last line, she says, "Somebody ought to examine my head!"

suspense: a feeling of excitement, anxiety, and curiosity about what will happen in a story or play. Suspense keeps readers going on until they find out what happens. In "Leiningen versus the Ants" (page 5), for example, readers are kept in suspense about whether Leiningen can save himself and his workers from total destruction by the ants.

*tall tale: (page 316) a story in which the personality, ability, and deeds of the main character are exaggerated to the point of impossibility. This exaggeration usually has a humorous effect. Sometimes the main characters in folktales are imaginary, such as Paul Bunyan. Others, such as Annie Oakley, were real people whose experiences have been exaggerated.

theme: (page 358) the main idea of a work of literature; the message the writer conveys. Except in unusual cases, such as fables, the theme is hardly ever expressed directly. Rather, it is implied in the story. A story does not always have a theme, and sometimes a story may have more than one theme. A theme for "Stranger on the Night Train" (page 215) might be: *It is difficult to judge whether people's actions are right or wrong unless we know the reasons behind them.*

*third-person-limited point of view: See **point of view.**

Index of Literary Terms

Glossary

The glossary includes unfamiliar words used in this anthology. In most cases words that are footnoted in the text are not included here. The order and kinds of information given in an entry are shown below:

1. The defined word is divided into syllables. For example: **ac·com·mo·da-tion.**

2. Pronunciation. When there are two common pronunciations of a word, both are usually given. For example: (*v.* är tik′ yə lāt, *adj.* är tik′ yə lit).

3. Accents. The mark ′ is placed after a syllable with primary or heavy accent, and the mark ′ after a syllable shows a secondary or lighter accent, as in **in·ge·nu·i·ty** (in′ jə nü′ə tē).

4. The part of speech and, when useful, information about the singular or plural form.

5. Usage labels. For example: **con·sta·ble** . . . BRITISH. policeman.

6. Definition. The words are always defined according to their use in the book; in addition, other commonly used meanings are frequently given.

7. Derivative parts of speech. Other commonly used parts of speech derived from an entry are frequently given. For example: **ag·ile** . . . **—agility,** *n.*

The following abbreviations are used:

adj.	adjective
adv.	adverb
n.	noun
pl.	plural
v.	verb

Pronunciation Key

a, hat, cap; ā, age, face; ä, father, far; b, bad, rob; ch, child, much; d, did, red; e, let, best; ē, equal, be; ėr, term, learn; f, fat, if; g, go, bag; h, he, how; i, it, pin; ī, ice, five; j, jam, enjoy; k, kind, seek; l, land, coal; m, me, am; n, no, in; ng, long, bring; o, hot, rock; ō, open, go; ô, order, all; oi, oil, voice; ou, house, out; p, paper, cup; r, run, try; s, say, yes; sh, she, rush; t, tell, it; th, thin, both; ŦH, then, smooth; u, cup, butter; u̇, full, put; ü, rule, move; v, very, save; w, will, woman; y, young, yet; z, zero, breeze; zh, measure, seizure; ə represents: a in about, e in taken, i in pencil, o in lemon, u in circus.

Y as in Fr. *du*; à as in Fr. *ami*; œ as in Fr. *peu*; N as in Fr. *bon*; H as in Ger. *ach*.

a·bate (ə bāt′), v. **1.** lessen in force or intensity; reduce or decrease. **2.** put an end to; stop.

ab·stract (adj. ab′strakt; v. ab strakt′; n. ab′strakt), adj., v., n. —adj. **1.** thought of apart from any particular object or actual instance; not concrete. **2.** naming a quality or idea rather than a particular object or a tangible thing. —v. **1.** summarize. **2.** take away; remove —n. a brief statement of the main ideas in an article or book; summary.

a·byss (ə bis′), n. **1.** a bottomless or very great depth. **2.** anything too deep or great to be measured; lowest depth. —**abysmal**, adj.

ac·cede (ak sēd′), v. **1.** give in; agree; consent. **2.** become a party (to) **3.** come, attain, or succeed (to an office or dignity).

ac·com·mo·da·tion (ə kom′ə dā′shən), n. **1.** anything that supplies a want or gives aid; help, favor, or convenience. **2.** lodging and sometimes food as well. **3.** willingness to help out.

a·cute (ə kyüt′), adj. **1.** acting keenly on the senses; sharp; intense. **2.** coming quickly to a crisis; brief and severe. **3.** crucial; critical. **4.** high in pitch; shrill. **5.** having or ending in a sharp point.

ad·ver·sary (ad′vər ser′ē), n. person or group opposing or resisting another or others; enemy; opponent.

af·firm (ə fėrm′), v. declare positively to be true; maintain firmly; assert.

af·flu·ent (af′lü ənt), adj. **1.** having an abundance of money or property; wealthy; rich. **2.** abundant; plentiful.

ag·gres·sor (ə gres′ər), n. one that begins an attack or quarrel, especially a country that starts a war.

---

hat, āge, fär; let, ēqual, term;
it, īce; hot, ōpen, ôrder;
oil, out; cup, pùt, rüle;
ch, child; ng, long; sh, she;
th, thin; ғн, then; zh, measure;

ə represents a in about, e in taken,
i in pencil, o in lemon, u in circus.

Pronunciation Key, respellings, and definitions in the Glossary are from SCOTT, FORESMAN ADVANCED DICTIONARY by E. L. Thorndike and Clarence L. Barnhart. Copyright © 1979 by Scott, Foresman and Company. Reprinted by permission.

a·ghast (ə gast′), adj. struck with surprise or horror; filled with shocked amazement.

ag·ile (aj′əl), adj. **1.** moving with speed, ease and elegance; lively; nimble. **2.** mentally alert; quick-witted. —**agility**, n.

ag·i·tate (aj′ə tāt), v. **1.** move or shake violently. **2.** disturb or excite very much. **3.** argue about; discuss vigorously and publicly. —**agitation**, n.

a·lac·ri·ty (ə lak′rə tē), n. **1.** brisk and eager action; liveliness. **2.** cheerful willingness.

al·lu·vi·al (ə lü′vē əl), adj. having to do with, consisting of, or formed by sand, silt or mud left by flowing water. A delta is an alluvial deposit at the mouth of a river.

a·men·i·ty (ə men′ə tē), n. **1.** something which makes life easier and more pleasant; agreeableness. **2.** amenities, pl. pleasant ways; polite acts.

an·i·mat·ed (an′ə mā′tid), adj. **1.** lively; vigorous. **2.** joyful.

an·ni·hi·la·tion (ə nī′ə lā′shən), n. complete destruction.

an·tic·i·pa·tion (an tis′ə pā′shən), n. **1.** act of looking forward to; expectation. **2.** enjoyment or celebration of an event or experience in advance.

ap·pa·ra·tus (ap′ə rā′təs), n. **1.** the tools, machines, or other equipment necessary to carry out a purpose or for a particular use. **2.** a political or party organization; an administrative machine.

ap·pa·ri·tion (ap′ə rish′ən), n. **1.** a supernatural sight or thing; ghost or phantom. **2.** the appearance of something strange, remarkable, or unexpected.

ap·pre·hen·sion (ap′ri hen′shən), n. expectation of misfortune; dread of impending danger; fear.

ap·pro·pri·a·tion (ə prō′prē ā′shən), n. sum of money or other thing set aside for a special purpose.

ar·dent·ly (ärd′nt lē), adv. **1.** in a manner glowing with passion; passionately. **2.** eagerly; keenly.

ar·dor (är′dər), n. **1.** warmth of emotion; passion. **2.** great enthusiasm; eagerness; zeal.

ar·du·ous (är′jü əs), adj. hard to do; requiring much effort; difficult; strenuous.

ar·id (ar′id), adj. **1.** having very little rainfall; dry. **2.** unfruitful because of lack of moisture; barren. **3.** uninteresting and empty; dull.

a·ris·to·crat (ə ris′tə krat), n. **1.** person who belongs to the aristocracy, a class of people having a high position in society. **2.** person high-class in tastes, opinions and manners. **3.** person who favors government by the upper class.

ar·ro·gance (ar′ə gəns), *n.* excessive pride with contempt of others; haughtiness.

ar·son (är′sən), *n.* the crime of intentionally and maliciously setting fire to a building or other property.

ar·tic·u·late (*v.* är tik′yə lāt; *adj.* är tik′yə lit), *v.*, *adj.* —*v.* **1.** speak distinctly; express in clear sounds and words. **2.** express oneself in words. —*adj.* **1.** uttered in distinct syllables of words. **2.** able to put one's thoughts into words easily and clearly.

as·cet·ic (ə set′ik), *n.* **1.** person who practices unusual self-denial or severe discipline over himself, especially for religious reasons. **2.** person who refrains from pleasures and comforts.

a·skance (ə skans′), *adv.* **1.** with suspicion or disapproval. **2.** to one side; sideways.

as·sail (ə sāl′), *v.* **1.** attack repeatedly with violent blows. **2.** attack with hostile words, arguments, or abuse.

as·set (as′et), *n.* **1.** something having value; advantage. **2.** assets, *pl.* all items of value owned by a person or business and constituting the resources of the person or business. Real estate, cash, securities, inventories, patents, and good will are assets.

as·tute·ness (ə stüt′nes), *n.* the quality of being shrewd, especially with regard to one's own interests; craftiness.

at·trib·ute (*n.* at′rə byüt; *v.* ə trib′yüt), *n.*, *v.* —*n.* an object or quality considered appropriate to a person, rank, or office; symbol; characteristic. —*v.* **1.** regard as an effect or product of; think of as caused by. **2.** think of as belonging to or appropriate to.

au·di·ble (ô′də bəl), *adj.* heard; loud enough to be heard.

au·ra (ôr′ə), *n.* **1.** a distinctive atmosphere surrounding a given source. **2.** a luminous radiation.

aus·tere (ô stir′), *adj.* **1.** stern in manner or appearance; harsh. **2.** severe in self-discipline; strict in morals. **3.** grave; somber; serious.

av·o·ca·tion (av′ə kā′shən), *n.* something that a person does besides his regular business; minor occupation; hobby.

be·fud·dle (bi fud′l), *v.* stupefy; confuse; muddle; perplex.

bel·lig·er·ent (bə lij′ər ənt), *adj.*, *n.* —*adj.* **1.** waging or carrying on regular recognized war; fighting. **2.** fond of fighting; tending or inclined to war; warlike. —*n.* **1.** nation or state engaged in war. **2.** a person engaged in fighting with another person. —**belligerently,** *adv.*

ben·e·fac·tor (ben′ə fak′tər), *n.* person who has helped others, either by gifts of money or by some kind act.

ben·e·fi·ci·ar·y (ben′ə fish′ē er ē), *n.* **1.** person who receives benefits. **2.** person who receives or is to receive money or property from an insurance policy or a will.

be·nev·o·lent (bə nev′ə lənt), *adj.* **1.** wishing or intended to promote the happiness of others; good will; kindly feeling. **2.** act of kindness; generous gift.

be·nign (bi nīn′), *adj.* **1.** kindly in feeling; benevolent; gracious. **2.** gentle; favorable; mild. **3.** not dangerous to health; not malignant.

be·rate (bi rāt′), *v.* scold sharply; upbraid.

be·siege (bi sēj′), *v.* **1.** surround by armed forces in order to compel surrender; lay seige to. **2.** crowd around. **3.** overwhelm with requests or questions.

boon (bün), *n.* **1.** great benefit; blessing. **2.** ARCHAIC. something asked for or granted as a favor.

bul·lion (bùl′yən), *n.* gold or silver in the form of ingots (blocks) or bars.

but·tress (but′ris), *n.*, *v.* —*n.* a support built against a wall or building to strengthen it. —*v.* support and strengthen.

cal·dron (kôl′drən), *n.* a large kettle or boiler. Also **cauldron.**

cam·ou·flage (kam′ə fläzh), *n.* a disguise or false appearance serving to conceal.

can·did (kan′did), *adj.* **1.** saying openly what one really thinks; frank and sincere; outspoken. **2.** fair; impartial.

can·ni·bal (kan′ə bəl), *n.* **1.** animal that eats others of its own kind. **2.** a person who eats human flesh.

cha·grin (shə grin′), *n.* a feeling of distress caused by humiliation, disappointment, or failure.

chap·e·rone (shap′ə rōn′), *n.* **1.** a person, especially a married or an older woman, who accompanies a young unmarried woman in public for the sake of proper behavior. **2.** an older person who is present at a party or other social activity of young people to see that good taste is observed.

chiv·al·ry (shiv′əl rē), *n.* **1.** qualities of an ideal knight in the Middle Ages; bravery, honor, courtesy, protection of the weak, repect for women, generosity, and fairness to enemies. **2.** gallant warriors or gentlemen. **chivalrously,** *adv.*

chron·ic (kron′ik), *adj.* **1.** lasting a long time. **2.** suffering long from an illness. **3.** never stopping; constant; habitual.

clap·board (klab′ərd), *n.* a thin board, usually thicker along one edge than along the other, used to cover the outer walls of wooden buildings. Each board is made to overlap the one below it.

co·her·ent (kō hir′ənt), *adj.* **1.** logically connected; consistent. **2.** sticking together; holding together.

com·mence (kə mens′), *v.* **1.** make a start; begin. **2.** begin (an action); enter upon.

com·mis·sar·y (kom′ə ser′ē), *n.* **1.** store handling food and supplies in a mining camp, lumber camp, army camp. **2.** deputy; representative.

com·pla·cen·cy (kəm plā′ sn sē), *n.* a state of being pleased with oneself or what one has; self-satisfaction.

com·punc·tion (kəm pungk′shən), *n.* **1.** uneasiness of the mind because of wrongdoing; pricking of conscience; remorse. **2.** a slight or passing regret.

con·ceiv·a·ble (kən sē′və bəl), *adj.* imaginable.

con·cus·sion (kən kush′ən), *n.* **1.** a sudden, violent shaking; shock. **2.** injury to a soft part of the body, especially the brain, caused by a blow, fall, or other physical shock.

con·fis·cate (kon′fə skāt), *v.* **1.** seize for the public treasury. **2.** seize by authority; take and keep.

con·sci·en·tious (kon′shē en′shəs), *adj.* **1.** careful to do what one knows is right; controlled by conscience. **2.** done with care to make it right; painstaking.

con·sta·ble (kon′stə bəl), *n.* **1.** a police officer, especially in a township, district, or rural area of the United States. **2.** BRITISH, policeman.

con·ster·na·tion (kon′stər nā′shən), *n.* great dismay; paralyzing terror.

con·stric·tion (kən strik′shən), *n.* **1.** a contracting, drawing together; compression. **2.** a feeling of tightness.

con·tem·pla·tive (kon′təm plā′tiv), *adj.* **1.** deeply thoughtful; meditative. **2.** devoted to religious meditation and prayer.

con·va·les·cence (kon′və les′ns), *n.* time during which one recovers from an illness.

cor·don (kôrd′n), *n.* **1.** line or circle of soldiers, policemen, forts enclosing or guarding a place. **2.** cord, braid, or ribbon worn as an ornament.

coun·sel (koun′səl), *n., v.* —*n.* **1.** lawyer or group of lawyers. **2.** act of exchanging ideas; talking things over; consultation. **3.** carefully considered advice. **4.** deliberate purpose; design; plan; scheme. —*v.* **1.** give advice to; advise. **2.** recommend. **3.** exchange ideas; consult together; deliberate.

cra·ni·um (krā′nē əm), *n.* **1.** the skull of a vertebrate. **2.** the part of the skull enclosing the brain.

cre·du·li·ty (krə dü′lə tē), *n.* a great readiness to believe.

cryp·tic (krip′tik), *adj.* having a hidden meaning; secret; mysterious.

daunt·less·ly (dônt′lis lē), *adv.* in a manner not to be frightened or discouraged; bravely.

de·ci·pher (di sī′fər), *v.* **1.** make out the meaning of (something unclear). **2.** interpret (secret writing) by using a key; change to ordinary language; decode.

de·crep·it (di krep′it), *adj.* broken down or weakened by use or old age; old and feeble.

def·er·ence (def′ər əns), *n.* **1.** a yielding to the judgment, opinion, wishes of another. **2.** great respect.

de·hy·drate (dē hī′drāt), *v.* take or lose water or moisture from; dry.

de·lib·er·a·tion (di lib′ə rā′shən), *n.* **1.** careful thought. **2.** discussion of reasons for and against something; debate. **3.** slowness and care.

de·men·tia (di men′shə), *n.* a partial or complete deterioration of mind.

de·mure (di myùr′), *adj.* **1.** artificially proper; assuming an air of modesty; coy. **2.** composed in demeanor; serious and sober.

den·i·zen (den′ə zən), *n.* **1.** inhabitant or occupant of a place or region. **2.** a foreign plant or animal that has been naturalized.

dev·as·tate (dev′ə stāt), *v.* make desolate; lay waste; destroy; ravage.

de·vi·a·tion (dē′vē ā′shən), *n.* **1.** act of turning aside; swerving. **2.** a difference from an ordinary policy or course of action. **—deviate**, *v.*, **—deviously**, *adv.*

hat, āge, fär; let, ēqual, tėrm;
it, īce; hot, ōpen, ôrder;
oil, out; cup, pùt, rüle;
ch, child; ng, long; sh, she;
th, thin; ᴛʜ, then; zh, measure;

ə represents *a* in about, *e* in taken,
i in pencil, *o* in lemon, *u* in circus.

640   *Glossary*

dex·ter·i·ty (dek ster′ə tē), *n.* **1.** skill in using the hands or body. **2.** skill in using the mind; cleverness.

di·a·bol·i·cal·ly (dī′ə bol′ik lē), *adv.* **1.** very cruelly or wickedly; devilishly; fiendishly. **2.** in a devil-like manner.

di·a·tribe (dī′ə trīb), *n.* speech or discussion bitterly and violently directed against some person or thing.

dic·tum (dik′təm), *n.* **1.** a formal comment; authoritative opinion. **2.** maxim; saying.

di·late (dī lāt′), *v.* **1.** make or become larger or wider. **2.** speak or write in a very complete or detailed manner.

dil·i·gent (dil′ə jənt), *adj.* **1.** hard-working; industrious. **2.** careful and steady.

dire·ful (dīr′fəl), *adj.* causing great fear or suffering; dreadful; terrible.

dis·arm (dis ärm′), *v.* **1.** take weapons or defenses away from **2.** remove anger or suspicion from; make friendly or harmless.

dis·con·cert (dis′kən sert′), *v.* embarrass greatly; confuse.

dis·con·so·late (dis kon′sə lit), *adj.* without hope; forlorn; unhappy.

dis·crep·an·cy (dis krep′ən sē), *n.* a difference; inconsistency.

dis·crim·i·na·tion (dis krim′ə na′shən), *n.* **1.** power of detecting distinctions or differences; good judgment. **2.** a difference in attitude or treatment shown to a particular person or class.

dis·pas·sion·ate (dis pash′ə nit), *adj.* free from emotion or prejudice; calm and impartial.

dis·perse (dis pèrs′), *v.* send or drive off in different directions; scatter.

doc·ile·ly (dos′əl lē), *adv.* **1.** in a manner easily managed or dealt with; obediently. **2.** easily taught; willing to learn.

dole·ful (dōl′fəl), *adj.* very sad or dreary; mournful; dismal.

do·mes·tic (də mes′tik), *adj., n.* —*adj.* **1.** of the home, household, or family affairs. **2.** not wild; tame. —*n.* servant in a household.

dom·i·nant (dom′ə nənt), *adj.* **1.** most powerful or influential; controlling; ruling; governing. **2.** rising high above its surroundings; towering over.

du·bi·ous·ly (dü′bē əs lē), *adv.* **1.** with doubt; uncertainty. **2.** hesitantly.

ed·dy (ed′ē), *n., pl.* **-dies**, *v.* —*n.* water, air, smoke moving against the main current, especially when having a whirling motion; small whirlpool or whirlwind. —*v.* **1.** move against the main current in a whirling motion; whirl. **2.** move in circles.

ef·fer·ves·cent (ef′ ər ves′nt), *adj.* **1.** giving off bubbles of gas; bubbling. **2.** lively.

el·o·quence (el′ə kwəns), *n.* **1.** flow of speech that has grace and force. **2.** power to win by speaking; the art of using language so as to stir feelings.

e·lu·sive (i lü′siv), *adj.* **1.** hard to describe or understand; baffling. **2.** tending to slip away or escape; evasive.

e·man·ci·pa·tion (i man′sə pā′shən), *n.* a release from slavery or restraint. —**emancipate**, *v.*

em·bel·lish (em bel′ish), *v.* add beauty to; decorate; adorn; elaborate.

em·boss (em bôs′), *v.* decorate with a design, pattern, etc., that stands out from the surface.

em·i·nent (em′ə nənt), *adj.* **1.** above all or most others; outstanding; distinguished. **2.** conspicuous; noteworthy. **3.** high, lofty. —**eminently**, *adv.*

em·phat·i·cal·ly (em fat′ik əl lē), *adv.* **1.** said or done with force or stress; strongly expressed. **2.** speaking with force or stress; expressing oneself strongly.

en·cum·ber (en kum′bər), *v.* **1.** hold back; hinder; hamper. **2.** block up; fill.

en·ig·mat·i·cal·ly (en′ig mat′ə kəl lē), *adv.* in a way that baffles or puzzles; obscurely.

en·rap·ture (en rap′chər), *v.* to fill with a strong feeling of delight or joy; transport.

en·sue (en sü′), *v.* **1.** come after; follow. **2.** happen as a result.

en·vel·op (en vel′əp), *v.* **1.** wrap or cover; enfold. **2.** hide; conceal. **3.** surround; encircle.

e·pit·o·mize (i pit′ə mīz), *v.* **1.** be typical or representative of. **2.** give an example of; summarize.

e·vade (i vād′), *v.* **1.** get away from by trickery; avoid by cleverness. **2.** avoid by indefinite or misleading statements.

ex·hor·ta·tion (eg′zôr tā′shən), *n.* strong urging; earnest advice or warning.

ex·ploit (*n.* ek′sploit, *v.* ek sploit′), *n., v.* —*n.* a bold, unusual act; daring deed. —*v.* make use of; make unfair or selfish use of.

ex·qui·site (ek′skwi zit), *adj.* **1.** very lovely; delicate. **2.** sharp; intense. **3.** of highest excellence; most admirable.

ex·u·ber·ance (eg zü′bər əns), *adj.* **1.** abundant; overflowing; lavish. **2.** profuse in growth; luxuriant.

3. abounding in health and spirits; overflowing with good cheer.

fas·tid·i·ous (fa stid′ē əs), *adj.* hard to please; dainty in taste; easily disgusted.

fath·om (faŦH′əm), *n., v.* —*n.* unit of measure equal to 6 feet, used mostly in measuring the depth of water and the length of ships' ropes or cables. —*v.* **1.** measure the depth of (water); sound. **2.** get to the bottom of; understand fully.

fath·om·less (faŦH′əm lis), *adj.* **1.** too deep to be measured; bottomless. **2.** impossible to be fully understood.

fa·tigue (fə tēg′), *n.* **1.** weariness caused by hard work or effort. **2.** a weakening (of metal) caused by long-continued use or strain.

fe·roc·i·ty (fə ros′ə tē), *n.* savage cruelty; fierceness.

fig·ur·a·tive·ly (fig′yər ə tiv lē), *adv.* **1.** in a manner using words out of their literal or ordinary meaning to add beauty or force. **2.** in a manner using many figures of speech; characterized by the use of metaphors, similes; poetically. **3.** symbolically.

filch (filch), *v.* steal in small quantities; pilfer.

fis·cal (fis′kəl), *adj.* of or having to do with finacial matters; financial.

foil (foil), *v.* **1.** prevent from carrying out plans or attempts; get the better of; outwit or defeat. **2.** prevent (a plan) from being carried out or from succeeding.

for·mi·da·ble (fôr′mə də bəl), *adj.* hard to overcome; hard to deal with; to be dreaded.

for·ti·tude (fôr′tə tüd), *n.* courage in facing pain, danger, or trouble; firmness of spirit.

fos·sil (fos′əl), *n.* anything found in the strata of the earth which is recognizable as the hardened remains or traces of an animal or plant of a former gelogical age.

fray (frā), *v.* **1.** cause to separate into threads; make ragged or worn along the edge. **2.** wear away; rub.

---

hat, āge, fär; let, ēqual, tėrm;
it, īce; hot, ōpen, ôrder;
oil, out; cup, pùt, rüle;
ch, child; ng, long; sh, she;
th, thin; ŦH, then; zh, measure;

ə represents *a* in about, *e* in taken,
i in pencil, *o* in lemon, *u* in circus.

fru·gal (frü′gəl), *adj.* **1.** avoiding waste; tending to avoid unnecessary spending; saving; thrifty. **2.** costing little; barely sufficient.

fur·tive·ly (fėr′tiv lē), *adv.* quickly and stealthily to avoid being noticed; secretly; slyly.

fu·til·i·ty (fyü til′ə tē), *n.* **1.** uselessness; ineffectiveness. **2.** unimportance. —**futile,** *adj.*

gam·ut (gam′ət), *n.* **1.** the whole range of anything. **2.** the whole series of notes on the musical scale.

gaunt (gônt), *adj.* **1.** very thin and bony; with hollow eyes and a starved look. **2.** looking bare and gloomy; desolate.

gen·teel (jen tēl′), *adj.* **1.** belonging or suited to polite society. **2.** polite; well-bred; fashionable; elegant. **3.** artificially polite and courteous.

ges·ta·tion (je stā′shən), *n.* **1.** period of pregnancy. **2.** formation and development of a project, idea or plan in the mind.

graft (graft), *n.* money dishonestly and improperly taken.

gro·tesque (grō tesk′), *adj., n.* —*adj.* **1.** odd or unnatural in shape, appearance, manner; fantastic. **2.** ridiculous; absurd. —*n.* painting or sculpture combining designs, ornaments, figures of persons or animals in a fantastic or unnatural way much used in the Renaissance.

har·ass (har′əs), *v.* **1.** trouble by repeated attacks; harry. **2.** distress with annoying labor, care, misfortune; disturb; worry; torment.

he·ret·i·cal (hə ret′ə kəl), *adj.* **1.** of or having to do with heresy, a religious opinion rejected by church authorities. **2.** characterized by a departure from accepted beliefs or standards.

hew (hyü), *v.* **1.** cut with an ax, sword, etc.; chop. **2.** hold firmly (to); stick fast or cling (to).

hol·o·caust (hol′ə kôst), *n.* complete destruction, especially by fire.

hom·age (hom′ij), *n.* dutiful respect; reverence.

id·i·om (id′ē əm), *n.* **1.** phrase or expression whose meaning cannot be understood from the ordinary meanings of words in it. **2.** the language or dialect of a particular area or group.

ig·no·min·i·ous·ly (ig′nə min′ē əs lē), *adv.* **1.** shamefully; disgracefully; dishonorably. **2.** contemptibly. **3.** humiliatingly.

il·lit·er·a·cy (i lit′ər ə sē), *n.* **1.** inability to read and write. **2.** lack of education; lack of cultural knowledge.

im·mi·nent (im′ə nənt), *adj.* likely to happen soon; about to occur.

im·mo·late (im′ə lāt), *v.* **1.** kill as a sacrifice. **2.** offer in sacrifice.

im·pas·sive·ly (im pas′iv lē), *adv.* in a manner without feeling or emotion.

im·pede (im pēd′), *v.* stand in the way of; hinder; obstruct.

im·per·a·tive (im per′ə tiv), *adj.* **1.** not to be avoided; that must be done; urgent. **2.** expressing a command or request.

im·per·il (im per′əl), *v.* put in danger; endanger; jeopardize.

im·pe·ri·ous·ly (im pir′ē əs lē), *adv.* **1.** in a haughty or arrogant manner; domineeringly; overbearingly. **2.** in a manner not to be avoided; necessarily; urgently.

im·per·turb·a·bly (im′pər tėr′bə blē), *adv.* in a manner not easily excited or disturbed; calmly.

im·pre·ca·tion (im′prə kā′shən), *n.* a calling down; cursing.

im·pro·vi·sa·tion (im′prə vī zā′shən), *n.* an act of making up (music, poetry, speech) on the spur of the moment.

im·pu·dent (im′pyə dənt), *adj.* shamelessly bold; very rude and insolent.

in·an·i·mate (in an′ə mit), *adj.* **1.** not living or alive; lifeless. **2.** without liveliness or spirit; dull.

in·ap·pli·ca·ble (in ap′lə kə bəl), *adj.* not applicable; unsuitable; irrelevant.

in·ar·tic·u·late (in′är tik′yə lit), *adj.* **1.** not uttered in distinct syllables or words. **2.** not able to put one's thoughts or feelings into words easily and clearly.

in·au·di·ble (in ô′də bəl), *adj.* unheard; not capable of being heard.

in·aus·pi·cious (in′ô spish′əs), *adj.* with signs of failure; unfavorable; unlucky.

in·cal·cu·la·ble (in kal′kyə lə bəl), *adj.* **1.** too great in number to be counted; innumerable. **2.** impossible to foretell or reckon beforehand. **3.** uncertain.

in·car·nate (*adj.* in kär′nit; *v.* in kär′nāt), *adj., v.* —*adj.* embodied in flesh, especially in human form; personified; typified. —*v.* **1.** embody. **2.** put into or represent in concrete form; realize.

in·co·her·ent·ly (in′kō hir′ənt lē), *adv.* in a manner having or showing no logical connection of ideas; disjointedly; inconsistently.

in·dig·nant·ly (in dig′nənt lē), *adv.* in a manner expressing anger at something unworthy, unjust, unfair, or mean.

in·dis·tin·guish·a·ble (in′dis ting′gwi shə bəl), *adj.* **1.** not clearly recognizable or understandable. **2.** indeterminate in shape or structure. **3.** lacking identifying or individualizing qualities.

in·duc·tion (in duk′shən), *n.* **1.** enrollment in military service. **2.** a reasoning from particular facts to general truths or principles. **3.** act or ceremony of installing a person in office. **4.** act of bringing into existence or operation; causing.

in·dulge (in dulj′), *v.* **1.** give in to one's pleasure; let oneself have, use, or do what one wants. **2.** give in to the wishes or whims of; humor. **—indulgent,** *adj.*

in·ef·fa·ble (in ef′ə bəl), *adj.* not to be expressed in words; too great to be described in words.

in·ev·i·ta·ble (in ev′ə tə bəl), *adj.* not to be avoided; sure to happen; certain to come.

in·ex·or·a·ble (in ek′sər ə bəl), *adj.* not influenced by pleading or entreaties; relentless; unyielding.

in·ex·plic·a·ble (in′ik splik′ə bəl), *adj.* incapable of being explained, understood, or accounted for; mysterious.

in·fuse (in fyüz′), *v.* **1.** introduce as by pouring; put in; instill. **2.** inspire.

in·ge·nu·i·ty (in′jə nü′ə tē), *n.* **1.** skill in planning or making something; cleverness. **2.** skillfulness of invention or design.

i·ni·ti·ate (i nish′ē āt), *v.* **1.** be the first one to start; begin. **2.** admit (a person) with formal ceremonies into a group or society. **3.** help to get a first understanding; introduce into the knowledge of some art or subject.

in·no·va·tor (in′ə vā tôr), *n.* a person who makes changes; one who brings in something new or creates new ways of doing things.

in·scru·ta·ble (in skrü′tə bəl), *adj.* **1.** not readily investigated or understood; hard to grasp. **2.** mysterious.

in·sid·i·ous (in sid′ē əs), *adj.* **1.** seeking to entrap or ensnare; wily or sly; crafty; tricky. **2.** working secretly or subtly; developing without attracting attention.

in·sin·u·ate (in sin′yü āt), *v.* suggest in an indirect way; hint.

in·stinc·tive·ly (in stingk′tiv lē), *adv.* following an inborn tendency; following a chain of unlearned, coordinated acts characteristic of a particular species or group of animals.

in·te·gra·tion (in′tə grā′shən), *n.* **1.** act or process of putting together, making into a whole. **2.** inclusion of people of all races on an equal basis in schools, parks, neighborhoods.

in·ter·mi·na·ble (in tėr mə nə bəl), *adj.* never stopping; unceasing; endless.

in·ter·mit·tent·ly (in′tər mit′nt lē), *adv.* **1.** during a pause. **2.** with pauses at intervals.

in·ti·mate (in′tə māt), *v.* **1.** suggest indirectly; hint. **2.** make known; announce; notify.

in·ti·mate (in′tə mit), *adj., n.* —*adj.* **1.** very familiar; known very well; closely acquainted. **2.** personal; private. **3.** far within; deepest; inmost. —*n.* a close friend.

in·tim·i·date (in tim′ə dāt), *v.* **1.** make afraid; frighten. **2.** influence or force by fear.

in·tol·er·ant (in tol′ər ənt), *adj.* **1.** unable or unwilling to grant equal freedom of expression especially in religious matters. **2.** bigoted.

in·tri·ca·cy (in′trə kə sē), *n.* **1.** a puzzling or entangled nature or condition; complexity. **2.** a thing or event that is puzzling, has many twists and turns, is complex; complication.

in·tro·spec·tive (in′trə spek′tiv), *adj.* characterized by examination of one's own thoughts and feelings.

i·tin·er·ant (ī tin′ər ənt), *adj.* traveling from place to place, especially in connection with some employment or vocation.

jad·ed (jā′did), *adj.* **1.** worn out; tired; weary. **2.** dulled from continual use.

ju·di·cial (jü dish′əl), *adj.* **1.** of or by judges; having to do with courts or the administration of justice. **2.** impartial; fair. —**judiciously,** *adv.*

knoll (nōl), *n.* a small rounded hill; mound.

---

hat, āge, fär; let, ēqual, tėrm;
it, īce; hot, ōpen, ôrder;
oil, out; cup, put, rüle;
ch, child; ng, long; sh, she;
th, thin; ₮H, then; zh, measure;

ə represents *a* in about, *e* in taken,
i in pencil, *o* in lemon, *u* in circus.

lab·y·rinth (lab′ə rinth′), *n.* **1.** number of connecting passages so arranged that it is hard to find one's way from point to point; maze. **2.** any confusing, complicated arrangement.

lack·a·dai·si·cal (lak′ə dā′zə kəl), *adj.* lacking interest or enthusiasm; languid; listless; dreamy.

lair (ler), *n.* **1.** den or resting place of a wild animal. **2.** secret or secluded retreat; hideaway.

lan·guid (lang′gwid), *adj.* **1.** without energy; drooping; weak; weary. **2.** without interest or enthusiasm; indifferent; listless. **3.** not brisk or lively; sluggish; dull.

la·tent (lāt′nt), *adj.* present but not active; hidden; concealed.

lay (lā), *adj.* of the people who do not belong to a particular profession, especially the clergy.

le·thal (lē′thəl), *adj.* causing death; deadly.

li·a·bil·i·ty (lī′ə bil′ə tē), *n.* **1.** state of being susceptible. **2.** state of being under obligation. **3.** something that is to one's disadvantage. **4.** liabilities, *pl.* debts or other financial obligations of a business.

lithe (li₮H), *adj.* bending easily; supple.

lop (lop), *v.* **1.** cut off. **2.** remove parts as if by cutting.

lu·cid (lü′sid), *adj.* **1.** marked by clearness of reasoning, expression, or arrangement; easy to follow or understand. **2.** clear in intellect; rational; sane. **3.** translucent; clear. **4.** shining; bright; luminous.

lu·di·crous (lü′də krəs), *adj.* causing derisive laughter; amusingly absurd; ridiculous.

lur·id (lùr′id), *adj.* **1.** lighted up with a red or fiery glare. **2.** shockingly terrible, repulsive; sensational; startling.

ma·ni·a (mā′nē ə), *n.* **1.** unusual or unreasonable fondness; craze. **2.** kind of mental disorder characterized by great excitement, elation, and uncontrolled, often violent, activity.

man·i·fest (man′ə fest), *v.* **1.** show plainly; reveal; display. **2.** put beyond doubt; prove.

mar·tyr (mär′tər), **1.** person who is put to death or made to suffer greatly because of a cause, principle, or religious belief. **2.** person who suffers great pain or anguish.

mar·tyr·dom (mär′tər dom), *n.* **1.** death or suffering on account of adherence to a cause and especially to one's religious faith.

ma·son·ry (mā′sn rē), *n.* **1.** wall, foundation, or part of a building built by a mason; stonework or brickwork. **2.** trade or skill of a mason.

max·im (mak′səm), *n.* **1.** a short rule of conduct expressed as a proverb. **2.** statement expressing some general truth.

may·hem (mā′hem), *n.* **1.** crime of intentionally maiming or injuring so that a person is less able to defend himself. **2.** any crime of violence which causes permanent physical injury. **3.** needless or willful damage.

mel·an·chol·y (mel′ən kol′ē), *n., adj.* —*n.* **1.** condition of sadness and low spirits; gloominess; dejection. **2.** sober thoughtfulness; pensiveness. —*adj.* **1.** depressed in spirits; sad; gloomy. **2.** causing sadness; depressing. **3.** thoughtful; pensive.

met·a·bol·ic (met′ə bol′ik), *adj.* of or having to do with the physiological processes by which an organism maintains life.

mil·i·tan·cy (mil′ə tən sē), *n.* warlike behavior or tendency; militant spirit or policy.

mod·i·fi·ca·tion (mod′ə fə kā shən), *n.* **1.** partial alternation or change. **2.** making less severe or strong; a toning down. **3.** a change in an organism resulting from external influences.

mo·nop·o·ly (mə nop′ə lē), *n.* the exclusive possession or control of something.

mo·rose (mə rōs′), *adj.* gloomy; sullen; ill-humored.

mor·tal·i·ty (môr tal′ə tē), *n.* **1.** mortal nature; condition of being sure to die sometime. **2.** loss of life on a large scale.

noc·tur·nal (nok tėr′nl), *adj.* **1.** of or in the night. **2.** active in the night.

nom·i·nal (nom′ə nəl), *adj.* **1.** existing in name only; not real. **2.** too small to be considered; unimportant compared with the real value.

ob·nox·ious (əb nok′shəs), *adj.* very disagreeable; offensive; hateful.

ob·sti·na·cy (ob′stə nə sē), *n.* **1.** stubborness. **2.** the state of being difficult to remedy, relieve, or subdue. —**obstinately,** *adv.*

om·i·nous (om′ə nəs), *adj.* **1.** being or exhibiting a bad omen; unfavorable; threatening. **2.** foreboding or foreshadowing evil.

o·paque (ō pāk′), *adj.* **1.** not letting light through; not transparent or translucent. **2.** not conducting heat, sound, electricity. **3.** not shining; dark; dull. **4.** hard to understand.

pa·cif·ic (pə sif′ik), *adj.* **1.** tending to make peace; making peace; peaceable. **2.** loving peace; not warlike. **3.** calm; quiet.

pal·at·a·ble (pal′ə tə bəl), *adj.* **1.** agreeable to the taste; pleasing. **2.** agreeable to the mind or feelings; acceptable.

pal·lor (pal′ər), *n.* lack of normal color from fear, illness, death; paleness.

par·a·dox (par′ə doks), *n.* **1.** statement that may be true but seems to say two opposite things. EXAMPLE. "More haste, less speed." **2.** statement that is false because it says two opposite things. **3.** person or thing that seems to be full of contradictions.

pa·thos (pā′thos), *n.* quality in speech, writing, music, events, or a scene that arouses a feeling of pity or sadness; power of evoking tender or sad emotion and pity.

pa·tron (pā′trən), *n., adj.* —*n.* **1.** person who buys regularly at a given store or goes regularly to a given restaurant or hotel. **2.** person who gives his approval and support to some person, art, cause, or undertaking. **3.** a guardian saint or god. —*adj.* guarding; protecting.

peer·less (pir′lis), *adj.* without an equal; matchless.

pell·mell (pel′mel′), *adv., adj., n.* —*adv.* **1.** in a rushing, tumbling mass or crowd. **2.** in headlong haste. —*adj.* headlong; tumultuous. —*n.* violent disorder or confusion.

pen·sive (pen′siv), *adj.* **1.** thoughtful; in a serious or sad way. **2.** in a sad frame of mind.

per·cep·tion (pər sep′shən), *n.* **1.** act of being aware through the senses. **2.** power of taking into the mind; power of observing or understanding.

pe·remp·tor·y (pə remp′tər ē), *adj.* **1.** leaving no choice; decisive; final; absolute. **2.** allowing no denial or refusal. **3.** dictatorial.

per·il (per′əl), *n., v.* —*n.* chance of harm or loss; exposure to danger. —*v.* put in danger. —**perilous,** *adj.*

per·pet·u·al (pər pech′ü əl), *adj.* **1.** lasting forever; eternal. **2.** lasting throughout life. **3.** never ceasing; continuous; constant. **4.** being in bloom more or less continuously throughout the year or the reason.

per·turb (pər tėrb′), *v.* **1.** disturb greatly; make uneasy or troubled; distress. **2.** cause disorder or irregularity.

pet·u·lant·ly (pech′ə lənt lē), *adv.* in little fits of bad temper; showing irritability over trifles; peevishly.

pil·grim·age (pil′grə mij), *n.* **1.** journey to some

sacred place as an act of religious devotion. **2.** a long journey.

pil·lage (pil′ij), v. **1.** rob with violence; plunder. **2.** take booty; plunder. —**pillage,** n.

plac·id·ly (plas′id lē), adv. in a pleasantly calm or peaceful manner; quietly.

plain·tive·ly (plān′tiv lē), adv. in a manner expressive of sorrow; mournfully; sadly.

pla·teau (pla tō′), n. **1.** plain in the mountains or at height considerably above sea level; large, high, plain. **2.** a level, especially the level at which something is stabilized for a period.

pom·mel (pum′əl), n., v. —n. **1.** part of a saddle that sticks up at the front. **2.** a rounded knob on the hilt of a sword, dagger. —v. strike or beat; beat with the fists.

pom·pous (pom′pəs), adj. **1.** trying to seem magnificent or very important; self-important. **2.** overly flowery or high-flown; inflated. **3.** characterized by pomp; splendid; magnificent.

pos·ter·i·ty (po ster′ə tē), n. **1.** generations of the future. **2.** all of a person's descendants.

prec·i·pice (pres′ə pis), n. **1.** a very steep or almost vertical face of a rock; cliff, crag, or steep mountainside. **2.** situation of great peril; critical position.

pre·cip·i·tate (pri sip′ə tāt), v., adj. —v. **1.** hasten the beginning of; bring about suddenly. **2.** throw headlong; hurl. **3.** be condensed as rain, dew, snow. —adj. **1.** very hurried; sudden. **2.** with great haste and force; plunging or rushing headlong; hasty; rash.

pre·cip·i·tous (pri sip′ə təs), adj. **1.** like a cliff; very steep. **2.** hasty; rash. **3.** rushing headlong; very rapid.

pred·e·ces·sor (pred′ə ses′ər), n. **1.** person holding a position or office before another. **2.** thing that came before another. **3.** ARCHAIC. ancestor; forefather.

pre·dom·i·nance (pri dom′ə nəns), n. a being powerful, having authority or influence; a superior being. —**predominate** (pri dom′ə nat), adj. —**predominate** (pri dom′ə nāt), v.

---

hat, āge, fär; let, ēqual, tèrm;
it, īce; hot, ōpen, ôrder;
oil, out; cup, pùt, rüle;
ch, child; ng, long; sh, she;
th, thin; ℄H, then; zh, measure;

ə represents a in about, e in taken,
i in pencil, o in lemon, u in circus.

pre·tense (prē′tens), n. **1.** make-believe; pretending. **2.** a false appearance. **3.** a false claim. **4.** anything done to show off.

pre·vail (pri vāl′), v. **1.** exist in many places; be in general use. **2.** be the most usual or strongest. **3.** be the stronger; win the victory; succeed. **4.** be effective. **5.** prevail on, prevail upon, or prevail with; persuade.

pri·mal (prī′məl), adj. **1.** of early times; first. **2.** chief; fundamental.

pro·cure (prə kyur′), v. **1.** obtain by care or effort; secure. **2.** bring about; cause.

pro·found (prə found′), adj. **1.** very deep. **2.** deeply felt; very great. **3.** going far deeper than what is easily understood; having or showing great knowledge or understanding.

prone (prōn), adj. **1.** lying face down. **2.** lying flat. **3.** having a tendency or inclination such as, *Man is prone to overlook such things.*

prop·a·ga·tion (prop′ə gā′shən), n. **1.** the breeding of plants or animals. **2.** a spreading; getting more widely believed; making more widely known. **3.** a passing on; sending further.

pro·pri·e·ty (prə prī′ə tē), n. **1.** quality or condition of being proper; fitness. **2.** proper behavior. **3.** proprieties, pl. conventional standards or requirements of proper behavior.

pros·trate (pros′trāt), v. **1.** lay down flat; cast down. **2.** make very weak or helpless; exhaust. —**prostrate,** adj.

ram·part (ram′pärt), n. **1.** a wide bank of earth, often with a wall on top as a fortification, built around a fort to help defend it. **2.** anything that defends; defense; protection.

rav·en·ous (rav′ə nəs), adj. **1.** very hungry. **2.** greedy.

ra·vine (rə vēn′), n. a long, deep, narrow gorge eroded by running water.

re·buke (ri byük′), v., n. —v. express disapproval of; reprove. —n. expression of disapproval; scolding.

re·coil (ri koil′), v. **1.** draw back; shrink back. **2.** spring back. **3.** react. —**recoil,** n.

re·gime (ri zhēm′), n. **1.** system, method, or form of government or rule. **2.** any prevailing political or social system. **3.** period or length of a regime. **4.** system of living; regimen.

re·it·e·rate (rē it′ə rāt′), v. say or do several times; repeat (an action or demand) again and again.

ren·e·gade (ren′ə gād), *n.* deserter from a religious faith, a political party; traitor.

re·nege (ri nig′), *v.* **1.** deny, renounce. **2** revoke. **3.** to go back on a promise or commitment.

re·per·cus·sion (rē′pər kush′ən), *n.* **1.** an indirect influence or reaction from an event. **2.** sound flung back; echo. **3.** a springing back; rebound; recoil.

re·pose (ri pōz′), *n., v.* —*n.* **1.** rest or sleep. **2.** quietness; ease. **3.** peace; calmness. —*v.* rest from work or toil; take a rest. **2.** depend; rely (on).

re·sil·i·ence (ri zil′ē əns), *n.* **1.** power of springing back; quality or nature of returning to original form; elasticity. **2.** power of recovering readily; buoyancy; cheerfulness. —**resilient,** *adj.*

res·pite (res′pit), *n., v.* —*n.* **1.** time of relief and rest; lull. **2.** a putting off; delay, especially in carrying out a sentence of death. —*v.* to put off; postpone.

re·splend·ent (ri splen′dənt), *adj.* very bright; shining; splendid.

re·tal·i·ate (ri tal′ē āt), *v.* pay back wrong, injury, etc.; return like for like, usually to return evil for evil.

ret·ro·spect. (ret′rə spekt), *n., v.* —*n.* **1.** survey of past time, events, etc.; thinking about the past. **2.** in retrospect, when looking back. —*v.* think of (something past).

rogue (rōg), *n.* **1.** a dishonest or unprincipled person; scoundrel; rascal. **2.** a mischievous person; scamp. **3.** animal with a savage nature that lives apart from the herd.

rue·ful (rü fəl), *adj.* **1.** sorrowful; unhappy; mournful. **2.** causing sorrow or pity. —**ruefully,** *adv.*

sac·ri·le·gious (sak′rə lij′əs), *adj.* injurious or insulting to sacred persons or things.

sa·dism (sā′diz′əm), *n.* **1.** an unnatural love of cruelty or delight in cruelty. **2.** excessive cruelty.

saf·fron (saf′rən), *n.* **1.** an orange yellow. **2.** an autumn crocus with purple flowers having orange-yellow stigmas. **3.** an orange-yellow coloring matter obtained from the dried stigmas of this crocus. Saffron is used to color and flavor candy and drinks.

sage·ly (sāj′lē), *adv.* **1.** in a manner showing wisdom or good judgment. **2.** wisely.

sal·u·ta·tion (sal′yə tā′shən), *n.* **1.** a greeting; saluting. **2.** something uttered, written, or done to salute. You begin a letter with a salutation, such as "*Dear Sir.*"

sate (sāt), *v.* **1.** satisfy fully (any appetite or desire).

2. supply with more than enough, so as to disgust or weary.

sa·vor (sā′vər), *v.* **1.** to enjoy the flavor of; perceive or appreciate by taste or smell. **2.** give flavor to; season. —**savor,** *n.*

scrim·mage (skrim′ij), *n.* **1.** a rough fight or struggle. **2.** the play in football that takes place when the two teams are lined up and the ball is snapped back. **3.** football playing for practice. —**scrimmage,** *v.*

se·clu·sion (si klü′zhən), *n.* **1.** a keeping apart from others; shutting off from others. **2.** a place shut off from others.

sed·en·tar·y (sed′n ter′ē), *adj.* **1.** used to sitting still much of the time. **2.** not migratory. **3.** fixed to one spot.

sham (sham), *n.* **1.** pretense; fraud. **2.** counterfeit; imitation. **3.** person who is not what he pretends to be. —**sham,** *adj., v.*

sheen (shēn), *n.* brightness; luster.

sim·u·late (sim′yə lāt), *v.* **1.** put on a false appearance of; pretend. **2.** act like; look like; imitate.

si·mul·ta·ne·ous (sī′məl tā′nē əs), *adj.* **1.** existing, done, or happening at the same time. —**simultaneously,** *adv.*

so·lic·i·tous·ly (sə lis′ə təs lē), *adv.* **1.** in a manner showing care or concern; anxiously; with concern. **2.** desirously; eagerly.

som·no·lent (som′nə lənt), *adj.* **1.** sleepy; drowsy. **2.** tending to produce sleep.

spec·trum (spek′trəm), *n.* **1.** the band of colors formed when a beam of white light is broken up by being passed through a prism or by some other means. A rainbow has all the colors of the spectrum: red, orange, yellow, green, blue, indigo, and violet. **2.** range; scope, compass, as *a broad spectrum of knowledge.*

spec·u·la·tion (spek′yə lā shən), *n.* **1.** careful thought; reflection. **2.** a guessing; conjecture. **3.** a buying or selling when there is a large risk, with the hope of making a profit from future price changes. —**speculate,** *v.*

spon·ta·ne·ous (spon tā′nē əs), *adj.* **1.** caused by natural impulse or desire; not forced or compelled; not planned beforehand. **2.** taking place without external cause or help; caused entirely by inner forces.

spo·rad·ic (spə rad′ik), *adj.* **1.** appearing or happening at intervals in time; occasional. **2.** being or occurring apart from others; isolated.

stag·nant (stag′nənt), *adj.* **1.** not running or flowing. **2.** foul from standing still. **3.** not acive; sluggish; dull.

stal·wart (stôl′wərt), *adj.* **1.** strongly built; sturdy; robust. **2.** strong and brave; valiant. **3.** firm; steadfast. —**stalwart,** *n.*

stealth·i·ly (stelth′i lē), *adv.* done in a secret manner; secretly; slyly.

ster·e·o·typed (ster′ē ə tīpt′), *adj.* **1.** lacking originality or individuality. **2.** fixed or settled in form; conventional.

stim·u·lus (stim′yə ləs), *n.* **1.** something that stirs to action or effort; incentive. **2.** something that produces a response.

stip·u·late (stip′yə lāt), *v.* **1.** arrange definitely; demand as a condition of agreement. **2.** make an express demand or arrangement.

strat·a·gem (strat′ə jəm), *n.* scheme or trick for deceiving an enemy; trickery.

stu·por (stü′pər), *n.* **1.** a dazed condition; loss or lessening of the power to feel. **2.** intellectual or moral numbness.

sub·lime (sə blīm′), *adj.* lofty or elevated in thought, feeling, language; noble; grand; exalted. —**sublime,** *n., v.*

sub·se·quent (sub′sə kwənt), *adj.* **1.** coming after; following; later. **2.** subsequent to, after; following; later than.

sub·stan·tial·ly (səb stan′shəl lē), *adv.* **1.** with substance; in actuality. **2.** with strength; firmly; solidly. **3.** in an important way; in a large amount. **4.** for the most part; in essentials, as *The stories were substantially the same.*

suc·ces·sor (sək ses′ər), *n.* **1.** person who follows or succeeds another in office, position, or ownership of property. **2.** person or thing that comes next after another in a series.

super·fi·cial (sü′pər fish′əl), *adj.* **1.** of the surface. **2.** concerned with or understanding only what is on the surface; not thorough; shallow. **3.** not real or genuine.

su·per·flu·ous (sù pėr′flü əs), *adj.* **1.** more than is needed. **2.** needless; unnecessary. **3.** extra; extravagant. **4.** marked by wastefulness.

sup·press (sə pres′), *v.* **1.** keep in; hold back; keep from appearing. **2.** put an end to; stop by force; put down. **3.** keep secret; refrain from disclosing.

sur·mise (sər mīz′), *n.* formation of an idea with little or no evidence; a guessing.

sur·rep·ti·tious·ly (sėr′əp tish′əs lē), *adv.* **1.** secretly. **2.** without authorization.

swarth·y (swôr′ᵺē), *adj.* **1.** being of a dark color, complexion, or cast. **2.** dusky.

syl·van (sil′vən), *adj.* **1.** living or located in the woods or forest. **2.** made, shaped, or formed of woods or trees. **3.** wooded.

sym·me·try (sim′ə trē), *n.* **1.** a regular, balanced arrangement on opposite sides of a line or plane, or around a center or axis. **2.** pleasing proportions between the parts of a whole; well-balanced arrangement of parts; harmony.

tact·ful·ly (takt′fəl lē), *adv.* diplomatically; dealing with people skillfully.

tan·gi·ble (tan′jə bəl), *adj.* **1.** that can be touched or felt by touch. **2.** real; actual; definite. —**tangible,** *n.*

tan·ta·lize (tan′tl īz), *v.* torment or tease by keeping something desired in sight but out of reach; holding out hopes that are repeatedly disappointed.

taunt (tônt), *v., n.* **1.** jeer at; mock; reproach; deride. **2.** get or drive by provoking. —*n.* a bitter or insulting remark; mocking; jeering.

taut (tôt), *adj.* **1.** tightly drawn; tense. **2.** in neat condition; tidy.

tem·pered (tem′pərd), *adj.* **1.** softened or moderated. **2.** treated so as to become hard but not too brittle.

te·na·cious (ti nā′shəs), *adj.* **1.** stubborn; persistent; obstinate. **2.** able to remember; retentive. **3.** holding fast together; not easily pulled apart. **4.** sticky.

teth·er (teᴛʜ′ ər), *n., v.* —*n.* **1.** rope or chain for fastening an animal so that it can graze or move only within a certain limit. **2.** at the end of one's tether, at the end of one's resources or endurance. —*v.* fasten or confine.

thresh·old (thresh′ōld), *n.* **1.** piece of wood or stone across the bottom of a door frame; doorsill. **2.** doorway. **3.** point of entering; beginning point.

---

hat, āge, fär, let, ēqual, tèrm;
it, īce; hot, ōpen, ôrder;
oil, out; cup, pùt, rüle;
ch, child; ng, long; sh, she;
th, thin; ᴛʜ, then; zh, measure;

ə represents *a* in about, *e* in taken,
i in pencil, *o* in lemon, *u* in circus.

thwart (thwôrt), *v.* prevent from doing something, particularly by blocking the way; oppose and defeat.

trans·verse (trans vèrs′), *adj.* lying across; placed crosswise; crossing from side to side.

trav·erse (trav′ərs), *v.* **1.** pass across, over, or through, diagonally. **2.** read, examine, or consider carefully. **3.** move sideways. **4.** oppose; hinder. **5.** turn on or as if on a pivot; swivel.

trib·u·la·tion (trib′yə lā′shən), *n.* great trouble; severe trial; affliction.

tu·mul·tu·ous·ly (tü mul′chü əs lē) *adv.* **1.** noisily or disorderly; violently. **2.** with great disturbance. **3.** roughly, stormily.

ty·rant (tī′rənt), *n.* **1.** person who uses his power cruelly or unjustly. **2.** a cruel or unjust ruler; cruel master. **3.** an absolute ruler. —**tyrannical,** *adj.*

un·can·ny (un kan′ē), *adj.* **1.** strange and mysterious; weird. **2.** so far beyond what is normal or expected as to have some special power.

un·con·gen·ial (un kən jē′nyəl), *adj.* **1.** having dissimilar tastes and interests; not getting on well together. **2.** not agreeable; not suitable.

un·couth (un küth′), *adj.* **1.** not refined; awkward; clumsy; crude. **2.** unusual and unpleasant; strange.

un·feigned (un fānd′), *adj.* **1.** not hypocritical. **2.** genuine; sincere.

un·mo·lest·ed (un′mə lest′ed), *adj.* not bothered, injured, troubled, disturbed or annoyed; not meddled with.

un·pro·fane (un pre fān′), *adj.* **1.** not characterized by contempt or disregard for God or holy things. **2.** not violating sacredness. **3.** clean and unpolluted.

ur·chin (ėr′chən), *n.* **1.** a small child. **2.** a mischievous child. **3.** a poor, ragged child.

va·grant (vā′grənt), *adj.* **1.** moving in no definite direction or course; wandering. **2.** wandering without proper means of earning a living. —**vagrant,** *n.*

val·id (val′id), *adj.* **1.** supported by facts or authority; sound or true. **2.** having legal force; legally binding. **3.** having force; holding good; effective.

van·quish (vang′kwish), *v.* **1.** conquer, defeat, or overcome in battle or conflict. **2.** overcome or subdue by other than physical means.

ver·ba·tim (vər bā′tim), *adv.* word for word; in exactly the same words.

vex (veks), *v.* **1.** worry; trouble; harass. **2.** anger by trifles; annoy; provoke. **3.** disturb by commotion.

vile·ly (vīl′lē), *adv.* **1.** in a manner that is very bad, foul, disgusting or obnoxious. **2.** in a manner that is evil; low; immoral. **3.** poorly; meanly; lowly. **4.** of little worth; trifling.

vin·di·ca·tion (vin′də kā′shən), *n.* a clearing from suspicion, dishonor, a hint or charge of wrongdoing; defense; justification.

vir·tu·os·i·ty (vėr′chü os′ə tē), *n.* character or skill of a person who is skilled in the techniques of an art, especially in playing a musical instrument.

vo·ra·cious (və rā′shəs), *adj.* **1.** eating much; greedy in eating. **2.** very eager; unable to be satisfied.

vul·ner·a·ble (vul′nər ə bəl), *adj.* **1.** capable of being wounded or injured; open to attack. **2.** sensitive to criticism, temptations, influences.

wel·ter·weight (wel′tər wā′), *n.* boxer who weighs more than 135 pounds and less than 147 pounds.

writhe (rīŦH), *v.* **1.** twist and turn; twist so as to distort. **2.** twist from or as if from pain or struggling. **3.** suffer mentally; be very uncomfortable. **4.** suffer keenly.

Index by Types of Literature

Index of Authors and Titles

Page numbers in italics indicate that a brief biography of the author is included.

Acknowledgments *continued from page iv.*

Houghton Mifflin Company for "Shirley Chisholm: College Years" from *Unbought and Unbossed* by Shirley Chisholm, published by Houghton Mifflin Company. Copyright © 1970 by Shirley Chisholm. Reprinted by permission. Also for the poem "A Song of Greatness" from *The Children Sing in the Far West* by Mary Austin, published by Houghton Mifflin Company. Copyright 1928 by Mary Austin. Copyright renewed 1956 by Kenneth M. Chapman and Mary C. Wheelwright. Reprinted by permission.

Liveright Publishing Corporation for the poem "Those Winter Sundays," which is reprinted from *Angle of Ascent,* New and Selected Poems, by Robert Hayden, with the permission of Liveright Publishing Corporation. Copyright © 1975, 1972, 1970, 1966 by Robert Hayden.

Macmillan Publishing Co., Inc., for the poem "Sea Fever" by John Masefield. Reprinted with permission of Macmillan Publishing Co., Inc. from *Poems* by John Masefield. Also for the poem "Advice to a Girl" by Sara Teasdale. Reprinted with permission of Macmillan Publishing Co., Inc. from *Collected Poems* by Sara Teasdale. Copyright 1933 by Macmillan Publishing Co., Inc., renewed 1961 by Guaranty Trust Co. of New York, Executor. Also for the poem "Sunset: St. Louis" by Sara Teasdale. Reprinted with permission of Macmillan Publishing Co., Inc. from *Collected Poems* by Sara Teasdale. Copyright 1920 by Macmillan Publishing Co., Inc., renewed 1948 by Mamie T. Wheless.

New Directions Publishing Corporation for the poem "An Easy Decision" by Kenneth Patchen, from *Collected Poems* of Kenneth Patchen. Copyright 1952 by New Directions Publishing Corporation. Reprinted by permission of New Directions.

W. W. Norton & Company, Inc., for the poem "Tree," which is reprinted from *Latest Will,* Poems by Lenore Marshall, with the permission of W. W. Norton & Company, Inc. Copyright © 1969 by Lenore Marshall.

Random House, Inc., for the excerpt "from *I Know Why the Caged Bird Sings*" by Maya Angelou. Condensed by permission of Random House, Inc. from *I Know Why the Caged Bird Sings,* by Maya Angelou. Copyright © 1969 by Maya Angelou. Also for the poem "in the inner city" from *Good Times,* by Lucille Clifton. Copyright © 1969 by Lucille Clifton. Reprinted by permission of Random House, Inc. Also for two poems by Langston Hughes: "Aunt Sue's Stories," Copyright 1926 by Alfred A. Knopf, Inc., renewed 1945 by Langston Hughes, and "Dream Variations," Copyright 1926 by Alfred A. Knopf, Inc. and renewed 1954 by Langston Hughes. Both reprinted from the *Selected Poems of Langston Hughes,* by Langston Hughes, by permission of Alfred A. Knopf, Inc. Also for the poem "New Mexican Mountain" by Robinson Jeffers. Copyright 1932 and renewed 1960 by Robinson Jeffers. Reprinted from *The Selected Poetry of Robinson Jeffers,* by Robinson Jeffers, by permission of Random House, Inc. Also for the poem "Sea Lullaby" by Elinor Wylie. Copyright 1921 by Alfred A. Knopf, Inc. and renewed 1949 by William Rose Benet. Reprinted from *Collected Poems of Elinor Wylie,* by Elinor Wylie, by permission of Alfred A. Knopf, Inc.

Charles Scribner's Sons for "Rattlesnake Hunt," excerpted from *Cross Creek* by Marjorie Kinnan Rawlings. Copyright 1942 by Marjorie Kinnan Rawlings; copyright renewal © 1969 Norton Baskin. Used by permission of Charles Scribner's Sons.

Simon & Schuster for excerpt from *Lame Deer: Seeker of Visions* by John Fire/Lame Deer and Richard Erdoes. Copyright © 1972 by John Fire/Lame Deer and Richard Erdoes. Reprinted by permission of Simon & Schuster, a Division of Gulf & Western Corporation.

Viking Penguin Inc., for "Battle by the Breadfruit Tree" from *On Safari* by Theodore J. Waldeck. Copyright 1940 by Theodore J. Waldeck, renewed © 1968 by JoBesse McElveen Waldeck. Reprinted by permission of Viking Penguin Inc. Also for the poem "Crossing" from *Letter from a Distant Land* by Philip Booth. Originally appeared in *The New Yorker.* Copyright 1953 by Philip Booth. Reprinted by permission of Viking Penguin Inc. Also for the poem "Death at Suppertime" from *Times Three* by Phyllis McGinley. Copyright 1948 by Phyllis McGinley, © renewed 1976 by Phyllis McGinley. Originally appeared in *The New Yorker.* Reprinted by permission of Viking Penguin Inc. Also for the poem "The Choice" by Dorothy Parker from *The Portable Dorothy Parker.* Copyright 1926, renewed 1954 by Dorothy Parker. Reprinted by permission of Viking Penguin Inc. Also for the poem "On the Death of the President" from *The Descent* by Ann Stanford. Copyright © 1970 by Ann Stanford. Reprinted by permission of Viking Penguin Inc.

Leonard Adamé for his poem "My Grandmother Would Rock Quietly and Hum." Copyright 1977, Leonard Adamé. Used by permission of the author.

Samuel W. Allen for his poem "American Gothic." Used by permission of the author.

Bolt & Watson Ltd, London, for "Stranger on the Night Train" by Mary Hocking, from *This Week* Magazine, October 20, 1957. Used by permission of the author's agent, Bolt & Watson Ltd.

Collier Associates for "Prairie Winter" by Rose Wilder Lane, abridged and slightly adapted from Chapter 4 of *Young Pioneers* (originally titled *Let the Hurricane Roar*), published by Bantam Books © 1933 by Rose Wilder Lane, © renewed 1961 by Roger Lea MacBride © 1976 by Wildrose Productions. Reprinted by permission of Collier Associates, agents for Roger MacBride.

Copp Clark Pitman, Toronto, for "The Black Stallion and the Red Mare" by Gladys Francis Lewis, from *All Sails Set,* © 1948, reproduced with permission of Copp Clark Pitman, Toronto.

E. I. Du Pont de Nemours & Co., for "Song of the Truck" from the radio play *Danger: Women at Work* by Doris Frankel, Cavalcade of America, copyright 1946.

Ann Elmo Agency, Inc., for the adaptation of "Leiningen versus the Ants" by Carl Stephenson. Copyright 1938 by Carl Stephenson. Reprinted by permission of Ann Elmo Agency, Inc.

Mari Evans for her poem "if you have had your midnights" from *Nightstar,* published by the Center for African American Studies, Berkeley, 1980, by permission of the author.

Barthold Fles Literary Agency for "The Life and Death of a Western Gladiator" by Charles G. Finney, which appeared originally in *Harper's* Magazine, October 1958. Used by permission of Barthold Fles Literary Agency.

Grove Press, Inc., for the poem "The Sleeper" by Edward Field from his book *Stand Up, Friend, with Me.* Reprinted by permission of Grove Press, Inc. Copyright © 1963 by Edward Field.

Evelyn Tooley Hunt for her poem "Taught Me Purple" from *Negro Digest,* February 1964. Used by permission of the author.

Johnson Publishing Company, Inc., for adaptation of "Pioneers in Protest"(Original title "Guerrilla in the Cottonfields") from *Pioneers in Protest* by Lerone Bennett, Jr., copyright, 1968, Johnson Publishing Co., Inc., Chicago. Used by permission of the publisher.

LULAC *News* for the poem "The Other Pioneers" by Roberto Félix Salazar. The poem appeared originally in the LULAC (League of United Latin American Citizens) *News,* July 1939. Used by permission.

Harold Matson Company, Inc., for "All Summer in a Day" by Ray Bradbury. Copyright © 1954 by Ray Bradbury. Reprinted by permission of the Harold Matson Company, Inc. Also for "The Torn Invitation" by Norman Katkov. Copyright © 1952 by Norman Katkov. Reprinted by permission of the Harold Matson Company, Inc.

Elliott Merrick for the adaptation of "Without Words" from his book *Frost and Fire.* Reprinted by permission of the author.

Toshio Mori for "Say It with Flowers" from *Yokohama, California* (Caxton Printers). Reprinted by permission of the author.

The New York Times for "I Have a Dream . . . " by Dr. Martin Luther King, Jr., as reported by James Reston, August 29, 1963. © 1963 by The New York Times Company. Reprinted by permission.

Hugh Noyes, England, for the poem "The Highwayman" from *Collected Poems* by Alfred Noyes. Reprinted by permission.

Richard Olivas for his poem "The Immigrant Experience." Reprinted by permission of the author and Professional Media Services.

Revista Chicano-Riqueña for the poem "piñones" by Leroy V. Quintana which was first published in *Revista Chicano-Riqueña,* Vol. 2, No. 2, copyright 1974. Reprinted by permission.

The Saturday Evening Post for "The No-Talent Kid" by Kurt Vonnegut, Jr., from *The Saturday Evening Post,* March 1975. Reprinted with permission from The Saturday Evening Post Company © 1975. Also for the poem "Midwest Town" by Ruth DeLong Peterson, from *The Saturday Evening Post,* November 13, 1954. Reprinted with permission from The Saturday Evening Post © 1954 The Curtis Publishing Company.

Saturday Review for the poem "A Spring Night" by Robert Beloof, from *Saturday Review,* July 22, 1961. Used by permission of Saturday Review.

The Society of Authors, London, for the poem "Silver" by Walter de la Mare. Reprinted by permission of The Literary Trustees of Walter de la Mare and The Society of Authors as their representative.

Robert Wallace for his poem "The Double Play." © 1960 by Robert Wallace. Reprinted by permission of the author.

Wesleyan University Press for the poem "A Blessing" by James Wright. Copyright © 1961 by James Wright. Reprinted from *The Branch Will Not Break* by permission of Wesleyan University Press. "A Blessing" first appeared in *Poetry.*

Albert Whitman & Company for "Pecos Bill Invents Modern Cowpunching" from *Pecos Bill—The Greatest Cowboy of All Time* by James Cloyd Bowman. Copyright © 1964, 1937 by Albert Whitman & Company. Reprinted by permission of the publisher.

Every effort has been made to trace the ownership of all copyrighted material in this book and to obtain permission for its use.

Footnote respellings and definitions are from *Scott, Foresman Advanced Dictionary* by E. L. Thorndike and Clarence L. Barnhart. Copyright © 1979 by Scott, Foresman and Company. Reprinted by permission of the publisher.

Credits

Design, Art Direction, Production, Photograph Research and Editing

DESIGN OFFICE / San Francisco

Illustration

KINUKO CRAFT / The Ugly Duckling
LYNN DENNIS / All You've Ever Wanted
JENNIFER DEWEY / Leiningen Versus the Ants; The Life and Death of a Western Gladiator
KEN HAMILTON / Paul Revere's Ride; The Torn Invitation; Going to Run All Night
ALETA JENKS / The No-Talent Kid
CHRISTA KIEFFER / Prairie Winter; The Redheaded League
JEN-ANN KIRCHMEIER / Johnny Appleseed; The Long Way Around
JAMES S. McCONNELL / Stephen's First Week
TERRENCE MEAGHER / A Measure of Freedom; Pecos Bill Invents Modern Cowpunching
WILLIAM S. SHIELDS / The Ransom of Red Chief

Photographs, Paintings, Prints, Drawings, Sculpture

COVER *detail from* "The Old Stage Coach of the Plains" Frederic Remington/ the Amon Carter Museum

Page

122   Library of Congress (BH823-145)
127   © Dennis Stock/Magnum
140   "The Sunny Side of the Street" by Phillip Evergood/The Corcoran Gallery of Art, Washington, D.C., Anna E. Clark Fund
141   © Dan McCoy/Rainbow
142   "Stone City, Iowa" by Grant Wood/Joslyn Art Museum, Omaha, Nebraska
154   Edward S. Curtis photo/Library of Congress
157   © Bob Adelman/Magnum
159   © Johnson Publishing Company
162   © Lee Goff/Magnum
167   American Foundation for the Blind
169   Library of Congress (LC-USZ62-13123)
186   LEFT © Owen Franken/Stock, Boston
186   RIGHT "Levels No. 452" by Wassily Kandinsky/The Solomon R. Guggenheim Museum, New York, photo by Robert E. Mates
187   TOP LEFT © Charles Harbutt/Magnum
187   CENTER RIGHT © Fred Bruemmer
211   "Sunrise IV," 1937 by Arthur G. Dove/Hirshhorn Museum and Sculpture Garden, Smithsonian Institution, Washington, D.C.
216   © Owen Franken/Stock, Boston
232   © Fred Bruemmer
252   © Charles Harbutt/Magnum
258   © Charles Harbutt/Magnum
265   © Charles Harbutt/Magnum
282   Roy King
287   "Conversations" 1958 by Ben Shahn, watercolor, 39¼ x 27 inches/ Whitney Museum of American Art, gift of the Whitney Museum of American Art
288   TOP RIGHT Drawing by Arthur Rackham © Barbara Edwards, Hampshire, England
288   BOTTOM Photo by Emma Coleman/Society for the Preservation of New England Antiquities (#7835-A)
318   "Ichabod Crane and the Headless Horseman" attributed to J. W. Wilgus/ National Gallery of Art, Washington, D.C.
321   Drawing by Arthur Rackham © Barbara Edwards, Hampshire, England
326   Drawing by Arthur Rackham © Barbara Edwards, Hampshire, England
328   Drawing by Arthur Rackham © Barbara Edwards, Hampshire, England
332   Drawing by Arthur Rackham © Barbara Edwards, Hampshire, England
347   Photo by Emma Coleman/Society for the Preservation of New England Antiquities (#7835-A)
361   © Marie Cosindas
362   BOTTOM Photo by William Clift, Seagram County Court House Archives/ Library of Congress
387   Photo by Geoff Winningham, Seagram County Court House Archives/ Library of Congress
412   Photo by William Clift, Seagram County Court House Archives/ Library of Congress
421   Photo by Stephen Shore, Seagram County Court House Archives/ Library of Congress
426   TOP © Nell Dorr
426   BOTTOM © Dan Morrill
427   TOP © Nicholas Sapieha/Stock, Boston
427   BOTTOM © Nicholas DeVore III/Bruce Coleman, Inc.
431   "The Scottish Horseman" by Gustave Moreau/The Gustave Moreau Museum, Paris, photo by Hans Hinz, Basel
438   "Cavaliers" fragment of a 15th century tapestry/Musée d'Arts Decoratifs, Saumur, France, photo by M. Decker
448   © Dan McCoy/Rainbow
450   © Chuck Kneyse/Black Star
451   © Chuck O'Rear/Woodfin Camp & Associates
453   "Moonlight, Wood's Island Light" by Winslow Homer, oil on canvas/ The Metropolitan Museum of Art, Gift of George A. Hearn

454   © David Cavagnaro
460   © Nicholas Devore III/Bruce Coleman, Inc.
467   "On A Lee Shore" by Winslow Homer/Museum of Art, Rhode Island School of Design, Jesse Metcalf Fund
472   © Ernst Haas
477   © Nicholas Sapieha/Stock, Boston
481   Library of Congress (LCUSF33-11602)
484   Alfred Eisenstaedt/Life Magazine © Time Inc.
488   © Owen Franken/Stock, Boston
490   © Nell Dorr
498   TOP Brown Brothers
498   BOTTOM © Steve Wilkings/Surfer Magazine
499   TOP Neil Leifer/Sports Illustrated ©Time Inc.
499   BOTTOM © Camilla Smith/Rainbow
502   Neil Leifer/Sports Illustrated © Time Inc.
510   © Jonathan T. Wright/Bruce Coleman, Inc.
517   The Bettmann Archive, Inc.
525   Brown Brothers
529   Laboratoire Curie de la Fondation Curie, Institut du Radium, Paris
536   © Camilla Smith/Rainbow
541   © Marvin Newman/Woodfin Camp & Associates
544   John Dominis/Life Magazine © 1965 Time Inc.
550   © Leo Hetzel
554   TOP © Nicholas Devore III/Bruce Coleman, Inc.
554   BOTTOM "Moonlight, Wolf" by Frederic Remington/Addison Gallery of American Art, Phillips Academy, Andover, Massachusetts
555   TOP Bancroft Library, Berkeley, California
555   BOTTOM © Fred Bruemmer
557   © James Quong
559   Bancroft Library, Berkeley, California
566   © Fred Bruemmer
570   Photo by Eric A. Hegg/Photography Collection, University of Washington Library
574   © Nicholas Devore III/Bruce Coleman, Inc.
576   Bancroft Library, Berkeley, California
584   © Fred Bruemmer
586   Bancroft Library, Berkeley, California
591   © Fred Bruemmer
601   © Nicholas Devore III/Bruce Coleman, Inc.
607   Bancroft Library, Berkeley, California
611   © Gary Milbur/Tom Stack & Associates
614   Photo by P. E. Larss/Alaska Historical Society

BCDEFGHIJ 0854321
Printed in the United States of America